Energy Manual

SUSTAINABLE ARCHITECTURE

HEGGER

FUCHS

STARK

ZEUMER

Birkhäuser
Basel · Boston · Berlin

Edition Detail
Munich

This book was compiled at the
Energy Efficient Building Design Unit, Darmstadt Technical University
Prof. Manfred Hegger
Department of Architecture, Darmstadt Technical University
www.tu-darmstadt.de/architektur/ee
in conjunction with the
Institut für internationale Architektur-Dokumentation GmbH & Co. KG,
Munich
www.detail.de

Authors

Manfred Hegger
Prof. Dipl.-Ing. M. Econ Architect
Energy Efficient Building Design Unit, Darmstadt TU

Matthias Fuchs
Dipl.-Ing. Architect
Energy Efficient Building Design Unit, Darmstadt TU

Thomas Stark
Dr.-Ing. Architect
Energy Efficient Building Design Unit, Darmstadt TU

Martin Zeumer
Dipl.-Ing.
Energy Efficient Building Design Unit, Darmstadt TU

Assistants:
Natascha Altensen; Hans Drexler, Dipl. Arch. ETH M. Arch. (Dist);
Laura Eckel; Alexandra Göbel, Dipl.-Ing.; Michael Keller, Dipl.-Ing.;
Nikola Mahal; Thomas Meinberg, Dipl.-Ing.

Drawing assistants:
Julia Kirsten Eisenhuth; Viola John, Dipl.-Ing.;
Geraldine Nothoff, Dipl.-Ing.; Johanna Wickenbrock

Editorial services

Project management & editing:
Julia Liese, Dipl.-Ing.
Steffi Lenzen, Dipl.-Ing. Architect

Editorial assistants:
Astrid Donnert, Dipl.-Ing.; Claudia Fuchs, Dipl.-Ing.;
Carola Jacob-Ritz, M.A.; Florian Krainer;
Nicole Tietze, M.A.

Editiorial assistant English edition:
Daniel Morgenthaler, lic. phil.

Drawings:
Marion Griese, Dipl.-Ing.; Daniel Hajduk, Dipl.-Ing.;
Caroline Hörger, Dipl.-Ing.; Claudia Hupfloher, Dipl.-Ing.;
Elisabeth Krammer, Dipl.-Ing.

Translation into English:
Gerd H. Söffker, Philip Thrift, Pamela Seidel

Proofreading:
Raymond D. Peat, Alford, UK

Production & layout:
Roswitha Siegler

Specialist articles:

Chris Luebkeman, Dr. sci. tech.
Arup Research + Development, London

Hermann Scheer, Dr. rer. pol., MdB
Eurosolar, Bonn

Robert Kaltenbrunner, Dr.-Ing. Architect
Federal Office for Building & Regional Planning, Bonn

Thomas Herzog, O. Prof. em., Dr. (Rome Univ.), Dr. h. c.,
Dipl.-Ing. Architect, Munich TU

Karl-Heinz Petzinka, Prof. Dipl.-Ing. Architect
Bernhard Lenz, Dipl.-Ing., Dipl.-Ing., MEng. Architect
Design & Building Technology Unit, TU Darmstadt

Scientific advisers, diagnosis system for sustainable building quality
(DSQ):
Brian Cody, Prof. BSc(Hons) CEng MCIBSE, Graz TU
Sabine Djahanschah, Dipl.-Ing. Arch., Deutsche Bundesstiftung Umwelt
Thomas Lützkendorf, Prof. Dr.-Ing. habil., University of Karlsruhe
Hansruedi Preisig, Prof. Dipl. Arch. SIA, Winterthur Polytechnic
Peter Steiger, Prof. em., Darmstadt TU

Library of Congress Control Number:
2008931674 (hardcover)/2008931739 (softcover)

Bibliographic information published by the German National Library
The German National Library lists this publication in the Deutsche
Nationalbibliografie; detailed bibliographic data are available on the
Internet at http://dnb.d-nb.de.

This book is also available in a German language edition
(ISBN 978-3-7643-8385-5)

Editor:
Institut für internationale Architektur-Dokumentation GmbH &
Co KG, Munich
www.detail.de

©2008 English translation of the 1st German edition
Birkhäuser Verlag AG
Basel · Boston · Berlin
PO Box 133, 4010 Basel, Switzerland
Part of Springer Science+Business Media

Printed on acid-free paper prod. from chlorine-free pulp. TCF∞

Reproduction: Martin Härtel OHG, Martinsried

Printing & binding: Kösel GmbH & Co. KG, Altusried-Krugzell

ISBN: 978-3-7643-8764-8 (hardcover)
ISBN: 978-3-7643-8830-0 (softcover)

9 8 7 6 5 4 3 2 1   www.birkhauser.ch

Contents

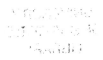

Preface

The *Energy Manual – Sustainable Architecture* not only adds one more title to the series of *Construction Manuals* but also a new dimension. For the first time it is not primarily concerned with fundamentals, a building material or a construction element group. This *Manual* approaches design and construction from apparently invisible qualities: the sustainability and energy-efficiency of buildings.

There is a whole range of arguments in favour of this way of looking at things. No other sector of industry uses more materials and energy, produces more waste and contributes less to material recycling than the building industry. For quite some time now, these themes have also dominated international public discussions and the process of forming political opinion. There are many reasons for this; some materials are becoming scarce and consequently more expensive, others have undesirable effects on the environment and users, and yet others fail to live up to people's expectations in the long-term. This applies just as much to conventional energy sources. They too are scarce and rapidly becoming more and more expensive; and, furthermore, they are considered to be one of the main causes of climate change and other environmental damage. Predictions of how long supplies of non-renewable energies such as natural gas and petroleum will last are shorter than the expected lifetime of many buildings, and not only the new ones. The global debate about reserves is coming to a head, fears about the safety of supply lines are only all too well founded. We are becoming increasingly aware of the finiteness of many resources and the consequences for humankind and the environment.

Architecture and building offer the greatest potential for a sustainable shaping of the environment. We will have to strengthen our efforts to increase materials- and energy-efficiency in construction and the use of buildings. Clever design and planning decisions could help us to use resources more sparingly, improve the durability of buildings and reduce environmental damage. In this way we can create and maintain lasting value and contribute to the sustainable progress of our society.

Sustainability affects the totality of the active planning and running of a building, social, economic and ecological concerns. It is a development where today's society considers the needs of future generations. Sustainability is defined not only in terms of the qualities of the object being built (object quality), but also by its position (location quality) and its development process (process quality). Efficiency in the use of energy and resources has become a key quality indication for a building. The instruments of materials- and energy-efficient building are at the same time architectural methods – lightness and mass, shelter and transparency, economical use of space and spatial effect.

There is a considerable difference between buildings and other objects in daily use. They already fulfil the requirements for the use of renewable energy sources. As a rule they are connected with the ground and are so near to the surface that they can benefit from the earth's even temperature level or from geothermal heat from deeper strata. They stand in an unimpeded airflow and can take advantage of differences in pressure and wind energy. They are exposed to daylight and can therefore tap directly into the main energy source available to us – the sun. Depending on location, further renewable energy sources are available: groundwater and rivers, biomass and biogas, to name but a few.

Despite having these possibilities so close at hand, where sustainability and energy-efficiency are concerned, we in the building trade are far from the state of development of other industry sectors. Yet we cannot go on procrastinating. Politics sees the need to step in and regulate because of foreseeable supply crises, conflicts and public opinion, globally, at the European level, nationally and locally. Architects and engineers have the chance to make their creative opinion-leadership socially effective. The potential for improvement is enormous and so far has hardly been exploited. The challenge of sustainable development in the building sector presents opportunities in a business sector that for a long time has not been particularly renowned for new ideas – including scientific, technical and design innovations, new export opportunities and once again as an impulse generator for long-term social developments.

The *Energy Manual – Sustainable Architecture* aims to provide a basis for this, to show examples and make suggestions. The overall structure follows the familiar pattern of Edition Detail *Construction Manuals*.

Part A, "Positions", concentrates on fundamental aspects of sustainable and energy-efficient building. Guest contributions dealing with global change and energy change provide the primary themes. The difficult relationship between architecture and sustainability are dealt with, also the scarcely used potential of solar architecture. Key issues such as efficiency and life cycles reveal the significance of considering sustainability in architecture. They elucidate the need for action and show what dynamics such a development in building could bring about.

Part B, "Fundamentals", on the other hand, is action-based. Starting off by illustrating the general basics of sustainability and energy, climate and comfort, the various planning and action dimensions of sustainable and energy-efficient building are dealt with. These include urban space and infrastructure, building envelope and building services and also choice of materials. Rapid developments in this field, especially in energy technology, made it necessary to revise this section again and again. The current standard of knowledge at the time of going to press has been clearly set out. The statements made in this part lead to instructions on how to act regarding development and energy concepts, and on the organisation of a planning process as a precondition for sustainable building and for evaluating sustainable building quality. Wherever possible, the statements are backed up by photographs or diagrams. In the last part of this section the DNQ system for diagnosing sustainable building quality is introduced and the most important assessment criteria for building in tune with the future are summarised. They make the

demands for sustainability, which up until now have only been expressed and devalued in a generalised manner – manageable and assessable.
The fundamentals of planning also provide relevant, comprehensive material on different ways of looking at the subject. They also show that we already have a wide selection of well-developed technologies at our disposal for using the resources efficiently which Earth offers us, without spoiling her beauty. It is left to the reader, however, to use this information to develop a solution that suits the place and the task, and which uses a minimum of means to achieve maximum benefits.

When selecting the "Case Studies" described in part C, it was always the interrelationship between a sustainable approach, an energy concept and an architectural position that was in the foreground. These are predominantly current projects that stand out thanks to their special architectural interpretation of building sustainability and energy-efficiency. The texts, diagrams and drawings portraying the buildings in each case add up an appraisal of the sustainability approach in accordance with the DNQ system for diagnosing sustainable building quality. The examples given make it clear that technologies for the efficient use of resources and energy open up new architectural potential – but at the same time it can be seen that the search for suitable architectural vocabulary for solving society's new tasks can by no means be considered as completed.

The *Energy Manual – Sustainable Architecture* goes far beyond that which the necessarily concise title of the book suggests. Energy is at the centre. The intention was, however, to examine this theme extending from urban planning und infrastructure beyond the object dimension into the forming of planning processes – but particularly within the wider context of the sustainable development of architecture and building.

Working on this book tied up a lot of energy, particularly human energy, from the team of authors, colleagues and the publisher. I would

like to thank most heartily all those institutions and people who worked competently with us, family members or friends who relieved us of chores, so that we could work on this project and those who so generously supported us with resources.
Perhaps our readers can sense this energy. The energy input will have been worthwhile if it mobilises further energy that takes up the social and professional challenges and thus encourages the development of architecture and building.

Darmstadt, August 2007
Manfred Hegger

Part A Positions

Fig. A   The Earth viewed from the moon

Global change

Chris Luebkeman

A 1.1

As far as the design and construction of the built environment are concerned, we can master almost everything technically. We are capable of erecting buildings that produce just as much energy as they use. We can create wonderful spaces and places where people enjoy being. We know how to produce materials that in theory will last forever – for instance titanium or glass – and the same applies to materials that degrade if we wish them to. We can fly faster than sound or even stop Brownian motion. And even so – although we can do all these things – we often look into the future nervously and wonder if we are doing everything right.

Drivers of change

The consulting engineers at Arup have carried out more than 10 000 projects worldwide and are renowned for their innovative ideas and multidisciplinary planning achievements [1]. From 1999 to 2002 I had the privilege of heading the research and development department. A team of 35 people with a great deal of knowledge about the built environment at their disposal advised engineers all over the world whilst the latter explored the bounds of feasibility. Straight after that, in 2003, I set up a department known by the name of "Foresight, Innovation + Incubation" (FII). Since then, this department has helped many clients – private individuals, firms and governments – to collect their thoughts about the future. The workshop series "Drivers of Change" was a part of this process and between 2003 and 2006 some 9500 people on five continents participated [2]. This involved every participant revealing what they believe the drivers of change to be, both at global and local level. The results show that there are various core themes such as climate, energy or geographical change, which are embedded in people's minds everywhere. At first glance this does not seem to be particularly remarkable. Bearing in mind the fact that nowadays we look more closely at geopolitical differences than at what people have in common, then finding a common global opinion is by no means a foregone conclusion. In the workshops, the STEEP system was used to evaluate the core themes [3]. In order to have an evenly matched dialogue about the future, each theme category is looked at individually. The individual categories such as demographic change, global nomadism or urbanisation are divided into five areas and analysed individually. This procedure allows a group to prioritise the individual drivers of change and then examine the correlating influences for each of the other four areas. Each "Drivers of Change" workshop was carried out using the same method. To start with, the groups were asked about the four global models for the future shown in Fig. A 1.4. Economic growth and global governance formed the two axes [4]. The participants were asked to draw a vector whose initial point showed the world today and whose terminal point showed what could be reality in the world in the next 20 years. The results were fascinating: the vectors did indeed vary according to where the participants came from. However, there was a clear tendency towards a world striving for economic growth but at the same time extremely separated and divided: a more differentiated world concentrating more on localis, than on globalism. In the second part of the workshop the participants were asked about their observations concerning the reasons for the change in each of the STEEP categories. It became apparent that there were some things in common globally, but also a few differing points of view on these themes.

Five theses

The built environment is the foundation of society. It allows social interaction between all levels. At the present time the world is "urbanising" at an unprecedented rate. Due to the enormous economic growth in China over the past 25 years, approximately 300 million people have moved to the towns and cities. This increase is expected to rise by 500 million by 2050 [5]. This represents the greatest mass migration in human history.

The cities are changing, developing further – using materials from all over the world; just about all the regions of the world come into contact with others some way every day. How can the built environment be defined in a world with ever-increasing dependencies? Who or what determines what should be built and how? And how does the "glocal" environment deter-

A 1.1 View of a power station in the Soweto district, Johannesburg (ZA)
A 1.2 Ubiquitous traffic chaos in Shanghai (CHN)

mine this [6]? Many questions, five fundamental assumptions:
- Change is constant; context is variable. A lot is said about change and that it is taking place at an ever-increasing speed. But it is far more interesting to observe the context of change, the integrated linking of certain epochs, the causality of successful innovations. This profound analysis of causes dependent on a particular time helps us to foresee how future contexts are interconnected with each other. It should help to work out projections for various future scenarios.
- Every person has three appraisal systems he or she can use: firstly, gut feeling, which provides information on a very low, almost animal level; secondly, the heart, which represents feelings and convictions; and finally, the head or analytical capabilities. The most intensive moments are those where all three are aligned.
- We have no choice but to learn how to get along with each other on this one planet. Our behaviour should therefore support the sustainable use of planet Earth's resources.
- In nature there are many containers but only people build boxes with walls and lids! For this reason, only people can remove the lids and leave their boxes. Symbolically, this stands for the necessity of thinking in an interconnected way rather than on separate planes.
- Anything we find inconvenient will not endure. Eliminating unpleasant conditions appears to have been one of the main causes of innovation and change throughout history. In order to find good ideas for the future, we must watch out for these inconvenient things.

Demographic change

Throughout the entire workshop series, demographic change was the most frequently mentioned topic. Its significance varies from place to place and from region to region. Nevertheless, almost everybody is concerned about the question of how the population is changing and how this change will influence the future. A pressing topic relates to the fact that in the built environment the majority of those currently in employment in the industrialised countries are about 12 years away from retirement [7]. Furthermore, too few young people are interested in the construction sector and its future. Soon the majority of those employed who have fundamental experience and specialised know-how will no longer be available. However, hope remains that – whilst the infrastructure around us ages with our society – interest in our built environment will increase again. In the richer part of the world, better living conditions and advances in medical care have contributed to a reduction in infant mortality and have prolonged life expectancy, resulting in long-term changes in the requirements for shaping the environment. The deterioration of those conditions in the less developed areas poses an enormous challenge. It is difficult to predict

which developments this discrepancy will give rise to. In 2020 there will very probably be one billion people in the 60+ age group; 75% of this group will live in the industrialised countries, and of those 16% will be US Americans, 20% Germans and 27% Japanese [8]. Who will look after this ageing population? How will they manage? What changes will we have to make in designing products and services, places and surroundings, to improve their living conditions?

As far as the ageing "baby boomer" generation of the post-war period is concerned, it seems probable that perceptions of what constitutes acceptable help will change and develop further. Those who resist getting caught up in technology by arguing that it is a foreign invasion will become fewer as more technology is integrated into their daily lives. Many people forget that a simple graphite pencil is an unbelievable piece of "technology". Human productivity is accelerating constantly. The baby boomers have already adjusted and prepared themselves for a progressive life situation. For instance, they accept medical solutions like artificial hips or knee joints and even cosmetic surgery to prolong their lives and raise their standard of living – in a way that previous generations knew only from science fiction. So probably in the foreseeable future our towns will be supporting us "proactively" in our daily lives.

Global nomadism

Since the 1970s interesting changes have been seen in the population density in various regions of the Earth. These are mainly based on the current availability of cheap fossil fuels and the widening global prosperity gap. A large number of people, both educated and uneducated, is on the move seeking work. This migration, from the farmer moving into the city to the highly qualified doctor leaving his home country, is taking place in different sectors in various parts of the world. The global economy is unexpectedly dependent on these international immigrants and emigrants. The illegal migrant workers in the USA, who over the last decade have fundamentally supported the economy there, are one example amongst others. Or medical staff who are lured from their own countries, where there is no money to be earned, to the rich nations with their ageing populations, whilst at the same time in their home countries there is a lack of vital specialists.

Further basic questions arise when we look at developments in the cities. How many international immigrants identify with their chosen homeland or place of refuge? Perhaps a new multi-nationalism is the solution with complex multiple obligations. Or maybe the need for a personal relationship with a local community will be replaced by a global attachment. In any case, this conflict between globality and locality will play a growing role in shaping our environment. Today, Europe is home to the the largest number of international immigrants, followed by

A 1.2

Asia and North America. We will probably develop slowly from state citizenship to world citizenship or transnational citizenship. Generally speaking, Europeans learn several foreign languages, spend longer in job training and enter the labour market later. Some 77% of students in the EU speak a foreign language well enough to take part in a conversation. The largest English-speaking population in future will be the Chinese. This poses the question of whether our cities, whilst undergoing systematic improvement and where every inhabitant will be identifiable, will be able to communicate with us in the language of our choice. Will we hear announcements in our mother tongue when we are using the London underground or the Hong Kong Metro? Which will be the first town to introduce a multimedia town guide with automated translation? The idea is being considered to provide resources for those people who do not speak any foreign language fluently, so that they can find their way around at airports, for example. Which language would we select? Many towns and cities are watching us already – how would we feel if they spoke to us too?

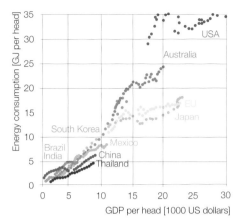

A 1.3

Energy and prosperity
The International Monetary Fund (IMF) research shows that there is a direct correlation between economic fluctuations and access to electricity. In Fig. A 1.3 the energy consumption per head for selected countries is shown in relation to their gross domestic product (GDP). This clearly shows that as an agricultural economy changes into a consumer society through industrialisation, energy consumption increases at the same time. During the process there seems to be a level at which a society "optimises", i.e. GDP rises and energy consumption remains unchanged. I think however that it has been more a case of shifting energy consumption from one country to another, i.e. a state imports the majority of its goods from another. A classic example for this is the United States: part of its energy consumption is transferred as it were, to China.

Two further aspects must be looked at critically regarding the chart: the first being that the nation shown to have the highest energy consumption per head has at the same time used up nearly all its energy resources. The second point is that the two most populous countries in the world, China and India, have the lowest gross domestic product and the lowest energy consumption per head. Both of these highly populated countries are currently striving to climb up the ladder. If every Chinese person drove a car then the current known world oil reserves would be exhausted within six months.

Nowadays traffic jams occur in every town in every country (Fig. A 1.2). Clogged up main arterial roads, the real motors of the economy, which pump development potential through every contemporary society, could drastically restrict our society's performance-capability. At some stage this clogging, this blockade, will reach a critical point. Energy production for the society of today has got to change. Industry is moving – albeit involuntarily – from the paradigm of the centralised Industrial Age towards a model which is divided and decentralised in a substantially more up-to-date way. This change is essential politically. If you look at the energy supply chain two thirds of the energy is lost during conversion and distribution. Electric

energy remains a fundamental requirement of today's society. It is the basis of almost everything we do today. Historically electricity was produced to further growth in small and large industries which were situated in the vicinity of energy sources. Over time the thirst for energy exceeded the capacity of local sources. For this reason large power stations emerged which were closer to supplies of raw materials than to consumers' infrastructure. Due to the emissions from the power stations these were built at some distance from the cities and the resulting enormous transmission losses were simply accepted as part of the system. However nowadays there are more and more possibilities to decentralise the production of electricity. Instead of one large power station there should be many small ones, spread

throughout a region. They would all be interconnected with each other and would be powered by small wind turbines, fuel cells in buildings, solar cells or small gas turbines. This system-wide approach increases the reliability of supply on the one hand and reduces the vulnerability of the electric power supply on the other hand due to the fact that the producer is far nearer to the consumers and end-users. This method has the added advantage of being able to draw on the great store of renewable energy.
Fig. A 1.1 shows the sun rising over a power station in the Soweto district in Johannesburg. As it was built during the apartheid period it originally only provided energy for a small group of the population – excluding all those living directly in that quarter. The power station

Block islands
· national economies recover at different speeds
· more frequent occurrence of regional economic or trade blocks
· political initiatives boost local / regional growth
· ideological differences affect global dynamics
· labour market reforms influence growth and employment
· technological progress and increase in productivity as the driving force for economic upturn

Reglobalisation
· Iran and USA announce new trade agreements
· United Nations restructured and revived, new members in Security Council
· terrorism and geopolitical instability checked
· booming world economy
· power and influence of WTO (World Trade Organisation) grows
· slow but constant inflation
· open national economies boost global dynamics

chaos — global — economic growth — governance — order

Failure scenario
· L-shaped path of the world economy, i.e. the economic situation hits rock bottom and hovers around without improving
· increasing tendency towards isolationism and protectionism
· countries like Switzerland and Japan serve as models for a growing number of national economies
· consumer climate sinks to an all-time low
· re-nationalisation of utilities by governments
· United Nations / World Trade Organisation on the verge of disintegration

Global yoyo effect
· W-shaped path of the world economy, i.e. phases of economic upturn alternating with downturn phases
· governments and business work closely together
· financial crises and terrorist attacks curb economic upturns
· national economies suffer due to inflated public sectors
· higher risk of a systemic shock for the global finance system with increasing risk premiums

A 1.4

A 1.5

A 1.3 "Prosperity ladder": Relationship between energy
consumption and gross domestic product of various countries in the period from 1970 to 1997
A 1.4 Global models of the future by 2026
A 1.5 Phoenix (USA) by night – the city as a densely
populated area

represented the centralisation of energy and power on many levels. Today, in a politically transformed and democratic South Africa, it produces energy for the whole of the population. Moreover the picture shows – perhaps even more significantly – the most important source of energy there is: the sun. Can we imagine the fact that all the energy the sun produces is renewable energy? What will happen when oil politics no longer determines the relationships between nations? Can we imagine no longer talking about shortages because producing renewable energies has become so efficient? Can we believe that every building produces so much energy that it repays the energy needed to build it?

Urbanisation

We are currently changing into an age in which, worldwide, more people live in cities than in rural areas. Nevertheless towns take up less than 2% of the earth's land surface. Urban populations are increasing at the rate of 180 000 people a day. The largest increases are occurring in less developed countries where it is predicted that urbanisation will increase by 50% by the year 2020 [9]. While more and more people are pouring into urban areas, and while over-development is destroying fertile land and at the same time encouraging higher consumption of non-renewable resources, we have to ask ourselves: Where does this path lead? What will the cities look like? How, for instance, will they be provided with food? In 2015, when there will probably be 23 metropolises each with over 10 million inhabitants, 19 of them in less developed countries, we will be faced with considerable problems with urban planning and infrastructure [10]. By the year 2030 approximately 60% of the world's population will live in cities. What sort of growth will this be? Is it possible to make a city centre CO_2-neutral? Is it possible to make new cities more plant-friendly? Is it possible for a city with one million inhabitants to function completely on the "One Planet Principle"[11]? Our future depends on how we control the growth of our cities and solve the problems which arise. It is time that the health of our cities went to the top of the global political agenda. We have to make sure that we are aware of the lim-

itations of our growth and that we do our best to develop within those limitations. It is the only effective way in the long-term.

Whilst looking into the future we are not allowed to forget the many thousands of years of history. In 1905 Studebaker, the American automobile producer from the Mid West, advertised for an engine type for the "horseless carriage". The car could be fitted out with an electric engine for town journeys and a petrol engine for overland journeys. It seems that even in those days car producers realised that certain fuels were more suitable for certain types of journey than others. They were providing hybrid vehicles 100 years before society recognised that these were not only a possibility but, in fact, a necessity. This is just one example of how we can learn from the past and benefit from what we have learnt. An American federal judge named Oliver Wendell Holmes said: "A hundred years after we are gone and forgotten those who have never heard of us will have to live with the consequences of our actions (...)." It would be good if we remembered this prescient sentence. The decisions we make every day – as the creators of the built environment – not only determine the places we live in today but also have an influence on our environment forever.

Hopeful developments

Population shifts, increasing scarcity and the wanton consumption of fertile land and natural – renewable and non-renewable – resources could turn out to be a significant global problem, a dilemma of disastrous proportions. We can only hope that global awareness of the fragility of our planet will grow. We appear to have reached a critical and sobering point in history. Despite setbacks and mistakes all is not lost. There is still time left for corrective steps. We as individuals in a "glocalised" society must heed the warning signs and we will thus be able to avoid falling into a downward spiral. How our future looks, and in whichever built environment we and future generations experience it, depends in many ways on our decisions. Ultimately it will not depend on technology and economics but on what we – people – decide. In the midst of uncertainty concerning the times which lie ahead of us one thing is sure: we are

the ones who will determine the future that we bequeath to our descendants – whether or not we take up the challenge.

References:
[1] Arup was founded in 1946 in London and today is one of the leading engineering companies worldwide, with over 80 offices and approx. 9000 employees. The company takes on multidisciplinary planning projects in all fields of structural and civil engineering.
[2] www.driversofchange.com
[3] STEEP stands for "social, technological, economic, environmental and political domains".
[4] Global Governance: a conceptual approach to answering the questions facing world politics in relation to the political controllability of world problems and globalisation tendencies.
[5] The Source of 5 February 2007
[6] "Glocal" is a combination of the words global and local.
[7] In the USA the average age of qualified employees in the building trade is 48 years according to the National Education Association. The "Engineering UK 2006" report gives 55 years as the average age for engineers.
[8] United Nations Population Information Network
[9] ibid.
[10] United Nations Population Division
[11] One Planet Principle: each city dweller has a certain global area, and a certain amount of resources at his disposal, calculated proportionally.

Energy change

Hermann Scheer

A 2.1

The term energy change is being discussed controversially in public more and more often. The term is, however, somewhat ambiguous. Which elements of the energy supply should be changed and in which direction? Is it a question of new sources of energy or only of the sparing and efficient use of the sources of energy currently in use? Is it about more internationally uniform or decentralised energy structures, or about more competition or a more ecological or sustainable energy supply? Usually, the term energy change is associated with sustainability, but that does not really make the term easier to understand. Meanwhile, even the use of nuclear power and fossil fuel is being labelled sustainable by the providers if those are a bit safer or more efficient than before. However, sources of energy whose primary resources are only available for a finite period – which applies to oil, natural gas, coal and uranium ore, and which, from their extraction right through to their conversion and use, cause severe environmental damage and leave residues – cannot justifiably be labelled sustainable. Energy change means energy *changeover*, i.e. replacing nuclear and fossil fuel sources with renewable ones. These are the only sustainable ones and – with the exception of biofuels – emissions-free and usable.

Solar or nuclear power – the fundamental conflict of the 21st century

With its generally still hesitant attitude to renewable energies, the world is still far short of what is possible and necessary. But on the other hand, it is living far beyond its means where nuclear and fossil fuels are concerned. The full spectrum of reasons for a changeover to renewable energies can be deduced from the following four elementary differences between nuclear and fossil energy on the one hand and renewable energies on the other:

• The use of nuclear and fossil fuels causes massive environmental interference with tectonic consequences starting with extraction and going on to emissions into water, air and the Earth's atmosphere. Renewable energies on the other hand can, in principle, be used without such consequences. Furthermore,

other than protecting the climate, there is also the general reason of environmental protection. Even if there were no climate problem, there would still be massive ecological reasons in favour of energy change.
• Fossil fuels are finite, which is why continuing to use them inevitably leads to rising costs and also supply bottlenecks and emergencies. Only the inexhaustible, renewable energies open the way for all people to have lasting, guaranteed energy supplies. This leads to another reason – permanent and certain availability.
• Nuclear and fossil fuel reserves are found in relatively few regions of the Earth; so using them requires long international supply chains (Fig. A 2.2). This inevitably leads to higher infrastructure expenditure, and to growing existential dependency and triggers economic, political and belligerent conflicts. Renewable energies on the other hand are available in a different form, as natural environmental energy everywhere, and can be obtained with technical assistance – with far fewer infrastructure requirements. This brings us to further reasons for changing to renewable energies, namely economic efficiency, political independence and preserving peace.
• Fossil and nuclear fuels are becoming more and more expensive as far as both direct and indirect costs are concerned due to the above mentioned conditions. Renewable energies on the other hand are becoming less and less expensive due to continuous technological improvements, industrial mass production, intelligent new applications and not least because (with the exception of bio-energy) there are no fuel costs involved. This results in social and economically strategic reasons for change.

Thus the subject of energy change is a question of renewable energies – the overwhelmingly huge and inexhaustible energy potential, which, however, is still underestimated. The key reason for this is that renewable energy sources only partially fit into current technical and economic structures for providing energy. For the most part they are incompatible with the energy sys-

A 2.1 Solar thermal electricity generation near Alice Springs (AUS)
A 2.2 Comparison of energy provider chains for the generation of electricity

tem already in place; in other words they are regarded as intruders and dismissed accordingly. They upset the calculations of the traditional energy business and common thinking on energy, too.

But what is stopping those people who are not directly or indirectly involved in the traditional energy system from insisting on changing to renewable energies, firmly and without being afraid of conflict? Why have there not been any political initiatives, intent on speeding up the use of renewable energies economically and concretely, just as this was possible for building railways, for space travel, nuclear technology and, only recently, information technology? Why are there still no European or international institutions for renewable energies, similar to the International Atomic Energy Agency (IAEA) or the European Space Agency (ESA) in their respective sectors? These questions concerning the players and the possible activities for and against renewable energies have to be addressed so as to identify how the energy change can be accelerated.

Enough energy for everyone – the full-scale potential of renewable energies

The structural diversity of renewable energies makes it so difficult for energy politicians, who for decades have been accustomed to the structures of fossil fuel consumption, to think their way into the potential of renewable energies. Whoever wants to recognise the economic and technical, cultural and political opportunities cannot and must not just compare the individual energy outputs with each other. Every isolated cost comparison with fossil fuel sources is an obstacle to viewing the broad spectrum of possible uses for renewable energies. What counts is the comparison in each case of the total energy supply chain, taking the constant and the variable factors into consideration. The constant factor is always the source, whereby with renewable energies the sources are not only considerably more diverse but also more widespread. The variable factors – within the scope of each proposed source – result from the varying and constantly improvable technical and thus economic effort involved for obtaining energy. As renewable energies can be found everywhere in the environment, there is the possibility of harvesting or collecting them and then using or converting them directly there in the same place, or at least in

the same area, where they will be used, something that has been more and more overlooked since the Industrial Revolution, and which is therefore unimaginable today. This means that for covering requirements using renewable energies, a much shorter energy supply chain is needed – if any at all. With the help of modern technology this in turn leads to regional or local self-sufficiency rather than global dependency on fossil fuel sources – an opportunity for new political, economic and cultural freedom.

The possibility of substituting regenerative for fossil resources widens the scope still further. It allows regions with suitable cultivation and climate conditions to establish their own natural resources base (Fig. A 2.1). In this way at least the natural resources base will be extended to considerably more countries, extensive shifts of industrial locations together with changes in world trade paths and a new, differentiated division of labour in the world economy could arise as a consequence.

At the same time, all of these changes mean the biggest step towards more energy efficiency due to a drastic reduction in enormous energy losses during the extraction, processing and transporting of primary nuclear and fossil fuels. The focus for investments in the energy business will shift from supplying energy to providing the

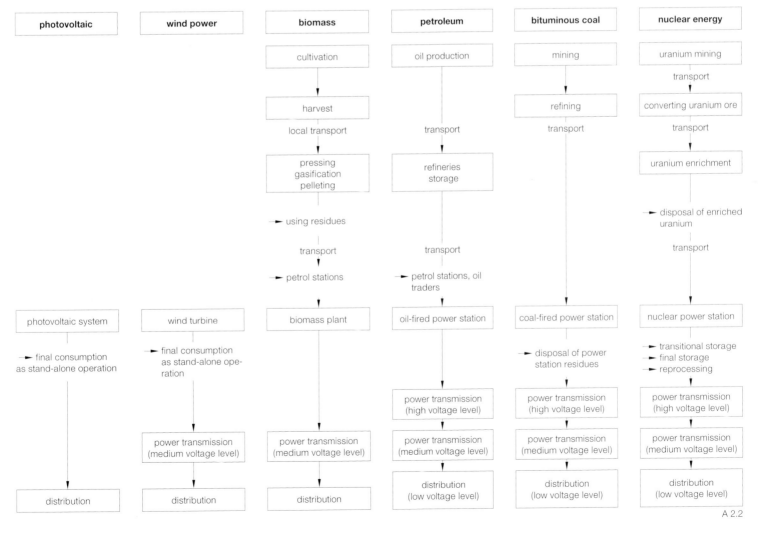

A 2.2

	heating and electricity from renewable energies with energy storage	biomass for energy and raw materials	nuclear / fossil energy provision
extracting energy	–	•	○
energy processing	–	•	○
energy storage	•	•	○
energy distribution	•	•	•
installation of energy conversion plants	•	•	○
operating of energy conversion plants	•	•	○
maintenance of energy conversion plants	•	•	○
designing of energy provision systems	•	•	○
municipal or regional tax revenues	•	•	○
regional credit institutions	•	•	○

• regional variation possible
○ regional variation not possible
– not applicable

A 2.3 Uniform regional distribution of economic activities in a comparison of solar and non-solar utilisation of resources
A 2.4 Avoidance of concentration and monopolisation of energy sources
A 2.5 Pipeline in Alaska (USA)
A 2.6 Theoretical potential of annual solar radiation on the Earth compared with annual energy consumption worldwide and also fossil and nuclear raw materials reserves

A 2.3

technical facilities for collecting renewable energies regionally and locally and also for converting them.

Decentralised structures
A solar plant is both a plant for collecting and for converting energy. This allows autonomous energy provision for buildings, housing estates, towns and regions. Either no work is necessary for energy distribution anymore or the channels are short. Instead of just a few external suppliers in the form of large energy companies, countless people become self-sufficient and there are many local or regional suppliers. This radically changes the ownership structure for energy plants. A seemingly irreversible monopolised concentration gives way to diverse decentralisation – brought about by the technology and sociology of renewable energies (Fig. A 2.3 and 4).
Those who think this is utopian should remember the development of information technologies. Up until the 1980s there were only mainframe computers in corresponding computer centres. The development of micro-technologies led to the introduction of radically decentralised and even individualised computers, which, however, need fixed networks and communication satellites. These are not absolutely necessary for the direct use of solar radiation for generating electricity and solar thermal energy for heating buildings. Solar houses and solar housing areas are no longer dependent on any commercial energy suppliers. They become solar thermal collectors both for electricity and heating requirements. After the costs for the necessary technology have been recouped, the energy used is free of charge. The more energy-efficiency you build in, the less expensive is the path to renewable energies.

The possibility of a complete energy changeover
By means of the natural potential of available technologies, which quantitatively outclass all traditional energy sources, and of the willingness to think creatively and practically, it can be argued plausibly that it is quite possible to replace traditional energies with renewable ones.

Example: electricity
According to the International Energy Agency, the annual commercial electricity consumption worldwide in 2001 was 15.5×10^{12} kWh. In order to produce this amount of electricity exclusively by wind power, 1.25 million wind power installations would need to be set up throughout the world – based on the use of 5 MW installations producing 12 million kWh per annum at average wind speeds. In order to produce the same amount of electricity using photovoltaic systems, based on a capacity of 75 kWh per m^2 of solar panels and per annum (which is a relatively low figure under German solar radiation conditions) – worldwide some 210 000 km^2 of solar cells would need to be installed. This is far less than the area covered by the built environment in the EU alone, where solar cells could be integrated in a variety of ways. For solar thermal collectors that would mean a collector area of 155 000 km^2 worldwide, based on a yield of 10 million kWh per hectare.

	nuclear energy	coal / gas petroleum	biomass	photovoltaic	wind power	small-scale hydropower	solar thermal power	large-scale hydropower/solar power stations	solar hydrogen (large-scale)	solar hydrogen (small-scale)
primary energy source	○	○	•	–	–	–	–	–	–	–
primary energy trade	○	○	•	–	–	–	–	–	–	–
energy processing	○	○	•	–	–	–	–	–	○	•
production of conversion technology	○	○	○	○	○	○	•	○	○	○
conversion in power stations	○	○	•	•	•	•	–	○	•	•
power transmission / secondary energy trade	○	○	•	•	•	•	–	○	○	•
financing of power stations	○	○	•	•	•	•	•	○	○	•

○ Concentration and monopolisation processes are preordained (except for cogeneration plants)..
• Concentration and monopolisation processes are technically and politically avoidable or impossible.
– not applicable

A 2.4

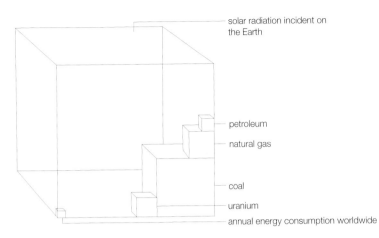

solar radiation incident on the Earth

petroleum

natural gas

coal

uranium

annual energy consumption worldwide

A 2.5

A 2.6

Example: heating
In order to satisfy the current thermal energy needs of the world's population using solar thermal power, based on the 2001 consumption level of 3.34 x 10^{12} kWh, 15 000 km^2 of solar collectors would be enough on the basis of only 225 kWh solar thermal yield per m^2 of collector area.

These calculations show only some of the options for renewable energies. The example for electricity clearly shows that each of these three options would be sufficient to cover worldwide requirements. Natural energy potential makes more extensive technical applications possible due to the fact that the sun, together with its derivatives wind, waves, water and biomass, supplies 15 000 times more energy per day than we are currently using in the form of atomic and fossil fuels (Fig. A 2.6). So there is neither a lack of energy potential nor any technical limitation. With the production volume required for plants we are looking at production capacities that have long been achieved in other sectors of industry. Here too, renewable energy can and will be used in the future.
So what is the basic stumbling block supposed to be? The calculations presented only serve to start people thinking. With every step towards a closer and more differential look at the natural and technical application potential, the practical attractiveness of renewable energies increases. The wide spectrum of possibilities presented here shows that, even with the growing energy needs in the developing countries, providing energy worldwide using only renewable energy sources is already feasible today. The ratios differ from country to country, region to region, community to community, house to house. Which combination is in fact implemented depends on many individual factors. These include the effects of saving energy to reduce requirements whilst simultaneously expanding the use of renewable energies. Another aspect is the varying geographic conditions and natural resources. Further factors include the extent of technological development, the degree of industrialisation and increasing costs, the receptiveness of companies

and, last but not least, political considerations and public awareness – social factors. The uniformity of the way the structures of energy providers and energy consumption based on fossil fuels have developed will be a thing of the past. Every country, every region will have a specific and at the same time diverse energy base. Providing the world with energy from renewable sources will be "multicultural". Of course many individual efforts will be necessary to bring about this vision, such as the German Renewable Energies Law (EEG). These requirements are, however, no more complex or costly than the development and production of satellite, aviation, communication, medical or weapons technology, and far less complex than nuclear technology. Claims that it is not possible to achieve full-scale energy provision using renewable energies is a discredit to the professionals such as physicists, chemists, engineers, architects, and their creative potential.

Opportunities for the building industry
The building sector with its many different trades could, together with agriculture, experience the greatest boom with the energy change if it took advantage of the opportunities offered by solar construction. Numerous new building materials and building methods – from glass, which provides both thermal insulation and electricity to energy-saving wooden constructions – could be used. In order to use free solar energy for heating and cooling optimally, every building must be adapted to suit the topography and the bioclimatic local conditions – each building being a solar design of its own.
Countless practical examples demonstrate that this is possible. Whether it be houses, including old buildings, prefabricated houses, schools, community buildings or offices, or even production plants, they can cover all their energy requirements – electricity and heating – autonomously with renewable energies and some of them, the so-called energy-plus houses, even produce surpluses. The majority of these property owners are average earners. Let us imagine more and more property owners rethinking in this way, and then in the end everybody else too, because it will have become a matter of

course socially. People could stop worrying about energy prices, the air in towns would be cleaner, and the number of sick people would fall. The towns would take on a different appearance, especially the roofs because instead of dull-looking roof tiles there would be crystal blue and other coloured solar panels. After all we are dealing here with a considerable part of the solution to the problem – the combined electricity, heating and cooling requirements in buildings.
Solar conversion for existing buildings and new solar buildings are "golden ground" for the building trades, architecture and the construction industry as a whole. The breakthrough in the construction industry will come with the number of commissions and the paradigm shift with architects.
More and more citizens will recognise the individual and social advantages of these developments and be guided by them. Since electricity, heating and cooling requirements in buildings account for about half of society's total energy needs, this new way of thinking is the most important factor of the energy change, of a fundamental change of system. This is unstoppable. The only remaining question is how long we will take before we achieve this readjustment? In view of the looming energy and environment crises there is no doubt at all that there is no time to waste. Readjusting is no longer a technological problem and if we get the calculations right it is not an economic problem either. It is a political and cultural one as the accelerating factors are politics and those society players who, within their own field of influence, decide for this energy change – both in their own and everyone else's interest.

Architecture and sustainability – a difficult relationship

Robert Kaltenbrunner

A 3.1

We probably do not think of Einstein first when sustainable architecture is mentioned. Yet his findings offer both an unusual and a necessary approach to this topic. Classical physics recognises the three core areas mechanics, electrodynamics and thermodynamics, which are still in existence today. However, since the mid-nineteenth century these three areas have slowly shifted in their interrelationship like continental plates. Albert Einstein's real achievement lies in the fact that he recognised what everyone else failed to see. He realised that, in the fault zones between the notional continents, problems occurred frequently at the boundaries, which the inhabitants of the separate continents only noticed marginally. It was only when they were considered from a non-specialist perspective that the extent of their explosiveness was revealed, which then led to the starting point of Einstein's scientific revolution.

"Crossing boundaries" like this is still necessary today. It is true that by now being environmentally aware has captured a firm place in society's canon of values and the obvious climate change is putting considerable pressure on politicians to act. But it still cannot be claimed that as a result all possible sectoral fields of action are totally trimmed for sustainability. There is still a yawning efficiency gap between what is economically expedient for business and what is necessary. It is high time that Aristotle's philosophy was applied to the construction sector, that living organisms should not be recognised by their appearance but by what they do and by their reactions to their environment.

Seen in this light, a different horizon quickly opens which goes over and beyond the individual building. One or two ecological measures here and there are not the same as ecological architecture; solar panels and passive use of the sun, greenhouses integrated into a house, green facades and thermal insulation are not far-reaching enough at all for real sustainable building. So far what we are seeing is more an optimising of – albeit important – isolated aspects rather than a total concept of sustainability-oriented planning principles. The current tendency is to concentrate on the individual building rather than on a whole housing project.

Sustainability just does not function like the automobile industry, which is forever proclaiming "state of the art" developments of all the systems.

Evaluation of the different approaches

Although clear criteria and, to some extent, measurable indicators for sustainability could be listed on the actual building level, the same can hardly be claimed from the point of view of urban planning and urban ecology. There is no indication here of a workable approach to defining and bringing about an optimum relationship between density, town size and environmental and life quality. The type or position of a building site alone can be crucial in changing the parameters for a sustainable construction project. For instance, individual economic location decisions taken by households and firms on moving nearer to the surrounding countryside lead to considerable uncovered subsequent costs or externalities – particularly in the areas of infrastructure, traffic, environment and urban planning. This involves social disadvantages, which so far have not been considered adequately in the balancing of the costs and benefits of suburbanisation (individually and from an overall economic point of view).

In this respect, the balance relating to the building process depends very much on the beholder's point of view, in fact it is a question of your view of the world. On the one hand, pressure from the constraints of circumstances is obviously juxtaposed to the crucial broad effects of sustainable building, and sometimes, as a result, quality standards that have already been achieved – particularly where the financing is private – tend to be cut back rather than used to set a general minimum standard. On the other hand, for special building projects, namely when paid for by the authorities – whether it be the Federal Office of the Environment in Dessau or Norman Foster's Commerzbank Tower in Frankfurt – a lot of emphasis is placed on "ecological correctness", if only for reasons of forward-looking marketing activities (Fig. A 3.2). This leaves an interpretative gap. Some people sing the hymn of success; sustainability is now a recognised objective in construction. Others complain that we are standing

A 3.1 Photovoltaic system in the roof surface, workshop building, Dresden (D) 2003, Haller Morgenstern Quincke
A 3.2 Federal Office for the Environment, Dessau (D) 2005, Sauerbruch Hutton

still or have even fallen back, believing that, technically, everything is feasible and controllable so that consequently the complexity of the task is not adequately taken into account. For the time being this ambivalence can hardly be resolved. Meanwhile, it is less a question of passing judgement than of drawing attention to some aspects that have perhaps been ignored so far.

Sustainable, ecological, conserving resources, environmentally friendly, biological or energy saving, no matter which heading we choose, building in such a way claims to be decentralised, integrated and self-sufficient. All these concepts have one thing in common, however – they all originated in the 1960s when the established system came under fire, above all from criticism by young people. So they stem from a social movement, not just from technical innovation. Freimut Duve once expressed on their behalf how far this belief went: "The centralistic large technological systems – traffic, utilities and television – are levelling off the historical cities. Ecological building, the quest for the lost human dimension in the city could give it back its face and singularity" [1]. An ambitious claim, then, which up until now, on its path to daily reality, has not always been fortunate.

In the discussions held here in Germany, sustainability – especially when innovation or high technology are concerned – seems like a truncated lady, cut off from cultural and social catalysts, without which not even the aseptically thought-out scientific discoveries would be conceivable, let alone their use in society [2]. Photovoltaic, passive-energy building standards, heat recovery – scientific, technical attempts alone are not enough, as the experts themselves complain from time to time: "The way civil engineers think is predominantly technical and rational and not geared enough to the complexity of human behaviour. The civil engineer lacks socio-political starting points and strategies to achieve his goals" [3]. But architects are also insufficiently prepared, as current architecture teaching demonstrates. It is either dominated by the primacy of the design or by a certain subcomplexity in which purely partial aspects are in the foreground.

Social cultural acceptance
The frequent reduction of sustainability to innovation, science and technology fails to recognise the extraordinary significance of conceptual inspirers, whose visionary work consisted of designing an overall view. This overall view suddenly put the countless individual findings from scientific and technological research into a different context. Richard Buckminster Fuller, who made history with his dictum "think global – act local", coined the expression "cosmic conceptioning" more than six decades ago. What is meant by that is the ability not only to recognise complex relationships for supporting and nurturing the basis of our livelihood, but also to have them take effect in thinking and in action. This involves precise modelling work on event patterns, their changes and transformations. Before the energy crisis, environmental damage and the global destruction of the ecosystem were ever heard of, Fuller was already working anticipatorily on concepts to solve these future problems. "The source of all powers", he diagnosed, "which man needs for operating all of his instruments – animate and inanimate – is the sun. … Designing dwellings on a scientific basis is closer to the stars than to the Earth." [4]

Buckminster Fuller's work had "How to make the world work" as a motto – as if somewhere in the wilderness he had been sent a box full of machine parts, whole ones and broken ones, which, together with the operating manual and improvisation, he has to assemble to make a functioning whole. The information from the parts for their functioning as a whole becomes the starting point for Fuller's "systems approach". The solution strategy begins with the integration of the individual functions. He sees the Earth as an integrally constructed machine that should be understood and used for the purpose of lasting performance capability as a whole. When Fuller calls his writing "Operating Manual" then he is particularly trying to point out its absence; mankind lives on Earth without having been given an operating manual for using the Earth correctly. Compared with the never ceasing accurateness with which all the details of "Spaceship Earth" have been defined *ab ovo*, it would seem that the operating manual has been deliberately and systematically excluded. This conscious exclusion does in fact have a positive effect. It forces us to "use our intellect, which is our highest ability and with which we can carry out our scientific experiments, and interpret the results of those experiments effectively. For the very reason that so far there has been no operating manual, we learn to anticipate which consequences would result from a growing number of alternatives to prolong our survival and growth satisfactorily – physically and metaphysically" [5]. It therefore follows that sustainable development and sustainable building only exist as a synthesis of technological engineering-type activity and socio-political value-based and value-oriented "demands".

In this canon of demands things such as mobility are not given enough consideration, although the history of the modern era is also the history of modern mobility. Building for the society of the future means accepting and shaping the interaction between mobility and modern times. To illustrate this briefly, let us consider Frank Lloyd Wright, who was one of the first to display this close relationship with his "Broadacre City"; and the uncompromising radicalism with which space is made for cars in Le Corbusier's "Ville Contemporaine" or "Plan Voisin" is still unparalleled. Yet within the European framework the arranged and open and later car-friendly town

A 3.2

A 3.3

A 3.4

A 3.3 Piazza XXIV Maggio, new layout, Cormons (I)
        1990, Boris Podrecca
A 3.4 Mature settlements, old quarter, Prague (CZ)
A 3.5 Passive energy houses, Salzburg (A) 2006,
        sps-architects

signalled what was to become the motive for future development; the car was advancing to become the *spiritus rector* of urban planning, and played a catalyst role where urban concepts became split and proved explosive for historical town structures. Where the 19th century, with its administrative buildings and educational institutions, only invaded existing areas insularly and even the Second World War could do nothing to upset the centuries-old pattern of parcelling out the land, such limits were literally run over by the dictates of the new urban planning paradigms. In the 1960s the connection between automobile and spatial structure as an urban reference value was ever-present. The forthcoming "liquefying" of space as a consequence of automobiles was rated a positive development and was encouraged through the extensive expansion of motorways and roads – thus began an upward spiralling correlation of available infrastructure and the degree of motorisation. Over recent years spatial proximity and the immediate neighbourhood have become less and less important while distance has now become predominantly a time category. And therein lies the dilemma; if mobility is the basis of social exchange processes and threatens, in practice, to be choking with traffic, then it is not just a nuisance but also something affecting the very substance.

What is meant by "more quality of life"?
The paradigm change in our society – away from one-sided economic growth and towards more quality of life – also plays a role that should not be underestimated, but not only a positive one. Together with this "more quality of life" the idea is expressed, for example, that families and households have a higher "desire for a place to live in" than they used to. Our society talks about sustainability and is using up more and more land. According to the Federal Statistics Office, in 2005 living space per head was 42 m² throughout the Germany. This subject very quickly brings us into the area of political and cultural values in our society, including private property, seclusion and our own private sphere. These values are inextricably linked with the hope for individual autonomy. Every attempt to stop the trend towards smaller

and smaller households and larger and larger living spaces or to put the brakes on using space for housing estates is therefore fighting not only against the ruthless exploitation of the countryside, pleasure-seeking consumerism and isolation in the cities, but also against the historic attainment of individual independence. An increasing need for living space poses a real concern and this requires a productive discussion of the term "sustainable building", i.e. systematically asking whether it could be that many people also have good reasons for wanting to hold on to their "harmful" way of living, those being their hopes for individual autonomy, for being spared toil and trouble. Only when we succeed in formulating a new identity-giving picture of building and living, where striving for a pleasant life is reconcilable with the limitations of life's natural fundamentals, can the ecologically essential be politically feasible and meet with the approval of the majority. This in turn implies two things. The first of these is the question of whether needs are affected in a non-state-controlled way. It is received wisdom in a market economy that supply determines demand and this seems to have become second nature in our society. It is hardly questioned anymore, as if demand was something fixed rather than the result of wishes, or needs, which are (can be) awakened again [6]. On the other hand, the question arises of whether the developments in the structure of housing estates in recent years really are sustainable. This has been denied with good arguments but altogether the developments reveal a necessary change in the function and meaning of a town in the 21st century by following neither dynamic nor normative laws. Urban planning has a difficult position per se since it demands that citizens, architects and politicians have a new awareness for what already exists, for sustainable, resource-conserving building, more preservation of historical monuments and less prosperity. Historical building stock, like the land, counts as one of the environmental resources that cannot be reproduced and certainly not repeated. What does the careful and gentle treatment of buildings already in existence signify other than a sustainable strategy that supposes adaptability and reusability as a principle and gives old

buildings a second chance? Despite all the progress already made on new buildings, we should not lose sight of the fact that the greatest ecological potential is to be found in upgrading what has already been built. A "clever" use of resources must lay the foundations for a paradigm change in architecture and urban planning, which is supported by society, away from the market economy-oriented, fast-moving lifecycle and over to a new appreciation of durability.
If one of the fundamental principles of sustainability is thinking in cross-linked interdependences, these interdependences, figuratively speaking, go beyond the borders of the grass verge and also include almost all our social, economic and political assessments. Sooner or later, sustainable building too will no longer be misunderstood as a non-binding lifestyle option with a private view of the world thrown in – and a fat wallet [7]. The approaches so far represent a first step, but are still not a solution. For years modern architecture dismissed ecological aspects, climate issues and the cost of heating as solvable problems and therefore attached negligible importance to them, but now better information and insulation in buildings are no longer an alternative but a must. Unquestionably, much has been achieved here, over and above "green glamour" as the expression of salving an individual's conscience. Architecture claiming to create something integrated, interconnected, environmentally aware would in the final analysis remain nothing but "indifferent technology, no matter whether hard or gentle, so long as subjective, semantic energies fail to complete the technical construction frame to form a picture of a different life" [8]. Planting trees, condensing boilers, solar panels, recyclable construction materials and comparisons of energy costs do not suffice. It is quite definitely more a question of willingness, awareness development and mental change. Architects and property developers, residents and business people have failed to ask themselves this question with the necessary intensity [9]. You need not be a follower of fatalism in the philosophy of history to foresee that this topic has not yet reached its full explosive potential.

Lack of sensivity is a problem

To be fair, it has to be admitted that rational, scientifically based findings on how sustainable construction should be structured are already available. Transferring these findings to the construction industry scarcely happens. Neither universities nor experts in the media seem very committed to this subject. A question seldom broached in public, yet nevertheless of immense importance, concerns form and appearance because they are fundamental. What does the architecture of sustainable building look like? Different relevant tendencies can be mentioned here. The most striking thing is that neither architects nor the media are particularly enthusiastic about it. This basic attitude speaks for itself, as for instance Peter Eisenman once said: "To talk to me about sustainability is like talking to me about giving birth. Am I against giving birth? No. But would I like to spend my time doing it? Not really. I'd rather go to a baseball game". [10] Sustainability seems to be a touchy subject for intellectuals or artistic people and "ecological architecture" a label that puts a lot of people off. This is probably attributable to the fact that early ecological architecture was associated with certain living arrangements and lifestyles (e.g. dropout forms, rural communes), which were contradictory to conventional forms. Perhaps what is being cultivated here is subconsciously, yet nonetheless perceptibly, the apparent opposite of sustainability and design.

In the search for a visual, aesthetic identity for ecological architecture, few concepts, basic rules, norms etc. have been very helpful so far. Including environment energies sensibly, directly or indirectly, when planning a building is bound to have an effect on the form of that building. The first signs are there that contemporary "architectural language" is picking up the notion of sustainable construction. We only have to look at the concept of "Natural Constructions" [11], at Munich architect Thomas Herzog with his intelligent and refreshing construction concepts. Yet this form of transferring ideas cannot really be regarded as groundbreaking, and there are no signs of this changing – and again the media are in no way blameless here. Despite all lip service to the contrary, sustainability has a hard time with them – considering the sensation-seeking market and effective selection mechanisms. You only need to point out that in our times definitions of what quality means are subjective, that tastes, to all intents and purposes, are lacking in objectivity. On the other hand, this freedom of subjectivity does not really make us happy; we want others to share our points of view. As a rule this usually means listening to those people to whom many others are listening. Tastes tend to undergo a certain homogenisation and conventionalisation. This is where the media come into their own. They channel public discussion determining what quality is. What is worth talking about in the media counts as architecture. As a conse-

quence, publishing has taken over the role of establishing a basic consensus when discussing arguments. And since sustainability is very complex and not very striking, other areas continue to dominate.

With sustainable construction, apart from anything else, the architects' self-image is on trial. Günter Moewes, for one, is of the opinion that much of what passes as "ecological construction" is only trying to give the impression of being environmentally compatible. "True ecological building resembles the 'conventional' building of the early 20th century more than today's decision-forming architecture claims as ecological". For example, Karljosef Schattner's conversions in Eichstätt or Otto Steidle's housing construction were "admittedly more ecological than many detached, short-lived 'green' wooden cottages in so-called ecological construction" [12]. A keyword for such an assessment is entropy. This term comes from physics and is based on the second law of thermodynamics. According to this law, in a closed system all processes flow in one direction only, from higher states to lower states. Entropy is the degree of this increasing mixing and diffusion; it is therefore a condition and not a process. The Earth too represents a more or less closed system since the only significant quantity entering is by incident solar radiation. Target energy can therefore only be achieved by a simultaneous increase in entropy in a different

A 3.5

A 3.6

place, as the example of the steam engine shows, whose power can only be produced by an unequally higher production of useless wasted heat. As our whole way of working functions like that – and only like that –, we are obviously faced with a serious problem caused, as it were, by the laws of nature. Instead of changing course now, architecture is just hastening things along. "This very craving for novelty, born of the mechanisms of public relations, leads into entropy, into the same mush everywhere from something different here and there. If everyone's on this individualist trip, then individuality is lost. Always the same mixture of extreme unique specimens – this would be the pinnacle of urban planning entropy [13].

The necessity of down-to-earth examples

We do not need such exceptionally eco-avantgarde projects to anchor the subject of sustainable building more firmly with the general public and in "normal" building – there are plenty of those already. Instead, practical examples should be demonstrated, the use of cost-effective, down-to-earth, already tried-and-tested technologies for the everyday lives of many should be proven and shown [14]. The so-called energy-saving houses at Lützowufer in Berlin were a type of experimental setup [15]. A further reference project is "Solar City" in Linz. We can draw fundamental experience from both projects. Assuming that architecture is supposed to "speak" to the beholder, the "ecological" part of the houses provided with this very attribute is not particularly eloquent. They stick within conventional frameworks, are "architecture parlante", only in as far as they work with well-known and well-recognised pictures of living spaces, if need be accentuated by a solar thermal collector as a special feature. This actually turns out to be an advantage. They clearly show that there is no "eco" style, not even an "energy-saving" one. Such buildings do not require any uniform aesthetics and no generally binding rules except that of behaving in a sensible way, which does not destroy (at least does not pollute) the environment. In this respect the popular contradiction between form and environmental claims is only a virtual one.

A central problem exists in the ratio of investment costs to operating costs, or in the fact that savings are only possible as a result of higher investments and building costs to start with. Property developers, buyers and the public authorities find it difficult to accept this. Amongst property owners who do not live in the property, and that usually is the case, there is very little enthusiasm to take action to tackle the running costs – electricity, water, heating. This part of the overheads will be passed on to the future tenants, who, on the other hand, are not involved in the primary discussions. Too little heed is paid to the fact that ecological effects become most apparent the more savings effects can be measured in euros and cents.

Many well-meant and innovative suggestions on the part of the architects obviously fail to recognise deep-seated habits. Here is an example. The concept of thermal zoning – warmer retreat areas at the centre of the house and sun lounges and other similar glass extensions on the south side of the building – presupposes adequate continuous use. If, due to lack of rooms,

the unheated sun lounge is used as a bedroom, it is clear that traditional values such as cosiness and comfort will, *de facto*, clash with energy concerns. In buildings with good thermal insulation, the user's behaviour has a decisive influence on energy consumption. Lack of knowledge, carelessness or technical ineptitude all have repercussions. If this is not continually borne in mind, or if it is too hard to regulate, the finest measures are of little use. Those who claim to build in a way that is in tune with the environment and its resources are not permitted to insist on closed, highly complicated technical systems where people would need a degree in engineering to be able to regulate this technology. Schumacher's axiom "small is beautiful" provides a guideline – less in the ideological sense than in the tendency to develop user-oriented (ergo: small) technologies that can be managed by the individual rather than large-scale technologies. If everybody took this requirement seriously and worked out a scheme accordingly, it would no longer only mean specialised division of labour for the working per-

A 3.7

A 3.8

son, but in fact more a changed view of people altogether. To do this it would perhaps be helpful to emphasize the enjoyable aspects rather than seeing it as a sacrifice where there is still always regimentation [16].

The nature of architecture is becoming less and less determined by its physical form. Materials are available in abundance, irrespective of local or regional conditions, and the same applies to the technology we can select. Admittedly, architecture claiming to be sustainable cannot just limit itself to technical or innovative building products. Recent history shows that, where sustainability is concerned, success is Janus-faced. This success provided the politicians with respectable arguments for their soothing tactics in the face of warnings about environmental catastrophes, without having to question the system at all. While technical solutions and product innovations were expanding to become a new business sector, they became part of the growth ideology from which the ecological movement was trying to escape with a counter-model, the reprocessing industry. Nevertheless, architecture, as a spatial system, is still responsible for the way things are arranged within society. It must, however, bear this responsibility in a new and far more complex way than before.

References:
[1] Duve, Freimut: Editorial. In: Schwarz, Ullrich (ed.): Grünes Bauen. Ansätze einer Öko-Architektur (Series: Technologie und Politik). Reinbek 1982, p. 6
[2] Indirectly, this touches on a core problem of the ecology movement: The notion of the unending natural cycle and its laws, to which people should humbly conform, can serve at best only to explain an ecological authoritarianism, the danger of which being that it would never find any limits itself anywhere. The notion of natural balanced conditions, out of which practical norms can be deduced, has something relieving about it in the face of conflicts of interest and society's political disputes. This probably explains its attraction.
[3] Scheelhaase, Klaus: Ist der Bauingenieur fit für die Zukunft? In: Deutsches Ingenieurblatt, Nr. 7/8 1999, p. 48
[4] Buckminster Fuller, Richard: Nine Chains to the Moon. Philadelphia, 1938, p. 67
[5] Buckminster Fuller, Richard: Einflüsse auf meine Arbeit. In: Bedienungsanleitung für das Raumschiff Erde und andere Schriften. Reinbek 1973, p. 32f. and p. 103
[6] In the system of the relationship between man and environment, both poles are the product of human history, i.e. variable in principle, and the possibilities this opens up can only be judged by standards that follow a desired rather than a natural way of life.
[7] cf. the section "Öko-Architektur – nur was für Reiche?" In: Beyel, Wolfgang; Nelles, Wilfried (ed.): Wirksame Energienutzung bei der Stadterneuerung – eine soziale und ökologische Notwendigkeit. ARCH+ 51/52. Aachen, 1980
[8] Schwarz, Ullrich: Ökologisches Bauen – Schritte aus dem grünen Schattenreich. In: Schwarz, Ullrich (ed.):Grünes Bauen. Ansätze einer Öko-Architektur (Series: Technologie und Politik). Reinbek, 1982, p. 7
[9] It is not only the needs of nature and caring for resources etc. that determine the direction and type of changes necessary. It is political objectives and cultural norms instead that decide how an ecologically responsible way of life should look.
[10] Hawthorne, Christopher: The Case for a Green Aesthetic? In: Metropolis. Oct. 2002, p. 113
[11] Applying the diverse building principles found in nature, whether they be diatoms or soap bubble film, to architectural loadbearing structures refers to the fundamental idea of "Nature as the master builder" or "Instructor". Today, a lot of work is carried out on developing this approach – in the area of bionics for dynamic-evolutionary adaptation processes as an indication of the potential of changes in nature.
[12] Moewes, Günther: Weder Hütten noch Paläste. Architektur und Ökologie in der Arbeitsgesellschaft – Eine Streitschrift. Basel / Berlin / Boston, 1995, p. 204
[13] ibid, p.167f.
[14] The real model of an ecologically sensible way of building and living was already put into practice in Berkeley in the 1970s (ct. Farallones Institute): The Integral Urban House. Self-Reliant Living in the City. San Francisco ,1979). Building should almost outpace itself here in affecting life; but whether and to what extent this pioneer project is still valid today is not clear.
[15] These were built within the framework of the IBA (International Building Exhibition) at the beginning of the 1980s. The urban planners' brief was "Restoration of the urban space on the south bank of the canal using a wall made of tightly grouped individual items". This gave rise to five cubes of about 15 × 15 m, whose energetic nonsense is highlighted still further by their joint pedestal – required to fulfil building regulations on account of ineduquate clearance from the boundary.
[16] Behne, Adolf: Der praktische Zweck mache das Haus zum Werkzeug, der Spieltrieb des Gestaltens zum Spielzeug. In: Der moderne Zweckbau Bauwelt Fundamente, vol. 10. Frankfurt a.M. / Berlin 1964, p. 11

Doing things right – on efficiency and sustainability

Manfred Hegger

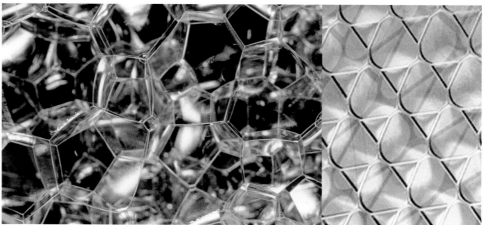

Research and development, new tools, innovative products and global economic development show us time and time again that our living conditions have been rapidly improving, especially since the beginning of industrialisation. Progress seems unstoppable. Mankind is clearly more and more successful in satisfying its basic needs. To do this they develop suitable technologies and appliances, networks and synergies. Nikolai Kondratiev's theory of the "grand supercycles" in social and economic development says that, since the beginning of industrialisation, in cycles lasting about 50 years we have succeeded in covering basic needs, and that this was always achieved by groundbreaking innovations. (Fig. A 4.4) [1, 2]. So far, in four long waves since the end of the 18th century, it has become possible to make work easier (1793–1847), to make resources available (1847–1893), to shape towns so they are worth living in (1893–1939) and also to foster individuality and mobility (1939–1989). Whereas at the beginning of every cycle it seemed as if the problems in question were unsolvable, by the end, generally speaking, it was possible to achieve ambitious aims, at least in the developed part of the world. That was the good news.

It is also correct, however, that a large part of the world hardly shares in these successes. In addition, solving a key problem usually causes several new ones. Inevitably, some of these become the problem to be solved in the next long development phase. Others are just left unsolved and are seen as unavoidable negative side issues. This is especially evident in the environmental damage resulting from industrial development and the depletion of natural resources.

What are the reasons for this? Is it enough to blame it on people's incapability to take a far-sighted view of things? Is the basic tenet of ecology – everything is connected to everything – too hard for our thoughts? Do we like always making new work for ourselves? Every one of these explanations is justified, but does not offer us any relief. In fact the "collateral damage" of our previous successful actions is now endangering our basic living conditions. We are aware of this. It is not in vain that Kon-

dratiev's theory, extended by a long wave, assumes that the fifth cycle, in whose boom phase our social and economic development obviously currently find themselves, does not see providing further material goods as a fundamental need, but rather the solving of the problems of the environment. Accordingly, tangible goods are shaping our future less than intangible achievements, such as knowledge networks. This development already seems to have progressed so far that we are faced with a shortage of transforming or of taking action rather than with a lack of knowledge.

Doing the right things or doing things right?

Our actions are mostly marked by an unconditional striving for success. Seen superficially, nothing can be said against this. Ultimately, we are trying to achieve a defined objective as perfectly as possible. But it depends how we achieve it. Here are some definitions of effectiveness and efficiency:

A course of action is effective if it achieves its stated objective, no matter how much effort is required for us to achieve this goal [3]. Being effective therefore means doing the right things without sparing any expense.

Efficient, on the other hand, is a way of behaving that leads to achieving the goal and at the same time keeping effort to a minimum. ISO 9000 defines efficiency as "the relationship between the result obtained and the means used" [4]. With efficiency it is not just a question of doing the right things, but of doing things right.

Economic and ecological considerations are increasingly questioning the principle of effectiveness, because this principle assumes that we have more or less unlimited resources at our disposal. Unfortunately, however, our society is largely dependent on non-renewable resources. And these are gradually becoming scarce. Our ability to obtain and burn oil and gas, to produce plastics and metals, and to create wealth, exceeds the supplies of limited natural resources. This in turn leads to shortages and high prices. Using non-renewable energies is changing our climate and the weather.

A 4.1 Efficient shell: soap bubbles – roof structure
A 4.2 Synergies from environmental protection and the economy
A 4.3 Efficient surface: butterfly wings – scaly metal facade
A 4.4 The grand supercycles of social and economic development according to Nikolai Kondratiev

Reduction in environmental damage	Reduction in costs
minimising energy consumption	lowering costs in the workplace
minimising use of materials	lowering costs in building and in the workplace
minimising toxic emissions	lower taxes, lower follow-up costs
	low liability risk
minimising waste and scrap	lowering costs on the building site
closing material cycles	long-term cost security
	long-term strategic competitive advantages
increasing the use of renewable resources	cost reductions in building and the workplace

A 4.2

A 4.3

The first logical steps have been taken since the first energy crisis in the 1970s and the recognition of the limits to growth. They affect our daily lives and are noticeable at first hand – deposits on bottles and the obligation to take the bottles back, refuse separation or meters to calculate energy costs. They also affect the economy – in the increasing use of renewable resources and superior recycling products, in new power station technologies and systems for using renewable energies.

Efficient thinking is replacing effectiveness more and more. This is particularly relevant where resources are scarce and the pressure of global competition dominates. This trend is especially visible with intangible products, which are influencing our lives more and more – databanks, multimedia, security and environmental technologies, or hardware for information systems. The efficiency potential is astounding; we only have to think of the longstanding so-called half-life period of computers, in which every 18 months computer capacity and memory capacity double. The use of materials and energy has attained a high degree of efficiency and it looks as if this can still be topped.

Many people in the building industry argue vehemently that similar efficiency leaps cannot be achieved there. The measures already taken to reduce the use of energy prove that those arguments are clearly unfounded. A house built before 1970 uses on average about 25–30 l of heating oil per m^2 floor space per year. If the current legal regulations on energy saving in Germany (EnEV) are applied, a new house is only allowed to use a maximum of 6–7 l of heating oil per m^2 floor space per year. Other countries have similar rules. The 4- and 6-litre houses are state of the art, and in Germany, if public grants are used, can be constructed at no extra cost. Over the past 10 years the 1.5-litre house, the so-called passive-energy house, has been built thousands of times. Compared with building the 6-litre house the costs were about 5% higher. Viewed as a whole this means that within fewer than 30 years development has led to a 20-fold increase in efficiency. At the same time there have been clearly reduced emissions and considerably improved climatic comfort.

Economy and Ecology

Efficiency is a primary economic category. Yet, as the examples mentioned have clearly shown, increasing efficiency and lowering costs often go hand in hand with less environmental damage. Fewer and fewer natural resources are being used up; less waste is produced, the air and the atmosphere are less polluted. In many areas the objectives of economy and ecology match up (Fig. A 4.2). Apart from this, there are benefits both for society and for the individual. They contribute to a change of values in society and to a model for sustainable development.

Today's wealth makes it possible to invest in efficient and environmentally friendly technologies. The early period of industrialisation was characterised by heavy industry and chimneys – resource-wasting. Today, the developed countries are rich and powerful, environmental damage is becoming noticeably less. This is also shown in Simon Kuznet's environment diagram. It can be seen that society's development is going from poor and dirty, then from wealthy and dirty, to wealthy and clean (Fig. A 4.6). Economic prosperity therefore leads to

Kondratiev cycles:	1st cycle	2nd cycle	3rd cycle	4th cycle	5th cycle
	steam engine, cotton	railways, shipping, steel	electricity, chemistry	mobility, petroleum, electronics	information technology, ecology
			analysis		projection
peak in development	1825	1873	1913	1966	2015 ?
fundamental needs	making work easier	making resources available worldwide	making urban life worthwhile	fostering individuality and mobility	solving problems for our contemporaries
comprehensive networks	trade networks	transportation networks	energy networks	communication networks	knowledge networks
groundbreaking applications	machines	locomotives, railway stations	lighting, cinema	telephone, car, television, data processing, missiles	intangible goods, information equipment and databases
groundbreaking technologies	steam	steel	electricity	electronics	multimedia
synergy applications	consumer goods	shipping	chemistry, aluminium	petroleum products	ecological problem solutions, traffic systems
technology applications	mechanics	large drives	large-scale plants	weapons systems	security and environment technologies
The grand supercycles of social and economic development					

A 4.4

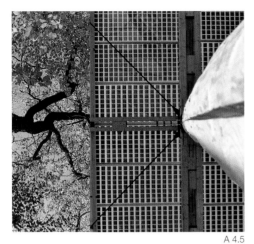

A 4.5

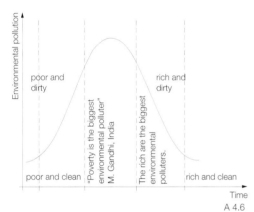

Time

A 4.6

A 4.5 Efficient loadbearing structure: tree – tree column
A 4.6 Environmental chart by Simon Kuznets
A 4.7 International comparison of office space per
      employee

Country	Average office space per employee in m²
Germany	30
Denmark	20
Italy	20
Netherlands	20
Switzerland	20
Sweden	18
France	17
Slovakia	15
Spain	15
UK	14
Poland	14
Russia	14
Belgium	12
Greece	12
Ireland	12
Austria	12
Hungary	12
Bulgaria	10
Estonia	10

A 4.7

an environmentally friendly structure change. It is understandable that it is the newly industrialised countries that are trying to copy this model. That is why they are building their own heavy industry and their own chimneys. But the model that produced our wealth is not reproducible. The once seemingly inexhaustible sources of raw materials are becoming scarce. The peak oil point seems to have been reached. The experts are only still debating whether oil will be depleted in 20 or in 50 years. The picture does not look much brighter for other resources, e.g. precious metals. We are coming up against limits with a lot of natural systems. The overhasty exploiting of resources is causing a noticeable change in climate, which is endangering the basis of our way of living. The ultimate limit will not necessarily be the scarcity of resources but the time still remaining for the Earth's climate system to be able to stabilise.

There are ways out and new models based on vastly increasing resource efficiency. At the Wuppertal Institute, for instance, they assume that by the middle of the century the same value can be created with only one-tenth of today's use of energy and resources, ultimately, worldwide, a tenfold "dematerialisation". This is an enormous challenge. Yet the scarcer, and thus dearer, raw materials become, the more it will be worth producing energy- and resource-efficient products, i.e. avoiding consumption and waste, closing material cycles, using renewable energies and raw materials and finally achieving a service-oriented economy. A third Industrial Revolution seems possible. Here too, as is so often the case, risks and opportunities are so close together.

And building?
Environmental and efficiency considerations have scarcely penetrated our building production and the buildings we already have. On the one hand it is hardly surprising. If building means ensuring the creation and preseration of our material environment, striving for "dematerialisation" seems at first glance to be out of place. Materials to ensure daily survival just cannot be replaced by immaterial services or even information.
On the other hand, architecture and building cannot remain aloof from a social development regarded as urgent. The example of energy saving shows that new requirements need not necessarily sound the death knell for architecture, as was still feared in the 1980s, but being able to promote energy-saving building forms and technologies. Another reason why it is not possible to remain apart from general developments is that building represents a considerable section of the economy. Almost 50% of the total invested capital in developed countries is tied up in the housing sector alone, approximately 70% in existing buildings.
Moreover, if you then consider the building industry's claims on resources, the pressure to act becomes even clearer:

• The building industry uses about 50% of all the raw materials processed in the world.
• In Germany, the building sector produces more than 60% of the total waste.
• Operating buildings in Germany requires approximately 50% of total energy use.

Building is an activity with long-lasting repercussions. Planning decisions that we have just taken move considerable resources. With the current usual lifetime of buildings, a building erected today will probably still be in use at the end of the oil and gas age. How can architecture and technology prepare for this?

Fields of action
The long timescales can preserve building from short-lived trends and fashions. At the same time, in times of fundamental changes, they put a lot of responsibility on architecture and technical services in order to guarantee usefulness, safety and comfort permanently. New objectives are necessary; the fields of action are diverse.

Energy
The level of technology we have reached allows high energy efficiency in building. Buildings fit for the future will exploit all the possibilities of energy efficiency – from the choice of site, shape and alignment of the building, choice of material and insulation, technical equipment and many other parameters. Maybe this will not be enough in a time when we are running out of fossil energy sources. We can suppose that in future two sectional markets will appear, buildings that are still reliant on fossil energy sources and those which make themselves completely independent. The possibilities for using site-specific, inexhaustible, renewable energy sources in building are diverse. Geothermal power via ground couplings and drilled wells, wind power via rotors on or in the building, solar energy through activation of the building envelope, and much more besides. Drawing on these energy sources today generally requires higher investment. But the cost of running them offers an advantage that should not be underestimated – the energy sources will remain safe and free of charge on a long-term basis.

Building materials and forms of construction
The use of materials for a building can be reduced considerably as a means of resource efficiency. One cubic metre gross volume of a house still weighs about 600 kg on average; a normal detached house with a volume of 500 m³ correspondingly ties up approximately 300 t of building materials. The possibilities to use materials efficiently and to integrate building materials in closed cycles are only being applied sporadically. Yet legal rulings are already in the planning stage. The federal government and the EU with their "sustainability strategy" and the "Construction Products Directive" (CPD) will formulate their requirements and, probably from 2010 onwards, demand proof of the environmental impact of building materials in accord-

ance with the life cycle assessments (LCA). It will be even more exciting to undertake creative steps to develop lighter architecture, not only architecture that seems lighter, and to be consistent in using reusable and renewable raw materials again and again. Using less materials increases the chance of being able to use high-quality building materials and thus reduces the danger of using substances that are damaging for homes or the environment.

Life cycle
Considering the normally long life of a building, it follows that durable and low-maintenance components should be used. Repairs, technical upgrades, and improving the form are, however, unavoidable turning points in the life cycle of a building. Components and materials for repairs and replacement should preferably be separable without destroying them, and reusable if reinstalled or removed. As already happens with appliances or in the automotive sector, there should be a comprehensive obligation in the building sector to take back building elements. An integral consideration of building costs and running costs, so-called life cycle costing (LCC), makes a considerable contribution with its holistic approach to improving the quality of building and processes and also to efficiency in building.

Adaptability
Before starting to build, a needs-analysis and a utilisation concept have to be worked out. Architects are often faced with integral layouts that are neither suitable for the future nor economical. Office buildings, for example, are usually arranged in a cellular way, highly differential and not very flexible. This type of space is very difficult to rent out nowadays because they are structured in such a small-format, inflexible way. The office space requirement per person in Germany is on average approximately 30 m², in other European countries it is below 20 m² (Fig. A 4.7) [5]. The basic spatial structure hinders not only communication and productivity, but also the adaptability and flexibility from a construction point of view to make it possible to continue using the building even if needs have changed. People often overlook the fact that the key to a building that combines high architectural quality with cost-effectiveness and environmental friendliness lies in the early planning phases. In order to achieve this, differentiated and carefully developed product specifications for buildings are required. These should include the organisation and foreseeable changes in the catalogue of requirements and go beyond generalisations and, ultimately, non-committal wishes.

Location and plot
The choice of location for building and redevelopment measures constitutes an increasingly important key factor for environmental friendliness and cost-effectiveness. More than half of the world's population already lives in towns and

cities. Living in towns and cities is ecological and environmentally friendly because density is efficient. The necessary technical infrastructure can only be guaranteed in the long run in densely populated areas. Access to all facilities is improved by nearness and a variety of commercial, social and cultural offers are then possible. Local public transport is only economically attractive in densely populated areas. The volume of traffic movement is reduced. It is imperative to ensure continuing density and thus avoid a downward spiral, particularly in regions with shrinking populations.

Individual and social advantages
The fields of action described can only give an indication of where action must be taken. The argumentation on the basis of primarily economic grounds is intended to show how closely interwoven with each other the areas of environment and economy have become. These fields of action also show that with ecological and economic advantages, the individual and social benefits increase too. Buildings and services improved from the point of view of sustainability also increase our quality of life, comfort and often our safety and security too. For example, an energy-saving building envelope offers not only thermal insulation in summer and winter, but also adds to users' wellbeing. Intelligent dimensioning and positioning of windows guarantee good daylight conditions and avoid overheating whilst saving energy and costs at the same time. The careful choice of materials that are safe from the health point of view and also environmentally friendly plays an important role in avoiding discomfort and "sick building syndrome", and avoids the need for the expenditure linked with premature disposal. The healthy and pleasant quality of the air in rooms presupposes good ventilation practices, which in turn are energy-saving and require robust, simple technology. Adaptable structures without barriers to communication guarantee high quality and long-lasting use. Density and varied possibilities of use create sustainable towns and buildings, and also facilitate both social contacts and individuality. In all of these aspects, economic criteria, environmental qualities and social effects go hand in hand.

Outlook
Because we are running up against the limits of many natural systems, the problems seem to be gaining the upper hand. Nine billion people want to be able to live well on our planet in the year 2050. Architecture is providing important requirements for this. Sustainable technologies are available. Improving the social conditions of the broad population on our planet seems feasible. We have the necessary money and sustainability is visibly paying off. The task is no less than reshaping the material basis of our civilisation.
The greatest barriers are in our minds – we still cannot imagine a sustainable future or sustain-

able building for the future. On a planet with enormous poverty, a lack of imagination is the greatest poverty of all. We must not become used to this poverty. Architects and engineers have the best chance to develop and envisage the building blocks for a better sustainable future and to demonstrate in the great global context, not as daydreaming, but how towns and houses as a whole and in detail could look.

References:
[1] Kondratiev, Nikolai: Die langen Wellen der Konjunktur. In: Archiv für Sozialwissenschaft und Sozialpolitik, Year 56/1926
[2] Nefiodow, Leo A.: Der sechste Kondratieff. Sankt Augustin, 2007
[3] Grauel, Ralf: Es werde Licht! In: Brand Eins. 10/2004
[4] DIN EN ISO 9000:2005: Quality management systems – Fundamentals and vocabulary
[5] Die Welt, from 3 August 2006, p. 20

Solar Architecture

Thomas Herzog

A 5.1

As far as using solar energy in architecture is concerned, there has been a change of position. Only a few years ago it was primarily a question of just using solar energy to save heating costs in the winter months or to produce hot water for domestic use. Since then there has been progress in both fields, regarding both the development of types of building – e.g. large glass surfaces on south elevations, well-insulated and closed north elevations, zoned plan layouts based on the thermal onion-skin principle, a favourable volume-to-surface ratio, orientation of the building, etc – and also in improving the active technology (higher efficiency and reliability).

This applies to heating systems and producing warm water, where, meanwhile, technology has reached the stage where even in Central Europe it is possible to obtain 60% and more of our domestic hot water requirements using solar thermal collectors.

Using solar energy

In the 1980s there was disagreement about the evaluation of the proportion of large glass surfaces on the south elevations of buildings; at the time, people were not even prepared to include solar gains in the data collection of an energy household. The experts working in the area of standardisation, and whose aim, they thought, was to draw up state regulations to reduce the use of fossil fuels, started off with the clear aim of reducing the U-value that defines the thermal transmittance through the outer walls of a building. The result was a primitive version of a thermos flask-type of building. In terms of method, this mono-causal approach fails to consider the fact that buildings as a whole comprise a highly complex interweaving of functional, technical and aesthetic aspects. Via the transparent, translucent and opaque parts of their envelope, energy always flows differently in both directions depending on both local conditions and the individual parameters of the building.

Bear in mind the following facts. Improving the thermal insulation where there are large glass surfaces can increase the problem of cooling in the summer months considerably – this often

applies to office buildings. Nowadays, in office buildings heating accounts for less than 10% of total energy costs on average, whereas costs for cooling have increased by 10 to 20%. At the same time, cooling requires about three times the amount of primary energy per kilowatt-hour, so that the energy requirements for cooling can be *de facto* between five and ten times higher. Variable g-values (total energy transmittance) are the aim therefore for outer wall construction as a possibility of reacting flexibly to climate change. The first experiments – e.g. the facade with light-directing elements in the office buildings in Wiesbaden – are proving very successful (Fig. A 5.6).

New active technologies like solar cooling systems are very promising since most energy is available when the energy requirements are at their highest. If, however, you reduce the transparent and translucent parts of the building envelope so that less daylight can enter the building, more additional artificial light is needed as a result. According to studies carried out at Cambridge University, lighting accounts for on average 30% of the energy requirements in office buildings. These conflicts demonstrate that many aspects play a role in the whole interrelationship.

"Smart" building technology

In relation to the running of buildings, we use environmental energies for natural lighting, for ventilation – so far as this is necessary physiologically or for maintenance reasons – for heat, for cooling and, where appropriate, with photovoltaic to generate electricity. Frequently, situations arise where these different uses conflict with each other. Depending on the season, the time of day and the weather conditions, the type of use, the period and the length of time within the individual building, different claims are made on the functions mentioned. It seems reasonable to expect "smart" buildings – a buzzword that has now become established – to be able to react properly to constantly changing conditions and situations.

It should be noted at this point that to a certain extent building control technology represents the brain and the nerves in such a system. It takes over the regulating and controlling func-

A 5.2

tions, which are linked to the changing conditions in such a way, both in the field of energy provision for the inside of the building (generating, distributing and emitting heat) and also in manipulating the building envelope (louvres are raised and lowered, the angle of inclination is adjusted, automatic switching of supplementary lighting, ventilation flaps as exhaust openings are opened or shut and the power of the humidifiers is varied, etc,).

Wide areas of our daily lives are determined by such technical processes, which are generally electronic controlling and regulating operations that react automatically to suit individual situations. The question of the correct balance arises. Compared with buildings, things like blind

approach flights in passenger planes in the fog, ABS or electronic traction control systems in vehicles do not seem to me to be suitable analogies. Extensive and often unnecessary automation involves considerable risks and alarming consequences such as vulnerability to technical system or component failures, higher building costs, avoiding the consequences of our own inappropriate behaviour, our growing dependency on newer technical systems and also on manufacturers and maintenance firms. In relation to its effects on the building sector and urban planning, however, it is necessary to encourage the right way of behaving and make people aware of certain things. Phenomena must be better understood so that the right way

of behaving can follow. Accordingly, electronic systems in a building should serve mainly to guide people and, at best, only cause conditions in the building envelope to change automatically to a limited extent.

So as not to become psychologically and mentally stunted, people must continue to try to be aware of their environment - and that includes the artificially created one too – with all their senses in the future too, instead of just manipulating virtual space with a few joysticks. The conscious and correct way of dealing with a building presupposes that you understand it.

So it would be important then for "smart systems" to show you, for example, whether your behaviour – such as leaving a window tilted open over a thermostat-controlled radiator in winter – is wasting thermal energy uselessly or whether by using certain apparatus electricity is being used unnecessarily. What use is the following year's electricity bill in this case? Nobody can then reconstruct what led to the bill being so high. Developing systems to do this is a high-level design task still facing us. In reality, on the other hand, we have electronic data processing tools for simulations in various areas:

Thermal
· administering climate data
· setting up usage profiles
· working out building technical and geometric variables

Light technology
· with multiple reflection, where, however, many things are still confusing in visualisation.

New components are in development, being tested or being used for the first time such as:

· vacuum insulation panels (VIP)
· glass types that react to changing solar radiation or can be switched to use special gas fillings to reach U-values of < 0.5
· electrochromic und thermotropic glass types with variable g-values
· ventilation components with pre-warming by solar radiation

A 5.3

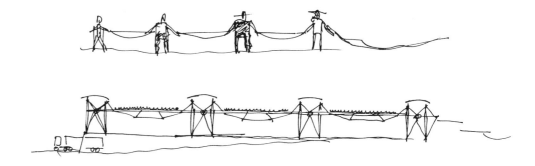

A 5.4

- disintegrated systems (with varying durability, varying technical processes within the combination)
- using (activating) internal masses through the heating and cooling of building components
- highly flexible photovoltaic modules
- large-format photovoltaic glass (up to 9 m²)

Some thoughts about the city

As far back as the first half of the 1960s we realised that as a result of the separation of urban functions – housing, production, leisure – not least due to the demands of the CIAM "Athens Charter" – there had been losses in quality for the modern city. However, our interest then centred on the characteristics of complexity, which we were supposed to try to regain. What we were thinking of was concentration, intertwinement, urban diversity and especially the effects on urban spaces as a result of changing usages. Young architects' hopes at the time were centred on large, variable structures, like first of all those designed by Yona Friedman for Paris, by Eckhard Schulze-Fielitz, e.g. for slag heaps in the Ruhr area, by Kisho Kurokawa for large single buildings and by Kenzo Tange for the Tokyo Bay project. In these plans suggestions were made for solving the rapidly increasing traffic problems – especially car traffic – going as far as keeping large traffic levels totally free under buildings. This traffic was never questioned but it was visible, not only in the models for the future but also in what was then noticeable in daily reality, caused by the intertwinement of the functions of the city already mentioned.

Today, we know that roughly a quarter of all fossil energies used flow into traffic processes with the well-known negative effects this entails. For this reason, our main task is not only to replace fossil fuels, or reduce their consumption in relation to individual transport cases, but also to reconsider the causes of increased traffic and correct them. It is not a question of extreme solutions but of combining urban operations – wherever it seems possible and sensible – since nowadays physically separating industrial and polluting processes from residential areas is no longer insisted on, as was often the case in the previous century.

In concrete terms this means that the mixing of functions should be integrated into building structures. Outstanding forerunners can be seen in the residential buildings of the second half of the 19th century long before people became stranded by mistakenly thinking that the optimum form of housing was on the basis of standardised space requirements, as was the case for decades after the Second World War. So we need building structures, which in their development, land use and use of space are considerably more neutral than is typically the case for most residential buildings – particularly the publicly funded ones. One of the consequences here would be to build as densely as possible. It is only when there is enough

purchasing power in an area and, in addition, the distances to facilities needed for daily needs are short enough for pedestrians that an effective mixture of operations is possible. At the same time, motor traffic can be reduced by a noteworthy order of magnitude. A reduction in land use and infrastructure costs naturally goes hand in hand with this, which is significant for the communities as regards investment and maintenance.

It is exactly here that new models are needed that are socially acceptable. The ideal of living in the countryside awakens the totally wrong impression of being an ecologically sensible strategy. Your own home on the edge of town in a low-density development does give you as

A 5.5

A 5.6

A 5.4 Design sketches for production halls in
       Bad Münder
A 5.5 Semi-detached houses, Munich-Pullach (D), 1989,
       Herzog + Partner
A 5.6 Office buildings, Wiesbaden (D), 2001,
       Herzog + Partner
A 5.7 Production halls, Bad Münder (D), 1992,
       Herzog + Partner
A 5.8 Apartment block, Linz (A), 1999, Herzog + Partner

an individual the feeling of being close to nature but makes you dependent on means of transport, increases fuel consumption and pollution, and in addition has devastating social repercussions. This is not really a new experience. After all, the catchword the "green widow" has been around for decades.

For the very reason that there is too little living space with real urban structure in our town centres – other than something resembling a housing estate – do we have millions of commuters every day. As building structures offer too little potential for change, we have millions of square metres of empty space, tied-up inefficient energy and material resources, which, on top of the opulent average of 40 m² of living space now available to every citizen in Germany, will all mean further expenditure. Whoever is worried that the density and spatial closeness, which we admire so much in the streets and lanes of southern countries, are bound to go hand in hand with undesirable social and hygienic developments similar to those in some urban developments of the past (cf. Heinrich Zille's Berlin "Milieu") is missing the point that the material conditions of our civilisation have fundamentally improved in these decisive categories. Anyone familiar with the relevant current technical state of the art – this concerns heating, ventilation, sanitation, daylight technology and constructional building physics systems – can confirm this.

The architect's profession is one of the few that is comprehensive in both its subject and its approach to work. Architects work holistically with complex systems from the theoretical concept, then the spatial dimensioning and arranging and after that the practical use of this large-scale object, the building. Their methods and working procedures and also their way of cooperating with specialists, whether it be in the scientific area or in putting things into practice materially, will, however, probably undergo fundamental changes over the next few decades.

Outlook

Very many of the problems we have today concerning natural resources and due to undesirable developments of civilisation are attributable to one-sided optimisations that failed to consider adequately their effects on other areas of life. Success certainly comes more easily if we ignore or close our eyes to unpleasant or disturbing adverse effects; if when looking for superlatives in achievements we look for swifter, higher, stronger; the highest possible buildings, the fastest building times, the fastest acceleration and the shortest braking time for sports cars; but not when the aim of our actions is harmony and balance. If this is what we want to achieve, one of the essential conditions related to the connection between technical processes, the ecological balance and social responsibility seems to be a stronger awareness of our long-term joint responsibility for the common wealth. It has become generally customary for us only to be committed to something with an eye to our own welfare. A society that wants to develop further in humane categories is more than the sum of self-centred individuals. A holistic way of looking at problems is becoming more and more important. This can only be achieved if we manage to intensify the interdisciplinary thinking and working approaches between natural, engineering, economic and social sciences and the arts – and if shaping the environment seriously is understood as a complex core discipline.

This text is a revised version of the original publication in Detail 3/1999.

A 5.7

A 5.8

Planning and building in life cycles

Karl-Heinz Petzinka, Bernhard Lenz

A 6.1

The term "life cycle" is already an indication that both natural and artificial systems are involved in a cycle of emerging and fading. So the lifecycle of a building describes the timespan between constructing and demolishing a building. The realisation that planning in tune with life cycles means a high savings potential is by no means new. This is seen in cost analyses made by the architects Philocles and Archilochos, who built the Erechtheion on the Acropolis in the 5th century BC [1].

For contemporary financing and planning models, e.g. public-private partnerships (PPP), life-cycle-oriented considerations, that means looking beyond the pure investment costs, are indispensable. With PPP projects, where financing, producing and running the property are usually all in the same hands, total cost benefits of 10% and more can generally be achieved. These stem not only from a less expensive building but also to a considerable degree from the cost-optimised running of the building.

As erecting a building naturally involves high investment, this only too often means that the investors and property owners only focus on examining the investment costs. The question of how they will finance future running cost is often ignored. Nevertheless, the costs of running a building can often be many times higher than the building costs. Striking economic and energy-saving potential can be gained from analyses in tune with life cycles.

Life cycle costs

In the life cycle costing (LCC) that goes with the life cycle, the costs for planning, constructing, running, maintaining, maintaining the value, demolishing and disposing of a building are compiled in the total cost calculation. The LCC stands therefore for a holistic approach to cost-optimised building planning. This is typically carried out in the form of a dynamic investment cost calculation, although the parameters, such as future prices and interest rate development, are hard to predict. Despite these uncertainties, you should not forego an LCC as it is an efficient instrument with which to compare competing one-stop solutions and evaluate them properly.

Often an LCC only refers to the individual components of a building, e.g. the facade elements. Simulation software available on the market also only considers individual components and assigns them a certain service life in accordance with their characteristics, from which in turn further costs for the building can be deduced. Life cycle cost calculations are also used when valuing property. However, there are no parameters such as quality of design, comfort, attractiveness and quality of the fixtures and fittings. As every building must as a rule yield a certain return, and as this is influenced by factors like *zeitgeist* and fashion, a calculation based only on technical aspects can hardly lead to a meaningful result.

Planning in tune with life cycles

Planning accomplishments are only judged by what it costs to carry them out; the running costs are not usually considered. With planning in tune with life cycles, the total lifetime of a building must be taken into consideration. As the running costs of a building, unlike constructing it, are hardly under pressure from competition, there is a certain discrepancy with the HOAI (approved fee scales for architects and engineers), which encourage planners to work cost-effectively but do not necessarily result in innovative, sustainable and cost-optimised solutions for maintaining the building. Investing in an optimised maintenance plan can lead to clearly reduced running, in-service and maintenance costs, and can thus result in noticeably lower total costs and contribute to clearly reduced energy consumption. Careful planning is crucial here as higher construction costs do not necessarily result in savings in the running costs. Particularly in the field of building services a lesser degree of technology can also contribute to lower running costs (Fig. A 6.2). The architect should pay attention as to which degree of mechanising is ideally justified in the building concerned and which technology is beneficial for microclimatic location factors. When determining which materials to use, bearing in mind the life cycle and the repair cycles due to ageing, choices have to be made between a technical and a reduced service life.

A 6.1 Redevelopment of the Centennail Hall, Bochum (D), 2003, Petzinka Pink Architects
A 6.2 Relationship between degree of technology and life cycle costs
A 6.3 Typical distribution of running costs for an office building
A 6.4 Refurbishment of the Nürnberger Hypothekenbank, Düsseldorf (D), 1998, Petzinka Pink Architects

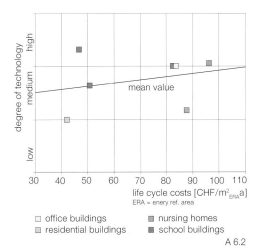

A 6.2

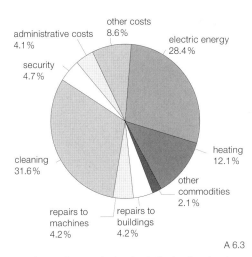

A 6.3

The technical service life describes the length of time a material, when used in a defined way, will still achieve full performance. Reduced service life on the other hand means the time period when the material will show signs of reduced performance yet still retain basic effectiveness. Determining the durability of individual materials therefore depends on the situation of the building and cannot be generalised.

The proper planning for materials for surfaces subjected to heavy wear and tear, like floor coverings, for example, should not be underestimated. Here the costs for cleaning and caring for surfaces in public buildings can quickly account for over 30% of the running costs – a cost factor that has a considerable effect on the total costs and, above all, is permanent (Fig. A 6.3). If a building is being designed to be particularly sustainable, it is necessary to consider the durability of the individual components and to adjust construction, maintenance and servicing accordingly.

As parts of a building do not age at the same pace, there is usually a very inhomogeneous picture. The study of costs and material flows within the framework of a life cycle analysis assumes that individual building components will be used for their entire lifetime and then replaced. Thus, if components remain in a building for a long time, the cumulative expenditure for maintenance and repairs falls in proportion. If a building part contains only a minimum of different building materials, this results in an improved total balance since there are fewer replacement cycles and these can be coordinated better. In the interests of sustainability and the economy, planning in tune with life cycles must have a structure that lends itself to repair and maintenance. This would involve piling the components on top of each other according to their differing lifetimes and also excluding unsolvable combinations. Typically, however, planning of this sort is scarcely feasible from an economic point of view, as the following example demonstrates. We have a reinforced concrete floor with a standard make-up (carpet, cement screed, PE sheeting, mineral wool, reinforced concrete grade C30/37, gypsum plaster). If you look at the varying life-

times of the different components in such a suspended floor construction, then you have the following problem; for the concrete and the PE sheeting you can assume a lifetime of about 100 years, the cement screed and the gypsum plaster will last for about 60 years, the mineral wool about 40 years and the carpet about 10 [2]. Renewing the mineral wool insulation would mean prematurely removing the cement screed and the PE sheeting. The PE sheeting must *de facto* be removed 60 years and the cement screed 20 years before the end of the technical lifespan as you cannot reach the mineral wool without damaging the other things and otherwise you could not replace the mineral wool. In a case like this the construction could be improved just by material synergies. If individual material layers took over some of the functions of the others, the durability of the whole system would increase and the number of layers necessary could be reduced. So, for example, mastic asphalt could be replaced by terrazzo, which provides a surface that can be used permanently. Of course, even with planning in tune with life cycles it can never be guaranteed that materials or components will not have to be replaced prematurely owing to changing legislation, increased intensity of use or technical progress.

In general, two opposing strategies can be distinguished in this type of life cycle planning. On the one hand, the architect can define long cycles which, if possible, include many components and involve more extensive investments at longer intervals which can be foreseen well in advance. On the other hand, it is possible to fix relatively short replacement cycles relating to individual function zones depending on component needs [3]. The latter approach ensures there is a constant high return on the structure but can mean that, if needs change, components that are still working perfectly have to be renewed or replaced. In the end unnecessary costs are incurred and there is an unreasonable waste of resources. For this reason this strategy is only suitable for buildings where it is assumed there will not be big changes in requirements. The most important advantage of long replacement cycles is that adaptations to the building because of changes in require-

ments can be carried out relatively simply when parts are being replaced, and material and energy do not have to be used unnecessarily.

Usage and follow-up costs

As facility management is becoming more and more important it seems imperative to consider future changes to a building right from the planning stage. It is not simple, however, to predict future developments in the vicinity of the building or with the potential users. For instance, no accurate predictions can be made about how often the tenants will change, what different things the building will be used for, how intensely and for how long it will be used. It is particularly difficult to make predictions concerning the long-term cost development of a building.

These factors are clearly illustrated in Fig. A 6.5, as it is especially in the early stage of the life cycle that the planning decisions taken can lead to serious changes. Generally, the life cycles of buildings can be subdivided into five different phases in which different parameters should be borne in mind:

- initiation
- planning

A 6.4

33

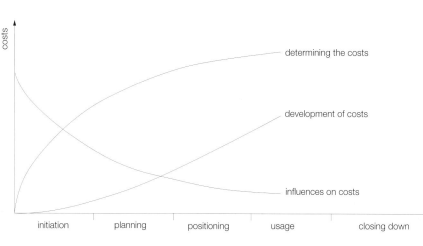

A 6.5 Planning dependencies in the various life phases
of a building
A 6.6 Conversion of the Centennial Hall, Bochum (D),
2003, Petzinka Pink Architects
A 6.7 Centennial Hall, Bochum, climate concept:
a principle of stratified ventilation system in winter
b principle of stratified ventilation system in
spring or autumn
c status quo in winter

determining the costs

development of costs

influences on costs

initiation   planning   positioning   usage   closing down   time

A 6.5

- realisation
- usage
- closing down

Only if the mutual dependencies and also the causal interrelationships are recognised and included in considering the life cycle is it possible to plan, build and operate precisely and sustainably.

As, owing to unclear future developments, in the end no accurate decisions can be taken but only ones based on what is presumed to be the way things will develop, those decisions taken during the initial phases of the life cycle (initiation/planning) must leave room for flexible reactions to various developments. With buildings we are looking at an asset with a long life, which is why cost prognoses and the probable figures for future monetary and consumption values are extremely complex. The cost-effective life, which is the starting point for profitability calculations for investors and owners, is based on the expected returns on the structure. This in turn means that the cost-effective and the technical lifetime of a building are not necessarily identical. If, despite the location of a building, only lower revenues are possible because the building cannot be let or only at a reduced rent, then the end of the cost-effective use of the building has been reached but not the end of the technical lifetime of the building or its components.

A crucial criterion in estimating the earnings is predicting the long-term use of the building. With residential buildings especially, the demographic changes in Germany will lead to noticeable upheavals in the housing market. By the year 2050 the population in Germany will have shrunk by more than 5%. In the former East Germany this population decline will be even higher than 16% according to scientific calculations compared with about 3.4% in the former West Germany. The proportion of people over 60, which in 2005 was about 25%, is expected to rise to over 29% by 2020 [4]. This means that various parameters must be considered in order to make a qualitative prediction about the use of buildings. For these reasons, with office buildings in an outstanding location for instance, we can assume a stable use structure and for

buildings in reconstruction areas a dynamic use structure. In the latter case the result is normally a simpler way of building based on a shorter period of payback on investments. Unlike buildings such as, for example, the Centennial Hall in Bochum, which are still being used decades after their predicted lifetime, there are also projects like the town of Wulfen, whose roughly 100 housing units were pulled down again after only 10 years of use, i.e. long before the stated lifetime. Apart from earnings it is often a lack of utilisation quality or technical deficits that lead to a premature partial or total dismantling of a building. An example of a building that was partially dismantled because of a faulty shell and also due to weaknesses in utilisation flexibility is the Nürnberger Hypothekenbank in Düsseldorf (Fig. A 6.4). The end of the cost-effective period in this case led to the demolition of some parts of the building before their technical life cycle had run out. After working out a flexible utilisation concept, which was supposed to guarantee a modern and forward-looking way of using the building, the massive parapets were demolished and the loadbearing structure was improved. Since the refurbishment work, heavier design loads, together with adaptable interior fittings and an innovative facade, have made it possible to react flexibly in future to changing developments in the surrounding area of the building. In this way the

building can, if necessary, be adapted without having to pull down parts of it before the end of their technical life cycle. In order to be prepared to react appropriately to changes in building services requirements, a ring-type installation, accessible from outside, was provided, in addition to the vertical shafts. In this way decisions can be made in a decentralised way, independently of the user; this is a great advantage in the rapidly changing requirements of media input.

One of the most important preconditions for sustainable building planning is a long, and if possible foreseeable, usage period since volume changes – which occur with new buildings – always entail a high consumption of resources and energy. Apart from the constructional biological aspects of efficiency and consumption of resources, the so-called soft skills especially – flexible characteristics of a building (e.g. variable layout possibilities) – are of fundamental importance. If a building has such parameters, it is possible to react to unforeseen changes and in so doing make an important contribution to sustainability.

The influence factors that can lead to adapting a building vary a great deal. For example, stricter legislation, energy-efficiency upgrade measures or adaptations because of changing use requirements can all interfere with the substance of the building.

A 6.6

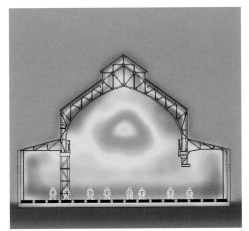
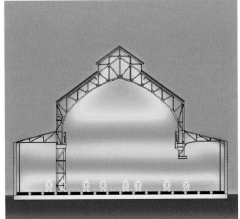
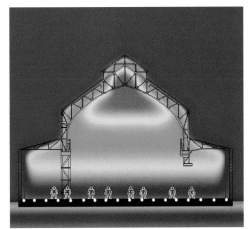

a   b   c   A 6.7

As over the next few years, and not only in Germany, building activity will concentrate more closely on repairs and the changing use of buildings, this development can and must be used as a starting point for thinking about which soft skills buildings must show. Only a building with flexible characteristics can be adapted optimally to changed surroundings and to the consequent demands made concerning structural conversions.

Metamorphosis and later usage

In nature adapted cyclical developments in the sense of a metamorphosis are quite common. Creatures that have to undergo a metamorphosis, for example, distinguish themselves at every stage by adjusting optimally to their environment. As the general conditions in our society, and consequently for our architectural surroundings, are constantly changing, our buildings must be convertible and adaptable to a certain extent. Only when this is the case does an architectural statement contain potential in the sustainability sense, which makes it possible for the building to progress into a new life cycle, after finishing the intended life cycle, without the total loss of the energy previously put into it. So long as a building has the right soft skills, such metamorphoses can be carried out easily without high energy and resource consumption – because "Energy can be substituted by good architecture" Richard Buckminster Fuller once said [5]. A striking advantage of such life cycles that supersede each other is without doubt to be found in the question of recycling. The standardised use of a building whose life cycle runs out is ideally connected with recycling the different raw materials, whereby, as a rule, to a greater extent this means "downcycling", i.e. a large proportion of the material contained in the building cannot be used again in the same quality, so only parts of primary and secondary building materials can be replaced. From the point of view of energy efficiency and sustainability. maintaining and then reusing the building substance is certainly preferable to demolishing it and then erecting a new building. A concept for using the building later in accordance with life cycles is in turn only feasible if buildings have the right soft skills.

An example of reusing in tune with life cycles in the sense of a metamorphosis is the conversion of Bochum's Centennial Hall into the so-called Montage Hall for art (Figs. A 6.1 and 6.6). This building was originally designed in the year 1902 in Düsseldorf for a fair trade taking place there and then transferred to Bochum one year later, to be used as an industrial plant. In 1968 this was closed down and until 2002 the building was used as a storage depot, then it was converted into a venue for plays and concerts with innovative building technology. This reusage in accordance with life cycles could be carried out because during the planning stage the building was designed flexibly. In order to ensure thermal comfort sustainably and efficiently in this ensemble of halls, the building was fitted out with a new stratified ventilation system, tried out there for the very first time ever, which worked on the principle of inversion weather conditions (Fig. A 6.7 a–c). So by using intelligent building services, it was possible to give the building a new function and a third life cycle. Considering soft skills in planning in tune with life cycles thus opens up a potential that makes it possible in future not only to plan, build and operate buildings more economically, but also in a more energy-efficient and sustainable way. As the French architect Philibert de L'Orme, working in the 16th century, once said "The good architect has three eyes, four ears and four hands at his disposal... What he has to say concerns the teachings of the past, observations of the present [and] foresight for the future" [6].

References:
[1] Wübbenhorst, Klaus: Konzept der Lebenszykluskosten. Darmstadt, 1984
[2] Herzog, Kati: Lebenszykluskosten von Baukonstruktionen. In: Darmstädter Nachhaltigkeitssymposium, 2003
[3] Swiss Federal Office for Economic Policy. Impulsprogramm IP Bau, Alterungsverhalten von Bauteilen. Bern, 1994
[4] Roth, Karin: Wo stehen wir? In: Der Lebenszyklus von Wohngebäuden. Ed.: German Federal Chamber of Engineers. Conference reports, Hamburg, Sept. 2006
[5] Tichelmann, Karsten; Pfau, Jochen: Entwicklungswandel Wohnungsbau. Wiesbaden, 2000, p. 230
[6] ibid., p. 218

Part B   Planning

1 Fundamentals

   Global boundary conditions
   Energy
   Climate and comfort

2 Urban space and infrastructure

   Land use
   Planning to suit the location
   Infrastructure and technical services

3 Building envelope

   Maintaining and gaining heat
   Avoiding overheating
   Decentralised ventilation
   Using the daylight
   Generating electricity

4 Building services

   Sustainable building services
   Heating
   Cooling
   Mechanical ventilation
   Optimising the artificial lighting
   Generating electricity

5 Materials

   Heat flow
   Embodied energy
   Materials in the life cycle

6 Strategies

   Energy concepts
   Politics, legislation,
   statutory instruments
   Planning process
   Sustainable architecture
   Diagnosis system for sustainable
   building quality (DSQ)

Fig. B   Aerial view of Venice (I)

Fundamentals

B 1.1

A solution to the energy problem is vital if we are to achieve a viable global development for our society. Safeguarding the standard of living we have reached today plus ongoing economic, technical and social developments are to a large extent dependent on improving the energy efficiency of all buildings and technical systems, also on sustainable energy supplies that do not damage the climate. Nobody doubts the urgent need for action. The exhaustion of the fossil fuels oil and gas is on the horizon. The battle for the distribution of the dwindling energy resources is becoming ever tougher; as a result, the laws of the market are forcing energy prices upwards. The consequences for the environment resulting from the use of non-renewable raw materials have been known for a long time. And the realisation that their unbridled use has triggered a long-term climate change now calls for swift action: the temperature at the Earth's surface is increasing everywhere, polar ice-caps and glaciers are melting, the oceans are warming up and becoming more acidic, sea levels are rising, extreme weather conditions are returning at shorter and shorter intervals. Global warming has in the meantime become a local threat and places mankind in an unprecedented situation. In order to avert the uncontrolled effects of temperature changes, our consumption and economic behaviour must change drastically over the next 10 to 20 years. The "theory of grand supercycles" states that social developments are always based on a technological change in energy, materials and/ or information flows (see "Doing things right – on efficiency and sustainability", p. 24). Accordingly, a paradigm change can be seen in the construction industry – with far-reaching effects for the design and building work of the future.

Buildings and structures are usually built to last and therefore individual decisions and measures have a long-lasting effect. In particular, the considerable mass flows plus the high consumption of resources and energy involved in construction work call for the formation of a new, viable concept for sustainable architecture. In other sectors of the economy, e.g. the automotive industry or agriculture, the efficiency and sustainability offensive is already further advanced. A direct comparison reveals the technological deficits in the building industry. The following aspects illustrate the need for action in architecture and construction:

Climate protection
- About 40% of the greenhouse gases result from the construction and use of buildings and hence make a major contribution to global warming.
- In the industrialised nations, approx. 40% of the total energy consumed goes into the operation of buildings. In addition to this, some 10% of the energy consumption is for the production of materials, construction processes and the transport of building materials.

Saving of resources
- The building sector consumes approx. 50% of all the materials extracted from the Earth.
- About 60% of all the waste produced comes from building and civil engineering work.
- The appetite for land for buildings and infrastructure has almost doubled in Germany over the past 40 years. Despite constant population figures, in Germany 129 ha of open land becomes part of the built environment every day [1] – the equivalent of about 164 football pitches.
- The average living space requirement per person rose in Germany from 19 m^2 in 1960 to 42 m^2 in 2005.

Safeguarding of supplies
- Our materials- and energy-intensive economies generate high dependencies – a multiple of that in countries with less stable governments, who in the future will be faced with the especially drastic effects of climate change. In the EU, at present 50% of the primary energy media required are imported; in Germany that figure is about 74%.
- Owing to the economic progress in the developing and newly industrialised countries, an increase in the global energy consumption amounting to about 60% is anticipated by 2030.

B 1.1 Satellite picture of the Earth by night
B 1.2 Study by the Club of Rome into the future of the world economy with a trend towards crisis-like states after the year 2020
B 1.3 Development of the average annual temperature (with 1950 as the reference year) and CO$_2$ concentration over the past 400 000 years
B 1.4 Intensive use of the land for housing
B 1.5 Demolition of an apartment block built in 1972 after a service life of just 17 years; St. Louis (USA), 1955, Minuro Yamasaki
B 1.6 Insufficient daylight, mechanical air-conditioning and polluted interior air are frequently the cause of sick building syndrome.

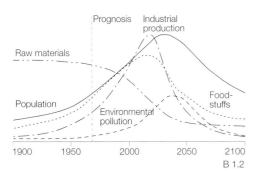

B 1.2

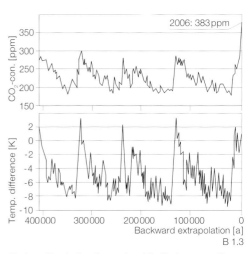

2006: 383 ppm

B 1.3

Reducing the operating costs
• Over the past 10 years, the cost of heating in Germany has increased by approx. 90%. This reduces the available income in private households and therefore has negative effects on the economy.
• For the rented housing market, increasing revenue by raising rents is hardly possible owing to rising operating costs.

Building stock and maintaining value
• In economic terms, buildings are the most valuable commodity of a society. About half of all capital investment in Germany is tied up in the housing market.
• Due to inadequate consideration of the possible energy efficiency, refurbishment measures currently achieve only about one-third of the economically profitable savings potential.

Incentives for the construction industry
• Some three-quarters of the housing stock in Germany is regarded as old and in need of refurbishment.
• Nevertheless, the volume of orders in the housebuilding sector sank by 57% over the past 10 years, although in 2005 the volume of investment in existing buildings (69%) was already clearly in excess of that for new building work (31%).

Health and comfort
• Around 80% of the people in Europe live in towns and cities and spend most of their time indoors.
• "Sick building syndrome" (SBS) is a symptom of about one-third of all new buildings.

Architects and engineers must face up to these considerable challenges. The task is to achieve the maximum overall economy, comfort and architectural quality with the minimum use of energy and resources.

Global boundary conditions

Our way of life has changed enormously since the onset of the Industrial Revolution. Prosperity in the industrialised countries of the world is based largely on the consumption of finite fossil fuels, in addition to unceasing innovation and new technologies. The satellite picture of the Earth by night demonstrates unequivocally the degree of resources consumption, plus the very uneven distribution of energy consumption (Fig. B 1.1). At the very latest, the first oil crisis of the 1970s showed just how dependent our economic growth is on fossil fuels. Even if the gloomy forecasts of the Club of Rome's *The Limits to Growth* [2] have not yet been seen, their scenarios – the interaction of population explosion, industrial production, resources consumption and environmental pollution – never-

theless illustrates the natural limits to our actions (Fig. B 1.2).

Climate change

The temperature of the Earth's surface rose over the last 100 years by about 0.8°C, and 11 of the past 12 years (1995–2006) have been among the hottest since records began. The global climate change – for a long time disputed owing to the complex interactions of individual factors – has in the meantime become acknowledged reality and endangers our very existence. The changes were initially perceived rather subjectively, primarily through the increasing frequency of extreme climate phenomena over recent years. But the documentary film "An Inconvenient Truth" (2006) by former US Vice-President Al Gore rudely awakened the public by showing the signs of the climate change already visible and the consequences to be expected.

The publication of the IPCC Fourth Assessment Report by the UN World Climate Council [3] in 2007 has intensified the public discussion. Since then, accelerated climate change has been generally acknowledged, even in politics. The IPCC Report establishes the unequivocal relationship between global climate change and the increasing emission of greenhouse gases by mankind. Since 1750 the carbon dioxide (CO_2) concentration in the atmosphere has increased by 36%, and is now 383 ppm (parts per million); this is probably the highest

B 1.4

B 1.5

B 1.6

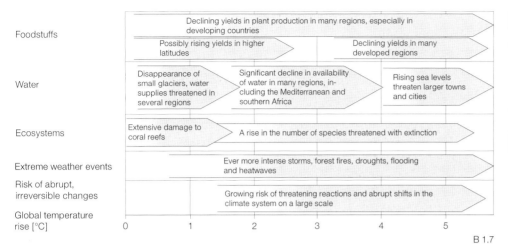

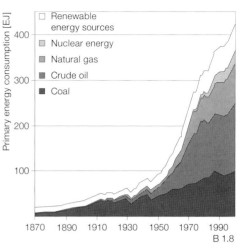

Foodstuffs	Declining yields in plant production in many regions, especially in developing countries
	Possibly rising yields in higher latitudes / Declining yields in many developed regions
Water	Disappearance of small glaciers, water supplies threatened in several regions / Significant decline in availability of water in many regions, including the Mediterranean and southern Africa / Rising sea levels threaten larger towns and cities
Ecosystems	Extensive damage to coral reefs / A rise in the number of species threatened with extinction
Extreme weather events	Ever more intense storms, forest fires, droughts, flooding and heatwaves
Risk of abrupt, irreversible changes	Growing risk of threatening reactions and abrupt shifts in the climate system on a large scale
Global temperature rise [°C]	0 1 2 3 4 5

B 1.7

B 1.8

level within the past 20 million years (Fig. B 1.3). Currently, the CO_2 concentration is increasing at a rate of 2.5 ppm every year. The climate debate has attained a new dimension. The question is no longer whether the higher CO_2 levels will have consequences for the global climate, but rather how much more carbon dioxide can the Earth's atmosphere soak up before risks appear for the survival of the human race? What measures are necessary? How much time do we have left in order to reform our economic behaviour fundamentally? Owing to the complexity of the climate system, the scientific predictions concerning the rise in temperature expected in our latitudes by the year 2100 (taking 1990 as our benchmark) range between 1.5 and 5.8°C. The Potsdam Institute for Climate Research notes in this context: "The figure of 1.5°C is already certain. The system is therefore already charged. The effects will be massive even in this case. And if the 6°C forecast becomes reality, our world will be a different place." [4] The World Climate Council is assuming a maximum tolerable temperature rise of a further 2.0°C before there is irreversible damage to the climate system (Fig. B 1.7). In order that we do not pass beyond this

"point of no return", the CO_2 concentration in the atmosphere by the end of the 21st century should not exceed 450 ppm (Fig. B 1.10). Furthermore, there is great uncertainty as to how especially sensitive regions and ecosystems may react to different temperatures and precipitation quantities. Climate researchers designate the melting of the Greenland ice sheet or the thawing of the Siberian permafrost as "tipping points". Self-perpetuating effects might possibly turn these into processes with an uncontrollable dynamic (Fig. B 1.9).

Repercussions for national economies
In the past, economic assessments and analyses of national economies pointed out the unbridgeable chasm between sustainable, ecologically responsible actions and the need for constant economic growth. However, it is increasingly becoming clear that the pricing of many products and services takes no account of the negative ecological and social effects (e.g. damage to the ecosystem) that result from conventional production and consumption processes. These are the "external costs" (externalities) that designate effects not borne directly by their originators. As a basis for sus-

tainable economies, companies will in future be asked to include the external costs in their market and price mechanisms by employing the "polluter pays principle".

The Stern Report
Shortly after its publication in 2006, the *Stern Report* [5] was seen to mark a new time period in the economic assessment of climate change. In the report, the former chief economist of the World Bank, Sir Nicholas Stern, puts figures to the risks and costs of global climate change, for the first time explicitly from the viewpoint of national economies. According to the report, further unrestrained emissions of greenhouse gases and the resulting climatic changes will in the medium-term lead to a decline in the annual global gross domestic product (GDP) of 5 to 20%. The knock-on effects of rising sea levels, declining harvests and massive migration would be comparable to the effects of the Great Depression of the 1930s (Fig. B 1.7). Stern concludes that the advantages of decisive and early action will by far outweigh the costs of inactivity. The calculations show that just 1% of the annual global GDP will be enough to prevent the most severe effects of

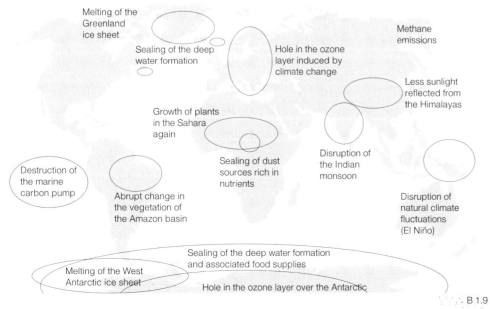

B 1.9

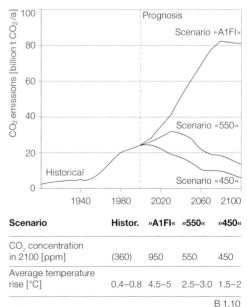

Scenario	Histor.	»A1FI«	»550«	»450«
CO_2 concentration in 2100 [ppm]	(360)	950	550	450
Average temperature rise [°C]	0.4–0.8	4.5–5	2.5–3.0	1.5–2

B 1.10

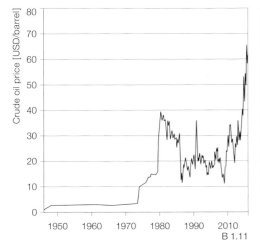

B 1.11

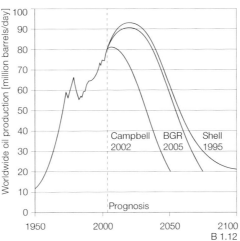

B 1.12

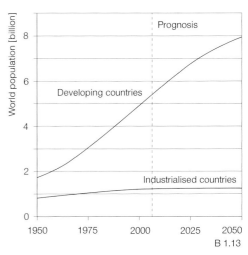

B 1.13

climate change. According to the *Stern Report*, the decisions and investments over the next 10 to 20 years will have a crucial effect on the climate in the second half of this century. This report written for the British government but essentially with a global relevance does not restrict its analysis to describing imminent risks, but also formulates recommendations for action to reduce those risks. Through the increased use of renewable energy sources, the deployment of low-carbon technologies and a marked rise in energy efficiency, Stern says that the drastic consequences of climate change ("the biggest market failure the world has ever seen") could be averted. According to the report, sustainable, ecologically responsible activity is no longer in conflict with economic growth, indeed forms the crucial basis for this in the long-term.

Fossil fuels economy
The industrialised world is to a large extent dependent on the availability of energy-giving raw materials. Non-renewable energy media currently account for 86% of the total primary energy consumption worldwide. In fact, in Germany this value is 95%! Mankind has consumed more fossil-fuel raw materials in the relatively short period of time since the end of World War 2 than in its entire prior history (Fig. B 1.8)! The rapid rise in energy prices in recent years herald the end of fossil raw materials (Fig. B 1.11); the gap between supply and demand is beginning to widen.
The Earth has in the meantime been explored so well that all the larger deposits of hitherto untapped energy media have probably been discovered. The statistical reaches of non-renewable energy reserves that can be tapped with conventional technology are as follows:

• crude oil, 41 years
• natural gas, 62 years
• coal, 200 years
• uranium, 40 years

Within these statistical reaches, constant extraction to exhaustion of all reserves cannot be maintained. The worldwide maximum oil production – the so-called Peak Oil – designates the crest where half of all crude oil

reserves obtainable with conventional techniques will be exhausted (Fig. B 1.12). The exploitation of deposits is progressing in the form of a bell-shaped curve. Once the Peak Oil point is reached, production will decline, slowly at first, then faster, and finally slowly again. This turning point is expected somewhere between 2008 and 2020. That will mark the end of the oil age; there will be an ever-growing gap between energy demand and maximum production capacity.
The mechanisms of the market economy stipulate that a price for a commodity rises until supply outstrips demand. The price levels of feasible crude oil substitutes (e.g. renewable energy sources, coal hydrogenation, etc.) plus a drop in demand through increased energy efficiency thus constitute the future market value for crude oil.
Furthermore, the countries of the EU are dependent on imports of oil and gas from regions that are often seen as politically unstable or are ruled by autocratic governments (Fig. B 1.14). Among those countries with the largest reserves of gas and oil are Saudi Arabia, Iran, Kuwait and the United Arab Emirates. From the point of view of availability, increasing the mining of coal would seem to be sensible; but the very high CO_2 emissions associated with this would once again exacerbate the climate change considerably.

B 1.7 The consequences of the global temperature rise according to the *Stern Report*
B 1.8 Development of the worldwide primary energy consumption from 1870 to 2000 and its coverage in terms of energy sources
B 1.9 The "tipping points" of the climate system
B 1.10 Comparison of various subscenarios for the development of energy-related CO_2 emissions plus their effects on CO_2 concentration and temperature rise in the atmosphere
B 1.11 Development of the nominal crude oil price in US dollars per barrel (= approx. 159 l oil) from 1946 to 2006
B 1.12 Development and prognosis of the worldwide maximum oil production ("peak oil") according to studies by Shell (1995), Colin J. Campbell (2002) and the Federal Institute for Geosciences & Natural Resources (BGR) (2005)
B 1.13 Prognosis of population growth up to 2050
B 1.14 The top 10 countries with the greatest known reserves of oil and gas (as of 2005)

Position	Country	Natural gas reserves in billion m³
1.	Russia	47 544
2.	Iran	27 484
3.	Qatar	25 768
4.	Saudi Arabia	6830
5.	United Arab Emirates	6068
6.	USA	5448
7.	Nigeria	5226
8.	Algeria	4542
9.	Venezuela	4284
10.	Iraq	3168

Position	Country	Crude oil reserves in million t
1.	Saudi Arabia	36 037
2.	Iran	18 022
3.	Iraq	15 646
4.	Kuwait	13 845
5.	United Arab Emirates	13 306
6.	Venezuela	10 847
7.	Russia	10 148
8.	Libya	5323
9.	Nigeria	4881
10.	Kazakhstan	4100

B 1.14

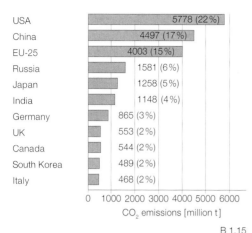

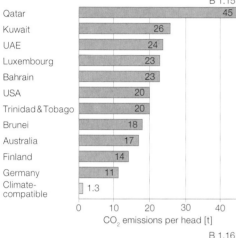

B 1.15

B 1.16

B 1.15 The countries with the highest CO_2 emissions (as of 2003)
B 1.16 CO_2 emissions per head of population in selected countries (as of 2003)
B 1.17 Target emissions changes and those achieved by 2002 within the scope of the Kyoto Protocol
B 1.18 Different forms of energy
B 1.19 The energy balance of the Earth

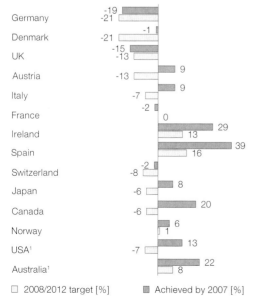

☐ 2008/2012 target [%]   ■ Achieved by 2007 [%]

[1] Original target, Kyoto Protocol not signed

B 1.17

Social effects

In the context of global warming, we must also ask ourselves whether our consumption behaviour is a viable proposition for the future. Climate change is also further aggravated by demographic developments; the population of the world is expected to increase from 6.6 billion people today to 9 billion in 2050, and stabilise at a figure of about 10 billion around 2100 (Fig. B 1.13). In order to provide a reasonable and sustainable basis for the lives of those additional 2.4 billion people, the resources available and their natural limitations plus the emerging consequences of climate change must be examined. The rise in the world's population is taking place primarily in the developing and newly industrialised countries. Leaving aside all efficiency efforts, by 2050 it is expected that the energy demand in Asia will have increased by about 40%, and that of Central and South America by 55%. Consequently, enormous investments in energy systems will be necessary in the newly industrialised countries in the coming years. These will define the energy infrastructure – and hence the levels of CO_2 emissions – for decades to come. In the light of the demographic, economic and climate developments, the IPCC Report is of the opinion that our window for action will only remain open until 2020 if we want to limit the global warming to max. 2.0°C through a significant reduction in greenhouse gases. As we have only 10 to 20 years left for serious changes, the majority of innovations must make use of existing technologies. Simply waiting and hoping for new technical solutions – in order to carry on business as before – will not be enough to deal with the tasks ahead.

The global challenges call for direct social innovations in addition to the technical ones. In the majority of the industrialised nations, current developments in social life can be characterised by the attributes individuality, anonymity and disunity. However, the historical experiences from the beginnings of the green movement shown that an altruistic people-environment relationship cannot be achieved through dogmatic or deterministic decrees. It remains to be seen to what extent "qualitative" growth – as a maxim for standard of living – can replace the doctrine of "quantitative" growth. The climate change therefore touches on ethical issues as well – both for political decision-makers and for every individual.

At the present time, every person, taken on a global average, produces 4.4 t of CO_2 annually. According to our current state of knowledge, the emissions per member of the world's population must drop by more than two-thirds, to a "climate-compatible" 1.3 t, by 2050. In the long-term, the industrialised countries of the world will not be able to claim more "pollution rights" than the developing and newly industrialised countries (Figs. B 1.15 and 1.16). Accordingly, in Germany the current per person emissions of almost 11 t will have to be cut to one-eighth of that figure! So the climate debate also results in embarrassing questions with respect to our own way of life: Will in future every person have the same right to 1.3 t of CO_2 emissions? Will we have to distinguish between "survival emissions" and "luxury emissions"? Will we also need to exercise restraint in some form? Will emissions rights also be traded individually in the future? In the end it seems that global warming will force us into a far fairer distribution.

Political goals

The current measures in international climate protection policies are essentially based on the results of the United Nations "Earth Summit" held in Rio de Janeiro in 1992, where more than 150 countries discussed general global environment themes for the first time without, however, stipulating any specific steps or targets. It was the Kyoto Protocol of 1997 that first specified binding targets for greenhouse gases on an international level. In that document, the industrial nations of the world pledged to cut their CO_2 emissions by a total of 5.2% (based on 1990 figures) by 2012. However, it took a further eight years before at least 55 of the countries that in 1990 were responsible for more than 55% of CO_2 emissions ratified the Protocol. So the Protocol first came into force in early 2005. According to the agreement, the amount of the reduction varies depending on the economic development in the individual countries. The EU has pledged to reduce greenhouse gases by a total of 8%, although once again the individual EU Member States must comply with different targets (Fig. B 1.17). Even if the Kyoto Protocol represents a milestone in international climate protection policies, the efforts according to our current state of knowledge are in no way sufficient to counteract the effects of global warming. Looked at globally, emissions of greenhouse gases are today some 25% higher than those of our 1990 reference year. The target of reducing greenhouse gases worldwide by 50% (compared to the 1990 level) by 2050 can be realised only when the industrialised countries cut their emissions by 60–80%!

In order to take on a leading function and model role on the international stage, the EU Commission recommends that the industrialised nations reduce their greenhouse gases by 30% by 2020. Without anticipating the next protocol, the EU Member States already intend to cut their emissions by at least 20% by 2020 and to increase the share of renewable energies in the energy supply chain to 20%.

Energy

Energy can be converted, stored or transported – and yet it is not a material. It evades our sensory perception, merely revealing its presence to our senses through outward characteristics (e.g. the heat of a fire) or its source (e.g. a log of wood). The origins of the word "energy" stretch back to ancient times. The Greek philosopher Aristotle called *energeia* (= activity, efficacy) the power through which the possible is transformed into the real. It was not until the 19th century that the term "energy" attained its current natural science significance. Since then, the physical definition of the term has been: "the work stored in the system or the capacity of the system to do work". Energy occurs in various forms and can be divided, for example, into mechanical, thermal or chemical energy in accordance with its physical properties (Fig. B 1.18).

It was in 1847 that Hermann Helmholtz formulated the decisive discovery for the understanding of energy conversion: energy cannot be created, merely converted from one form to another. This law of energy conservation at the same time gave rise to the first law of thermodynamics, according to which the quantity of energy in a closed system is always constant. In terms of physics, the designation "energy consumption" therefore designates the transformation from one form of energy into another and can be described as follows:

energy = exergy + anergy = constant

Exergy is the quantity of energy in a system that can do work for a necessary energy service, whereas anergy represents the portion of energy not capable of doing work. For example, when heating buildings, the chemical energy of a fuel is converted into thermal energy through combustion. The total energy here is made up of the usable portion (exergy) plus the unusable portion (anergy) due to waste heat and conversion losses. In contrast to energy, exergy is therefore not conserved, but is instead devalued through the transformation into anergy.

The physical laws with respect to possible energy conversions are described in physics with the term "entropy" (= change, transformation). It was in 1865 that Rudolf Claudius defined the second law of thermodynamics, according to which the entropy of a closed system always remains constant or increases. In the case of irreversible processes, there is always an increase in entropy like, for example, with the depletion of resources. If the known reserves of copper are almost fully used up, then what this really means is that the copper is more or less evenly distributed over the entire earth and the entropy has increased through this uniform distribution. Restoring the original situation (low entropy) can only be achieved through the use of energy. From this it follows that systems without energy input from outside always tend towards a state of greater disorder. Human

beings cannot stop the increase in entropy through efficient use of energy and resources; they can at best only slow it down. Only the sun is able to lower entropy because it feeds energy into the system "Planet Earth" from outside.

The energy balance of the Earth

All of the energy flows available on the Earth are fed principally from three sources:

- Geothermal energy: the creation of the planet released huge quantities of energy, which together with the natural decay of isotopes make up the so-called geothermal energy.
- Gravitation: planetary movements in conjunction with the gravitational attraction between the Earth and the Moon cause the tides.
- Solar radiation: thermonuclear conversion in the sun causes solar radiation to reach the Earth's atmosphere and also its surface.

The quantities of energy from these three sources vary considerably. By far the largest is solar radiation, which accounts for more than 99.9% of the total quantity of energy available to us. The second-largest source is geothermal energy, which accounts for about 0.02%. And the contribution of the tides due to planetary gravitation and movements is 10 times smaller

than that. In the sense of a closed energy system, we can assume that the Earth is in a state of energy equilibrium. This means that the amount of energy fed in is equal to the amount taken out. Almost one-third of the solar radiation that reaches the planet, with a specific value of 1367 W/m² (solar constant), is reflected by the Earth's atmosphere. Owing to the interactions with atmospheric constituents, only about half the radiation actually reaches the Earth's surface with its land masses and oceans (Fig. B 1.19). This energy is then available for convection, evaporation and radiation, and after conversion is radiated back into space as long-wave heat radiation. Only a relatively small part remains on the Earth – converted via photosynthesis into organic substances.

This storage in the form of biomass means that the energy input is marginally greater than that re-radiated back into space. If the organic substances are not converted directly into energy, they are transformed into fossil biogenic energy media over extremely long periods of time. Together with the fossil mineral substances in the form of bonded nuclear or radiation energy, these form the energy reserves of the planet. However, the intensive use of fossil raw materials over the past 150 years has disrupted the energy equilibrium because it is now the case

Form of energy	Occurs as (example)...	Technical energy conversion
Mechanical energy/potential energy	Reservoir	Reservoir-fed hydroelectric power plant
Mechanical energy/kinetic energy	Flowing water	Run-of-river hydroelectric power plant
Thermal energy	Hot water	District heating
Electrical energy	Electricity	Heat pump
Radiation energy	Sunlight	Solar collector
Chemical energy	Natural gas	Gas-fired condensing boiler
Nuclear energy	Nuclear fission	Nuclear power station

B 1.18

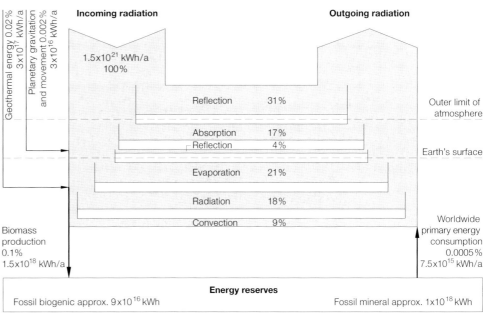

B 1.19

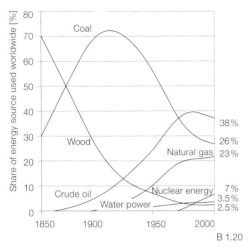

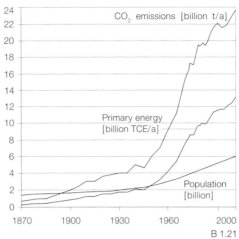

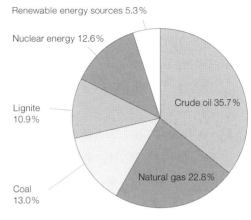

B 1.20

B 1.21

B 1.22

that more energy is released than can be fed into the Planet Earth system, or rather be used to form new energy reserves.

This is where the definition of renewable energy begins – energy media that are continuously fed from the three aforementioned sources and hence on a human scale can be regarded as inexhaustible. The renewable primary energy media are the aforementioned primary resources but also energy forms derived from these, e.g. wind or water power. The availability of secondary or final energy, e.g. solar power from a photovoltaic installation, depends entirely on the functional capabilities of the technical installation for conversion.

Forms of energy

As described above, the energy of the Earth consists of three primary energy sources – solar radiation, geothermal energy, gravitation – and makes itself felt in various ways and forms. These are supplemented by the non-renewable energies stored in atomic nuclei. Likewise, the fossil forms created over immense periods of time by the solar radiation of the past are on the human scale non-renewable. Fig. B 1.23 shows the energy sources and their various forms on the Earth. Only the essential relationships are shown here because the individual forms cannot always be unequiv-

ocally assigned to a certain source. For example, wind power results from the interaction between atmospheric movements, solar radiation and the rotation of the Earth. We can therefore define the following forms:

- Nuclear power, which can be used in the form of nuclear fission or nuclear fusion
- Fossil fuels (coal, oil, gas) – the products of the solar radiation of the past
- Geothermal energy – the heat of the Earth deep below the surface
- Tidal energy caused by gravitational effects

However, the majority of forms result from the current solar radiation, which is available in direct and diffuse form and heats up the ground near the surface, the atmosphere and open water masses. As a result of this temperature rise, modified energy forms such as wind, ocean currents, waves and rivers appear. And solar radiation is, of course, the basis for biomass production too.

The development of energy consumption

A study of developments in the worldwide energy provision up to the present day reveals that the usage of the various energy sources and types takes place in certain cycles. Following start and growth phases, all fossil raw materials

– with an increase in the amount extracted, or rather consumed – reach their peak and finally a phase of declining importance (Fig. B 1.20). Beginning with wood and coal as the dominant energy media of the 19th century, the structural composition in the 20th century is characterised by a broad energy mix. Also interesting in this context is the fact that in the past there has always been a direct relationship between population growth, energy consumption and CO_2 emissions (Fig. B 1.21). The largest proportion (in percentage) of the worldwide energy provision is currently still met by crude oil. The use of coal had already reached its peak by the start of the 20th century, but even today still plays a key role in energy provision. The proportions of natural gas and nuclear energy are growing, whereas wood and water power, the traditional renewable energy sources, play only a subsidiary role.

In contrast to the worldwide trend, primary energy consumption in Germany over recent years is on the decline; the energy mix nevertheless exhibits a similar structure (Fig. B 1.22), and even German energy provision is dominated by crude oil. The use of coal is declining continuously, but still represents an important energy source for electricity generation. Natural gas, on the other hand, is showing signs of growth. The proportion of renewable energy

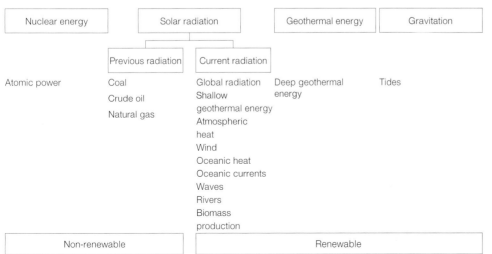

B 1.23

B 1.20 Structural development of energy sources worldwide from 1850 to 2000
B 1.21 Comparison between population growth, energy consumption and CO_2 emissions from 1870 to 2000
B 1.22 Share of energy sources in primary energy consumption in Germany (as of 2006)
B 1.23 The energy sources of the Earth and their form of occurrence
B 1.24 Current scenarios for the global primary energy consumption for 2050 assuming the world's population increases to 9–10 billion
    WBGU: possible development path (2003)
    Shell SCA: Spirit of the Coming Age (2001)
    WEC A3: Growth (1999)
    Shell DAS: Dynamic as Usual (2001)
    WEC B: Business as Usual (1999)
    RIGES: Renewable intensive scenario (1993)
    SEE: Solar Energy Economy (2003)
    WEC C1: Ecological priority (1999)
    Faktor 4: Efficiency revolution (1999)

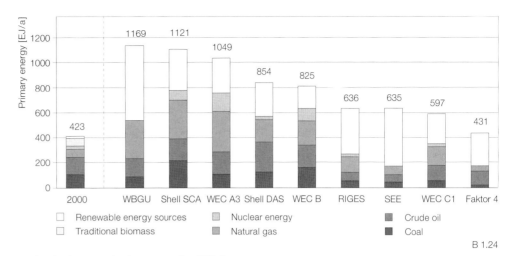

☐ Renewable energy sources	▨ Nuclear energy
☐ Traditional biomass	▨ Natural gas

▨ Crude oil
▨ Coal

B 1.24

sources has increased considerably since 1995 through the increase in the number of wind power installations.

The forecasts with respect to the future development of global energy consumption are burdened with uncertainties (Fig. B 1.24). All the scenarios assume, however, that an increasing world population plus the rise in the gross national products (GNP) of the developing and newly industrialised countries will result in a considerable increase in energy consumption over the coming years. At present, more than 20% of the world's population does not have access to electricity and 40% cover their energy needs in essentially traditional ways through the use of biomass. Owing to this backlog in development, most studies anticipate a three- to four-fold growth in the worldwide GNP by 2050.

Fossil energy

Some 80% of the world's energy supplies are currently based on the fossil energy media coal, oil and gas, plus atomic energy. As the creation periods for fossil energy media by far exceed the human scale, current consumption clearly outstrips their re-creation. Fossil energy reserves were formed from organic material at various times in the Earth's history through biochemical and chemical conversion processes. The creation periods for such energy media are as follows:

- Crude oil and natural gas: 20–440 million years
- Coal: 10–370 million years

In order to moderate climate changes, the advocates of the fossil energy industry are placing their hopes on storing future CO_2 emissions underground. Carbon dioxide sequestration involves separating CO_2 from the waste gases of power stations and industrial plants, compressing it and finally forcing it under high pressure into salt-water aquifers at a depth of about 1000 m. By the year 2015, a dozen pilot plants in Europe should begin operations. However, there are still considerable uncertainties regarding the safety and economy of this method. Forcing the carbon dioxide into the rocks could cause water containing salt or heavy metals to escape through cracks and contaminate groundwater reservoirs. With larger leaks there would be the risk of large quantities of emissions escaping into the already over-loaded atmosphere. Furthermore, CO_2 sequestration is expected to result in a loss of efficiency of up to 20% at power stations, which in turn would increase consumption of resources, dependence on imports and costs.

Nuclear energy

The use of nuclear energy is the subject of a heated debate among politicians and the public. Although nuclear power stations do not generate any CO_2 emissions while in operation, considered over their entire life cycle, the construction and demolition of reactors, the mining of uranium, waste disposal and safety and security risks do result in considerable costs and impacts. Nuclear energy currently accounts for approx. 17% of global electricity generation, but contributes less than 7% to the total energy provision. The risks and benefits of zero-carbon electricity generation from nuclear energy must be weighed up against this background. And for the reactor technology in widespread use today, there is also a resources problem. Cheap uranium for light-water reactors (LWR) will only be around for another 40 years or so. Breeder reactors, which in addition to generating electricity also create further fissile material, are not in permanent operation in any country. And the plutonium created as a waste product increases the nuclear threat through its suitability for use in weapons.

Intensive research into the realisation of nuclear fusion reactors has been in progress since the 1960s. Theoretically, nuclear fusion could generate large amounts of electricity with a comparatively low fuel consumption and little radioactive waste. However, the development of nuclear fusion reactors requires huge investments; the commercial use of this technology – if indeed it is feasible at all – is not expected for another 50 years.

The extraction, use and disposal of radioactive substances results in extremely high health risks. As the half-life of uranium 235 exceeds 700 million years, it takes an enormous technical and logistics setup to monitor such substances and shield them from the environment.

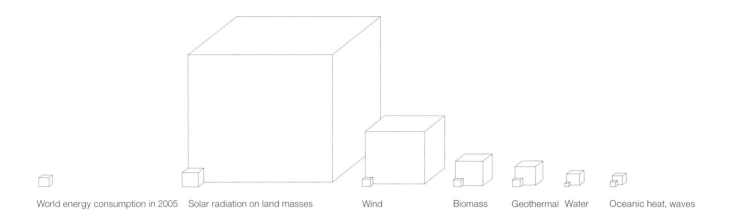

World energy consumption in 2005   Solar radiation on land masses   Wind   Biomass   Geothermal Water   Oceanic heat, waves

B 1.25

Renewable energy

Apart from the centuries-old ways of using biomass, wind and water power, as the prices for fossil fuels began to rise in the mid-1970s, renewable energy sources started to be given more attention. And in the wake of the reactor disaster at Chernobyl in 1986, the motivation behind such efforts was multiplied. Measurable effects have been noticeable since about 1990. As a result of favourable political framework conditions, we have seen a small but continuous growth in the use of renewable energy media. Developments in Germany show that the increase is in the first place based on the increased use of wind power plus gaseous and liquid biomass (Fig. B 1.26). Germany has in the meantime become the world-leader in the generation of energy from wind power and solar thermal energy, and the amount of electricity generated from solar power is higher only in the USA and Japan.

If we consider the structure of energy provision from renewable sources, the use of solid biomass in the form of the burning of wood is the most significant factor, although it should be mentioned that owing to decentralised structures, the statistics are mainly based on estimates. Solid biomass together with the use of wind and water power accounts for more than 75% of the contribution made by renewable sources. The other energy sources in the form of solar thermal power, solar electricity (photo-voltaic) and geothermal energy are currently only minor players. Together, all renewable energy sources account for approx. 6% of primary energy provision and about 12% of electricity generation in Germany.

Potential
Detailed analyses of the potential in renewable energy sources have been carried out in recent years, but the results exhibit a relatively large scatter. The theoretical potential contains the entire physical availability of a certain energy source over a defined area and within a defined time period, e.g. the solar radiation incident on the area of Germany over a period of one year, the annual kinetic energy of the wind in a certain region, or the entire energy content of the biomass of a country which is replenished each year. The possible yields here are based solely on the natural energy supply, which, however, is subject to fluctuations, e.g. the varying annual solar radiation.

The technical potential is part of the theoretical potential, and involves considering the technical restrictions necessary for practical usage (Fig. B 1.25). It varies depending on the underlying technology and the degree of efficiency of that technology. Furthermore, we distinguish between technical generation potential at the start of a defined stage in the conversion chain and technical substitution potential with respect to final, secondary or primary energy (see p.

50). Whereas the theoretical potential has little practical relevance, the technical potential is highly important.

The economic potential is in turn that part of the technical potential that is economically advisable for the time under investigation. Here, however, diverse boundary conditions, e.g. the costs of fossil fuels, interest rates, depreciation periods and operational or national economy considerations, influence the profitability considerably. If in future we were to include the external costs of the fossil energy economy (e.g. global warming, extreme weather events) in the overall economic calculation, the economic potential of renewable energy would look much better.

The achievable potential describes the contribution to energy supplies that can actually be expected under current boundary conditions. Owing to production capacities, the existence of competing systems, lack of information, legal or administrative hurdles, etc., this currently lies below the economic potential. Grants and subsidies can, however, help the achievable potential to exceed the economic potential.

Development scenario for Europe
If we define governing variables for energy demand, e.g. economic and demographic developments, technical progress and anticipated price rises for energy, we can derive scenarios for future energy consumption and

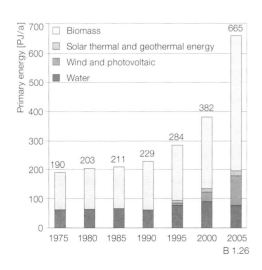

B 1.26

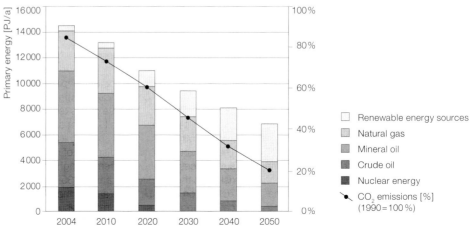

Renewable energy sources
Natural gas
Mineral oil
Crude oil
Nuclear energy
CO_2 emissions [%]
(1990 = 100 %)

B 1.27

B 1.25 Theoretical annual potential (large cube in background) and technical potential (small cube in foreground) in comparison with the world energy consumption as of 2005

B 1.26 Contribution of renewable energy sources to the primary energy supplies in Germany from 1975 to 2005

B 1.27 Scenario for the development of the primary energy consumption and CO_2 emissions in Europe up to 2050

B 1.28 Contribution of renewable energy sources to electricity generation in Germany from 1990 to 2005

B 1.29 Technical potential and use of renewable energy sources in Germany as of 2005

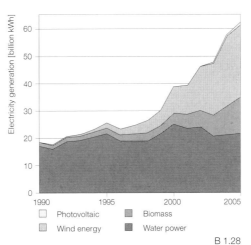

Photovoltaic
Wind energy
Biomass
Water power

B 1.28

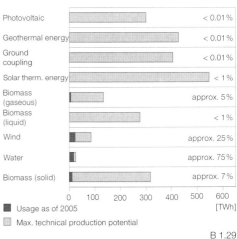

Usage as of 2005
Max. technical production potential

B 1.29

how we can cover those requirements. Most forecasts – in contrast to developments hitherto – expect a continuous decline in primary energy consumption in Europe up until 2050, in particular due to efficient thermal insulation for buildings plus a constant increase in the proportion of renewable sources in the provision of energy (Fig. B 1.27). The intention is that by the middle of the 21st century, renewable energy sources will cover half the energy requirements owing to the much reduced total demand. Further assumptions are a drop in the proportion of coal in the equation and a probable significant reduction in electricity generation by nuclear energy [6].

The forecasts for electricity supplies assume that water and wind will continue to make substantial contributions in the coming years, and that these will be joined by biomass conversion after 2010 plus significant contributions by geothermal and photovoltaic installations after 2020. In addition, large quantities of electricity generated from renewable energy sources could be imported, e.g. from solar thermal power stations near the equator. With the exception of water power, all energy sources exhibit considerable potential for expansion.

In electricity generation above all, the use of renewable energy sources instead of conventional energy media exhibits one important characteristic: by far the largest part of the potential for generating activity is based on solar radiation and wind, both highly fluctuating resources. If these are in future expected to replace real power station output to a large extent, a considerable redesign of the current supply structures with respect to load management, storage of reserves and power station control will be required.

The generation of heat is will initially continue to be based on individual installations for incinerating biomass. Significant changes are expected here via concepts for group heating systems through central biomass heaters, geothermal power stations and, in particular, large solar collector installations.

Technical systems for viable future energy supplies
Studies carried out for Germany reveal that the use of biomass has on the whole the greatest

technical potential. The generation of low-temperature heat can be achieved with solar power, but also by exploiting the heat near the surface (ground coupling and external air) or the heat at greater depths (geothermal energy). These sources exhibit very high efficiencies which up to now have remained virtually untapped. When it comes to electricity generation, besides water and wind, it is primarily the photovoltaic conversion of solar radiation that represents an important alternative to conventional forms of generation. At the same time, photovoltaics combines the greatest reservoir of energy with the lowest rate of use to date. In contrast to this, the use of hydroelectric power has already reached its limits. Bringing wind turbines on line has experienced enormous growth rates in recent years, and the upward trend continues (Fig. B 1.28).

On the whole, Germany has considerable options for using renewable energy sources. In total, the achievable potential for renewable energy media has already reached the order of magnitude of the current final energy requirement when considered in terms of today's boundary conditions (Fig. B 1.29). This also applies to the other European countries, albeit with a different mix.

Using the chances offered by renewable energies depends mainly on the system technologies available. The technologies for energy provision in buildings are discussed in detail in the chapter entitled "Building services" (pp. 110–145). The next section explains the fundamental global perspectives for a sustainable energy economy.

Global radiation
In order to be able to use the global radiation actively, we have generally two alternatives at our disposal: the conversion into heat or electricity. Solar thermal installations have been around since the 19th century, and the systems common today have proved themselves over decades. Besides solar thermal power stations for generating electricity in countries with particularly high levels of sunshine, there are small-format solar thermal installations in use for the provision of hot water and as a backup for space heating. To date, more than 30 million m²

of collectors have been installed worldwide. Such collectors can be separate additions to buildings or may be integrated into the building envelope (see p. 93). Despite the different radiation levels at different locations, solar thermal power is today worthwhile virtually everywhere in Germany.

With some reservations, this also applies to photovoltaic systems for generating electricity. Their modular design permits a very wide range of installed capacity, and they can also be installed directly in the building envelope (see p. 106). The system technology is based on developments that have taken place since the middle of the 20th century, and are of a high technical standard. More than 300 MW of installed capacity has already been realised in Germany, corresponding to an area of some 3 million m².

Solar chimney power stations represent another option for the large-scale exploitation of global radiation. The engineering consultants Schlaich, Bergmann & Partner set up the first trial installation in Manzanares, Spain, in 1989 in order to gather experience for practical operations. The principle behind the operation of this type of power station is very simple (Fig. B 1.35): air heated below a transparent collector roof rises up a central chimney as a result of the thermal currents. At the base of a chimney, one or more turbines convert the airflow into electricity. The first 200 MW power station, near Mildura, Australia, is due to go on line in 2010.

Biomass
Although the options for exploiting the energy in biomass are extremely diverse, the burning of wood currently represents the commonest use of renewable energy worldwide. In principle, solid, liquid and gaseous biomasses can be incinerated for producing heat or used for the co-generation of heat and electricity via motorised CHP (combined heat and power) plants (see pp. 115 and 143). The well-developed system technology achieves high degrees of efficiency with low emissions. The output ranges from a few kilowatts to several megawatts.

Costs [ct/kWh]

☐ Global warming effect
■ Atmospheric pollutants

PV: Photovoltaic
SPS: Steam power station
G&S: Gas and steam power station

Lignite SPS 40% · Lignite G&S 48% · Coal SPS 43% · Coal GG&S 46% · Natural gas G&S 57% · PV (today) · PV (2030) · Hydro-electric power · Wind onshore · Wind offshore

B 1.30

Ground coupling

Solar radiation stored in the topmost strata of the Earth's crust and in groundwater can be utilised through a ground coupling (underground heat exchanger) and systems of drilled wells, together with heat pumps, for space heating and hot-water provision (see p. 121). The technology for this was developed back in the 19th century and ground couplings can be used anywhere in Europe. More than 300 000 heat pump systems are now installed in Europe every year.

Geothermal energy

As we go further into the solid crust of the Earth, so the temperature rises markedly. The high temperatures in the deeper strata can be utilised by geothermal power stations. This is achieved by using deep heat sondes or the hot dry rock (HDR) method, which draws thermal energy from depths approaching 7000 m. The water extracted from the ground, or rather heated by the ground, with temperatures between 100 and 300°C, is used in a power station at ground level for producing electricity via steam processes, or is fed into group or district heating networks. The technology required for geothermal energy has been available in Europe for a number of decades.

Atmosphere

Heat pumps also allow the thermal energy contained in the external air to be used for space heating and hot-water provision. This is, in principle, the same system technology as for a ground coupling, but in this case it is the thermal energy in the air that is extracted via a air-to-air heat exchanger. For heating, however, there is an unfavourable correlation between the temperature level of the external air (e.g. -10°C) and the heating requirement (e.g. +20°C). The efficiency of heat pumps diminishes as the temperature difference increases.

Wind

Using the wind as a source of energy is a method with a long tradition. For example, in the 17th and 18th centuries, there were about 9000 windmills in the Netherlands. At the moment, wind energy in Germany is primarily used for generating electricity, and currently accounts for more than 5%. In regions with particularly high yields, with average wind speeds exceeding approx. 3 m/s, wind turbines with capacities of up to 5 MW are possible. The first concepts for integrating wind power systems into buildings are at the planning stage (Fig. B 1.34).

Hydroelectric power

Water power is another method that has been used throughout history. We distinguish between low-pressure installations (run-of-river hydroelectric power stations) and medium- or high-pressure installations (reservoir-fed hydroelectric power stations). Nearly 6000 hydroelectric power stations are in operation in Germany, which supply more than 4% of the net electricity requirements. By far the greatest number of these are small hydroelectric power plants with an output of less than 1 MW, and many of these are privately owned.

Ocean currents

The balancing currents of the world's oceans, caused by different temperatures, different salt concentrations or the changing tides, can be used to drive underwater rotors and thus generate electricity. To do this, however, specific current dynamics are essential, which in Europe are found, in particular, off the coasts of the British Isles. According to estimates of the technical potential, the United Kingdom could generate 10–20% of the electricity it needs with power stations driven by the currents (Fig. B 1.31).

In principle, the breaking of waves on the shore could also be used in combination with suitable power stations for generating electricity. One of the simpler systems, for example, converts the kinetic energy of the breaking waves into potential energy by way of a appropriately designed collector. The actual electricity generation then functions in the same way as a reservoir-fed power station.

Tides

The tides, primarily caused by gravitational effects and comparable with the energy of breaking waves, could be converted into energy. However, this requires an average tidal range of at least 3 m, a value that is not reached on the German coast. A number of such power stations have already been built elsewhere in the world, but the total potential is probably quite low.

Waves

Wave energy is in the first place induced by wind energy. In contrast to a tidal power station, the electricity generation in a waves-driven power station results not from the tides, but rather from the continuous movement of the waves. According to calculations by the World Energy Council (WEC), there is considerable potential for such power station technology.

B 1.31

Oceanic thermal energy

Like groundwater, the seas and oceans can also store energy, which with a suitable temperature difference exceeding about 20 K between the water near the surface and the water in the depths can be used for generating electricity in a suitable power station. However, besides problems with storing and transporting the energy, there are still many technical questions to be answered and therefore a commercial use of this technology is not expected in the near future.

The economics of renewable energy

The overall cost to society of providing fossil and nuclear energy supply systems lies considerably higher than calculations have revealed up to now.

In order to obtain an all-embracing economic evaluation, in future the considerable environmental damage caused by fossil energy conversion – the "external costs" – must be included in the economic calculations. A study carried out by the Federal Ministry for the Environment, Nature Conservation & Nuclear Safety (BMU) shows that CO_2 emissions play a key role here [7]. The BMU study estimates the cost of the damage to be € 70 per tonne of CO_2. Accordingly, these external costs amounting to, for example, 6–8 ct/kWh in the case of electricity generated using coal and lignite, should be added to the current electricity production costs of 3–4 ct/kWh for fossil fuel-fired power stations. On the other hand, the consequences of obtaining electricity from renewable energy sources – including the construction and deconstruction of the plants required – are much lower (Fig. B 1.30).

The true external costs of the fossil energy sector, e.g. damage to ecosystems, impairment of biodiversity, uncertainty of supplies plus geopolitical risks, are currently not (yet) taken into account because of the uncertainties in the financial evaluation of the damage.

Whereas the market prices for fossil and nuclear energy will continue to rise because of their limited availability, proposed CO_2 surcharges, uncertainty of supplies and "risk factors", the production costs for renewable energy are falling steadily owing to the decline in the technical and commercial costs (economies of scale). It should therefore be only a matter of time before renewable energy sources cause lower operating costs than energy from finite sources.

The BMU study (2007) comes to the conclusion that if the price of conventional energy supplies continues to rise substantially, renewable energy will probably reach the price level of the finite energy sources in 2025 (Fig. B 1.32). From that point on, they will help to stabilise energy costs, which without renewable energy sources would continue to rise unstoppably [6]. The expansion of energy supplies with future viability is becoming an ever more important economic factor. Domestic sales in Germany have been exhibiting growth rates of approx.

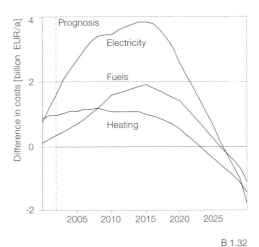

B 1.32

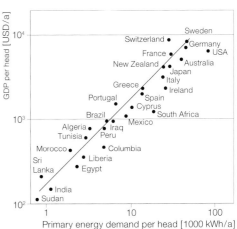

B 1.33

20% for a number of years. Hardly any other branch of industry has created a similar number of new jobs.

Efficient use of energy

The energy policies of the past always considered sustainable energy supplies to be in conflict with economic growth. There was seen to be a causal relationship between gross domestic product (GDP) and primary energy demand (PED). According to that, every economic upturn requires a rise in energy consumption. In 1970 countries with a low GDP also had a low PED. By contrast, the industrialised countries exhibited a high GDP and a high PED. The GDP/PED ratio was therefore considered to be an indicator of the respective standard of living (Fig. B 1.33).

Triggered by the oil crisis at the start of the 1970s, the development of national economies was uncoupled from the energy consumption. In Germany, the PED has changed very little since 1980, whereas the GDP has continued to rise (Fig. B 1.36). In 2000 the Germans could

maintain the same standard of living as in 1970 with just two-thirds of the PED of that time. The inverse of the aforementioned GDP/PED ratio, i.e. the PED/GDP ratio, therefore expresses how efficiently a nation uses energy. The higher the GDP in comparison to the energy consumption, the better is the value creation with the energy consumed.

Energy provision chain

Huge losses ensue in the processes for converting, in particular, primary energy media (e.g. coal) into the actual energy service, e.g. light (Fig. B 1.39). The energy provision chain can be defined as follows (Fig. B 1.38):

- Primary energy is the theoretically usable energy content of fossil, nuclear and renewable energy media that occur in nature and have not yet been converted or prepared.
- Secondary energy is obtained – with corresponding energy losses – from primary energy as the result of conversion processes; secondary energy media include, for example, petrol, coal briquettes and heating oil.

B 1.34

B 1.35

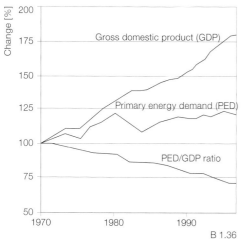

B 1.36

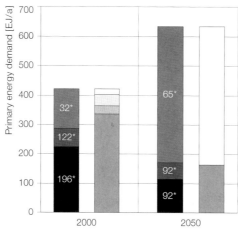

Consumption according to country groupings

■ Developing countries

■ CIS, Eastern Europe, Middle East

■ OECD countries

* per head consumption

average per head consumption$_{world}$=70 GJ/a

Coverage of demand according to energy sources

☐ Renewable energy sources, excl. traditional biomass

☐ Traditional biomass

☐ Nuclear energy

■ Fossil energy sources

B 1.37

· Final energy is equal to the proportion of secondary energy after subtracting the transport, line and/or transformation losses of users.

· Net energy is the quantity of energy actually used for the energy service, e.g. space heating.

In total, about two-thirds of the primary energy obtained from nature is currently lost through conversion and/or transmission; accordingly, the current energy utilisation systems provide the user with only about one-third of the energy available in the natural raw materials. Amory Lovins, head of the Rocky Mountain Institute, has coined the term "negawatt" for this situation, the hypothetical unit of saved energy. According to Lovins, preventing losses will represent the most important energy source in the future.

Strategies for a sustainable energy industry

Conservation of energy and resources, environmental protection and safety and security policies are increasingly perceived as a single element. Today's energy industry sees itself essentially having to face four problems: risks for the climate, rising prices for fossil raw materials, uncertain supply situations and more and more geopolitical distribution conflicts involving energy. Several parallel strategies are necessary for reconfiguring the energy industry [8]:

· Efficiency:
The rational conversion and use of energy enables the desired energy services, e.g. a pleasant interior or transportation from A to B, to be provided much more efficiently for the same effect.

· Consistency:
Owing to the consumption of finite energy resources and the accumulation of hazardous emissions in the atmosphere, the current energy system is "open". The creation of a "closed" energy system, which provides energy virtually without consumption of raw materials, can only be achieved by using renewable energy sources.

· Sufficiency:
The energy consumption is mainly determined by ways of life and consumer behaviour. A sustainable use of resources presumes that consumers, through responsible actions, refrain from using energy-intensive products and services.

A viable energy industry can only be achieved by pursuing these strategies with their complementary interactions. A clear reduction in energy consumption as a result of efficiency and sufficiency measures forms the prerequisite for covering the remaining demand through the use of renewable energy.

The "ideal scenario" of achieving a sustainable global energy supply by 2050 is founded on these strategies and includes the following key data (Fig. B 1.37): The current average per head energy consumption of 70 GJ/a, with its very irregular geographical distribution, will be evened out by the middle of the century. To do this, the industrialised countries must more or less halve their current energy consumption of 196 GJ/a, whereas the developing countries will be able to double theirs. In addition, there will have to be a 50% reduction in the use of fossil fuels, the abandonment of nuclear energy and a 24-fold increase in the use of renewable energy sources. The technical potential is readily and widely available, but considerable efforts are still required. In order to achieve this "ideal scenario", the market share of renewable energy must increase over the next 50 years by 6–7% annually.

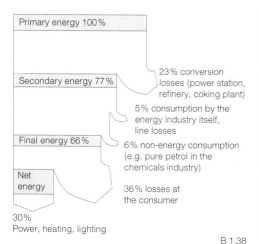

B 1.38

B 1.39

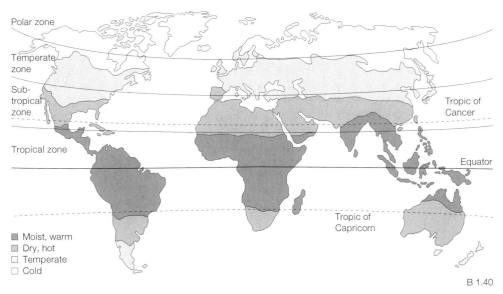

Moist, warm
Dry, hot
Temperate
Cold

B 1.40

Climate and comfort

Human beings first started to spread across our planet some 200 000 years ago, in the African savannah. At a rate of, on average, some 400 m/a, *Homo sapiens* finally reached the Atlantic coast on the Iberian peninsula about 40 000 years ago. However, the human organism is, even today, designed for a life under the original, ideal climatic conditions of Africa. As a result of the population explosion and hence the settlement of almost all the land masses on the planet, human beings have developed strategies for living in, for example, polar regions with average temperatures as low as -25°C, or tropical regions with average temperatures that reach +26°C. Clothing as a second skin and the building envelope as a third take over the task of compensating for fluctuations in the climate and thus ensuring comfort.

Prior to industrialisation, when the level of comfort was much lower than that which we expect and enjoy today and there were only a few technical options for creating an interior climate not dependent on the ambient conditions, it was primarily the components of the building envelope that were directly influenced by local conditions. The realisation of the prevailing climatic factors and elements forms the prerequisite for being able to develop energy-efficiency design concepts and, at the same time, optimum comfort conditions.

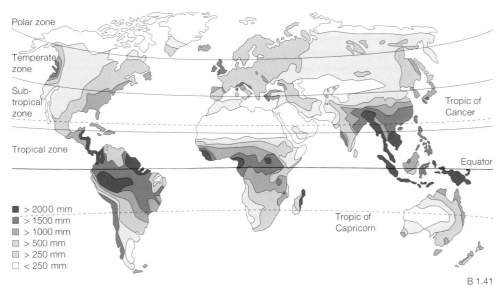

> 2000 mm
> 1500 mm
> 1000 mm
> 500 mm
> 250 mm
< 250 mm

B 1.41

Climate

The term "climate" designates the local state of the atmosphere that can be described by means of meteorological variables. We employ time dimensions in order to distinguish between the weather and the meteorological conditions:

- Weather: momentary state of the atmosphere; one hour to a few days.
- Meteorological conditions: character of the weather over a few days to one week, in the extreme a whole season.
- Climate: average state of the Earth's atmosphere over 30 to 40 years.

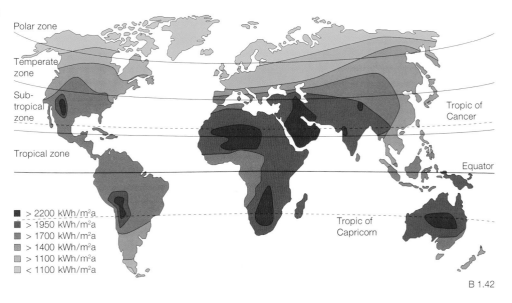

> 2200 kWh/m²a
> 1950 kWh/m²a
> 1700 kWh/m²a
> 1400 kWh/m²a
> 1100 kWh/m²a
< 1100 kWh/m²a

B 1.42

Climate zone	Climate elements	Fundamental building requirements
Polar zone (cold)	• Low solar radiation, very low seasonal annual average temperatures (0–6°C) • Low daily temperature differences (summer: many hours of daylight; winter: many hours of darkness) • High annual temperature differences for continental locations (e.g. Siberia 45–60 K) • Moderate/low annual temperature differences for coastal locations (e.g. Iceland, Norway 11–15 K) • Low relative humidity, especially in winter • Long periods of frost (5–9 months), partly permafrost deeper in the ground • Low precipitation (e.g. approx. 250 mm/a in the Arctic borders)	• Protection against cold for most of the year • Protection against strong winds and storms, mainly in the cold months • Best-possible use of the sun's warmth during the short summer
Temperate zone (temperate)	• Very diverse solar radiation intensities (e.g. in central Europe a high proportion of diffuse radiation and frequent cloud cover, in the transition zones to the tropics sometimes more direct radiation) • High annual temperature differences (e.g. central Europe approx. 18–20 K on average) • Moderate to low daily temperature differences (e.g. central Europe approx. 6–8 K on average) • Moderate to high relative humidity (e.g. central Europe approx. 80%) • Moderate precipitation (e.g. in central Europe approx. 800–1000 mm/a, in the transition zones to the tropics approx. 300–400 mm/a)	• Protection against overcooling in winter • Protection against overheating in summer • Protection against occasional, in some regions frequent, precipitation
Subtropical zone (dry, hot)	• Intensive direct solar radiation • Low relative humidity (approx. 10–50%) • Very low average precipitation (approx. 0–250 mm/a), but occurs as sporadic short periods of heavy rainfall • High daytime temperatures (max. temperature approx. 35–38°C as annual average, individual temperatures in continental desert regions > 50°C) • Moderate, sometimes low night-time temperatures (min. temperature approx. 16–20°C as annual average, individual temperatures as low as 0°C possible) • High daily temperature fluctuations (20 K on average) • Diverse, sometimes severe winds, in the form of sandstorms/dust-storms in desert regions • Low cloud coverage, usually clear skies, sometimes a high dust content in the atmosphere	• Protection against the loads of high heat absorption due to direct solar radiation and high temperatures • Protecting building components and building materials against direct solar radiation, plus their selection and use taking into account the high, short-term temperature differences
Tropical zone (moist, warm)	• High direct solar radiation with a cloudless sky, otherwise mostly tempered by cloud cover • High relative humidity (60–100%) • High precipitation (1200–2000 mm/a, in extreme cases up to 5000 mm/a) • Low daily and annual temperature differences (daily average: approx. 7 K; annual average: approx. 5 K) • Max. daytime temperatures approx. 30°C as an annual average • Min. night-time temperatures approx. 25°C as an annual average • High frequency of cloud cover, i.e. high proportion of diffuse radiation • Low air pressure • Often only light winds, but sometimes stormy gusts during rainfall • Tropical storms (cyclones, typhoons, hurricanes) in certain regions	• Relief from the unfavourable influence of heat and moisture (humid conditions) by using air circulation to promote heat dissipation via transpiration • Protecting buildings and building components against direct solar radiation and undesirable heat storage-through shading and the right choice of building form and orientation • Protecting building components against permanent saturation through well-controlled rainwater drainage and good ventilation

B 1.43

The term climate is often substituted by "global climate". As, however, global climate trends and average values for localities can be considerably different, we divide the spatial dimension into three scales:

• The microclimate describes the meteorological conditions of layers of air about 2 m above the surface for specific locations and their direct surroundings. Various influencing factors such as the characteristics of the ground or terrain, the position on a slope, valley or plain, vegetation, shading and the neighbouring buildings must be taken into account. The microclimate is influenced by landscaping and/or building measures; its effects on the climate inside a building and human well-being are crucial.
• The mesoclimate, also called the local climate, refers to the conditions over a few hundred metres to a few hundred kilometres. The different microclimates of a certain place (e.g. valley, settlement, island) are grouped together for this.
• The macroclimate can extend for more than 500 km and is made up of oceanic and/or continental effects. According to the macroclimate, the Earth is divided into four climate zones, whose special features form the overriding framework for energy-efficient design and construction.

Climate factors, climate elements
The processes and conditions that determine the climate of a place are known as the climate factors. These include the geographical latitude (e.g. incident solar radiation), the position with respect to the sea (e.g. precipitation, lower temperature fluctuations at sea level), the altitude or position with respect to mountains (e.g. drop in temperature with increasing height, precipitation depending on position with respect to prevailing winds) and ground coverage (e.g. low temperatures in forests, higher temperatures in built-up areas).
Climate elements, on the other hand, represent meteorological variables that identify the measurable properties of the climate system. The following elements are crucial to the conceptual design of buildings:

• solar radiation (direct and diffuse)
• air temperature and its daily/seasonal fluctuation
• air pressure
• air humidity
• wind (strength and direction)
• precipitation (quantity and annual distribution)
• evaporation

The climate factors therefore influence the daily weather, whose characteristics can be determined by measurable climate elements. Considered over a period of 30 to 40 years, the average values of these variables determine the climate as a whole.

Climate zones
The (approximately) spherical shape of the Earth, resulting in different angles of incidence for solar radiation, plus the tilt of the Earth's axis are responsible for the wide range of temperatures on the planet. In addition, the Earth's rotation is a central factor determining both the weather dynamic in the atmosphere and also the climate zones.
Many existing climate classification systems are based either on the global wind circulation systems or are derived from the effects on the Earth's surface. The most widely used is the "eco-climatic classification" dating from 1923 [9]. It divides the Earth into four different climate zones by means of certain meteorological variables (e.g. temperature, precipitation):

• polar zone (cold)
• temperate zone (temperate)
• subtropical zone (dry, hot)
• tropical zone (moist, hot)

These zones are further subdivided into climate types (e.g. elevated or frost-free tropics) or vegetation zones (e.g. tundra, steppe or tropical rainforest). The four climate zones listed above stretch from north to south in approximately parallel belts around the planet (Figs. B 1.40 and 1.41). As the distance from the equator or from the nearest ocean increases, so the seasonal temperature fluctuations of the respective zone increase as well. Their charac-

B 1.43   Correlation between climate zones, climate ele-
          ments and fundamental building requirements
B 1.44   Average annual global radiation in Europe
B 1.45   Average annual global radiation in Germany

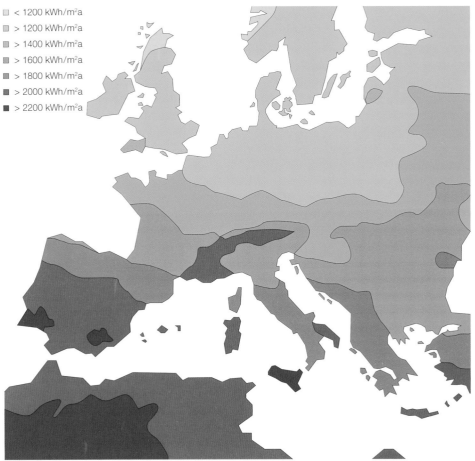

  ☐ < 1200 kWh/m²a
  ☐ > 1200 kWh/m²a
  ☐ > 1400 kWh/m²a
  ☐ > 1600 kWh/m²a
  ☐ > 1800 kWh/m²a
  ☐ > 2000 kWh/m²a
  ☐ > 2200 kWh/m²a

B 1.44

teristic climate elements plus the resulting
requirements for building work are given in
Fig. B 1.43 [10].

Solar radiation

Solar radiation is a critical factor for the passive
and active use of solar energy in buildings. The
sun emits radiation as it converts hydrogen into
helium. This radiation has an intensity of approx.
63 000 kW/m² at the surface of the sun, where
the temperature is about 6000°C. The intensity
of this radiation output is 1367 W/m² on the
edge of the Earth's atmosphere (solar constant).
The radiation components that reach the Earth's
surface after penetrating the atmosphere are
broken down as follows:

• Direct radiation, reaching the surface directly
  and unobstructed.
• Diffuse radiation, reaching the surface after
  being scattered in the atmosphere (e.g. by
  clouds, or water and dust particles).

Together, these two radiation components are
known as global radiation. Owing to the varying
angle of incidence, there is a variation in the
intensity and the seasonal fluctuation of the
available solar radiation as we move further
away from the equator. Whereas the global
radiation at the equator is about 2200 kWh/m²a,
solar gains in Central Europe are on average
only 1100 kWh/m²a (Fig. B 1.42). If we compare
the radiation profile of northern or southern
Europe with that of the Sahara Desert, besides
the increasing seasonal differences as we go
further north, we also see a difference in the
diffuse and direct radiation components (Fig.
B 1.48). In principle, both types of radiation can
be exploited for energy purposes, but solar
energy yields are mainly based on the direct
radiation component.
Furthermore, the length of a sunlit day and the
hours of sunshine have a considerable influence
on the solar gains (Fig. B 1.44). In Europe the
number of hours of sunshine annually is 1400–
2500 on average. The differences between
Mediterranean regions, countries with a continental climate or tall mountains therefore amounts
to approx. 40%. In Germany the annual number
of hours of sunshine fluctuates between 1400

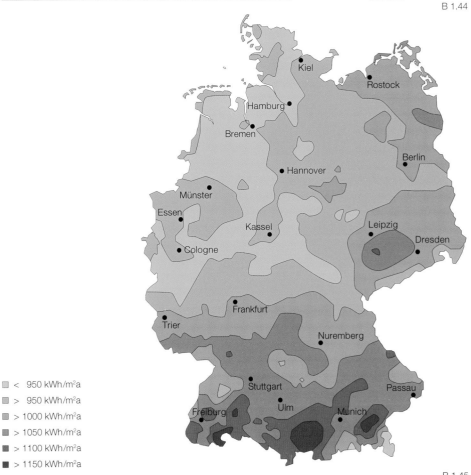

  ☐ < 950 kWh/m²a
  ☐ > 950 kWh/m²a
  ☐ > 1000 kWh/m²a
  ☐ > 1050 kWh/m²a
  ☐ > 1100 kWh/m²a
  ☐ > 1150 kWh/m²a

B 1.45

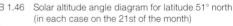

B 1.46   Solar altitude angle diagram for latitude 51° north
         (in each case on the 21st of the month)
B 1.47   Annual trajectory of the sun over the northern
         hemisphere
B 1.48   Comparison of mean values for diffuse and direct
         radiation in different regions
         a Northern Europe: London (GB), latitude 51° north
         b Southern Europe: Almeria (E), latitude 36° north
         c Africa: Sahara, latitude 20° north
B 1.49   Systematic representation of comfort factors
B 1.50   Selected climate data for Berlin (D)

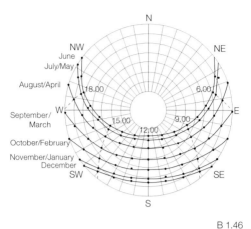

B 1.46

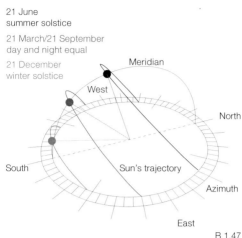

B 1.47

and 1800, with approximately equal amounts of direct and diffuse radiation. The global radiation lies between about 900 and 1150 kWh/m²a, with about three-quarters of this incident radiation arriving in the six hottest months (Fig. B 1.45). The exploitation of solar energy through passive measures or active systems calls for details regarding the intensity and number of hours of sunshine plus the angle of incidence and the trajectory of the sun (Fig. B 1.47). The natural lighting conditions, the duration of sunlight and shading, can be determined for a certain geographical location with the help of a solar altitude diagram (Fig. B 1.46).

Climate data
Optimum use of the local natural energy reserves requires specific climate data corresponding to the geographical location (Fig. B 1.50, for further data see p. 260). In addition to the global radiation, the temperature, humidity and wind are the most important factors.

Temperature
The temperature of the external air is dependent on the available solar radiation and the altitude of the place above sea level. The temperature drops by approx. 1°C for every 200 m rise in altitude. The average air temperature has a distinct effect on the transmission or ventilation heat losses in winter and the possible overheating in summer. The frequency of

extreme temperatures must be considered in conjunction with the efficiency and design of passive measures plus the sizing of HVAC systems. If, for example, night-time cooling is to be used to the full, the external air temperatures at night must generally remain on the low side. In Germany the average annual temperature is about 8.4°C (16.5°C in summer, 0.9°C in winter). The fluctuations between day and night are around 5–10 K.

Humidity
The humidity of the air is a measure the quantity of water vapour in the atmosphere. It affects the health and well-being of human beings just as it much as it does statements as to whether regions tend to be foggy or rainy. The maximum quantity of water vapour that the air can accommodate is influenced by the temperature. The unit of measurement "absolute humidity" reflects the quantity of water vapour actually present in the air in g/m³. This is important for the escape of moisture from rooms through diffusion. The "relative humidity" is specified as a percentage and indicates the ratio of the current water vapour content in the atmosphere to the maximum possible water vapour content.

Wind
Directional air movements in the atmosphere ensue as a result of the different air pressures of masses of air. Air particles from regions with

high pressure conditions flow into regions with low pressure conditions until the pressure differences are evened out. Besides the wind loads relevant for the structural design of buildings, the development of natural ventilation concepts need information on the prevailing wind direction plus the pressure and suction conditions. With a skilful arrangement of ventilation inlets and outlets, the wind can be used to ventilate a building, although this does depend on the depth and height of the building as well. In Germany the average wind speed in the north with a prevailing wind direction of west to south-west is approx. 5 m/s, and about 2 m/s in the south.

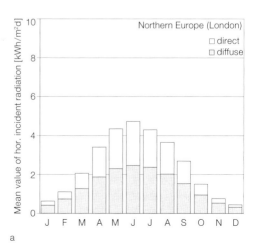

a

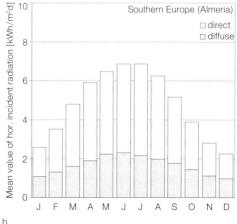

b

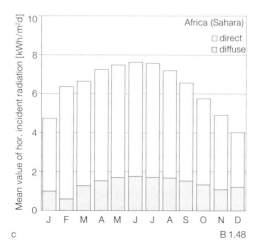

c

B 1.48

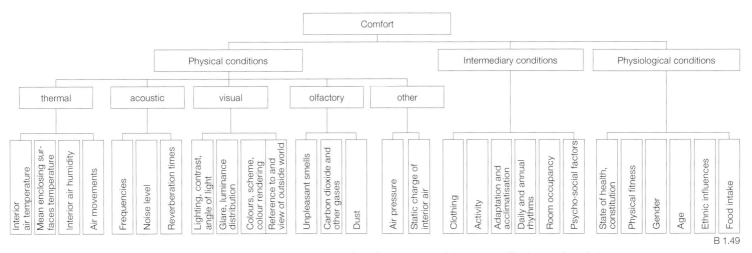

B 1.49

Comfort

The well-being of a person is based on his or her subjective perception of a number of external influences. Besides standardised, physically measurable ambient conditions (e.g. temperature of interior air, intensity of lighting, level of noise), certain individual, physiological criteria (e.g. age, gender, constitution) and intermediary conditions (e.g. clothing, activity) affect our well-being (Fig. B 1.49). Comfort is therefore not a factor that can be quantified exactly, but instead represents individual empirical values at which a human being experiences his or her surroundings as agreeable.

Levels of perception

The primary sense for human beings is the sense of vision. Some 80–90% of our data input is based on what we can see. However, the human brain cannot fully process all the information that arrives via our sense of vision. The quantity of data is therefore reduced, supplemented with our own experiences and assembled to form a complete picture. Every person generates his or her image, i.e. perception, of the world in this way. Users develop an understanding for their spatial environment, insert this into their wealth of experience and at the same time transfer the specific context of each a situation to their current perception. Besides the sense of vision, our sense of touch, hearing and smell, plus the feeling of hot or

cold are important functions for perceiving architecture and act as a means for concretising the things we have perceived primarily visually. Concordance, harmony and superimposition between the visual impression and other levels of perception therefore condense to form an overall picture.
Human beings store the information they have received by linking the perception with the respective experience. Each additional sensory link increases the chance of "recalling" a memory. The linking strategies can be demonstrated by way of a simple example, e.g. a Finnish sauna. If we initially think of a simple timber construction (visual), the feeling of moisture plus the warmth of the benches or the smell of the resinous wood are then recalled as well. The stimulation of many senses creates a higher chance of lasting memories of specific places or buildings.

Interior climate

The factors crucial for the interior climate are derived from a person's prevailing levels of perception. In order to arrange pleasant living and working conditions, an interior climate that is agreeable in terms of thermal, acoustic, visual and olfactory aspects must be guaranteed. And thermal comfort is the most important factor here. It influences the human heat balance and also has a direct effect on the energy consumption of a building.

The human heat balance

A heat balance with a basic body temperature around 37°C over the whole body is a fundamental prerequisite for well-being and efficiency. If the ambient temperature drops, the body first allows the extremities to cool in order to protect the functions of the brain, heart and other vital organs (Fig. B 1.51). The human organism generates heat to maintain its bodily and metabolic functions, which it obtains by converting the chemical energy contained in nutrients. To guarantee a constant temperature, it is necessary to transfer the internal heat generated to the environment. Our bodies use the following mechanisms for this (Fig. B 1.52):

- evaporation of water via breathing and the skin (transpiration)
- convection of heat from the surface of the body to the ambient air
- conduction of heat from the body to immediate objects (floor, chair, etc.)
- radiation of heat to the surfaces enclosing the room and to nearby objects

At low temperatures, the heat loss takes place mainly via convection, conduction and radiation. In an excessively cold environment, the blood circulation in the skin is initially restricted and heat is generated by movement (starting with shivering). As the temperature rises, the evaporation component in the heat loss starts

Berlin		Min.	Month	Max.	Month	Annual mean
Air temperature	[C°]	-0.6	Jan	18.5	Jul	8.9
Mean daily max. temperature	[C°]	1.7	Jan	23.8	Aug	13.1
Mean daily min. temperature	[C°]	-3.5	Jan	13.3	Jul	4.7
Absolute max. temperature	[C°]	13.0	Jan	37.8	Jul	37.8
Absolute min. temperature	[C°]	-26.0	Feb	5.7	Jul	-26.0
Mean relative air humidity	[%]	66.0	May	88.0	Dec	78.0
Mean precipitation	[mm]	31.0	Mar	70.0	Jul	581.0
Max. precipitation	[mm]	85.0	Feb	230.0	Jul	803.0
Min. precipitation	[mm]	1.0	Apr, Sept–Nov	16.0	Jan	381.0
Max. daily precipitation	[mm]	20.0	Dec	125.0	Aug	125.0
No. of precipitation days	[d]	12.0	Mar, Sept	17.0	Jan	166.0
Evaporation	[mm]	0	Jan–Feb	125.0	Jul	615.0
Mean No. of sunshine hours	[h]	36.0	Dec	244.0	Jul	1818.0
Radiation	[Wh/m²d]	607.0	Jan	5436.0	Jun	2805.0
Mean wind speed	[m/s]	2.8	Aug–Sept	3.8	Mar	3.2

[1] Annual total of incoming radiation (horizontal) = 1010 kWh/m²a

B 1.50

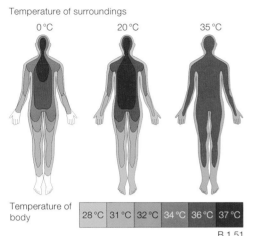

Temperature of surroundings

0 °C   20 °C   35 °C

Temperature of body

| 28 °C | 31 °C | 32 °C | 34 °C | 36 °C | 37 °C |

B 1.51

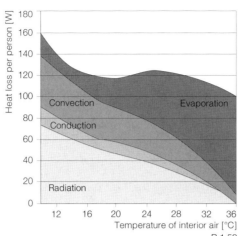

Temperature of interior air [°C]

B 1.52

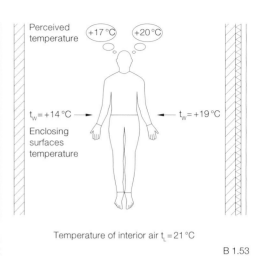

Temperature of interior air $t_L = 21$ °C

B 1.53

to increase markedly. Once the ambient temperature is perceived as too hot, the blood circulation is initially increased in order to cool the surface of the skin through increased evaporation (transpiration). This thermal regulation of the human body has such fine mechanisms that the metabolic rate can change by approx. 20% for every 1.5 K increase or decrease in temperature.

There is also a close relationship between the heat production of the human body and the type of activity (Fig. B 1.54). The quantity of heat generated increases with physical activity. When performing uncomplicated office work in an interior air temperature of 20°C, a person of average constitution and size generates a heat output of 125–170 W. But strenuous physical work can increase this heat output to 360–490 W. Hence, the limit of the perception of humid conditions lies between 19.5 and 28°C, depending

on the degree of activity, the limit for the perception of cool conditions between 14.5 and 18°C, and the range of thermal comfort extends from 17 to 24°C. In recent years it has become accepted for the design of production and office premises in particular that optimum interior climate conditions improve the efficiency and satisfaction of employees – and that leads to economic benefits.

Thermal comfort

Assuming optimum physiological boundary conditions and other physical factors (e.g. velocity and humidity of the interior air, average external temperature) and a person with a normal physical constitution, investigations into the frequency of accidents and the efficiency of sedentary workers have shown that the range of thermal comfort is not very wide (Fig. B 1.55). If the temperature of the interior air is too high or too low, the risk of accidents increases and manual dexterity, productivity and mental abilities decrease rapidly. DIN 1946-2 defines the thermal comfort for humans as being when the temperature, moisture and movement of the surrounding air are agreeable and neither hotter nor colder, drier nor moister interior air is desired. A thermally comfortable environment is therefore primarily due to physical influencing factors such as the temperature of the inte-

Values for one person		Type of activity								
		Complete rest Lying down Basic metabolic state		Minimal activity Sitting		Light work		Light physical work		Strenuous physical work	
		Child	Adult	Child	Adult	Child	Adult	Child	Adult	Child	Adult
Energy consumption required per day	[kJ/d] [kcal/d] [kWh/d]	5900 1410 1.6	7500 1790 2.1	8000 1910 2.2	9700 2320 2.7	8800 2100 2.4	10500 2510 2.9	10100 2410 2.8	12600 3010 3.5	11300 2700 3.1	14700 3510 4.1
Total heat loss (inc. evaporation)	[W]	50–65	65–85	60–80	75–100	100–130	125–170	170–225	215–295	280–380	360–490
thereof dry heat loss (convection, conduction, radiation)	[W]	35–45	50–65	45–60	60–75	70–95	95–130	120–160	165–220	200–275	280–370
Water vapour production per hour	[g/h]	21–28	23–32	25–34	27–38	41–57	46–62	70–95	78–108	117–160	130–180
Oxygen requirement per hour	[l/h]	9–12	12–16	10–14	14–19	17–24	24–32	30–41	40–51	50–68	65–90
Exhaled CO_2 per hour (concentration in the air 0.03–0.05% by vol.)	[l/h]	7–10	10–13	9–12	12–16	15–20	19–26	25–34	32–43	46–56	55–75
Fresh-air rate required when CO_2 is max. 0.10% by vol.	[m³/h]	12–17	17–21	15–20	20–26	25–33	32–42	42–57	55–72	70–93	90–130
Boundary of humid conditions with respect to interior air temperature	[°C]	28	28	26	26	24	24	21.5	21.5	19.5	19.5
Equilibrium = comfort	[°C]	24	24	22	22	20.5	20.5	19	19	17	17
Boundary of feeling of coolness	[°C]	18	18	17	17	16	16	15.5	15.5	14.5	14.5

B 1.54

rior air and the average temperature of the external air (not too cold, not too hot), the humidity of the interior air (not too dry, not too humid) and the movement of the air (no draughts). Even though these parameters have a mutual influence on each other and a person's well-being is always founded on subjective perceptions, it is nevertheless possible to specify a few guiding values for an agreeable environment: interior air temperature 20–22°C (in summer up to 26°C), interior air humidity 35–60%, and interior air movements up to 0.15 m/s. But even with optimum conditions, 100% satisfaction among users or occupants can never be achieved owing to the diverse parameters and individual factors (e.g. type of clothing, physical activity, age, gender, etc.).
In order to take account of these individual, subjective, varying human factors, the thermal perception is specified in terms of the PMV (Predicted Mean Vote) value (Fig. B 1.57). From this value it is then possible to determine the PPD (Predicted Percentage of Dissatisfied) value – the number of people who can be expected to be unhappy with the prevailing interior climate. Due to the individual evaluation of the interior climate conditions, even with a PMV value of 0 (comfortable), the number of dissatisfied persons will still be 5% (Fig. B 1.56).

European standards
The methods contained in DIN 1946-2, CEN report CR 1752 and DIN EN ISO 7730 are currently the most popular methods for evaluating the thermal interior climate. These assessment methods, however, are primarily intended as an aid for designing HVAC installations; there is no separate directive or standard for assessing the climatic comfort with natural ventilation.
In DIN 1946-2 [11] the guide values for the "operative" temperature – also called the perceived temperature – are always related to the concurrent external air temperature (Fig. B 1.65). A rapid rise or fall in the external air temperature must therefore be compensated for by the HVAC installation. The new edition of DIN EN 13779 [12] refers to the recommendations of DIN EN ISO 7730 for non-residential buildings with HVAC installations. DIN EN ISO 7730 [13] can be used to create new and assess existing ambient climates. It is based on the PMV model and recommends maintaining a comfort range between -0.5 < PMV < +0.5 (Fig. B 1.56), which corresponds to a PPD of 10%. As these ambient conditions can only be achieved through the use of HVAC installations, the planned new edition of the standard will permit higher temperatures – similar to Fig. B 1.58, category C – in the case of natural ventilation. CEN report CR 1752 [14] defines interior quality categories (A–C). Whereas there are very tight limits for rooms with demanding specifications (category A, PPD < 6%), greater temperature fluctuations are permitted in rooms with less demanding specifications (category C, PPD < 15%).

Interior air temperature and average enclosing surfaces temperature
The level of comfort in a building is essentially determined by the interior air temperature and the average enclosing surfaces temperature. On average, these values correspond roughly to the perceived temperature, which should lie between 19 and 20°C. Within certain limits, the surface and air temperatures can compensate for each other. The smaller the difference between these temperatures (in the ideal case no more than 3 K), the more comfortable people will feel in their surroundings. An excessively asymmetrical thermal profile, which can occur, for example, in rooms with large windows and poor thermal insulation, leads to discomfort. As can be seen in Fig. B 1.59, good thermal insulation to the building envelope therefore forms the foundation for creating comfortable conditions through high surface temperatures, and at the same time reduces the energy consumption. When planning coil heating in particular, it is important that with room temperatures of around 20°C, the temperature of the floor should not exceed 27°C and that of the ceiling 34°C (Figs. B 1.60 and 1.61).

Interior air humidity
With ambient temperatures of 20–22°C, the relative humidity of the interior air may fluctuate between 35 and 70% and still be perceived as agreeable (Fig. B 1.62). In this comfort range, the perceived room temperature of a human being rises by 0.3 K for every 10% increase in the humidity. Above 70% r.h., there is a risk of condensation and mould growth on cold external components without good thermal insulation (Fig. B 1.64). A relative humidity below 35%, on the other hand, promotes dust accumulation and electrostatic charges in components, which can be very unpleasant in the case of floor finishes and metal items with which people come into contact. As a result, the recommended value for the interior air humidity is 40–60%. In order to rule out a "barracks climate" – ambient conditions regarded as disagreeable due to high temperature and moisture fluctuations – right from the planning phase, adequate thermal masses are required for interiors (see p. 158).

Air movements
The movement of the air in a room also exerts a noticeable influence on a person's heat balance and hence his or her well-being. DIN EN ISO 7730 includes recommended values for air velocities in conjunction with the degree of turbulence of the airflow because airflows with changing directions and velocities reinforce the feeling of draughts. At an interior air temperature of 20°C, air velocities as low as 0.15 m/s may be regarded as unpleasant (Fig. B 1.63). If, however, the interior air temperature is above 23°C, a higher air velocity can help to generate a pleasant environment by dissipating body heat. Draughts in the finished building can be avoided by ensuring – during the planning

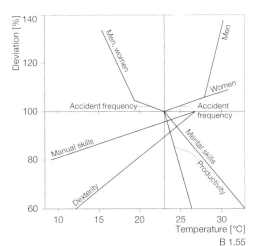

B 1.55

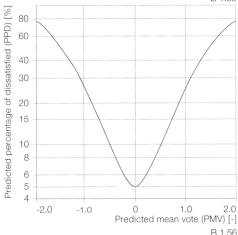

B 1.56

Perception	Predicted mean vote (PMV)
Cold	-3
Cool	-2
Acceptably cool	-1
Neutral (comfortable)	0
Acceptably warm	1
Warm	2
Hot	3

B 1.57

	Summer (cooling period)	Winter (heating period)
CEN CR 1752		
Category A	24.5°C ±1.0	22.0°C ±1.0
Category B	24.5°C ±1.5	22.0°C ±2.0
Category C	24.5°C ±2.5	22.0°C ±3.0
DIN EN ISO 7730	24.5°C ±1.5	22.0°C ±2.0

B 1.58

B 1.51 Temperature distribution in the body for different ambient temperatures
B 1.52 Heat losses from the body for different interior air temperatures (office work)
B 1.53 Perceived temperature for different enclosing surfaces temperatures
B 1.54 Recommended values for the human air, heat and moisture balance
B 1.55 Accident frequency and productivity in relation to the interior temperature for sedentary activities
B 1.56 PPD value in relation to PMV value
B 1.57 Assessment scale for the predicted mean vote (PMV)
B 1.58 Requirements regarding the operative interior temperature for sedentary activities

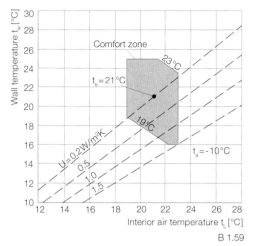

B 1.59

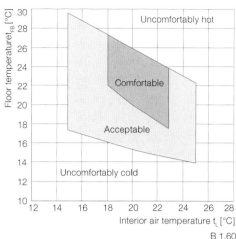

B 1.60

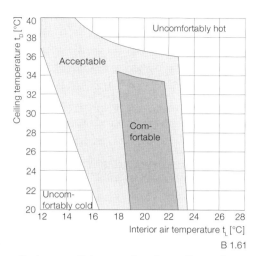

B 1.61

phase and particularly during construction – that all details are airtight.

All the factors that influence the thermal comfort also have a direct effect on the energy consumption of buildings. Low flow velocities in ventilation systems save energy and improve the well-being of occupants. Higher internal surface temperatures brought about by good thermal insulation measures improve the well-being of people and prevent transmission heat losses (Fig. B 1.53). External components with low U-values allow the interior air temperature to be lowered without compromising comfort; the heating requirement decreases by approx. 6% for every 1 K reduction in temperature. Current studies show that the type of ventilation has a critical influence on the well-being of occupants [15]. In buildings with natural ventilation, an average of 20% of users experience the interior climate as unpleasant; this figure rises to 34% in buildings with partial conditioning of the interior air, and 54% in fully air-conditioned buildings. Furthermore, persons who regard the interior climate as unhealthy are 2.6 times more likely to suffer from sick building syndrome.

The possibility of influencing the interior climate, to adapting it to individual needs, represents another important factor that influences the satisfaction of users. These possibilities include:
- opening windows
- individually controlled sunshades and glare protection
- fans (used locally in summer)
- thermostat valves
- regulation of the interior air

In a comparison of mechanically and naturally ventilated rooms, the aforementioned studies reveal that people in a naturally ventilated environment accept a wider range of temperatures; the statutory comfort limits can therefore be expanded.

Visual comfort
Visible perception generates the formation of an identity via the unmistakability of the design. If the information users require is easily available, well-being, orientation abilities, productivity and

the feeling of safety and security all improve. But the physical boundary conditions of our power of sight also contribute substantially to our well-being. The human eye perceives the electromagnetic radiation of sunlight over a range of wavelengths from approx. 380 nm (violet light) to approx. 780 nm (red light). Above all, the visual cortex in the brain processes the excitation patterns coming from the eye as a result of its reaction to light and colour. Optimum visual comfort for working areas is guaranteed when the luminance at the place of work (ambient luminance) is geared to the respective visual task (direct luminance). This can be accomplished, in principle, with daylight, artificial light or a combination of both. However, natural daylight creates more comfortable conditions because it includes all the colours of the spectrum. Visual comfort is influenced by a number of factors with relevance for energy consumption.

Illuminance
The luminous flux is measured in lumens [lm]. It describes the entire light output emitted by a light source. On the other hand, the illuminance, measured with the unit lux [lx], describes the luminous flux incident on a certain surface. The directives specifying recommended illuminance levels are in each case derived from the most difficult visual task is to be expected.

Glare
Besides a reasonable illuminance, appropriate contrast is also necessary for agreeable conditions. The luminance [cd/m²] defines the luminous flux emitted from an illuminated surface. Absolute glare in humans is the result of excessive luminance (> 104 cd/m²), whereas relative glare is caused by excessive contrast. Ideally, the luminance conditions for a specific visual task, the immediate surroundings and the wider environment should not exceed a ratio of 10:3:1. Bright wall and ceiling surfaces increase the reflections from the surroundings and reduce the risk of relative glare by creating a more consistent distribution of the luminance (Fig. B 1.67).

Angle of light and contrast
The colour of the light, the colour rendering, the direction of the light and the colour of surfaces

affect our spatial perception depending on the angle of incidence or reflection of the light. Light striking bright materials at a shallow angle can cause them to take on a sculpted look, whereas dark surfaces tend to appear two-dimensional owing to the minimal contrast. Due to their better reflection properties, bright surfaces improve the lighting efficiency and optimise the effects of both daylight and artificial lighting.

Colours
The colours of surfaces in a room promote associative references. Warm colours are stimulating and allow a facade, a room or an object to appear smaller. In contrast to this, cold colours create distance and enlarge the impression of space. We perceive colours not only visually, but also subjectively – our perception of hot and cold can be influenced noticeably by the colours of our surroundings. For example, tests have established that rooms painted in a cold colour, e.g. blue-green, reduced the temperature perception of test persons by approx. 3°C. A room painted orange, on the other hand, raised the subjective temperature perception. This can be explained by the physiological effects of the colour on the human organism, leading to a marginal increase in pulse rate and blood pressure. A uniform, monotonous colour scheme based on a simple, physiological colour effect should, however, be avoided. Only a composition made up of harmonising colours leads to an overall impression that will be regarded as pleasant.

Colour rendering
The visual perception of the human being is calibrated to natural sunlight. The changing spectrum of the light over the course of a day controls, for example, the daily rhythm and the functions of the organs. Distorting the spectrum can have detrimental effects on our perception and well-being. The prevailing colour of the light for normal activities should therefore be natural or nearly natural. The glazing should not alter the frequency pattern of the light any more than is unavoidable (see p. 155, and Fig. B 5.25).

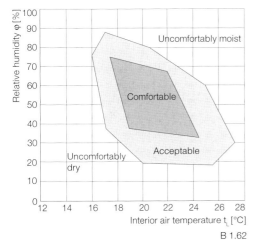

B 1.62

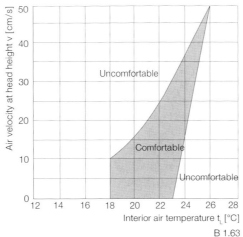

B 1.63

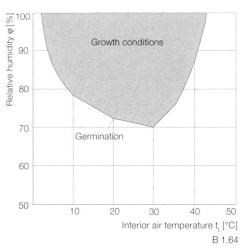

B 1.64

Acoustic comfort

Our auditory perception is based on the transmission of vibrations of the ambient air (airborne sound) or solid bodies (structure-born sound). Noise pollution can even occur at low sound pressure levels, disturbing sleep and relaxation, and impairing productivity. The acoustic comfort of a room depends on a number of parameters, e.g. the sound level of external noise, the sound reduction index of the building envelope, noises from the building services, the shape and/or size of a room, and the surface characteristics of the enclosing surfaces and the furniture.

Sound

Sound is propagated as a result of the smallest pressure and density fluctuations in an elastic medium (e.g. air, solid body). We distinguish between infrasound (< 20 Hz), audible sound (20 – 20 000 Hz), ultrasound (20 Hz – 1 GHz) and hypersound (> 1 GHz), with the human being best being able to perceive the sounds in the range from 1000 to 5000 Hz. Like light, sound is transmitted in the form of absorption, reflection and dissipation (conversion into heat). In addition, we distinguish between noise and sounds, the former being regarded as disturbing acoustic events (e.g. traffic noise) and the latter being able to awaken associations and hence have a positive influence on our acoustic well-being.

Acoustic power, weighted sound pressure level

The sound pressure level [Lp] represents a logarithmic scale for describing sound events and is specified in decibels [dB]. The measurable range of sound pressure levels stretches roughly from 0 to 160 dB. A sound pressure level difference of 3 dB can be readily perceived at moderate to high volumes and frequencies. Differences of 10 dB are perceived as being roughly "twice as loud". In order to emulate the human perception of loudness as closely as possible, the sensory impression of the frequency response is taken into account by using the weighted sound pressure level [dB(A)] instead of the straightforward sound level [dB]. Specific maximum dB(A) values are specified for disturbing noise depending on the

type of use, e.g. 25 dB(A) for recording studios or opera houses, 35 dB(A) for offices.

Reverberation times

The reverberation time describes the acoustic properties of a room. A minimal reverbertion time (up to 50 ms) helps ensure legibility of speech. In the case of music, a medium reverberation time (approx. 80 ms) improves clarity, whereas long reverberation times favour a voluminous sound (Fig. B 1.66).

Olfactory comfort

The human sense of smell, besides allowing us to recognise food that is no longer edible, primarily serves us in our social communications, for controlling our vegetative or hormonal processes. The mucous membrane responsible for smell in the upper nasal cavity has more than 350 different types of receptor at its disposal, which can separate out the odour molecules from the air and register them chemically. As our sense of smell can differentiate between several thousand odours (but cannot name them all completely), we distinguish between seven main odour categories: flowery, ethereal, musklike, camphor-like, putrid, sweaty and pungent. Besides the three main constituents of the air, nitrogen (78%), oxygen (21%) and argon (0.9%), there are many other trace elements (e.g. carbon dioxide, hydrogen and other noble gases) plus foreign substances. The quality of the interior air is influenced by various factors, e.g. the composition of the external air, furnishings, fittings and building materials plus the usage-related contamination by people. Guaranteeing pleasant and healthy interior air calls for an adequate supply of fresh air plus the extraction of CO_2, moisture, pollutants and odours. Owing to the high importance of the air quality for health and productivity, the maximum workplace concentration values stipulate appropriate recommended values for the maximum permissible quantities of hazardous substances. Since 2005 further statutory values have also been valid in Germany: the workplace limit value and the biological limit value.
When assessing the interior air, both the CO_2 concentration and the indicators olf and decipol [dp] are relevant. The CO_2 production

B 1.59 Comfort in relation to interior air temperature, average enclosing surfaces temperature and U-value of building envelope
B 1.60 Comfort in relation to interior air and floor temperatures
B 1.61 Comfort in relation to interior air and ceiling temperatures
B 1.62 Comfort in relation to interior air temperature and relative humidity
B 1.63 Comfort in relation to interior air temperature and air velocity near the body
B 1.64 Conditions for mould growth
B 1.65 Permissible temperature ranges to DIN 1946-2 for the design of HVAC installations
B 1.66 Recommended reverberation times according to room function
B 1.67 Recommended degrees of reflection for surfaces to EN 12464-1

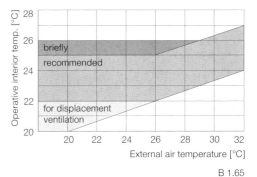

B 1.65

Room function	Reverberation time [ms]
Office	35
Classroom	40–60
Opera house	130–160
Organ music	250–300

B 1.66

Building component	Degree of reflection
Ceiling	60–90 %
Wall	30–80 %
Work surface	20–60 %
Floor	10–50 %

B 1.67

59

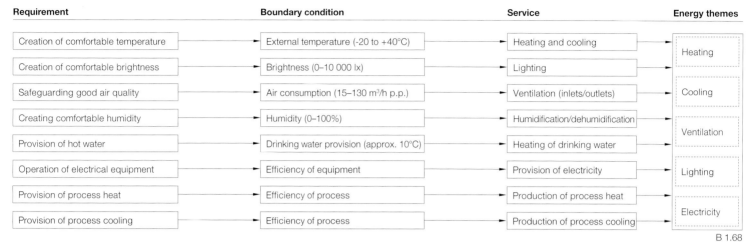

Requirement	Boundary condition	Service	Energy themes
Creation of comfortable temperature	External temperature (-20 to +40°C)	Heating and cooling	Heating
Creation of comfortable brightness	Brightness (0–10 000 lx)	Lighting	
Safeguarding good air quality	Air consumption (15–130 m³/h p.p.)	Ventilation (inlets/outlets)	Cooling
Creating comfortable humidity	Humidity (0–100%)	Humidification/dehumidification	
Provision of hot water	Drinking water provision (approx. 10°C)	Heating of drinking water	Ventilation
Operation of electrical equipment	Efficiency of equipment	Provision of electricity	
Provision of process heat	Efficiency of process	Production of process heat	Lighting
Provision of process cooling	Efficiency of process	Production of process cooling	Electricity

B 1.68

of a person fluctuates, depending on activity, between 7 and 75 l per hour and is a major factor in the deterioration of the interior air quality. It was back in the 19th century that the hygiene expert Max Josef von Pettenkofer defined the recommended value of 0.1% by vol. for the CO_2 content, a value that is still valid today as a measure of agreeable interior air conditions. Legislation covering CO_2 concentrations plus details of the air change rates required can be found in the chapter entitled "Building services" (see p. 133). The indicators olf and decipol can also be used to assess the quality of the air. Whereas the olf identifies the strength of odour sources (e.g. people, animals, plants, emissions from materials, etc.), the decipol – a measure of the perceived odour emissions – also includes the airflow. The quality of the air in a room lies between 0.7 and 2.5 dp depending on the usage requirements. Besides the quality of the air in interiors, emissions of pollutants from building materials can have a considerable effect on the health and well-being of users or occupants. Further information can be found in the chapter entitled "Materials" (see p. 171).

Energy services
The creation of comfortable living or working conditions and satisfying the aforementioned comfort conditions calls for intelligent planning of buildings with a much higher energy efficiency. Nevertheless, an energy input will remain necessary in most climate zones. The magnitude of the energy consumption during the period of use must be considered in addition to the design of the building and building envelope, the climatic boundary conditions, the technology employed and, of course, the comfort demands plus the behaviour of occupants and users.

Demands and needs
The energy requirement in a building is principally due to boundary conditions and user-related requirements, which trigger, directly or indirectly, energy-relevant services that are in the first place independent of architectural parameters (Fig. B 1.68).
In Central Europe, the temperature of the external air varies between -20 and +40°C. The user-related comfort requirements strive, how-

ever, to maintain a certain temperature range, which results in the corresponding services "heating" and, possibly, "cooling" too. Likewise, the brightness varies from virtually 0 lx in the night to about 100 000 lx on a sunny day, which results in the need for the service "lighting". The use of enclosed interiors by human beings results in a certain "air consumption" because of corresponding emissions. The aim is, however, to maintain a constant, high air quality in the ideal case. This calls for a specific exchange of air by way of the service "ventilation" (inward and outward airflows). If the humidity of the air is to remain between certain limit values, the service "humidification and dehumidification" is necessary.
Normally, the temperature of fresh-water supplies to buildings is about 10°C. In order to create agreeable usage conditions, especially for personal hygiene purposes, this drinking water has to be heated accordingly. And there is also the need to operate electrical equipment, e.g. escalators and lifts, tools and machines, telecommunications, household appliances, etc. For industrial users, these requirements are supplemented by process-related heating and cooling requirements.
Whereas the climatic boundary conditions specific to the location can hardly be influenced, there is considerable leeway in the user-related requirements. For example, the maximum permissible air temperature in summer has a decisive influence on the extent of the energy service "cooling". Likewise, the behaviour of users with respect to heating, ventilation, lighting or the use of hot water has a decisive influence on the use of energy-relevant services. In this respect, a fundamental questioning of needs is indispensable – in cooperation with the users. Deviations from the technically feasible optimum are sensible; users should, however, explicitly agree to restrictions based on economic and/or ecological reasoning (e.g. natural ventilation).
In order to create comfortable conditions and be able to handle the needs of users and utilisation properly, we must distinguish between five different energy themes: heating, cooling, lighting, ventilation and electricity (Fig. B 1.69).
In terms of the thermal balance, the provision of heating must ensure that heat is not lost and

hence is retained for as long as possible. As – despite all efforts – the provision of heat is necessary in many instances, the efficient production, storage, distribution and transfer of heat must be guaranteed. In all these areas, but especially in the production, there is the potential to realise a low-CO_2 or even a neutral-CO_2 overall concept by using renewable energy sources. Numerous technologies are available for using biomass, solar thermal systems and heat pumps in a variety of ways.
When it comes to cooling, the initial aim should be to plan building and construction measures such that overheating of habitable rooms is avoided. If cooling is nevertheless necessary, requirements and options here are similar to the provision of heat. It is primarily the systems that use the cooling potential of the ground and groundwater, also solar-powered cooling systems, that offer the most favourable perspectives for the cooling of buildings.
In order to guarantee an appropriate air quality, an easily regulated natural exchange of air should be the first priority. Usage-related situations and measures for reducing the heating and cooling energy requirements can, however, render it necessary to provide a mechanical backup for ensuring a supply of fresh air. Early coordination between ventilation requirements and building measures (e.g. exhaust air channelled through an atrium or double-leaf facade) for the fresh-air supply will result in synergy effects. In many cases technical components for heat recovery contain considerable potential for savings.
The primary challenge for the lighting theme is to improve the use of daylight. The technical optimisation of artificial lighting is another worthwhile factor, e.g. through differentiation in the illuminance levels, the installation of low-energy lighting and good controls.
Electrical power requirements in addition to those required for operating artificial lighting and HVAC systems are essentially determined by the needs of users and the amount of electrical equipment installed in the building. However, a considerable influence can be exerted on the energy-efficiency targets during the planning process. Furthermore, there is great potential embodied in decentralised electricity

Energy themes	Minimising energy requirement	Optimising energy supply
Heating	Maintaining heat	Efficient heat gains
Cooling	Avoiding overheating	Efficient heat dissipation
Ventilation	Natural ventilation	Efficient mechanical ventilation
Lighting	Use of daylight	Optimising artificial lighting
Electricity	Efficient use of electricity	Decentralised electricity generation

B 1.69

generation through co-generation plants and building envelopes with active solar energy systems.

Level of technology
The question regarding the extent to which energy services need to be provided by way of technical systems depends on the type of utilisation and the level of requirements, and, critically, on the building form, the building envelope and the choice of materials as well. Two different strategies can be pursued here:
One is centred around the respective technological means to guarantee optimum functioning, although numerous energy installations, flaps, valves, sensors, etc. enable an adaptive behaviour. These are controlled by a complex computer program which guarantees the optimum regulation strategy depending on the climatic boundary conditions and the behaviour of users. Comfortable interior conditions can be achieved through optimised technical building services in nearly every building and at any location.
The other strategy aims to design the building in such a way that through urban planning stipulations, a building form and envelope optimised for the energy needs, the layout and choice of materials, the desired conditions – if necessary with minor compromises with respect to the optimum – can be achieved with a minimum of technology.
The expressions "high-tech" and "low-tech" respectively have been become established for these two strategies. As neither of these theories can be implemented alone, as with most things in life, a coordinated interaction of both strategies, which gives priority to the so-called passive or cybernetic (self-regulating) systems, usually produces the best result.

References:
[1] Status as of 2000
[2] Meadows, Donella; Meadows, Dennis; Zahn, Erich; Milling, Peter: The Limits to Growth. A Report for the Club of Rome's Project on the Predicament of Mankind. New York, 1972
[3] Intergovernmental Panel on Climate Change (IPCC): Fourth Assessment Report. Summary for Policymakers (AR4). 2007
[4] Schellnhuber, Joachim, cited in Lebert, Stephan: Ein Mann läuft Sturm. In: Die Zeit, 37/2005
[5] Stern, Nicolas: The Economics of Climate Change. A report prepared on behalf of the UK Treasury. 2006
[6] Nitsch, Joachim: Leitstudie 2007. Aktualisierung und Neubewertung der Ausbaustrategie Erneuerbare Energien bis zu den Jahren 2020 und 2030 mit Ausblick bis 2050. Study carried out on behalf of the Federal Ministry for the Environment, Nature Conservation & Nuclear Safety (BMU). 2007
[7] Federal Ministry for the Environment, Nature Conservation & Nuclear Safety (BMU): Renewable energy sources in figures – national and international development. 2007
[8] Federal Ministry for the Environment, Nature Conservation & Nuclear Safety (BMU): Renewable Energies – Innovation for the Future. 2004, p. 15
[9] Lauer, Wilhelm: Klimatologie. Braunschweig, 1995
[10] Schütze, Thorsten; Willkomm, Wolfgang: Klimagerechtes Bauen in Europa. Planungsinstrumente für klimagerechte, energiesparende Gebäudekonzepte in verschiedenen europäischen Klimazonen. Hamburg Polytechnic research project, with a focus on interdisciplinary research into "Planungsinstrumente für das umweltverträgliche Bauen", Department of Architecture & Civil Engineering, final report, 2000
[11] DIN 1946-2: Ventilation and air conditioning; technical health requirements (VDI ventilation rules). 1994
[12] DIN EN 13779: Ventilation for non-residential buildings – Performance requirements for ventilation and room-conditioning systems. 2005
[13] DIN EN ISO 7730: Ergonomics of the thermal environment – Analytical determination and interpretation of thermal comfort using calculation of the PMV and PPD indices and local thermal comfort criteria. 1995
[14] CEN report CR 1752: Ventilation for buildings – Design criteria for the indoor environment. 1998
[15] Hellwig, Runa Tabea: Thermische Behaglichkeit. Unterschiede zwischen frei und mechanisch belüfteten Bürogebäuden aus Nutzersicht. Dissertation, Munich Technical University, 2005

B 1.68 Boundary conditions, requirements, services and energy themes
B 1.69 The 10 components of energy-optimised building according to energy themes

Urban space
and infrastructure

Buildings must always be considered in conjunction with their surroundings. Numerous factors such as climate, landscape, topography, neighbouring buildings, traffic and infrastructure have an effect on every building or structure and determine the urban context plus the energy available. In addition, architecture is usually incorporated into a complex network of supply and disposal systems. And this networking covers not just the technical infrastructure, but also social and cultural amenities that guarantee mobility, communication and other services. This is consistent with the technical and economical rationale plus the nature of human beings as social creatures who rely on neighbourhoods, on social and cultural services. Finally, the high division of labour in our employment structures render necessary the need for access to workplaces, trade and industry. Dense urban structures are generally best suited to the energy-efficient, economic provision of services and operation of buildings. Besides planning to suit the location and the provision of the technical infrastructure, the efficient use of land is critical for the energy-related optimisation of buildings and urban spaces.

Land use

The use of the land, as a finite resource, has always been characterised by various interests and the demand for efficient utilisation. In terms of land use, buildings and infrastructure have to compete with the production of foodstuffs and energy, the supply of raw materials, the conservation of nature, the landscape and diversity of species, plus many other functions. Within built-up areas, further uses and issues compete for space. These are driven by social notions of value and technical requirements, by public or individual economic interests. Always playing a central role in this with regard to efficiency is the pattern of development with respect to the land use. The prototypical models of urban spaces organised along monocentric, polycentric and sectoral lines, or the so-called *Zwischenstädte* ("neither city nor landscape" – Thomas Sieverts) provide only initial reference points. Falling populations and smaller households call for other models of urban life and generate a changing structure with respect to demands.

The history of land use

In the towns of the Middle Ages, work was carried out on the ground floor of the house and the upper floors were used as living accommodation. Farmers working in the surrounding region were often integrated into the urban structure. The town grew by transferring operations requiring considerable space, e.g. farmyards, beyond the town's borders.

Industrialisation and the associated growth in the populations of the towns resulted in a rapid increase in demand for space, which led to dense grid layouts that still dominate whole urban districts even today. In doing so, open and public spaces were reduced to a minimum. Such small-format space efficiency gave rise to, typical in Berlin for example, the large rooms in the corners of these perimeter housing block + inner courtyard layouts which, however, suffered from a lack of daylight. Although this very high-density development covered housing needs, hygiene requirements were virtually ignored.

The value of open spaces and recreational functions became obvious. The ideal image of living in the countryside initially gave rise to new "garden cities", which were situated outside the towns themselves and created the first neighbourhood centres in the urban spaces. As an answer to overpopulated structures, poor health conditions and the lack of open spaces, the slogan "air, light and sun" became the proclamation of the urban planners and architects of the 1920s. For example, clearances between buildings were defined so that all habitable rooms had access to sunlight, and the first courtyard clearances of perimeter blocks took place (Fig. B 2.29).

The CIAM "Athens Charter" dating from 1933 was an attempt to solve the problem through a comprehensive restructuring of towns and cities. In particular, the demands for generous open areas for citizens, a strengthening of the individual functions and an increase in the order in the system formed the basis for urban-planning objectives (Fig. B 2.4). The neigh-

B 2.1 Reflection creates the illusion of a larger space, residential development as infill development and to close off a perimeter block, Paris (F), 2000, Herzog & de Meuron
B 2.2 Development of the heating energy requirement of buildings according to year of construction and their proportion in the German building stock
B 2.3 Energy consumption in Germany according to sector (2005)
B 2.4 Pictorial representation of the demands of the CIAM "Athens Charter", 1933
B 2.5 Relationship between density of building and energy consumption for selected cities

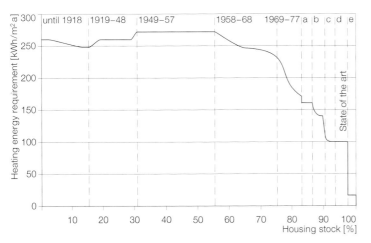

a   1st Thermal Insulation
    Act, 1977
b   2nd Thermal Insulation
    Act, 1984
c   3rd Thermal Insulation
    Act, 1995
d   Energy Conservation
    Act (EnEV), 2002,
    revised 2007
e   Passive-energy house
    standard

B 2.2

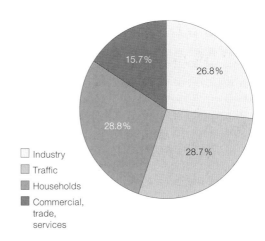

☐ Industry
☐ Traffic
■ Households
■ Commercial,
   trade,
   services

B 2.3

B 2.4

bourhood centres themselves became towns, which were given functional designations, e.g. residential estates.

However, the clear demarcation of uses contradicts the structural concept of the urban system as such. Synergies between the individual uses can no longer form, structures have to be doubled, needs met in duplicate. Traffic is the result, which wastes space, time and energy (Fig. B 2.5). Secondary effects are the increasing environmental impacts in urban developments and the lower quality of life for inhabitants. The decrease in the consumption of land creates density, enables a compact town, where everything is within reach, and an efficient use of energy. Sensibly sized small centres cover daily needs, special constructional requirements such as museums can also serve exotic requests. With such an image of its ideal, the town is clearly demarcated from the surrounding open spaces, which are responsible for foodstuffs, nature and energy supplies. These open-space qualities at the same time represent high usage qualities. Land use optimised for energy and space requirements also ensures a sustainable development of the space through diverse qualities.

Energy and space
Biogenic energy sources enable the re-establishment of local jobs in rural areas, the diversification and stabilisation those areas, the creation of additional sources of income and the closure of the life cycles of diverse materials. The production of energy is no longer reduced to a centrally controlled coverage of needs, but instead allows specific solutions based on local circumstances.

This represents a breakthrough in the way of looking at rural and urban areas common hitherto – frequently reduced to agglomerations. These areas, very different in terms of their structures and layouts, achieve equivalence through this approach, without losing their own identity. Every space occupies a certain central function in the supply chain.

This does not imply a romanticised "back to nature" attitude. Even contaminated sites and wasteland can achieve new qualities. For example, the "landmarks" for reinforcing local

identity at IBA Emscher Park or the new lakes landscape near Cottbus (D) at IBA Fürst-Pückler-Land on the one hand pursue the use of energy normal up to now, but on the other create images of a new future (see "Materials", p. 167). They are the symbols of energy-efficient and sustainable development in which the negative consequences of earlier activities are processed and transformed into a new added-value.

Density and energy
A comparison of the per head energy consumption of various cities reveals a clear relationship between density and energy efficiency. Densely populated cities exhibit an energy consumption reduced by a factor of eight. But with more than 75 persons per hectare, the effect of density on energy consumption begins to weaken, and when the population density exceeds 150 persons per hectare, only a small saving is still possible (Fig. B 2.5).

New building work and energy
In principle, a high-density form of construction should therefore be encouraged for new building work. The energy requirements of a building increase, however, with its height. Increased structural requirements reduce the internal space available and increase the amount of energy tied up in the building materials. Energy-consuming means of access (e.g. lifts) and the need for mechanical ventilation consume additional space and energy.

Building stock and energy
Existing buildings represent a long-term resource in urban areas which attracts about 80% of building investments at present. It would seem obvious to reduce their energy consumption in the course of such measures in the building stock. The savings potential can be increased by a factor of 10 for residential buildings (Fig. B 2.2), even more for special uses such as swimming pools.

Refurbishment (adapting to the current technical standards) and modernisation (increasing the market value) have a mutual influence on each other. Energy-efficiency upgrades result in a simultaneous increase in the standard of comfort, which without the simultaneous improve-

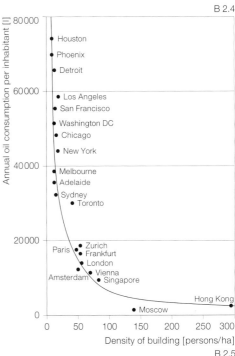

B 2.5

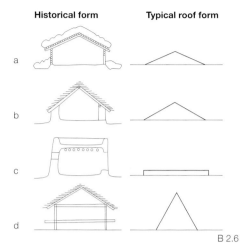

Historical form   **Typical roof form**

a

b

c

d

B 2.6

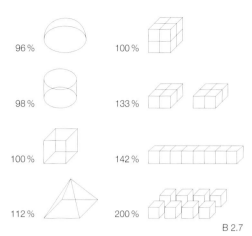

96 %   100 %

98 %   133 %

100 %   142 %

112 %   200 %

B 2.7

B 2.6   Traditional building typologies according to climate zones:
      a   Cold
      b   Temperate
      c   Dry, hot
      d   Moist, warm
B 2.7   Transmission heat losses of various three-dimensional shapes with the same volume
B 2.8   Schematic drawings of infill development arrangements for housing
B 2.9   Orientation of the building for passive use of solar energy, apartment block, Berlin (D), 1997, Assmann Salomon & Scheidt
B 2.10   Orientation of the building for active use of solar energy, apartment block, Dornbirn (A), 1999, Roland Gnaiger, Udo Mössler
B 2.11   Dense housing development, Hamburg (D), 1998, Atelier 5
B 2.12   Schematic presentation of the uses and proportions of a building according to climate zones

ment to the energy standard, cannot be fully effective. The following approaches are possible:

- Modernisation:
  Modernisation enables an existing building with an old-fashioned interior layout to be adapted to existing standards of comfort. In energy terms, modernisation is based on optimising the building envelope (see p. 82) and the building services (see p. 110).
- Conversion:
  Reusing buildings preserves the established picture of the town and at the same time the energy tied up in the building materials. If related to usage, conversion results in a better coverage of needs in urban areas and can contribute to increasing the utilisation density.
- Infill development:
  Infill development satisfies the same requirements as conversion and also creates additional living and working spaces (Fig. B 2.1). It can close up the boundaries of plots, exploit the depth of plots better, or raise the height of existing structures and contribute to preserving the density of population with a higher standard of living and falling household sizes (Fig. B 2.8).

Sustainable space development

The urban space can only function due to the interaction of building functions, open spaces and the networking with neighbouring spaces. Urban spaces are these days very heterogeneous – in terms of both their use of the land and their supply structures. Strengthening the heterogeneity and individuality increases the appeal of the space on energy, usage and social levels. A sustainable development is based on bringing together different requirements and interests in order to cover overriding needs in an integrative way and to preserve local qualities.

Energy integration

The "big shot" in efficiency desired most of all by large-scale industry – with respect to a energy supplies solution reduced to technology (e.g. in power station technology the concept of CO_2 sequestration) – is not possible owing to the diversified nature of the problems. All existing

structures for energy supplies must be examined to establish the options for converting them to renewable energy media. Although the coordination of decentralised and centralised energy production does bring with it an increased need for technical controls, it does lead to greater reliability of supplies thanks to the variety of the products and services on offer. Added to this is the merger of the consumption development and energy production which today are still essentially separate. Within the building, the passive and active use of energy sources must in future be coordinated (Figs. 2.9 and 2.10). However, energy flows and needs cannot remain restricted to just single buildings. In the medium-term, the boundaries of the audits must be expanded to groups of buildings, even whole city districts.

Usage integration

The provision of services is crucial for the sustainable development of urban structures. Mixed usage always has a positive effect on energy consumption because traffic can be avoided. If a demand cannot be met locally (local traffic), people travel to another urban space in order to meet that demand (regional traffic). Large supermarkets, for example, have catchment areas that can extend up to 200 km. Regional traffic in excess of 20% leads to energy, resources or economic strength being lost from a region [1]. The attractiveness of an area, in the end decided by the people themselves, is therefore necessary for its economic survival. "Business Improvement Districts" (BID), which since 2007 have also been anchored in Germany's Federal Building Code, try, for example, to strengthen inner-city zones through a stronger coupling between needs and users. On the other hand, the aim is to preserve ecological qualities like, for example, biodiversity. Open spaces linked to each other and helping to define the urban area merge habitats for flora and fauna and at the same time improve the recreation and leisure opportunities for inhabitants.

Social integration

In order to preserve and improve the attractiveness of the urban space, certain reactions are necessary with respect to demographic developments and changing social requirements. These result in new objectives for building work:

- Accessibility:
  Barrier-free buildings enable all people to use them without any help from others.
- Identity:
  Urban spaces and buildings with an individual character promote identity. They preserve and strengthen local characteristics and contribute to spatial diversity. Private, semi-public and public spaces enable the formation of identities on different levels (Fig. B 2.11).
- Integration:
  The ever-greater segregation within social structures can, for example, be counteracted by diverse, mixed, adaptable housing styles linked via neighbourly help. Places for meeting and communication indoors and outdoors encourage the social exchange.
- Co-determination:
  Attractiveness, diversity of spaces and, above all, identification are founded on the chances for those involved to exert their influence. Planning processes must therefore be designed with the necessary openness (see "Strategies", p. 188).

Extra storey   Expansion   Extension

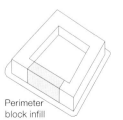

Perimeter block infill   Inner courtyard infill

B 2.8

B 2.9

B 2.10

B 2.11

From the definition of sustainability according to Gro Halem Brundtland it becomes clear that property means not only wealth for the coming generations, but also problems [2]. Buildings are objects that outlive generations and should therefore offer long-term useful value. The ability to adapt to changing needs and the planned changeability of buildings must be taken into account accordingly and be seen as potential added-value. And that applies not only to function and usage, but, in particular, to building services and energy supplies as well.

Planning to suit the location

The prevailing climate at the site determines the energy available and hence also the design options (see "Fundamentals", Fig. B 1.43). Energy can be provided for buildings in various ways. The building envelope serves to protect against the negative effects of the climate and, if necessary, to obtain energy for the building from the environment (see "Building envelope", p. 85).

Macroclimate

Depending on the climate zone, the macroclimate creates different conditions for human well-being. The prevailing climate factors have led to typical forms of construction in the individual climate regions over the history of building (Fig. B 2.6):

- Polar zone (cold):
  Traditional building forms in the cold climate zones frequently use the insulating effect of wood. Roofs generally have a shallow pitch, which offers protection against cold winds and in winter allows the snow to be retained as an additional layer of insulation. Compact forms of construction are generally preferred in the cold and temperate zones so that the ratio of the external surface area to the internal volume is as small as possible (A/V ratio, Fig. B 2.7).
- Temperate zone:
  In temperate climates, transmission heat losses and draughts require special attention. Undesirable thermal effects are reduced by building dense, well-insulated walls, backed up by thermal masses. Roofs have a medium pitch, which allows precipitation to drain away but at the same time offers little resistance to the wind. The higher the energy losses through the thermal envelope, the greater is the relevance of the compactness of the building.

- Subtropical zone (dry, hot):
  The high day-night temperature fluctuations are compensated for by heavyweight buildings with high thermal masses, e.g. made from stone or loam. The dense form of construction typical in towns enables buildings to shade each other and cuts overheating due to solar gains. The roof surfaces collect the low rainfall; excess water contributes to cooling via evaporation. Small windows allow only minimal solar radiation into the interior. The principal rooms are usually located on the ground floor, on the cool ground slab.
- Tropical zone (moist, warm):
  The permanently moist climate with its low temperature fluctuations over the course of the day renders integral thermal masses virtually ineffective. The conventional forms of construction in the tropics are therefore usually elevated, lightweight, timber structures. On the one hand, they protect against the infiltration of moisture, on the other, they enable a cooling effect by way of the high air change rate. Roofs are steep and have generous eaves to protect against rain and also to provide shade. Solid walls would hinder the circulation of cooling air and therefore they are replaced by airy openings or lattice forms of construction.

	Positioning of ancillary spaces	Positioning of areas with solar gains	Optimum aspect ratio length:width	Positioning of heavyweight parts of the building	Use of atria a as solar trap b for ventilation and cooling	Energy-related market value for atria
Cold			1:1		a	a
Temperate			1:1.6		a	
Dry			1:2		b	b
Tropical			1:3		b	

B 2.12

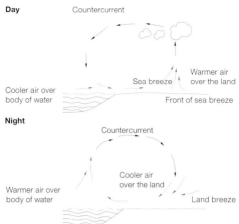

B 2.13

B 2.14

B 2.15

Even if traditional building typologies are often no longer in the position to satisfy today's needs, they still supply valuable design inspiration and potential solutions. For example, the typical positions for access, active solar surfaces, orientation, thermal masses or atria can still be derived for contemporary buildings (Fig. B 2.12).

Mesoclimate

Different intensities of solar radiation cause local temperature differences at the Earth's surface and in the layers of air near the ground. Pressure differences ensuing as a result of those temperature differences generate areas of high and low pressure, whereupon air starts to flow from a high-pressure area to a low-pressure one in order to balance this difference. Sea breezes, airflows due to the topography or local thermal currents are the outcome.
The governing factors are the solar absorption and thermal capacities of the Earth's surface, which become apparent in the extensive "maritime climate" conditions on the coast or around large lakes. Water exhibits a very low albedo (global radiation reflection component) of approx. 5%, i.e. it absorbs virtually all the incident energy (Fig. B 2.18). Owing to its high thermal mass and the ensuing evaporative cooling effect, water heats up only very little during the day. Land masses heat up very much more rapidly and therefore the rising air (thermal currents) over the land leads to a low

pressure; the cool air over the water then flows towards the land. At night, the temperature on the land drops markedly, but not over the water – the process reverses (Fig. B 2.14).
Similar effects, albeit much less significant, can be experienced in the case of land masses with different surface features. A rougher terrain results in lower wind speeds and more wind turbulence at ground level (Fig. B 2.19). The particular topography can give rise to increased exposure to or shading from the sun on certain surfaces, e.g. valley and mountain breezes (Fig. B 2.15). Together, these factors form the central components of a local wind system.

Urban climate

The urban climate is relevant for the majority of construction projects (Fig. B 2.17). The high roughness of the built environment results in lower wind speeds in the atmosphere over towns and cities; the various types of usage and the different surfaces increase the quantity of dust, which bonds more and more water vapour. This is why more rain falls on urban areas than on rural districts, especially on the leeward side of the town. The increase in precipitation for Central European towns and cities is approx. 10%. In addition, the risk of summer thunderstorms is higher.
Owing to the increased adiabatic cooling effect available, urban areas should, theoretically, be cooler than the surrounding countryside. But in

fact, towns and cities exhibit measurably higher temperatures than those of their environs. These are caused by the – compared to the surrounding countryside – higher degree of absorption of urban surfaces and also by the fact that precipitation is drained away (in pipes) from urban spaces before it can evaporate locally. This means that the groundwater is not replenished and so urban areas usually exhibit a lower water table. For urban areas, an unhindered supply of fresh air especially and the retention of precipitation are therefore important for the urban system.

Supply of fresh air
The cooler air flowing from the surrounding countryside into the town near ground level requires defined "flow channels" with less rough surfaces. Such flow channels can be provided by, for example, river or stream courses, low or flat ground, traffic routes or open spaces. Buildings and structures and the intervening open spaces therefore define the system of urban ventilation. A green belt around the city centre (e.g. London) or open spaces radiating out from the city centre (e.g. Hamburg) have proved particularly useful (Fig. B 2.16). The increasing density of development towards the city centre promotes the local wind system through the increased buoyancy. Some towns and cities are experiencing more and more inversion weather conditions, i.e. a colder layer of air gathers on top of the heated urban

B 2.13 Central Park, New York (USA)
B 2.14 Sea breeze over the course of the day
B 2.15 Local winds over the course of the day
B 2.16 Schematic presentation of urban systems for introducing fresh air using the example of Wiesbaden (D)
B 2.17 Structure of the urban atmosphere plus principal dependencies within the system
B 2.18 Albedo values of various surfaces
B 2.19 Wind speeds in relation to roughness α of terrain and height above ground level
B 2.20 Schematic drawing of precipitation drainage in the Kronsberg district of Hannover (D)
B 2.21 Body of water for part of the water supply and adiabatic cooling of the outside air, motorway service station near Abbeville (F), 1998, Bruno Mader

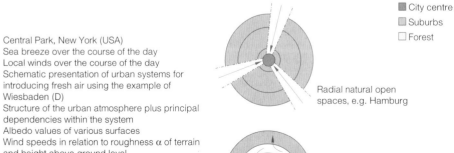

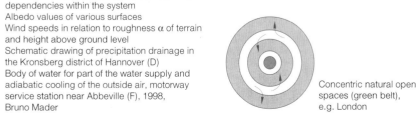

Radial natural open spaces, e.g. Hamburg

Concentric natural open spaces (green belt), e.g. London

B 2.16

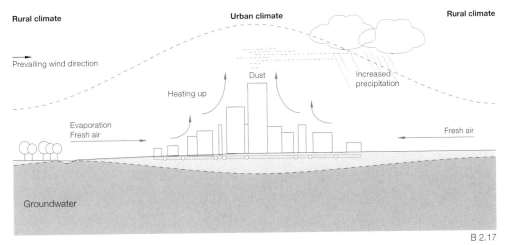

Rural climate
Urban climate
Rural climate

Prevailing wind direction

Dust

Heating up

Increased precipitation

Evaporation
Fresh air

Fresh air

Groundwater

B 2.17

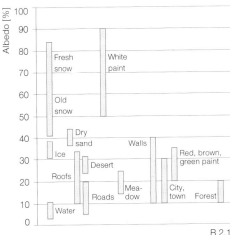

B 2.18

atmosphere and virtually halts the exchange of air with the surrounding countryside. To counteract this, surfaces with different degrees of absorption, which deliberately create thermal air movements, are necessary.

Large parks and gardens within the urban area have a positive ventilating effect (e.g. Central Park in New York, Fig. B 2.13), which can be further assisted by a network of interlinked natural open spaces. The incoming fresh air from the surrounding countryside or parks contains a higher proportion of biogenic suspended matter such as pollen. But linking traffic routes and fresh-air channels results in a problem with ultrafine particles emitted from vehicle exhausts (e.g. oxides of nitrogen or sulphur), with the exhaust particles becoming attached to the pollen and converting these into allergens.

The hydrological cycle

In the case of heavy rainfall, surface waters and drainage systems cannot cope with the quantities of water involved, especially where ground sealing is widespread. In such situations, larger pipe cross-sections and the construction of expensive rainwater retention basins are often believed to be indispensable. However, altering the layout of open areas and buildings can render such highly expensive technical systems more or less unnecessary (Figs. B 2.20 and 21). This approach includes all measures that interrupt the hydrological cycle only marginally, delay the draining of

water, retain water as a local potential and have a positive effect on the town's microclimate by way of increased evaporation (Fig. B 2.17):

• Water retention:
  Water can be retained centrally in basins or decentrally in cisterns, using man-made structures or natural features. Decentralised retention at the same time helps to reduce the consumption of drinking water by using rainwater. Buffering quantities of water on green roofs or in shallow bodies of water improves the microclimate, prevents temperature peaks and cuts the amount of dust in the atmosphere. Along rivers, generously sized flood relief channels provide the opportunity of increasing the storage capacity of shallow bodies of water, alleviating high-water peaks and improving the soil.

• Restoration of unsealed ground:
  Wherever possible, surfaces within urban areas should be permeable to water. However, any possible contamination of the groundwater through pollutants (oils etc.) carried into the ground with the water must be taken into account. The degree of permeability is defined by means of so-called run-off coefficients (Fig. B 2.22).

• Seepage surfaces:
  Precipitation that is not fed back directly via the surfaces into the hydrological cycle

should be allowed to seep away. The type of seepage surface depends on the type of soil. Infiltration ponds can be provided for seepage, the size of which should be roughly 10–20% of the area to be drained. Gravel- or ballast-filled trenches with large void ratios are frequently used as well. Such arrangements reduce the area required, increase the short-term storage volume and enable a constant seepage capacity (Figs. B 2.24 and 2.25).

• Evaporation:
  In urban areas, shallow bodies of water and vegetation, through their evaporation capacity, help to reduce the quantities of waste water and also lower the temperature. At the same time, they can be used for landscaping purposes and therefore improve the general quality of life locally.

Microclimate

As part of a local, microclimatic appraisal, protecting buildings against undesirable climate effects specific to the locality is an important aspect. But the options for tapping environmental energy are also important.

Solar exposure

High global radiation and long hours of sunshine indicate a very good potential for exploiting energy gains, but also the possibility of overheating in buildings. In Germany the global radiation incident on horizontal surfaces amounts

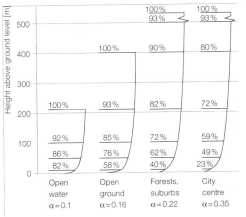

B 2.19

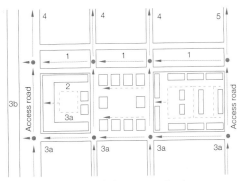

1 Drainage and retention in the avenues on the slope
2 Storage
3a Seepage   3b Retention areas at bottom of slope
4 Regulated system of drains

B 2.20

B 2.21

67

Surface	Run-off co-efficient [-]
Roofs with pitch ≥ 15°	1.0 [1]
Concrete and asphalt surfaces	0.9
Paved surfaces	0.75
Gravel roofs, courtyards, promenades	0.5
Concrete paving, joints allowing seepage	0.40 [2]
Granite paving, joints allowing seepage	0.33 [2]
Rooftop gardens	0.3
Play areas and sports grounds	0.25
Grass paving, chippings in joints	0.22 [2]
Private gardens	0.15
Allotments	0.05
Parks/amenities adjacent to bodies of water	0

[1] Corresponds to 100% water run-off
[2] According to research findings

B 2.22

B 2.23

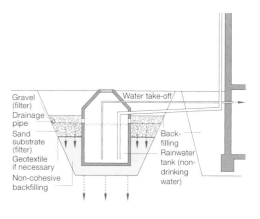

Gravel (filter)
Drainage pipe
Sand substrate (filter)
Geotextile if necessary
Non-cohesive backfilling
Water take-off
Back-filling
Rainwater tank (non-drinking water)

B 2.24

to approx. 1000 W/m². The particularly beneficial direct radiation component accounts for about 50% of this total incident radiation in Central European latitudes, but only approx. 20% in Scandinavia. These values can vary considerably depending on the climate zone (see "Fundamentals", p. 54).

The microclimate conditions for construction change depending on the location of the building within its topographical surroundings, the vegetation and the neighbouring structures (Fig. B 2.27). Shading caused by other parts of the same building or by neighbouring buildings can be appraised by way of solar altitude angle models. Such a model enables the efficiency of both active and passive solar energy applications to be determined, the exposure to sunlight of rooms and open areas to be checked, and the necessary shading measures to be designed.

The design of external surfaces in the immediate vicinity of the building can help to reinforce the radiation on the building because reflective surfaces help to direct radiation and daylight into the building. Suitable solutions here are light-coloured pavings or bodies of water, the

reflection from which depends on the angle of incidence. The shallower the angle of the incoming radiation, the higher is the reflection component.

Water as a microclimate regulator

Water stores the component of the solar radiation that is not reflected. A pond next to the building, for instance, can help to regulate the inflow of fresh air, reducing temperature peaks and ultimately leading to a reduced energy requirement in the building (Fig. B 2.23). Generally, water retention and seepage, through enhanced adiabatic cooling capacity and storage capacity, has a positive effect on the microclimate. For example, the temperature over green roofs in summer is approx. 35°C, over gravel roofs up to 70°C.

Soil

The soil near the surface absorbs the incident solar radiation. Its mass and water content make it an efficient storage medium. As we go deeper into the ground, so the temperature remains more and more constant over the year, and so the soil, just like the groundwater, can

be used to operate heat pumps all year round with a good degree of efficiency, provided unshaded surfaces are available.

Wind exposure

Buildings particularly exposed to the wind suffer from higher energy losses via their external walls and roofs. Typical wind directions and speeds can be determined in a wind analysis. The wind effects that occur can also be established through flow simulations or wind tunnel tests. Trees, hedges or walls, positioned at a certain distance ahead of the building in the prevailing wind direction, can help to reduce the wind speeds acting on the building itself (Fig. B 2.28). Direct planting on the facade has only a low savings effect, amounting to approx. 0.5% of the heating energy requirement. However, such planting does reduce the ambient temperature around the building owing to the enhanced adiabatic cooling capacity, lowering the risk of overheating in summer and thus improving the interior comfort.

The pressure differences on different elevations mean that the wind can contribute to the natural ventilation of a building. In addition, various constructional and technical options are available for using the wind, e.g. night purging (see "Building envelope", p. 101).

Building design

Energy losses can be minimised and energy gains maximised through the design of the building itself. The type and degree of use define the corresponding requirements. For example, in housing, rooms and uses can be arranged according to compass orientation (Fig. B 2.29) and with sensible window areas (see "Building envelope", p. 90) in order to achieve the desired solar gains and lighting requirements. Microclimate factors in conjunction with usage requirements can help to structure the building in diverse ways.

Seepage through the surface

Open gravel-filled trenches

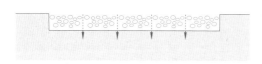

Buried gravel-filled trenches with discrete inlets

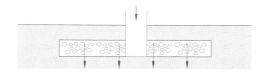

Infiltration pond

Infiltration pond plus gravel-filled trenches

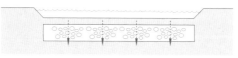

Infiltration pond plus gravel-filled trenches

B 2.25

Zoning in buildings

Usage zones can be arranged according to, for example, temperature or daylight requirements, or even the preferences of users or occupants. Thermal zoning is the most effective from the energy point of view: primary uses are thermally insulated by adjacent buffer spaces or ancillary floor spaces (Fig. B 2.12). There are three principal zoning options for buildings with a high heating requirement (e.g. residential buildings) (Fig. B 2.26):

- Concentric zoning:
  Concentric zoning enables generous building depths. Uses that need to be protected from the climate, that require stable thermal conditions, are placed in the centre of the building.
- Linear zoning:
  Linear zoning is based on the orientation with respect to the sun. The rooms with the greatest lighting and heating requirements are positioned to face south, east or west, those with lower or only sporadic heating requirements should face north.
- Storey zoning:
  In a storey zoning approach, the rooms with high thermal requirements are normally placed in the middle of a stack of storeys.

Positioning thermal masses

The advantages of climatic zoning can be further improved by paying special attention to the positioning of the thermal masses (Fig. B 2.36). If a building is at risk of overheating due to changing external loads, the positioning and activation of thermal masses (e.g. floors exposed to sunlight) can be used to buffer temperature peaks effectively. If a building suffers from internal loads particularly (e.g. offices), thermal masses can also be activated indirectly via convection.

An exact appraisal of external influences and internal requirements can help to check known building typologies critically and to develop new ones. In doing so, the fundamental energy- and usage-related considerations can be brought together (Fig. B 2.33).

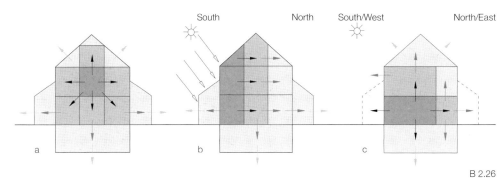

B 2.26

	Open location (reference)	Protected location	Depression, cold-air pool	South-facing slope	Hilltop location
Difference in ambient temperature	± 0 °C	no data	-3 °C	+2 °C	-1 °C
Heat losses	± 0 %	no data	+25 %	-17 %	+10 %
Heat losses due to wind	± 0 %	-50 %	no data	+100 %	+100 %

B 2.27

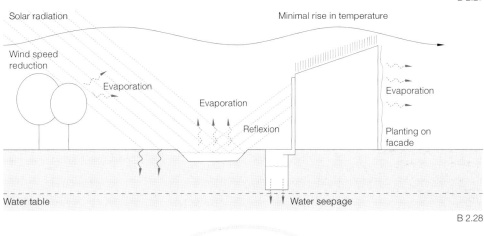

B 2.28

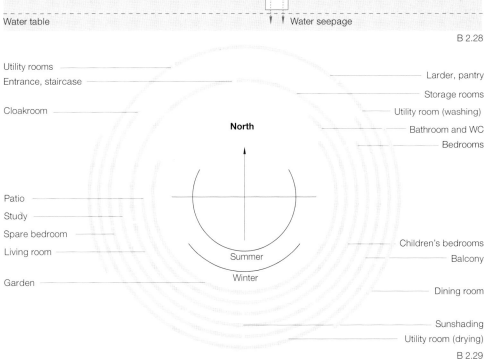

B 2.29

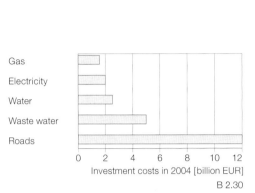

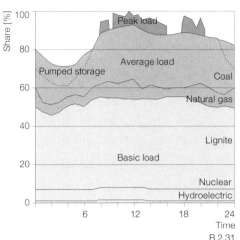

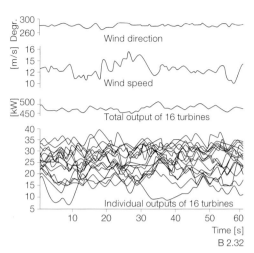

B 2.30

B 2.31

B 2.32

Infrastructure and technical services

Buildings are not isolated objects; during their operation, they are integrated into networks of overriding technical infrastructures. They consume drinking water as well as energy, create waste water as well as waste, and require transport connections.

In Germany the technical infrastructure accounts for between 40 and 45% of the total area of land covered by the built environment, with most of this being used for transport purposes. Every year, 10–15% of the gross domestic product is used for its maintenance and upgrading (Fig. 2.30).

Striving to achieve more efficient supplies of energy and resources also changes the boundary conditions for the infrastructure – on both the user and the supplier side. And this applies not only to increasing requirements, but to decreasing requirements, too, because partial utilisation of the infrastructure can lead to a lower efficiency in the system and result in "stretched infrastructures". The German Council

for Sustainable Development (RNE) therefore comes to the following conclusion:
"In the future we will require an integrated management of the technical infrastructure, including the preservation of the building stock, investment and deconstruction plus the social infrastructure from public transport to ... fundamental provisions and the cultivation and preservation of natural resources." [3]
The relationship between urban and rural areas is particularly evident here. On the one hand, infrastructure for integrating rural areas is an expensive undertaking. But on the other, with the increasing use of renewable energy sources they could regain some of their supply functions.

Networks
Even if buildings should be designed to use far fewer resources in the future, they will generally continue to remain dependent on the inflow of external energies and resources. To date, the technical networks necessary for this have been set up mainly as one-way, purely supply structures (Fig. B 2.31).

As decentralisation increases, so the infrastructure can no longer be regarded as a one-way, tree-like, branching distribution structure (Fig. B 2.40). Only with the interaction between supply and demand – a two- or even multi-way flow – can the technical infrastructure really take on the qualities of a network. Energies and resources flow from a high to a low.

Reliability of supplies
The magnitudes of renewable energy sources such as the wind and the sun are not wholly predictable. They reduce the demand for fossil fuels in electricity generation without themselves being able to guarantee total reliability of supplies. For this reason, further electricity generation providers must contribute to ensure reliability of supplies, and the energy supplies or the consumption figures must be calculable. In the case of wind power, prognosis models for supplies have been developed whose forecasts 24 hours in advance deviate by only 8–10% from the reality. This enables a better estimate of the energy yield and a reduction in

Typological comparison		Detached house		Terrace house		Apartment block		High-rise building		Stepped arrangement	
Orientation: north-south Building volume: 4320 m³ Proportion of windows: north 20% east 30% west 30% south 50%											
A/V ratio	[1/m]	0.78		0.65		0.43		0.49		0.78	
Total area of outer surface	[m²]	3384		2808		1848		2104		3384	
Area in contact with external air	[m²]	2664		2088		1608		2024		2124	
Area in contact with soil	[m²]	720		720		240		80		1260	
Net roof area for solar energy	[m²]	720		720		240		80		720	
Ratio of external air to soil	[-]	3.7 : 1		2.9 : 1		6.7 : 1		26.3 : 1		1.7 : 1	
Proportion of windows	[%]	23		21		27		30		20	
Thermal losses through outer surface [$H_t{'}$]		0.49		0.46		0.56		0.63		0.45	
Specific heating energy rqmt. q_h	[kWh/m²a]	72	(100%)	60	(83%)	48	(66%)	56	(77%)	66	(9%)
Total primary energy rqmt. Q_p	[kWh/a]	168000	(100%)	136000	(81%)	113000	(67%)	126000	(75%)	146000	(87%)
Lighting		+		o		o		+		–	
Open areas available for thermal uses		+		o		o		o		o	
Specific energy-related aspects		High A/V ratio, high space requirements		Low A/V ratio for same solar energy area		Lowest A/V ratio		High space requirements for building services, increased air velocity on facade		Large area in contact with soil, water drainage requirements	

B 2.33

the additional technical controls required (Fig. 2.32).

Non-controllable supplies can be compensated for by storable energy media (e.g. biogas, biogenic fuels or energy storage media) (Fig. B 2.37). The possibility of being able to switch energy on or off to suit our requirements, to compensate for surplus and shortfall capacities, can be achieved by increasing storage capacities and is one of the key tasks for reliable supplies of energy in the future.

Many applications in buildings, especially heating requirements (e.g. for hot-water provision) and large electrical consumers (e.g. freezers), could themselves act as a kind of storage because the periods of their power consumption can be shifted considerably. They could be switched off at peak times and switched on again during periods of surplus capacity. But to do this we need a controllable link between consumption and energy provision.

Energy infrastructure
On both a regional and international level there are different availabilities of energy media and energy forms. The resulting differentiated energy supplies will in future enable a greater networking of the individual energy subsystems (Fig. B 2.35).

Energy relocation and distribution result in losses which can be quantified by way of the primary energy factor (see "Building services", p. 114). This describes, as a cumulative value, that part of the energy losses that occurs outside the building, in the entire "external chain" (Fig. B 2.34). Networks with high losses are therefore only suitable for solutions with a local coverage (e.g. heating networks), whereas networks with low losses enable a wide coverage (e.g. electricity grids). In principle, we distinguish between networks for energy media (e.g. gas) and networks for energy forms (e.g. electricity, heat).

Networks for energy media
Networks for energy media exhibit low energy losses. The provision of the medium itself, e.g. crude oil, consumes about 10% of its calorific value, but the main losses occur during transport. In the case of solid biomass, these losses

Transport losses	10 km	100 km	1000 km
Energy form			
Electricity			
380 KV	0.15%	1.5%	15%
800 KV	0.05%	0.5%	1.5%
Heat [1]			
130°C	~3%	~13%	–
70°C	~1.5%	~6.5%	–
Energy medium			
Wood, oil [2]	0.08%	0.8%	8%
Gas	no data	no data	no data

[1] Heat transport is heavily dependent on the flow velocity; district heating networks exhibit losses of up to 40%.
[2] Based on transport in road tankers

B 2.34

amount to about 20% owing to the many treatment processes required because wood has to be, for example, processed to form chippings or pellets, dried and then transported to the consumer.

Gas networks
The sole energy medium network covering virtually the whole of Central Europe is the gas network. In 2004 some 47.2% of all German households were using gas for heating. A total of 42 underground gas storage installations, using either subterranean caverns or porous rock strata with a gastight enclosure, result in a storage capacity of max. 75 days for the total system.

Up until now, the EU has supplied approx. 60% of its natural gas requirements from its own sources; 40% is imported. However, it is estimated that supplies from EU sources will fall to 25% by 2020. Major investment in the overriding gas infrastructure is therefore planned.

The gas network can contribute to renewable energy supplies in the medium-term. As the principal chemical component of natural gas, mine gas, wood gas and biogas is methane (CH_4), like with the electricity grid, a pool of different suppliers could be set up. The other constituents of the gas – especially with respect to the moisture saturation and the hydrogen sulphide (H_2S) content – differ depending on the source. As both these factors cause corrosion of the pipes, the "raw gas" must be converted into "product gas" before being fed into the pipes. The first pilot plants for supplying biogas and wood gas are already in operation. In Germany today, biogas plants that benefit from the remuneration payable under the Renewable Energy Sources Act are already profitable when operated as a combined heat and power (CHP) plant (Fig. B 2.38).

Networks for energy forms
After production, energy forms, in contrast to energy media, can only be stored at great cost. Networks for energy forms are therefore more heavily dependent on the need for the production of energy in line with demand than is the case for energy media. In addition, CHP technology forces us to look at electricity and heat-

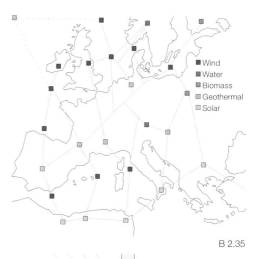

Wind
Water
Biomass
Geothermal
Solar

B 2.35

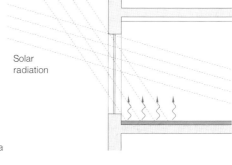

Solar radiation

a

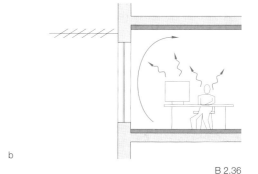

b

B 2.36

B 2.37

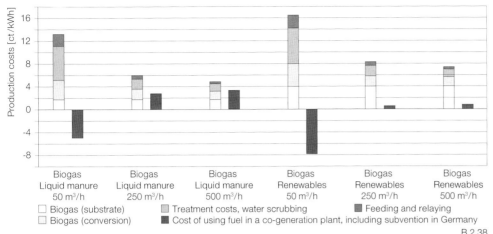

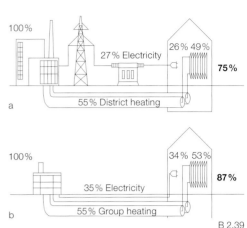

B 2.38

B 2.39

ing requirements in combination (Fig. B 2.39). Owing to its relatively low losses over longer distances, electricity is suitable for the distribution of energy over wide areas. Heat, on the other hand, suffers from high line losses, but can be used to cover the heating requirements of buildings with low-cost technology.

Electricity network
More usually called the electricity grid, this network consists of a hierarchy of distribution levels that branch cascade-like down to the consumer (Fig. B 2.40). The length of all public electricity lines in Germany adds up to about 1.6 million km.
Losses ensue as a result of the resistance (R) of the electrical conductors, which is dependent on the current (I) and the voltage (U): R = I/U. If we increase the voltage and decrease the current, it is possible to transmit the same power (P = I·U) with a reduced resistance. High voltages are therefore used for energy transmission, low voltages for the safe use of that energy. Transformer substations are necessary at the transitions between the distribution levels, which take up considerable amounts of land (Fig. B 2.40). The conversion of the alternating current results in high electromagnetic loads in the local environment. And line losses, too, cause the emission of electromagnetic waves. The maximum value of 5 kV/m recommended by the World Health Organisation (WHO), and also included in DIN VDE 0848,

applies in Germany. The optimised value of 2.5 kV/m recommended by building biologists would mean a minimum distance of 30–60 m between a 380 kV overhead power cable and a building. Mass reduces the effects of electromagnetic fields. In the meantime, approx. 71% of all power lines in Germany are routed underground – and the trend is growing.
The electricity grid possesses only minimal storage capacity. Additional power stations are kept on standby to cope with peak loads and are switched on line as required. In the case of short-term voltage fluctuations or in order to maintain the voltage in the grid locally (< 1 min), flywheels, e.g. the rotors of wind turbines, are suitable. Longer storage is usually provided by pumped storage power stations (see "Building services", p. 145).
The 380 kV grid has been expanded to provide wide coverage on a European scale. About 1.5% of the transported energy is lost over a line length of 100 km. High-voltage direct-current (HVDC) transmission networks employing a voltage of 800 kV enable lower induced currents and smaller losses (0.5% line losses over 100 km) plus a reduced materials requirement. Such lines form part of the planned electricity supply network extending beyond the borders of Europe (Fig. B 2.35).
According to a study by the German Energy Agency (dena), the trend towards decentralised electricity generation will not require many new transmission lines in Germany [4]. How-

ever, the growing number of customers feeding electricity into the network will render more technical controls necessary. In the medium-term, the electricity grid will require an additional information channel, the use of which will be expressed in the "grid codes", the rules for a network. Once this channel is installed, the controls can develop over the medium-term to such an extent that even individual consumers (e.g. washing machines) will be able to indicate their requirements via a "peer-to-peer network", which will then regulate their operation.

District and group heating networks
In 2005 the proportion of residential buildings in Germany heated by such networks was 14%, and the total length of the lines was approx. 50 000 km (Fig. B 2.41). Heating networks are only local, do not cover wide areas and are not interconnected. Some 84% of the energy from heating networks is generated in combined heat and power (CHP) plants. Various studies of future energy supplies assume an increase in more efficient, decentralised electricity generation on the basis of CHP (Fig. B 2.43). The constant generation of electricity results in the constant production of heat as a "waste product" (Fig. B 2.39).
The energy losses of a heating network depend on the length of the pipes and their operating temperature. The lower the temperature of the heat transfer medium, the lower are the thermal losses from such a system. At the same time,

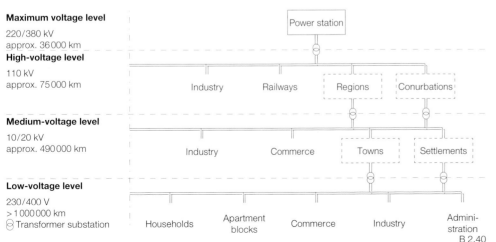

B 2.40

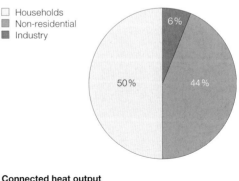

Connected heat output

Year	2000	2001	2002	2003	2004	2005
[kWh]	53 606	51 649	52 162	52 112	52 264	52 729

B 2.41

District heating network, Basel

Length:	198.2 km
Heat production:	100340 Mio. kWh/a
Network losses:	10%
Flow temperature:	170°C
Peak output:	309 MW
Customers:	Hospitals, public buildings, industry and commerce, approx. 40 000 housing units

• Heating plant   0 |_|_|_|_| 1 km

B 2.42

however, the maximum quantity of energy that can be transmitted, or rather the pumping capacity in the system, must be increased. Many heating networks are therefore operated at a high temperature (> 100°C), mostly using water or steam as the heat transfer medium. The maximum transport distance from the plant to the most distant consumer is seldom more than 20 km. Nevertheless, district heating networks can exhibit system-related losses of up to 40%. There is no clear dividing line between a group and a district heating network (Figs. B 2.42 and 2.44). The terms relate to both the size of the network and the type of energy production, i.e. centralised or decentralised. The decentralised production of biogas clearly shows where the sensible boundaries between gas and heating networks lie (Fig. B 2.50). Heating networks are therefore particularly interesting for high energy consumers in the area to be served. Heat as an energy form cannot be universally employed and that reduces its sales potential, being used mainly for space heating, in individual cases also for space cooling (Fig. B 2.41). Falling energy demands thanks to buildings with better thermal insulation reduce the sales potential still further. At the same time, there is often an insufficient demand for the heat supply during the summer. Many networks therefore require densification of the supply structure and connections to new energy consumers. Regulation of the heating requirement over the course of the year

can make use of options such as the integration of industrial users who require process heating and an increased cooling requirement via sorption chillers, e.g. by means of cheaper tariffs for the purchase of heat in summer (see "Building services", p. 130).

Solar-powered group heating networks
Apart from producing heat for group heating networks through the incineration of fuels, it is also possible to generate the heat by means of solar energy installations with short- or long-term heat storage. If there is a high, constant hot-water requirement, like in apartment blocks, hotels, homes, hospitals or residential estates with more than 30 housing units, systems with short-term heat storage are suitable. Like with traditional drinking water provision, the heat is retained in hot-water tanks. These days, such systems are optimised mainly for a coverage of approx. 50%. In terms of the German Energy Conservation Act (EnEV), approx. 20% of the primary energy requirement for residential buildings can be covered in this way (Fig. B 2.48). In solar-assisted systems with long-term heat storage, water or the ground is employed (Fig. B 2.47). Such systems have a coverage potential of 40–60% of the primary energy requirement and owing to the considerable technical input are only economical for upwards of 100–250 housing units (Fig. B 2.46; see also "Building services", p. 124).

Cooling networks
In comparison to heating networks, cooling networks exhibit low losses because their operating temperature is usually only slightly different to that of the ambient temperature. On average, the cooling requirements of most buildings are lower than their heating requirements. Certain production plants, laboratories or shopping centres represent some of the exceptions. Up until now, only a few public cooling networks have been built, e.g. in Chemnitz (Fig. B 2.45). The current length of lines in Germany is just 43 km [5]. Cooling networks function either as a closed system or as a secondary part of a heating network. Sorption chillers link the production of heating and cooling energy. In the medium-term, such chillers achieve not only a high efficiency on the cooling side, but on the heating side as well.

High thermal loads can occur briefly within the networks, e.g. in the case of large events, and that means the installations must be sized accordingly right from the start. The integration of storage media into the system reduces these requirements markedly and can contribute to better utilisation of the chillers.

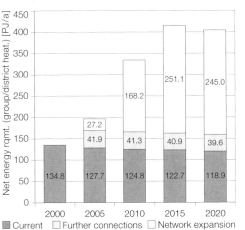

Net energy rqmt. (group/district heat.) [PJ/a]

	2000	2005	2010	2015	2020
Network expansion			168.2	251.1	245.0
Further connections		27.2			
		41.9	41.3	40.9	39.6
Current	134.8	127.7	124.8	122.7	118.9

■ Current □ Further connections □ Network expansion

B 2.43

Salach paper plant

Length:	1.35 km (incl. house connection lines)
Heat production:	no data
Network losses:	no data
Flow temperature:	70–90°C
Peak output:	approx. 1 MW, 610 kW for paper plant
Customers:	approx. 150 housing units (planned for final phase in 2010)

• Heat source   0 |_|_|_| 50 m

B 2.44

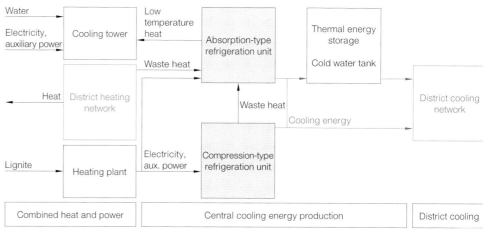

B 2.45

Sizing of long-term storage

Hot-water thermal storage

- 1.5–2.25 m³ per m² collector area

Gravel/water thermal storage

- 2.5–4.0 m³ per m² collector area

Borehole thermal storage

- 8.0–10.0 m³ per m² collector area
- borehole spacing: 1.5–2.5 m, max. 3.0 m in rock
- borehole depth: 20–80 m

Aquifer thermal storage

4.0–6.0 m³ per m² collector area

B 2.46

Sizing of group heating network with long-term storage

Min. number of housing units

- approx. 200–500 housing units each with 70 m² floor space, or 100–120 detached houses

Collector area

- 0.14–0.20 m² collector area per m² floor space
- 1.25–2.5 m² collector area per MWh of annual total heating requirement (lower values apply to locations with high levels of sunshine and highly efficient collectors)
- annual solar energy yield: 300–450 kWh/m²a

Storage volume (water-equivalent)

- 1.5–2.25 m³ per m² collector area (lower values apply to a larger ratio between available solar energy and heating energy requirement)
- The type of storage depends, in the first place, on the local circumstances, especially the geological and hydrological conditions.

Solar energy contribution

- approx. 40–50% of annual heating requirement
- up to approx. 60% for low-energy houses

B 2.47

Sizing of group heating network with short-term storage

Collector area

- 0.7 –1.0 m² collector area per person (approx. 0.02–0.03 m² collector area per m² floor space)
- 0.4–0.5 m² collector area per person for solar preheating systems (solar energy contribution 25–40%)
- annual solar energy yield: 300–450 kWh/m²a

Storage volume

- 0.05–0.06 m³ per m² collector area (flat-plate collectors)
- 0.06–0.08 m³ per m² collector area (vacuum-tube collectors)

Solar energy contribution

- approx. 50–60% of energy requirement for hot-water provision
- approx. 10–15% of annual heating requirement, up to approx. 20% for low-energy houses

B 2.48

Water

Although roughly two-thirds of the Earth's surface is covered by water, this life-giving liquid in its form as drinking water is a resource that threatens to become scarce. At the same time, water is a critical energy medium in the climate system.

The humid climate of Central European latitudes offers the chance of enhancing surface water or groundwater reservoirs and producing drinking water – but the necessary boundary conditions are not available everywhere. Drawing off excessive amounts of water leads to a drop in the water table, which can have a considerable detrimental effect on local ecosystems. The consumption of drinking water and the quantities of waste water that occur should therefore be limited through suitable constructional and technical measures (e.g. water-saving taps). In addition, in many instances it is preferable to use rainwater or "grey water" (water already used once but not seriously contaminated).

Water treatment

The consumption of drinking water per head has dropped steadily in Germany over recent years thanks to water-saving technologies and a change in the behaviour of users, although local, marked differences are evident. Even on the international scale, there are major differences (Fig. B 2.51). Whereas the daily per head consumption in Germany in 1990 was 147 l, it had dropped to 128 l by 2005.

Untreated water can be obtained from groundwater, springs and surface waters, by collecting precipitation (e.g. cisterns) or by means of sea-water desalination in dry coastal regions. To maintain quality, certain regions are designated as groundwater protection areas. In Germany it is groundwater that supplies most of the drinking water (65%), followed by bank filtrate, which consists of groundwater plus surface water; sandy banks promote the mechanical pretreatment of the water.

In order to produce drinking water from untreated water, it is cleaned and sterilised in a central plant according to DIN 2000 and, if necessary, dissolved ions (e.g. iron or salts) are removed or added. The adjustment of pH value and conductivity plus the addition of chlorine are necessary not only to achieve the desired water quality but also because of the quality of the existing network of pipes.

High-level tanks, pumping and boosting stations are used to maintain the pressure in the network of pipes, which in turn results in high costs and considerable technology for construction and maintenance. Operators must guarantee a constant flow of water in the network. Every water supply network has leaks; across the EU, the losses in the water supply range between 8% in Germany and 27% in Italy [6].

Dimensions [m]	h x w x d 1.5x1.1x0.6
Weight	approx. 130kg
Capacity	500 l in total
Pressure [bar]	max. 4.7 min. 1.7
Power supply	230 V, 50 Hz
max. output	1 kW
Power consumption	0.6 kWh/d

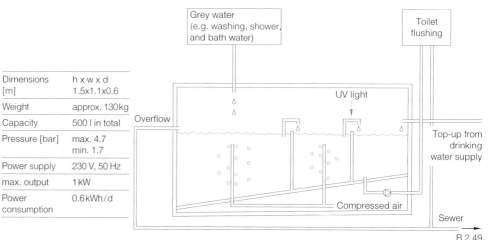

B 2.49

Distance	Most efficient form of transport for biogas energy
< 1.5 km	Group heating network
> 1.5 km	Own gas network
> 5 km	Gas treatment and feeding into the gas network

B 2.50

Country	Drinking water consumption per head and day [l]
Basic requirement (WHO)	50
Europe	
Belgium	122
Germany	128
Austria	145
France	151
Sweden	188
Italy	213
Switzerland	237
India	25
Japan	278
USA	295

B 2.51

Waste-water usage

In order to be able to use our water resources efficiently, water can be used more than once for certain applications (Fig. B 2.52). Rainwater, for example, can first be used as "grey water" and later as "black water" (containing faecal material), which corresponds to a slowed down-cycling process.

Rainwater can be used, for example, for flushing toilets and watering gardens, but also as a transfer medium for cooling purposes. The filtering required before use can be assisted by planting in the rainwater collecting areas.

Grey water is especially useful for flushing toilets. As the daily water consumption for baths and showers is roughly equivalent to the water needed for flushing toilets, water consumption can be cut by approx. 30%. Grey-water installations filter and clean the water, and the addition of UV-light treatment sterilises it. Such systems require separate grey-water pipework within the building and a grey-water tank (Fig. B 2.49).

New on the market are technical solutions that isolate usable partial flows from the water by means of a materials-flow analysis. It is possible, for example, to use rainwater in the building services, e.g. for cooling, with both low-tech solutions for open bodies of water and even high-tech solutions for air-conditioning systems already available. Vacuum toilets are also based on a materials-flow analysis; they collect concentrated black water, possibly separated into brown and yellow water, and store it in tanks, where it is then available for other uses (Fig. B 2.52). Upcycling thus becomes possible as well. Such systems can reduce a building's waste water to zero or near-zero.

Waste-water drainage

If the waste-water is drained away via a combined system, all waste-water flows are collected in one system of pipes and fed to waste-water treatment plant. During heavy rainfall, the flow rate can reach 100 times the quantity of waste water during dry periods. Only rarely can sewage systems and sewage plants cope with such large amounts of water, which can mean that waste water is not properly treated. This is why separate systems are generally used, with waste water and rainwater being drained away in two separate systems (Fig. B 2.72). Pipes can therefore be made smaller and the operation of waste-water plants optimised.

Waste-water treatment

We distinguish between three treatment stages for processing the waste water:

- Mechanical treatment (first treatment stage): Large foreign matter is removed by screens; heavy, later also light, suspended matter is deposited in the grit chamber and primary settlement tank due to the reduction in the flow velocity.

- Biological treatment (second treatment stage): Micro-organisms are introduced into the waste water to eliminate nitrogen; the high level of nutrients helps the micro-organisms to grow and they themselves become suspended matter. The activated sludge method requires considerable oxygen. The ensuing sewage sludge is afterwards removed mechanically.
  Mechanical and biological treatment remove about 90% of the biologically degradable contamination in the waste water (Fig. B 2.53).

- Chemical treatment (third treatment stage): A third treatment stage – used only rarely – employs various elaborate methods, which require considerable energy and resource inputs, to remove virtually any chemical from the waste water as required.

Waste-water treatment plants require an area of 0.5–2 m^2 per inhabitant (Fig. B 2.57). A drop in water consumption in conjunction with the smaller household sizes these days plus the increase in the living space requirements per person have resulted in reduced waste-water flows.

The ensuing residues lead to flow problems and an increase in maintenance and treatment costs for centralised waste-water treatment plants. In Germany the cost of waste-water treatment in large-scale plants is much greater than the cost of treating drinking water. And with a consumption of 4400 GWh/a, waste-

Flow	Treatment	Usage options	Further uses
Rainwater	Simple filtration (gravel)	Irrigation	Groundwater supplement
	Filtration	Cooling (technical refrigerant)	–
		Shower, washing machine	Grey water
		Toilet flushing	Yellow and black water
	Biological treatment	Water supply	
Grey water	Sterilisation	Washing machine	Grey water
		Toilet flushing	Yellow and black water
	Filtration, biological treatment	Irrigation	Groundwater supplement
	Biological treatment	Water supply	
Yellow water	Sterilisation through storage and drying	Manure production	
	Storage	Raw material for chemicals industry	
Black water	Anaerobic fermentation	Biogas production	Humus and manure production
Kitchen and organic waste	Composting	Humus and manure production	

B 2.52

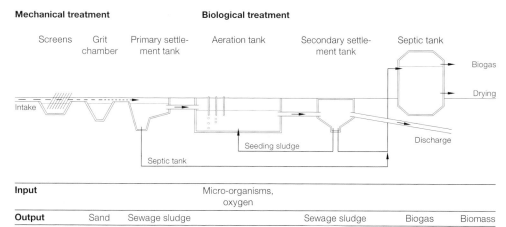

Mechanical treatment   **Biological treatment**

Screens Grit chamber Primary settlement tank Aeration tank Secondary settlement tank Septic tank

Biogas

Drying

Intake

Seeding sludge

Discharge

Septic tank

Input			Micro-organisms, oxygen			
Output	Sand	Sewage sludge		Sewage sludge	Biogas	Biomass

B 2.53

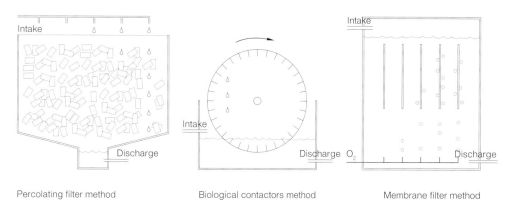

Intake

Intake

Discharge

Intake

Discharge O_2

Discharge

Percolating filter method Biological contactors method Membrane filter method

B 2.54

Pretreatment Treatment by way of root-bed medium

Suitable plants:
various reed, bulrush, and grass varieties

Multi-compartment digestion chamber Pumping chamber   Weir and inspection chamber

Intake

Coarse gravel Sand and gravel or cohesive soil Synthetic liner 2% fall Discharge

B 2.55

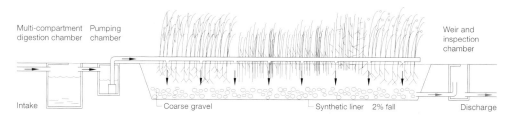

Multi-compartment digestion chamber Pumping chamber   Weir and inspection chamber

Intake

Coarse gravel Synthetic liner 2% fall Discharge

B 2.56

water plants consume more energy than all German schools put together [7]! The energy requirement is mainly due to the aeration, circulation and transportation of the waste water to be treated. The biological treatment stage accounts for two-thirds of the area required for the whole waste-water treatment plant.

Owing to the high cost of such centralised plants, decentralised waste-water treatment offers an alternative. Besides the large-scale activated sludge method, the following methods are also available for the biological treatment (Fig. B 2.54):

- In the percolating filter method, the waste water trickles through support media made from synthetic or mineral materials. The cleaning micro-organisms are located on the enlarged surface area of the support media, which at the same time ensures good aeration.
- In the biological contactors method, the biological film of a fixed film reactor is partially immersed in the flow of waste water to be treated; the supply of oxygen to the micro-organisms is achieved by continuous rotation.
- In contrast to other methods, the small-scale variation of the activated sludge method, the membrane filter method, does not require a secondary settlement tank. The membrane is cleaned by rotation, rinsing and the rising air bubbles.

The biological treatment methods often preferred these days are those in which the waste water is treated virtually naturally in waste-water lagoons or constructed wetlands to DIN 4261. The majority of smaller plants are particularly suitable for domestic or similar waste water and a typical catchment area of up to approx. 200 inhabitants. Treatment can be carried out horizontally or vertically.

A horizontal constructed wetland with beds 60–80 cm deep requires a treatment area of 3–10 m² per person, depending on whether only grey water or the entire waste water is to be treated (Fig. B 2.55).

A vertical constructed wetland achieves a more effective depth of 80–120 cm with a more consistent utilisation of the volume and thereby reduces the area of land required. Between 1.5 and 5 m² is required per person (Fig. B 2.56).

B 2.57

B 2.53 Schematic diagram of a traditional waste-water treatment plant with mechanical and biological treatment stages
B 2.54 Schematic diagram of alternative aeration techniques for the biological treatment stage
B 2.55 Schematic diagram of a horizontal constructed wetland
B 2.56 Schematic diagram of a vertical constructed wetland
B 2.57 Aerial view of a waste-water treatment plant in Germany's Ruhr region
B 2.58 Functional design for an entrance area, with waste collection station, Ochsenanger Estate, Bamberg (D), 2000, Melchior Eckey Rommel
B 2.59 Landfill quotas for various types of waste in Germany
B 2.60 Ecological evaluation and prognosis of developments for waste management in Germany
B 2.61 Materials flows and their further use within the waste sector

B 2.58

Waste from operations and usage

Waste is regarded as a raw material. A maximum recycling quota is therefore desirable. According to German legislation, waste should be reused whenever possible and disposal should only be considered when this is unavoidable. A large portion of waste in Germany is already recycled; the landfill quotas, apart from building debris, have declined enormously (Fig. B 2.59). In energy terms, the recovery of materials – reuse, recycling, further use – offers the greatest savings potential (see "Materials", p. 174).

Waste collection

Domestic waste is the most heterogeneous type of waste. Special collection depots for hazardous waste (e.g. batteries containing heavy metals, paints, varnishes, etc.) enable such waste to be removed from general waste streams.

Separate collection enables waste streams to be segregated right at the point where the waste is created. Individual waste streams are, however, vulnerable to contamination, which has to be dealt with in subsequent sorting stages, which results in an additional energy requirement for transportation. Whether centralised mechanical sorting or local pre-sorting represents the more advantageous solution in terms of energy, depends on the particular situation. Well-planned waste collection depots readily accessible to the public can have a crucial

influence on the function of the system and users' behaviour.

Waste collection in the public sector is suitable for high-quality, mass-produced or hazardous waste streams. Separate collection systems have been put in place for paper, glass, biomass, plastics, textiles, metals, electrical appliances and used oil, for instance. Such collection depots can be at or below ground level. Although the underground variety is more expensive, they are easier to integrate and use less land. On the other hand, there is a higher risk of misuse and vandalism. Positioning these on well-used pathways helps the collection of private waste. The local significance of the "waste" theme is evident in the valuation of properties: in the assessment of the quality of the location, the siting and layout of waste depots are seen as important criteria (Fig. B. 2.58). Certain types of usage (e.g. gastronomy) may generate special waste streams that require specific measures.

Waste treatment

One major load on the climate is due to the anaerobic decomposition of biological components in landfilled waste, which produces the so-called landfill gas (methane) so damaging to the climate. However, the methane can be collected and used for energy purposes in co-generation plants.
In order to reduce methane emissions from landfill sites, treatment of waste has been com-

pulsory in Germany since 2005: biological-mechanical pre-treatment treats the waste initially mechanically – separating out reusable raw materials (Fig. B. 2.61). The mechanisms of the sorting plants are based on, for example, the size, colour, magnetism or weight of the waste to be processed (Fig. B. 2.62). The biological residues can be composted or, like sewage sludge, anaerobically fermented, which cleans up the residue and also produces usable biogas.

Thermal treatment involves all types of incineration. The ensuing heat is converted into electricity via generators but can also be used for group and district heating networks. Pyrolysis involves changing the chemical composition of the waste through high temperatures and simultaneous exclusion of oxygen. This method can be used to produce a gas that can be fed into the gas network, but a slag residue is also produced.

The targets of the Federal Ministry for the Environment, Nature Conservation & Nuclear Safety (BMU) for 2020 require 1% of energy needs in Germany to be met by thermal waste treatment (Fig. B 2.60).

Traffic

In a society with a division of labour, traffic represents a necessary prerequisite for the economy and for individuals. As mobility between buildings is the norm, the structure of that traffic and its energy consumption are closely linked

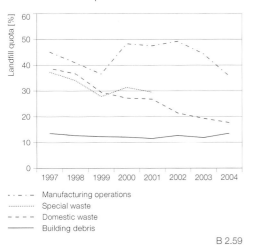

Manufacturing operations
Special waste
Domestic waste
Building debris

B 2.59

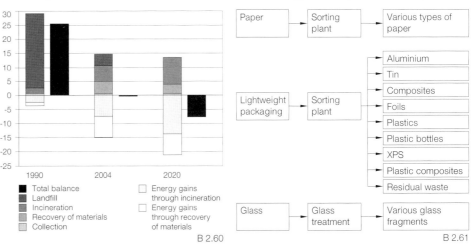

B 2.60 / B 2.61

B 2.62

Means of transport	Work W/km [%]	Typical utilisation [%]	Typical catchment radii [km]	Typical journey distances			Means of transport utilisation [%]		
				[km]	[min]	[km/h]	Total	Rural areas	Urban areas
Walking	100	100	–	1.4	21.1	4.3	22	21	24
Bicycle	30	100	–	3.3	22.3	10.6	9	11	9
Bus and train	420	20–25[1]	[2]	12.6	39.6	18.1	8	5	12
Car	930 (overland) 2700 (town)	–	25–30	14.1 –	20.7	32.8[3]	61 (D: 45 P: 16)	63 (D: 46 P: 18)	55 (D: 40 P: 15)
Aircraft	830	60	>200 km	n.d.	n.d.	no data	no data	no data	no data

[1] Coach: 60%; high-speed train: 45%
[2] Bus and tram: 400 m; rapid transit rail system: 500–1000 m
[3] Values for driver; passenger: 15.4 km/22.0 km/31.6 km

D = driver
P = passenger

B 2.63

with the urban-planning and architectural circumstances, and, after all, are triggered by these. In Germany traffic is the sector with the second-highest energy consumption (Fig. B 2.3). Constructional measures and systems of incentives create the conditions for transferring private vehicular traffic to more efficient public transportation, also walking and bicycles. Basically, we can divide the total volume of traffic into passenger and goods traffic (Fig. B 2.65).

Traffic infrastructure
The road and rail networks represent full-coverage traffic infrastructures. The network of public roads in Germany has a total length of about 626 300 km and covers approx. 1.2% of the total area of the country; 63.1% of this is attributable to local, minor roads (Fig. B 2.66). The German rail network totals approx. 43 800 km. Converting the traffic infrastructures into a pro head land requirement, then the figure of about 50 m² is higher than the average per head living area (see "Architecture and sustainability – a difficult relationship", p. 18). In terms of land use and transport performance, the rail network is roughly twice as efficient as the road network. Boats and ships transfer goods traffic to lakes, rivers and canals. The low land requirements for air traffic are placed in perspective by the widespread noise pollution and environmental impacts.

Means of transport
Three key factors influence the energy requirements of transport systems: efficiency of the means of transport, speed and utilisation. Whereas maximum values are always desirable for efficiency and utilisation, the optimum speed depends on the distance to be travelled. An ideal system speed for long-distance journeys across Central Europe is, for example, 250–300 km/h. As a rule, decreasing the speed leads to a saving in energy. In urban public rail transport, for example, decreasing the maximum speed from 70 to 50 km/h reduces the energy requirement by 50%. Efficiency, accessibility and speed therefore result in catchment radii typical for the type of technology (Fig. B 2.63). Railways and waterways are especially energy-efficient transport systems for goods traffic. Goods transport by road, on the other hand, ensures an optimised distribution of the goods, but consumes considerably more energy (Fig. B 2.67). For passenger traffic, too, railways represent the most energy-efficient technology. The high energy requirements of private vehicles are caused, in particular, by the low utilisation (25–30%) and low energy utilisation plus the high total transport weight in relation to the number of people to be transported. An increase in the level of utilisation in passenger transportation would require the introduction of further local public transport alternatives, car sharing schemes and car rental stations. The most efficient means of transport is the use

of our own muscles, and travelling by bicycle uses 70% less muscle power than walking. Another important factor when assessing the different means of transport is their effect on the climate. The water vapour produced during combustion is, for example, of little importance near the ground, but in higher atmospheric strata it plays a significant role in the climate change. So aircraft represent the means of transport that has by far the greatest impact on the climate.
Within towns and cities, the use of electric cars is one of the measures being promoted in the name of climate protection because on the urban scale they are essentially neutral in terms of their environmental impact. However, the primary energy balance and hence the environmental effect can only be evaluated on the basis of the electricity generation.

Mobility needs
Every day, mobility accounts for, on average, 75–85 min of a person's time, regardless of which forms of transport are available to us and the national or regional contexts in which we find ourselves [8]. But whereas the time taken for mobility is obviously undergoing little change, our radius of movement and hence the destinations achievable with the means of transport at our disposal are increasing. This is accompanied by a rise in the volume of traffic. Both are expressions of the ever more marked increase in flexibility of our lifestyles [9].

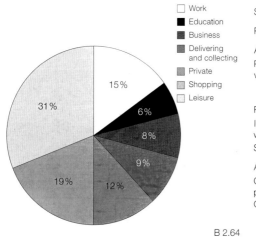

Work
Education
Business
Delivering and collecting
Private
Shopping
Leisure

31%
15%
6%
8%
9%
12%
19%

B 2.64

Scheduled traffic | 8662
Rail traffic | 2131
Air traffic | 146
Private vehicles | 56140

Passengers transported [million/a]

Rail traffic | 317.3
Inland waterways | 236.8
Sea-going ships | 281.0
Air traffic | 2.9
Crude oil pipelines | 95.5
Goods vehicles | 2765,0

Goods transported [million t/a]

B 2.65

Road	Length [km]	Proportion [%]
Motorways	11 786	1.9
Trunk roads	41 228	6.6
A-roads	86 838	13.9
B-roads	90 996	14.5
Local roads	395 400	63.1

B 2.66

Means of transport for goods traffic	Efficiency- [t km/MJ]
Air	0.3
Road	1.7
Rail	3.3
Sea	4.3

B 2.67

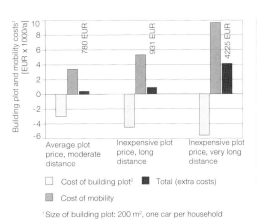

Cost of building plot[2]   Total (extra costs)

Cost of mobility

[1] Size of building plot: 200 m², one car per household
[2] Difference in cost in relation to a city-centre building plot

B 2.68

B 2.69

People undertake, on average, 3.5 journeys per day and 50% of those journeys are shorter than 3 km.

Urban traffic

If we include the fact that we spend approx. 90% of our time indoors in the mobility equation, then traffic can be described as movement between buildings.

One of the most frequent journeys we undertake is that between home and work (Fig. B 2.64). Taking the example of Hamburg, it can be shown that despite the cost of land being up to seven times higher, living in the city is more economic than living in an equivalent home in the suburbs because of the mobility costs that are saved (Fig. B 2.68). This relationship can be regarded as essentially universal. Added to this are savings because fewer cars are required or journey times are shorter (up to a factor of five). Comparing the energy requirements, an older building with an energy consumption of 200 kWh/m²a and a floor space of 150 m² is roughly equivalent to a passive-energy house plus car travel amounting to 10 000 km/a, for example. The energy balance for a family can be up to four times less in town than it is in the country.

The best way of avoiding traffic is to provide a dense form of construction coupled with a range of interesting, local open spaces, diverse spatial situations and close proximity between supply and demand. Short distances to shops, schools, workplaces, recreational and other amenities reduce traffic and hence the associated energy consumption (Fig. B 2.69).

Urban spaces exhibit a higher proportion of local public transport plus journeys on foot and by bicycle than in rural settlements. Systems of incentives can achieve a further shift away from private vehicles and on to public transport. Easy accessibility, frequent services and a better feeling of safety can help here. Districts develop differently depending on access for private vehicles, which can restrict the behaviour of users to a greater or lesser degree (Fig. B 2.73).

In choosing a location, good local public transport connections will become a decisive factor. And in designing spaces, the clarity and legibility of the corresponding transport interchanges will also be important to users. In principle, travellers much prefer single-level situations (Fig. B 2.70 a–c). For underground locations, bright, well-lit interiors provide a degree of compensation, especially for low passenger numbers and at night. Underground systems do reduce the use of land in urban areas, but require a high energy input for ventilation and lighting where direct lighting and ventilation from outside is not possible (Fig. B 2.71). Attractive paths and cycle tracks with safe, priority routing and easily accessible cycle parks should be included in every mobility concept for gaining access to the immediate surroundings.

a

b

c

B 2.70

B 2.71

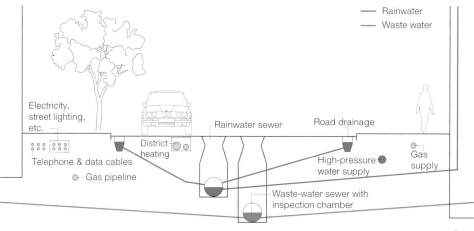

B 2.72

Urban street design

Within settlements, the public traffic infrastructure occupies 39% of the land on average. In the light of this high land use, measures for efficient use of the spaces, a reduction in the space required and the conversion of any poorly used traffic infrastructure would seem to be sensible (Fig. B 2.72).

Different forms of traffic result in different mobility speeds within urban streets. These may impair each other or represent potential dangers. Safety can be improved by harmonising the various speeds or by separating the forms of traffic. The latter is, however, associated with a considerable amount of land use and can lead to a loss in urban qualities.

Appropriate design measures can improve the attention of road users at those points where speeds change. The deceleration of the traffic in the streets, e.g. by way of a traffic-calming

open-space design, at the same time contributes to enhancing the standard of living in the urban area (Fig. B 2.73).

Fast, high-volume traffic has negative effects on the social environment. It has been shown that a rise in segregating traffic flows is associated with a decrease in contact between local residents.

Around the building there are spaces for parked vehicles which should take into account the orientation with respect to and accessibility of the building from its access roads. The provision of cycle parks, wherever possible a compact arrangement of car parking spaces and a reduction in the number of parking spaces to encourage the changeover to local public transport foster the change to energy-efficient forms of mobility. Systems of incentives such as tickets that cover all forms of local public transport can help here.

Stationary traffic

Mobility is always linked with non-mobility. On average, a car spends only about 1% of its useful life in motion [1]! Besides their requirement for a mobility infrastructure, cars also demand a large amount of space for parking. The land requirement for parking spaces for all the cars registered in Germany corresponds to approx. 20% of the residential floor space in the country. In the case of ground-level parking, this leads to a conflict between high-quality usage and low-quality parking spaces (Fig. B 2.76). In this context, space-saving parking options should be considered:

· Parking areas:
  The right arrangement of parking spaces can reduce the land required by up to 35% (Fig. B 2.77). In residential districts the use of so-called double- and triple-decker garages

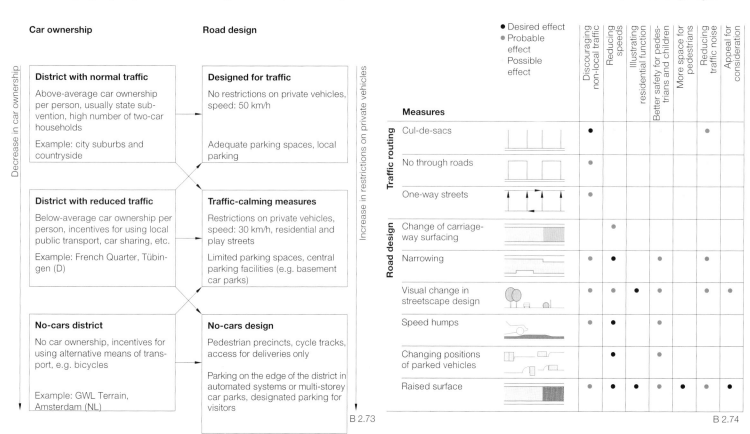

B 2.73

B 2.74

B 2.71 Daylighting in the underground tram station "Rathaus-Süd", Bochum (D), 2006, Pahl + Weber-Pahl
B 2.72 Schematic section through an urban street
B 2.73 Relationships between car ownership, parking requirements and usage restrictions
B 2.74 Measures and effects for local traffic
B 2.75 Schematic section through the basement car park of an office building, Wiesbaden (D), 2001, Thomas Herzog
B 2.76 Aerial view of the centre of Houston, Texas (USA)
B 2.77 Space requirements for various parking arrangements
B 2.78 Schematic sections through various automated parking systems:
   a "Parksafe"
   b "Flurparker"
   c Double-decker garage
   d Triple-decker garage

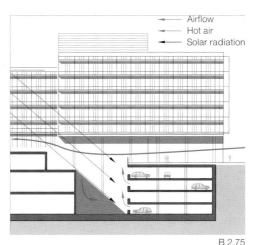

B 2.75

B 2.76

(Fig. B 2.78 c–d) is one way of reducing the overall area required. The height-adjustable platforms require a parking space height of 3.50–4.95 m for double-decker garages.

· Multi-storey car parks:
Stacking parking spaces vertically can reduce the land use in urban areas. However, access requires almost the same area as the parking space itself (Fig. B 2.77). In residential districts local parking options in the form of multi-storey or basement car parks can help to clear parked vehicles from public spaces, create additional local meeting places (social consequence) and generate a good feeling of safety among users.

· Basement car parks:
Underground car parks are expensive to build and operate. The energy requirement for permanent artificial lighting and mechanical ventilation can exceed the heating requirement of a building. Natural lighting and ventilation must therefore be considered, especially as this also improves the feeling of safety among users (Fig. B 2.75). The benefit of underground facilities is that they release land for amenities above ground in heavily built-up areas.

· Automated parking systems:
These are based on the principle of stacking cars mechanically in a type of "shelving system", which may be above or below ground, or integrated into a building. As drivers do not need access to the parking spaces, the overall space required is much less than that needed for directly accessible parking spaces. However, the operating costs are higher (Fig. B 2.78).

In energy terms, parked cars represent unused power stations with an extremely low degree of efficiency for mobility (approx. 18%). If we take the number of cars in Germany (approx. 46 million) and assume an average engine output of 60 kW, this adds up to a mechanical capacity of 2.8 TW! As a motorised object, it contains, in principle, all the components necessary for a decentralised combined heat and power plant! As our cars stand stationary for 8600 hours every year, they could generate 24 000 TWh of electricity! Gross electricity generation in Ger-

many is about 550 TWh – only approx. 2% of this theoretical potential! In addition, the generating process would create thermal energy amounting to approx. 50 000 TWh, which corresponds to about 20 times the annual final energy requirement or 575 times the annual district heating output in Germany!

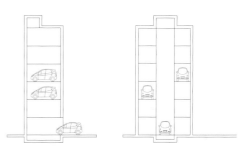

Possible number of spaces per 100 m road length	34	40	68	80
Possible number of spaces per 100 m²	4.4	3.2	4.4	5
Space requirement per parking space, incl. access m²	22.5	30.8	22.5	20

B 2.77

References:
[1] Knoflacher, Herrmann: Stehzeuge. Vienna/Cologne/Weimar, 2001
[2] Hauff, Volker: Unsere gemeinsame Zukunft. Der Brundtland Bericht der Weltkommission für Umwelt und Entwicklung. (Our Common Future. Report of the World Commission on Environment and Developments. Greven 1987
[3] Mehr Wert für die Fläche: Das "Ziel-30-ha" für die Nachhaltigkeit in Stadt und Land. German Council for Sustainable Development (RNE) (ed.). Berlin, 2004
[4] Planning of the grid integration of wind energy in germany onshore and offshore up to the year 2020 (summary of the "dena Grid Study"). German Energy Agency (ed.). Cologne, 2005
[5] Meyer, Franz: Kältespeicher in großen Kältenetzen. In: Projektinfo 10/05. Bine Informationsdienst, 2005
[6] Wasser-Wissen, RWE AG
[7] Steigerung der Energieeffizienz von Kläranlagen. Presentation at the BMU/UBA conference on energy efficiency in sewage treatment plants, Ingenieurberatung für Abwassertechnik Bernd Haberkern. Bonn, 2007
[8] Steierwald, Gerd: Stadtverkehrsplanung. Berlin/Heidelberg/New York, 2005
[9] Tully, Claus J.; Baier, Dirk: Mobiler Alltag – Mobilität zwischen Option und Zwang. Vom Zusammenspiel biographischer Motive und sozialer Vorgaben. Wiesbaden, 2006

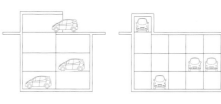
a Cross-section   Longitudinal section

b Cross-section   Longitudinal section

c Cross-section   d Cross-section
B 2.78

Building envelope

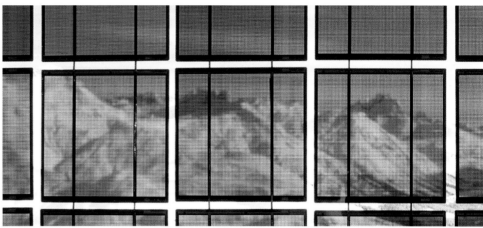

B 3.1

The outer shell of a building defines the boundary between inside and outside. It dominates the external appearance of the building and enters into a dialogue with its surroundings. The history of the building envelope is therefore dominated by features and attributes that govern appearance, proportions, choice of materials and cultural aspects. Its primary function is to protect the building against wind, precipitation and solar radiation. As comfort demands have grown, however, the building envelope has taken on a more complex, climate-regulating function.

The increasing importance of energy consumption in buildings has led to more and more attention being focused on the building envelope – the facade design especially – with respect to architectural and technical considerations. The external surfaces of a building have a considerable effect on its energy efficiency. This applies to both the optimisation of the heat transfer between inside and outside, and also to the decentralised energy production via the building envelope (Fig. B 3.1).

At the same time, our awareness of the need for a sustainable use of resources is on the increase. The choice of materials for the building envelope defines to a considerable extent both the energy requirements for constructing the building in the first place, and also those of the follow-up period, e.g. for operating the building, cleaning or maintenance (see "Materials", p. 165). Further aspects of sustainability are privacy requirements and sound insulation, the durability of the materials and the deconstruction options.

Factors determining the design

Numerous demands are placed on the building envelope as the energy interface between the ambient conditions and the internal climate needs of users and occupants (Fig. B 3.2). Often, the resulting tasks lead to a conflict of aims between, for example, the view out, the use of daylight and shading measures. Besides architectural ideas and economic criteria, the design of a building envelope is subjected to complex conditions that must be optimised for each structure. Generally speaking, these conditions fall under the following headings:

Usage
The task of the building envelope is to create safe, secure, healthy and agreeable interior conditions for the respective type of use, although some of the boundary conditions differ considerably. Housing, for example, requires a totally different specification to that for offices or museums, theatres or manufacturing facilities. Just the usage alone can have an effect on the design of the building envelope, e.g. through mandatory stipulations regarding a higher air change rate or level of illumination.

The desired degree of comfort involves a subjective perception which is determined by a number of influencing factors (see "Fundamentals", p. 55). In all the deliberations regarding the energy-efficiency optimisation of the building envelope, users' specific requirements are both the elementary condition and the objective. A viable concept contains the synthesis of all relevant parameters and places the user at the focus of the investigation. It is necessary and also permissible to question the subjective demands of users, especially in the case of a building whose energy concept is based on a close interaction with the external influences. For example, a deviation from the ideal values for a limited period of time is often sensible if this enables a reduction in the auxiliary air-conditioning installation. Moreover, static interior conditions not dependent on the weather do not necessarily represent the ideal situation for human well-being.

Climatic aspects
In the early days of the history of building, building forms and types of construction developed in the different climate zones of the planet which were closely related to the local, specific climatic conditions. Contrasting with that, the architecture of the International Style is in many instances characterised by the fact that extensive technical systems can guarantee the desired interior conditions at any place – with the corresponding energy input. The planning of energy-efficient buildings calls for a sensitive understanding of the specific macroclimatic and microclimatic conditions. Besides the savings to be made on technical systems and the reduced energy demand, it is, in particular,

B 3.1 Semi-transparent solar cells in the facade, cable-car station, Lech am Arlberg (A), 2002, Hans Riemelmoser
B 3.2 Building envelope: influencing factors, properties and functions

better comfort that forms the focus of attention. The technical and materials-related properties of the external surfaces take on a key role here. An accurate analysis of the climate data is therefore an important prerequisite for designing a building envelope to suit a specific location.

Construction
The configuration of the building envelope can be influenced by the design of the remainder of the building. One critical aspect here is whether the outer shell is to provide loadbearing functions or is to be relieved of any primary structural requirements. Accordingly, choice of materials and design language are mutually influential. Whereas in housing solid external walls with their climate-regulating effect are generally preferred, many contemporary office buildings keep the loadbearing and enclosing functions separate, often resulting in the large-scale use of glass. Transparent surfaces call for special care during planning because they normally have to satisfy many functions, and unwanted side-effects can manifest themselves. In order to deal with these effects, such facades are mostly supplemented by systems such as opening elements, sunshades, glare protection, etc.

One increasingly important aspect is integrating decentralised building services into the building envelope. A compressive selection is now available, including servo-motors for automatic night-time cooling, fully automatically regulated sunshading systems, facade-mounted ventilation units and active solar modules. The different service lives of the building envelope materials and the technical components should be taken into account. And subsequent improvements to the energy-efficiency properties are coupled with high costs when the building envelope is involved. For both new building works and refurbishment projects it is therefore sensible to estimate the ongoing trends in comfort demands and to implement the highest standards possible.

Legislative stipulations
The planning work is increasingly affected by legislation. Numerous documents contain specifications and recommendations with respect to the energy-efficiency properties of the building envelope. In Germany the corresponding legislation is drawn up at national or federal state level and often forms the basis for further statutory instruments. Statutory instruments help to focus the legislation and also refer to numerous standards. One German example is the Energy Conservation Act (EnEV), which is based on the Energy Conservation Directive (EnEG) and provides specific information regarding the maximum permissible primary energy requirements of buildings (see "Strategies", p. 183). The statutory instruments and standards relevant to the building envelope are listed in the appendix (see p. 268).

Historical developments
In warm climate zones, buildings have always been broken down into loadbearing structure (e.g. wooden poles) and enclosing elements (e.g. animal skins). Contrasting with this, in the temperate and cold climate zones it was better to build solid external walls that provided loadbearing functions at the same time (e.g. masonry). Such forms of construction permitted only small openings but introduced a large thermal mass, and both these factors had a substantial influence on the interior climate.

It was the natural scientists of the 19th century in particular who contributed to the further development of building envelope functions by explaining their building physics aspects. Around 1820 the Frenchman Jean Fourier postulated a theory about heat conduction in solid bodies, and his use of the terms "heat flux", "temperature gradient" and "thermal conductivity" still dominate the language today. In 1828 another Frenchman, the physicist Jean Claude Eugène Péclet, introduced the k-value (now known as the U-value, measured in W/m^2K, see "Materials", p. 150, Fig. B 5.12) as a coefficient for a body's permeability to heat [1]. In the sense of energy, the building envelope consists of six surfaces in the simplest case. These must be considered separately according to

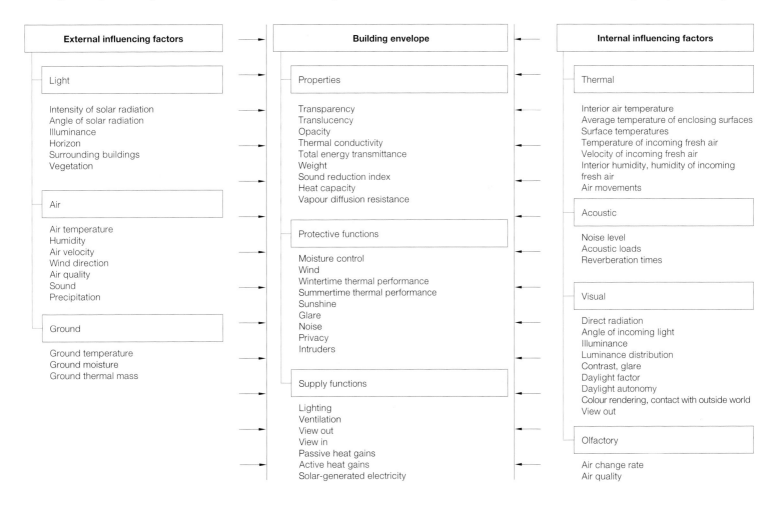

External influencing factors	Building envelope	Internal influencing factors
Light	**Properties**	**Thermal**
Intensity of solar radiation Angle of solar radiation Illuminance Horizon Surrounding buildings Vegetation	Transparency Translucency Opacity Thermal conductivity Total energy transmittance Weight Sound reduction index Heat capacity Vapour diffusion resistance	Interior air temperature Average temperature of enclosing surfaces Surface temperatures Temperature of incoming fresh air Velocity of incoming fresh air Interior humidity, humidity of incoming fresh air Air movements
Air	**Protective functions**	**Acoustic**
Air temperature Humidity Air velocity Wind direction Air quality Sound Precipitation	Moisture control Wind Wintertime thermal performance Summertime thermal performance Sunshine Glare Noise Privacy Intruders	Noise level Acoustic loads Reverberation times
Ground	**Supply functions**	**Visual**
Ground temperature Ground moisture Ground thermal mass	Lighting Ventilation View out View in Passive heat gains Active heat gains Solar-generated electricity	Direct radiation Angle of incoming light Illuminance Luminance distribution Contrast, glare Daylight factor Daylight autonomy Colour rendering, contact with outside world View out
		Olfactory
		Air change rate Air quality

their respective internal and external requirements. Whereas roof and ground slab have been almost exclusively designed from the functional viewpoint, the facade, as a "communicating system", has always been designed taking into account architectural aspects. In this context, in European architecture it was primarily the developments in glass technology and the production of iron that were important. One of the landmarks in glass architecture, the Crystal Palace in London, was a product of the mid-19th century. More or less at the same time, the first patent for insulating glass units was granted in the USA. That part of the building envelope that frequently goes unnoticed is crucial in this context: surfaces in contact with the soil. Unimportant for the external appearance, they are crucial to the thermal balance of a structure.

Thermal insulation to the external walls had already become an important theme in the 19th century in the sense of thermal comfort in the interior. The building physics function, protecting the components, became relevant with the development of multi-layer building envelopes made from different materials. Only later did thermal insulation attain the economic and ecological importance it enjoys today in conjunction with energy consumption (Fig. B 3.3).

The 20th century

Architectural developments at the beginning of the 20th century were characterised by a striving for filigree constructions and the use of glass on a grander scale, as, for example, Walter Gropius demonstrated impressively at his Fagus Works (Fig. B 3.4) and Ludwig Mies van der Rohe formulated in his vision for a glass tower in Berlin. At the start of the 20th century, it was the engineer Ludwig Dietz who enabled a differentiated appraisal of the building envelope by defining an average k-value for multi-layer and inhomogeneous components [1]. However, the desire for large expanses of glass to optimise the amount of daylight in the interior mostly resulted in a worsening of the thermal comfort owing to the insufficient knowledge about the physical properties of glazing at that time. Furthermore, high transmission heat losses during the winter and excessive

heat gains during the summer led to a high energy consumption. The inadequately insulated opaque external components also contributed to the high heating energy requirements. The consequence of this in Germany was the adoption of the Energy Conservation Directive (EnEG) in the 1970s, which formed the basis for the 1st Thermal Insulation Act (1977). For the first time, legislation defined mandatory maximum k-values for the external components of heated buildings. At the same time, people once again started looking at using the energy of the sun more and more for space heating requirements. The elementary rules for the passive use of solar energy resulted in an era of experimental housing during the 1980s, with a south-facing orientation, large amounts of glass and large thermal masses – "solar architecture". It quickly became clear, however, that maximising the passive solar gains could not achieve the desired outcome by itself. Much greater successes were achieved with measures aimed at minimising heat losses through the building envelope, which in the end allowed the heating energy requirement to shrink to the smallest item in the net energy balance. This was demonstrated, for example, by the first passive housing in Germany in the early 1990s (Fig. B 3.5).

Current trends

At the same time as the research projects were being built in the 1980s, software programs were being written to accompany and influence the entire planning process, from drawing up simple energy balances to simulating complex energy and flow situations. Heat conduction, radiation and convection are three-dimensional phenomena and can be visualised with several zones, taking into account dynamic changes in the internal and external boundary conditions. This has made a decisive contribution to being able to develop and design the thermodynamic system "building envelope" with a high degree of reliability (Fig. B 3.6). Such options take on a special significance in the case of energy-efficiency upgrades for existing buildings, where there is a substantial backlog. Energy-efficiency upgrades for existing building envelopes represent one major task in the meaning of sustain-

B 3.4

B 3.5

B 3.6

able development. This is where the greatest savings potential can be tapped in the short-term because the few energy-efficient new buildings are far outweighed by the building stock, which will determine the energy requirements for the coming decades (see "Urban space and infrastructure", p. 63, Fig. B 2.2).

Energy-efficient building envelopes
The energy-efficiency planning of the building envelope means guaranteeing that the interior climate conditions necessary can be maintained over the whole year with low energy requirements and, wherever possible, essentially without any costly energy supply technologies. Such planning presumes an accurate analysis of the climatic boundary conditions and the usage profile in conjunction with all the aforementioned aspects. A building envelope optimised for energy aspects has a maximized passive capacity and hence represents the foundation for viable energy concepts in the future.

Furthermore, by integrating active solar technology, it can make an important contribution to a building's energy supply. The building envelope should therefore be devised in close conjunction with the energy supply technologies. These days, designers of energy-efficient building envelopes have a large number of materials, systems and technologies at their disposal. Taking the 10 components of energy-optimised building as our starting point (see p. 61, Fig. B 1.69), the individual targets, concepts and measures are explained in the following (Fig. B 3.7). These are divided up according to the five energy themes – heating, cooling, ventilation, lighting, electricity – and hence provide a structured overview of the optimisation approaches possible in principle.

B 3.3 Brief chronology of the building envelope aspects relevant to energy
B 3.4 Fagus Works, Alfeld a.d. Leine (D), 1911, Walter Gropius
B 3.5 First passive house in Germany, Darmstadt (D), 1991, Bott, Ridder, Westermeyer
B 3.6 Semi-detached houses, Mühlheim (D), 2005, Pfeifer Roser Kuhn
B 3.7 Targets, subtargets, concepts and measures for the energy-efficiency optimisation of building envelopes

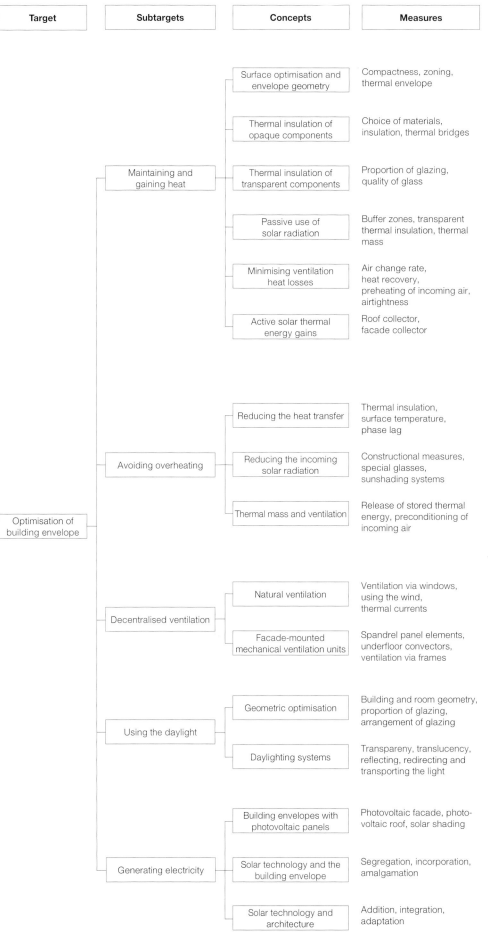

B 3.7

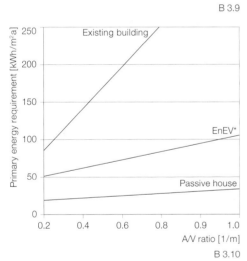

Transmission heat losses	Heating requirement
Insulation of opaque components	e.g. active use of solar radiation
Insulation of transparent components	
	passive solar gains
Ventilation heat losses	internal gains
Losses	**Gains**

☐ Areas where the building envelope may have an influence

B 3.8

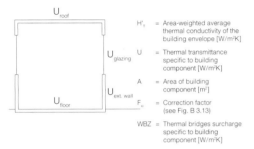

U_{roof}

$U_{glazing}$

$U_{ext. wall}$

U_{floor}

H'_T	=	Area-weighted average thermal conductivity of the building envelope [W/m²K]
U	=	Thermal transmittance specific to building component [W/m²K]
A	=	Area of building component [m²]
F_{xi}	=	Correction factor (see Fig. B 3.13)
WBZ	=	Thermal bridges surcharge specific to building component [W/m²K]

$$H'_T = \frac{h_t}{A} \qquad H'_T = \Sigma \, (U \cdot A \cdot F_{xi}) + WBZ \cdot A$$

B 3.9

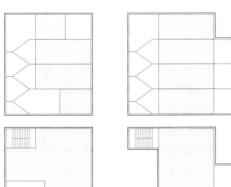

Primary energy requirement [kWh/m²a]

Existing building

EnEV*

Passive house

A/V ratio [1/m]

B 3.10

——— Building volume   ——— Heated volume

B 3.11

Maintaining and gaining heat

In the temperate and cold zones of the Earth it is particularly important to guarantee agreeable interior conditions by way of appropriate measures when outside temperatures are low. The primary aim is to keep as much heat within the building by constructing an optimised building envelope. A thermal balance can be drawn up for the building in order to analyse the heat flows, specifying the relationship between heat losses and heat gains throughout the year (Fig. B 3.8).

When assessing the loss factors, we distinguish between transmission and ventilation heat losses. On the gains side, there are internal heat sources (waste heat produced by lighting, people and electrical appliances) and energy gains due to solar radiation entering through transparent sections of the building envelope (passive use of solar energy). The properties of the building envelope should contribute to evening out this balance as far as possible. The difference between the two sides of the equation determines the heating requirement that must be provided via technical means, and forms the basis for calculating the primary energy requirement in the meaning of the Energy Conservation Act (see "Strategies", p. 185, Fig. B 6.26). As the internal heat sources are, first and foremost, determined by the type of use, the optimisation potential of the building envelope lies in minimising the losses and maximising the solar gains. The average thermal resistance of the enclosing surfaces contributing to the heat transfer (H'_T in W/m²K, Fig. B 3.9) can serve as the target variable for assessing the passive thermal performance of a building via its outer shell. This figure provides an indication of the transmission heat losses to be expected. In addition to this, the provision of fresh air from outside at low temperatures represents another loss factor which becomes more significant as the air change rate increases. Finally, the proportion of glazing with respect to the orientation expresses the potential for the passive use of solar radiation. Besides the direct thermal energy flow via the building envelope, active solar thermal systems for supplying heat are growing in importance. Components in the building envelope are particularly relevant here (see p. 93). In order to improve the thermal performance of the building envelope in winter, the following elements must be harmonised with each other:

· Surface optimisation and envelope geometry
· Thermal insulation of opaque components
· Thermal insulation of transparent components
· Passive use of solar radiation
· Minimising ventilation heat losses
· Active solar thermal energy gains

Surface optimisation and envelope geometry

Decisive criteria for energy-efficiency optimisation are laid down as early as the preliminary design phase through the shape of the building and the layout of the usable floor spaces.

Compactness
Selecting a form for a building has a substantial influence on its energy requirements. The volume of a building is normally mainly determined by the internal layout and economic considerations. In addition, construction and planning legislation stipulations with respect to site occupancy index and plot ratio, which define the permissible total volume, must be taken into account. However, there is usually some leeway for the architectural design of the building envelope. Surface areas of different sizes have a direct effect on the heat losses: the smaller the envelope area required for a given volume, the lower is the building's heating requirement. And vice versa: the larger the envelope area for a given volume, the greater the thermal insulation requirements will be. This relationship becomes directly visible in the design and can be quantified via the concept of compactness. The variable for assessing compactness is the ratio of the heat-transferring enclosing surface area (A) to the heated volume of the building (V) (= A/V ratio). From the geometrical point of view, a sphere represents the ideal form; but in terms of an orthogonal structure, a cube is best. Deviations from these optimum forms lead to differences with respect to the heating requirement of a building (Fig. B 3.10). Unheated circulation zones, utility and storage rooms, garages, etc. are not counted as part of the heated volume and therefore must be thermally separated from the heated volume(s). From the energy point of view, it is not the compactness of the gross volume that is relevant, but rather the volume of the heated part(s) of the building (Fig. B 3.11). A small facade surface area also has a positive effect on the construction costs. But striving to achieve a high compactness does have its limits – where daylight conditions and visual contact with the outside world are impaired (see p. 102). In principle, the degree of compactness improves as the volume increases. For example, large units in apartment blocks exhibit much lower transmission heat losses than detached houses with the same floor space (see "Urban space and infrastructure", p. 70, Fig. B 2.33).

Thermal zoning
Energy-efficiency optimisation potential can also be achieved in the layout of the building by way of thermal zoning. This means apportioning the internal spaces according to their different temperature requirements. It is important to consider the underlying climatic conditions for the orientation of the different rooms. Accordingly, it is advisable to locate areas with a high heating requirement on the south side,

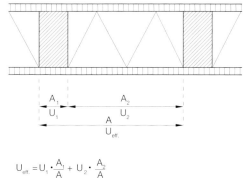

$$U_{eff.} = U_1 \cdot \frac{A_1}{A} + U_2 \cdot \frac{A_2}{A}$$

B 3.12

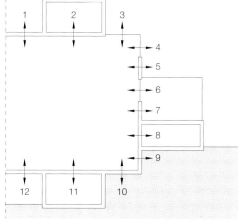

Component	Temperature correction factor [F_{xi}]
1 Opaque floor/roof against outside air	1.0
2 Opaque floor/roof against unheated room	0.8
3 Transparent floor/roof against outside air	1.0
4 Transparent wall against outside air	1.0
5 Opaque wall against outside air	1.0
6 Transparent wall against glass extension	–
7 Opaque wall against glass extension	–
8 Opaque wall against unheated room	0.5
9 Opaque wall against ground	0.6
10 Ground floor against ground	0.6
11 Ground floor against unheated room	0.6
12 Ground floor against outside air	1.0

B 3.13

unheated rooms or those with a low heating requirement, also rooms with high internal heat loads, on the north side, to act as a thermal buffer.

Furthermore, thermal optimisation of the building is possible through a specific arrangement of zones without heating requirements – either through the use of unheated ancillary rooms or, in particular, by adding an outer leaf of glass. The traditional conservatory can achieve this effect just as well as modern double-leaf facades or atria. Transferred to a larger scale, the consequence of further development is a private climatic envelope (see p. 92).

Thermal insulation of opaque components

The magnitude of transmission heat losses through opaque building envelopes is essentially determined by the thermal conductivity of the components enclosing the heated volume. It depends on the specific properties of the materials and the construction of the components involved. The parameter for the thermal quality of a building component is the thermal transmittance (U-value) measured in W/m^2K. It describes the heat flow under static conditions and is calculated as the heat output per square metre for a difference of 1 K between the two surfaces of the component, usually between inside and outside. The lower this value, the better is the thermal performance of a component (see "Materials", p. 149). In a highly insulated building such as a passive house, an

average U-value of less than 0.15 W/m^2K is required. During the planning work, we must distinguish between different components and their requirements. As an energy appraisal also takes into account the heat transfer from the building component to the outside, the same wall constructions can exhibit different U-values depending on the particular situation (e.g. in contact with the outside air or soil) (Fig. B 3.13).

External walls
In most cases the external walls form the largest area of the building envelope, and their significance increases with the height of the building. The thermal quality of the opaque external walls therefore has a considerable influence on the transmission heat losses of a building. In the case of single-leaf masonry external walls, highly perforated clay bricks achieve thermal conductivities as low as 0.08 W/mK (Fig. B 3.14). This means that with a wall thickness of 360 mm, U-values as low as approx. 0.2 W/m^2K are possible. Alternatively, combining loadbearing calcium silicate masonry with insulating autoclaved aerated concrete can reduce the U-value to approx. 0.12 W/m^2K for the same thickness of wall. Even solid concrete walls, if constructed from autoclaved aerated concrete, can achieve U-values as low as 0.3 W/m^2K for a thickness of 400 mm (Fig. B 3.16). However, lowering the thermal conductivity of a building component also reduces its loadbearing capacity. In many cases the requirements placed on external

walls are so high that a monolithic construction with a reasonable material thickness can no longer achieve a thermal performance that satisfies modern requirements.

A multi-layer or multi-leaf construction makes use of additional layers of thermal insulation. The range of suitable materials ranges from natural products such as cork or hemp to the ubiquitous mineral wool and extruded foams, and the latest vacuum insulation panels. Choosing the right insulating material depends on the application and the specific requirements, e.g. compressive strength, moisture resistance or fire protection (see "Materials", p. 151). Figs. B 3.16 to 3.23 show examples of different wall constructions. Furthermore, there are many different types of construction and many different types of material that can be used for facades. External walls that must satisfy high thermal specifications can be broken down into the following principal insulation typologies: external insulation, cavity insulation, internal insulation and frame construction.
To achieve the ideal sequence of layers in terms of the building physics, the insulating material should be placed on the outside of solid external walls (e.g. masonry, concrete). This places the wall construction on the warm side where its mass can have a favourable effect on the interior climate. One widely used system for insulating external walls is the external thermal insulation composite system (insulation + render). This solution represents

Building material	Thermal conductivity λ [W/mK]
Timber	
Structural timber, hardwood, $\rho = 700\,kg$	0.18
Structural timber, softwood, $\rho = 500\,kg$	0.13
Materials with mineral binders	
Normal-wt. conc. w. 1% reinforcement	2.30
Ltwt. conc. w. expanded clay agg., $\rho = 500\,kg$	0.16
Aerated concrete, $\rho = 500\,kg$	0.16
Aerated concrete, $\rho = 350\,kg$, ltwt. mortar	0.09
Masonry (including mortar joints)	
Calcium silicate bricks, $\rho = 1600\,kg$	0.79
Solid clay bricks, $\rho = 1600\,kg$	0.68
Vert. perf. clay bricks, $\rho = 550\,kg$, ltwt. mortar	0.27
Insul. clay bricks, $\rho \leq 600\,kg$, perlite fill., ltwt. mortar	0.08
Metal	
Mild steel, Fe 360 BFN	56.90

B 3.14

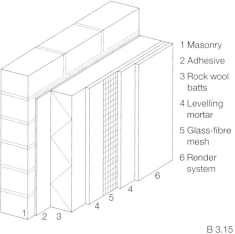

1 Masonry
2 Adhesive
3 Rock wool batts
4 Levelling mortar
5 Glass-fibre mesh
6 Render system

B 3.15

an efficient, high-quality thermal optimisation for an external wall and at the same time provides protection from the weather (Figs. B 3.15 and 3.18).

Thermal insulation composite systems are bonded to the outside of a solid wall, additional mechanical fixings only being required in the case of higher structural requirements. Such systems can be used with virtually any substrate and are therefore also ideal when installing extra insulation in refurbishment projects. Alternatively, the weather protection layer can be detached from the insulating layer. This arrangement requires an air space behind the outer leaf in order to drain any moisture and lends itself to a wide spectrum of facade materials and design options (Fig. B 3.20). Fixing the outer leaf to the loadbearing wall usually penetrates the layer of insulation, a fact that must be taken into account when calculating the U-value.

In a double-leaf solid wall construction (e.g. facing masonry, fair-face concrete), it is possible to position the insulation between the two leaves (Fig. B 3.17). An air space is not usually necessary. Mineral-fibre and rigid foam boards, but also loose materials, can be used for the insulation. Like with a facade with a ventilation cavity, there must be structural connections between the outer leaf and the inner loadbearing leaf, which inevitably leads to the fixings penetrating the thermal insulation. The clearance between the leaves and hence the maximum thickness of insulation possible is limited to approx. 150 mm in standard systems. Thicker insulation calls for custom solutions.

If external insulation is not possible (e.g. when refurbishing facades protected by preservation orders), it may need to be attached to the inside (Fig. B 3.21). This solution, however, places a "thermal break" between the thermal mass of the wall and the interior. In addition, the mounting of items on the wall internally is then limited because the insulating material is not usually rigid enough and fixings that penetrate the vapour barrier behind, which is normally necessary, lead to building physics problems. Great care must be taken with moisture

control measures when installing the insulation internally. As the amount of internal insulation increases, so the surface temperature of the inner face of the loadbearing wall construction decreases. In order to avoid condensation, the design must ensure that water vapour in the air does not drop below the dew point temperature at any point, especially within the layer of insulation. The thickness of internal insulation is therefore restricted to approx. 60–100 mm. Furthermore, a vapour barrier (a membrane impermeable to water vapour) must be attached to the inside of the insulation in order to prevent the transport of moisture from the interior into the layer of insulation. Alternatively, it is possible to employ insulating materials that can absorb large quantities of water vapour and release it again (e.g. boards of calcium silicate foam). With such a solution it is important to ensure that the moisture can be dissipated through the normal exchange of air in the interior.

In frame construction, linear vertical elements (studs, posts, columns of timber or metal) provide the structural functions. Timber stud construction is very popular for housing. Frame construction enables the loadbearing and insulating layers to be combined in one plane and therefore a good U-value can be achieved with a thinner wall (Fig. B 3.19). The inhomogeneous wall construction means that the U-value is calculated as the average value according to the proportions of the areas of the insulating and loadbearing components (Fig. B 3.12). In non-residential work, the structure is normally of reinforced concrete or steel. Post-and-rail systems are then normally used for the separate building envelope. A good thermal break in the facade system is important here. The infill elements for opaque parts of the building envelope can be designed as cold facades with insulation to solid components (e.g. concrete spandrel panel) or as highly insulated panels (Fig. B 3.22). Vacuum insulation panels (VIP) can be used to achieve excellent insulating values with thicknesses only marginally greater than those of glazing elements (Fig. B 3.23).

Roofs

The roof represents a significant area for losses through heat transfer, especially in low-rise buildings. We distinguish between heavyweight slabs, couple or purlin roofs and lightweight constructions. Figs. B 3.24 to 3.26 show examples of different roof structures.

- Flat roofs are usually in the form of heavyweight constructions, normally of reinforced concrete. In terms of optimising their thermal performance, they are comparable to solid external walls. When choosing the insulating material, the compression loads should be taken into account, especially in the case of trafficable surfaces or rooftop planting (Fig. B 3.24). Rigid foam elements are the norm here, designed as a warm or cold deck. To achieve U-values < 0.15 W/m^{2}K, insulating thicknesses exceeding 200 mm are necessary. The resulting depth of the roof finishes should be taken into account when designing parapets.
- Pitched roofs for housing are usually in the form of couple or purlin roofs. In principle, the same conditions apply here as for a timber stud wall. It is particularly important to ensure that the vapour barrier is installed carefully and completely on the inside. In addition to a continuous layer of insulation, it is also possible to fill the spaces between the rafters with insulation (Fig. B 3.25). If insulation is not installed between the rafters, e.g. so that the roof structure can be left exposed internally, the continuous layer of insulation must be sufficiently thick, which can lead to a very deep roof construction. In highly insulated forms of construction, both insulating principles are combined, but the thing deep roof construction must be properly dealt with when designing the eaves.
- Steel structures frequently employ lightweight sheets (e.g. trapezoidal profile steel sheeting) for the roof. These require external insulation similar to solid reinforced concrete roofs (Fig. B 3.26). As an alternative to the layer-by-layer construction, insulated sandwich panels can be attached directly to the loadbearing construction.

Components for rooms with a temperature difference

Components adjacent to unheated rooms or those with low heating requirements must be considered with respect to the heat transfer. This concerns, for example, the topmost suspended floor slabs beneath unheated roof spaces, floor slabs over unheated basements, floors or walls adjacent to garages and unheated staircases. Owing to the low temperature differences, the thermal insulation requirements are reduced in such instances. In the refurbishment of existing buildings, such insulation generally proves to be very economical because it achieves good savings for a low capital outlay.

B 3.16 Solid wall of autoclaved aerated concrete, private house, Chur (CH), 2003, Patrick Gartmann
B 3.17 Fair-face concrete with cavity insulation, "House of Tranquillity", Meschede (D), 2001, Peter Kulka with Konstantin Pichler
B 3.18 External thermal insulation composite system, private house, Zweibrücken (D), 2006, dd1 Architekten
B 3.19 Timber stud wall, private house, Seekirchen (A), 2003, Ebner Grömer
B 3.20 Metal facade with ventilation cavity, research centre, Bonn (D), 2002, BMBW Architekten + Partner
B 3.21 Refurbishment with internal insulation, private house, Constance (D), 2003, Schaller + Sternagel
B 3.22 Post-and-rail facade with insulating panels, office building, Düsseldorf (D), 2005, Gatermann + Schossig
B 3.23 Timber stud facade with vacuum insulation panels, experimental facade project, Würzburg (D),1999, Michael Volz

Autoclaved
aerated concrete

B 3.16

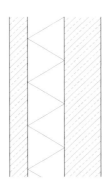

Reinforced concrete
Cavity Insulation
Reinforced concrete

B 3.17

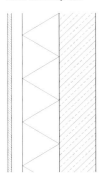

Thermal insulation
composite system
Solid masonry wall

B 3.18

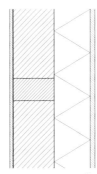

Cladding
Air space
Timber stud wall/
insulation
Lining

B 3.19

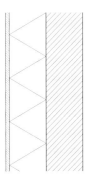

Facade panel
Air space
Insulation
Solid wall

B 3.20

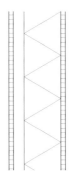

Render
Timber frame
Internal insulation
Plasterboard

B 3.21

Post-and-rail construction/
insulating panel
Glass

B 3.22

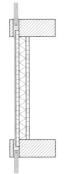

Glass panel
Vacuum insulation panel
Hardboard

B 3.23

Components in contact with the soil
The lower temperature fluctuations in the soil mean that components in direct contact with the soil exhibit a more favourable thermal behaviour than components in contact with the outside air. Thermal insulation below ground is usually attached outside the waterproofing to the structure. Rotproof materials are essential and they must able to withstand moisture and compression loads (see "Materials", p. 151). The more favourable temperature boundary conditions mean that the layer of insulation required is usually thinner than that for wall elements exposed to the outside air. When specifying the dimensions, however, it should be remembered that subsequent improvements to the thermal quality of buried components is not normally possible.

Thermal bridges
Avoiding thermal bridges is a very important aspect when insulating building components. Thermal bridges are local disruptions to the insulating enclosure at which – compared with the surrounding surface – a higher heat flow from inside to outside takes place, e.g. at cantilevering balcony slabs, fixings for facade panels or housings for roller shutters (Fig. B 3.29). We distinguish here between geometrical and constructional thermal bridges. In principle, from the thermal point of view, we should try to achieve an insulating envelope that is as homogeneous as possible. It is helpful here to fix the

positions of the layers of insulation and the insulating glazing units at an early stage in the design process. In new construction work, careful planning can result in the avoidance of thermal bridges. But for those thermal bridges that cannot be eliminated and for refurbishment projects, the building physics of the corresponding weak spots should be critically analysed and taken into account as causes of losses when calculating the heating requirement. Thermographic images can be used to back up the analysis. Such images provide information on the surface temperatures and therefore allow conclusions to be drawn concerning the thermal transmittance (Fig. B 3.27). Thermal bridges can be taken into account by means of general surcharges or by way of detailed calculations [2]. The significance of thermal bridges increases with the quality of the thermal insulation to the building envelope. In very well-insulated buildings, even minor constructional thermal bridges can cause high heat losses. In addition, they lead to a lower surface temperature on the inside compared to the surrounding components, which means there is a risk of condensation and subsequent moisture damage. Careful planning of those areas at risk is therefore extremely important if later damage to the building is to be prevented.

Thermal insulation of transparent components
When planning transparent components, numerous requirements such as daylight utilisation, the views in and out, freedom from glare, etc. must be considered. In well-insulated structures, transparent surfaces usually exhibit a poorer thermal performance than opaque components because of the materials used. The size and arrangement of areas of glazing therefore have a great influence on the transmission heat losses. In this respect, the significance of transparent components increases with the area of glazing. We speak of a high proportion of glazing when the transparent area of a facade exceeds 30% for residential buildings or 50% for buildings with other functions. As the height of the glazing increases, the body of cold air descending on the inside of the cooler glass surfaces can lead to draughts. Such effects must be counteracted by heating.

The quality of the glass
Just like with the opaque building components, the thermal quality of different types of glass varies considerably. Depending on climate zone and building function, systems from single glazing right up to highly advanced insulating units with different coatings and gases can be employed (see "Materials", pp. 152 and 155). The standard today in temperate climate zones is low E double glazing. The U-value of the window (U_W) is made up of the specific values for the glass (U_G) plus the frame (U_F).

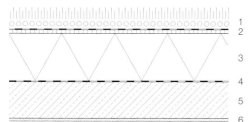

1 Green roof, waterproofing
2 Wood-based board product
3 Thermal insulation
4 Vapour barrier
5 Reinforced concrete slab
6 Plaster

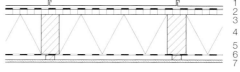

1 Sheet zinc
2 Separating layer
3 Decking
4 Thermal insulation/rafters
5 Vapour barrier
6 Battens
7 Plasterboard

1 Photovoltaic modules
2 Waterproofing, wood-based board product
3 Thermal insulation
4 Vapour barrier
5 Trapezoidal profile steel sheeting
6 Steel beam

B 3.24

B 3.25

B 3.26

Triple glazing is being increasingly used for housing, and even quadruple glazing with U-values as low as 0.3 W/m²K is now available on the market. Vacuum glazing, which should guarantee an extremely high level of thermal insulation with very thin units, is still undergoing development.

The optimum quality of glass required can be determined on the basis of a heating requirement calculation depending on the proportion of glazing and the orientation plus the desired efficiency of the building envelope. Fig. B 3.30 illustrates how the quality of the glazing influences the heating requirement.

Multi-leaf arrangements
Further optimisation potential can be achieved through the use of multi-leaf arrangements; these range from coupled windows to double-leaf facades. However, the thermal aspect is usually of only secondary importance in these systems. They can prove economically viable if other performance requirements, e.g. sound insulation or natural ventilation in tall buildings, are of prime importance in the planning (see p. 99). Double-leaf facades in particular must be guaranteed adequate ventilation in the cavity so that the desired buffering effect during the winter months does not lead to thermal loads during the summer.

The double-leaf principle can also represent a sensible alternative for energy-efficient upgrades to existing buildings. Combining the existing building envelope surfaces with a second leaf of glass will increase the total thermal quality substantially. Such a solution presents the chance of reusing the existing glazing and frames.

This approach also considerably diminishes the effects of existing thermal bridges. In addition, facades worthy of preservation can be protected from the weather and are given a new look without altering their existing structure.

Temporary thermal insulation
As during the night there is no daylight and a view through the windows is mostly unimportant, transparent components provide the chance of temporarily reducing the heat trans-fer with the help of various types of thermally insulating elements placed in front of or behind the glass temporarily. Typical elements are folding and sliding shutters, insulated roller shutters or vertical or horizontal louvres that can be closed completely (Fig. B 3.33).

Passive use of solar radiation
Up until now, so-called solar architecture has been characterised by positioning buildings to suit the available sunlight, large openings on south-facing elevations, mainly closed surfaces to the north, roof overhangs to protect against overheating in summer while still allowing plenty of sunlight into the interior in the winter, and an interior layout based on thermal zoning. Glass plays a decisive role in these designs because it enables thermal separation but at the same time still permits the use of daylight and visual contact with the outside world. Furthermore, its specific physical properties allow it to be used specifically as a "heat trap" for heating the interior.

This effect is based on the following principle: the short-wave solar radiation (ultraviolet radiation) from the sun is absorbed by materials and converted into long-wave heat radiation (infrared radiation). Glass possesses the property of being permeable to short-wave radiation but impermeable to long-wave heat radiation. This characteristic, known as the greenhouse effect, can be used to optimise the thermal use of solar radiation through a combination of transparent areas and absorbent materials. Such a simple form of gaining energy should be assessed as particularly positive because the heat absorption takes place by way of the building components that are provided anyway and therefore does not employ any moving parts and is completely free from emissions and noise. This energy potential is, however, subjected to certain limits owing to the constants of the sun's trajectory, which we cannot influence (and hence the resulting "passivity"). There is thus a conflict between energy needs and energy availability in many situations. Sunshades and thermal masses play an important role in this context. Thermal masses can compensate for brief fluctuations in the day and night rhythm efficiently.

B 3.27

B 3.28

B 3.24 Reinforced concrete slab with rooftop planting, mixed residential and commercial development, Vienna (A), 2002, Delugan Meissl
B 3.25 Couple roof with sheet metal covering, apartment block, Dortmund (D), 2005, ArchiFactory.de
B 3.26 Flat roof on steel structure, private house "R128", Stuttgart (D), 2000, Werner Sobek
B 3.27 Thermographic image of the Centre Georges Pompidou, Paris (F)
B 3.28 Example of isotherms at a constructional thermal bridge (plinth of building)
B 3.29 Typical thermal bridges
   a in an existing building
   b example of refurbishment: reducing thermal bridges
   c example of new building work: avoiding thermal bridges

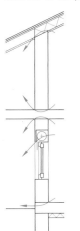

Thermal bridges surcharges according to Energy Pass

in accordance with DIN 4108-6:
surcharge = 0.05 W/m²K

not in accordance with DIN 4108-6:
surcharge = 0.1 W/m²K

with internal insulation
surcharge = 0.2 W/m²K

a

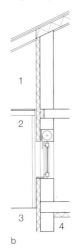

1 Thermal insulation composite system

2 Separate balcony construction in front of facade

3 External insulation below ground

4 Insulation beneath floor over basement

b

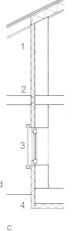

1 Continuous layer of insulation

2 Thermally isolated construction (e.g. Isokorb)

3 Functioning elements positioned outside e.g. sliding shutters)

4 External insulation below ground

c

B 3.29

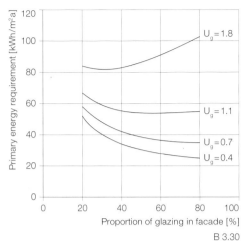

B 3.30

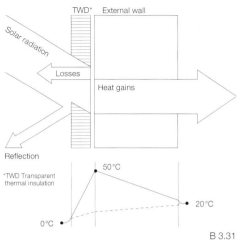

B 3.31

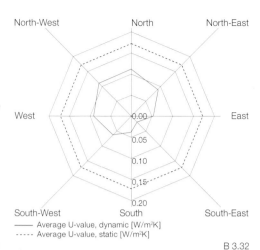

— Average U-value, dynamic [W/m²K]
---- Average U-value, static [W/m²K]

B 3.32

The passive use of solar radiation via the windows is, in principle, always available (even those facing north – by way of diffuse solar radiation). The solar gains via the glazing should be taken into account accordingly in the heating requirement calculations. The magnitude of these energy gains can be influenced decisively by the design of the building plus the size and arrangement of the transparent surfaces. It is, in particular, the orientation of transparent surfaces with respect to the solar radiation that plays a key role. The thermal effect of glazing in the heating period is calculated as the difference between the transmission heat losses and the solar gains. On elevations facing away from the sun, the losses prevail, whereas those facing the sun can generate heat gains to be entered into the calculation. Accordingly, for an energy-efficient optimisation, both the proportion of glazing and the thermal quality should be determined separately depending on the orientation. Optimum passive use of solar radiation starts with establishing the size, geometry and orientation of the transparent areas in the building envelope necessary for visual contact with the outside world and the provision of daylight. Important in all approaches aimed at an increased use of solar radiation is, however, that the advantages during the cold months do not lead to negative consequences during the hotter part of the year (see p. 95). The usable solar potential also differs markedly depending on the use of the building. For example, passive

solar optimisation is normally sensible for residential buildings, whereas in offices the overheating problem in summer generally outweighs because of the higher internal loads.

Solar buffer spaces
Besides direct energy gains from solar radiation, a further concept that can be used is to provide solar buffer spaces, so-called sunspaces. These range from the traditional conservatory and glazed atria right up to complete climatic envelopes. The main idea here is always to create an intermediate space between interior and exterior which is heated exclusively by solar radiation and where the temperature is higher than that of the outside air. This reduces the transmission heat losses of the interior which, however, must be verified by way of simulation calculations. The external shell is generally in the form of single glazing. The buffer space is not heated, but should always be linked with some form of usage (Fig. B 3.34).
Synthetic membranes can be used instead of glass. In a triple-layer, air-cushion design, U-values ≤ 1.7 W/m²K are possible. The outer and middle membranes can be printed with patterns, one a reverse of the other. The position of the middle membrane can then be adjusted manually (by varying the air pressure in the cushion) to alter the total energy transmittance (g-value) of the membrane roof depending on requirements (Fig. B 3.35).
On a large scale, a transparent climatic enve-

lope offers new opportunities for energy-efficiency optimisation and also creates a special space that provides a good-quality climate compared to the outside, especially on cool days (see example 11). The investment required for the additional envelope can be compensated for by the lower requirements placed on the internal envelope. In the refurbishment market, this approach can generate interesting alternatives to conventional energy-efficiency upgrades.

Transparent thermal insulation
Various materials, elements and facade systems that permit the use of solar radiation even via opaque components, e.g. transparent thermal insulation, have been developed for the building envelope over recent decades (Fig. B 3.31). The underlying principle is that during the heating period solar radiation can pass through a layer of insulation and heat up the outer surface of a solid wall. If the temperature is the same as the internal temperature, no transmission heat losses ensue.
Translucent elements with integral storage materials can be used instead of opaque systems (Figs. B 3.38 and 3.39). Various types of latent heat storage systems (e.g. PCM, see "Materials", p. 158) can be used. Furthermore, glass elements with inexpensive honeycomb or lamella structures are also possible. Overheating is avoided in these systems by using special types of glass or a special geometric struc-

B 3.30 Example of how the proportion of glazing and the quality of the glass affect the primary energy rqmt. of a private house (S : W/E : N = 3 : 2 : 1)
B 3.31 Schematic diagram showing the function of TI
B 3.32 Dynamic U-value of a timber stud wall (180 mm insulation + 50 mm TI)
B 3.33 Folding shutters as temporary sunshades and thermal insulation, apartment blocks, Innsbruck (A), 2000, Baumschlager & Eberle
B 3.34 Double-leaf facade, Aschrott home for senior citizens, Kassel (D), 1931, Otto Haesler
B 3.35 Atrium roof with membrane cushions, kindergarten, Wismar (D), 2005, Institut für Gebäudetechnik + Energie + Licht Planung (IGEL)
B 3.36 Lucido® facade, Wildhaus (CH), 1999, Architheke
B 3.37 Solid timber wall with glass elements, joinery workshop, Ehrenkirchen (D), 1999, Pfeifer Kuhn
B 3.38 TI with integral thermal mass
B 3.39 Facade with TI, sheltered housing, Domat/Ems (CH), 2004, Dietrich Schwarz

B 3.33

B 3.34

B 3.35

B 3.36

B 3.37

ture so that the incident solar radiation can penetrate as far as the absorber surface in winter, but is reflected in summer because the sun is high in the sky and the angle of incidence is steep (Fig. B 3.36).

Combinations of solid timber walls with a glass outer leaf are also possible (Fig. B 3.37). In addition to the passive functions, such an arrangement offers the chance of solar preheating of the incoming fresh air.

As a rule, this "dynamic insulation" has a lower U-value than high-quality opaque insulation, at least when considered in a static calculation. Whether it offers advantages taken as a whole over the year, can be determined only through dynamic thermal building simulation and monitoring (Fig. B. 3.32).

Minimising ventilation heat losses

More attention will have to be paid to ventilation heat losses if a good-quality building envelope has been provided. This applies especially to buildings whose uses require guaranteed high air change rates. Four aspects are essentially relevant to this topic of minimising ventilation heat losses:

- The design and construction of the building envelope should ensure a high airtightness in order to prevent an uncontrolled exchange of air. To achieve this, careful detailing of the many junctions and connections is necessary. The so-called blower-door test can be used to check the airtightness of a building (Fig. B 3.41). By creating an overpressure or a partial vacuum, the fan output required to maintain a certain pressure (50 Pa) in the building is determined, which in turn allows the actual air change rate per hour (1/h) to be calculated. A guarantee of high airtightness is especially important for buildings with mechanical ventilation in order to ensure their proper functioning and the efficiency of the heat recovery. Values < 0.6/h are usual here.
- In buildings with ventilation via the windows only, the choice and arrangement of opening lights can help to achieve energy-efficient user behaviour. For example, an opening light without a tilt function will prevent continuous ventilation while the heating is in operation, which leads to the cooling of thermal

masses and a considerable increase in energy consumption (see p. 100, Fig. B 3.70).
- Natural ventilation concepts can make use of fresh air preheated via various systems such as double-leaf facades, atria or special air collectors (Fig. B 3.40).
- Heat exchangers in conjunction with ventilation systems with mechanical assistance can help to avoid up to 90% of the heat losses (see "Building services", p. 135). Very efficient buildings (e.g. passive houses) require mechanical ventilation with heat recovery in order to achieve a low heating energy requirement.

Active solar thermal energy gains

In contrast to the passive use of solar energy, the active use of solar thermal energy via collectors does not depend on the interior climate. Active solar energy systems in conjunction with efficient storage technology mean that solar energy can be used essentially irrespective of the momentary incident solar radiation conditions. Well-developed technologies and concepts are already available (see "Building services", p. 118).

At the heart of the planning there is the collector for converting the incident solar radiation into thermal energy for generating heat. The collector is both part of the building services and a building envelope component. Its technical and architectural integration represents a special challenge, but at the same time this synergy effect brings economic advantages.

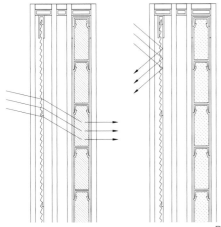

B 3.38

B 3.39

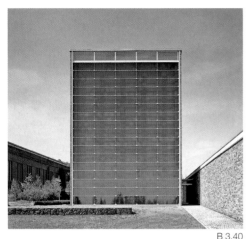

B 3.40

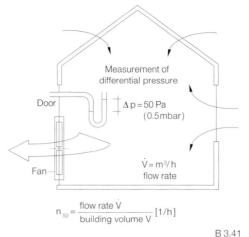

Measurement of
differential pressure

Door

$\Delta p = 50$ Pa
(0.5 mbar)

Fan

$\dot{V} = m^3/h$
flow rate

$$n_{50} = \frac{\text{flow rate } \dot{V}}{\text{building volume } V} \quad [1/h]$$

B 3.41

B 3.42

B 3.43

B 3.44

Solar facades

Solar thermal collectors are these days mainly produced as standard products with fixed dimensions and technical specifications. However, the solar activation of building envelopes calls for custom solutions that up until now have been available from only a few manufacturers. Flat-plate collectors are ideal for integrating into facades or roofs. Both the formats and the horizontal and vertical divisions in the collector surfaces can be customised to suit the grid of the building design (Figs. B 3.40 and 3.42). Even the colour of the absorber and the optical properties of the glass cover can be modified. But for reasons of efficiency, the great majority of solar thermal flat-plate collectors use a covering of highly transparent glass. But in principle, any conceivable design is possible by using different types of glass (e.g. patterned, tinted, etc.). Collectors can be prefabricated to a large degree and are available in sizes up to 30 m². For the integration into a facade, we must distinguish between flat-plate, air and vacuum-tube collectors.

On a solid external wall, the flat-plate collector can be attached like external cladding, with a ventilation cavity between collector and wall (Fig. B 3.45). It can therefore replace conventional cladding materials and at the same time provide weather protection to the building. This arrangement does not affect the wall construction – apart from avoiding the thermal bridges that can ensue due to the fixings. Alternatively, collectors can be integrated into the wall construction without a ventilation cavity. This approach achieves a greater degree of synergy because the insulation required for the collector itself can also function as the thermal insulation to the external wall. Another positive effect is that even diffuse solar radiation leads to high temperatures behind the absorber, which reduce the heat flow to the outside. Like with transparent thermal insulation, this can lead to external walls without heat losses. Care needs to be taken with the direct integration of collectors (i.e. no ventilation cavity) that the heat conduction from outside to inside during the summer does not lead to increased heat loads in the interior, i.e. collector and wall must have high levels of insulation. Moreover, the

total wall construction must be carefully checked with respect to moisture diffusion or condensation. Solar thermal flat-plate collectors can also be added to existing buildings (Fig. B 3.43). Without a ventilation cavity, the collector surface also improves the passive thermal performance and can therefore replace other insulating measures. In the case of timber stud construction without solid components, the external wall can be built directly in the form of a collector (Figs. B 3.42 and 3.45). This results in a very efficient external wall with a minimal wall construction. For the building physics, the requirements of a non-ventilated collector apply with respect to heat transfer and moisture.

If there is a large demand for low-temperature heat (< 40°C, e.g. as a heat source for heat pumps), metal elements without a glass cover can be designed as thermal collectors too. This makes use of a heat exchanger, which enables the solar activation of metal or roofs and facades.

In energy concepts with warm-air heating systems, there is the possibility of preheating the fresh air with solar energy via air collectors integrated into the facade. This can be achieved via a corresponding facade construction, e.g. solid external wall plus glass elements, or prefabricated air collectors can be installed. The principle of the air collector is the same as the flat-plate collector containing water pipes, except that the absorber is constructed with a shallow duct structure through which external air passes. Integration can be similar to flat-plate collectors, but the air intakes must be properly considered (Fig. B 3.48).

The constructional and architectural integration of vacuum-tube collectors has not played a major role to date. Although they have a high aesthetic potential, the geometrical and architectural options are severely limited. Fig. B 3.44 shows an interesting application in which the vacuum-tube collectors double as safety barriers. Synergy effects for sunshade applications are also possible.

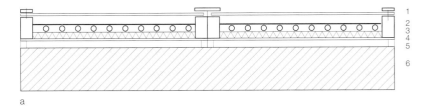

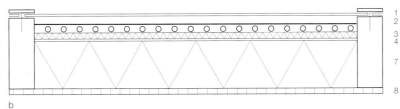

a

b

1
2
3
4
5
6

1 1 Solar glass
2 2 Absorber
3 3 Collector insulation
4 4 Rear wall of collector
5 Ventilation cavity
7 6 Wall
7 Thermal insulation
8 8 OSB

B 3.45

B 3.46

B 3.47

B 3.48

B 3.49

Solar roofs

In most cases, roofs are ideal for solar thermal activation. On flat roofs most collector installations hitherto have been mounted above the roof surface, but vacuum-tube collectors can also be laid horizontally without a drop in yield provided the absorber in the tubes is properly aligned. The constructional and architectural integration of flat-plate collectors is relatively straightforward on pitched roofs. Like on the facade, they can also take on the functions of the roof covering (Figs. B 3.46 und 3.47). Prefabrication in the form of complete roof elements is possible for large roof surfaces. In principle, the technical and building physics conditions apply as for solar collectors on the facade. Vacuum-tube collectors can be integrated into the construction and the architecture by using them, for example, as sunshades (Fig. B 3.49). Owing to the different incident radiation conditions, roof and facade collectors exhibit different energy yields. In Europe, facade collectors have to be about 20–25% larger than properly aligned roof collectors in order to achieve the same annual energy yield. However, when using solar thermal energy, it is not the annual yield that is primarily important, but rather the solar coverage (see "Building services", p.119), which depends on the operative load profile. If collectors are used for generating heating energy, a vertical installation may be more effective because the yields during the heating period are greater and the risk of overheating of the collector fluid in summer is reduced.

Avoiding overheating

Like the thermal performance in winter is intended to protect occupants and users against unpleasant, low temperatures, protection against excessive temperatures in the building must be guaranteed during the summer. In the light of global warming, the secure knowledge about the relationship between the operative room temperature and human efficiency plus higher comfort demands means that summertime thermal performance is becoming more significant. Deviations from the ideal temperature are generally less in summer than they are in winter, but human beings can protect themselves much better against low temperatures than against high temperatures (Fig. B 3.50). In addition, the generation of heat, from the physical point of view, is connected with a small effort and can make use of a wider technological spectrum than cooling, which, after all, can only take place through the removal of heat (see "Building services", p. 128).
Even in summer, buildings, as climate-regulating systems, have to guarantee pleasant interior temperatures if at all possible. Attention focuses here on the building envelope, the construction and materials of which can be coordinated such that overheating is avoided without the use of expensive, elaborate technical systems. In buildings with a proportion of windows > 30%, the Energy Conservation Act calls for proof of the summertime thermal performance. This is based on solar gain data determined statically, which may not exceed a permissible value (Fig. B 3.66). In buildings with a very high proportion of glazing, it is recommended to investigate the thermal behaviour of rooms with a high thermal load in detail by means of a dynamic simulation. Besides determining the cooling load and the cooling energy requirement, such a simulation can calculate the temperatures over the course of the day and the year. One widely used parameter for assessing the summertime thermal performance is the resulting number of hours in which the maximum permissible operative interior temperature is exceeded.

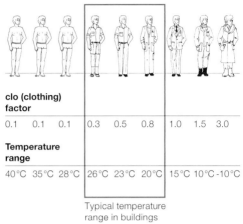

clo (clothing) factor								
0.1	0.1	0.1	0.3	0.5	0.8	1.0	1.5	3.0

Temperature range								
40°C	35°C	28°C	26°C	23°C	20°C	15°C	10°C	-10°C

Typical temperature range in buildings

B 3.50

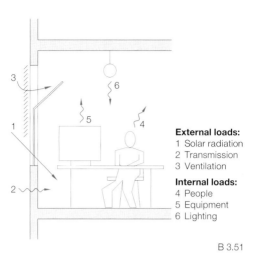

External loads:
1 Solar radiation
2 Transmission
3 Ventilation

Internal loads:
4 People
5 Equipment
6 Lighting

B 3.51

Area	Influencing variable	Relevance
Location	Air temperature	+
	Intensity of radiation	++
Form of construction	Room geometry	+
	Thermal transmittance (U-value)	++
	Heat capacity of room surfaces	+++
	Heat capacity of insulating material	+
	Temperature amplitude ratio	+
Ventilation	Type of ventilation	+
	Intensity of ventilation	++
Glazing	Proportion of glass	+++
	Orientation	++
	Total energy transmittance (g-value)	++
Sunshading	Effectiveness (f_c value)	+++

B 3.52

Thermal loads

The room temperature is influenced by the effective thermal loads. We distinguish here between internal and external thermal loads (Fig. B 3.51). The internal thermal loads depend on the type of use and are generally caused by people, lighting and electrical appliances. Efficient technologies (e.g. low-energy bulbs, power-saving computers, etc.) result in low levels of waste heat.

The factors that can be influenced by the building envelope concern the external thermal loads. These can be divided into heat transfer, incoming solar radiation and ventilation heat gains. In order to optimise the interior temperatures in summer, numerous influencing variables are available to the planner (Fig. B 3.52).

Reducing the heat transfer

If the outside air temperature is higher than the room temperature, a heat transfer takes place from outside to inside. To avoid this type of heat transfer, the same principles apply as for thermal insulation in winter. A building envelope optimised with respect to minimising transmission heat losses (= low U-value) at the same time therefore provides good protection against overheating in summer. This applies to both opaque and transparent surfaces. Fig. B 3.55 shows an example of how the thermal transmittance of the building envelope influences the heat gains in the interior. Important here, besides the thermal transmittance, is the sur-

B 3.50   Use of clothing to protect against excessive high and low temperatures
B 3.51   Internal and external heat loads in office buildings
B 3.52   Variables that influence the summertime room temperatures and their relevance
B 3.53   Solar radiation intensities for various building envelope surfaces using the example of Stuttgart (D)
B 3.54   Temperature amplitude ratio (TAR) and phase lag △t
B 3.55   How the quality of the glass affects the heat gains due to transmission
B 3.56   How the quality of the facade affects the heat gains due to radiation
B 3.57   Possibilities for reducing the solar radiation
B 3.58   Typical day and night radiation levels for Stuttgart (D)
B 3.59   Typical radiation levels at the summer solstice for Stuttgart (D)

face temperature of the outermost layer. A low heat absorption (e.g. by way of light colours) or a ventilation cavity behind the outer layers has a favourable effect on the transmission heat flow. Special attention must be paid to this aspect when planning rooms that have a high proportion of roof surface; they suffer from an often considerable proportion of heat transfer through the roof, or the topmost floor, in addition to the facade. Rooftop planting has a positive effect in this context because the localised evaporative cooling keeps surface temperatures down.

Another parameter for assessing the summertime thermal performance of opaque building components is the temperature amplitude ratio (TAR), which specifies the period of time it takes for a temperature rise on the outside of the wall to be passed on to the inside (phase lag/shift, Fig. B 3.54). The TAR improves with increasing thermal insulation, and the time of the phase lag depends on the thermal mass. Optimising these parameters allows the heat to be released into the interior once other thermal loads are no longer effective or can be easily dissipated (e.g. ventilating with cool night air).

Reducing the incoming solar radiation

In the majority of cases, the heat gains through transparent building elements represent the largest component in the summertime heat balance for a room. The planning of areas of glazing must therefore be carried out especially

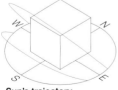

Sun's trajectory

Summer's day
Quantity of energy [kWh/m²]

Annual incident radiation
Quantity of energy [kWh/m²]

Winter's day
Quantity of energy [kWh/m²]

carefully. The trajectory of the sun and the intensity of the radiation are important parameters for assessing the nature of the solar heat gains. Areas of the building envelope subjected to thermal loads can be determined for a specific project based on an analysis of the shading. The shading caused by neighbouring structures can lead to differing situations for different storeys, even different rooms.

For a simplified estimate of the shadows, it is sufficient to consider the incident solar radiation on three days: 21 December, 21 March and 21 June. When calculating the summertime thermal performance, the intensity of the incident solar radiation on 21 June is important. It should be remembered that in Central Europe the sun's trajectory means that the east and west facades attract much more radiation than southern facades, and that the maximum radiation intensity is measured on horizontal surfaces (Figs. B. 3.58 and 3.59). Moreover, shading on east and west elevations due to the low solar altitude angle is usually linked with a considerable loss of daylight and external views. Fig. B 3.53 shows the sun's trajectory and gives examples of the solar radiation values for various surfaces of the building envelope.

Proportion of glazing

Transparent surfaces always represent a weakness with respect to summertime thermal performance. Even with optimised sunshading, the heat gains are generally several times higher

Surface	Summer's day	Winter's day
Horizontal		
Azimuth angle	55–305°	130–230°
Horizontal angle	0–63°	0–17°
Hours of sunshine	16h	8h
East/West		
Azimuth angle	55–180°/ 180–305°	130–180°/ 180–230°
Horizontal angle	0–63°	0–17°
Hours of sunshine	7.5h	3.5h
South		
Azimuth angle	90–270°	130–230°
Horizontal angle	33–63°	0–17°
Hours of sunshine	9h	8h

B 3.53

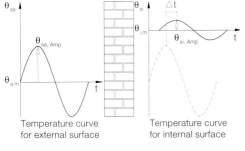

$$TAR = \frac{\theta_{si, Amp}}{\theta_{se, Amp}}$$

TAR = temperature aptitude ratio
θ_{se} = surface temperature, external
θ_{si} = surface temperature, internal

B 3.54

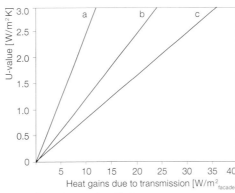

Room temperature: 24·C
External temperature: a: 28° b: 32° c: 36°

B 3.55

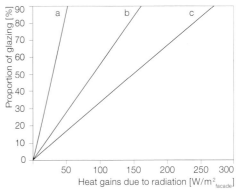

Glazing g-value: 0.6
Radiation incident on facade: 500 [W/m²]
Reduction factor for sunshade f_c: a: 0.2 b: 0.6 c: 1.0

B 3.56

than those for an opaque wall. A large area of glazing thus always results in an increase in the thermal loads. Fig. B 3.56 shows the maximum solar gains for three typical glazing qualities in relation to the area of glazing. From the energy view point, transparent surfaces should be planned in relation to their orientation. Considering all the functions of glazing such as passive solar energy gains, visual contact with the outside world, daylight, etc., a proportion of max. 50% has proved sensible for south-facing facades. On east and west facades, proportions > 30% are regarded as critical. The north facade plays only a subsidiary role in summertime thermal performance.

Sunshades
There are many ways of optimising the thermal quality of transparent surfaces (Fig. B 3.57). The first group of measures involves the constructional design of the facade. Overhangs, returns or favourable angles of inclination can protect transparent areas against direct sunlight during the summer months. Deep window surrounds have proved worthwhile, e.g. as *brise-soleil* for southern elevations (Fig. B 3.60). The constructional measures can be very easily optimised for extreme solar altitude angles, although this means they are often less useful in the spring and autumn. In order to reduce the amount of radiation entering a building through glazing, special solar-control glasses can be used (see "Materials", p. 157). Thanks

to optimised coatings or printing, such glasses can achieve low energy transmittance values (g-values), which mean that in the best cases only about 20% of the incoming heat energy is released into the interior. The downside of this is a high degree of reflection, greater colour distortion and hence reduced transparency (Fig. B 3.61). This also applies to types of glass in which the cavity between the panes is filled with reflective or absorbent materials. In addition, the fixed parameters of such components lead to lower solar energy gains in the winter. From the energy viewpoint, the preferred glazing systems are those that can react flexibly to changing incoming radiation quantities and interior conditions, e.g. by using movable louvre blinds in the cavity between the panes, a solution that is already available for double glazing units. Such systems achieve very good values that are almost equal to those of external sunshades. At the same time, the blinds are protected against soiling and wind. However, such products place high demands on the stiffness of the facade, and the entire insulating unit must be replaced in the case of defects. Variations on this principle can be realised in multi-leaf systems (coupled windows), where the sunshade is fitted between the outer and middle panes. Switchable glasses, which use electrical or chemical processes to achieve different g-values, represent another form of sunshading, but such products are still at the development stage.

Besides constructional aspects and special glazing products, shading systems represent the third group of optimisation measures for summertime thermal performance. The range of systems available is very broad and can be categorised according to various criteria such as fixed or movable, single- or twin-axis tracking systems, opaque or translucent, horizontal or vertical, etc. From the energy point of view, however, it is the position of the sunshade that is significant. We distinguish here between internal and external systems. Basically, external systems provide the best shading effect (Fig. B 3.62). One of the advantages of external systems is that the windows can still be opened inwards even when the sunshades are in use. One popular form is the louvre blind, which can be readily adjusted to deal with different lighting situations. Closed louvres in conjunction with insulating glazing units can achieve effective g-values below 0.1. Louvre blinds are, however, vulnerable to the wind and are therefore often unsuitable for tall buildings. In order to guarantee their operation despite this drawback, an additional pane of glass is sometimes added simply to protect against the wind (double-leaf facade). The alternative is to attach the sunshades on the inside, behind the glazing, a solution that protects the sunshade against soiling and wind. A highly reflective sunshade will reflect a certain proportion of the incident solar radiation back to the outside, but the heat energy absorbed by the sunshade will intro-

Element	Shading by...
Construction	Overhang
	Return
	Inclination
Glazing	Coating
	Printing
	Fixed elements in cavity between panes
	Movable elements in cavity between panes
	Switchable glasses
Sunshade	Internal
	External, rigid and flexible
	Fitted in double glazing, rigid and flexible

B 3.57

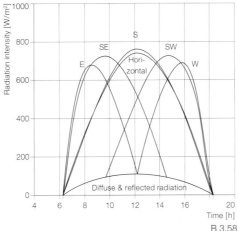

B 3.58

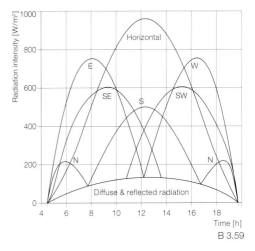

B 3.59

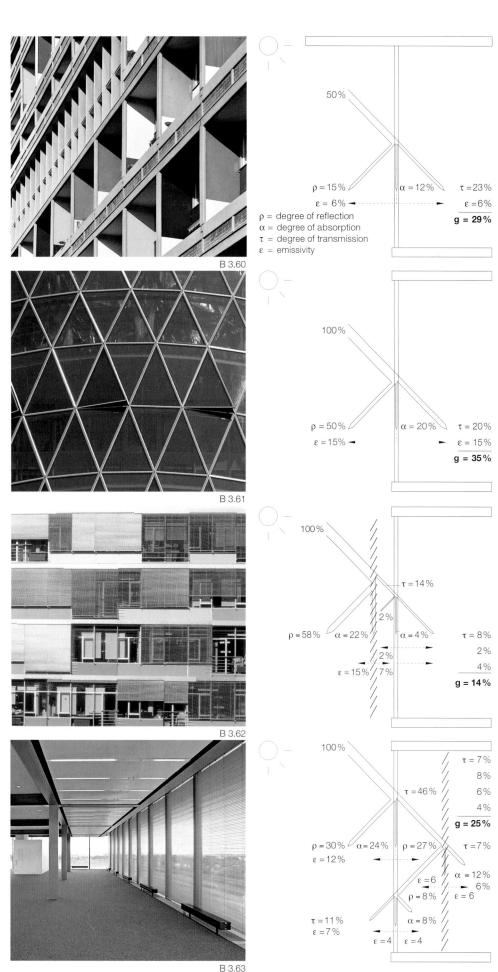

ρ = degree of reflection
α = degree of absorption
τ = degree of transmission
ε = emissivity

B 3.60

B 3.61

B 3.62

B 3.63

duce a further thermal load into the interior. In addition, some of the reflected solar radiation is absorbed by the glazing and reflected back into the room. Internal sunshades therefore do not usually achieve such good figures as external ones. Due to their interaction with the glass, their effectiveness is particularly dependent on the properties of the glass (Fig. B 3.63).

Solar gain index
The solar gain index can be used to obtain a rough estimate of the effectiveness of a sun-shading system (Fig. B 3.66). This is the sum of the heat gains through the glazing related to the floor area of the room. The critical factor here is the effective g-value of the total system (g_{total}), which is the product of the g-value of the glazing and the reduction factor f_c for the shading system (Fig. B 3.64). Fig. B 3.65 lists the DIN 4108 reduction factors that can be used in calculations if more accurate figures are not available. The majority of building products, however, achieve considerably better values so users are recommended to refer to the manufacturer's data whenever possible. The parameters for the cooling load related to the usable area for various shading situations are given in Fig. B 3.67. The importance for the cooling load of the solar radiation entering via the glazing and the resulting requirements for optimising the transparent building envelope are evident here.

Thermal mass and ventilation
The heat capacity of the enclosing components and the ventilation measures are further important parameters for avoiding overheating in summer. A lack of thermal mass leads to the heat gains causing an unpleasant rise in the temperature of the interior air. If sufficient thermal mass is available, e.g. in the form of solid soffit, wall and floor components, a part of the heat gains can be temporarily stored in those components, which, however, must be discharged at a later time. Suitable measures are therefore necessary to guarantee the release of that stored thermal energy (e.g. ventilation with cool night air). Critical for the effectiveness of thermal masses is their direct thermal link with the interior. Cavity floors, suspended ceilings and inner linings to the walls prevent the flow of heat between interior air and thermal mass, meaning that the heavyweight components cannot fulfil their function. The thermal activation of thermal masses often has consequences for the design of the interior and the room acoustics, e.g. fair-face concrete soffits and walls. Such parameters must be considered accordingly in the interior design.
Besides transmission and incoming solar radiation, unwanted heat flows can occur in conjunction with the indispensable exchange of air. This is the case when the external air lies above room temperature and is fed directly into the room. The air in the cavity of a double-leaf facade can be subjected to an extreme thermal

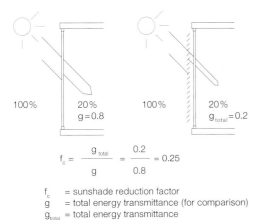

$$f_c = \frac{g_{total}}{g} = \frac{0.2}{0.8} = 0.25$$

f_c = sunshade reduction factor
g = total energy transmittance (for comparison)
g_{total} = total energy transmittance (including sunshade)

B 3.64

Sunshading system	f_c [%]
Without sunshading system	1.0
Internal or between the panes	
White/reflective surface with low transparency	0.75
Light colours or low transparency	0.8
Dark colours or high transparency	0.9
External	
Pivoting louvres, with ventilation cavity	0.25
Louvres/fabric blind with low transparency, with ventilation cavity	0.25
Louvres, general	0.4
Roller shutters, window shutters	0.3
Canopies, loggias, free-standing louvres	0.5
Awnings, with ventilation at top and sides	0.4
Awnings, general	0.5

B 3.65

$$S = \frac{\Sigma_i (A_{W,i} \times g_{total,i})}{A_G}$$

S	[-]	Solar gain index
$A_{W,i}$	[m²]	Area of windows in room
g_{total}	[-]	Total energy transmittance of glazing, including sunshading ($g_{total} = g \times f_c$)
f_c	[-]	Reduction factor for sunshading
A_G	[m²]	Floor area of room

B 3.66

situation. Optimising the exchange of air can take place via thermal preconditioning (e. g. ground coupling, evaporative cooling, heat or cooling energy recovery). In the majority of cases, mechanical assistance with a corresponding energy requirement is necessary. A combination of natural and mechanical ventilation is advisable. The mechanical ventilation is used only during periods of extremely low or extremely high temperatures (in Europe approx. 30% of the year) and the rest of the time the building is ventilated naturally without placing thermal loads on the interior. Furthermore, mechanical ventilation can be employed to increase the efficiency of night-time ventilation. Fig. B 3.68 shows a typical daily rhythm for an office building on a summer's day. This schematic diagram shows the principal boundary conditions for summertime thermal performance.

Decentralised ventilation

Good-quality air in buildings calls for a regular exchange of air that depends on the type of use and the number of persons. Modern forms of construction render possible a high airtightness; an uncontrolled exchange of air via joints and cracks is to a very large extent prevented. This demands careful planning of ventilation systems, which can be realised via the building envelope or by building services (see "Building services", p. 133). From the sustainability viewpoint, a maximum amount of natural ventilation should be the aim. This means that the air change rate for habitable rooms is achieved by way of thermal currents or differing pressures due to the wind. Electrical ventilation leads to a considerable increase in the energy consumption; on average, a specific electrical power of approx. 2500 W is necessary per m³ of air per second. Owing to the long operating hours of ventilation systems, there is a substantial potential for savings in energy consumption and operating costs if mechanical ventilation can be avoided. In addition, the horizontal and vertical ducts of many ventilation systems occupy considerable valuable floor space. In a high-rise building, the omission of fresh- and exhaust-air ducts will result in a considerable saving in the overall height of the building.

Natural ventilation

The planning of natural ventilation systems calls for an accurate analysis of the climatic and usage-related requirements. Pressure differences caused by temperature differences always result in a natural circulation of the air. In macroclimate terms, this energy is available as a wind, in microclimate terms as thermal currents (Fig. B 3.72). In principle, natural ventilation can take place by way of a direct exchange of air via the building envelope or via special systems that generate a natural airflow by way of concentrated thermal- or wind-induced pressure differences.

Ventilation via the windows
Opening a window allows the user to regulate the exchange of air himself exactly as required. In addition to the supply of fresh air, the direct contact with the outside air triggers further sensations such as the warmth of the unfiltered sunlight, smells and acoustic stimuli, all of which can have a positive effect on the quality of the habitable room. Natural ventilation systems are therefore particularly user-friendly from the emotional viewpoint. Habitable rooms should therefore always include the possibility of opening the facade. In many cases the glazing is designed to be opened for cleaning purposes and the daylight acquisition, visual contact the outside world and ventilation functions are all accomplished via one and the same component. Exposed or concealed ventilation

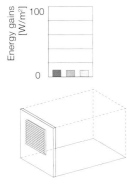

Proportion of glazing: 30%
g-value of glazing: 0.6
Sunshading:
external louvre blind f_c=0.2

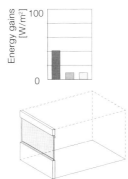

Proportion of glazing: 60%
g-value of glazing: 0.6
Sunshading:
internal louvre blind f_c=0.5

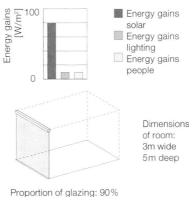

Proportion of glazing: 90%
g-value of glazing: 0.3
Sunshading:
none

■ Energy gains solar
▨ Energy gains lighting
□ Energy gains people

Dimensions of room:
3m wide
5m deep

B 3.67

B 3.60 Brise-soleil, Unité d'Habitation, Berlin (D), 1958, Le Corbusier
B 3.61 Office building, Frankfurt am Main (D), 2003, Schneider + Schumacher
B 3.62 Office building, Stuttgart (D), 1998, Behnisch, Behnisch & Partner
B 3.63 Company headquarters, Senden (D), 2007, Gerken Architekten + Ingenieure, Braun-Gerken
B 3.64 Determining the reduction factors for sunshading systems
B 3.65 DIN 4108 reduction factors for sunshading systems
B 3.66 Calculating the solar gain index S to DIN 4108
B 3.67 Examples of cooling loads, related to the floor area, for different facade arrangements

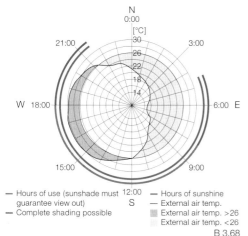

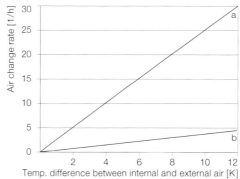

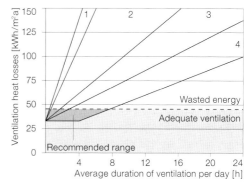

— Hours of use (sunshade must guarantee view out)
— Complete shading possible
— Hours of sunshine
— External air temp.
■ External air temp. >26
□ External air temp. <26

B 3.68

Window size: 1.2 m²
Room size: 30 m²
a: open window
b: tilted window (10 cm opening)

B 3.69

1 Window fully open
2 Window half open
3 Window tilted with cross-ventilation
4 Window tilted without cross-ventilation

B 3.70

flaps independent from the glazing are another option (Fig. B 3.75). The type of opening element should generally permit many different adjustments so that the ventilation can be individually regulated as required. With an opening on one side only, the exchange of air takes place by airflows in and out of the same opening (Fig. B 3.73). The movement of the air and hence the air change rate that can be achieved differs depending on the temperature difference between the internal and external air. Fig. B 3.69 shows the air change rates for different window openings in a typical room. In winter the high temperature, and hence pressure, difference means that the window need be open for only a few minutes in order to replace the air in the room once completely (Fig. B 3.70). If, however, the internal and external temperatures are similar, natural ventilation on one side only results in only a limited air change rate. The airflow can be improved by employing cross-ventilation, a situation in which wind movements have a considerable driving effect. With good flow conditions, very high air change rates of up to 50/h can be achieved. In principle, it is advisable to place exhaust-air outlets as high as possible and fresh-air inlets as low as possible in order to maximise the effective thermal height. Prerequisites for natural ventilation are favourable room geometries and an adequate number of large opening elements. In Germany, the Places of Work Directive stipulates limiting values for room depths and open-

ing elements in offices where ventilation via the windows is usually adequate (Fig. B 3.71). However, natural ventilation can lead to unpleasant effects:

• Extremely low temperatures in winter and extremely high temperatures in summer can be a problem. Natural ventilation does not permit any heat recovery, which leads to unwanted ventilation heat losses during the heating period. In addition, the direct inflow of cold outside air can be unpleasant. In Central Europe, however, natural ventilation is suitable for the temperatures experienced over about 70% of the year.
• High wind pressures on the facade can lead to a serious increase in the air change rates and draughts. Furthermore, there is a risk that pressure or suction forces could be transferred to interior components, making it difficult, for example, to open a door. High-rise buildings are particularly affected by this. Natural ventilation is possible if additional "windbreaks" are positioned in front of the opening elements (e.g. coupled windows, double-leaf facade, etc.). It should be ensured that there is adequate ventilation in the cavity during the summer months in order to avoid heating up the incoming fresh air excessively (Fig. B 3.74).
• High noise pollution from the direct environs. Additional panes of glass assist the natural ventilation in this situation. Alternatively,

sound-insulated air inlets can be incorporated in the facade. As a rule, these require mechanical assistance owing to the high pressure resistance (extract system).
• Polluted outside air, e.g. on busy roads. In such situations it is advisable to draw in the fresh air for the interior mechanically from less polluted areas. Filters can be used to improve the quality of the fresh air further.

Besides purely manual operation, the elements in the natural ventilation installation can also be controlled electronically. In addition to the protective function (e.g. automatic closure during rainfall or opening to allow smoke and fumes to escape in the event of a fire) and climate functions (e.g. automatic ventilation with cool night air), it is also possible to improve the level of comfort by fitting temperature- and wind pressure-regulated controls to the fresh-air inlets (Fig. 3.76).

B 3.68 Factors influencing the summertime thermal performance in an office building over the course of a day
B 3.69 Air change rate for ventilation via the windows in relation to the temperature difference
B 3.70 Ventilation heat losses in relation to the duration and type of ventilation to VDI 2067
B 3.71 Ventilation cross-sections for natural ventilation according to the German Places of Work Directive
B 3.72 The principle of air movements due to wind and thermal currents
B 3.73 Window ventilation, mixed residential and commercial development, Berlin (D), 2001, Grüntuch Ernst
B 3.74 Horizontal louvres, high-rise office building, Hannover (D), 1999, Herzog + Partner
B 3.75 Ventilation flaps, office building, Senden (D), 2007, Gerken Architekten + Ingenieure, Braun-Gerken
B 2.76 Vertical louvres, office building, Kronberg (D), 2000, Schneider + Schumacher

System	Max. perm. room depth [m]	Inlet/outlet cross section per m² of floor area [cm²]
One-sided ventilation with openings in one external wall	2.5 × H	200
Cross-ventilation with openings in external walls	2 × H	120
Cross-ventilation with openings in external walls and duct	2 × H	80
H = Height of room		

B 3.71

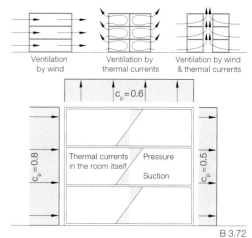

Ventilation by wind
Ventilation by thermal currents
Ventilation by wind & thermal currents

$c_p = 0.6$
$c_p = 0.8$
Thermal currents in the room itself
Pressure
Suction
$c_p = 0.5$

B 3.72

Natural ventilation by way of wind forces
Wind flows around a building lead to forces acting on the buildings, which are essentially influenced by climatic conditions, topography and the surrounding buildings. Pressure and suction forces are the result, the magnitude and distribution of which are influenced by the height and geometry of the building itself. An individual analysis is necessary in each case. On tall buildings, a double-leaf facade with appropriately designed opening elements can control the wind forces to such an extent that natural ventilation is possible via the inner leaf. Specially shaped components can generate a partial vacuum from the movement of the wind, and by linking this to the interior, it is possible to provide natural ventilation even for large internal spaces (e.g. exhibition halls, atria, etc.). If the suction forces are directed into an exhaust-air duct, it is possible to extract the air adequately from several adjoining rooms. The application of these principles requires careful planning of the make-up air inlets. In order to compensate for fluctuations in the temperature and wind conditions, exhaust-air ducts can be supplemented by mechanical ventilation in order to guarantee continuous operation.

Natural ventilation by way of thermal currents
Wind movements are not the only way of creating a suction effect. Such an effect can also be established via thermal currents, which can be employed as the driving force for extracting air from the interior. The strength of this suction effect depends on the temperature difference and the effective height (Fig. B 3.78). Tall buildings are therefore particularly suited to a ventilation concept making use of thermal currents. Three basic principles apply to the constructional implementation of this type of system:

· Buildings with a double-leaf facade can make use of the thermal currents induced by the higher air temperature in the cavity to establish a ventilation concept. The double-leaf facade can, for example, serve as an exhaust-air duct in the summer for extracting air from the interior.
· Using the same principle, glazed atria can be employed for removing the exhaust air. Owing to the ensuing high air temperatures beneath the atrium glazing (heat build-up), the atrium must be higher than the adjoining structure in order to reduce the thermal load on the topmost floors.
· Furthermore, thermal currents can be used as an alternative or supplementary driving energy for shaft-type ventilation. This system is also known as a "solar chimney", and by integrating such a system into the roof or facade, its dark absorber surfaces can exert a considerable influence on the architecture (Fig. B 3.79).

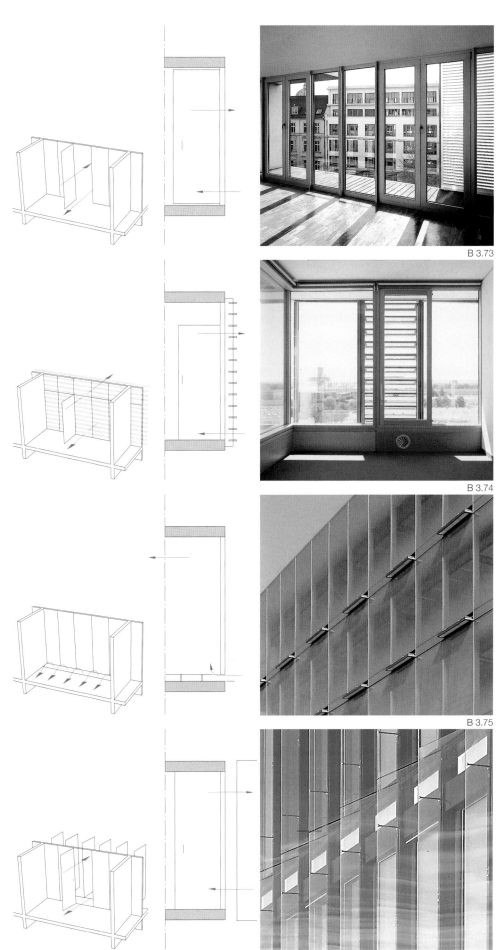

B 3.73

B 3.74

B 3.75

B 3.76

B 3.77 Exhaust-air expelled via rooftop ducts, office building, Solihull (GB) 2000, Arup Associates
B 3.78 Natural ventilation via "venturi spoiler", trade fair hall, Hannover (D), 1999, Herzog + Partner
B 3.79 "Solar chimney", residential building, Boston (USA) 2003, Office dA
B 3.80 The principles of systems for decentralised mechanical ventilation: a unit mounted in facade, b unit mounted on spandrel panel, c unit in frame, d unit under floor
B 3.81 Typical temperature increases in the incoming fresh air, compared with the external air, for certain types of facade and the case of high incident solar radiation in Europe
B 3.82 Pros and cons of decentralised mechanical ventilation compared to central ventilation systems
B 3.83 Facade elements with integral ventilation units, Capricorn House, Medienhafen, Düsseldorf (D), 2006, Gatermann + Schossig

B 3.77

B 3.78

B 3.79

Facade-mounted mechanical ventilation units
The operation and efficiency of natural ventilation systems depend on the external climatic conditions. Considerable fluctuations in the flow rates and air change rates therefore occur. If a constant air change rate is desired, additional mechanical ventilation is necessary. Numerous systems with different types of air feeding and air treatment are available (see "Building services", p. 133). Decentralised mechanical ventilation via the building envelope enables a constant air change rate without ventilation ducts – which leads to space savings, greater flexibility in the event of a change of usage and high efficiency thanks to the individual, demand-driven form of operation (Fig. B 3.82). If used to supplement natural ventilation, such a system, besides securing the flow rate, can compensate for other disadvantages inherent to natural ventilation:

- In the case of excessive outside noise, ventilation can still be provided with the windows closed to provide the necessary sound insulation.
- The use of air filters improves the quality of the incoming fresh air.
- Systems responsible for fresh air and exhaust air can reduce the ventilation heat losses during the winter quite markedly through integral heat recovery.
- The inclusion of heating or cooling batteries enables the fresh air to be preheated or precooled as required. These systems can therefore be used to provide heating and cooling capacity as well.

Facade-mounted ventilation units draw in the fresh air directly from the vicinity of the facade – so care must be taken to ensure good-quality air. A rise in temperature next to the facade in summer can therefore have a negative effect on operation (Fig. B 3.81). The units can be integrated into a cavity floor or suspended ceiling. Moreover, there is the option of incorporating them in spandrel panels or frame elements (Fig. B 3.80). The flow rates of facade-mounted ventilation units are limited. The use of such units is particularly useful in offices of low depth. Furthermore, facade-mounted ventilation units can also be retrofitted, for instance, within the scope of building refurbishment projects.

Using the daylight

Daylight is a key factor for pleasant interior conditions. Natural light stimulates the human organism and controls a number of bodily functions. It is critical for our visual perception and has a considerable influence on the efficiency of our work.
Transparent or translucent building components are necessary if we wish to make use of daylight. However, such components always lead to solar heat gains in the interior, which are undesirable in summer. But if daylight reduces the reliance on artificial lighting, besides reducing the electricity requirement for the lighting, the internal heat loads are diminished as well because artificial lighting generates more heat than daylight for the same level of illumination.
As glazed areas generally exhibit a higher thermal conductivity than opaque walls, a large expanse of glazing weakens the wintertime thermal performance of a building envelope. Daylight planning is therefore always closely tied to the summertime and wintertime thermal performance. In particular, it is always necessary to weigh up the energy required for removing the heat caused by excessive incoming daylight and the energy-savings brought about by the shorter period of operation of the artificial lighting (Fig. B 3.84).

Daylight
Daylight is made up of direct and indirect (diffuse) components, which differ considerably depending on the location (see "Fundamentals", p. 54, Fig. B 1.48). Daylight can be transmitted, absorbed, reflected and refracted. It is basically the case that diffuse radiation results in a better illumination of interiors, but direct radiation can be steered into the farthest corners of an interior by way of additional elements. An important parameter for the quantitative assessment of the daylight in a room is the daylight factor, which describes the ratio between the illuminance of a horizontal, unshaded surface in the open air under an overcast sky to the illuminance of a horizontal interior surface, usually taken to be 0.85 m above the floor. Crucial to the visual comfort, besides the illuminance, is the avoidance of glare caused by excessive contrast. Whether a room has a consistent illumination can be assessed by the ratio between the maximum and minimum daylight factor values. This ratio should not exceed 1:6 in the case of daylight entering via the walls, or 1:2 if coming from overhead.
In buildings with specific requirements for the illuminance (e.g. office workplaces), the daylight factor for a certain point can determine the degree of "daylight autonomy" (Fig. B 3.90). This value, expressed as a percentage, represents the proportion of a typical period of usage during which the lighting requirements are guaranteed exclusively by daylight. Although universally applicable, this factor is employed almost only for offices and relates to typical

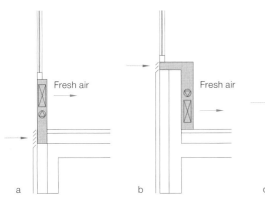

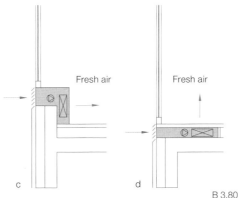

B 3.80

	Temperature increase	
	typical	maximum
Layer of air adjacent to facade, without wind	5 K	10 K
Layer of air adjacent to facade, with wind	2 K	5 K
Absorbent facade surface	10 K	15 K
Coupled window	5–15 K	20 K
Coupled window optimised for sound insulation	5–20 K	30 K
Non-segmented double-leaf facade	5–20 K	30 K
Controllable double-leaf facade	5–10 K	20 K
Shading louvres	2–5 K	10 K
Awning	5–10 K	15 K

B 3.81

working hours (weekdays, 8 a.m. to 6 p.m.). On average, office buildings should have a daylight factor of 3% (which results in approx. 50% daylight autonomy for office workplaces). As there are no defined figures for illuminance in residential buildings, it is not possible to determine the daylight autonomy. Adequate illumination for a living room lit from one side is assured when the daylight factor in the middle of the room and 1 m in front of the two side walls is at least 0.9% on average.

Geometric optimisation
Owing to the path of the sun across the sky, daylight is a dynamic variable, in terms of both its daily and its annual trajectory. Accordingly, the planning of a building must be considered in terms of its specific location. For instance, an analysis of the sun's trajectory and the shading by neighbouring buildings or vegetation is an important fundamental parameter. In order to establish the daylight potential of a building, three geometric parameters are required: horizon angle, vertical shade angle and lateral shade angle (Fig. B 3.88). The surfaces of the neighbouring buildings and the open areas also influence the daylight situation, so daylight planning begins outside the building; light-coloured or reflective external surfaces (e.g. water features) increase the amount of daylight available at the facade.
The principal influencing variables for the geo-metric optimisation of daylight can be divided into three areas: building, interior and glazing.

Building
The form of the building has a considerable influence on the potential scope for using daylight. A high proportion of envelope area in relation to the building volume is advantageous. Daylight optimisation therefore stands in direct conflict with wintertime thermal performance, where maximum compactness is an advantage. Low compactness, on the other hand, provides ample surface area for transparent or translucent components. Buildings with a compact overall volume can optimise their use of daylight by including an internal courtyard or an atrium. In many situations such measures enable rooms to be lit from two sides, which helps to provide a consistent level of illumination.
The intensity of the light entering rooms adjacent to an atrium diminishes quite noticeably as we approach the ground floor, but at the same time the percentage of diffuse radiation increases. The facades of the lower storeys therefore enjoy a more even luminance distribution (Fig. B 3.87). The dimensions of the atrium, the form of the roof construction and the type of shading can, however, reduce the amount of incoming light to such an extent that the minimum daylight factor for offices is not reached in the bottommost storeys.

Large single-storey buildings, e.g. production buildings, sport halls, can receive daylight via the roof. Even quite small openings are adequate here because in Central Europe the illuminance for horizontal surfaces is about three times that for vertical ones.

Interior
The layout and geometry of the interior spaces also influences the daylight potential. Rooms with high lighting requirements or those used intensively during the day should therefore be positioned near the facades, rooms with low lighting requirements in the middle of the building.
In terms of the form of the interior spaces, tall rooms and low room depths are more favourable, likewise light-coloured surfaces with a high reflection component.
Natural lighting to circulation zones can be achieved via transparent or translucent partitions, glazed doors or continuous high-level windows in the partitions.

Glazing
The design of the building envelope is critical for the use of daylight, defining the usable daylight potential principally by way of the proportion of glazing. However, the proportions of windows in the facades and daylight autonomy do not exhibit a linear relationship. For example, with a proportion of facade glazing exceeding

---

Decentralised ventilation systems

Advantages	Disadvantages
• Low space requirements for ducts, plant rooms and suspended ceilings	• Specific capital outlay equal to or marginally higher than that for a central ventilation plant with constant flow rate
• Low energy requirement for transporting external (e.g. < 1 W$_{elec}$/(m³/s)	• No humidification
• Low energy requirement for post-treatment of external air thanks to proper ventilation (e.g. three switchable, fixed fresh-air flows)	• With no dehumidification, the dew point temperature limits the cooling capacity
• Variable fresh-air flows	• Higher maintenance costs
• Upgrade options and good adaptability for variable room uses	• Usage conflicts when servicing units in office spaces
• Popular with users thanks to individual controls	• Higher operating noise in the case of high fresh-air flows
	• Greater control requirements in order to compensate for wind pressure, to limit the temperature of the incoming air and to protect against frost
	• An air intake directly on the facade may lead to higher air temperatures

B 3.82

B 3.83

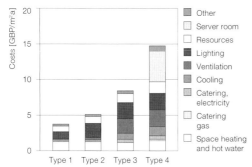

Type 1: Row of separate offices with natural ventilation
Type 2: Continuous open-plan office with natural ventilation
Type 3: Standard air-conditioning
Type 4: Higher standard of air conditioning

B 3.84

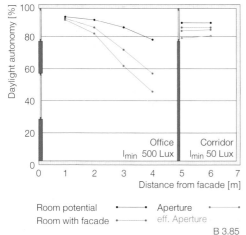

Room potential ●———● Aperture
Room with facade ●———● eff. Aperture

B 3.85

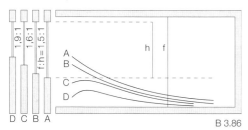

B 3.86

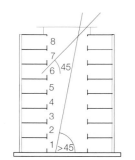

about 50%, the effects on daylight autonomy diminish drastically; increasing the proportion of glazing from, say, 70 to 90% has no noticeable effect on the quality of daylight in the interior. In residential buildings, a proportion of windows equal to between 20 and 30% of the room area is necessary in order to guarantee the basic needs with respect to natural lighting and visual contact with the outside world. DIN 5034 describes a simplified method for calculating the minimum window sizes for one-sided lighting to habitable rooms.

Besides the ratio of the area of glazing to the volume of the room, the orientation of the glazing is also important. In Central Europe, south-facing elevations enjoy a high illuminance which can lead to considerable differences in the luminance near the facade owing to the steep angle of incidence. On facades facing east and west, the low position of the sun and the shallow angle of incidence must be taken into account. Adequate protection against glare must be assured in both instances. Beneficial for daylight utilisation is the almost exclusively diffuse light that falls on northern elevations. Another aspect to be considered is the storey in which a room is located. For example, the availability of daylight over the facade differs considerably in the case of heavily built-up surroundings with tall buildings. Such a situation might dictate the need for different amounts of glazing in different storeys.

Furthermore, the arrangement of the glazing influences the efficiency of the daylight utilisation. Positioning the glazing at the top of a wall – ideally also in the lintel region – results in better illumination of the room, whereas glazed spandrel panels have hardly any effect on the daylight factor. Several individual glazed elements illuminate the interior better than one central element. If rooms are lit from more than one side, the level of illumination is noticeably more consistent and the better subjective impression of the room has a considerable, positive influence on how users perceive the interior and the daylight. Finally, the quality of the glass is a very important factor in the use of daylight. The most important parameter for assessing transparent components is the light transmittance (τ-value), which describes the

amount of light passing through the glass as a percentage. There is a close relationship between this value and the sunshading effect of glass (g-value, see "Materials", p. 154), and it exerts an almost linear influence on the daylight factor: glazing with a τ-value of 0.4 achieves over the full depth of the room only 50% of the daylight factor of glazing with a τ-value of 0.8.

Generally speaking, in order to comply with the requirements of the Places of Work Directive (300/500 lx), offices illuminated from one side only can be lit naturally up to a depth of 5 m without any additional artificial lighting.

Daylighting systems

Systems that redirect the light can improve the availability of daylight quite considerably and achieve a consistent, higher level of daylight even with lighting from the side and in deeper rooms. Moreover, some systems can redirect the light via roof glazing to illuminate even very tall or narrow spaces (e.g. atria).

The multitude of different solutions possible can be divided to static and controllable systems (Fig. B 3.93). We also distinguish these systems according to their positioning (roof, rooflight, window and spandrel panel) plus their location with respect to the glazing (outside, in the cavity between the panes or inside). The light-redirecting systems described below function in one of the following three ways:

- Scattering the light: diffuse light is introduced into the interior and produces an even level of illumination.
- Redirecting the light: light is shone into the depth of the room via reflective surfaces.
- Transporting the light: light is conveyed into dark external areas, interior areas remote from windows or windowless interiors via fibre-optic or other elements.

Horizon angle [°]	South	East/ West	North	Vert. shade angle [°]	South	East/ West	North	Lat. shade angle [°]	South	East/ North	West
0	1.00	1.00	1.00	0	1.00	1.00	1.00	0	1.00	1.00	1.00
10	0.94	0.92	0.99	30	0.93	0.91	0.91	30	0.94	0.91	0.99
20	0.68	0.75	0.95	45	0.80	0.79	0.80	45	0.86	0.83	0.99
30	0.49	0.62	0.92	60	0.60	0.61	0.65	60	0.74	0.75	0.99
40	0.40	0.56	0.89								

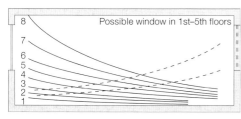

B 3.87

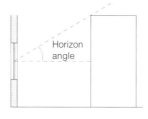

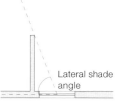

B 3.88

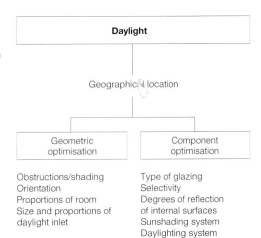

B 3.89

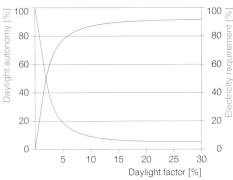

—— Daylight autonomy
—— Electricity requirement for artificial lighting

B 3.90

Light-scattering glasses

A glass designed to scatter the incoming light has either a special surface or, in the case of insulating units, the cavity between the panes can be filled with various materials in order to scatter direct sunlight and hence produce illumination without glare (Figs. B 3.95e and f). Light-scattering fillings made from translucent thermal insulation achieve a similar effect. They, too, guarantee an even distribution of light across the interior and, through absorption, exhibit a higher luminance at the facade in comparison to transparent glass.

Holographic optical elements (HOE)

Transmission holograms can be embedded in laminated glass in the form of a transparent foil. In order to avoid splitting the incoming daylight into the colours of the spectrum, which can be disturbing and can happen when redirecting the light, white-light holograms are used, which allow the diffuse light to pass through unhindered while bending the direct sunlight depending on its wavelength and redirecting it in the desired direction (Fig. B 3.96b).

The holographic effect, owing to its diverse application options, enables a combination of daylight redirection, sunshading (total reflection) and energy gains (focusing and redirecting the light to photovoltaic modules).

Light-redirecting glasses

Incorporating zero-maintenance light-redirecting elements in the cavity between the panes of insulating units means that such glasses are equally suitable for facade and roof applications. In vertical glazing, sunlight entering at a shallow angle is reflected up to the ceiling, which enables an enhanced light transmission that decreases as the angle of incidence increases. Installed horizontally, the direct radiation is reflected and the diffuse radiation allowed to pass through (Fig. B 3.95c).

Light Shelves

Direct sunlight can be reflected onto the ceiling by light shelves (Figs. B 3.94 and 3.96a). A light shelf is best positioned in the upper third of a wall, either on the inside or outside of a transparent element. Light shelves also help to protect against direct sunlight directly adjacent to the facade.

Laser-Cut-Panels (LCP)

LCPs consist of perspex panes with thin, parallel incisions or air inclusions (Fig. B 3.95d). Depending on the solar altitude angle, the light striking the horizontal incisions is subjected to single or multiple reflection and is directed up to the ceiling or scattered across the depth of the room. As laser-cut panels restrict the visual contact with the outside world, they are mainly used for high-level windows and rooflights.

Louvres

Horizontal louvres and louvre blinds are used primarily as sunshades, but they can also be employed to redirect the incoming daylight. Of the many systems and designs available (adjacent to the glass or within the cavity, rigid, pivoting, Venetian blinds, narrow or wide louvres, aluminium or glass sections, etc.), the following types are especially relevant:

- Horizontal pivoting louvres at high-level in front of the glass cut out the direct radiation in summer and reflect the daylight into the farthest corners of the room in winter (Figs. B 3.96c and d).
- Venetian blinds positioned at high level can deflect the incoming light up to the ceiling of the room, but positioned at a different angle in the windows or spandrel panels can guarantee effective shading (Fig. B 3.95a).
- Special light-redirecting louvres (louvres with a retroreflective coating) have selective properties: a W-shaped outer edge to the louvre cuts out the sunlight with a steep angle of incidence, whereas the shape on the inner edge allows the light at a shallow angle to be reflected up to the ceiling. The design of these louvres is such that even when they are in use, they still permit a view through the window (Fig. B 3.95b).

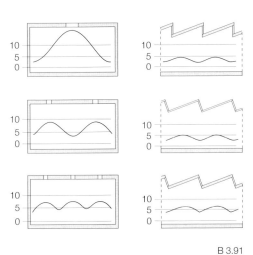

B 3.91

a

b

B 3.92

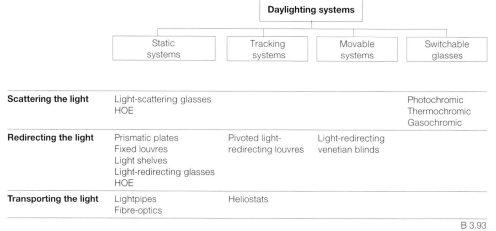

	Static systems	**Tracking systems**	**Movable systems**	**Switchable glasses**
Scattering the light	Light-scattering glasses HOE			Photochromic Thermochromic Gasochromic
Redirecting the light	Prismatic plates Fixed louvres Light shelves Light-redirecting glasses HOE	Pivoted light-redirecting louvres	Light-redirecting venetian blinds	
Transporting the light	Lightpipes Fibre-optics	Heliostats		

B 3.93

Heliostats and lightpipes
Heliostats consist of tracking parabolic mirrors rotating about one or two axes which convey daylight, especially direct radiation, from unshaded surfaces into deep lightwells or underground structures (Fig. B 3.97). If the heliostats track the sun constantly over the course of the day, and are possibly assisted by additional fixed mirrors for further distribution, then an adequate level of direct radiation produces virtually natural lighting conditions in the interior. When used in combination with pipes with a highly reflective lining, so-called light-pipes, or fibre-optic elements, heliostats can redirect daylight over great distances to internal, windowless areas (Fig. B 3.98).

Switchable glasses
Electrochromic glass is either transparent (liquid crystals arranged) or translucent (liquid crystals disarranged) depending on the electric voltage applied. This enables them to scatter the light accordingly (Figs. B 3.95g and h). Further types of switchable, or smart, glass are described in "Materials", p.157.

Selection criteria
The many different daylighting systems available on the market differ considerably with respect to the cost of their installation and upkeep, and exhibit specific features. Answering the following questions will help the designer make the right choice [3]:

- Will the view through the glass be restricted or interrupted?
- At what angle of incidence is the daylight directed into the interior?
- To what extent is the level of illumination in the farthest corners of the room improved?
- Is protection from glare guaranteed?
- Could thermal problems occur, e.g. due to multiple reflection and absorption by elements in the cavity between the panes?
- Does the system react "generously" to a change in the angle of incidence or is tracking necessary?
- What intervention and regulation options are there for users?

Generating electricity

Photovoltaics technology enables electricity to be generated via the building envelope without any mechanical wear, emissions or noise. Alongside solar thermal energy, this is the second way of exploiting solar radiation actively (see p. 93). Whereas solar thermal systems have always been closely tied to the planning of buildings, developments in photovoltaics technology began fairly recently; only since the early 1980s have photovoltaic elements been integrated into the building envelope. Many different photovoltaic modules are now available (see "Building services", p. 138). Besides the generation of electricity, these modules are

taking on more and more additional functions and are hence achieving numerous synergy effects: photovoltaic panels can provide protection from the weather, sunshading and privacy functions, or, as insulating units, even constitute the thermal envelope itself. In addition, they can also characterise the architecture (Fig. B 3.102).

Building envelopes with photovoltaic panels
Photovoltaic modules are mainly available in the form of laminated glass or plastic elements and should therefore be employed like glazing components. Numerous special modules are available for special applications (e.g. solar roof tiles, solar membranes, etc.). In principle, virtually all conventional planar building components can be provided with photovoltaic functions and this enables electricity to be generated over the entire building envelope, provided the surfaces are exposed to an adequate amount of solar radiation. However, in contrast to solar thermal applications, in photovoltaics even relatively little shading of the solar cells can lead to a considerable reduction in the energy yield (see "Building services", p. 140, Fig. B 4.113). An unshaded surface is therefore an absolute priority, and an accurate analysis of the location and the building is essential during the planning (Fig. B 3.103).
In addition, it is important to plan the routing of the cables carefully, a matter that is especially important with transparent components; but is

B 3.94

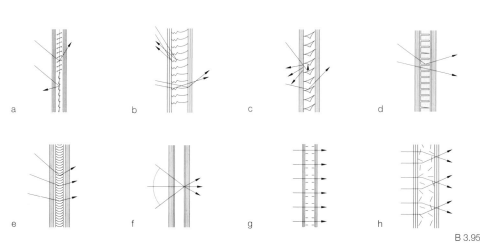

B 3.95

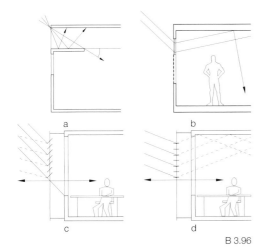

a   b

c   d

B 3.96

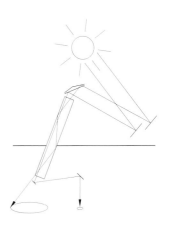

B 3.97

B 3.98

usually possible to route the cables in suitable facade sections. In such cases, the electrical connections to the modules must be fitted on the side, and not on the rear as is usually the case (see "Building services", p. 140).
The positions and arrangement of the inverters (DC-AC converters) necessary must also be taken into account in the planning. Short distances from the photovoltaic modules to the inverters are desirable, and the latter must be accessible for maintenance. The heat given off by the inverters in operation is another aspect that must be considered when deciding on their positions.

Photovoltaic roofs
On pitched roofs, photovoltaic modules can be used directly as the water run-off layer and therefore as a replacement for conventional roof coverings, e.g. roof tiles (Fig. 3.100). South-facing monopitch roofs or sawtooth roofs have proved to be ideal.
On flat roofs, there is the option of mounting the modules clear of the roof surface similar to when installing them on open ground, which permits optimum orientation of the panels and guarantees a high efficiency. However, the solar radiation conditions in Europe mean that the panels tend to throw shadows on each other and so must be installed at considerable spacings, which reduces the area of roof surface available for electricity generation quite substantially. The modules can therefore also

be installed over the entire roof surface at a very shallow angle, almost horizontal. Although this does reduce the specific yield of each module, the overall energy yield in relation to the area of the building envelope is, however, maximised (Fig. B 3.99).
On opaque flat roofs, active solar waterproofing elements represent yet another alternative. Even curved surfaces such as arched metal roofs or membrane structures can be fitted with photovoltaic installations.

Photovoltaic facades
Facades provide further potential surfaces for generating electricity from the sun. Although the amount of incident radiation on vertical surfaces is lower than that on inclined surfaces, facades do offer considerable energy-generating and economic potential if conventional high-quality components, e.g. metal panels or natural stone, are replaced by photovoltaic panels. When used as architectural features and when they provide other functions as well as energy generation, the use of photovoltaic modules in facades is justified, even if they do not achieve their maximum efficiency.

B 3.93	Systematic presentation of systems for redirecting daylight
B 3.94	Light optimisation with light shelves, office building, Schweinfurt (D), 1998, Kuntz + Manz
B 3.95	Schematic drawings of light-redirecting glazing elements:
	a Venetian blind
	b Light-redirecting louvres
	c Reflective sections
	d Laser-cut panel
	e, f Light-scattering glasses
	g, h Electrochromic glazing
B 3.96	Schematic drawings of light-redirecting systems:
	a Light shelf
	b Holographic optical element
	c, d Pivoting louvres
B 3.97	The principle of the heliostat
B 3.98	The principle of heliostat + lightpipe
B 3.99	Solar yields of photovoltaic systems for horizontal surfaces in relation to the angle of inclination (location: Frankfurt am Main)
B 3.100	Photovoltaic modules as roof covering, solar housing, Schlierberg, Freiburg (D), 2000, Rolf Disch
B 3.101	Pivoting photovoltaic louvres as sunshades, office building, Schwerin (D), 1999, Roland Schulz

Inclination of module surface [°]	Usable solar area [%]	Specific incident rad. [%]	Usable incident rad. [%]
0	100	100	100
10	75	106	80
20	61	111	68
30	53	113	60
40	48	113	54

B 3.99

B 3.100

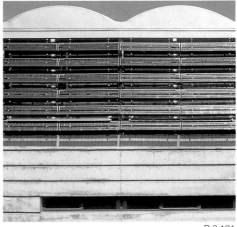

B 3.101

Requirements placed on building envelope	Influence of active solar energy usage
Thermal separation	o
Weather protection	+
Privacy	+
Sunshading	+
Glare protection	o
Noise protection	o
Security	o
Daylight utilisation	–
Views in and out	–
Architecture	+
Passive solar energy usage	–

o neutral   + symbiosis   – conflict

B 3.102

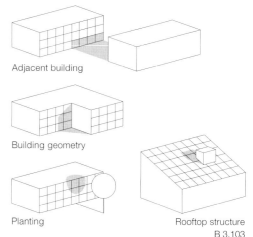

Adjacent building

Building geometry

Planting

Rooftop structure

B 3.103

Solar shading

Shading elements, owing to their function, are generally exposed to direct solar radiation and are therefore ideal for integrating into a photovoltaic installation. This applies to both fixed and movable elements, where solar modules can replace opaque or translucent materials, e.g. metal panels, printed glass (Fig. B 3.101). Photovoltaic modules can also be used directly as shading glazing elements. The desired g-value of the components can be influenced by the extent of the active cell area. What should be considered here, however, is the high heat radiation towards the inside caused by the heat build-up at the solar cells. Nevertheless, in a dense installation, very good outputs are achievable. And this means that, for example, roof glazing allowing good daylight exploitation can at the same time achieve a generous shading effect (Fig. B 3.107).

Solar technology and the building envelope

The building envelope, the loadbearing structure and the technical services represent the energy subsystems in a building. They have mutual effects on each other and can be interlinked in different ways, described by the terms segregation, incorporation and amalgamation [4] (Fig. B 3.110). This becomes clear when considering the possible connections between the building envelope and the loadbearing structure:

Whereas a solid, loadbearing external wall represents a clear amalgamation between loadbearing structure and enclosing envelope, a frame construction is also perceived as one element, but the loadbearing and enclosing functions can be allocated to the individual components frame and infill respectively – an incorporation of the functions. The third stage is the frame construction with a suspended facade, where there is a clear segregation of the functions.

This classification is also obvious with respect to the possible ways of using photovoltaic modules or solar thermal collectors on or in the building envelope. These strategies are explained below using the example of photovoltaics, but they also apply to solar thermal systems (see p. 93).

Segregation

The segregation of solar elements and building envelope is when the solar components are perceived as autonomous elements and are clearly demarcated from the envelope subsystem. One widespread segregation method is the rooftop mounting of solar modules on residential buildings with tiled roofs. The normal reasons for segregation are the need for an inexpensive, usually retrofitted installation and a clear separation of trades with corresponding warranties. The multiple functions of the solar elements possible are limited here to shading and visual appearance (Fig. B 3.104).

Incorporation

Incorporating solar elements into a building envelope as the outer leaf or layer, thus replacing conventional materials and forming the weather protection to the building, represents an incorporation of the technical services into the building envelope subsystem. In this case the building envelope could not function without the solar elements because they provide one indispensable function of the building envelope. This type of integration calls for a careful coordination of dimensions and details between photovoltaic modules and facade system plus an exact coordination of the different trades (Fig. 3.105).

Amalgamation

Amalgamation is achieved when the solar elements can fulfil all the functions normally provided by the building envelope. One example of this is the photovoltaic panel the form of an insulating glass unit, which besides generating electricity can also provide the thermal separation between inside and outside plus shading, privacy, sound insulation and weather protection functions, and at the same time possesses a high architectural potential. The solar element represents a fusion between the technical services and building envelope subsystems (Fig. B 3.106).

B 3.104

B 3.105

B 3.106

Solar technology and architecture

In addition to the constructional integration, the architectural treatment of active solar components, right up to the form of the building, will become especially important for future developments in solar architecture. After all, it is the harmony between building and solar technology and the attractiveness of the ensuing architecture that, to a large extent, will govern the level of acceptance and the success of these technologies.

It is necessary to distinguish between three design strategies in this context: addition, integration and adaptation (Fig. B 3.110). In considering a strategy, it is irrelevant as to how the solar elements are fitted into the building envelope.

Addition

The principle of addition stands for a design attitude in which the building is, in principle, planned without the use of solar technology. Accordingly, when adding any solar technology, the architectural and geometrical configuration of the building envelope is ignored. The building is merely a supporting structure for the solar technology. The lack of an architectural integration can lead to the solar technology components appearing alien to the building and this may have a detrimental effect on the appearance. This becomes evident when retrofitting solar technology installations to existing buildings. As a rule, an additive approach results in an unsatisfactory solution, even if the elements are incorporated into the building envelope at great expense.

Integration

In this approach the solar elements are consciously incorporated in the architectural concept of the building envelope and the building; their proportions, patterns of horizontal and vertical joints and surfaces do not appear alien. The solar elements therefore fit in with the three-dimensional form of the building, but this can lead to a reduction in the exploitation of the available solar radiation. This is justified, however, by the additional functions and the high visual compactness (Figs. B 3.107 and 3.108).

Adaption

If components for the active use of solar radiation, with their specific requirements regarding orientation and freedom from shadows, are integral to and dominate the design concept, this will entail adapting the planning in many senses, possibly even changes to the form of the building and the building envelope. To a large extent, the building or parts thereof will need to be adapted to suit the requirements of the solar elements, to assist in optimising their energy efficiency. The use of solar energy then becomes a primary criterion of the architectural language for the entire building (Figs. B 3.109 and 3.111). The building and the solar elements are mutually dependent on each other. This form of integration embodies a high potential for developing new forms of architectural expression based on the active use of solar radiation.

References:
[1] Usemann, Klaus: Entwicklung von Heizung und Lüftung zur Wissenschaft, Oldenbourg-Verlag, Munich, 1993.
[2] Without an analysis, a thermal bridges surcharge of 0.1 W/m²K should be applied according to the Energy Conservation Act (EnEV). When carrying out the planning work according to DIN 4108 supp. 2, this value can be reduced to 0.5 W/m²K. Alternatively, a simplified analysis is possible according to DIN EN 10211.
[3] After: Köster, Helmut: Tageslichtdynamische Architektur. Grundlagen, Systeme, Projekte, p. 96, Basel, 2004
[4] System developed at the Institute for Building Construction & Design, Chair 2, University of Stuttgart

B 3.107

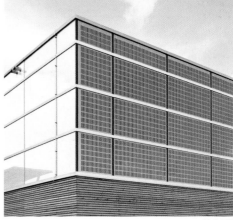

B 3.108

B 3.109

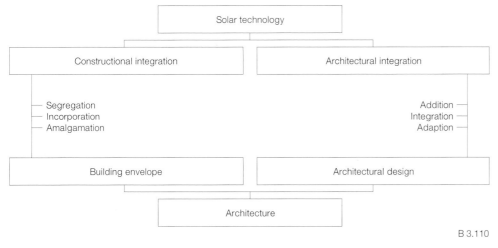

B 3.110

B 3.111

Building services

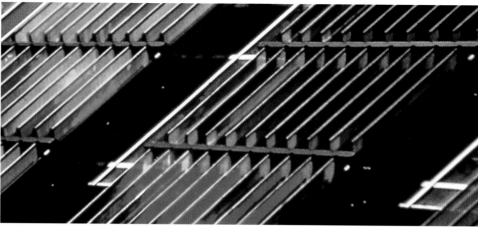

The key issue in energy-efficient building is the attempt to use constructional measures to accomplish a convenient, comfortable use of the building with the minimum use of energy. This is achieved in the first place through designing the building and building envelope, and choosing the materials, to suit the climate. In addition, buildings in many climate zones require a controllable energy supply. The technologies necessary for this have a considerable influence on user comfort and also the environmental impact of the structure. The latter can be assessed by calculating all the energy requirements that occur during operation, as is now stipulated by the EU Directive on the Energy Performance of Buildings for space heating, hot water, cooling, ventilation, lighting and their respective auxiliary power requirements. And extending the calculation to the primary energy requirement means that the environmental impacts related to the technology and specific to certain energy media are also ascertained. Building services are consequently an integral constituent of the overall energy concept of a building.

Sustainable building services

In essence, three aspects are critical for sustainable building services:
Firstly, special attention must be paid to the ecological consequences of the technical systems. When using fossil and nuclear energy sources, dwindling resources should be used as sparingly as possible in order to minimise the environmental problems caused by their usage. In addition to guaranteeing a high energy efficiency, is also necessary to achieve extensive use of renewable energy sources for the energy supplies to buildings. For the ideal case this means complete CO_2 neutrality (i.e. zero carbon emissions on balance), and the boundaries of the CO_2 audit could even be extended beyond an individual building to cover a building complex, a whole community, even regional or national structures. However, the use of renewable energy sources calls for investment in the technology. Besides the embodied primary energy, the further ecological effects of

the materials used must be taken into account. And last but not least, a high consumption of energy media results in corresponding logistics costs, e.g. when using biomass.
Secondly, at the same time building services affect the architecture in many instances. They interact with the design and should therefore take full account of the constructional boundary conditions and users' specifications. When considering sustainability, building services cannot be simply assembled from technical components straight out of the catalogue and installed according to statutory instruments and standards. Accordingly, the system components cannot be seen as add-ons provided in the sense of a "technical fitting-out" to make a building usable. Instead, it will be necessary to provide a technical concept integrated into the design which provides the optimum solution for the specific demands of the project. Building simulations for energy purposes will enable the technical planning to proceed without excessive safety margins – and they also have the potential to provide considerable impetus for the building design itself. This is especially significant with photovoltaics and solar thermal energy. Furthermore, building services influence user behaviour. Extensive and intuitive control options promote sustainable usage.
Thirdly, building services always tie up capital – in terms of both production and the cost of operation (cost of energy media plus service and maintenance). Optimisation is therefore only possible when considering the entire life cycle. One key aspect here is the careful planning required when using components whose technical service lives may be totally different. The easy replacement of technical components is an important planning criterion.
Renewable energy sources promise environmentally compatible energy usage. So when using energy supplies exclusively from renewable sources we could come to the conclusion that the energy consumption is no longer relevant. However, the use of such sources is always coupled with a high cost, which is revealed in the cost of the energy conversion (e.g. geothermal energy) in particular. Reducing losses, increasing efficiency and using renewable energy sources therefore represent

B 4.1   Active solar installation with holographic shading elements, terrace house, Stuttgart (D), 1993, Hegger Hegger Schleiff
B 4.2   Example of passive air management and evaporative cooling from Arabian architecture, 2nd century BC
B 4.3   Hypocaust heating for a Roman bath, c. 3rd century AD
B 4.4   Solar power plant at the World Exposition in Paris (F), 1878, Augustin Mouchot
B 4.5   Milestones in building services

1 Living room, winter
2 Water basin
3 Living room, summer
4 Cooling wind

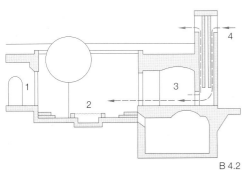

B 4.2

hollow bricks (*tubuli*)

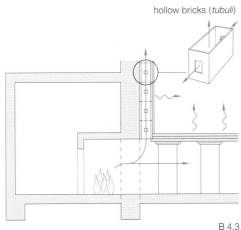

B 4.3

B 4.4

mutually beneficial aims. Besides measures to reduce demand, the choice of energy source and the ensuing building services must be given equal weight in the planning (see "Strategies", p. 176).

Historical development

Building services first became a separate discipline in the 20th century, although the majority of principles and many of the technologies can look back on a longer period of evolution. Numerous historical examples from the realm of Arabian culture bear witness to the intelligent coupling of technical systems and natural climatic boundary conditions in order to ensure a comfortable interior climate. Fig. B 4.2 shows an example of the use of wind, the evaporation of water and thermal currents to cool the supply of fresh air to a building. In Roman building culture, long before the birth of Christ, it is remarkable how intelligent systems of ducts were installed in bathing facilities to create central heating systems in which the heat was released via the floors and walls (Fig. B 4.3). But it was not until the 18th century or thereabouts that people began to have specific ideas about heating buildings and guaranteeing agreeable interior conditions. One of the earliest documents on the subject was written, rather surprisingly, by a German clergyman, Johann Georg Leutmann, in 1720 – a treatise on the "calculation of heating requirements in buildings". In this document, he establishes that "the size of the oven must depend on the chamber to be heated" [1].

19th century

The demonstration of the first solar thermal power machine by Augustin Mouchot at the 1878 World Exposition in Paris (Fig. B 4.4) shows that renewable energy technology was already playing an important role in the 19th century. The motivation behind the development of this machine was an appeal by the French king to discover alternative sources of energy because of the dwindling reserves of coal. We can certainly speak here of an early global energy crisis! A quote by the physicist Clausius dating from 1885 shows that, right at the beginning of the age of fossil fuels, it had already been realised that these energy sources

were finite: "We have discovered that coal deposits from ancient times lie within the earth, which have accumulated over such long periods of time that all of mankind's history is negligible by comparison … We are consuming these now and in doing so behave like laughing heirs enjoying a rich inheritance. It is dug out of the earth … and consumed as if it were inexhaustible … Once this supply is consumed, … mankind will have to rely on the energy that the sun will continue to supply through its rays for many years to come" [2].

After the Association of German Engineers (VDI) was founded in 1856, the German physicist Schinz carried out further calculations on the heating requirements of buildings, the results of which led to the introduction of the expression "heat losses due to transmission and ventilation". Towards the end of the 19th century, the extensive practical work of Hermann Rietschel laid the foundation for our current calculation of the heating requirements of buildings, work that was published in the first manual and textbook for heating engineers. All the technological systems common today have their origins in the scientific studies and findings of the 19th century. For instance, the physicist Alexandre Edmond Bequerell had already discovered the photovoltaic effect by 1839, and this still forms the basis of all current systems for generating electricity from sunlight. Worthy of note in this context is that the need for active solar surfaces and the resulting use of facades and roofs for the large-scale development of photovoltaics was already known in the 19th century. This is evident in a quote by the American physicist Charles Fritt dating from 1880: "Photovoltaics only has a chance if it can be harmoniously integrated into the architecture." The first prototypes in the field of thermodynamics also date from this period – prototypes in which compression and decompression could be used to influence the heating potential specifically via a transfer medium. The vast majority of our present refrigeration plants and heat pump systems are based on these findings. Absorption and adsorption technologies also have their roots in the 19th century, and they are enjoying a comeback in current developments for solar cooling.

1700	• First calculations for the heating requirements of buildings
	• Energy crisis in Europe owing to the scarcity of coal
1750	• First solar thermal high-performance system
1800	• Introduction of the terms heat flow, temperature gradient and thermal conductivity
	• Introduction of the k-value as a means of measuring the thermal transmittance (today: U-value)
	• Invention of the heat pump
	• Discovery of the photoelectric effect
	• Discovery of the sorption principle
1850	• Crystal Palace in London (GB) (Paxton)
	• Introduction of the terms transmission and ventilation heat losses
	• Patent for insulating glazing
	• First ideas about integrating photovoltaics into the building envelope
	• Numerous patents granted for solar thermal collectors
1900	• Fagus Works, Alfeld a.d. Leine (D) (Gropius)
	• Boom in the USA for solar thermal installations
	• Vision of the glass tower (Mies van der Rohe)
	• MIT solar houses
	• Insulating glazing ready for the market
1950	• First photovoltaic modules ready for the market
	• Solar house with Trombe wall
	• Worldwide oil crises
	• Comeback for passive solar architecture
	• First photovoltaic facade
	• First passive houses
	• Self-suffficient solar house in Freiburg (D)
2000	

B 4.5

111

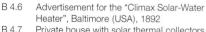

B 4.6

B 4.7

B 4.8

20th century

By the end of the 19th century, numerous patents had been granted for solar thermal collectors. In the USA it would be fair to speak of a "solar boom" in thinly populated regions (Figs. B 4.6 and 4.7). Architects were now thinking about energy technology, and that was the reason behind the book written by the German professor of architecture Richard Schachner in 1926, the first "comprehensive book on building services for the construction industry" [1]. Just three years later, the latest information was incorporated in the new DIN 4701 standard, "Rules for calculating the heating requirements of buildings and for calculating boiler and radiator sizes in heating installations". This 47-page publication included the climate tables of the Prussian Meteorological Institute, advice on natural ventilation by exploiting the leaks around doors and windows, and a list of thermal insulation values (in those days expressed as k-values) for various building components. The subject of energy was first introduced into the university education of architects in 1940 by including compulsory lectures on "technical fitting-out" in the foundation studies in architecture [1]. As industrialisation took hold in the building industry and numerous technical developments in the areas of building materials, design and systems appeared, so the buildings in the highly industrialised countries were increasingly characterised by very sophisticated machinery for conditioning the interior air totally irrespective of the external conditions. These developments called for a marked increase in technology requirements for the use of buildings, a fact reflected by the addition of the term "air conditioning" to the VDI "Building Services" study group in 1967. At that time, photovoltaic modules were already being used by satellites, but their integration into architecture was not yet foreseeable.

During the 1940s and the 1960s, many research and pilot projects in housing were aimed at achieving the maximum use of solar thermal systems for space heating and hot water. Among those developments were passive applications such as the Trombe wall and active solar thermal systems with long-term storage such as the MIT solar house (Fig. B 4.8). A major breakthrough was, however, not forthcoming because at that time the costs of conventional energy supplies were at a very low level. The turning point for further development was the first oil crisis of 1973. Besides the ecological aspects, the driving force was now primarily the effort to reduce dependence on uncertain energy supplies. Since the 1980s, important progress has been made in the efficiency of building services, e.g. the great improvements in boilers through the introduction of condensing technology and more efficient heat pumps, making them viable alternatives to conventional heating systems. Work was undertaken to improve, for example, the operational reliability of and controls for solar thermal systems so that today a wide range of fully developed components is available. In addition, photovoltaic installations for generating electricity have been integrated into building envelopes since the 1980s (Fig. B 4.9). And the vision of the self-sufficient building, i.e. not requiring any external energy supplies, finally became reality in 1992 (Fig. B 4.10); its operation was made possible primarily through a solar water circuit, photovoltaic elements and fuel cells.

B 4.6 Advertisement for the "Climax Solar-Water Heater", Baltimore (USA), 1892

B 4.7 Private house with solar thermal collectors, Pamona Valley (USA), c. 1910

B 4.8 MIT solar house, research project with integral collector roof (USA), 1939

B 4.9 First building with integral photovoltaic installation, residential development, Munich (D), 1982, Herzog + Partner

B 4.10 Self-sufficient solar house, Fraunhofer ISE research project, Freiburg (D), 1992, Planerwerkstatt Hölken & Berghoff

B 4.11 Targets, subtargets, concepts and measures for the energy-efficiency optimisation of building services

B 4.9

B 4.10

Current trends

Natural gas has been the dominant fossil fuel in Europe since the 1990s. Condensing boilers have in the meantime become standard in this sector. The main developments are now taking place in technologies for the use of renewable energy. The thermal use of biomass – primarily in the form of wood pellets – has become established thanks to efficient technology. Solar thermal systems for hot-water provision and for assisting the space heating are now standard products, and photovoltaic modules can be custom-made for any project. Heat pumps and decentralised combined heat and power (CHP) plants are viable alternatives. Currently undergoing development are, in particular, new storage technologies, concepts for building automation, fuel-cell technology and systems for solar cooling and solar thermal electricity generation. From the technical point of view, many fully developed technologies are therefore already available for using energy efficiently and for using renewable energy. Through the use of biomass, CHP plants, customised photovoltaic modules, solar thermal collectors plus efficient storage systems and control technology it is now possible to operate a building with a neutral CO_2 balance without incurring any significant extra costs. Taking the 10 components of energy-optimised building (see "Fundamentals", p. 61) as a starting point, the individual technologies will be explained on the following pages. Fig. B 4.11 provides a structured overview of the five energy themes and the systems feasible in principle. The operation of the individual technologies is explained and together with advice on relevant planning criteria this should serve as a basis for the development of an overall energy concept (see "Strategies", p. 177).

Heating

The provision of heat is one of the most important functions of building services. Heat guarantees agreeable interior temperatures when the passive capacity of the building can no longer offer this. As the majority of people on the earth need some form of heating system, there is a huge potential for avoiding negative environmental impacts embodied in heating technology. The extent and duration of heating supplies are essentially influenced by the climatic boundary conditions, users' specific requirements and the thermal quality of the building envelope. The basis for planning heating installations is the so-called (standard) heat load (formerly: heating requirement), which specifies the amount of heat that must be fed into the building, or individual rooms, in the most unfavourable situation in order to guarantee the required interior temperature (Fig. B 4.12). In principle, the calculation is based on the same method as that used to determine the annual heating requirement according to the German Energy Conservation Act (EnEV). However,

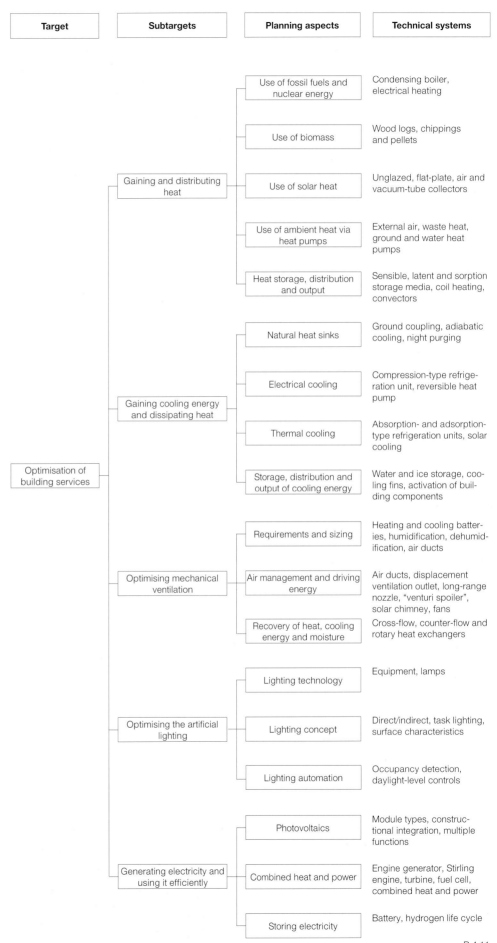

Target	Subtargets	Planning aspects	Technical systems
Optimisation of building services	Gaining and distributing heat	Use of fossil fuels and nuclear energy	Condensing boiler, electrical heating
		Use of biomass	Wood logs, chippings and pellets
		Use of solar heat	Unglazed, flat-plate, air and vacuum-tube collectors
		Use of ambient heat via heat pumps	External air, waste heat, ground and water heat pumps
		Heat storage, distribution and output	Sensible, latent and sorption storage media, coil heating, convectors
	Gaining cooling energy and dissipating heat	Natural heat sinks	Ground coupling, adiabatic cooling, night purging
		Electrical cooling	Compression-type refrigeration unit, reversible heat pump
		Thermal cooling	Absorption- and adsorption-type refrigeration units, solar cooling
		Storage, distribution and output of cooling energy	Water and ice storage, cooling fins, activation of building components
	Optimising mechanical ventilation	Requirements and sizing	Heating and cooling batteries, humidification, dehumidification, air ducts
		Air management and driving energy	Air ducts, displacement ventilation outlet, long-range nozzle, "venturi spoiler", solar chimney, fans
		Recovery of heat, cooling energy and moisture	Cross-flow, counter-flow and rotary heat exchangers
	Optimising the artificial lighting	Lighting technology	Equipment, lamps
		Lighting concept	Direct/indirect, task lighting, surface characteristics
		Lighting automation	Occupancy detection, daylight-level controls
	Generating electricity and using it efficiently	Photovoltaics	Module types, constructional integration, multiple functions
		Combined heat and power	Engine generator, Stirling engine, turbine, fuel cell, combined heat and power
		Storing electricity	Battery, hydrogen life cycle

B 4.11

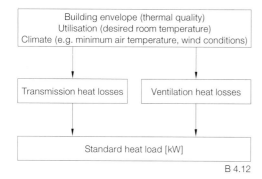

Building envelope (thermal quality)
Utilisation (desired room temperature)
Climate (e.g. minimum air temperature, wind conditions)

↓ ↓

| Transmission heat losses | Ventilation heat losses |

↓ ↓

Standard heat load [kW]

B 4.12

Rough heat load calculation

$$Q\,[W] \sim Q_{spec} \cdot GFA_{heated} \cdot f_{temp}$$

GFA: gross floor area
TIA: Thermal Insulation Act
ECA: Energy Conservation Act

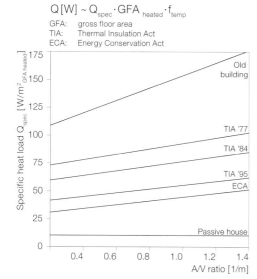

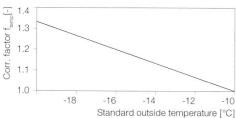

Examples   **Standard outside temp./annual average**

Hamburg	-12°C/8.5°C	Hof	-18°C/3.0°C
Berlin	-14°C/9.5°C	Stuttgart	-12°C/10.2°C
Cologne	-10°C/8.1°C	Munich	-16°C/7.9°C

B 4.13

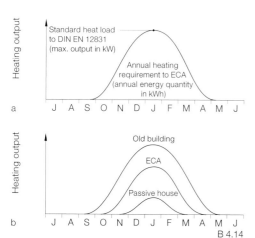

B 4.14

whereas the latter determines the quantity of energy per year, for the heat load only the most unfavourable case is relevant. Variable energy gains such as internal heat sources or solar gains are left out of the equation. As we continue to optimise the building envelope, so we reduce not only the heat load, but also shorten the heating period considerably (Fig. B 4.14). The heat load forms the starting point for sizing the heating plant (boiler, heat pump, etc.) and the heat output elements (radiators, fresh-air heating battery, etc.). DIN EN 12831 is used when accurate calculations are required, but a rough estimate for residential buildings can be obtained by using the usable floor space, specific heat load values and surcharges (Fig. B 4.13). The most important heating installations, arranged according to their energy sources, are explained below. Systems for combined heat and power can be found in a separate section on p. 143.

Use of fossil fuels and nuclear energy
Worldwide, energy supplies are mainly met by fossil fuels in the form of coal, oil and natural gas. The finite nature of these energy resources was properly recognised right at the start of the "fossil-fuel age", but not the equally serious problem of damaging greenhouse gases and the resulting global climate change (see "Fundamentals", p. 39).
The – in terms of technology – simple principle of combustion and its period of development mean that very well-developed heating systems are now available for buildings. Thanks to low-temperature technology and electronically controlled, modulating systems, the originally simple boiler is now capable of very efficient combustion. And in the meantime, advanced condensing-boiler technology enables virtually the entire energy content of oil or natural gas to be converted into useful heat. The efficiency is improved by exploiting the latent heat energy stored in the water vapour in the exhaust gases. The water vapour condenses due to the cooler return from the heating circuit and the heat released raises the temperature of the return pipe. The acidic condensate is handled appropriately and drained away. As the degree of efficiency of a boiler is related to its calorific value (without exhaust-gas heat), condensing-boiler technology that includes the use of exhaust-gas heat can achieve values exceeding 100% (Fig. B 4.18)!
Nevertheless, even extremely efficient conversion does not alter the underlying problem that fossil fuels are finite and cause CO_2 emissions, aspects that from the sustainability viewpoint that must be considered as negative.

Electrical heating
Electricity began to be used for space heating and hot water more and more in the second half of the 20th century. In the case of small amounts of energy (e.g. decentralised hot-water requirements), an electric instantaneous heating appliance can be used; storage tanks are included for greater energy requirements,

which means that a time buffer is possible in order to detach the use of the electricity from the use of the heat (e.g. for using low-cost night-time electricity). Electric heating systems require neither a chimney nor a separate plant room because there is no combustion. When assessing the ecological quality of electricity as a secondary energy medium, the energy sources for generating the electricity are important. These can be determined for each country. In Germany, for example, the electricity mix consists of 88% fossil fuels and nuclear energy (as of 2006). Owing to their dependence on uranium, even nuclear power stations face the problem of the finite resources of this raw material. In terms of CO_2 emissions, nuclear power is better than other fossil fuels when generating electricity, but the highly problematic and as yet unsolved international problem of disposing of the radioactive waste, also the security issues, weigh heavily on the downside of this technology (see "Fundamentals", p. 45).
With high conversion losses in electricity generation from fossil fuels, the direct use of electricity for heating has a particularly unhelpful effect on the primary energy balance of a building (Fig. B 4.15). Heating with electricity is generally only advisable when, firstly, an efficient system such as a heat pump can be used. In such a system the use of ambient heat can achieve ecological advantages over generating heat from fossil fuels (Fig. B 4.48). Secondly, electricity is a good choice for extremely low heating requirements, e.g. decentralised hot-water provision in office buildings. Thanks to the simple technology and the avoidance of line losses, efficient heating is possible when considering the system as a whole.
In principle, electricity should be generated – in central or decentralised installations – completely from renewable energy sources.

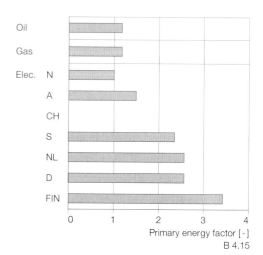

B 4.15

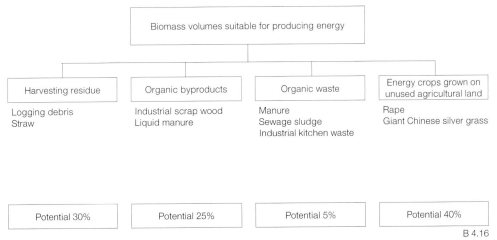

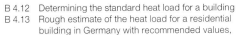

| Potential 30% | Potential 25% | Potential 5% | Potential 40% |

B 4.16

Use of biomass

Vegetable biomass is a renewable raw material that has the potential to guarantee an energy provision life cycle that does not produce additional amounts of carbon dioxide because when incinerated it releases only the quantity of CO_2 that was taken up by the plants during their growth (Fig. B 4.17). Biomass is therefore considered to be a "CO_2-neutral" energy source – provided the management of its growth and use is sustainable. The primary energy input in the chain from growth to usage must be considered in the overall calculation. The fossil primary energy value of biomass is therefore not zero. However, the permanent availability is an advantage and so the potential for optimisation lies mainly in easy provision, highly efficient conversion and minimising pollutants during combustion. The problem of ultrafine particles is the main problem here because in future developments, both generally and for biomass in particular, definitions and limiting values plus more advanced technologies are necessary in order to reduce emissions and avoid health risks.

The term "biomass" describes a very wide range of energy sources. In biological terms it covers basically all substances of organic origin (materials containing carbon) and hence all plants and animals and their residues (e.g. animal droppings), dead but not yet fossilised plant mass, and, in the broadest sense, all media produced through conversion or use of

a substance (e.g. paper, organic domestic waste, vegetable oils, biogas, etc.). The boundary between biomass and fossil fuels is marked by peat. From the energy viewpoint, biomass can be divided into primary and secondary products. Primary products are in the first place created by direct photosynthetic conversion of solar radiation (e.g. wood, grass, straw, etc.). Secondary products are energy media that require energy for their production (e.g. wood chippings, wood pellets, vegetable oils, etc.) and also materials created by the decomposition or conversion of organic substances from organisms (e.g. liquid manure, sewage sludge, etc.). In the literature biomass is often employed as a synonym for "renewable raw materials". Here again, there is no generally applicable definition. One way of distinguishing this is that the term "raw material" means a material for use by mankind, which does not generally apply to biomass. At the other end of the scale we have the boundary with foodstuffs. The use of biomass for energy purposes focuses on the aspect of "stored solar energy", which can be rendered useful via suitable conversion systems. Which materials are specifically suitable for this is also a question for ethics, e.g. deciding whether the use of cereals or animal carcasses may be used to produce energy.

Biomass forms

Biomass occurs in various forms and is influenced by countless factors such as the presence of water, temperature, type of soil, nutrients, etc. Solar radiation and the photosynthesis process are responsible for the growth of organic substances, which is why vegetable biomass is also referred to as stored solar energy. The substances produced by photosynthesis are cellulose (approx. 65%), hemicellulose (approx. 17%) and lignin (approx. 17%), which together make up about 99% of the global increase in biomass every year. Ligneous plants constitute the greatest potential here. In terms of the forms that can be used for energy purposes, biomass in Europe can be divided into four areas (Fig. B 4.16):

• Harvest residues – including solid biogenic energy sources from the direct management of forests (logging debris, low-strength wood), landscaping and road maintenance in addition to those from agricultural operations.
• Organic by-products – residues that occur due to a primary treatment process; typical examples are scrap wood from industrial woodworking or liquid manure from commercial animal husbandry for the production of biogas.
• Organic waste – biogenic secondary energy sources that remain as residues after final usage, e.g. sewage sludge, landfill gas.
• Energy crops – the greatest potential for

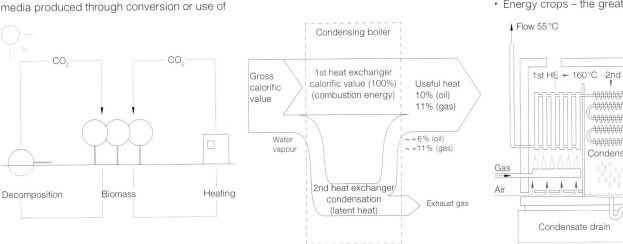

B 4.17　a

b　B 4.18

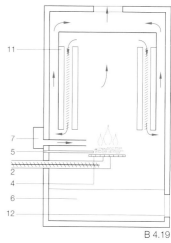
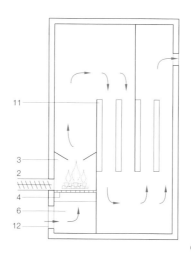
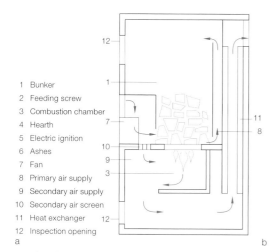

1 Bunker
2 Feeding screw
3 Combustion chamber
4 Hearth
5 Electric ignition
6 Ashes
7 Fan
8 Primary air supply
9 Secondary air supply
10 Secondary air screen
11 Heat exchanger
12 Inspection opening

a   b   c   B 4.19

using by biomass for providing energy; fields
not used for other agricultural operations are
specially managed and used exclusively for
cultivating such crops, which include plants
containing oil (rape, sunflowers, soya, etc.),
fast-growing grasses with a high cellulose
mass and hedges and trees with very low
cultivation requirements.

Provision of biogenic energy media
In order to be able to use biomass for heat supplies in buildings, it must be turned into energy
media. Biomass passes through several phases
from its creation to its thermal use. Cultivation
and harvesting, or recovery, together form the
so-called production and supply phase. This is
followed by the provision phase, which spans
the time between the supply of the biomass
and its use for energy purposes, and which
includes the transport, storage and, first and
foremost, the treatment processes. Biogenic
energy sources can be categorised as follows:
In the case of solid fuels we distinguish between
ligneous and culmiferous biomass. The production locations and supply options for wood
fuels are very diverse. Typical biogenic solid
fuels are logging debris, scrap wood from
woodworking operations and wood from plan-
tations with short cutting cycles. The treatment
to provide materials ready for energy purposes
is primarily by way of the sawing and splitting
of trunks (logs), mechanical chipping of all species of wood (chippings) or the compression of

sawdust (pellets, Figs. B 4.20 and 4.26).
The main liquid energy fuels made from biomass are vegetable oils and alcohols. Soya,
and in particular rape, are the important vegetable oils. When fully mature, the seeds of the
rape plant have a crude fat content of about
44% and by way of pressing or additional
extraction in large-scale plants can be turned
into an energy source (rapeseed oil). In a further
stage, it is possible, via ester interchange, to
refine the rapeseed oil into rape methyl ester
(RME). This energy source known as "biodiesel"
can be used in conventional diesel engines.
Alcohols obtained through the fermentation of
plants containing starch (e.g. sugar cane,
maize, potatoes, etc.) have played only a subsidiary role in the European energy sector up
until now. New developments are expected
here, particularly by way of the "biomass-to-
liquid" process. Using this process, many different types of biomass can be converted into a
very high-quality and universally applicable oil
whose properties correspond to those of the
ubiquitous crude oil products. Instead of direct
combustion in oil-fired boilers, the oils are used
almost exclusively as fuels for engines in combined heat and power plants and for vehicles
(see p. 143).
Under favourable boundary conditions, methane
can be obtained from biomass through fermentation processes under exclusion of air. Suitable substrates are, for example, liquid manure
from animal husbandry, organic waste from

households, horticultural operations and industry, or sewage sludge. Feeding biogas into
existing supply networks is currently being tried
out in a number of pilot projects prior to large-
scale usage.

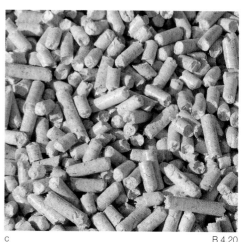

a   b   c   B 4.20

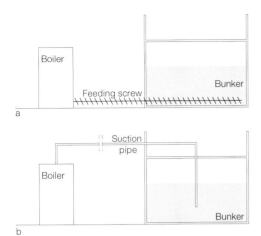

Boiler

Feeding screw

Bunker

a

Suction pipe

Boiler

Bunker

b

Boiler

Suction pipe

Silo

c

Suction pipe

Boiler

Under-ground tank

d

B 4.21

Filling nozzle DN 100

Suction nozzle DN 100

max. 30 m to road

Baffle plate

Boiler

B 4.22

Combustion systems for buildings
A number of firing principles are available for incinerating biogenic energy media and these depend on the form of energy used. Those suitable for decentralised supplies in buildings will be explained here (Figs. B 4.19 and 4.23): The burning of wood (logs) is the oldest method of turning biomass into energy. An open fire, however, achieves only a very low degree of efficiency and the uncontrolled inflow of air results in exhaust gases with a high pollutant content. Special burners for logs are now available which enable an automated incineration process with degrees of efficiency of up to 90%. Advantageous here are the simple preparation of the fuel and the manual feeding of the burner. The ashes must be cleaned out at regular intervals. Processing wood to form wood chippings enables a suitable heating plant to be fed automatically. Owing to the minimisation of the moisture content (large surface area), this fuel should not be stored too long, which is why short delivery intervals – normally two weeks – are preferred (Fig. B 4.24). Besides adequate storage facilities, properly planned logistics are necessary for the deliveries, which usually take place in tipper trucks. Plants fired with wood chippings can achieve good economics because of the low cost of the raw material (minimal processing). Owing to the relatively high maintenance and feeding costs, wood chippings are primarily suitable for larger, centralised heating plants.

Wood pellets enable a particularly high-quality incineration of biomass. DIN 51731 defines the essential properties of this fuel, such as size (40 mm long, 6 mm diameter), density, water and ash content, etc. This enables them to be matched to the system technology exactly, which leads to degrees of efficiency of well over 90% and very low emissions at the same time. However, the production requires additional operations which in terms of primary energy represent 10–20% of the energy content. Pellet installations are available with manual or automatic feeding (via feed screws or suction pipes). Storage over several months is also possible, which means that in the case of low heating requirements (e.g. detached house), the fuel for a complete heating period can be stored (Figs. B 4.21 and 4.25). With the exception of cleaning out the ashes, a pellet-burning installation with automatic feeding is in terms of footprint and comfort requirements comparable with a conventional oil-fired boiler. Owing to the growing popularity of pellets for heating, an economic supply of wood pellets is now guaranteed throughout Europe. Pellets are delivered in road tankers just like heating oil. Suction pipes up to 30 m long are used to discharge the pellets into a bunker (Figs. B 4.21 and 4.22).

B 4.19 Wood-burning installations (selection):
a for logs
b for chippings
c for pellets
B 4.20 Wooden energy media:
a Logs
b Chippings
c Pellets
B 4.21 Storage options for bulk biomass products:
a Bunker with feeding screw
b Bunker with suction pipe
c Silo with suction pipe
d Underground tank with suction pipe
B 4.22 Plan of typical wood pellet bunker with feeding screw
B 4.23 Range of supplies and typical outputs for biomass-burning installations
B 4.24 Calorific value of ligneous energy media plotted against moisture content
B 4.25 Estimate of the storage space required for a defined annual energy requirement
B 4.26 Pelletising machine

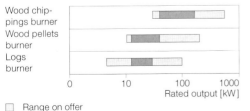

Wood chippings burner

Wood pellets burner

Logs burner

Rated output [kW]

□ Range on offer
▪ Typical output

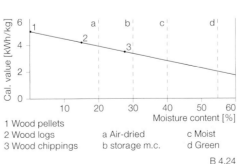

Cal. value [kWh/kg]

Moisture content [%]

1 Wood pellets
2 Wood logs
3 Wood chippings
a Air-dried
b storage m.c.
c Moist
d Green

B 4.24

Energy medium	Unit	Calorific value [kWh]
Crude oil	1 m³ = 1000 l	10 000
Wood logs	1 m³ (bulk)	1700
Wood chippings	1 m³ (bulk)	800
Wood pellets	1 m³ (bulk)	3200

B 4.23

Rough sizing

· per 1 kW heat load = 0.9 m³ space (incl. empty space)

· usable storage space = 2/3 of storage room volume

· 1 m³ pellets = 650 kg

B 4.25

B 4.26

117

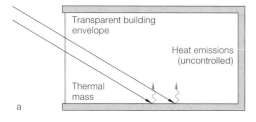

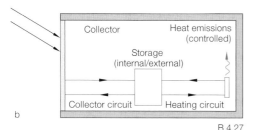

a

b

B 4.27

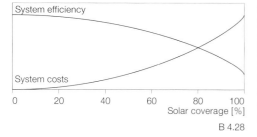

B 4.28

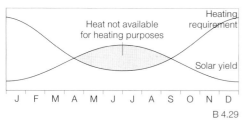

B 4.29

B 4.30

Use of solar heat

Converting solar radiation into heating energy is known as a solar thermal application. All bodies exposed to solar radiation absorb this to different degrees and convert it into heat radiation by way of the photothermal effect (Fig. B 4.33). For buildings, this effect is included in the planning in principle as "passive use of solar energy". The so-called active use of solar energy is described below; the differentiation between this and passive use is not always clear.

Active solar thermal energy systems are characterised by the fact that the functions of solar energy absorption, conversion and storage are not carried out exclusively by the building or building components (Fig. B 4.27). Such systems generally consist of collector, heat transfer medium, transport system and means of heat storage so that the heat output can be controlled properly. The aim of the majority of active systems for providing heat is to decouple the use of the heat from the occurrence of the solar radiation as much as possible (Fig. B 4.29). A means of storage combined with controls play a crucial role within the overall system (see p. 124). Besides the heat load profile and the collector orientation, the efficiency of a solar installation is mainly influenced by the solar radiation levels at a particular location. This differs considerably across Europe and reaches values of approx. 850–1750 kWh/m²a for horizontal surfaces (see "Fundamentals", p. 53). As the available solar radiation is subjected to a time limit, a correspondingly high material input is necessary for the technology required for converting and storing the energy. Solar thermal installations produce no emissions apart from during their production and – unless they operate on the gravity principle – in connection with the operation of pumps (auxiliary energy). Active solar thermal heating systems have in the meantime reached a high technological standard. The developments are characterised by constant improvements to individual components and, in particular, by optimised system concepts and electronic control strategies. The focus in the future, however, will be the constructional and architectural integration of thermal solar collectors into the building envelope (see "Building envelope", p. 94).

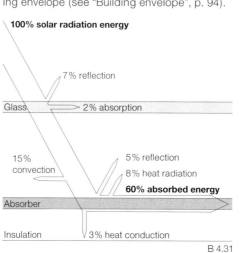

100% solar radiation energy

7% reflection

Glass → 2% absorption

15% convection

5% reflection

8% heat radiation

60% absorbed energy

Absorber

Insulation → 3% heat conduction

B 4.31

How the system works

The basic principle of solar thermal applications is the conversion of short-wave solar radiation into long-wave heat radiation. This process takes place when light strikes a material and its intensity depends on the absorption properties of that material (see "Materials", p. 158). In an ideal absorber, reflection and transmission are minimised and at the same time the heat energy absorbed should not be re-radiated, but rather transferred, as far as possible through conduction, to the transfer medium. This has led to the development of selective absorber materials, which for technical reasons are mostly dark blue to black in colour. Other colours are possible, but this reduces the efficiency (Fig. B 4.30). Owing to diverse losses, the heat absorbed is not equal to the total global radiation incident on the absorber (Fig. B 4.31). In order to reduce the convection losses to the surroundings, absorbers are formed into collectors that are insulated on the side facing away from the sun and covered with highly transparent special glass on the side facing the sun. A heat transfer medium flows through the collector in order to carry away the usable heat. The difference between the energy of the incoming and outgoing transfer medium represents the heat flow. One important criterion for the quality of the collector is its degree of efficiency, which is the ratio of the heat flow in the heat transfer medium to the global radiation incident on the collector. This is heavily dependent on the temperature difference between exterior air and absorber (Fig. B 4.34). Besides the collector's efficiency, the "solar coverage component" is particularly important for the whole system, and describes, expressed as a percentage, the share of the usable energy provided by the solar system with respect to the total heating energy requirement of the building. This is particularly influenced by the discrepancy between the time of the supply of the solar radiation and the demand for usable energy, and the ensuing unusable solar radiation (storage media at maximum temperature) plus line and storage losses (Fig. B 4.35). Owing to the aforementioned boundary conditions, it is generally true that as the solar coverage component increases, the size of the installation

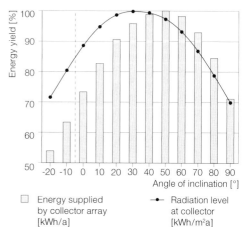

☐ Energy supplied by collector array [kWh/a]

━•━ Radiation level at collector [kWh/m²a]

B 4.32

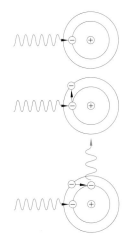

Light energy excites
the electron

Excited electron jumps
to a higher energy level

Excited electron
returns to lower
energy level and
emits heat energy

B 4.33

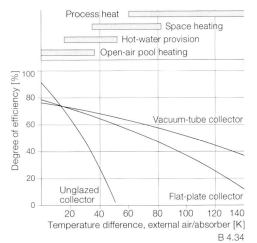

B 4.34

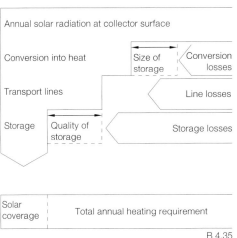

B 4.35

(absorption area and storage volume) mush-rooms disproportionately, whereas the efficiency of the system per unit area drops (Fig. B 4.28).

Technical system components
A solar thermal system consists of several components required for the primary functions of heat absorption, heat transport and heat storage. The solar thermal converters, normally called collectors, are the chief elements in a solar thermal installation. Various types of collector are used in practice, and the most common types are shown in Fig. B 4.36. The collector array is the part of the installation visible externally. The architectural and functional integration places considerable demands on the planning because the orientation of the active solar thermal surfaces has a great influence on the efficiency (Fig. B 4.32). From the technical point of view, solar thermal collectors can be divided into five categories:

• Unglazed collectors represent the simplest type of solar thermal converter. But their high thermal losses mean that their degree of efficiency is low. They are used for heating swimming pools or as a heat source for heat pumps.
• In a flat-plate collector, insulation is attached to the rear of the absorber and a special glass cover is fitted on the side facing the sun. Flat-plate collectors are the most popular type of collector for supplying heat to

buildings. Their construction allows them to be very easily integrated into the building envelope (Fig. B 4.37). Occasionally, the air space in the collector is filled with a noble gas to minimise convection heat losses.
• As an alternative to the flat-plate collector containing water pipes, air collectors are used to preheat the air for a warm-air heating system. Such collectors are constructed in a similar way to flat-plate collectors. However, the heat absorbed is not transported via pipes filled with water, but instead via the air flowing past the absorber.
• In vacuum-tube (or evacuated-tube) collectors, a flat or curved absorber is fitted into an evacuated glass tube (Fig. B 4.41), which prevents convection heat losses almost completely. Depending on the form of construction, the degree of efficiency of such collectors per unit area can be increased by using integral or external reflective surfaces. Vacuum-tube collectors achieve the best degree of efficiency and the highest operating temperatures. The individual tubes of many products can be rotated to suit the incoming solar radiation, which means that these collectors also achieve a good level of efficiency on horizontal or even very steep surfaces.
• The use of special lenses or reflective surfaces enables collectors to reach very high temperatures (> 300°C) when exposed to direct radiation. Concentrating collectors are employed for supplying heat to production

processes and for solar thermal electricity generation (see p. 144).

In principle, either gases or liquids can be used as a transfer medium, although liquid-filled systems are more common. To avoid frost damage, the collector circuit is separated from the actual usable water circuit and filled with a water/glycol mixture. Pipes, typically made from copper or polyethylene, join collectors and storage tanks. In the case of vacuum-tube collectors, the liquid either flows directly through the collectors, like the flat-plate variety, or the tubes contain a liquid separated from the brine circuit which via evaporation and condensation effects the heat transport from collector to brine circuit ("heat-pipe principle"). Air collectors are generally connected directly to the system of warm-air ducts.
Storage options for solar thermal energy (solar storage tanks) enable the energy needs of users to be decoupled from the energy generation, which is dependent on the incoming solar radiation. Storage has a considerable influence on the limits of solar energy utilisation. For a simple hot-water supply, storage can be built into the collector if the risk of freezing is only low (combined collector and storage tank). However, in the majority of applications separate heat storage is used (see p. 124).
The function of controls is in the first place to regulate the operation of the collector circuit. Typical designs use temperature sensors at

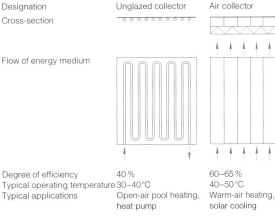
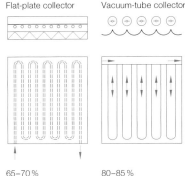
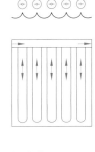

Designation	Unglazed collector	Air collector	Flat-plate collector	Vacuum-tube collector
Cross-section				
Flow of energy medium				
Degree of efficiency	40 %	60–65 %	65–70 %	80–85 %
Typical operating temperature	30–40 °C	40–50 °C	60–90 °C	70–130 °C
Typical applications	Open-air pool heating, heat pump	Warm-air heating, solar cooling	Hot-water provision, space heating, solar cooling	Hot-water provision, space heating, solar cooling, process heat

B 4.36

B 4.37

a

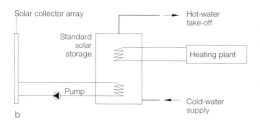

b

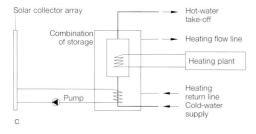

c

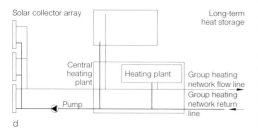

d

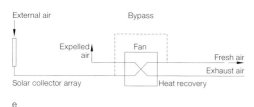

e

B 4.38

collectors and storage tanks to control the pumps depending on the temperature difference. At the same time, the control monitors the limiting temperature values in brine circuit and storage tank.

Solar system concepts for buildings
In Europe, decentralised solar thermal energy is principally used in the temperature range up to approx. 120°C. The applications include hot-water provision, heating of swimming pools, space heating and, via suitable chillers, cooling as well (Fig. B 4.38, see also p. 131).
Up until now, a solar thermal installation for hot-water provision was the most popular application. The size of the system is influenced by the hot-water requirements and the desired solar coverage. Typical installation sizes for four-person households are approx. 5 m² collector area and a storage volume of 0.3–0.4 m³, covering approx. 50–60% of the annual needs (Fig. B 4.39). In the case of a higher annual hot-water requirement, e.g. apartment blocks, hospitals, hotels, installations with collector arrays totalling several hundred square metres and correspondingly larger storage tanks are possible. Flat-plate collectors are mostly used, but also vacuum-tube collectors with higher degrees of efficiency. Solar thermal heat generation is the ideal solution for heating public and private open-air swimming pools because the heat is required in the hotter months of the year anyway. Only minimal technical requirements are placed on the installation and the system components, which are usually unglazed collectors. As the volume of water in the swimming pool renders interim storage unnecessary, very economical operation is possible. Generally, if limited temperature fluctuations are accepted, additional heating plant will not be required at all. In Central Europe, the area of the absorbers should be equivalent to about 50–80% of the area of the pool.
When solar thermal energy is to be used to assist the space heating in addition to providing hot water, the installation must be enlarged in accordance with the desired solar coverage. Typical values for a four-person household in Germany are a collector area of 10–20 m² and a storage volume of 0.7–2.0 m³. With an energy-

efficient building, this allows between 20 and 30% of the total heating requirement to be covered by solar thermal energy. The interim storage for the heating circuit can be designed as additional to the hot-water tank or a single combination tank can serve both space heating and hot-water systems. For a detached house, appropriate sizing of the collector area and storage volume, which is located within the thermal envelope, permits a solar coverage of up to 100% for the total heating requirement (Fig. B 4.40). The efficiency of the installation presumes a low heating requirement and a low temperature level in the heating circuit. Combining a warm-air installation with an air collector enables the incoming fresh air to be preheated. Group heating networks can be fed from solar thermal installations with long-term heat storage. The discrepancy between the high level of radiation in the summer and the maximum heating requirement in the winter can be compensated for to a large extent (approx. 50% solar coverage of total heating requirement) through seasonal storage. Sensible sizes for a solar-powered group heating network with long-term heat storage are residential estates with upward of about 100 housing units. The heat gain in the collectors is transported via appropriate lines to the central plant and distributed directly to the buildings as required. The excess solar heat in the summer is fed into the long-term storage system (see p. 125). During the heating period, the heating energy is retrieved from the store and supplemented by further central heat generation as required. The collector arrays can be located centrally or distributed over various building roofs or facades. Besides the planning of the buildings themselves, the urban planning of the area served by the group heating network is also important. The sizing of such installations depends on the individual circumstances such as total size of settlement, specific heating requirements, type of long-term storage, temperature level, etc. As a guide, approx. 1.5 m² collector area and 3 m³ storage volume per MWh of annual heating requirement can be assumed. Further information on sizing can be found in "Urban space and infrastructure" (see p. 74).

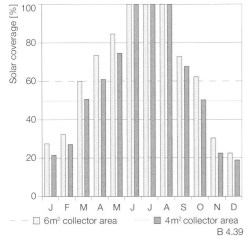

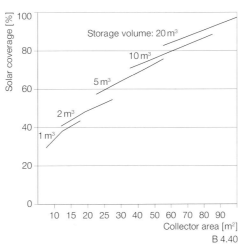

B 4.39

B 4.40

B 4.41

Use of ambient heat via heat pumps

The term "ambient heat" covers both the atmospheric strata near the earth's surface, up to an altitude of about 100 m, and also the soil strata down to a depth of approx. 200 m (soil, groundwater and surface waters). Both media obtain their energy content primarily from the absorption of solar radiation and are therefore available as energy stores for indirect use of solar energy. The third type of ambient heat is waste heat from production processes, waste water or expelled air.

The temperature of these heat sources is normally too low for supplying heat directly to a building. In order to exploit the energy content, however, technical devices are used to prepare the ambient heat (Fig. B 4.42). The principle can be reversed both physically and technically and thus used for cooling, too (see p. 130). Despite this twin application possibility, we still generally speak of a heat pump.

Heat sources

In terms of technical exploitation, we distinguish between the following heat sources:

- External air in the direct vicinity of the heat pump or the building
- Soil, which is tapped by constructional measures
- Groundwater or surface waters
- Waste heat in the form of cooling water, waste gases, expelled air, etc.

The external air is available as a source of heat at all times and in unlimited quantities. It is either fed via fans directly to the evaporator of a heat pump or transferred via a heat exchanger indirectly to a fluid heat transfer medium. The external air is cooled by a few kelvins at the evaporator. Using this method, heat can be extracted from very cold air (even below freezing). The low energy density calls for a high air circulation, which leads to a marked cooling in the vicinity of the air/air heat exchanger and brings with it the risk of disturbing noise. One major disadvantage of using the external air as a heat source is the considerable temperature fluctuations over the day, over the seasons. In particular, the conflicting nature of external temperatures and heating requirements over the year have an unfavourable effect on the energy efficiency of the system as a whole. When the heating requirement is high, the energy content of the external air is very low, and during the summer the heat remains virtually unused (Fig. B 4.43). The upshot of this is that heat pumps using air as a heat source are generally used only where a low capacity is required, or they are operated in conjunction with a further heat exchanger.

In principle, there are two approaches relevant in practice for tapping the heat of the ground: shallow and deep ground couplings. The former requires a horizontal grid of brine-filled pipes to be laid at a depth > 1.5 m in the ground. The heat absorbed is essentially temporarily stored solar energy with corresponding seasonal fluctuations, which, however, are considerably smaller than those of the external air (Fig. B 4.43). The heat flow from the ground is generally < 1 W/m², the extraction capacity varies from approx. 20 to 40 W/m² of ground coupling depending on the moisture content of the soil. This method of tapping the heat can be realised inexpensively as part of new building measures, but does require large areas. Alternatively, the heat potential of lower strata can be exploited via vertical boreholes. The seasonal temperature fluctuations in the ground decrease with the distance from the earth's surface. Below a depth of approx. 30 m, an almost constant temperature corresponding to the average annual temperature for that region prevails throughout the year (about 12°C in Central Europe). The boreholes are normally approx. 100 m deep. The brine-filled plastic pipes, in the form of a pair of U-pipes or pipe-in-pipe arrangement, and contact with the ground over their full surface area is assured by using a suitable backfilling material (Fig. B 4.44). The extraction capacity varies depending on the properties of the ground and the flow of groundwater, and in Central Europe approx. 40–80 W can be expected per metre depth of borehole. To minimise the risk of mutual interference, the pitch of the boreholes should not be less than 6 m. An alternative to the borehole is the so-called solid absorber – normally solid concrete elements required for structural purposes anyway (e.g. pile foundations) which are activated thermally via brine-filled pipes.

The thermal energy stored in bodies of water above or below ground can also be exploited for heating buildings. At suitable locations with open bodies of water or a water table near the surface, the thermal potential tied up in the water can be used to operate heat pumps. Here, the water is pumped up directly via bored wells and hence itself becomes the heat transfer medium. When using the groundwater, corresponding quantities of water are pumped via the production well (depth approx. 15 m) to the evaporator of the heat pump and fed back into the ground via a separate, re-injection well at another position – provided there is a continuous flow of groundwater. When using the ther-

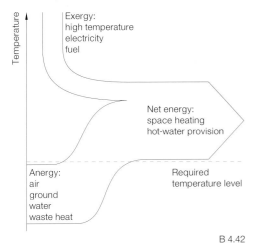

B 4.42

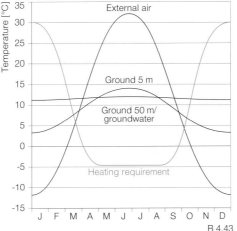

B 4.43

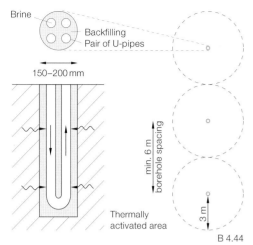

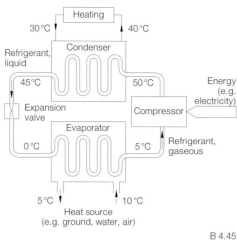

B 4.44

B 4.45

B 4.46

mal potential of groundwater directly, chemical and microbiological processes can lead to negative phenomena such as corrosion of installation components or deposits in the system. The geological boundary conditions and the quality of the water must therefore be analysed in advance of the planning.

In Europe, groundwater exhibits a relatively constant temperature of approx. 7–12°C over the year and the output capacities during the heating period are about 5–6 kW/m³ groundwater per hour. When using bodies of open water, it is normally possible to pump out the water directly. Higher temperature fluctuations of approx. 2–25°C are possible here. The extraction capacities during the heating period are typically 3–4 kW/m³ water per hour. Owing to the effective heat extraction, using the groundwater is a very economic method for large capacities. In addition, the groundwater, like the borehole method, can also be used as a powerful heat sink for cooling purposes (see p. 128). Extra special care must be taken when using groundwater in order to prevent contamination of this valuable fundamental resource.

Many production processes produce considerable waste heat that can be sensibly used for heating buildings. If the temperature level is too low for a direct link to the heating circuit, the energy potential can be used as a heat source for a heat pump. Another application for using waste heat on a small scale is in systems for controlled ventilation with heat recovery. If the heating requirement is minimal (the case with passive houses in particular), the heating requirement of the building can be accomplished with a heat pump integrated into the ventilation system (see p. 135). In this situation the expelled air, which has a higher temperature than the external air even after heat recovery, can be employed directly as a heat source for the heat pump process.

Heat pump technology

Heat pumps use driving energy (exergy) to raise the temperature of a heat source by way of a thermodynamic cyclic process (Fig. B 4.42). In doing so, the latent energy potential in the form of "anergy" can be made available for heating the building (see "Fundamentals", p. 43). From the technological viewpoint, there are, in principle, two ways of realising this process:

In a sorption heat pump the thermodynamic process is driven by the inflow of thermal energy. This technology is of only minor significance for heating buildings and is used in the case of waste heat (also district heating) or when cooling is required (see p. 130).

As an alternative to the sorption process, the rise in temperature required can be achieved via compression. In principle, any type of motor can be used as the drive unit, but electric compression heat pumps are used almost exclusively for building heating requirements.

	Ground coupling, grid of pipes	Ground coupling, borehole	Ground-water	Air	Solid absorber
Availability	Preferably open areas	Anywhere	Depends on local availability	Anywhere	New construction works
Space requirement	High	Low	Low	Low	Low
Average temperature in winter	-5 to +5°C	0 to 10°C	8 to 12°C	-25 to +15°C	-3 to +5°C
Permit required	No	Almost always	Always	No	No
Typical energy efficiency ratio (EER) for heat pump	4.0	4.5	4.5	3.3	–

B 4.47

How the compression heat pump works

The basic ingredient for the heat pump process is a liquid with a very low boiling point which is known as a refrigerant. This liquid passes through four stages in one cycle (Fig. B 4.45): In the evaporator the refrigerant is initially in a liquid state. Feeding in energy from the heat source raises the ambient temperature of the evaporator beyond the boiling point of the refrigerant corresponding to the respective pressure. This cools the heat source by approx. 4–6 K. The refrigerant, now in vapour form, is compressed in the next stage, a process that requires a considerable amount of energy to be fed into the system. In the case of an electric compressor, the quantity of electricity required has an effect on the primary energy balance. The enormous pressure increase also raises the temperature of the refrigerant by up to 70 K. The highly compressed, high-temperature refrigerant now passes to the condenser where it is in contact with the water circuit for the heat output (heating circuit) via a second heat exchanger. The temperature of this flow of water is lower than that of the condensation temperature of the refrigerant corresponding to the respective pressure, whereupon it cools and condenses. The heat of condensation released is transferred to the heating circuit. In order that the cycle can begin again, the pressure of the refrigerant must be relieved via an expansion valve, which causes the temperature to fall again. As it re-enters the evaporator, the initial pressure and temperature have been restored and the process can begin again.

Parameters

Like with the degrees of efficiency of boilers, heat pumps also have parameters to enable an energy assessment (Fig. B 4.49). The coefficient of performance (COP) for a heat pump frequently specified in manufacturers' documentation designates the ratio of the energy released at the condenser to the electrical power of the drive motor for the compressor. It is therefore only an assessment of the quality of the heat pump cycle and is always related to a certain operating situation. It should always be specified in conjunction with the primary boundary conditions (e.g. S5W35 = brine temperature 5°C, heating circuit flow temperature 35°C). Critical for the evaluation of the complete system is the energy efficiency ratio (EER) – the ratio (for a whole year) of the thermal energy released to the total amount of electrical energy consumed. The fundamental assumption for heat pumps is: the lower the temperature difference between heat source and usage, the more efficient is the operation of the system. The flow temperature of the heating system is therefore just as important as finding a suitable heat source. Coil heating, e.g. in floors or walls, is effective here because such installations require only low flow temperatures. The essential criterion for the ecological assessment of heat pump systems is the magnitude of the possible primary energy savings compared to

fossil fuel-fired heating systems. Critical here is the source of the electricity for the driving energy. Fig. B 4.48 compares the energy flows in a heating system with a gas-fired condensing boiler and a heat pump installation. In the gas installation, the preparation and transport of the energy medium and the annual degree of utilisation of the boiler result in only low losses (in percentages) in the primary energy input. By contrast, in the heat pump system, some 60 to 80% of the final energy stems from a renewable heat source (e.g. geothermal energy), but the electrical driving energy required results in, in Germany, for example, a correspondingly high primary energy consumption due to the high cost of generating the electricity. In addition, the use of refrigerants containing fluorocarbons results in the emission of CO_2-equivalent substances. To achieve a noticeable reduction in carbon dioxide compared to a gas-fired condensing boiler, more favourable operating conditions must be presumed (e.g. a high EER). It therefore seems obvious to include decentralised electricity generation using renewable sources in the planning alongside an efficient heat pump system (see p. 138).

Typical installation concepts

The output of heat pumps ranges from mini installations with just 1 kW to large systems supplying several hundred kilowatts. The arrangement and type of components vary depending on the heat source (Fig. B 4.52). Up until now, more than 90% of new heat pump installations have been in residential buildings, but they are being increasingly used for other types of building as well. To cover the enormous requirements of office buildings, for instance, several heat pumps can be operated in parallel. And as they are also suitable for cooling, they represent an interesting alternative for buildings with high cooling requirements. In principle, heat pumps can be integrated just like boilers, although it is normal to include some form of interim storage in order to avoid high cycle rates and to bridge over the periods between special heat-pump electricity rates (see p. 125). Special plant rooms are not required and so heat pumps can be set up anywhere. Even a chimney is unnecessary. Only the noise of operation has to be considered. There are various operating concepts for using heat pumps for space heating and hot-water provision. If the heat pump is used as the sole heating plant, we speak of monovalent operation. This is usually only possible with heat sources that also provide a sufficiently high temperature level even on extremely cold days (e.g. ground, groundwater). An electric heating element can be used to assist the heat pump operation on very cold days. As electricity is the only energy medium used, this represents a mono-energy operating mode. And finally, the heat pump can also be used in bivalent operation, in combination with a second heating installation (e.g. boiler). In this setup, the heat pump is used to cover the basic load and the other heating installation handles the peak loads.

B 4.44 Pair of U-pipes in borehole for exploiting geothermal heat
B 4.45 Schematic diagram showing how an electric compression heat pump works
B 4.46 Cascaded heat pumps for high performance and use of groundwater
B 4.47 Comparison of different heat sources for heat pumps
B 4.48 Comparison of typical energy and CO_2 audits (assumptions: natural gas 0.2 kg/kWh, CO_2 emissions for electricity 0.57 kg/kWh, energy efficiency of heat pump 3.5):
  a Gas-fired condensing boiler
  b Compression heat pump operated with conventional electricity, CFC refrigerant
  c Compression heat pump operated with electricity from renewable sources, zero-CFC refrigerant
B 4.49 Parameters for heat pumps

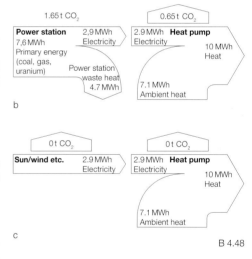

B 4.48

	Meaning	Statement
Coefficient of performance (COP) ε	The ratio of the specified heat output to the consumed electrical drive power at a certain time and for certain temperature conditions.	Efficiency of heat pump under test conditions
Energy efficiency ratio β	The ratio of the heat energy supplied per year (Q) to the energy input required (W), for determining operational fluctuations etc.	Efficiency of total heat pump heating installation
Seasonal perform. factor	The inverse of the EER designates the ratio of the energy iinput to the heat energy supplied.	Efficiency of total-heat pump installation to VDI 4650

B 4.49

123

Capacity of heat source

$$\phi_{source} = \frac{\phi_i}{\beta} \cdot (\beta - 1)$$

ϕ_{source} = Capacity [kW]
ϕ_i = Standard heat load [kW]
β = Energy efficiency ratio

Rough sizing per kW ϕ_{source}

Ground coupling, grid of pipes	30 m²
Ground coupling, boreholes	20 m
External air	300 m³/h
Groundwater	0.15 m³/h

B 4.50

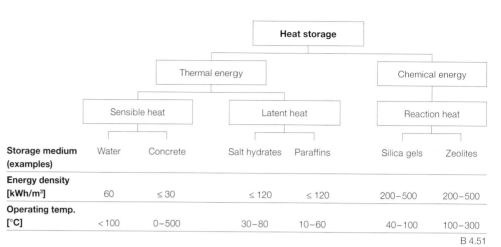

	Heat storage				
	Thermal energy			**Chemical energy**	
	Sensible heat		Latent heat	Reaction heat	
Storage medium (examples)	Water	Concrete	Salt hydrates	Paraffins	Silica gels	Zeolites
Energy density [kWh/m³]	60	≤ 30	≤ 120	≤ 120	200–500	200–500
Operating temp. [°C]	< 100	0–500	30–80	10–60	40–100	100–300

B 4.51

Besides distinguishing between method and operating mode when designating heat pumps, we also make a distinction between the types of heat source and heat output media. For example, a heat pump with ground coupling and integral hot-water heating circuit is known as a brine/water heat pump, and one driven by external air for warm-air heating is known as an air/air heat pump. Depending on requirements, it feeds the buffer tank for the heating or hot-water circuit. Electric pumps are used almost everywhere in the world because their maintenance requirements are very low. The market has been evolving since the 1990s – with high growth rates; the total number of heat pump systems operating in Europe, however, accounts for only a small share of the heating market – except for a few countries (e.g. Switzerland). The sizing of the heat source can be estimated via certain parameters (Fig. B 4.50).

Heat storage, distribution and output

Providing a means of storage for thermal energy enables the energy to be used at different times to the production of that energy and in the case of solar thermal installations permits their use over the entire year. Storing the heat also allows the installed (power plant) output to be reduced because the useful heat can be gradually "accumulated". Likewise, storage can also be used to reduce the cycle times (switching on and off at short intervals) of the heating plant.

Storage principles
We can divide heat storage, in principle, into thermal and chemical storage (Fig. B 4.51). In sensible (= measurable with thermometer) heat storage the incoming energy causes a proportional increase in the temperature of the storage medium. This is the most common type of heat storage (e.g. water tank, solid concrete walls as thermal mass, etc.).
In latent (= not measurable with thermometer) heat storage, in addition to the measurable rise in temperature, the state of the aggregate in the storage medium undergoes a change (solid to liquid or liquid to gaseous). During this phase, thermal energy is absorbed without a rise in temperature, which leads to a very high storage density at a low temperature level and has a favourable influence on storage losses (Fig. B 4.53). Moreover, the temperature range of the phase transition can be influenced during manufacture. Latent heat storage media are known as phase change materials (PCM) because of the way they function; typical materials are paraffins or salt hydrates. Up until now they have been primarily used as wall or ceiling elements for optimising the storage capacity of rooms. In future they will also be employed in storage technology for increasing the storage density (e.g. for solar installations).
Thermochemical heat storage makes use of reversible chemical reactions to control the flow of heat. Silica gel and water are examples of the media used for this type of storage. The

water is bonded and expelled by adsorption and desorption, and these reactions enable heat to be either absorbed or released (Fig. B 4.54). In contrast to sensible or latent heat storage, the time of the reaction can be determined as required. Furthermore, there are no heat losses when the materials are separate. Such systems therefore offer, in principle, excellent conditions for seasonal heat storage. The materials used must be checked with respect to their ecological compatibility.

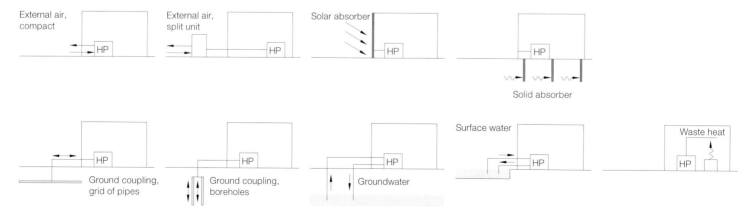

B 4.52

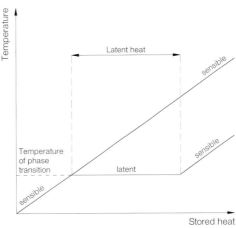

B 4.53

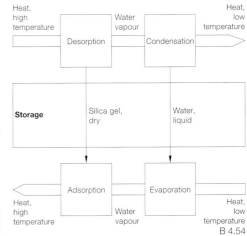

B 4.54

Storage typologies

Besides the quantity of thermal energy and the temperature level, the time periods are especially important for the practical application of heat storage media. We therefore distinguish between short- and long-term heat storage. Short-term heat storage makes use of systems with which thermal energy can be stored for periods ranging from a few hours to more than several days. One common method of short-term storage is via the building components when exploiting passive solar energy gains and to help the summertime thermal performance (e.g. thermal activation of thermal masses, night-time cooling, etc.). Water is the most frequently used type of technical short-term storage (Fig. B 4.57) – in a tank with a volume of about 0.2–2.0 m³ and normally made from a corrosion-resistant material such as stainless steel or mild steel with a heat-resistant or enamel finish, with an insulating jacket and internal heat exchangers. They are used as buffer tanks for the heating circuit, e.g. for heat pumps or co-generation plants, for storing hot water or as a component in solar thermal systems. In the simplest case these are the same as conventional storage media with an additional heat exchanger for the solar circuit. Their efficiency is improved when specific charging and discharging gives rise to a vertical temperature stratification. Another type of storage principle frequently used is the tank-in-tank principle in which the hot-water tank is integrated

into a buffer tank for the heating circuit, which means that the water for space heating benefits from heating losses in the heating period. Care must be taken with hot-water storage to ensure that no legionella bacteria can thrive.

In order to be able to store solar thermal energy over a period of several months, long-term heat storage media must be used, which are also known as seasonal storage systems. Such installations exploit the physical property that the ratio of surface area to volume of a body improves disproportionately as the volume of that body increases. This leads to significantly lower heat losses and when used together with good thermal insulation enables the production of the heat to take place at a different time of year to its usage. Long-term heat storage is mainly used for separate buildings with a very high solar coverage (> 50%) and in concepts for solar-powered group heating (Figs. B 4.55 and 4.58; see also "Urban space and infrastructure", p. 74). In addition to water tanks with a volume of up to 12 000 m³, it is possible to activate natural, enclosed aquifers to act as heat storage media, or a mixture of gravel and water sealed off from the surrounding soil, or ground strata connected via vertical boreholes (Fig. B 4.56). As the heat losses are very high with water-based long-term storage, low-losses thermochemical storage media will play a major role in future developments.

Heat distribution

Heating installations for space heating are these days housed almost exclusively in separate plant rooms. The thermal energy must therefore be distributed via a suitable system to the various interior areas where it is required. A transfer medium is required to transport the heat. The following systems have proved themselves in practice:

- Heat distribution via pipes with hot water as a medium (hot-water heating) is the method used most frequently for space heating. The water heated up by the heating plant is pumped via pipes to the heat output components (flow), where it cools and then flows back to the heating plant (return).
- The heating requirement of a room can be provided by incoming fresh air. Owing to the low heat capacity of air, however, favourable constructional conditions must be established to minimise the heat losses. Otherwise, high temperatures or high flow rates are necessary. Distributing the heat entirely by way of air can be advisable if some form of air conditioning is provided anyway and low heat loads mean that low fresh-air temperatures are possible, or fast heating for flexible usage is required, e.g. for industrial workshops or sports halls. In these cases the incoming air is preheated via an integral heating battery which is connected via a hot-water circuit to the heating plant. Alternatively,

B 4.55

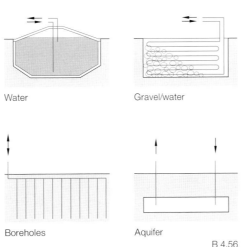

Water Gravel/water

Boreholes Aquifer

B 4.56

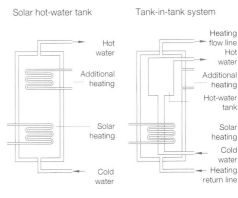

Solar hot-water tank Tank-in-tank system

B 4.57

125

B 4.58 Apartment block with integral long-term heat storage and 100% solar heating coverage, Oberburg (CH), 2007, Aeschlimann + Willen
B 4.59 Size of heating area in relation to flow temperature
B 4.60 How the various heat output systems work
B 4.61 Room temperature profile depending on heat output system
B 4.62 Systematic presentation of heat output systems
B 4.63 The principle of building component activation throughout the year
B 4.64 Typical arrangements for the thermal activation of a suspended reinforced concrete floor slab

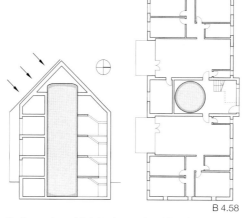

B 4.58

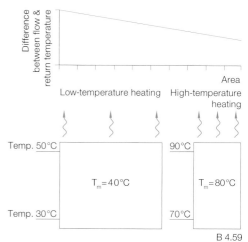

B 4.59

gas burners can be integrated into special wall or ceiling elements with recirculated air ventilation.

- Using steam as the heat transfer medium enables thermal energy to be transported at very high temperatures (> 100°C). This method is usually employed in industry for production processes (e.g. heating of acid baths).

Three aspects are essentially critical for the energy-efficiency evaluation of the heat distribution:

Firstly, the heat distribution pipes must be insulated (lagged) in order to minimise heat losses during transport. Distribution within the heated building envelope should be preferred for all horizontal and vertical lines in order to benefit from the inevitable heat losses. This also applies to the distribution of hot water. Additional circulation lines are often installed in residential buildings in order to prevent the hot water cooling during phases where hot water is not required and also to cut the waiting time once hot water is required. However, the additional line losses and pumping requirements also increase the energy requirement. This disadvantage must be weighed against the advantage that the water consumption is generally reduced when such circulation lines are installed.

Secondly, electric pumps are installed to transport the hot water as and when required. The capacity of a recirculating pump increases with

its flow rate, which is determined by the temperature difference between flow and return. The greater this difference, the lower is the flow rate. Modulating control to suit requirements is important in addition to the use of efficient electric pumps. Another option is to cut back the heating operation automatically during the night: a timer switches the room temperature to a lower level (just a few kelvins) during the night to reduce transmission heat losses.

Thirdly, the temperature level of the heat distribution is essentially influenced by the configuration of the total system. Typical values for flow and return are (in °C): 90/70 (old buildings), 70/40, 50/30 and 35/28. A low temperature level (low-temperature heating, max. 50/30°C) often results in a higher efficiency for the heating plant (e.g. condensing boiler, heat pump, solar thermal energy). In addition, the line losses can be reduced. It should be remembered here, however, that as the flow temperature drops and the temperature difference shrinks, so the sizes of the heat output components must increase (Fig. B 4.59).

Heat output systems

Radiators or coil heating are necessary for transferring the heat energy to the interior spaces (Figs. B 4.60 and 4.62). They form the interface between building services and architecture. The type and arrangement of heating components influence the thermal comfort of a room. One of the tasks of planning is to ensure that, in conjunction with the design of the building envelope, the surface temperatures are as homogeneous as possible (see "Fundamentals", p. 56).

The heat output always takes place simultaneously by way of conduction, radiation and convection. Whereas the conduction is negligible, the proportions of radiation and convection differ considerably depending on the type of heat output system. We distinguish here between radiators (individual components) and coil heating (integrated into building components). Radiators are heating components in which a high proportion of the heat output is by way of radiation (> 30%). Water flows through the metal housing and transfers heat to the room via its surface. Most radiators are in the form of ribbed components, manufactured in sizes to suit the output required. One variation on this is the flat radiant panel – two flat metal housings joined by thin plates. Radiators exhibit good heat output values over a wide range of temperatures and can be used virtually anywhere. They are normally positioned on outside walls directly below windows, but with a well-insulated

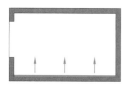

Underfloor heating

Wall heating

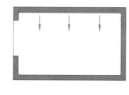

Ceiling heating

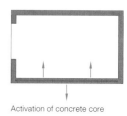

Activation of concrete core

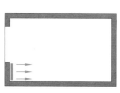

Radiator

Convector

Underfloor convector

B 4.60

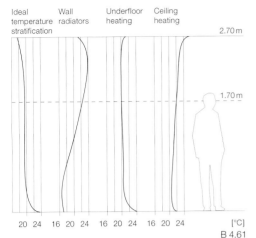

B 4.61

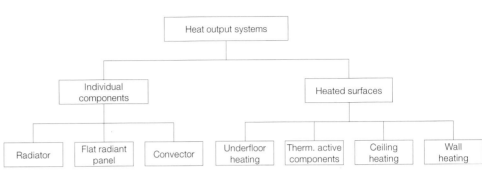

B 4.62

building envelope, other positions are also possible.

The heat output from convectors is almost exclusively by way of convection. This is achieved with a multitude of sheet metal lamella that are connected to the heating pipe. Owing to the large surface area, the air between the lamella heats up to create a thermal current. Such systems require a much higher temperature than the interior air, which means that flow temperatures of at least 50°C are necessary.

Various types of convector are available. Like radiators, they can be fitted to outside walls, in wall recesses (also concealed) or along the base of a wall. Their high proportion of convection means that they are suitable for tall glazing that extends down to the floor and, especially in the case of inferior thermal insulation, they can prevent a body of cold air descending down the glazing. In conjunction with very tall glazing (e.g. atria, indoor swimming pools), additional convectors can be fitted part-way up the facade.

One variation of this type of space heating is the underfloor convector, which is fitted flush with the floor beneath large expanses of glazing. Very low models are available (min. approx. 75 mm high). To increase the output, an underfloor convector can be fitted with an electrical recirculating air fan. However, the noise of operation and the auxiliary energy requirement must be taken into account in the

planning. Underfloor convectors with fans and a connection to the outside air can also be used for decentralised ventilation (see p. 132 and "Building envelope", p. 103).

Radiant ceiling panels have a metal plate element that is thermally activated by being connected to the heating pipes. This radiates heat into the room and can be combined with other functions (interior design, sound insulation) in a suspended ceiling.

The thermal activation of the floor can be achieved by laying pipes, normally of plastic, in the screed. The screed is heated up and the large surface area means that low flow temperatures (generally 35/28°C) usually suffice for underfloor heating. The heating output can be increased locally (e.g. adjacent to floor-level glazing) by reducing the pitch of the pipes. However, the large thermal mass has the effect that the regulation of the heat output is more sluggish than with radiators. The very high proportion of radiation and the method of heating the room from the bottom upwards results in a particularly agreeable temperature profile in the room (Fig. B 4.61). Care should be taken with the choice of floor covering because it should not prevent the heat exchange. Wooden floors in particular require an adequate thermal conductivity and resistance to dynamic temperature fluctuations (fissures).

Wall surfaces can also be used for the heat output in a similar way to underfloor heating. Warm wall surfaces are regarded as particularly

pleasant and again require only very low flow temperatures. The (very narrow) plastic pipes are laid in the plaster or integrated into special wall elements. Restrictions on the use of the rooms must be taken into account because the wall surfaces may not be screened off (e.g. by cupboards) and drilling holes in the wall is practically impossible.

One variation of wall heating is facade heating. Systems employing post-and-rail construction can be suitably modified so that hot water can flow through the hollow sections. Advantageous here is the invisible integration of the heating system into components that are necessary anyway. But with inadequate thermal insulation around the sections, the heat losses to the outside can be very high.

The solid components required for structural purposes (e.g. reinforced concrete suspended floors) can be thermally activated by building in heating pipes (Figs. B 4.63 and 4.64). In conjunction with the high storage mass, such a system can achieve a basic temperature during the heating period with flow temperatures only marginally higher than the required temperature of the room. The activation of building components is therefore ideal for exploiting ambient heat. The high inertia and the low specific heat output generally require a supplementary heating system that can respond quickly to users' needs (e.g. convectors). It must be remembered here that an undisturbed exchange between the surfaces of the compo-

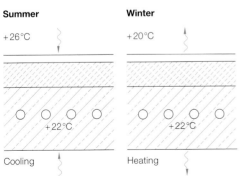

B 4.63

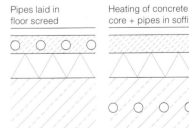

B 4.64

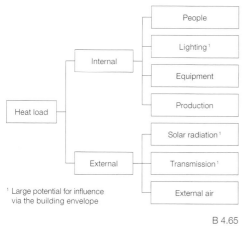

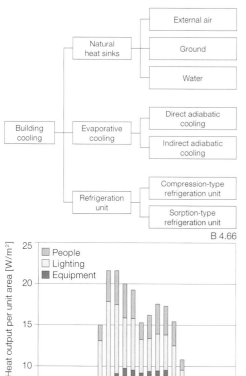

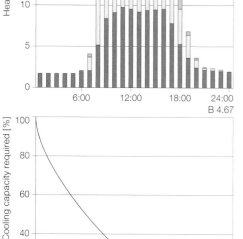

¹ Large potential for influence via the building envelope

B 4.65

B 4.66

B 4.67

B 4.68

nents and the interior air must be able to take place. So suspended ceilings or cavity floors have a detrimental effect on the performance of such systems. The soffit design in particular must be coordinated with other requirements, e.g. room acoustics, when considering thermal activation.

Cooling

Besides the supply of heat, limiting high temperatures is another important aspect for thermal comfort in buildings. We distinguish between internal and external causes of undesirable heat sources, the so-called cooling loads (Fig. B 4.65). The most significant internal cooling loads are caused by people (high occupancy density), lighting and electrical equipment (e.g. computers). The external energy sources can be divided into solar radiation, heat transmission from outside to inside and the heating potential that loads the interior via the exchange of air.

In the majority of cases, buildings, especially in the cold and temperate zones of the earth, can be operated without active cooling, provided the energy efficiency has been optimised in the planning. Designing the building envelope to minimise external cooling loads is therefore a top priority (see "Building envelope", p. 195). However, certain work processes require specific climatic boundary conditions, or especially high, usage-related cooling loads may require the provision of cooling, more properly expressed as the need for a "heat sink". Like with the heating requirement, the cooling requirement is determined for the most unfavourable situation. The maximum permissible room temperature (e.g. 26°C in office buildings) is a significant factor. A minor compromise, e.g. agreeing a number of hours per year during which the maximum temperature may be exceeded, will lead to considerable savings (Fig. B 4.68). Remembering the needs of sustainable development, it should be ensured that this energy service is provided with a high efficiency and maximum use of renewable energy sources. The systems and concepts for cooling requirements are explained below (Fig. B 4.66).

Natural heat sinks

In the ideal case, the heat load in a building can be dissipated via natural cooling potential, or rather heat sinks, without the need for active cooling. Favourable temperature levels in the air, ground and water can be useful here.

External air
In most situations the cooling requirement occurs at the same time as high external air temperatures. Nevertheless, there are situations over the course of a day or year in which the external air can be integrated into the building services concept as a heat sink.
Firstly, because of their high internal heat loads, certain uses (e.g. theatre auditorium) have a

cooling requirement even when the external air temperature is low. In these cases the external air can be used directly (direct cooling) or via an air/air heat exchanger (e.g. recooling unit) to dissipate the heat loads.
Secondly, during periods with high external air temperatures, potential heat sinks are available during the night most climate zones which are useful for the thermal discharging of buildings (night-time cooling, Fig. B 4.69), provided there is sufficient thermal mass that can be thermally activated to achieve a phase lag (Fig. B 4.70). The transport of energy can take place directly via an exchange of air (natural or mechanical) or via a water-filled system (e.g. activation of building components) with natural recooling. Purely natural night-time ventilation is very efficient but difficult to control, and is often impossible for security reasons. The higher the local difference between maximum daytime temperature and minimum night-time temperature, the higher is the cooling capacity that can be achieved. To realise effective cooling during the night, it should be ensured that the room temperature in the night drops below the maximum permissible temperature by at least 5 K for several hours [3].

Ground
The temperature level in the ground becomes more constant as we go deeper, and beyond a depth of approx. 30 m corresponds to the average annual air temperature. There are essentially two concepts for using the temperature level of the ground as a heat sink.
Buildings with mechanical ventilation can divert the incoming fresh air via a ground exchanger to achieve a drop in the air temperature amounting to several kelvins. In most cases further cooling is then unnecessary (Fig. B 4.71). The ground exchanger also helps to preheat the incoming air when the outside temperatures are low, which means that the system can be operated economically over the whole year. The principle of using the temperature of the ground for ventilating the building is very old. A "method for cooling and preheating the air with the help of geothermal heat" was registered with the German Imperial Patent Office as long ago as 1877 [4]! The cooling capacity depends on the average annual temperature and the dimensions of the ground exchanger (Figs. B 4.72 and 4.73). The range of materials and cross-sections is considerable and extends from plastic pipes with a diameter of 150 mm to accessible concrete ducts and complete basements with walls forming an underground labyrinth for the air. Plastic pipes approx. 300 mm in diameter laid at a depth of 2–4 m have proved to be particularly economic [4]. There are several ways of building such a ground exchanger. If the air flow rates are low, e.g. detached houses, flexible pipes laid in the ground are usually sufficient. For larger buildings, correspondingly larger pipe cross-sections or the use of several parallel lines will be necessary. Materials with smooth surfaces are

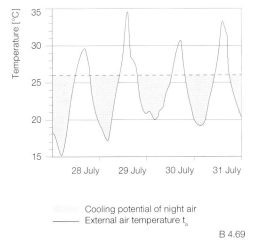

Cooling potential of night air
External air temperature t_a

B 4.69

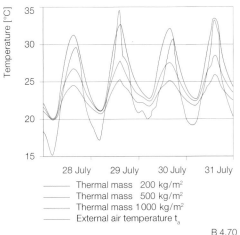

—— Thermal mass   200 kg/m²
—— Thermal mass   500 kg/m²
—— Thermal mass 1000 kg/m²
—— External air temperature t_a

B 4.70

recommended in order to reduce the flow resistance and optimise hygiene. Suitable inspection openings must be included to enable cleaning if the ground exchanger is not large enough for direct access. As condensation can collect, pipes or ducts should be laid to a suitable fall so that the water can drain to an outlet. Considerable experience has been gained with ground exchangers and it is clear that the economic efficiency of such systems (taking into account preheating of the incoming air during the heating period) must be verified for each project. Combined with night-time cooling (activating a bypass around the ground exchanger), high heat loads can be dissipated passively. As an alternative to ground exchangers, boreholes (similar to heating applications) or solid absorbers in the ground as heat sinks can also be used for cooling. This multiple usage accelerates the regeneration of the ground and leads to a better economy of the total system. The prerequisite for this is a liquid heat transfer medium with corresponding absorption surfaces and a heat transfer in the interior of the building that makes cooling by just a few kelvins below the room temperature necessary (e.g. activation of building components). An air/water heat exchanger can be used to integrate the brine circuit into the ventilation system. The cooling capacity of boreholes is approx. 20 – 40 W/m in Central Europe. Where the passive cooling is insufficient, a heat pump can also be employed as an active chiller unit (see p. 130). The great

popularity of ground-coupled heat pumps in North America is founded on this option.

Water
Groundwater or surface waters also offer a great potential for cooling buildings in addition to their possible use as a heat source for heat pumps. If sufficient quantities of water with a temperature level < 20°C are available, the water can be integrated directly into the building services concept as a heat sink (Fig. B 4.74). The high heat capacity of water means that the energy density is very high for a thermal discharge. If the water is also used as a heat source for heat pumps, economic energy supplies can be realised to meet high requirements.

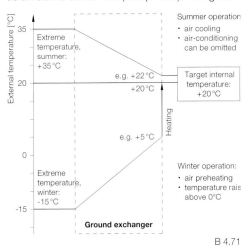

B 4.71

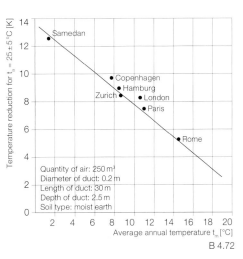

B 4.72

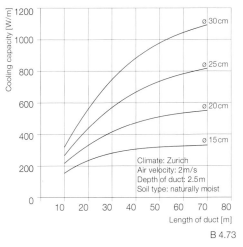

B 4.73

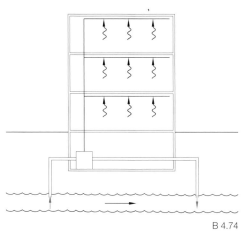

B 4.74

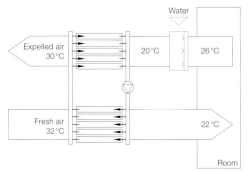

Heat or cooling energy recovery   Humidification of air or fine water spray

B 4.75

B 4.76

Evaporative cooling

Cooling by the evaporation of water is a very old principle, and we experience this ourselves through transpiration via the skin. Energy is required to accomplish the transition from the liquid to the gas state and this is obtained from the surroundings (adiabatic cooling). It is possible to reduce the temperature of the fresh-air supply to a building directly or indirectly in a similar way.

Direct adiabatic cooling involves humidifying the incoming air directly, which reduces the temperature of the air. Such a cooling effect can be achieved via, for example, open bodies of water, plants or a fine spray of water (Fig. B 4.76). Generally, it should not be forgotten that evaporation always increases the humidity, and humidity can cause a rise in the perceived temperature (see "Fundamentals", p. 57). Direct adiabatic cooling is therefore particularly advisable in dry, hot climate zones.

In order to reduce the temperature without increasing the humidity of the air, adiabatic cooling can be employed indirectly by humidifying the exhaust air (Fig. B 4.75). The prerequisite for this is mechanical ventilation with heat recovery. Here, the incoming air transfers a large part of its heat potential, via a heat exchanger, to the cooled (and moist) outgoing air without changing the absolute humidity. The efficiency is, however, limited and depends, in particular, on the moisture content of the external or exhaust air. The efficiency can be improved by combining direct and indirect adiabatic cooling with dehumidification of the incoming air (Fig. B 4.80).

Electrical cooling

Buildings that place a high demands on the efficiency or controllability of the cooling can employ refrigeration plant. Depending on the technology used, they are integrated either via a water-filled cooling system (activation of building components, cooling fins, etc.) or via a cooling battery in the ventilation system. Refrigeration plants can generate very low temperatures, and the incoming air can be dehumidified via air-conditioning plant if required.

Compressor-type refrigeration plant

Electric compressor-type refrigeration plant is the most common method of generating a cooling effect. They are often simply referred to as chillers and are used for small capacities (e.g. refrigerator, freezer, etc.) as well as for building cooling or industrial applications. The technology corresponds to the principle of a heat pump (see p. 122), but used in reverse, the chiller extracts heat from the building cooling circuit via the evaporator. The waste heat that ensues at the condenser must be allowed to escape. This process is usually achieved via a recooling unit or a cooling tower, where – provided they are positioned in an unobstructed airflow – the heat can be dissipated directly to the outside via a further water circuit by way of evaporative cooling.

Reversible heat pump

If a heat pump system is used for heating the building, it can be used simultaneously for providing cooling needs because heat pumps and electrical chillers use the same technology in principle. Twin usage as a "reversible heat pump" can represent an economic solution, provided heating and cooling energy are not required at the same time.

Electrical cooling has been fully developed and can be used for many different capacities; parameters can be used to estimate the space required for compressor-type refrigeration plant (Fig. B 4.81). The electrical energy required has an unfavourable effect on the primary energy balance of the building. And to achieve CO_2 neutrality in the energy supply, it is therefore necessary when using electrical cooling to ensure the use of electricity generated from renewable sources – just like with the heat pump. For example, solar-powered cooling can be achieved by combining a reversible heat pump with a photovoltaic system. High solar yields and the simultaneous increase in cooling requirements brought about by external loads turn this into a sensible solution (Fig. B 4.77).

Thermal cooling

Like with heat pumps, thermal methods can be used for cooling as well. This is made possible by a reversible chemical process.

Sorption-type refrigeration plant

Sorption-type refrigeration systems are older than the electrical systems preferred today. They are used primarily in industry for exploiting waste heat. Sorption-type refrigeration systems are already widespread in the USA and Japan, where they make use of the spare capacity in the gas network during the summer. There are sorption chillers available for producing cold water in a closed refrigerant circuit which use solid sorption media (e.g. water/silica gel) and the principle of adsorption, or liquid sorption media (e.g. ammonia/water) and the principle of absorption. These two methods can be used just like the more popular electric compressor-type refrigeration systems (Fig. B 4.78). The main quality feature of sorption-type refrigeration plant is the ratio of the cooling capacity generated per unit of driving energy (i.e. heat) (COP = coefficient of performance); typical values lie between 0.7 and 1.3. Thermally driven cooling processes achieve an ecological advantage over electrical systems primarily when heat generated from renewable sources can be used directly as the driving energy.

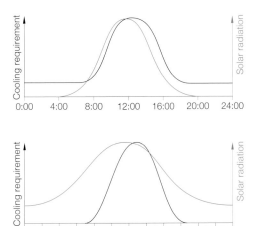

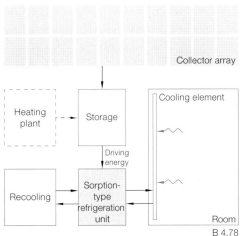

Collector array

B 4.77

B 4.78

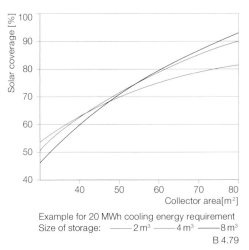

Example for 20 MWh cooling energy requirement
Size of storage: ——2 m³ ——4 m³ ——8 m³

B 4.79

Use of waste heat

One interesting application for sorption-type refrigeration plant is in the use of waste heat from the decentralised supply of heat and power in co-generation plants, or district heating. In the ideal case, renewable energy media (e.g. vegetable oil) are used as the fuel for the co-generation plant – renewable combined heat and power. Combined heat and power plus additional thermal cooling enables economical operation throughout the year.

Solar cooling

If the driving heat is mainly obtained from solar thermal systems, we speak of solar cooling. If cooling loads and solar gains occur simultaneously, the cooling requirements can be met without high storage capacities. Fig. B 4.78 shows a typical layout for solar-powered cooling with closed adsorption-type refrigeration plant. In future, such systems will also enable cooling for small capacities (< 100 kW) and with a low driving temperature (< 100°C) in order to guarantee efficient use of solar radiation. All types of collector, apart from the unglazed collector, are suitable for solar cooling (see p. 119). Generalisations regarding the sizing of solar cooling systems are not possible owing to the lack of experience; the solar coverage recommended as economic is approx. 75% of the thermal driving energy.

One important aspect of solar cooling is how the remaining heating requirements are covered. If they are provided by fossil fuels, the ecological advantage over electrical compressor-type refrigeration plant – depending on the primary energy input for the electricity – only occurs with a very high solar coverage (e.g. for Germany > 70%, Fig. B 4.79).

Alternative methods with an open refrigerant circuit can be used for cooling purposes where the incoming air is conditioned directly in combination with air-conditioning plant. Up until now, most of the systems installed use a solid sorption medium (silica gel) – in revolving sorption wheels, which operate according to the principle of sorptive dehumidification of the air plus evaporative cooling (desiccant and evaporative cooling, DEC). This therefore represents a further development of pure evaporative cooling in which the incoming air is initially dried via the sorption medium, which in addition to heat recovery enables the fresh air to be humidified directly. Heat is required to regenerate the sorption medium, and this can be provided by solar radiation (Fig. B 4.80). Solar thermal cooling is currently at the stage of advanced technical development. To date, approx. 100 installations have been built in Europe. Standardised design methods and control concepts are currently being devised in pilot projects in conjunction with scientific research.

Storage of cooling capacity

Similar to heat energy, potential cooling capacity can be stored, too. Storage can help to optimise the complete system in situations with high cooling requirements and severely fluctuating supplies. One important factor for the storage density, and hence for the economic efficiency, is the feasible temperature difference between temperature of usage and temperature of storage. Cold-water tanks cannot be cooled down below 0°C, which, for example, with a cold-water flow temperature for an air-conditioning plant of 6°C means a difference of just 6 K. Good results have been achieved with ice storage systems, where the latent heat of the ice formation is stored in addition to the sensible heat and so storage densities some 10 times higher are feasible. Like with heat storage, this is incorporated in the system via a network of cold-water pipes.

Distribution

The heat already present in a room must be removed in order to lower the room temperature or maintain it, and this can be achieved with air- or water-filled systems (Fig. B 4.82). Regulating the temperature by way of a controlled exchange of the interior air requires a cooling battery to be integrated into the air-conditioning plant. Introducing cooled fresh air and extracting the heated waste air enables the

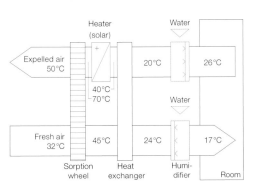

B 4.80

| Rated cooling capacity [kW] | Minimum space rqmts. for... | | Height of room [m] |
	piston compressor [m²]	turbo-compressor [m²]	
20	8	–	2.20
50	12	–	2.50
100	20	–	3.00
250	30	50	3.50
500	45	60	4.00
750	–	70	4.20
1000	–	80	4.50
1500	–	100	4.80
2000	–	110	5.00

Apart from access to all sides for maintenance work, a space about 0.8 times the length of the unit should be reserved adjacent to the unit for extracting the pipe battery.

B 4.81

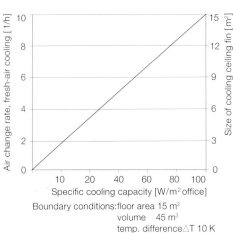

Boundary conditions: floor area 15 m²
volume 45 m³
temp. difference△T 10 K

B 4.82

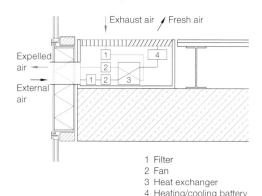

1 Filter
2 Fan
3 Heat exchanger
4 Heating/cooling battery

B 4.83

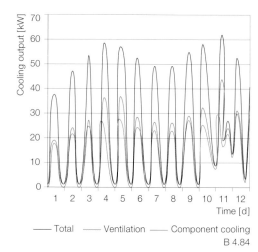

—— Total —— Ventilation —— Component cooling

B 4.84

interior climate to be controlled. A copious flow of air is required, especially in the case of high cooling loads, and this has repercussions for the sizing of the system (driving energy, costs, space requirements).

Air cooling is sensible when high air change rates are required for hygiene purposes anyway (e.g. theatre auditorium). In addition, the integration of cooling requirements into the air supply enables the fresh air to be dehumidified and the use of adiabatic cooling.

Alternatively, or in addition, cooling energy can be distributed via a network of water-filled pipes, just like for heating. These pipes, too, must be insulated in order to prevent condensation due to the low temperatures. Water-filled systems are common in office buildings.

Cooling output

Even though in physical terms the cooling of a building requires the dissipation of heat, we still speak of cooling output when describing the interface in the room. Like with the distribution of heat, it is important to make sure that no noticeable radiation asymmetry or draught phenomena occur which could impair the thermal comfort. Air or water cooling is possible depending on the type of distribution.

Air cooling

To avoid cold draughts, great care must be taken with the routing, distribution and velocity of

cooled fresh air when introducing it into a room. Two concepts have become established for air cooling: mixing and displacement ventilation (Fig. B 4.93).

In mixing ventilation (also known as dilution ventilation), the fresh air is introduced into the room via highly inductive air inlets (e.g. ceiling outlets, long-range nozzles) so that the high entry velocity causes it to mix thoroughly with the existing air in the room. The positioning and design of the inlets should be chosen so that all the air in the room is moved by way of gentle turbulence – without any unpleasant draughts. Extraction is usually at floor level. Very high cooling rates of more than 60 W/m² are possible with this system.

Where the cooling loads to be handled by the fresh air are low (< 30 W/m²), displacement ventilation represents an alternative. This way of introducing the fresh air enables higher thermal comfort demands to be met. The fresh air is fed in at floor level with a very low velocity (low flow rate). It warms up due to the heat loads in the room and rises gently upwards, where it is extracted. For higher cooling loads, displacement ventilation can be combined with a water-filled system.

Water cooling

In principle, the same requirements apply to heat output surfaces with water cooling as for heat output. For cooling, the surface tempera-

tures (approx. 15–18°C) must always lie above the dew point temperature of the interior air in order to avoid condensation. This means that the achievable cooling capacity is limited. The following cooling output systems are available:

· Cooling fins
· Convector fans
· Underfloor heating
· Activation of building components

Cooling fins are very frequently employed to dissipate cooling loads via water-filled pipes. They mostly consist of flat metal plates connected to the network of cold-water pipes. The cool surface undergoes a radiation exchange with the interior and enables heat to be dissipated without air circulation. Cooling fins are normally installed at soffit level and can be integrated into suspended ceiling systems. Convectors, too, can be used for cooling the interior. When fitted at floor level (e.g. underfloor convectors), a fan is necessary to force the air cooled in the convector into the room, either by way of recirculating air operation or with a connection to the outside air (Fig. B 4.83). Underfloor heating can instead be used to dissipate heat in the summer. In principle, this has the same effect as the cooling fin, although the capacity is much lower. In addition, cooling the floor is not so good for thermal comfort as cooling the ceiling.

	Reducing the air treatment
	Minimising the quantity of air
Optimising mechanical ventilation	Optimising the air management
	Optimising the driving energy
	Recovery of heating or cooling energy

B 4.85

Usage	Examples	External air flow rate per person per m²	
		[m³/h]	[m³/h]
Working	Separate office	40	4
	Open-plan office	60	6
Places of assembly	Concert hall Theatre Conference room	20	10–20
Residential	Apartment	no data	no data
	Hotel bedroom	no data	no data
Educational	Classroom	30	15
	Lecture theatre	30	15
	Reading room	20	12
Spaces accessible to the public	Sales area	20	3–12
	Restaurant	30	8

B 4.86

Usage		Air change rate [1/h]
Office		4–8
Computer centre		> 30
Restaurant	- smokers' area	6–12
	- non-smokers' area	4–8
Indoor swimming pool	- pool area	3–6
	- showers	10–15
	- changing rooms	8–10
Lecture theatre, conference room		6–8
Canteen		6–8
Cinema, theatre		4–8
Hospital	- patients' rooms	3–5
	- operating theatres	5–20
Industrial kitchen		15–30
Shop, sales area		4–8
Museum		4–6
School (classroom)		4–5
Sports hall		2–3
Residential		0.5

B 4.87

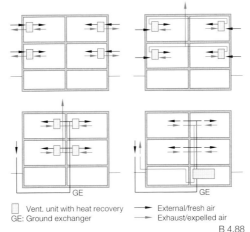

Vent. unit with heat recovery ⟶ External/fresh air
GE: Ground exchanger ⟶ Exhaust/expelled air

B 4.88

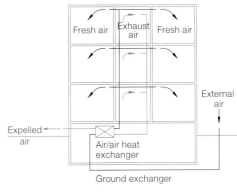

B 4.89

Activation of building components has become standard in recent years, especially for office buildings. Incorporating grids of pipes in solid components (mostly reinforced concrete suspended floors) enables a very high thermal mass to be activated for conditioning the interior climate (see p. 127). The cooling capacity is, however, limited (< 50 W/m²) and this system reacts very sluggishly owing to the large thermal mass. With an optimised building envelope design and low internal loads, cooling solely via activation of building components can, however, prove adequate, provided night purging is possible. In addition, the system can be supplemented by, for example, local cooling fins or cooling of the incoming air in the case of high loads (Fig. B 4.84).

Mechanical ventilation

Ventilation systems are designed to guarantee optimum air quality in buildings with minimum use of technical apparatus and energy. Wherever possible, natural ventilation should be used – coordinated with the needs of users and occupants (see "Building envelope", p. 99). The reasons for installing mechanical ventilation are diverse and range from statutory requirements to comfort demands and energy efficiency (heat recovery). There are several approaches that can be employed for the energy-efficiency optimisation of mechanical ventilation systems (Fig. B 4.85):

- Reducing the air treatment
- Minimising the quantity of air
- Optimising the air management
- Optimising the air feeding
- Recovery of heating or cooling energy

Requirements and sizing

In principle, there are four types of technical air treatment: heating, cooling, humidifying and dehumidifying. Only when all four types of treatment are available do we speak of air conditioning. As every air treatment method involves an energy input, the level of requirements must be discussed in detail with the user, explaining the associated consequences, when designing an optimum system. Heating

the incoming air is advisable in most cases, cooling, too, if the specification demands this. Regulating the humidity is especially important from the energy viewpoint because in conventional systems electrical evaporation or electrical cooling to below the dew point leads to a considerable electricity consumption. Limited humidification of the fresh air – with only minimal energy input – is also possible via moisture recovery. If a compromise is therefore made with respect to adhering to specified limiting values for the air humidity, which is possible in many cases (and also advantageous from the hygiene viewpoint), substantial savings are feasible. The key question here concerns the type of heating or cooling provision. The aim is to provide unavoidable energy services as far as possible completely through renewable energy sources.

Air flow rates

DIN EN 13779 specifies various methods for calculating the flow rate required. Parameters can be used for the incoming air flow rate in order to guarantee good interior air quality (Fig. B 4.86). The hourly air change rate is related to the number of persons or the usable floor area, but an hourly air change rate related to the volume of the interior space can be specified (Fig. B 4.87). These are not stipulations, but rather empirical values that have proved sensible. Another criterion for determining the flow rate is

Flow rate [m²]	Height of room [m²]	Supply and extract system[1] H[2] [m³/h]	HC[2] [m]	HCHu[2] [m²]	Extract air w/o[3] [m²]
10 000	3.00	30	50–60	65–75	20
25 000	3.50	35–40	65–80	85–100	25
50 000	4.00	50–60	90–110	120–140	35–40
75 000	4.50	65–80	120–145	155–180	40–55
100 000	5.00	80–100	150–180	190–220	50–70
150 000	6.30	110–140	210–250	260–300	70–100

[1] The higher values for space requirements apply when there is only one unit in the room; the lower values apply when there are several units in one room.
[2] H = heating; C = cooling; Hu = humidifying
[3] w/o = without thermodynamic air treatment
[4] Designations used for air velocities:
in room: v [m/s], in duct: w [m/s]

Calculation of duct cross-section

$$A = \frac{V_h}{w \cdot 3600}$$

A = duct cross-section [m² = 10 000 cm²]
w = air velocity in duct [m/s]
V_h = flow rate (quantity of air) [m³/h]

$$A = \frac{d^2 \cdot \pi}{4}$$

$$A = b \cdot h$$

Max. air velocity at inlet grille

Positions of air outlets	Air velocity v [m/s] [4]
near the floor	0.2–0.3
at head height	≤0.15
Ceiling outlets height of room = 3.0 m	≤2.0
height of room = 3.5 m	≤2.5
height of room = 4.0 m	≤3.0

Air velocities in ducts		
Low-pressure system	Air velocity w [m/s] [4] for comfort	for industry
External air	2–3	4–6
Main ducts	4–8	8–12
Branch ducts	3–5	5–8
Exhaust/recirculating air grille	2–3	3–4

B 4.90

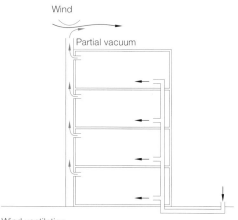

Wind

Partial vacuum

Wind ventilation

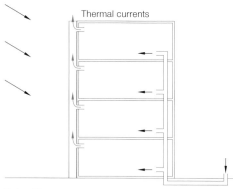

B 4.91

Thermal currents

Solar chimney

B 4.92

the perceived air quality in decipol or the concentration of hazardous substances in the interior air (workplace limit values). Careful, detailed planning of the interior areas and the fitting-out can lead to a reduction in the air flow rate necessary. The CO_2 content of the interior air is another important parameter for the flow rate. Ventilation control related to the CO_2 value can be advisable for flexible usage with a high occupancy density (e.g. schools) in particular. As the capacity of the ventilation system increases, so does its space requirements as well. Rough sizes for the duct cross-sections and the space requirements for the ventilation plant resulting from the air flow rates required can be estimated with parameters (Fig. B 4.90).

Conditioning
An air-conditioning installation can be used to maintain temperature and humidity limit values in addition to a given air change rate. The size of the installation required depends on the heating and/or cooling requirements. The air flow rate necessary is determined from the thermal requirements taking into account the specific heat capacity of air. Depending on those requirements, this can lead to a very high air flow rate, which has a direct effect on the size of the installation and the corresponding energy consumption. Therefore, the aim should be to limit the air flow rate to that required for hygiene purposes. Heating and cooling requirements that cannot be covered by this can then be supplied by supplementary systems (e.g. radiators, cooling fins, etc.).

Air management and driving energy
One essential feature of mechanical ventilation is the predetermined air management, which takes place in suitable ducts. In principle, a defined air change rate must be guaranteed by the system, which can be accomplished in various ways by different technical and constructional measures.
An extract-only system is the simplest variation. Here, an exchange of air is guaranteed by make-up air flowing via inlets into the ensuing partial vacuum in the interior (e.g. bathroom ventilation). Carefully planned inlets for make-

up air in the facade can guarantee a good distribution of air for an extract system, but preheating of the incoming fresh air, e.g. in a ground exchanger, is not possible. The opposite of this, a supply-only system, is also conceivable. Here, an exchange of air is guaranteed by an overpressure, like ventilation in cars. Concepts employing mechanical fresh-air management can include filters, which leads to better air quality but entails regular maintenance and cleaning or replacement of the filters. A controlled combination of the two systems is installed in the majority of instances. In residential buildings, such systems supply air only to living rooms, bedrooms, workrooms, etc. (Fig. B 4.89). The air flows via door or wall openings into the sanitary and kitchen areas, from where the exhaust air is extracted. Ventilation units for apartments or small detached houses can be accommodated in wall cupboards or behind suspended ceilings in hallways or corridors. Various concepts with respect to number and positioning of ventilation units are possible in multi-occupancy residential buildings (Fig. B 4.88).
Numerous air management options are possible for non-residential buildings, which range from central plants to decentralised, facade-mounted units (Fig. B 4.93). Besides user requirements, conceptual boundary conditions such as building depth, atrium or double-leaf facade play a major role in deciding on a solution (see "Building envelope", p. 101). A decentralised ventilation concept via the facade minimises, for example, the costs for air management. Such concepts mean that vertical shafts are usually unnecessary and in high-rise buildings in particular this leads to much better use of the floor space. in some circumstances the omission of horizontal ducts can mean that additional floors are possible without increasing the height of the building. On the other hand, a high number of individual units and the associated servicing costs can be a disadvantage. And decentralised systems cannot be linked to a ground exchanger. The positioning of the air intakes must be carefully planned; the outside air should be drawn in from areas with permanently good air quality which are also shaded

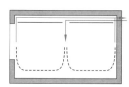

Mixing ventilation, tangential

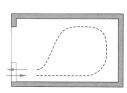

Mixing ventilation, radial

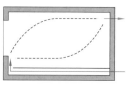

Displacement ventilation, single inlet/outlet

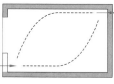

Facade-mounted ventilation unit with central extraction

Facade-mounted ventilation unit with decentralised extraction

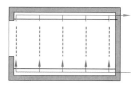

Displacement ventilation, multiple inlets/outlets

B 4.93

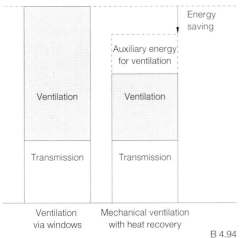

Ventilation via windows | Mechanical ventilation with heat recovery

B 4.94

1 Fan
2 Air condenser
3 Evaporator
4 Compressor
5 Additional heating
6 Water condenser
7 Coil (heat exchanger)
8 Expelled air
9 Exhaust air
10 External air
11 Fresh air
12 Air/air heat exchanger

B 4.95

B 4.96

in summer to minimise solar cooling loads. Likewise, the exhaust-air outlets must be positioned so that no disturbing noises or odours ensue and there is no airflow "short-circuit" between outlets and inlets.

Actuating the ventilation
Various methods can be employed to induce a flow of air. They differ considerably with respect to the energy requirements and architectural repercussions:

• Wind
• Thermal currents
• Fans

High-rise buildings can make use of natural wind movements to actuate the building ventilation. This requires a suitable building form or elements that create a partial vacuum due to wind suction. Various principles, e.g. "wind towers" or "venturi spoilers", can be used (Figs. B 3.78 and 4.91).
Exploiting thermal currents is a very old method of inducing air circulation. The pressure differences between cold and hot air lead to airflows that can be used specifically for the building ventilation. This effect is amplified as the temperature gradient and height of the building increase. Tall internal spaces, e.g. atria or double-leaf facades, where high air temperatures can be reached in the upper zones, are ideal for

exploiting thermal currents. The integration into a system of air ducts calls for a high, constant partial vacuum, which can be achieved with a solar chimney, for example (Fig. B 4.92). The inclusion of thermal masses enables a phase lag between solar radiation and thermal currents, which thus prolongs the period of use. Electric fans are generally used to guarantee constant, fully controllable air circulation. Several types are available, which differ – sometimes considerably – in terms of their efficiency: radial, axial and cross-flow fans. The radial (or centrifugal) fan is the most common, offering high efficiency, high capacity and diverse installation options. The flow characteristics of the duct system have a considerable influence on the fan output required. Large, round or rounded cross-sections, smooth surfaces and few changes of direction result in a low resistance to the flow. The energy requirements for fans can represent a considerable factor in the total energy balance because the full-load hours of a ventilation system can reach high figures. The use of efficient motors, bypass circuits and controls that reflect users' requirements are therefore important optimisation parameters.

Recovery of heat, cooling energy and moisture
Ventilation heat losses normally represent a significant item in the energy balance of a building. During the heating period, considera-

ble heating potential is lost through ventilation via the windows or via extract-air systems; in well-insulated buildings, the ventilation heat losses account for the majority of such losses (Fig. B 4.94). Energy-efficient ventilation therefore demands a controlled supply and extract system with integral heat exchanger (Fig. B 4.96). With degrees of efficiency sometimes exceeding 90%, the ventilation heat losses can be almost completely avoided. In non-residential buildings, high air change rates make heat recovery especially important. When cooling is required, a heat exchanger can "recover the cold" from the exhaust air. There are various methods for the technical implementation of heat recovery (Fig. B 4.97):

• In a cross-flow heat exchanger the fresh air and expelled air are fed through special, adjacent systems of ducts with a large surface area, which results in a heat flow from the cold to the warm airflow without the two being mixed.
• The counter-flow heat exchanger has a somewhat higher degree of efficiency because the use of larger contact surfaces leads to a prolonged heat exchange.
• If fresh air and expelled air do not coincide, the heat potential of the exhaust air can also be recovered indirectly via an extract-air heat pump. Alternatively, the heat transfer can be achieved over long distances by using an

Designation	Cross-flow heat exchanger	Counter-flow heat exchanger	Run-around coil	Rotary heat exchanger with/without hygroscopic storage mass
Arrangement				
Heat recovery	up to 60%	up to 90%	up to 50%	up to 80%
Moisture recovery	no moisture exchange	no moisture exchange	no moisture exchange	up to 70%

B 4.97

B 4.91 Use of wind energy for building ventilation, office building, Hertfordshire (GB), 1996, Feilden Clegg Architects
B 4.92 Solar chimney integrated into facade for building ventilation, Oeste de San Fermin, Madrid (E), 2003, Mario Muelas Jimenez & Agustin Mateo Ortega
B 4.93 Types of mechanical ventilation for offices
B 4.94 Potential savings through the use of heat recovery in residential buildings
B 4.95 Compact ventilation unit for a residential building, with heat recovery, integral air heat pump and water tank
B 4.96 Supply- and extract-air unit with cross-flow heat exchanger
B 4.97 The principles for heat recovery in ventilation systems

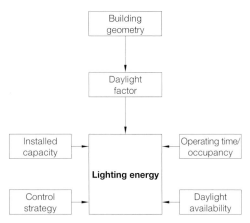

B 4.98

Variable Symbol	Designation Relationship	Unit Abbreviation
Luminous flux Φ	output of light source	lumen lm
Luminous efficacy $\eta = \Phi/P$	$\dfrac{\text{luminous flux}}{\text{electrical power}}$	lumen/watt lm/W
Quantity of light $Q = \Phi \cdot t$	$\dfrac{\text{luminous flux}}{\times \text{ time}}$	lumen-hour lm-h
Illuminance $I = \Phi/\omega$	$\dfrac{\text{luminous flux}}{\text{solid angle}}$	candela cd
Luminous intensity E	$\dfrac{\text{luminous flux}}{\text{size of area}}$	lux $lx = lm/m^2$
Luminance L	$\dfrac{\text{illuminance}}{\text{visible area}}$	candela/m² cd/m²
Degree of reflection	reflection of light	%

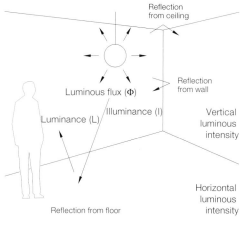

B 4.99

additional brine circuit, a so-called run-around coil; the degree of efficiency is, however, much lower than with direct heat recovery owing to the doubling of the heat exchange mechanism (air/brine and brine/air).

- The heat transfer in a rotary heat exchanger is by way of a revolving thermal mass which revolves alternately in the fresh-air and expelled-air ducts. Employing hygroscopic materials in this system enables moisture recovery as well.

Optimising the artificial lighting

The objective of planning the lighting is to achieve maximum daylight autonomy through the conceptual optimisation of the building (see "Building envelope", p. 102). Furthermore, it must also be possible to use the building irrespective of the amount of daylight available. In some cases the use of daylight is impossible or even undesirable, and in those situations it is important to guarantee artificial lighting adequate for the type of usage which at the same time uses as little energy as possible (Fig. B 4.98).
Numerous computer programs, which can simulate the daylighting and artificial lighting conditions in the building with considerable accuracy, are available to assist with the planning. Important factors here are colour distortion,

freedom from glare and good contrast (see "Fundamentals", p. 58). In essence, three levels of planning are relevant for energy-efficiency optimisation of the lighting concept: lighting technology, lighting concept and lighting automation.

Lighting technology

Human beings perceive their surroundings primarily via their sense of vision and this is ideally assisted by sunlight. The aim of lighting technology is therefore to emulate this quality as closely as possible by converting electrical energy into electromagnetic oscillations that upon striking a material are reflected into the human eye to be perceived as light.

Parameters
The following parameters are particularly important for describing and evaluating lighting systems (Fig. B 4.99):

- The luminous flux describes the effectiveness of a light source and specifies the total lighting power emitted in all directions; this value forms the basis for all further parameters.
- The luminous efficacy describes the ratio of the luminous flux to the electrical power used and hence specifies the efficiency of the light source.
- The quantity of light represents the luminous flux emitted over a defined period of time.

- The illuminance (illumination) specifies the luminous flux incident on a defined surface (e.g. desktop).
- The luminous intensity (candela) is the proportion of luminous flux related to a defined direction of emission and angle. It therefore depends on the structure of the light source and, if applicable, on influencing layers (e.g. diffusing etc.). For an assessment, the distribution of luminous intensity of a light source can be projected graphically onto a surface.
- The luminance describes an observer's impression of brightness of a light source or an illuminated surface; it is the quotient of luminous intensity and surface area.

Lamps
Artificial light sources are called lamps (also bulbs). The choice of lamp has a decisive influence on the electricity requirements. The efficiency (luminous efficacy) in lumens per watt of connected power can differ considerably (Fig. B 4.101). Added to this is the fact that a low luminous efficacy at the same time means a large heat development with a corresponding influence on the internal heat load of a building. Furthermore, the technical service life is significant for an ecological and economic assessment.

Use of room, activity	$\overline{E}_m$ [lx]
Circulation zones and general areas in buildings	
Circulation areas and corridors	100
Canteens, tea kitchens	200
Sanitary facilities	500
Storage rooms	100
Offices	
Filing and copying, circulation zones	300
Writing, reading, data processing	500
Technical drawing	750
Offices	
Storage rooms	50–200
Offices, oriented for daylight	300
Offices, standard	500
Open-plan offices	750–1000

Use of room, activity	$\overline{E}_m$ [lx]
Retail premises	
Sales areas	300
Public areas	
Parking zones	75
Entrance halls	100
Kitchens	500
Conference rooms	500
Educational establishments	
Playrooms, nursery rooms	300
Classrooms in primary and secondary schools	300
Lecture theatres, classrooms for evening classes and adult education	500
Libraries: bookshelves	200
Libraries: reading areas	500

B 4.100

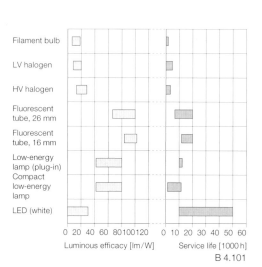

B 4.101

Light fittings

Light fittings are systems designed to accommodate lamps. Besides their function as an electrical interface, light fittings influence the lighting technology characteristics of the lamp to a considerable extent. As yet there are no standardised energy-efficiency classes for complete lighting systems. The light fitting efficiency factor is used for the assessment, which, similar to the luminous efficacy, specifies the luminous flux (in lumens) that the total system emits per watt of electrical power. Alternatively, the degree of efficiency for the operation of the light fitting can be used for the assessment, which is an indication of the energy efficiency of a light fitting and takes into account lamp, electronics, lampholder, reflectors and housing properties. The meaningfulness of this is, however, limited because the direction of the light beam is ignored. A lamp with a high degree of efficiency for the operation of the light fitting can, for example, be inefficient in terms of energy if it supplies purely indirect lighting. In order to assess this, the quotient of the connected power should be compared with the illuminance.

Lighting concept

The lighting in buildings has a great influence on the quality of the interior (Fig. B 4.100). For working situations in particular, a good level of illumination has a positive effect on our power of vision and efficiency. An important parameter for the energy requirement of artificial lighting is the installed lighting power with respect to the usable floor space (in W/m²). Clear differences are evident in practice. The installed lighting power has a huge impact on energy requirements owing to the, usually, high number of full-load hours. Minimising this to a compulsory, necessary level reduces not only the energy consumption, but also the building costs. We distinguish here between the following types of lighting concept:

• Amenity lighting for a homogeneous illumination of functional areas without any special demands (e.g. circulation zones, basic lighting for areas with variable usage)
• Task lighting for specific functions with defined requirements (e.g. working places)
• Decorative lighting, which often does not supply any lighting power needed for lighting purposes, but is required simply to influence the interior atmosphere or to highlight individual zones.

Direct and indirect lighting

We distinguish between direct and indirect lighting plus a combination of the two when describing the type of lighting. Indirect lighting has a positive effect on the interior and is frequently perceived as agreeable because it results in a lighting situation with fewer shadows and less glare. But in order to achieve the desired illuminance, a much higher installed

lighting power is necessary than is the case with direct lighting, which leads to a correspondingly higher energy consumption. A sensible solution for working places is therefore a combination of indirect general lighting and local, direct lighting of the working area itself (Fig. B 4.104). This also helps to create an interesting lighting situation and reduce the fatigue phenomena associated with uniform illumination.

Interior surfaces

An interior design with bright and/or reflective surfaces assists the lighting concept. The reflection component, or vice versa the loss of luminance due to absorption by surfaces, varies greatly depending on material and colour. Appropriate planning can help to achieve the necessary illuminance with a lower installed lighting power, which is particularly important in the case of a large amount of indirect lighting.

Task lighting

Differentiated artificial lighting with zones having different illumination levels is frequently regarded as adequate for work situations and less fatiguing. Planning for task lighting also enables the installed lighting power to be minimised and hence has a positive influence on the energy consumption. However, the high specification should be coordinated with demands for flexible usage.

Lighting automation

The primary aim of automation is to improve the convenience for users. But in addition, automation can help to achieve good savings in the electricity consumed by the lighting by reducing the number of full-load hours (Figs. B. 4.102 and 4.103). The degree of automation will always represent a compromise between energy savings and user satisfaction. Optimised controls respond sensitively to the needs of users and prevent the impression of a controlling body. It is advisable to differentiate between zones for general or public use (e.g. circulation areas, sanitary facilities, etc.) and those for individual usage with a need for manual control (e.g. offices for one or two persons).

Occupancy-related automation

The lighting can be controlled automatically depending on the presence of persons, e.g. by movement detectors. This technology offers considerable potential savings for areas used purely temporarily (e.g. circulation zones, sanitary facilities) in particular.

B 4.98 Factors affecting the energy requirement for artificial light
B 4.99 Parameters for lighting technology
B 4.100 Recommended luminous intensity levels for different uses to DIN EN 12464-1
B 4.101 Comparison of the luminous efficacy and service lives of various lamps
B 4.102 Diagram for the rough calculation of the full-load hours for lighting in offices
B 4.103 Examples of measurements to determine how lighting automation affects the energy consumption
B 4.104 Office situation with indirect amenity lighting and direct light source for the workplace, office building, Stockholm (S), 1998, Jakob Zeilon Architekten

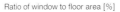
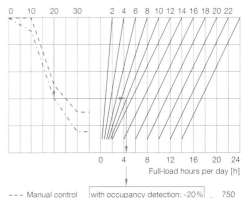

- - - Manual control
- · - Daylight control

with occupancy detection: -20%
working days per year: 200

750 h/a

B 4.102

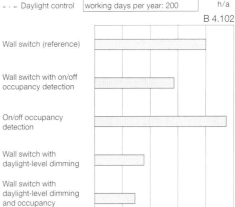

Wall switch (reference)
Wall switch with on/off occupancy detection
On/off occupancy detection
Wall switch with daylight-level dimming
Wall switch with daylight-level dimming and occupancy detection

Annual lighting energy requirement [%]

B 4.103

B 4.104

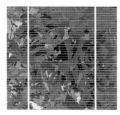
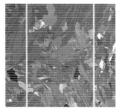

B 4.105

B 4.105   Examples of colours for polycrystalline solar cells
B 4.106   Primary energy requirement for residential and
          office buildings
B 4.107   Schematic diagram of electricity generation
          a   central
          b   decentralised
B 4.108   How a crystalline solar cell works
B 4.109   Structure and possible sequences of layers in
          photovoltaic modules
B 4.110   Solar cells available on the market and their
          parameters

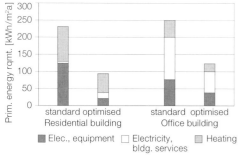

Elec., equipment   Electricity,   Heating
                   bldg. services

B 4.106

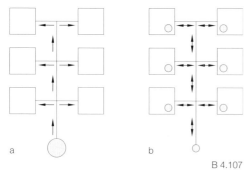

○ Electricity generation
□ Electricity consumption

a   b

B 4.107

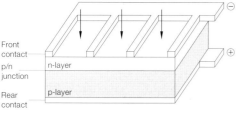

Front
contact
p/n   n-layer
junction
Rear   p-layer
contact

B 4.108

Brightness-related automation
Alternatively, or in addition, the lighting can be controlled automatically depending on daylight levels. The lighting power can be regulated radically (on/off) or gradually (dimming, daylight supplement lighting). The effects are severely limited in places of work with a very high daylight component and in areas without any daylight, but the opportunities are very good for those zones with an average amount of daylight.

Generating electricity

In physical terms, electricity is the highest form of energy because it can be converted into all other forms of energy (force, heat, etc.). Its diverse applications have made it indispensable in virtually all facets of modern life. And this is particularly true for the operation of buildings (Fig. B 4.106). Its rational use is verified in Europe by determining the total energy efficiency of a building – up until now only in the form of auxiliary energy for providing heat in the case of residential buildings, but for lighting, ventilation and cooling as well in non-residential buildings (see "Strategies", p. 184).
Throughout the world, electricity generation is mainly carried out in central power stations fired by fossil fuels or nuclear energy. Distribution is by way of corresponding networks (grids) with different voltage levels. The electricity sector is undergoing a period of upheaval, especially in Europe, which is promoting the expansion of renewable energy in the sense of sustainable energy provision. Besides hydroelectric power, wind power has evolved into another pillar of electricity generation in recent decades, which, on the whole, has led to a restructuring of the energy sector – towards more decentralised energy production. An electricity industry based on renewable energy therefore has a large number of small, different energy producers at its disposal. Through its distribution function, the electricity grid can assume a management task and coordinate the balance between generation and consumption (Fig. B 4.107). The planning of buildings plays a decisive role in this context. Besides minimising the electricity requirements, every building must be checked as to whether and to what extent the building itself could generate electricity. Instead of being a pure consumer, it can become a productive element for the energy sector. In the ideal case, the building can generate its entire electricity requirements. And the prime consideration here is not to operate the building independently of the electricity grid, but rather to achieve a balanced energy audit for the whole year (Fig. B 4.118). Photovoltaics and combined heat and power represent fully developed systems that can be used for decentralised electricity generation in direct connection with the planning of the building. There are also other important technologies that up to now have not been incorporated in buildings but exhibit valu-

able potential for future developments (see p. 144).

Photovoltaics

Photovoltaics designates the process of generating electricity directly from sunlight. The term is derived from the Greek word *phos*, meaning light, and the Italian physicist Alessandro Graf von Volta, who gave his name to the unit of electrical voltage. The discovery of the "photovoltaic effect" can be traced back to the 19th century and the work of the physicist Alexandre Edmond Becquerel. Nevertheless, it was not until the middle of the 20th century that workable photovoltaic systems were developed, and then initially only for applications in outer space. The first terrestrial pilot installations were built in the 1970s. The focus of photovoltaic applications for buildings is their constructional and architectural integration into the building envelope. The aim of these developments is to achieve harmonious overall concepts in which that part of the building services visible externally (photovoltaic module) also provides important building and aesthetic functions (see "Building envelope", p. 108).

How the system works
Photovoltaic electricity generation is based on the so-called photoelectric effect. This means the transfer of energy contained in the photons of sunlight to electrons in physical matter. This gives rise to a voltage in specially prepared semiconductor materials which can be used in an electric circuit. The electrical conductivity of a material is defined by the size of the energy gap between the valence and conduction bands, which is a criterion defining which external energy effect is required for a flow of electrons in a body. In conductive materials (e.g. copper), the conduction band is either only partly occupied (electrons can move freely within the body) or the valence and conduction bands overlap. If the energy gap is more than 5 eV (electron volt), the specific electrical resistance is so great that we speak of an insulator. The semiconductor materials for solar cells occupy an area between these two extremes. They are potential conductors which, however, develop the ability to allow a flow of electrons only under certain conditions (Fig. B 4.108).

Solar cells
Solar cells are divided into various categories and designated according to their structure and the materials used (Fig. B 4.110). Silicon (Si) is a suitable material for solar cells, and the majority of those in use today are made from this. We make a basic distinction between crystalline cells, which have been produced since the 1950s, and the newer thin-film cells. The classical way of producing monocrystalline cells is to cut a specially produced silicon rod (boule) into thin circular wafers. In order to distribute the cells more effectively over an area, they are usually trimmed to form hexagons or squares. Other methods of manufacture, in

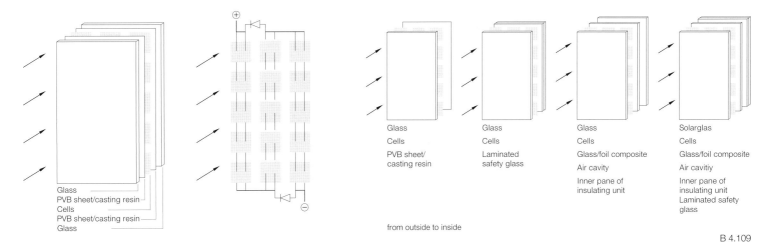

Glass
Cells
PVB sheet/
casting resin

Glass
Cells
Laminated
safety glass

Glass
Cells
Glass/foil composite
Air cavity
Inner pane of
insulating unit

Solarglas
Cells
Glass/foil composite
Air cavitiy
Inner pane of
insulating unit
Laminated safety
glass

Glass
PVB sheet/casting resin
Cells
PVB sheet/casting resin
Glass

from outside to inside

B 4.109

which the silicon is cast into blocks, produce square formats directly. The cooling process produces many individual crystals, which is why these are known as polycrystalline cells. The size of crystalline cells depends on their thickness. With a minimum cell thickness, dimensions between 100 x 100 mm and 150 x 150 mm have proved practical. Changes to the anti-reflection coating mean that crystalline solar cells can now be produced in colours other than blue and black, which do, however, produce the maximum yield (Fig. B 4.105). Solar cells made from amorphous silicon led to the development of thin-film technology in the 1970s. The material is applied directly to a backing of glass, metal or plastic, which means that considerable amounts of materials and energy can be saved during manufacture. Recently, further semiconductor compounds, e.g. cadmium-telluride (CdTe) or copper-indium-selenium (CIS), have been used. Using this thin-film technology, the size and form of these cells is no longer dependent on the dimensions of the backing material and the desired electrical properties can be chosen to suit, which results in huge design freedoms. Owing to the existing manufacturing capacities, crystalline solar cells will continue to play a dominant role, but the significance of thin-film technology will grow owing to the low materials requirements and the high cost-savings potential (Figs. B 4.114 and 4.116).

Parameters
One essential selection criterion for solar cells is their degree of electrical efficiency, which specifies (as a percentage) how much of the solar radiation incident on the cell is converted into electrical current. The degree of efficiency is heavily dependent on material and cell structure. As the energy content of the photons in the spectrum of sunlight differs considerably depending on the frequency, some photons do not have the energy required to cross the energy gap, whereas other photons have more energy potential than is necessary, which also remains unused. Therefore, for physical reasons, it is not possible to convert the entire incident solar radiation into electricity. Depending on the cell material and the energy gaps, a theoretical maximum degree of efficiency of approx. 30% is possible for silicon, for instance. Using a multi-layer structure, higher degrees of efficiency could be achieved. Conventional solar cells achieve values between about 8% (amorphous silicon) and 17% (monocrystalline silicon). The degree of efficiency in operation is also dependent on the temperature of the solar cell, with a higher temperature leading to a lower degree of efficiency.

As solar cells are always combined to form suitable powerful modules, it is only the degree of efficiency of the module that counts in practice. Once again, this depends on the cell technology, but also on the number of cells per unit area in particular. The "performance ratio" is used to assess the total system – the ratio of the energy generated to the rated output of the modules based on the incident radiation.

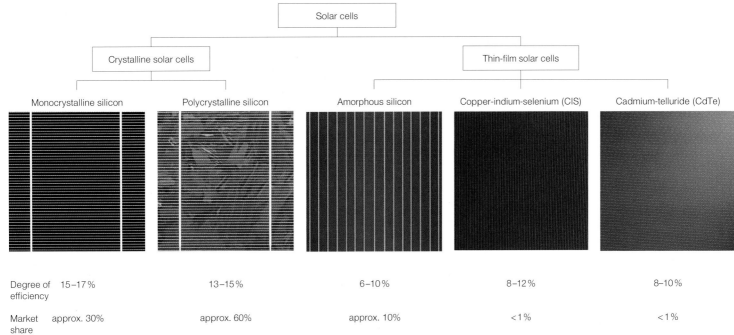

	Monocrystalline silicon	Polycrystalline silicon	Amorphous silicon	Copper-indium-selenium (CIS)	Cadmium-telluride (CdTe)
Degree of efficiency	15–17 %	13–15 %	6–10 %	8–12 %	8–10 %
Market share	approx. 30%	approx. 60%	approx. 10%	< 1 %	< 1 %

B 4.110

139

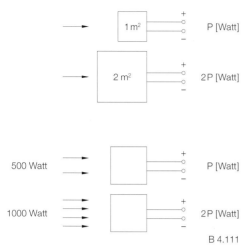

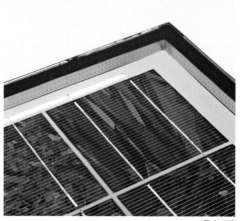

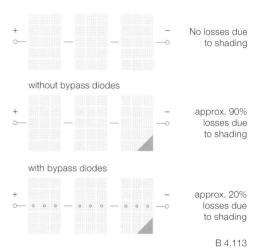

B 4.111

B 4.112

B 4.113

Photovoltaic modules

The output of a single solar cell is inadequate for most applications. In order to achieve sizes relevant for practical applications, they are connected – like batteries – in series and parallel and fitted with so-called bypass diodes to bridge over any (partially) shaded areas. To protect against mechanical damage and the vagaries of the weather, solar cells are embedded between covers front and back (Fig. B 4.109). This glass-glass or glass-plastic composite construction is then called a photovoltaic module. Solar cells are handled differently according to their method of manufacture:
Crystalline cells can be arranged as single pieces almost at random in the module, but

there must be a minimum insulating distance between them. Thin-film cells are produced together with a backing material and are normally arranged to cover a whole area. The cell structure required and the electrical circuitry is carried out directly during the coating process. Most module manufacturers produce standard modules in sizes from about 0.5 to 1.5 m², always with fixed dimensions and output ratings that are conceived for a maximum energy output per unit area. Their fixed dimensions and forms mean, however, that their suitability for building envelopes is limited. Specialist companies can provide modules for demanding architectural integration concepts which can be manufactured according to the architect's geo-

metrical and design specifications (Fig. B 4.115). In principle, the shapes, sizes and technical parameters possible are the same as those for conventional glasses for the building sector. The technology used means that the maximum size of a photovoltaic module with crystalline solar cells is currently limited to approx. 6 m². Individual thin-film modules can be made in sizes up to about 1 m² at present and can be joined together in laminated glass units to form larger components.

Photovoltaic modules in the form of building components can take on many different additional functions and their appearance opens up a whole wealth of design options. Their colour can be changed, too. Maximum-yield standard crystalline cells are dark blue to black in order to achieve maximum sunlight absorption. But the anti-reflection coating can be changed to produce crystalline cells in other colours (Fig. B 4.105). Generally speaking, the lighter the colour, the greater is the (negative) effect on the output. The range of colours for thin-film cells is still limited: amorphous silicon is reddish brown, the CIS cell is black, the CdTe cell blackish green (Fig. B 4.110).
Flexible modules offer further options for the architectural integration. Metal foils, plastic films or transparent synthetic resins serve as backing materials. Bending radii as tight as 1.5 m are possible with crystalline solar cells mounted on such materials. Thin-film technology enables cell material to be applied directly to metal foils or plastic films, which enables very flexible modules to be produced (Fig. B 4.114). A special visual effect can be achieved with semi-transparent modules. Combining these with a backing of coloured glass or light-scattering or light-redirecting glasses enables such elements to influence the amount of incoming light and its distribution. Semi-transparent modules inevitably exhibit a lower output because of their permeability to light. There are essentially three methods for producing semi-transparent modules:

· Crystalline solar cells can be simply mounted at a larger spacing on the module so that light can pass between the cells. The amount of incoming light can be controlled by vary-

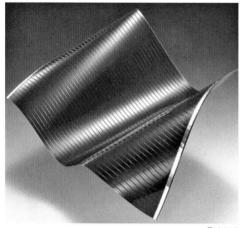

B 4.114

B 4.115

B 4.116

B 4.117

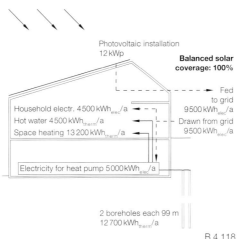

Photovoltaic installation
12 kWp

Balanced solar coverage: 100%

Household electr. 4500 kWh_elec/a
Hot water 4500 kWh_therm/a
Space heating 13 200 kWh_therm/a

Fed to grid 9500 kWh_elec/a
Drawn from grid 9500 kWh_elec/a

Electricity for heat pump 5000 kWh_elec/a

2 boreholes each 99 m
12 700 kWh_therm/a

B 4.118

ing the spacing. Such an arrangement means that the glazing can be used to provide daylight as well as generate electricity (Fig. B 4.117). The shadows cast in the interior are structured and rich in contrast – corresponding to the shape and layout of the cells.
- A mechanical method can be used to produce tiny perforations in the crystalline solar cells so that the cells themselves become semi-transparent. The light passing through the cells is diffuse.
- Thin-film modules made from amorphous silicon can be produced in a semi-transparent form by introducing fine lines or dots without cell material. The normal degree of light transmittance is approx. 20%. From a distance of a few metres, these modules appear like a completely uniform surface.

Inverters
In a photovoltaic installation connected to the electricity grid, the function of the inverter is to convert the direct current generated by the array of modules into alternating current suitable for the electricity grid. The geometry and arrangement of the photovoltaic modules determine the choice of inverter concept. Central inverters are only advisable for completely unshaded installations with a homogeneous orientation. Common today are modular inverter systems in which – taken to the limit – each

module has its own inverter and so failure of one module has no effect on the output of the other modules. The lengths of DC cabling in the building and the space requirements for one or more inverters, including access for maintenance, depend on the inverter system selected. The conversion of energy with an inverter is associated with losses, which in the best case are only 5%, at worst up to 15%. The positions of inverters should be specified at an early stage in order to guarantee access to them for maintenance and replacement during the life of the building.

Installation concepts
When designing the installation, it is important to know whether the building will be connected to the public electricity grid. We thus distinguish between stand-alone and grid-connected systems. Whereas the stand-alone system is intended to guarantee an autonomous electricity supply over the whole year, a building with a grid-connected system is also supplied with electricity from the public grid. The technical components required and the planning work differ depending on the type of system. In a stand-alone system, interim storage of electricity is necessary to cope with the fluctuating energy yield and consumption. In addition, the photovoltaic installation may need to be supplemented by other energy sources.

If a public electricity grid is available, interim storage is unnecessary. Excess electricity generated by solar power is then fed into the grid (for which the building owner is credited) or electricity is drawn from the grid as usual in the case of deficits. Almost all the photovoltaic systems installed throughout Europe are of the grid-connected variety. This simplifies the installation to two components: generator array (= sum of photovoltaic modules) and inverter(s) for converting the electricity generated into alternating current suitable for the grid. If the photovoltaic installation generates more electricity than is required in the building, the excess electricity is fed into the grid; the building becomes an energy supplier. If more electricity is required than can be generated by the building's photovoltaic system, the electricity required to make up the difference is drawn from the grid in the usual way. So electricity supplies are guaranteed at all times. In the event of generous financial remuneration for electricity produced by solar systems (e.g. in Germany guaranteed by the Renewable Energy Sources Act), the entire electricity yield is normally fed into the grid. The size of the photovoltaic installation in such a situation need not be matched to the requirements of the building, but instead could be designed according to geometrical, economic or architectural criteria. A comparison between generation and con-

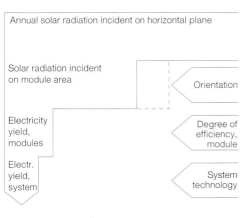

Annual solar radiation incident on horizontal plane

Solar radiation incident on module area

Orientation

Electricity yield, modules

Degree of efficiency, module

Electr. yield, system

System technology

Fed to grid

a

Solar cell technology	Solar electricity generation [kWh/m²_module a]		
	Oslo	Berlin	Thessaloniki
Crystalline monocrystalline polycrystalline	90-100	95-110	125-140
Thin-film CIS CdTe	60-75	65-80	90-110
Thin-film amorphous silicon	35-55	40-60	55-80
Translucent modules:	reduction according to light transmittance		

b

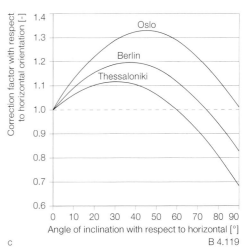

c

B 4.119

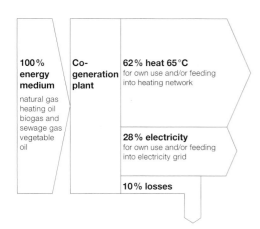

| 100% energy medium | Co-generation plant | 62% heat 65°C for own use and/or feeding into heating network |
| 28% electricity for own use and/or feeding into electricity grid |
| 10% losses |

natural gas
heating oil
biogas and
sewage gas
vegetable
oil

B 4.120

		i. c. engine	Diesel engine	Stirling engine	Fuel cell	Gas turbine
Electrical output	[kW]	1–5000	5–20000	1–40	1–250	30–250000[1]
Total degree of efficiency	[%]	up to 90	up to 90	up to 85	up to 90	up to 85
Elec. degree of efficiency	[%]	25–42	28–44	10–30	30–47	25–30
Power-to-heat ratio	[-]	0.4–1,1	0.5–1,1	0.4	0.3–0.7	0.3–0.6
Part-load behaviour		good	good	not so good	very good	not so good
Status of technology		proven	proven	small series	pilot plants	proven
Normal fuel		biogas, natural gas	vegetable oil, diesel	solar, wood	hydrogen, gas	biogas, natural gas

[1] Micro gas turbines up to approx. 200 kW

B 4.121

sumption – and hence the solar coverage feasible – is carried out here not physically but instead by way of an annual audit (Fig. B 4.118).

Yields
The yield per unit area depends in the first place on the incident solar radiation (location and orientation of modules) and the degree of efficiency of the photovoltaic installation as a whole. Depending on the type of cell and the number of cells per unit area, installations in Central Europe free from shade and with an ideal orientation can achieve annual specific yields of about 40 kWh/m² with semi-transparent thin-film modules. Using a maximum number of monocrystalline cells per unit area, annual yields of up to 130 kWh/m² are possible. Fig. B 4.119 shows the chain of losses in a photovoltaic system and parameters to enable rough estimates of the solar yields. Besides the orientation of the modules, freedom from shading is another crucial aspect. As solar cells and modules are wired in series, there is always a disproportionate decrease in yield even if only part of the array is in the shade (Fig. B 4.113).

Ecological aspects
The manufacture of photovoltaic elements requires high amounts of energy and so the energy-related payback time is an important ecological criterion. The main materials used when producing modules with cells made from silicon are glass and quartz sand, with installa-

tions using crystalline cells requiring considerably more than thin-film modules for the same energy output. Plastics have so far played a subsidiary role. Owing to the composite form of construction, the materials used are notoriously difficult to recycle. In an energy audit, the cumulative energy requirement for manufacture and operation is balanced against the usable energy yields of an installation. The energy-related payback times differ depending on type of cell, installation situation and location, and range from six months (thin-film technology, high yields) to four years (crystalline technology, moderate yields). The only emissions associated with photovoltaic installations are those associated with their manufacture. When integrating photovoltaic modules into the building envelope, the production energy of the materials used is considered as an energy "credit".

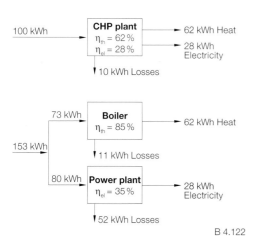

B 4.122

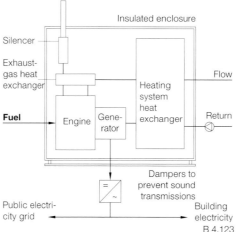

B 4.123

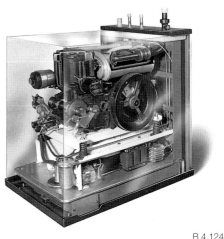

B 4.124

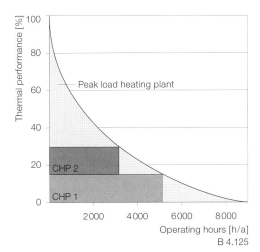

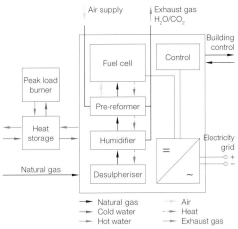

a

b

B 4.126

B 4.125

Combined heat and power

Combined heat and power (CHP) fuses generation of electricity and production of heat into one process (Figs. B 4.120 and 4.122). This principle grew out of electricity generation, where the conversion process inevitably leads to large quantities of waste heat, which can seldom be used in large power stations and entails additional cooling requirements with their corresponding negative ecological impacts such as raising the temperature of rivers etc. Only under favourable boundary conditions can the waste heat be fed into a district heating network.

An alternative popular at the moment is to arrange for the electricity to be generated decentrally, directly at the consumer. This approach enables CHP to be incorporated directly into the energy concept of a building or neighbourhood. Excess electricity is, like with photovoltaic systems, fed into the public electricity grid. Technologies based on various energy media are available for decentralised CHP (Fig. B 4.121). From the ecological viewpoint, renewable energy sources should be used whenever possible, e.g. biomass, hydrogen, waste heat or solar radiation.

Electricity from biomass

An electricity generator driven by a small engine is the most popular solution for decentralised CHP with biomass. The heat given off is integrated into the heating circuit via a heat

exchanger (Fig. B 4.123). Such setups are known as co-generation plants. Small plants (< 50 kW$_{elec}$), are referred to as mini co-generation plants (Fig. B 4.124). Internal combustion, diesel or gas engines can be used as the drive units. Rapeseed and soya oil have become established as fuels for modified diesel engines in biomass applications. One important parameter for CHP, besides the overall degree of efficiency, is the power-to-heat ratio. This specifies the amount of electrical energy generated per kilowatt-hour of heat emitted. A typical value for a decentralised co-generation plant is 0.5, i.e. 0.5 kWh of electricity is generated per kilowatt-hour of heat. In principle, a co-generation plant can be integrated for electricity or heating purposes. To improve the overall degree of efficiency, the control is usually based on the heating requirement. As co-generation plants are associated with a high capital outlay, many hours of operation per year should be the target. For this reason, they are not usually designed to cover peak loads on their own, but rather are designed for the basic heating load. Other heating plant is then required which can react flexibly to load fluctuations (Fig. B 4.125). Owing to their function as an electricity generator, in some cases a co-generation plant can replace an emergency generator unit required for safety or security reasons, which can improve the economic efficiency quite considerably.

Electricity from hydrogen

Besides the engines borrowed from the automotive industry, in future the fuel cell will become more significant for CHP setups. The fuel cell generates electricity by way of an electrochemical process, using hydrogen as the energy medium. With a decentralised application, the ensuing heat can be fed into a heating circuit just like in the case of a co-generation plant. The fuel cell requires hydrogen for its operation, which in the ideal case is produced using renewable energy and must be stored. As no suitable infrastructure exists for this, fuel cells are mainly operated using hydrogen obtained from natural gas at the moment (Fig. B 4.126). The hydrogen production/storage/usage chain is burdened by very high losses. Heating appliances powered by fuel cells exhibit excellent part-load behaviour. However, only prototypes have been built to date; a market launch is expected in the near future.

Electricity from waste heat/solar energy

Another possibility for decentralised CHP is the Stirling engine, which can convert a heat potential into electricity. As the provision of heat can be carried out externally, the engine can be combined with various heating plants. Biomass systems are suitable for renewable CHP; a coupling with a Stirling engine enables the waste heat to be used for energy purposes (Fig. B 4.127). Alternatively, solar radiation can be employed to drive the system. As reasonable degrees of efficiency call for a high tempera-

B 4.120 The principle of combined heat and power (CHP)
B 4.121 Combined heat and power (CHP) systems available on the market
B 4.122 Comparison of decentralised combined heat and power (CHP) and separate energy production
B 4.123 Incorporating decentralised CHP in the building heating system
B 4.124 Mini co-generation plant for operation with vegetable oil
B 4.125 Example of the integration of decentralised CHP for covering the basic load
B 4.126 Fuel-cell heating plant
     a Diagram of function
     b Prototype with natural gas reformer
B 4.127 Boiler with integral Stirling engine
B 4.128 Comparison of separate energy production and decentralised combined cooling, heating + power
     a Energy flow with electrical cooling
     b Energy flow with thermal cooling by means of CHP plus absorption-type refrigeration unit

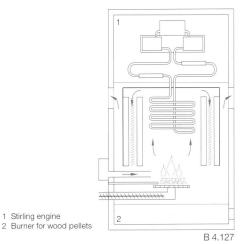

1 Stirling engine
2 Burner for wood pellets

B 4.127

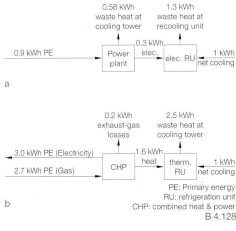

a

b

PE: Primary energy
RU: refrigeration unit
CHP: combined heat & power

B 4.128

143

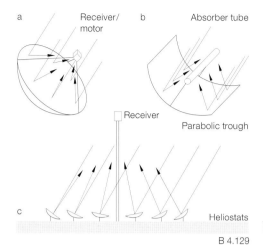

a Receiver/ motor
b Absorber tube
Receiver
Parabolic trough
c
Heliostats

B 4.129

Tower

500 – 1000 m

Electricity generator

Glass roof

B 4.130

B 4.129 Options for concentrating solar radiation for electricity generation:
a Parabolic dish
b Parabolic trough collector
c Central receiver system
B 4.130 How a solar chimney power plant works
B 4.131 Parabolic dish
B 4.132 Solar power plant with parabolic trough collectors
B 4.133 Jacobi mini hydroelectric power plant, Sarmigstein (A), 2005, Designstudio Juland
B 4.134 Parameters for different types of electricity storage

ture level (> 600°C), however, only concentrating thermal systems at locations with high levels of solar radiation are feasible.

Combined cooling, heating and power
If the CHP installation is supplemented by a machine that can generate cooling power from the waste heat, we speak of combined cooling, heating and power. Like with solar cooling, sorption-type refrigeration units are the norm here (see p. 130). Adding a heat consumer to the system results in improved utilisation of the co-generation plant outside the heating period, which improves the economics considerably. From the energy viewpoint, combined cooling, heating and power has significant advantages over electrical cooling (Fig. B 4.128).

Other technologies for generating electricity
Numerous other technologies, in addition to photovoltaics and decentralised CHP, are available for using renewable energy sources for generating electricity. There is not usually a direct connection between these systems and the planning of the building, or even an architectural integration. Nevertheless, these technologies offer interesting options for future developments.

Solar thermal electricity generation
Besides photovoltaic electricity generation, it is also possible to generate electricity via the thermal use of solar radiation. Very high tem-

peratures are needed to achieve reasonable degrees of efficiency. Up until now, concentrating solar systems and solar chimney plants are the only forms that have been put into practice. Concentrating solar collectors using lenses or mirrors can achieve very high operating temperatures at locations with a very high proportion of direct radiation. On the whole, three concepts have proved worthwhile (Fig. B 4.129):

• A parabolic dish can be used to focus the sun's rays exactly onto a receiver (absorber) (Fig. B 4.131). Such a system must include twin-axis tracking of the sun.
• Alternatively, a number of heliostats can be focused on to a central receiver in order to achieve large outputs. The max. 1000-fold concentration leads to temperatures well in excess of 1000°C.
• The parabolic trough collector represents a simpler construction. The approx. 100-fold concentration of the sunlight can achieve temperatures up to about 400°C (Fig. B 4.132), which is adequate for generating solar electricity via a steam power plant. This type of system has already been in use for more than 20 years for commercial electricity generation.

The economics of the individual concepts must be determined separately for each case and depend quite decisively on the location. The potential for electricity generation worldwide is

enormous and the relatively low materials requirements result in particularly favourable parameters in comparison to the energy output.

Solar chimney power plant
The first solar chimney power plant was built back in 1989 in southern Spain as a research project and a plant in Australia is expected to start generating electricity on a commercial scale in the near future (see "Fundamentals", p. 49, Fig. B 1.35). The concept exploits the effect of thermal currents for driving one or more turbines to generate electricity (Fig. B 4.130). It is necessary to coordinate the heated surface area (glass roof) and the chimney in order to generate sufficient thermal currents.

Wind power
The enormous developments in the use of wind energy for generating electricity have in the meantime resulted in highly developed technologies in virtually all output classes. High-rise buildings and windy locations in particular can offer interesting options for generating electricity with wind turbines integrated into buildings or infrastructure facilities. To date, only a scaled-down pilot project has been realised at the University of Stuttgart. The project has shown that optimising the form of the building can help to increase the wind speeds around the turbine, but the noise of such an installation must be considered.

B 4.131

B 4.132

B 4.133

		Supercapacitor	Superconducting magnetic energy storage (SMES)	Flywheel (status quo)	Battery	Pumped storage	Compressed-air storage	Hydrogen storage
Coefficient of performance (COP)	[s]	≤1	1–20	10–30	>1000	≥1000	≥1000	≥1000
Energy density	[kWs/kg]	5–20	<5	15–200	100–800	–	–	–
Mechanical storage density	[kWh/m³]	–	–	–	–	0.22	1.59	1.82
Chemical storage density	[kWh/m³]	–	–	–	–	0.00	0.00	69.72
Total storage density	[kWh/m³]	–	–	–	–	0.22	1.59	71.54
Power	[kW]	≤10	≤7000	≤15000	≤500	approx. 500 000	approx. 500 000	≤10
Service life	[No. of cycles]	>1 000 000	approx. 1 000 000	approx. 1 000 000	≤1000	no data	no data	no data
Efficiency	[%]	>95	approx. 90	85–90	70–85	approx. 81	approx. 72	27
Standby losses	[%]	0.1–0.2/h	Cooling capacity	3–20/h	<0.01/h	<0.01/h	<0.01/h	no data

B 4.134

Hydroelectric power

Hydroelectric power
Water power has been an important factor in electricity generation for a long time. As a rule, its use is linked with certain geological boundary conditions (running water, waterfall) or calls for massive intervention in the landscape (dam, reservoir). On a small scale, however, linking architecture or constructional infrastructure with the use of water for generating electricity is conceivable at suitable locations. Up until now, hydroelectric power stations have been purely utility structures built specifically for that purpose. Linking constructional measures that are required anyway with the creation of additional utilisation options opens up new perspectives (Fig. B 4.133).

Storing electricity

It is not usually necessary to store electricity in countries with an extensive electricity grid. The aim is not to operate more and more buildings autonomously in the future, but rather to expand the number of suppliers to the grid, which will result in increased flexibility in electricity generation and better safeguarding of supplies. Nevertheless, in certain cases it may be sensible to store electricity for longer periods, especially when the expansion of renewable energy for generating electricity calls for interim storage due to the fluctuations in the energy sources. In regions without an electricity grid, storage to ensure permanent electricity supplies is indispensable, especially when generating electricity from solar radiation or the wind.
Various methods are available for storing electricity (Fig. B 4.134). Capacitors are very efficient at storing electricity directly. The storage density feasible is low, however. Capacitors are principally employed in electronic components. The alternative is to store electricity indirectly by converting it into another form of energy in order to store larger quantities of energy over longer periods of time.

Batteries
This very well-known form of storage employs a chemical conversion process. Batteries are the most widely used form of electricity storage and various materials can be used. Whereas efficient materials are now being used in electrical and electronics applications (e.g. lithium-ion batteries), supplies for buildings not connected to the electricity grid mainly use lead-gel batteries, which are very reliable and economic. However, from the ecological viewpoint, they are unsatisfactory owing to their short service life and the problems of disposal.

Hydrogen
As an energy medium, hydrogen has the potential to take on a key role in energy storage. The electrolysis method enables hydrogen to be produced from water using electrical energy. The fuel cell makes the stored electrical energy available again. However, hydrogen has to be handled extremely carefully if it is to be used for storage purposes because of its chemical and physical properties (highly explosive in contact with the air). The challenge for the future is therefore to develop suitable storage options using hydrogen and to realise an integrated overall concept (hydrogen life cycle).

Flywheel energy storage
Another option for storing electricity is to convert it into kinetic energy. So-called flywheel energy storage (FES) represents an interesting option here. The electricity is used to start turning a flywheel mounted in magnetic bearings. The extremely fast rotation (> 50 000 rpm) and the virtually frictionless mounting enable the kinetic energy to be stored for longer periods. Slowing down the flywheel via a dynamo enables the electricity to be recovered.

Compressed-air storage
Storing electricity by way of compressed-air storage is another alternative. To do this, the electrical energy is used to compress air in an enclosed volume. The ensuing compressed air can be converted back into electricity by relieving the pressure. This principle is simple to implement, cost-effective and requires little maintenance. As the heat generated during compression cannot normally be used, the degree of efficiency is, however, rather low (approx. 50%).

References:
[1] Usemann, Klaus: Entwicklung von Heizung- und Lüftungstechnik zur Wissenschaft. Munich, 1993
[2] Mener, Gerhard: Bemühungen um die Sonnenenergie in Frankreich und Deutschland 1860–1924. Munich, 1997
[3] Zimmermann, Mark: Handbuch der passiven Kühlung. Stuttgart, 2003
[4] BINE Project Information 2/2000: Raumluftkonditionierung mit Erdwärmetauschern

Materials

B 5.1

The built environment is a material environment. It ties up a large proportion of both renewable and non-renewable resources that are removed from the earth for the well-being of the human race. With the forms of construction common these days, we can assume that one cubic metre of enclosed space in a heavyweight building consumes about 650 kg of materials, a lightweight building about 450 kg. It is therefore not surprising to discover that, worldwide, the building sector is the greatest consumer of resources (see "Doing things right – on efficiency and sustainability", p. 27).

The decision in favour of certain materials is governed by many aspects (Fig. B 5.5). Objective, definable aspects, e.g. physical or chemical properties, dimensions or costs, play a large part in the decision-making process. Our perception of materials is, however, essentially individual and subjective. A material interacts with the observer via its surface and is in each case experienced and appraised in a totally individual way (Fig. B 5.1); people and their well-being are the focus of attention (see "Fundamentals", p. 55).

On the other hand, technical and functional performance determines whether the use of a material really does satisfy the demands placed on it and the need for safe and durable usage. Building physics places demands on the properties of a building material, e.g. fire protection, sound insulation, moisture control, and for loadbearing components, it is the structural calculations that lay down the requirements. It is often the case that one material alone cannot satisfy all the demands placed on a component; in this situation, multi-layer constructions are used, with each individual layer responsible for one or more defined functions.

Over the course of a component's lifetime, further requirements – not foreseeable at the time of the planning – can occur. There is growing recognition of the fact that the choice of materials defines the health and hygiene boundary conditions for users and occupants, has a considerable effect on energy requirements and the environment, and can promote or prevent subsequent usage. For many types of use, the aim is to ensure flexibility, to keep open the options over the life of the building. Many well-known architects have evolved their own views on this; Alvar Aalto, Carlo Scarpa or Peter Zumthor, to name just a few, use materials in a way that shapes their architecture.

History
Historical, vernacular types of construction – apart from prestigious structures and those with a cultural importance – were always forced to use the scarce energy and resources available in an efficient way. Besides the responsible use of characteristic, locally available materials (e.g. stone or wood), scarcity was usually the prerequisite for the careful use of a material. The decisive breakthrough came with the Industrial Revolution; energy and raw materials were now available in seemingly unlimited abundance. Thereupon, architecture gradually broke away from natural circumstances and influences to pursue the ideal of "anything is feasible". On the other hand, technological progress brought innovation with it, e.g. in materials or in the optimisation of forms of construction and building processes. The full capabilities of materials were first exploited in engineering structures, e.g. railway stations, bridges. Joseph Paxton's Crystal Palace, optimised technically right down to the smallest detail, inaugurated a revolution in building (Fig. B 5.4). An engineering- and materials-related revolution in architecture now took place on a broad front, which was particularly evident in the fast-growing cities of North America. Here, steel played a key role as a construction material, uniting high material performance with rapid construction.

In the early days of the modern movement, impetus in materials research came from the need to meet the huge demand for new buildings, but also the desire for transparency, light, air and sunshine. This gave rise to ideas of constructional prefabrication, like Le Corbusier's "Dom-Ino" system of 1917. In the 1930s, Le Corbusier's interest in the vernacular architecture of North Africa led to other elements being incorporated into construction and architecture. One of these was the *brise-soleil*, a low-tech sunshading and loadbearing element optimised in terms of construction and energy efficiency (Fig. B 5.2).

B 5.1 Experimental House, Muuratsalo (FIN), 1954,
Alvar Aalto
B 5.2 Le Corbusier's sketches for his *brise-soleil*
B 5.3 "Dymaxion House" prototype, 1928,
Richard Buckminster Fuller
B 5.4 Crystal Palace, London (GB), 1851,
Joseph Paxton
B 5.5 Aspects of material selection

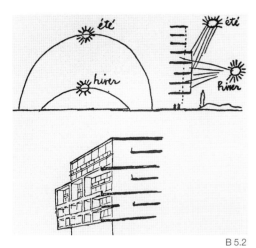

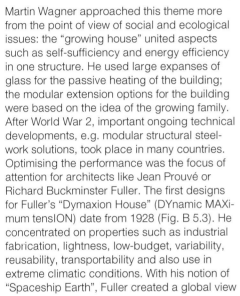

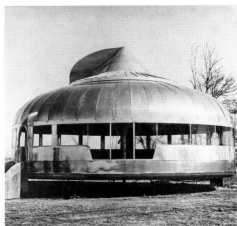

B 5.2

B 5.3

B 5.4

Martin Wagner approached this theme more from the point of view of social and ecological issues: the "growing house" united aspects such as self-sufficiency and energy efficiency in one structure. He used large expanses of glass for the passive heating of the building; the modular extension options for the building were based on the idea of the growing family. After World War 2, important ongoing technical developments, e.g. modular structural steelwork solutions, took place in many countries. Optimising the performance was the focus of attention for architects like Jean Prouvé or Richard Buckminster Fuller. The first designs for Fuller's "Dymaxion House" (DYnamic MAXimum tensION) date from 1928 (Fig. B 5.3). He concentrated on properties such as industrial fabrication, lightness, low-budget, variability, reusability, transportability and also use in extreme climatic conditions. With his notion of "Spaceship Earth", Fuller created a global view

of building, but also the operation of buildings in the sense of a service concept.
Engineers such as Pier Luigi Nervi dedicated themselves to optimising construction with concrete; his structural shells in double curvature trimmed the consumption of materials (Fig. B 5.7). Frei Otto and Günter Behnisch developed construction techniques even further by considering functional requirements such as "loadbearing" and "waterproofing" separately. The outcome was even lighter structural systems that encouraged the use of materials that up to that time were unusual in building: steel cables and plastics, e.g. the roof to the Olympic Stadium in Munich.
Fritz Haller took modular construction a step further. He created rigorous, rational systems whose prefabricated modules took account of spatial as well as technical requirements, e.g. by integrating pipes and cables. His structures could be dismantled just as easily as they

could be assembled – promoting the idea of reuse. The precise definition of requirements and their targeted implementation created an autonomous, constructional aesthetic. Environmental aspects started to play a role as development progressed. For Thomas Herzog, the "development of constructional systems with the use of renewable energies" and "product developments" are central issues in his work. His goal is the active promotion of energy efficiency in building and, in particular, to use it to help configure the building envelope (see "Solar architecture", p. 28). The experimental use of building materials creates the basis for the industrial manufacture of wood-based products, thermal mass concepts and many low-tech material solutions.
One interpretation of this movement regarded as particularly efficient in terms of materials is the "Eden Project" – the minimal use of materials to construct a lightweight structure with an

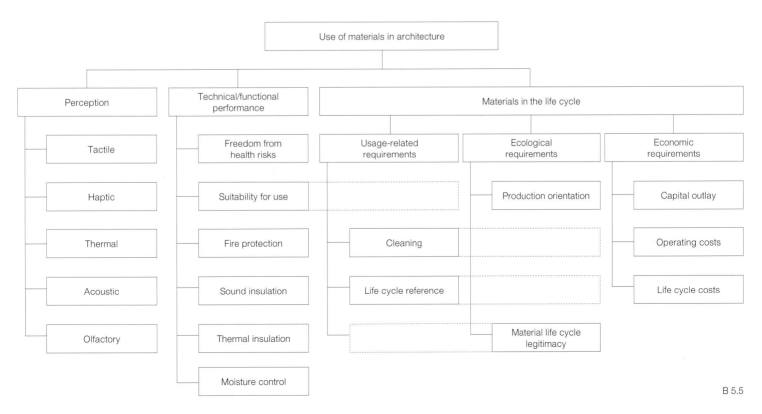

B 5.5

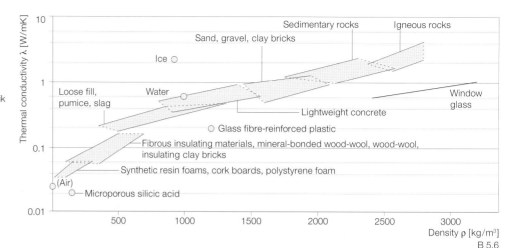

B 5.6

B 5.7

B 5.8

B 5.9

envelope made from pneumatically stabilised, multi-layer plastic sheeting. Extremely thin, lightweight and transparent, nevertheless long-lasting ETFE material has been used for the three-layer air-filled cushions. The boundaries between engineering and architecture are gradually becoming more and more blurred (Fig. B 5.8).

Other, new solutions are appearing in the pre-fabrication of building components. In particular, timber construction is undergoing a major upheaval with the advent of frame and panel techniques. New, lightweight methods of construction are opening up new opportunities for construction, e.g. existing roof landscapes (Fig. B 5.9).

Materials and energy
Energy and sustainability considerations overlap when choosing a material. So considering the energy processes does not mean just looking at one area, but rather is always integrated into an overall view of the sustainability theme (Fig. B 5.5). The material, via physical processes, has a decisive influence on the energy performance of a building. Basically, three themes are relevant here:

- Building materials minimise the flow of heat. They therefore enable a clear reduction in the energy consumption of the whole building, save operating energy and contribute to better economy. Energy consumption goes mainly hand in hand with ecological consequences, e.g. CO_2 emissions, acid rain, excessive fertilisation, "summer smog". A lower consumption reduces these environmental impacts. In addition, the material regulates the flow of heat and transfers or stores energy. It absorbs energy where it is needed, or dissipates it in the case of a surplus of energy. This means that economical and ecological advantages, e.g. cost-savings and a reduced environmental impact, can be achieved and the efficiency of the building improved.
- The production, maintenance and deconstruction activities surrounding the material tie up energy, which is known as "grey" or "embodied" energy and is quantified in the form of the primary energy input (PEI). The produc-

tion in particular results in a multitude of irreversible environmental impacts. The rational use of materials or the creation of material life cycles, for example, can help to reduce these effects.
- Finally, materials can trigger secondary energy processes during their usage, especially through their care and maintenance. Such processes have substantial energy-related, ecological and economic effects over the entire lifetime of a material. And these effects can only be analysed when considering a material over the entire life cycle of the building and not, as has been the case hitherto, just in relation to the as-built condition.

It is therefore necessary to appraise the effects of the application of a material differentiated according to energy, environment and sustainability. A life cycle analysis looks at material chains, reveals the energy-related and ecological effects of materials, and hence creates the basis for selecting building materials responsibly.

Heat flow

The thermal insulation of a building is of vital importance in cutting the energy requirements of that building. The better the thermal insulation, the lower are the energy losses in the case of temperature differences between inside and outside, and the smaller is the difference between the respective surface and air temperatures. Besides reducing the transmission heat losses in winter, the thermal insulation provided by the material also serves to

- improve thermal performance in summer,
- protect the construction against condensation and frost,
- improve the sound insulation if applicable.

Thermal conductivity
The thermal conductivity λ [W/mK] is at the very heart of energy-efficiency material optimisation measures (Fig. B 5.6). It describes the heat flow from a heat surplus to a heat sink that takes place as a movement of atoms or as a wave. A heat flow can take place in the form of

transmission, radiation and convection (Fig. B 5.11). In the case of transmission, the atoms transfer their energy through collisions with each other. In the case of radiation, they emit energy that can be absorbed by the next atom without the need for a intervening material. And in the case of convection, the internal temperature and density differences are converted into motion; this process, only possible in liquid or gaseous media, constitutes the heat transfer mechanism.

Heat transfer always involves all three processes, albeit to different extents. Each of these processes can be optimised in different ways (Fig. B 5.10). It is generally true that the lower the thermal conductivity of a material, the lower is the energy loss through a component made from that material. In the past it was usual to assign materials to thermal conductivity groups (WLG) which defined the thermal conductivity to an accuracy of 0.05 W/mK.

This method has now been replaced by the so-called thermal conductivity design value (e.g. WLG 040 – λ = 0.04 W/mK), which enables a more accurate classification of insulating materials (to 0.001 W/mK).

Transmission
The transmission of a material depends on its mass and internal structure. Fig. B 5.6 shows the thermal conductivities of materials depending on their density: the lower the density of a building material, the lower is its thermal conductivity, too. This is because of the higher proportion of air per unit volume of the material. Lightweight materials with a high proportion of pores, e.g. cork (Fig. B 5.10a), are therefore preferred as insulating materials. Air, with a thermal conductivity of 0.024 W/mK, is one of the best-known thermal insulators. However, air is only effective as insulation when the convection remains low. This is guaranteed by the formation of small voids, e.g. as in foams. Noble gases have thermal conductivities even lower than that of air; argon (0.016 W/mK), for instance, is used as standard for filling the cavity in double glazing made from low E glass. Moisture in a building component always increases the transmission because the thermal conductivity of water is 0.6 W/mK. Normally present in the air in the form of water vapour, it infiltrates the insulation and owing to the temperature difference can condense there, which reduces the insulating effect and can lead to mould growth, corrosion, decomposition of the insulating material or frost damage. Insulating materials should therefore always be moisture-repellent or should be protected against moisture by a vapour barrier (inside) and water-proofing materials (outside). Materials such as glass or a number of plastics have an amorphous structure that reduces the thermal conduction within the building material itself.

Convection
Air, a mixture of gases, is the energy media in convection processes, irrespective of insulating capacity. The thermal insulation effect of a layer of air is not linear, but instead reaches a maximum at about 60 mm (Fig. B 5.11). Both thinner and also thicker layers of air exhibit a lower insulating effect. In order to reduce convection, insulating spaces can be filled with noble gases, which are heavier than air and so the convection process begins later.

There is no convection in a vacuum. A vacuum insulation panel (VIP) exploits this fact by enclosing a rigid core, made from fibres, open-cell foam or pyrogenic silicic acid, in a gastight foil composite (Fig. B 5.10b). Owing to its very fine, open pores, pyrogenic silicic acid places the lowest demands on the tearing strength and imperviousness of the enclosing foil. But despite this, the gas pressure within a VIP increases by approx. 2 mbar every year, which means that heat convection processes eventually begin again and the thermal conductivity gradually rises:

- 0.004 W/mK vapour-tight (< 5 mbar gas pressure)

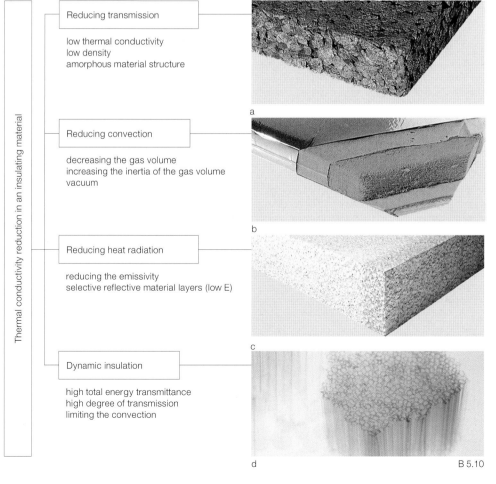

Thermal conductivity reduction in an insulating material

Reducing transmission

low thermal conductivity
low density
amorphous material structure

a

Reducing convection

decreasing the gas volume
increasing the inertia of the gas volume
vacuum

b

Reducing heat radiation

reducing the emissivity
selective reflective material layers (low E)

c

Dynamic insulation

high total energy transmittance
high degree of transmission
limiting the convection

d   B 5.10

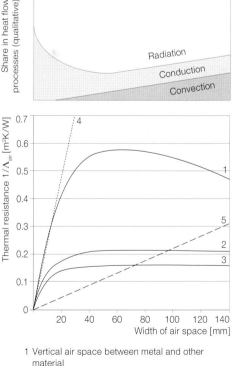

Share in heat flow processes (qualitative)

Radiation
Conduction
Convection

Thermal resistance $1/\Lambda_{air}$ [m²K/W]

Width of air space [mm]

1 Vertical air space between metal and other material
2 Vertical air space between building materials (horizontal heat flow)
3 Horizontal air space between building materials (upward heat flow)
4 Mineral fibre insulating material (λ = 0.04 W/mK)
5 Clay bricks (λ = 0.4 W/mK)

B 5.11

149

$$U = \cfrac{1}{R_{si}} + \cfrac{1}{s_n \cdot \lambda_n} + \cfrac{1}{R_{se}}$$

U Thermal transmittance [W/m²K]
R_{si} Internal surface resistance [W/m²K]
s_n Thickness of material [m]
λ_n Thermal conductivity of material [W/mK]
R_{se} External surface resistance [W/m²K]

B 5.12

Building component	max. U-value [W/m²K]	min. insulation thickness[1] [mm]
External wall	0.45	82
Renewed external wall[2]	0.35	106
Window	1.70	20
Pitched roof	0.30	126
Flat roof	0.25	152
Floors and walls in contact with unheated area or soil	0.40	94

[1] Assumptions: thermal conductivity of insulating material λ = 0.04 W/mK, thermal insulation solely responsible for energy efficiency
[2] Various exceptions possible according to Energy Conservation Act Annex 3

B 5.13

Building component	DIN 4102 building materials class required[1]		
Type of building	1–2 storeys	> 2 storeys, max. 22 m high	> 22m high
Curtain wall	B2	B1	A
Supporting construction	B2	B1	B1
Fixings	A	A	A
Thermal insulation	B2	B2	B1

[1] According to German Model Building Code; deviations in federal state building codes plus new standards must be taken into account; other solutions must be checked in each individual case.

B 5.14

B 5.12   Calculating the U-value of a construction to DIN 4108
B 5.13   Energy Conservation Act requirements for the U-value of a building component and the resulting theoretical minimum insulation thickness
B 5.14   Building materials classes (fire protection) required for parts of facades according to the German Model Building Code
B 5.15   Schematic wall construction for transparent thermal insulation in the form of a solid wall system
B 5.16   Physical parameters of selected insulating materials

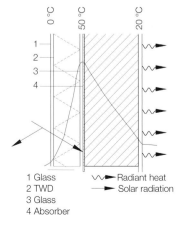

1 Glass   ∿∿ Radiant heat
2 TWD   → Solar radiation
3 Glass
4 Absorber

B 5.15

- 0.01 W/mK with low pressure difference (< 100 mbar gas pressure)
- 0.025 W/mK without pressure difference

However, at the end of this process the thermal conductivity is still lower than that of conventional insulating materials. According to the current standard (with aluminium foil or multi-layer, metallised plastic film), we can assume that a VIP will last 30–50 years.

Heat radiation
The radiation transmission can be influenced by reducing the passage of infrared radiation, the so-called emissivity. To do this, selective, reflective layers can be applied to a material – usually invisible, thin metallic coatings applied by vapour deposition. The effect remains independent of the visible radiation component and so is particularly suitable for transparent elements. This technique was first applied in the glass industry and led to improvements in U-values of about 25%. As this technology is to large extent not dependent on the backing material, it has also been used in the production of standard insulating materials, e.g. in the form of a modified expanded polystyrene (EPS) with a thermal conductivity of 0.032 W/mK (Fig. B 5.10c) (standard EPS: λ = 0.04 W/mK).

Solar gain systems
The three reduction options described above enable the thermal conductivity to be reduced to very low values. If we also consider the solar radiation, then the insulating effect of both opaque and transparent components can be increased to enable even temporary gains. To maximise solar gains, we need transparent materials with a high total energy transmittance (g-value [%]), which is the case, for example, with special elements such as quartz glass or transparent thermal insulation. The g-values of plastics and typical float glass are more or less equal; a polycarbonate sheet has a g-value of 87–89%. Translucent plastics (e.g. PMMA, PC), however, have much lower thermal conductivities (about 0.18 W/mK), are easier to shape and are usually less expensive. Horizontal capillary tubes or honeycomb structures allow the solar radiation to pass through the insulating material virtually unimpeded. At the same time, the structure of the sheets or the form of the cross-section reduces the convection (Fig. B 5.10d). A similar performance can be achieved with double- and triple-wall panels or cardboard honeycomb products. The Trombe wall – a solid storage wall behind a transparent facing – is also based on this principle. Such walls are cheap to build, but achieve only a low degree of efficiency.
Common to all dynamic forms of insulation is the fact that their insulating effect is not defined by a material parameter λ, but rather by the thermal transmittance, the U-value (U = unit of heat transfer), of the entire construction (Fig. B 5.12). There are three systems classified according to their method of function:

- Direct gain systems:
Windows and transparent thermal insulation elements integrated into the facade allow daylight into the interior, distribute the energy into the depth of the room and activate any thermal masses available.
- Solid wall systems:
These are a combination of direct gain system and thermal mass, which in order to increase the degree of efficiency is usually a dark surface that absorbs the incident energy and transfers this to the interior after a delay. Energy gains of 50–150 W/m²a can be achieved depending on orientation and type of system (Fig. B 5.15)
- Coupled/switched systems:
The disadvantage of direct gain and solid wall systems is that energy can penetrate them at all times, even when the building should actually be releasing heat. Coupled or switchable insulation systems have therefore been developed which are intended to regulate the heat flow between transparent thermal insulation elements and storage masses using water or air as a transfer medium, plus further functional layers if necessary. In the insulating state, these systems achieve U-values of 0.2–0.3 W/m²K, but in the "heat-release mode", e.g. for night-time cooling, can reach U-values as high as 10 W/m²K.

Insulating opaque components
According to DIN 4108, building materials with a thermal conductivity < 0.1 W/mK are regarded as insulating materials. This means that even lightweight solid timber, e.g. spruce, could be included in the group of insulating materials. On the whole, designers have a multitude of materials at their disposal. Fig. B 5.16 shows a selection and their typical parameters. In practice, these should be compared with the actual product values.

Product designations of insulating materials
Generally speaking, it is not the energy-related material qualities that govern the choice of an insulating material, but rather the constructional boundary conditions. The following list contains just some of things that may need to be considered:

- General requirements: product dimensions, product appearance
- Strength: compressive stress at 10% deformation, compressive strength under constant loading, tensile strength, shear strength
- Dimensional stability: in the case of moisture and temperature fluctuations
- Moisture control: water vapour diffusion, water absorption, hydrophobic properties
- Fire protection: building materials class, combustibility (Fig. B 5.14)
- Sound insulation: dynamic stiffness, sound impedance
- Health issues and environmental protection: volatile organic compounds (VOC) and synthetic mineral fibres (Fig. B 5.83)

- Durability: ageing resistance, UV resistance
- Economy

The product designations of insulating materials to DIN 4108-10 are based on the product properties and their applications (Figs. B 5.20 and 5.22).

Requirements placed on insulating components
The minimum thermal requirements for Germany are laid down in the Energy Conservation Act (EnEV) and DIN 4108-9 (Fig. B 5.13). They refer to complete building components and not to individual layers of insulation. The thermal transmittance [W/m^{2}K], which is the quantity of heat passing through a building component with a surface area of 1 m^2 for a temperature difference of 1 K, including losses due to the transfer of energy to the ambient air, is defined in Fig. B 5.12. A low heat flow through a building component is reflected in a low U-value. The given U-values can be converted into corresponding minimum layer thicknesses for each particular insulating material. The Energy Conservation Act prescribes an insulating standard for new buildings that would result in a layer thickness of 82 mm for a thermal conductivity of 0.04 W/mK.
The U-value calculation according to the Energy Conservation Act also includes surcharges for thermal bridges, i.e. conductive components usually required for constructional purposes (see "Building envelope", Fig. B 3.29).

The following applies here:

- when using the standard details to DIN 4108 supp. 2: +0.05 W/m^{2}K
- in the case of constructions not complying with the state of the art: +0.1 W/m^{2}K
- for internal insulation: +0.2 W/m^{2}K

Designing the thermal insulation
In order to avoid condensation within the construction (interstitial condensation), a vapour diffusion analysis should be carried out and the thermal insulation should be attached to the cold side of the construction. However, it is not always possible to install the layer of insulation on the outside, e.g. in the case of an energy-efficiency upgrade to an existing building. In such instances the insulation is placed on the inside, which, however, results in a considerable loss of floor space. The unavoidable thermal bridges in the form of floor and wall junctions reduce the theoretical U-value by another 30–50% and impair the thermal comfort. The increased risk of condensation calls for a careful analysis of the moisture gradient within the construction. This usually results in the need for an internal vapour barrier, the function of which, throughout the life of the building, may not be impaired in any way.
The new calcium silicate insulating boards can obviate the need for an internal vapour barrier. Their high moisture absorption capacity permits short-term storage of any moisture in the

building component, but as yet no long-term experience has been gained with this product. Energy problems ensue with inhomogeneous components, e.g. a timber stud wall with insulation between the timber members. The thermal conductivity differs within the building component because the structural materials result in a higher energy loss; in addition, there can be a negative impact on the moisture gradient within the material. The calculation of an average U-value for such a form of construction is carried out according to DIN EN ISO 6946 (see "Building envelope", Fig. B 3.12). Constructions made from wood-based products, e.g. an I-section or a box section filled with insulation, can reduce the thermal transmittance. At the same time, they enable longer spans when used as floor beams, or rather result in a lower material consumption.
The efficiency of the thermal insulation offers better comfort and a gain in floor space with low material usage. Thermal insulation with better thermal conductivity reduces the thickness of the layer required and so increases the available floor space. A U-value $\leq$ 0.15 W/m^{2}K is necessary in order to reach passive house standard, which with standard insulating materials means a total wall thickness exceeding 500 mm! Compared to this, vacuum insulation panels (VIP) can achieve a similar performance with a wall thickness of just 190 mm (Fig. B 5.18). In the private house shown in Fig. B 5.19, the use of VIPs resulted in a gain in floor space of

Insulating material	Density [kg/m^3]	Thermal conductivity design value λ_B [W/mK]	Vapour diffusion resistance index μ [-]	Building materials class/combustibility class[1] [-]	Product standard	Product forms
Inorganic						
Calcium silicate	115–290	0.045–0.070	2/20	A1–A2/up to A1	[2]	Board
Glass wool/rock wool	12–250	0.035–0.050	1/2	A1–B1/up to A1	DIN EN 13162	Board, blanket, caulking material
Cellular glass (CG)	100–150	0.040–0.060	virtually vapour-tight	A1/A1	DIN EN 13167	Board, loose fill
Expanded perlite board (EPB)	60–300	0.050–0.065	2/5	A1–B2/up to A1	DIN EN 13169	Board, loose fill
Expanded clay	260–500	0.100–0.160	2	A1/A1	DIN EN 14063	Loose fill
Vermiculite (expanded mica)	60–180	0.065–0.070	2/3	A1/A1	[2]	Loose fill
Organic						
Polyester fibres	15–45	0.035–0.045	1	B1–2/up to B	[2]	Blanket
Polystyrene, expanded (EPS)	15–30	0.035–0.040	20/100	B1/up to B	DIN EN 13163	Board
Polystyrene foam, extruded (XPS)	25–45	0.030–0.040	80/250	B1/up to B	DIN EN 13164	Board
Polyurethane rigid foam (PUR)	$\geq$ 30	0.020–0.035	30/100	B1–2/up to B	DIN EN 13165	Board, in situ foam
Cotton	20–60	0.040–0.045	1/2	B1/up to B	[2]	Batt, blanket, caulking/blown material
Flax	25	0.040–0.045	1/2	B1/up to B	[2]	Board, batt, blanket, caulking mat.
Hemp	20–70	0.040–0.045	1/2	B2/up to D	[2]	Board
Wood fibres (WF)	45–450	0.040–0.070	1/5	B2/up to D	DIN EN 13171	Board
Wood-wool board (WW)	360–570	0.065–0.090	2/5	B1/up to B	DIN EN 13168	Board
Coconut fibres	50–140	0.045–0.050	1/2	B1–B2/up to B	DIN 18165-1/-2	Batt, blanket, caulking material
Insulation cork board (ICB)	80–500	0.040–0.055	5/10	B1–B2/up to B	DIN EN 13170	Loose fill, board
Sheep's wool	20–80	0.035–0.040	1/2	B1–B2/up to B	[2]	Batt, blanket, caulking material
Cellulose fibres	30–100	0.035–0.040	1/2	B1–B2/up to B	[2]	Blown material, board
"Innovative" insulating materials						
IR absorber-modified EPS	15–30	0.032	20/100	B1/up to B	DIN EN 13163	Board
Transparent thermal insulation	[4]	0.02–0.1[3]	virtually vapour-tight	[4]	[2]	Panel
Vacuum insulation panel (VIP)	150–300	0.004–0.008	virtually vapour-tight	B2 [2]	[2]	Panel

[1] The combustibility classes given here represent guidelines; they should be checked against the actual product data.
[2] With national technical approval.
[3] The insulating material exploits the static insulating effect plus solar gains. The values given here include solar gains averaged over a heating period in Germany. Distinct differences can occur depending on climate and orientation of insulation.
[4] Depends very much on the actual product.

B 5.16

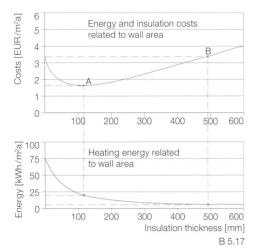

B 5.17

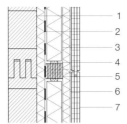

1 Solid spruce, 80 mm
2 Wood fibreboard, 22 mm
3 Vacuum insulation panel, 40 mm
4 Peripheral compressible strip
5 LVL battens, 40 x 45 mm
6 Wood fibreboard, 22 mm
7 3-ply core plywood, 22 mm
U-value: 0.14 W/m²K
Total thickness: 190 mm

B 5.18

B 5.19

about 5% without increasing the volume of the building. The use of VIPs can also be sensible for existing buildings, e.g. in order to retain a reasonable floor-to-ceiling height in basements when insulating the underside of the ground floor slab.

Fixings
Any fixings necessary contribute to heat conduction and therefore represent a constructional thermal bridge. We distinguish between three types of fixing depending on the type of product (Fig. B 5.16):

• No fixings: The loose insulating materials are tipped, stuffed or blown in. They require a firm base or a volume enclosed on both sides. This type of installation avoids constructional thermal bridges but can lead to uninsulated voids, e.g. caused by settlement of the insulation, which must be subsequently filled (and so must be accessible).
• Point fixings: Insulating materials in the form of blankets, batts or boards are nailed, screwed, anchored or glued at individual points. Penetrating metal components, e.g. fixings for an outer leaf, are especially dis-

advantageous. Annex D of DIN EN ISO 6946 specifies the exact calculation of the ensuing heat loss.
• Continuous fixings: Insulating materials in the form of blankets, batts or boards can be glued over their entire area, e.g. using mortar or bitumen, to form a structural bond with the substrate.

Payback time
Even those insulating materials whose production consumes large amounts of energy, e.g. cellular glass, pay back their cost within a few years, and organic insulating materials such as straw and even mineral fibre insulating materials usually within 12 months. Based on this payback calculation, demands for insulation up to 500 mm thick have been made for Germany (Fig. B 5.17). For an economic payback, the material thickness stipulated in the Energy Conservation Act for new buildings represents the minimum economic insulation thickness. According to that, the thicknesses of standard insulating materials (thermal conductivity λ = 0.04 W/mK) are generally 120–160 mm. If we assume that during an energy-efficiency upgrade, the scaffolding and labour make up

the lion's share of the costs, a solution equivalent to the standard of new building work should also be considered here.

Low E glazing
The use of light-permeable building components is coupled with the desire to exploit the incoming daylight and the incoming energy, and to create a visual link with the outside world. Light-permeable building components are therefore mainly transparent and made of glass or plastic, less often translucent.
The glass industry has improved its products enormously in recent decades. Since the 1970s, the U-values of insulating glasses have improved by a factor of 10 from the approx. 3.6 W/m²K customary in the old days.
If we include the solar gains through areas of glass in the calculation, then the insulating qualities of low E glazing – when considered as part of an energy-efficiency drive – are equal to or even better than those of standard insulating materials (Fig. B 5.29). This is due to the so-called greenhouse effect: the radiation enters the room, strikes a surface and is converted into heat radiation with a longer wavelength; the permeability of the glass for this wavelength

Product property	Abbreviation	Description	Examples
Compressive strength	dk	No compressive strength	Insulation to cavities and voids, between rafters
	dg	Low compressive strength	Residential and office areas below screed
	dm	Moderate compressive strength	Non-habitable roof space with waterproofing
	dh	High compressive strength	Trafficked roofs and terraces
	ds	Very high compressive strength	Industrial floors, parking decks
	dx	Extremely high compressive strength	Heavily loaded industrial floors, parking decks
Water absorption	wk	No requirements regarding water absorption	Internal insulation to residential and office areas
	wf	Absorption of water as liquid	External insulation to external walls and roofs
	wd	Absorption of water as liquid and/or through diffusion	External basement insulation, upside-down roof
Tensile strength	zk	No requirements regarding tensile strength	Insulation to cavities and voids, between rafters
	zg	Low tensile strength	External insulation to wall behind cladding
	zh	High tensile strength	External insulation to wall behind render, roof with bonded waterproofing
Sound insulation properties	sk	No requirements regarding sound insulation properties	All applications without sound insulation requirements
	sg	Impact sound insulation, low compressibility	Floating screed, party walls
	sm	moderate compressibility	Floating screed, party walls
	sh	Impact sound insulation, high compressibility	Floating screed, party walls
Deformation	tk	No requirements regarding deformation	Internal insulation
	tf	Dimensionally stable under moisture and thermal loads	External insulation to wall behind render, roof with waterproofing
	tl	Deforms under loads and thermal effects	Roof with waterproofing

B 5.20

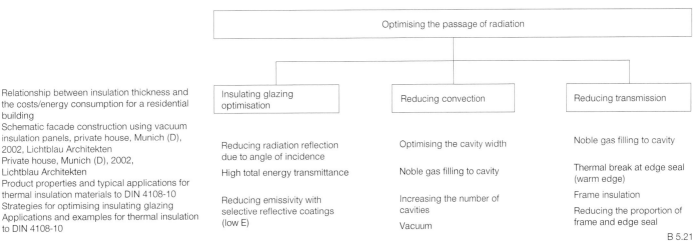

B 5.21

is lower than that of visible light and this forces a build-up of heat in the room. With a favourable orientation, the energy gain of this "heat trap" can even exceed the transmission losses through the glass – it becomes a passive energy gains system for the building.

Glass manufacturers can exploit a number of system advantages within the sequence of layers to improve the energy efficiency of their products. High-quality low E glasses behave according to the principles of dynamic insulation. Like with insulating materials, the systematic reduction of transmission, convection and radiation through glazing contributes to the energy performance of the building components. However, the property of transparency involves certain special features in the case of the passage of radiation, e.g. reflection and transmission. The goal of optimisation is the transmission of light depending on the incoming radiation and the heat losses (Figs. B 5.21 and 5.23).

Besides energy losses and gains through the area of glass, the amount of daylight entering the building is decisive for the use of glass. Increasing the proportion of daylight in the room leads to a lower energy requirement for artificial lighting and hence to a significant energy-saving.

But an energy gain via transparent components is not always desirable. As the thermal insulation improves, so the solar gains, especially in buildings with high internal loads (e.g. offices), have to be reduced, or at least the regulating and control options have to be improved. Sunshading and glare protection can be implemented through the use of certain materials or by adding special components (see "Building envelope", p. 102).

Types of glazing

We distinguish the possible applications depending on the type of glazing. Parameters for glazing are always stipulated with reference to the defined system or the system parts. They can be specified for the entire window (w), the frame (f) and the glazing (g).

· Single glazing can have a U_g-value between 3.6 and 5.2 W/m²K. Such glazing is only suitable for unheated rooms, as a facade material or for internal applications.
· Insulating glazing consists of two or more panes of glass that together with a hermetic edge seal provide a gastight enclosure for a filling of gas. Insulating glazing units improve both the thermal and the acoustic properties.
· Insulating glazing units can be provided with one or more low E coatings on the glass. Standard for low E double glazing is a U_g-value of 1.1 W/m²K. Triple glazing products with a noble gas filling and two low E coatings currently achieve U_g-values as low as 0.4 W/m²K. The most important parameters of glazing products currently on the market are listed in Fig. B 5.30.
· Glasses with a U_g-value of 0.8 W/m²K or less are known in Germany as "warm windows" according to DIN EN 10077. The lower transmission heat losses result in surface temperatures close to the desired interior air temperature. Compared to other types of glazing, there is a higher heat radiation from the surface, which leads to a higher thermal comfort.

Application	Abbreviation	Examples
Floor, roof	DAD	External insulation to suspended floor or roof, protected from the weather, insulation below roof covering
	DAA	External insulation to suspended floor or roof, protected from the weather, insulation below waterproofing
	DUK	External insulation to roof, exposed to the weather (upside-down roof)
	DZ	Insulation between rafters, double-skin roof, accessible but non-trafficked topmost suspended floor
	DI	Internal insulation to suspended floor (underside) or roof, insulation below rafters/structure, suspended ceiling, etc.
	DEO	Internal insulation to suspended or ground floor (top side) below screed, without sound insulation requirements
	DES	Internal insulation to suspended or ground floor (top side) below screed, with sound insulation requirements
Wall	WAB	External insulation to wall, behind cladding
	WAA	External insulation to wall, behind waterproofing
	WAP	External insulation to wall, behind render
	WZ	Cavity insulation to double-leaf walls
	WH	Insulation to timber-frame and timber-panel forms of construction
	WI	Internal insulation to wall
	WTH	Insulation between party walls with sound insulation requirements
	WTR	Insulation to separating walls
External basement insulation	PW	External thermal insulation to walls in contact with the soil (on outside of waterproofing)
	PB	External thermal insulation below ground floor slab in contact with the soil (below waterproofing)

B 5.22

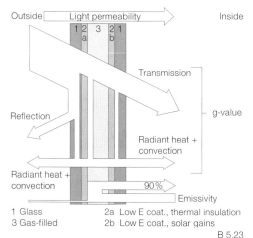

Outside — Light permeability — Inside

Transmission

Reflection — g-value

Radiant heat + convection

Radiant heat + convection — 90% — Emissivity

| 1 | Glass | 2a | Low E coat., thermal insulation |
| 3 | Gas-filled | 2b | Low E coat., solar gains |

B 5.23

B 5.23 Schematic presentation of the passage of radiation through a double glazing unit

B 5.24 Thermal transmittance values for various gas fillings in the cavity between the panes of glass

B 5.25 Hermetic edge seal systems and their effects on the U-values of glazing units

B 5.26 U_g-value in relation to the g-value of a glazing unit

B 5.27 Glazing with pyrogenic silicic acid filling, office building, Munich (D), 1994, Herzog + Partner

B 5.28 Light permeability parameters for various types of glazing

B 5.29 Dynamic U-values of various types of glazing according to orientation

B 5.30 Parameters of selected transparent building components

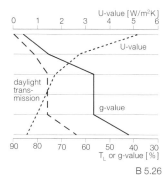

Single glazing (float glass)
Double glazing (air)
Double glazing (air/IR)
Double glazing (argon/IR)
Double glazing (krypton/IR)
Triple glazing (krypton/IR)

U-value [W/m²K]

daylight transmission

g-value

T_L or g-value [%]

B 5.26

B 5.27

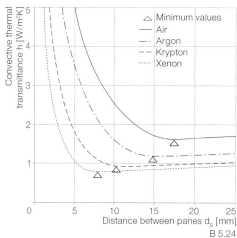

Convective thermal transmittance h [W/m²K]

△ Minimum values
— Air
—·— Argon
— — Krypton
······ Xenon

Distance between panes d_s [mm]

B 5.24

Optimising the passage of radiation

Transparency is the outstanding quality of glass – and also a number of plastics. Like all materials, glass absorbs radiation. This absorption, however, takes place in a range beyond the spectrum of visible light. The three coefficients absorption (A), reflection (R) and transmission (T) occur in a relationship that is specific to each material and add up to 100%. The important parameters in this context are (Fig. B 5.23):

• Degree of transmission τ
• Total energy transmittance g
• Emissivity ε

Absorption involves converting the radiation into heat, which is then transported through the structure of the material and emitted from the surface of the material in the form of long-wave radiation. Reflection means bouncing the radiation off the surface and back into its surroundings. The shallower the angle of incidence of the radiation, the higher is the reflection component, and in the case of glass this is usually significant for angles greater than about 60°.

A large proportion of the radiation passes through the material without undergoing any physical change. This process corresponds to transmission (T), which is specified by the degree of transmission τ; the effect of this is to make the glass appear particularly transparent. In contrast to our understanding of heat theory, the degree of transmission designates the radiation permeability and not the energy transfer by means of thermal conduction.

In the case of special glasses (e.g. for solar panels), the degree of transmission can be up to 98%. But even with normal window glass, the aim is to keep absorption and reflection low while raising the transmission. However, other factors such as colour rendering play a role here. Glass is not equally transparent in every part of the spectrum. Natural lighting and colours, however, determine depth and comfort. The colour rendering Ra to DIN EN 410 must therefore also be specified for glasses in addition to the daylight transmission TL. For this variable expressed as a percentage, values

Hermetic edge seal	Edge [mm]	TBC Ψ [W/mK]	U-val. for perim. length of glass [W/m²K] 1.0 m	2.0 m
Aluminium, exposed	0.5	0.115	0.999	0.883
Steel	0.5	0.112	0.991	0.879
Stainless steel	0.5	0.105	0.973	0.867
Stainless steel 0.2	0.2	0.096	0.950	0.853
Plastic, exposed	1.0	0.068	0.877	0.808
Aluminium PU10	0.5	0.056	0.846	0.789
St. steel 0.2 PU10	0.2	0.049	0.827	0.778
Aluminium PU30	0.5	0.035	0.791	0.756
St. steel 0.2 PU30	0.2	0.031	0.781	0.749
Plastic PU30	1.0	0.024	0.762	0.738

The thermal bridge coefficient (TBC) is related to the length of the thermal bridge.

B 5.25

> 90% represent very good, values > 80% good colour rendering. Nevertheless, colour distortion can occur due to increased light refraction at the edges of the glass even with values over 90%. The colour rendering value should be higher than 97% for special applications such as daylighting in museums (Fig. B 5.28).

The total energy transmittance g designates the sum of direct transmission, solar radiation and heat emissions into the interior due to radiation and convection. Float glass single glazing has a degree of transmission of approx. 90% and a g-value of 85–87% (Fig. B 5.30). The g-value decreases as the number of panes increases. Triple glazing thus has an energy transmittance of only 40–50%. At the same time, however, the Ug-value falls (Fig. B 5.26). Besides the energy gains from outside, there is also an energy flow in the opposite direction at the glazing. That part of the physical transmissions in the range of infrared radiation (heat) is measured in the form of emissivity ε. This value describes the ratio of the thermal radiation penetrating the body to the heat radiation incident on the body. The emissivity of float glass single glazing is about 89%. Metallic coatings made from silver or titanium reduce the emissivity of glass. These ultra-thin coatings applied by way of vapour deposition reflect most of the infrared radiation generated in the interior back into the building. The selective, aligned coatings have only a small influence on the g-value, but reduce the emissivity substantially – up to 2% with certain products. Silver-coated low E glasses represent the state of the art. They can be produced virtually free from any colouring. A low E coating reduces the U-value of a double glazing unit from 3.0 to about 1.6 W/m²K. As the position of the coating within the insulating unit is relevant, care should be taken to install such glazing units according to their labelling. Single glazing with a low E coating is also available, with a U-value of approx. 3.6 W/m²K.

So-called hard coatings are characterised by their toughness and can therefore be placed on the inner face of a glazing unit without any further protection, which increases the energy efficiency. This is a particularly worthwhile fea-

Technical values of various insulating glass units		Low E glazing					Solar-control glazing			
		Double glazing, 1 pane coated			Triple glazing, 2 panes coated		Quadruple glazing, 4 coatings	Double glazing, 1 pane coated		
Dimensions (pane/cavity/pane) [mm]		4-15-4			4-12-4-12-4		6-12-6-12-6-12-6	6-16-4	6-16-4	6-16-4
		$\varepsilon \leq 0.05$			$\varepsilon \leq 0.05$		$\varepsilon = 0.02$	colourless[1]	blue[1]	green[1]
Cavity filling (gas concentration $\geq$ 90%)		air	argon	krypton	argon	krypton	krypton	argon	argon	argon
U_g-value to EN ISO 10077-1	U_g [W/m²K]	1.5	1.2	1.1	0.8	0.5	0.3[1]	1.1	1.1	1.1
Total energy transmittance[1]	g [%]	64	64	64	52	52	38[1]	37	24	28
Light permeability[1]	T_L [%]	81	81	81	72	72	59[1]	67	40	55
Light reflection[1]	R_L [%]	12	12	9	14	14	18[1]	11/12[2]	10/33[2]	9/12[2]
Colour rendering[1]	R_a [%]	98	98	98	96	96	no data	96/94[2]	95/70[2]	86/88[2]

[1] Typical manufacturers' data
[2] Values valid for internal/external

B 5.28

ture for refurbishment work. Existing windows can be upgraded in this way (secondary glazing, coupled window).

Convection and low E glasses
The cavity between the panes is generally between 8 and 20 mm in order to reduce the convection processes in the gas. The width is not dependent on the gas used (Fig. B 5.24). Dividing the cavity into several layers can reduce the convection still further and improve the insulating properties of the glazing unit. In triple glazing, the middle pane is at the same time used as a backing for a second low E coating. U_g-values as low as 0.4 W/m²K can be achieved by filling the cavity with krypton or xenon gas. However, the g-value of the pane drops to about 0.4. Quadruple glazing units are now available, but such units are considerably thicker and heavier.
As an alternative, there are forms of construction in which the middle panes are replaced by plastic film (Fig. B 5.33). This reduces the thickness of the component to 23 mm; the g-value is 0.43, the U-value 0.45 W/m²K.

Transmission and transparent components
Glass has an amorphous structure and hence exhibits lower transmission compared with building materials of similar weight, e.g. concrete. Nevertheless, owing to its density, the value of about 0.8 W/mK is relatively high compared to the approx. 2.1 W/mK of concrete (Fig. B 5.6).
In order to reduce the conductivity of the construction, noble gases such as argon, xenon or krypton, which have a lower conductivity than dry air, are used in the cavity between the panes (Fig. B 5.24). Compared to a filling of air, the U-values of double glazing units improve by about 0.3 W/m²K. Owing to its good availability and hence easier production, argon is used most frequently. Xenon and krypton have better thermal properties but are only available in small quantities, which makes their production process very elaborate and costly.
A vacuum in the cavity reduces the heat conduction still further. The insulating effect of the vacuum is not dependent on the distance between the panes, which means that a spacing of < 1 mm is technically possible. A partial vacuum of about 10^{-3} bar then prevails in the cavity. As the vacuum causes the panes of glass to deflect inwards, either allowing them to touch or even breaking them completely, spacers between the panes of glass are necessary. These can be discrete points or cover the whole area, e.g. made from pyrogenic silicic acid or an adhesive. A spacer across the whole area results in a certain specific optical effect owing to the ensuing translucency (Fig. B 5.27). Vacuum double glazing can achieve Ug-values as low as 0.5 W/m²K, vacuum triple glazing 0.3 W/m²K. Better values have not been achieved so far because the dense, stabilising hermetic edge seal always constitutes a thermal bridge. The glued metal hermetic edge seal, the form most often encountered in practice, consist of a double seal, a metallic spacer and an integral desiccant for absorbing any moisture (Fig. B 5.25). The linear thermal transmittance Ψ of such a construction lies between 0.9 and 2.2 W/mK. Condensation can therefore collect around the edges of the pane. The better the actual insulating effect of the glazing and the smaller the window, the greater are the negative effects of the hermetic edge seal. For a 2 x 2 m window with a U-value of 0.4 W/m²K in the middle of the pane, the U_g-value of a construction with an aluminium hermetic edge seal is only 0.58 W/m²K, i.e. a 45% decrease. A hermetic edge seal with a thermal break, on the other hand, leads to a decrease of only approx. 22%, i.e. corresponding to a U_g-value of 0.49 W/m²K (Fig. B 5.36).
As the surface temperatures of the glazing with such a construction do not drop severely at the edges and corners, as used to be the case, we speak here of a "warm edge". This prevents condensation collecting around the edge of the glass. The spacers required are made from a UV-resistant, gastight plastic.
The window frame is a significant energy loss factor. It normally exhibits a poorer U-value

Type of glazing	Light transmission	South U_{eq}	East/West U_{eq}	North U_{eq}
Double glazing, U_g-value = 1.8, g-value = 0.70	0.81	0.12	0.540	0.960
Double glazing, U_g-value = 1.3, g-value = 0.62	0.77	-0.188	0.184	0.556
Double glazing, U_g-value = 1.1, g-value = 0.58	0.76	-0.292	0.056	0.404
Triple glazing, U_g-value = 0.7, g-value = 0.40	0.60	-0.260	-0.020	-0.020
Quadruple glazing, U_g-value = 0.3, g-value = 0.38	0.59	-0.612	-0.384	-0.156

B 5.29

Transparent building component		U_g-value to DIN EN 673	Daylight transmission	g-value to DIN EN 410
Single glazing	Float glass	5.8	0.90	0.85
	Float glass with low E coating	3.8	0.67	0.62
	Extra-clear glass	5.8	0.92	0.92
	Laminated glass with sunshading film as interlayer	5.8	0.75	0.52
Double glazing	Low E glass, air filling	1.4	0.80	0.63
	Low E glass, argon filling	1.1	0.80	0.63
	Neutral solar-control glass, argon filling	1.1	0.70	0.41
	Neutral solar-control glass, argon filling	1.1	0.62	0.34
	Neutral solar-control glass, argon filling	1.1	0.51	0.28
	Neutral solar-control glass, argon filling	1.1	0.40	0.24
	Neutral solar-control glass, argon filling	1.1	0.30	0.19
Triple glazing	Low E glass with 2 coatings, argon filling	0.7	0.72	0.50
	Low E glass with 2 coatings, krypton filling	0.5	0.72	0.50
Quadruple glazing	Low E glass with 4 coatings, krypton filling	0.3*	0.59*	0.38*
Twin-wall panel	Polycarbonate	1.5*	0.70	0.60*

*Manufacturer's data

B 5.30

Material	Thermal conductivity [W/mK]	U_f-value [W/m²K] [1]		U_w-value [W/m²K] [1]	
		typical	feasible	typical	feasible
Wood	0.12	1.5	1.3 [2]	1.1	0.9 [2]
Aluminium	220	1.5	1.2 [2]	1.1	1.0 [2]
Plastic	0.16	1.3	1.0	1.0	0.8

[1] Based on triple glazing, related to an average frame proportion of 25%.
[2] Lower values can be achieved only with additional layers of insulation in the form of secondary glazing, which means that U_f-values as low as 1.0 W/m²K and Uw-values as low as 0.8 W/m²K are achievable for all materials. Composite materials for aluminium are wood, wood-based products or plastic. Composite wood-plastic frames are also possible.

B 5.31

B 5.32

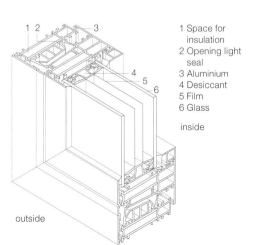

1 Space for insulation
2 Opening light seal
3 Aluminium
4 Desiccant
5 Film
6 Glass

inside

outside

B 5.33

than the glazing itself and reduces the area available for solar gains.

Window frames can be made of wood, plastic or metal (Fig. B 5.31). As a raw material, wood exhibits the best thermal properties, with U_f-values between 1.5 and 2.1 W/m²K. However, the simple production of thermally optimised extruded sections means that these days plastic frames are usually better in terms of their energy performance. Metal window frames are a disadvantage in thermal terms, but their particularly slender sections and hence smaller thermal loss surface areas outweigh their disadvantage to a certain extent. They are especially weather-resistant and therefore very long-lasting.

The need for energy-efficiency improvements has led to the appearance of more and more thermally optimised wood-plastic composite frames on the market. The insulating layer is either attached to the outside of the frame, with the appearance determined by a fascia panel, or the layer of insulation is in the same plane as the glass, between the inner and outer parts of the frame. Assemblies insulated with PUR foam enable the use of better loadbearing and stiffening frame materials made from steel or glass fibre-reinforced polyolefin sections (Fig. B 5.32). The thermal and constructional optimisation of the component can, however, restrict the later recycling options.

If the U-value of the frame is poorer than that of the glazing, a larger edge cover dimension will improve the U_w-value. Setting blocks with a thermal break reduce the Uw-value of a window yet further. "Warm windows", like those used in, for example, passive houses, can thus achieve U_f-values well below 1.0 W/m²K.

The creation of larger window areas with a smaller frame proportion results in further energy-efficiency optimisation potential.

Radiation balance for glazing

The total thermal transmittance U_w for a glazing element is calculated according to EU norm CEN/TC89/W67 (Fig. B 5.34). This parameter considers, however, only the energy losses through a window.

The dynamic U_{eq}-value can be calculated from the U_g- and g-values. This parameter intro-duced by Gerd Hauser and Lothar Rouvel is an attempt to consider, roughly, the potential of the energy gains via the glazing in the U-value. It is therefore specific to the incident radiation and hence the location and is only valid for Germany. It can be shown by way of this value that for Central European latitudes, triple glazing compared to double glazing with a higher g-value on the south side of a building results in hardly any extra energy gains. On the east and west sides, and especially on the north side, however, triple glazing exhibits considerable advantages (Fig. B 5.29). If we add the DIN 4108-6 shading factors (F) into the equation, the effect of the true building surroundings can be taken into account in the assessment (Fig. B 5.35).

Light-redirecting glasses

Glare can be prevented by diffusers. One simple way of increasing the amount of diffuse light in a room is to use obscured glass. Cellular structures, like those of transparent thermal insulation, generate a similar effect.

A directed lighting effect can also improve the illumination in the interior. Perspex prismatic panels installed in the cavity of a double glazing unit exploit the higher angular selectivity of the material. The direct incoming light is reflected depending on the angle of incidence, either outwards or onto the ceiling of the room; but the diffuse light passes through unhindered. Reducing the size of the prisms enables a better view of the outside world but that does diminish the protection against glare. Laser cut panels (LCP) are available on the market but must be produced specifically for a particular location and particular angle of incidence. Optical lenses can direct light specifically into the depths of a room. But as such components are expensive and solar-tracking systems require maintenance, they can be replaced by holographic optical elements (HOE) which apart from their light-redirecting properties can also be used as sunshades or four focusing the light onto photovoltaic modules (Fig. B 5.37; see also "Building envelope", p. 104).

$$U_w = \frac{A_g \cdot U_g + U \cdot \Psi + A_f \cdot U_f}{A_g + A_f}$$

U_w Total thermal transmittance of glazing [W/m²K]

A_g Area of glazing [m²]

U_g U-value of glazing [W/m²K]

U Perimeter length of glazing [m]

Ψ Linear thermal transmittance of edge seal [W/mK]

A_f Area of frame [m²]

U_f U-value of frame [W/m²K]

B 5.34

$$U_{eq} = U_g - (g \cdot S)$$

U_g U-value of glazing [W/m²K]

g g-value of glazing [-]

S Radiation gains in relation to orientation:

south	2.4 W/m²K
east/west	1.8 W/m²K
north	1.2 W/m²K

$$U_{eq} = U_g - (g \cdot S \cdot F_h \cdot F_o \cdot F_f)$$

F_h Partial shading coefficient, horizon angle

F_o Partial shading coefficient, vertical shade angle

F_s Partial shading coefficient, lateral shade angle

B 5.35

		for $U_{\text{mid-pane}}$ [W/m²K]		
		1.3	0.9	0.4
Dimen-sions	Spacer Material	U_w-value incl. edge seal		
0.6 × 0.6 m	Aluminium	1.61	1.27	0.76
	with thermal break	1.48	1.12	0.58
1.0 × 1.0 m	Aluminium	1.56	1.21	0.70
	with thermal break	1.45	1.08	0.55
2.0 × 2.0 m	Aluminium	1.46	1.09	0.58
	with thermal break	1.39	1.01	0.49
3.0 × 3.0 m	Aluminium	1.41	1.03	0.53
	with thermal break	1.36	0.98	0.46

B 5.36

Solar-control glasses

In addition to sunshading systems, solar-control glasses are another way of reducing the energy gains via areas of glass (see "Building envelope", p. 98, Fig. B 3.61).
Simple forms make use of enamelled or printed glass surfaces to diminish the energy gains. Reflective coatings on the outer pane can also help to shade the interior of a building from the sun; the transparency effect of the glazing is, however, lost (Fig. B 5.38).
Selective coatings, e.g. low E coatings facing outwards, enable the energy gains to be limited without any loss of transparency. As can be seen from Fig. B 5.28, however, the colour rendering characteristics of the glasses must be checked when using solar-control coatings.

Smart glazing

Glasses with changeable properties open up new applications. The most important products in this field are:

• Electrochromic glasses
• Liquid crystal glasses
• Gasochromic glasses
• Phototropic or thermotropic glasses

These glasses react to environmental influences – controlled by automatic or manual means – and change from a light- and radiation-permeable state to a light-scattering, darkening or reflective state.

Electrochromic coatings consist of a polymer film about 1 mm thick which regulates the total energy transmittance of the glass. Upon applying an electric current, the glass changes from transparent to a deep blue colour. The energy transmittance can be reduced to max. 20% with such a coating. Electrochromic glasses are therefore suitable for use as sunshades or glare protection (Fig. B 5.39).
Coatings made from microencapsulated liquid crystals (LC) behave similarly. They vary the transmission between 76% in the transparent state and 48% in the diffuse, light-scattering state, when they take on a milky appearance.
Gasochromic glasses change to a blue colour due to the inclusion of catalytically generated hydrogen and lose this colour again when air is introduced. The light transmission values of the two states vary between 15 and 60%. One controlled gas supply unit is required for every 10 m² of glass area.
Phototropic and thermotropic glasses do not require any form of control. The changes in phototropic glasses are based on metallic (e.g. silver) ions and the changes take place depending on the ultraviolet radiation. Thermotropic glasses are based on a two-component layer that segregates above a certain temperature. The glass then scatters the incoming sunlight as diffuse light and appears translucent.

Regulating the heat flow

Overheating effects ensue either as a result of high energy gains through transmission and ventilation, or as a result of high internal heat loads. Basically, the summertime thermal performance is regulated room by room according to DIN 4108-2 (see "Building envelope", p. 95). Materials present us with three ways of regulating the heat flow by way of three physical processes: absorption, specific heat capacity and phase lag. In this way they contribute to smoothing out the temperature amplitude, which signifies better thermal comfort in the interior (Fig. B 5.41).
Depending on the type of use, however, it may also be sensible to reduce the thermal masses. The corresponding capacity must then be ensured with technical systems. This strategy may be advisable for places of assembly with high, sudden internal loads.

Absorption and reflection

A material soaks up heat energy by way of absorption; the rest of the energy is reflected back into the room. The darker the colour of the material, the greater is the absorption and radiant heat. The choice of colour therefore affects the speed of the energy absorption and emission. The quantity of heat that can be absorbed by and stored in a building material therefore increases over time. It is possible to optimise a surface in energy terms by way of its degree of absorption, by its colouring (Fig. B 5.40). In

B 5.37

B 5.38

B 5.39

Surface	Heat absorption degree [%]
Aluminium, polished	0.20
Asphalt	0.93
Leaves, green	0.71 – 0.79
Roofing felt, black	0.82
Iron, galvanised	0.38
Iron, rough	0.75
Gold, polished	0.29
Copper, polished	0.18
Copper, oxidised	0.70
Marble, white	0.46
Slate	0.88
Snow, clean	0.20 – 0.35
Silver, polished	0.13
Clay bricks, red	0.75
Zinc, white	0.22

B 5.40

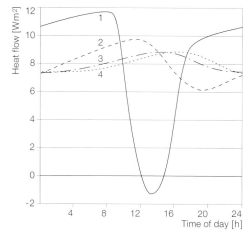

1 Insulation

2 Render, insulation, masonry, plaster

3 Render, masonry, insulation, air space, masonry, plaster

4 Render, vertically perforated clay bricks, plaster

B 5.41

Central European latitudes, the feasible energy-savings can amount to up to 8% of the heating energy requirements. If energy gains are undesirable, light colours should be chosen for the surface as far as possible, as are common in the countries bordering the Mediterranean, for example.

Specific heat capacity
The lower the thermal mass of a building, the quicker an unpleasant, hot and stuffy atmosphere builds up inside, with high temperature and humidity fluctuations. Materials with a high specific heat capacity enable overheating effects to be temporarily buffered. The capacity of a building component to store heat depends on its specific heat capacity and density. Pre-standard DIN V 4108-6 contains a method for calculating the effective heat capacity (Fig. B 5.46).
Heavyweight materials such as stone or concrete exhibit good storage characteristics owing to their high densities, but even timber is suitable for storing heat. Organic materials have a higher specific heat capacity than solid mineral building materials, i.e. they can generally absorb more thermal energy per kilogram of material (Fig. B 5.49).
A better storage capacity, essentially irrespective of the mass, can be achieved by integrating a phase change material (PCM). In a PCM, heat is converted into chemical energy at the phase transition – from solid to liquid, liquid to

gas – of the material. The material changes its internal structure as this happens. The enhanced storage capacity created in this way is, however, only available at the phase transition and hence only over a limited temperature range. Paraffin, a long-chain hydrocarbon, is the raw material for the majority of latent storage materials used in building (Fig. B 5.42). It prevents overheating in summer in particular, but can also prevent brief overcooling of a building by presetting the temperature of the phase transition to a certain level. PCMs can be incorporated into a building as separate volumes, but they are mostly used in microencapsulated form added to other building materials, e.g. plasterboard or wood fibreboard.

Phase lag
Stored heat is emitted from the material after a certain time, essentially in the form of radiant heat. As one component of the perceived temperature, this can achieve a drop in the temperature of the interior air in some circumstances. The time between energy absorption and emission is known as the phase lag or shift. This delay can be well exploited by the material, especially where the energy balance is primarily determined by external factors (e.g. residential buildings). Components such as solid walls or suspended floors can absorb solar energy and release it into the interior later, and this is how the concept of night-time cooling works (Fig. B 5.43).

The phase lag is particularly high when a material has a high effective heat capacity but at the same time a low thermal conductivity. A low thermal diffusivity indicates a high phase lag for a material (Fig. B 5.48). But insulating and storage effects in one material essentially cancel each other out, although one exception is wood fibreboard, which is ideal for insulating between conditioned and energy-gain zones, e.g. atria, conservatories. Furthermore, wood fibreboard can be used in areas with low storage masses, e.g. roof spaces converted into habitable rooms.

Sorption capacity
Materials have an influence not only on the heat flow, but also on the moisture balance. As the humidity of the air has an effect on the perceived room temperature for human beings (in the comfort range every 10% increase in humidity raises the perceived room temperature by 0.3°C), sorption also plays a role in energy terms. Its principal benefit lies, however, in the improved comfort.
Every building material has its own equilibrium moisture content, which is normally represented by way of sorption isotherms in relation to temperature and humidity. When a material possesses a large internal surface area, i.e. a high proportion of very fine pores, the sorption of water vapour from the air is particularly significant (Fig. B 5.44).

B 5.40 Heat absorption degrees of various surfaces
B 5.41 Heat flow through various wall constructions
B 5.42 PCM facade, home for senior citizens, Domat/Ems (CH), 2004, Dietrich Schwarz
B 5.43 Loam storage wall, information centre, Wangelin (D), 2002, Günter zur Nieden
B 5.44 Moisture absorption of various wall coatings in the case of a sudden moisture increase from 50 to 80%
B 5.45 Water vapour adsorption potential of various loam plasters in relation to their thickness
B 5.46 Calculating the effective heat capacity to pre-standard DIN V 4108-6
B 5.47 "Ecological rucksacks" (embodied materials flows) of various materials
B 5.48 Calculating the thermal diffusivity
B 5.49 Technical comparison of building materials with a capacity to store heat

B 5.42

B 5.43

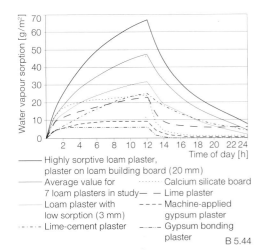

Highly sorptive loam plaster, plaster on loam building board (20 mm)
Average value for 7 loam plasters in study
Loam plaster with low sorption (3 mm)
Lime-cement plaster
Calcium silicate board
Lime plaster
Machine-applied gypsum plaster
Gypsum bonding plaster

B 5.44

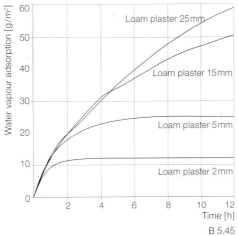

B 5.45

$$C_{eff} = \Sigma \, (c_i \, \rho_i \, d_i \, A_i)$$

C_{eff} Effective heat capacity
c Specific heat capacity [J/kgK]
ρ Density [kg/m³]
d Thickness [m]
A Area of component facing the room [m²]

i contains all the layers with thickness d up to 100 mm total wall thickness over area A that are not separated from the room by a layer of insulation ($\lambda < 0.1$ W/mK, $R \geq 0.25$ m²K/W).
Building components activated from both sides are included with only half their values.

B 5.46

In the case of loam, wood or gypsum, the process of adsorption can gradually change to capillary action, which also activates deeper layers of the building material for sorption (Fig. B 5.44). The selection of sorptive materials should take into account climatic (e.g. typical climate fluctuations) and use-related factors (e.g. a sudden rise in moisture content due to a large number of people). For example, a 2 mm coat of loam plaster requires only about two hours to reach its equilibrium moisture content when the relative humidity rises from 50 to 80%, but a 15 mm coat can regulate the internal atmosphere for more than 12 hours (Fig. B 5.45).

Embodied energy

We need substances to protect the operation of the building against excessive energy consumption or to regulate the flow of heat. Those substances are converted into building materials or building components by using energy. The production of building materials and components and the construction work itself tie up a considerable proportion of the total energy requirement of a building (see "Strategies", p. 187, Fig. B 6.29). Even though the building industry generally produces long-lasting products, it still remains by far the largest consumer of resources. It is in this context that questions arise as to the choice of a suitable material when considering energy consumption and environmental impacts. This choice should be linked with a notable reduction in quantities of materials and hence mass flows for the construction process.

Entropy
Entropy represents the interface between consumption of resources and consumption of energy. Entropy ensues when raw materials components and materials flows merge during the production processes and can only be separated again with a high energy input (see "Fundamentals", p. 43). The aim is therefore to generate fewer materials flows and keep them separate as far as possible in order to minimise the entropy.
For example, in the production of aluminium, a

material with one of the highest energy contents, besides the high energy consumption, a great amount of water is also needed for treating and enriching the bauxite. And the waste water in turn contains highly toxic heavy metals. On the other hand, aluminium is very durable and can be readily recycled.
There are various ways of reducing the entropy within the production:

- Local extraction or processing
- Reuse of scrap material or production waste
- Clear separation of process chains, e.g. through the production of recyclable, sorted by-products
- Minimal packaging
- Short transport distances

Entropy is also influenced by the way a material is used, or rather by the form of construction. In modern thermal insulation composite systems, the layer of insulation is frequently bonded to the substrate and then protected by a complete surface covering bonded to the insulation. It is therefore no longer possible to separate the individual material layers.

Grey energy
The energy used during manufacture and hence tied up in the material is known as "grey energy" or "embodied energy". This defines the quantity of energy required for the production, transport, storage and disposal of a product. Looked at in absolute terms, the grey energy of the existing building stock in Germany is – at a rough estimate – equal to 20 times the annual energy requirement for operating the buildings. As the energy efficiency of the building envelope and the building services improves, so the quantity of grey energy in the materials is increasing only marginally. But its proportion of the total energy consumption seen over the entire lifetime of a building is rising drastically. For a passive house, up to 50% of the total energy consumption remains embodied in the materials over a 50-year lifetime (see "Strategies", p. 187, Fig. B 6.29). Efficiency improvements in the operation of buildings must therefore always follow efficiency improvements in the use of materials (Fig. B 5.50).

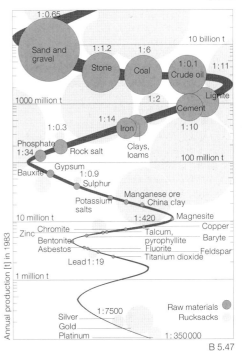

B 5.47

$$a = \lambda / \rho \, c$$

a Thermal diffusivity
λ Thermal conductivity [W/mK]
ρ Density [kg]
c Specific heat capacity [J/kgK]

B 5.48

Building material	Density ρ [kg/m³]	Spec. heat capacity c [kJ/kgK]
Stone	2700	1.0
Concrete	2300	1.0
Wood-chip concrete	1100	1.2
Structural timber	500	1.6
PCM – micro-encapsulated wax	approx. 600[1]	2.1[2]
Water, liquid	1000	4.2

[1] Bulk density (density approx. 1000 kg/m³)
[2] Plus 110 kJ/kg enthalpy of fusion in the temperature range 3–4°C

B 5.49

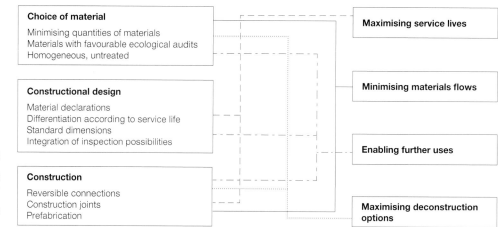

B 5.50

Primary energy input for building materials

The primary energy input (PEI) describes the grey energy in a building material (see "Fundamentals", p. 50). This parameter, which is specified for various reference units (normally kg or m³), makes a distinction between renewable and non-renewable energy consumption. The unit of measurement is the megajoule [MJ]; 100 MJ is equal to a calorific value of 2.8 l of oil, and 3.6 MJ is equal to 1 kWh.

The energy required for the manufacture of a building material can differ by a factor of more than 2000 – based on the weight of the material. High-energy materials are, for example, metals, glass and plastics; low-energy materials are, for example, loam and gypsum. Armed with PEI data, the architect can investigate alternative building materials and will preferably choose those that offer the same performance for a lower proportion of grey energy. The transportation of products makes a contribution to the primary energy input which varies and should not be underestimated (Fig. B 5.51).

Functional equivalent

With respect to the primary energy input, it should always be remembered that building materials exhibit different efficiencies. Polytetrafluoroethylene (PTFE), also known as Teflon, is a synthetic material with one of the highest energy inputs. Owing to its surface properties,

it is employed as a sealant and coating, e.g. as an alternative to bitumen sheeting, which has a very much lower energy input. However, the high energy input must be considered in conjunction with the fact that PTFE is used in much thinner layers. The functional equivalent eases the comparison of different building materials because it specifies the material thickness for the same performance (see "Appendix", p. 262). One particularly good example for the consideration of the functional equivalent is the typical structural materials timber, concrete, steel and aluminium. They are sized according to the forces in the components; the ability to carry tension or compression forces plus the elastic modulus therefore represent the governing design criteria (Fig. B 5.52).

Environmental Product Declaration (EPD)

Data on the primary energy input of a product will in future be specified as part of the type III Environmental Product Declaration (EPD). This information is based on ISO 14025 "Environmental labels and declarations" and is drawn up by independent bodies using information provided by manufacturers. The standard defines the standardised environmental statements required and therefore guarantees that all the relevant environmental impacts of a building material can be presented in an understandable manner. Product groups have

been set up to ensure compatibility between products. The following groups have been set up so far for Germany:

- Construction metals
- Mineral wool insulating materials
- Wood-based products
- Calcium silicate bricks
- Aerated concrete
- Clay bricks
- Lightweight concrete
- Calcium silicate insulating materials
- Lightweight aggregates
- Mineral premixed mortar
- Metal pipes

Renewable raw materials

A comparison of the parameters in Fig. B 5.53 reveals that renewable raw materials like wood have a high calorific value compared to all other building products. A large part of this energy is embodied in the tree during its growth. For an assessment, the primary energy input must therefore be expressed in terms of renewable and non-renewable energy sources plus the calorific value. In this case an increase in efficiency means using renewable energy sources to cover a large proportion of the PEI. By burning the wood after using the building product, this embodied energy can be converted back into usable energy. But as the combustion

Type of transport	PEI non-renewable [MJ/t km]	PEI renewable [MJ/t km]
HGV, 22 t perm. laden weight, 14.5 t payload, 85% utilisation	1.50	0.00031
Canal-going ship, approx. 1250 dwt, no currents	0.47	0.001
Goods train	0.40	0.053
Container ship, approx. 27 500 dwt, ocean-going	0.17	0.00004

B 5.51

Material	PEI [MJ/m³]	PEI/compression [J/kNm]	[%]	PEI/tension [J/kNm]	[%]	PEI/elastic modulus [J/kNm]	[%]
Concrete							
C 35/40 grade concrete	1764	50	83%	551	100%	0.05	76%
Reinforced concrete (2% steel reinforcement)	4098	60	100%	551	100%	0.07	100%
Masonry							
Calcium silicate bricks	2030	169	280%	–	–	–	–
Clay bricks	1663	139	229%	–	–	–	–
Timber							
Structural timber, pine	609	72	118%	87	16%	0.06	80%
Glued laminated timber	3578	358	592%	421	76%	0.33	469%
Metals							
Steel (FE 360 B)	188400	554	916%	554	101%	0.89	1281%
Weathering steel (WT St 27-2)	204100	454	750%	498	90%	0.96	1388%
Stainless steel (V2A)	411840	824	1362%	824	149%	1.96	2827%
Aluminium (EN AW-7022)	753380	1838	3038%	1838	333%	10.76	15513%
Float glass	35000	50	83%	1167	212%	0.50	721%

B 5.52

Material	Ref. value	Calorific value [MJ]	PEI non [MJ]	PEI renew. renew. [MJ]	GWP global w. potential [kg CO_2eq]
Stone					
Granite (long transport distances), polished, ρ = 2750 kg/m³	1 m³		9837	332	626
Marble (moderate transport distances), polished, ρ = 2700 kg/m³	1 m³		6749	249	422
Slate (local), ρ = 2700 kg/m³	1 m³		4608	165	286
Sandstone (local), sawn, ρ = 2500 kg/m³	1 m³		4099	153	253
Loam					
Compacted loam, ρ = 2200 kg/m³	1 m³		158	1	9.7
Loam bricks (sun-dried), ρ = 1200 kg/m³	1 m³		1257	4	74.0
Building materials with mineral binders					
Mortars and screeds					
Anhydrite mortar/screed, comp. strength class 20, 2350 kg/m³	1 m³		655	11.0	43
Magnesia mortar/screed, comp. strength class 20, 2000 kg/m³	1 m³		2439	9.9	348
Cement mortar/screed, comp. strength class 20, 2250 kg/m³	1 m³		2161	27.0	389
Gypsum mortar, class P IVa, ρ = 1300 kg/m³	1 m³		1477	9.6	177
Lime-cement mortar, class P IIa, ρ = 1500 kg/m³	1 m³		2675	28.0	448
Masonry units					
Calcium silicate, ρ = 1800 kg/m³	1 m³		2030	117	247
Concrete (paving), ρ = 2500 kg/m³	1 m³		1990	46	310
Aerated concrete, ρ = 400 kg/m³	1 m³		1484	81	186
Lightweight concrete, ρ = 600 kg/m³	1 m³		787	35	97
Concrete					
In situ concrete (C 25/30), ρ = 2340 kg/m³	1 m³		1549	17	251
In situ concrete (C 35/45), ρ = 2360 kg/m³	1 m³		1764	23	320
Precast concrete element, 2% steel (FE 360 B, C 35/45), ρ = 2500 kg/m³	1 m³		4098	86	455
Boards					
Fibre-cement board, ρ = 1750 kg/m³	1 m³		26839	116	2200
Gypsum wallboard (type A), ρ = 850 kg/m³	1 m³		2655	251	150
Ceramic materials					
Vertically perforated clay bricks, external wall, ρ = 670 kg/m³	1 m³		1485	638	95
Clay bricks, internal wall, ρ = 750 kg/m³	1 m³		1663	715	107
Solid engineering bricks (KMz), ρ = 1600 kg/m³	1 m³		4776	39	301
Glazed stoneware, ρ = 2000 kg/m³	1 m³		6322	0.060	393
Unglazed stoneware, ρ = 2000 kg/m³	1 m³		7160	0.070	445
Bituminous materials					
Pure straight-run bitumen (B 100-B 70)	1 kg		45.6	0.010	0.37
Polymer-modified bitumen (PmB 65 A)	1 kg		35.3	0.020	0.50
Wood and wood-based products					
Sawn timber					
Pine, 12% m.c. (local), oven-dry density 450 kg/m³	1 m³	8775	609	9512	-792[1]
Western red cedar, 12% m.c. (North America), o.-dry density 630 kg/m³	1 m³	12285	4485	14359	-907[1]
Teak, 12% m.c. (Brazil), oven-dry density 660 kg/m³	1 m³	12870	3217	13435	-1013[1]
Wood-based products					
Glued laminated timber, 12% m.c., oven-dry density 465 kg/m³	1 m³	9300	3578	13870	-662[1]
3-ply core plywood, 12% m.c., oven-dry density 430 kg/m³	1 m³	8618	2617	9387	-648[1]
Veneer plywood (BFU), 5% m.c., oven-dry density 490 kg/m³	1 m³	10175	4729	15041	-636[1]
Particleboard (P 5, V 100), 8.5% m.c., oven-dry density 690 kg/m³	1 m³	13998	5818	12614	-821[1]
Oriented strand board (OSB), 4% m.c., oven-dry density 620 kg/m³	1 m³	12555	4593	16479	-839[1]
Medium density fibrebd. (MDF), 7.5% m.c., o.-dry density 725 kg/m³	1 m³	15843	9767	12495	-515[1]
Metal					
Ferrous metals					
Cast iron, casting (GG 20; secondary), GJL	1 kg		10	0.49	0.97
Structural steel, hot-rolled section (FE 360 B)	1 kg		24	0.54	1.70
Steel mesh as concrete reinforcement (secondary)	1 kg		13	0.24	0.83
Weathering steel, cold-rolled strip (WT St 37-2), 2 mm	1 kg		26	0.56	2.00
Stainless steel (V 2 A, X 5 CrNi 18-10), 2 mm	1 kg		54	6.30	4.80
Non-ferrous metals					
Aluminium alloy (EN AW-7022 [AlZn5Mg3Cu]), sheet, 2 mm	1 kg		271	38	22.0
Lead, sheet, 2 mm	1 kg		34	1.9	2.3
Titanium-zinc (pure zinc Z1, 0.003% titanium), sheet, 2 mm	1 kg		45	3.8	2.6
Copper, sheet, 2 mm	1 kg		37	4.6	2.5
Glass					
Float glass, ρ = 2500 kg/m³	1 kg		14	0.08	0.88
Synthetic materials					
Polyethylene (PE-HD), film	1 kg	41	75	0.09	1.82
Polyvinyl chloride (PVC-P), compound for waterproof sheeting	1 kg	17	61	2.10	2.28
Polymethyl methacrylate (PMMA "Perspex"), panel	1 kg	24	87	0.29	3.39
Polytetrafluoroethylene (PTFE "Teflon"), coating	1 kg	8,3	295	2.50	16.20
Polyester resin (UP)	1 kg	32	115	0.45	4.68
Epoxy resin (EP)	1 kg approx. 30		137	0.78	6.47
Chloroprene rubber (CR "Neoprene"), bearing	1 kg approx. 25		96	0.96	3.65
Silicone (SI), sealing compound	1 kg approx. 25		91	30.0	4.07

B 5.53

process simply releases the carbon dioxide that was tied up in the wood during its growth, renewable raw materials are also known as carbon sinks. From this point of view, the greater use of renewable raw materials should be seen as positive.

However, these days most timber or wood-based products no longer undergo a natural drying process, but rather an artificial one making use of heating plant. This shortens storage times and increases the productivity of the resource in microeconomic terms, but the CO_2 emissions caused by this process can cancel out the positive effect of the overall balance (Fig. B 5.54). Product forms similar to the raw material plus fewer technical processing steps increase the energy value of renewable raw materials.

The problem of availability and the assessment of the obtaining of the raw materials still remains, however, and is particularly obvious in the case of timber, wood-based products or cellulose. We assume that these renewable raw materials can be permanently regenerated. This premise is correct in the context of a temperate climate like that of Central Europe because such a humid climate enables a high biomass productivity per unit area. But even renewable raw materials are subject to a maximum production speed that limits the supply to the market. This speed is especially relevant in the case of scarce resources or slow-growing organic resources, as the severely depleted stocks of red cedar in North America bear witness to, for example.

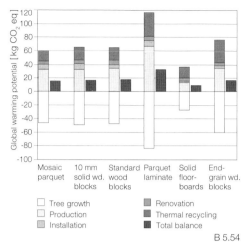

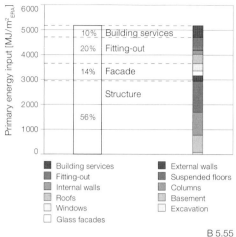

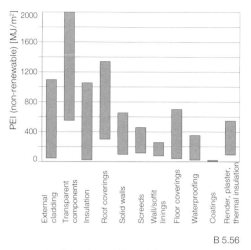

B 5.54

B 5.55

B 5.56

Embodied energy of building components

Building materials must always be considered in a functional context. They are joined, connected, assembled and bonded in many different ways. They thus form functional layers that can be compared with one another. For example, the cladding to a facade cannot be properly assessed without taking into account its fixings and the necessary supporting construction. In contrast to the building material assessment, the functional assessment per square metre results in differences of "only" a factor of max. 100.

In principle, we divide functional layers into two groups: invisible components, which are required to satisfy specific requirements in the building, and visible components, which besides functional requirements also have to satisfy aesthetics and the perceived value of the structure. Invisible functional layers can be optimised by comparing their embodied energy. Among the non-structural elements, these include:

- Insulation
- Solid walls
- Screeds
- Roof waterproofing
- Waterproofing

But there is also potential in visible components such as facades. Such components include:

- Cladding to external walls
- Transparent elements
- Roof coverings
- Floor coverings
- Wall and soffit finishes
- Plaster and render
- Coatings

There is potential for optimisation without placing restrictions on the aesthetics, provided the quantities of materials are reduced. In terms of the as-built condition, it is mostly the functional parts of a layer, e.g. fixings, that offer the greatest optimisation possibilities.

This can be demonstrated using the example of floor coverings, where omitting the adhesive normally used to bond the covering to the substrate results in a vital energy-saving (Fig. B 5.60).

Building component groups

The various building component groups of a building tie up different amounts of primary energy (Fig. B 5.56; see also "Appendix", p. 262). In virtually all buildings, the largest part of the embodied energy is usually that in the load-bearing structure. Other building component groups with large amounts of embodied energy are the facade and the internal fitting-out. This statement is demonstrated by the "Chriesbach Forum" (see Example 15, pp. 240–42), where the structure accounts for 56% of the grey

energy, the facades 14% and the internal fitting-out 20% (Fig. B 5.55).

Optimising the design is a particularly good way of reducing the grey energy. Durable, lightweight forms of construction are generally preferable to heavyweight forms. Every additional kilogram of building material employed increases the usage of resources, the associated environmental impact and the energy consumption.

Embodied energy in the life cycle

The weighting of building components with respect to energy requirements shifts over the life cycle because the components remain in the building for different lengths of time, i.e. have different service lives. The necessary process of renewal entails further energy requirements during the period of use.

Fig. B 5.61 shows the embodied energy of a typical suspended floor construction. In the as-built condition, 37% of the grey energy is found in the structure and 40% in the floor covering. However, if we consider this component over a defined period of 100 years, certainly not unusual for a building, then – in contrast to the loadbearing construction – the floor covering will be replaced several times during that period. The accumulated cost of the floor covering over 100 years therefore accounts for many times the cost of the initial floor covering; over this period, it accounts for about 80% of the

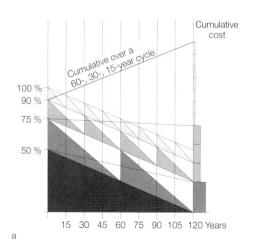

a

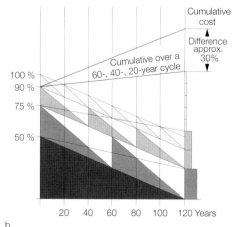

b

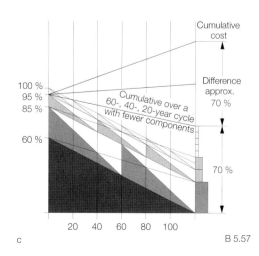

c

B 5.57

total embodied energy. The more frequently a building component is renewed, the more significant is its contribution to the grey energy of the total building.

This represents a starting point for low energy demands in the life cycle. In terms of optimising the choice of materials, the nature and progress of the life cycle therefore takes on a key role alongside the material properties. The aim is to match the choice of materials and the constructional assembly to the planned lifetime, type of use and anticipated usage processes. Energy optimisation processes then usually go hand in hand with financial savings.

Durability

In theory, durability describes the potential for a building material to maintain the function(s) assigned to it for a certain length of time. To determine durability, we compare the lengths of time for which building components survive undamaged in a defined usage situation. This depends, for example, on specific potential risks or the building context. The outcome is a normal distribution curve, which describes the upper and lower limits of a typical usage period for probabilities from 50 to 90%, divided into time periods (Fig. B 5.59). The durability is therefore specified as a timespan corresponding to usage influences and the associated risk factors. The lower value describes the durability for standard planning and usage, the higher value relates to optimised planning and usage contexts.

Sawtooth model

One way of illustrating the durability of building materials and building components is the so-called sawtooth model, which shows the different durabilities of building components. The model assumes that building components are used right up to the limit of their durability before being replaced. The cumulative cost of this is also shown (Fig. B 5.57a). If building components last longer and can therefore remain in the building for longer, the cumulative cost is reduced considerably (Fig. B 5.57b). If we use fewer different building materials, this usually results in a better overall balance because the material-related replacement cycles coincide more often.

The sawtooth model therefore reveals the energy efficiency and the economic potential of material optimisation with respect to the durability. Three general statements are relevant for design and planning:

- Separation of layers according to durability
- Material synergy
- Maintenance intervention

Firstly, technical, functional building components or fitting-out layers with different service lives should be joined together in such a way that they can be renewed without impairing or damaging adjacent components. Such types of construction normally decrease the amount of

embodied energy – demonstrated using the example of floor coverings (Figs. B 5.60 and 5.62). The especially durable layers within the construction should therefore be arranged accordingly. Modern facade constructions illustrate the problem of separating the layers. It is not always possible to design all the layers in order of their durability. For example, a layer of insulation is much less durable than a waterproofing layer, so the insulation should thus be readily accessible. No reliable durability values are available as yet for certain layers such as bonded vapour barriers and airtight membranes. Detachable connections permit inspection and, if necessary, replacement of such layers. Secondly, individual building components can in some circumstances fulfil not only the functional requirements assigned to them, but also some of the requirements of other layers; this is another way of reducing the embodied energy (Fig. B 5.57c). For example, a mastic asphalt subfloor can be replaced by a terrazzo screed, which results in a very hardwearing surface. If the number of layers is reduced, this usually results in energy-efficiency and economic benefits. Fig. B 5.66 shows the ESO Hotel in Chile, a building in which the wearing surfaces are – where appropriate – mostly the surfaces of the loadbearing construction.

Thirdly, high-maintenance building components – building services elements especially – must be readily accessible (Fig. B 5.88). Leaving the building services exposed results in optimum accessibility. Otherwise, ducts and shafts, systematic routing and zoning permits the straightforward installation of new technology media and the necessary flexibility. The lifespans of building services are frequently overestimated, and the fact that upgrading and technological overhauls may be necessary within a few years is often overlooked. Outdated building services components then frequently lose their benefits, but can be incorporated into the building services in a new context, like, for example, defunct chimneys, which although no longer used as flues for exhaust gases can nevertheless be used as shafts for electric cables or heating pipes.

"Disrupting factors" in the sawtooth model

It is not always technical- or material-related deficiencies that trigger a process of renewal. It is often also building services, safety, security and aesthetic factors or a change of function that make replacement necessary.

Changes to statutory instruments and regulations and also technical progress are not always wholly foreseeable. And in Europe, EU legislation now constitutes the overriding criteria. EU legislation formulates the approximate direction, which is subsequently implemented in concrete terms via national legislation. Gaining an overview of current trends, especially with respect to building services and the energy-efficiency quality of buildings, is useful when planning for future needs.

B 5.58

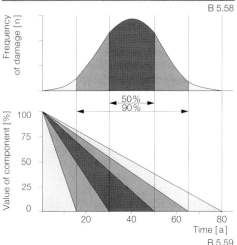

B 5.59

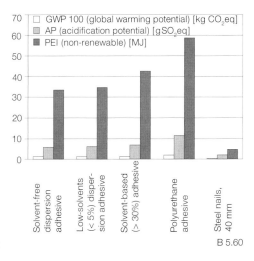

B 5.60

B 5.54 CO₂ balance of various wooden floor coverings over their life cycles

B 5.55 Primary energy input (PEI) (= embodied energy) of the "Chriesbach Forum" according to building component groups

B 5.56 Primary energy input (PEI) (= embodied energy) of various functional layers

B 5.57 Durabilities of various functional layers in the form of a sawtooth model

B 5.58 Private house in timber, Bregenzerwald (A), 1999, Dietrich Untertrifaller

B 5.59 Calculating durabilities based on the probability of damage to the material

B 5.60 Energy parameters of various floor covering fixing methods

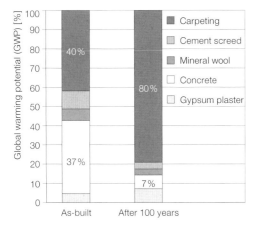

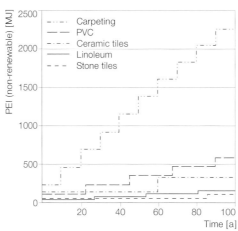

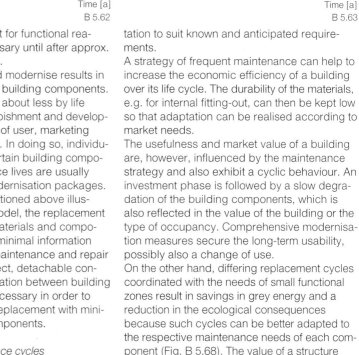

B 5.61

B 5.62

B 5.63

The intensity of usage cannot always be defined in advance during the planning phase and can turn out to be much higher or lower than predicted. Designers are recommended to use robust forms of construction and better-quality building components when designing buildings for the general public.

Market demands and trends have always been and still are the reasons for building activities. Planners do not just satisfy a demand, but rather create needs, set fashions and form styles through their activities. Appraisals should be seen very much in the light of the time in which they were made. If the high durability of building components really is to be exploited, a too fashionable, trendy design can easily lead to premature renewal of components even before the expiry of their technical service lives owing to "visual wear". On the other hand, lucid, high-quality but nevertheless contemporary architectural statements retain their aesthetic value over a long period. For example, the Alt-Erlaa residential development in Vienna, built between 1973 and 1985, is very popular among its present occupants despite the fact that similar buildings erected during that same period are today viewed highly critically (Fig. B 5.64).

Even on the level of individual building components, service lives are often subjected to certain cycles that reflect certain tastes. An analysis of the number of replacement processes for a WC reveals that replacement after 25 years takes place primarily for reasons of fashion,

even though replacement for functional reasons would not be necessary until after approx. 55–70 years (Fig. B 5.63).

The need to upgrade and modernise results in the replacement of many building components. Modernisation is brought about less by life cycles and more by refurbishment and development schemes, changes of user, marketing problems or other events. In doing so, individual measures involving certain building components with different service lives are usually combined into larger modernisation packages. The sawtooth model mentioned above illustrates, as a theoretical model, the replacement processes for building materials and components, but supplies only minimal information with regard to sensible maintenance and repair procedures. In that respect, detachable connections and clear separation between building component layers are necessary in order to guarantee renewal and replacement with minimal damage to other components.

Optimisation of maintenance cycles
Two opposing strategies can be worked out for optimising maintenance: long cycles with extensive, one-off measures, or short cycles with many small measures.

Joint replacement cycles encompassing only a few building components entail a predictable, high investment and high energy input at defined times. Such maintenance can also include conversion measures to enable adap-

tation to suit known and anticipated requirements.

A strategy of frequent maintenance can help to increase the economic efficiency of a building over its life cycle. The durability of the materials, e.g. for internal fitting-out, can then be kept low so that adaptation can be realised according to market needs.

The usefulness and market value of a building are, however, influenced by the maintenance strategy and also exhibit a cyclic behaviour. An investment phase is followed by a slow degradation of the building components, which is also reflected in the value of the building or the type of occupancy. Comprehensive modernisation measures secure the long-term usability, possibly also a change of use.

On the other hand, differing replacement cycles coordinated with the needs of small functional zones result in savings in grey energy and a reduction in the ecological consequences because such cycles can be better adapted to the respective maintenance needs of each component (Fig. B 5.68). The value of a structure therefore remains on a constant level, which also ensures a constant return on investment (ROI). The components can be optimised for especially long service lives and renewed in small packages of measures. However, the ensuing ongoing process of replacement restricts the usage flexibility of the building, and in the case of a comprehensive change of use, many still usable components will also have to be replaced.

B 5.64

B 5.65

B 5.66

B 5.67

B 5.68

If the planning remit presumes a defined, short timespan, like with temporary structures or the internal fitting-out for retail premises, the durability of the materials can be chosen to suit the intended lifespan (Fig. B 5.65).

The longer the expected period of use of a building, the more important it is to consider the usage phase. If there is a long-term requirement for a certain type of interior space, as is usually the case with residential buildings, high durability in conjunction with smaller packages of measures is usually the best solution. The quality of the internal fitting-out and the small-format usage increase the materials and energy requirements (Fig. B 5.68).

In buildings with variable requirements, growing usage expectations and correspondingly better internal fitting-out mean that long-lasting components are not fully exploited. In such cases the planning should take into account renewal processes and, if applicable, secondary uses for components and materials (Fig. B 5.67).

Materials in the life cycle

Considering the embodied energy in materials reveals the importance of the life cycle model. Besides the energy consumption, every use of every material triggers environmental impacts due to the resulting flow of resources. Starting with the need for a building, such flows can only be reduced, not eliminated (Fig. B 5.70).

Consumption of resources

The availability of raw materials was critical for the development of prosperity in the industrialised countries. It was only through the exploitation and processing of those materials that industrial prosperity became possible at all. According to the rules of the marketplace, dwindling resources makes a commodity expensive; and permanent availability of other resources is not guaranteed, as the disputes involving gas, oil and water are already proving. Worldwide, buildings consume about 50% of all resources in their construction and operation. They represent *the* critical factor for dwindling resources and environmental problems. On the

other hand, owing to their low-tech status and high material consumption, building materials are predestined for considerable improvements in efficiency. Other sectors, like the automotive or electronics industries, have pledged themselves to saving resources and increasing efficiency, and derive competitive advantages from that. Without new impetus from within the building sector, new developments or comparable pledges, political demands for similar objectives in the construction industry are certainly only a matter of time. In order that materials remain available permanently, open materials chains, especially those for non-renewable raw materials, must be closed wherever possible.

Life cycle approach

Considering the life cycles of materials represents a new and to a certain extent not yet comprehensively defined approach which brings together knowledge from various social and economic sectors. However, the total life cycle cannot be fully predicted and planned. So it is therefore often the need to guarantee options, e.g. adaptation to suit actual usage requirements that is important. "Flexible fit" strategies are suitable here: increased durability to prolong the potential period of use, simpler internal fitting-out to enable changes to the internal layout, reversible connections between components to ease deconstruction, and recovery of materials for the building materials life cycle.

Considering the embodied energy alone can force a decrease in the use of materials (Fig. B 5.50). Complying with constructional necessities, e.g. through comprehensive exploitation of material capacities, simple assemblies, adapted durability, use of renewable materials, leads to a much lower consumption of both energy and resources.

However, further factors come into play in the life cycle approach, e.g. secondary emissions due to cleaning or changes to the interior air due to emissions from materials. Many of these factors can only be considered and described as potential factors. They are not necessarily triggered by negative aspects and indeed do not have to be used positively, but they are key

elements in viable planning for the needs of the future. And it is precisely here that we find the potential for innovation provided by the advance planning of the life cycle.

Life cycle analysis methods

Life cycle analyses are used to evaluate the complex influences. They balance the entire lifespan of a building material, building component or whole building. To do this, all the stages – obtaining the raw material, production, processing, transport, usage, subsequent usage, disposal – are evaluated. In principle, there are two different methods: looking at the required material inputs or the resulting environmental effects (Fig. B 5.71).

Materials-flow analysis

The MIPS (Material Input Per Service unit) concept introduced by Friedrich Schmidt-Bleek in 1994 adds up the material inputs necessary for producing and using a building product or component. All natural materials required for the production are collated as "material intensities". They form the material input related to the self-weight of the material, measured in kilogram input per kilogram output. The unit of measurement used for energy is the kilogram per megajoule [kg/MJ].

Material intensities are distinguished according to sources of resources as follows:

- abiotic resources [kg]
- biotic resources [kg]
- soil [kg]
- water [l]
- air [m^3]

The total material input, also known as the "ecological rucksack", is the sum of the self-weight of the product and its material intensities (Fig. B 5.72).

This procedure reveals materials flows and identifies the main resources used per unit of mass (Fig. B 5.47).

The MIPS concept takes into account all the conversion steps necessary for the production and offers planners the chance to join up existing materials flows. The use of just a few recyclable, flexible materials in the material concept

B 5.69   Process flow chart for drawing up a life cycle
         assessment (LCA)
B 5.70   The life cycle of a building and the associated
         planning activities
B 5.71   Input/output relationship within the production
         chain of a building material
B 5.72   Schematic presentation and calculation of a
         building material according to the MIPS concept
B 5.73   Apportionment of emissions using the example
         of the global warming potential
B 5.74   Apportionment of LCA parameters by country to
         form a cumulative single value

LCA framework

Goal and scope definition

Inventory analysis

Impact assessment

Evaluation

Checking completeness, sensitivity, consistency

Determining the key statements

Assessment

Conclusions

Recommendations

Presentation of results

Application

Development and improvement of products

Strategic planning

Public decision-making processes

Marketing

B 5.69

increases the potential for subsequent usage. In global terms, building materials thus accumulate in the construction industry over time. This means that closed life cycles are possible to a large extent, which promotes the cradle-to-grave economy.

However, materials-flow analyses are limited in their options for identifying the harmful environmental effects of individual processes. The analyses cannot be broken down according to the different effects of climate change, loss of biodiversity or human toxicity, for instance.

Life cycle assessment
DIN EN ISO 14040-44, which came into force in 2000, defines the life cycle assessment (LCA). Taking materials flows as its starting point, the LCA converts these into effects (e.g. emissions). The LCA can be applied not only to building products, but also to every process, e.g. a service, a production procedure or an economic unit (e.g. a company in general). An LCA generally comprises three parts interconnected via defined iteration loops (Fig. B 5.69):

- The inventory analysis determines which materials and energy conversion processes are necessary for a product and its production. The limits for the audit, the so-called cut-off criteria, are normally set to at least 1% material mass and primary energy consumption. The cut-off criteria should be checked in the case of materials known to cause environmental problems (e.g. plasticisers in synthetic materials).
- The impact assessment compiles the emissions of all materials and energy conversion steps. For this assessment, the various emissions are collated in groups with the same environmental effects (e.g. global warming potential) and expressed as an equivalent of a dangerous substance known to be heavily responsible for that harmful effect (Fig. B 5.73).
- The assessment is divided into steps for determining the core statements plus evaluation and presenting the results. Data relevant to the assessment but not included in the audit, e.g. emissions during use or durability, can also be presented. In addition, recommendations for the use of the product can be derived.

The "Round Table on Sustainable Construction" initiated by the Federal Ministry of Transport, Building & Urban Affairs, has specified (for Germany) the following categories for the verification of environmental effects caused by building materials:

- Primary Energy Input, renewable/non-renewable (= embodied energy), PEI [MJ]
- Global Warming Potential, GWP 100 [kg CO_2 eq]
- Ozone Depletion Potential, ODP [kg CCL_3F eq]
- Acidification Potential, AP [kg SO_2 eq]
- Eutrophication (= excessive fertilisation) Potential, EP [kg PO_4^{3-} eq]
- Photochemical Ozone Creation Potential, POCP [kg C_2H_4 eq]

The results of the LCA for a building material will in future be given in the type III European Product Declarations (EPD) to form a useful design aid (see p. 161). In contrast to the MIPS concept, however, the effects of the individual categories cannot be added together to form a generally applicable total value. This is why there is a problem with the weighting of the

individual parameters; an overall interpretation is difficult. Some European countries have developed standards that enable an LCA to be expressed as an overall parameter. For this, the modelling and the weighting of the parameters have been specified in legislation and are consequently not necessarily scientifically precise (Fig. B 5.74).

In Germany, the Federal Environment Agency has devised a method for classifying and prioritising the impact categories. In this method, the extent of the impact (global – local; permanent – temporary), the current environmental status for the impact category (harmful – harmless) and the contribution of the impact category to the total burden in Germany (large – small) form part of the evaluation.

The results of an LCA and the conclusions that can be drawn may change depending on the limits chosen for the audit. The embodied energy described above is a central element in an LCA. There are three levels to be considered here: building materials, functional layers and building elements.

Operation

Energy requirements
Facility management
Servicing
Maintenance/cleaning
Repairs

Modernisation

Upgrading
Adaptation/extension
Conversion
Refurbishment

Commissioning

Acceptance
Documentation
Energy performance certificate

Construction

Site supervision
Recycling of waste
Quality control

Deconstruction

Recycling
Disposal

Project development

Location
Usage
Existing building fabric
Financing
Period of use

Planning

Preliminary design

Detailed design
- energy minimisation

Selection of materials
- production of materials
- dangerous substances
- durability
- deconstruction options

Planning the works
- minimising materials

Specification
Handover

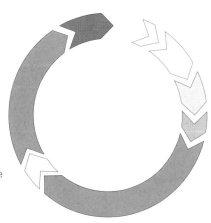

B 5.70

If we summarise the statements of the LCA, we discover which building components cause the greatest emissions. The areas in which our planning activities can unfold their greatest effectiveness are revealed (Fig. B 5.78). Furthermore, an LCA helps us to make decisions regarding forms of construction and types of material.

Materials and production

The energy and resources productivity in Germany should have increased to such an extent by 2020 that our current standard of living will be safeguarded for the future without the consumption of additional natural resources. Besides increasing the proportion of renewable raw materials in construction, production-oriented optimisation can choose between two strategies: Firstly, using materials produced locally creates employment locally, but can sometimes lead to higher costs. The shortening of transport routes and the (usually) better controllability of the environmental impacts can contribute to a high resources efficiency and result in less pollution. Secondly, the main focus when using materials procured on the global building materials market is not the individual construction itself, but rather the increased efficiency of the materials employed. These should then turn out to be particularly optimised, low-resources forms of construction. The more efficient use of such materials must then outweigh the increased environmental impact due to, for example, transport.

Obtaining raw materials
The quarries and mines supplying mineral and metallic raw materials entail the consumption of land and/or subsequent settlement, the negative economic and ecological repercussions of which should be minimised. The relationships are readily apparent in open-cast mining, e.g. the stone quarries of Carrara. But even the deepest German open-cast lignite mine (Hambach) reveals the negative ecological effects: the ratio of excavated soil to lignite extracted is 7.2:1. Open-cast mining calls for a lowering of the water table. For every 1 t of lignite there is 4–7 t of water; so on average 11 t of material must be moved to obtain 1 t of lignite. Flora and fauna change in the vicinity of the open-cast mine, and the stability of the ground, embankments in particular, is impaired.
The evaluation of such consequences reveals both ecological and economic conflicts. For instance, open gravel pits can offer rare animals new habitats, and whole landscapes can be given a new appearance through such open-cast mining, e.g. the former industrial landscape at IBA Fürst-Pückler-Land near Cottbus (D). However, the subsequent use of a quarrying or mining area should always be guaranteed and, furthermore, restoration and rehabilitation concepts should be specified in advance.
Only the LCA takes account of secondary pollutant emissions and their relevance for the

environment, e.g. sludge containing heavy metals in the mining of bauxite and the subsequent accumulation in hydrological and foodstuffs cycles. So an LCA evaluates not only the raw materials extraction itself, but also the type of extraction. In the case of stone, the ecological rucksack is low according to the MIPS concept – a ratio of 1:1.2 (Fig. B 5.47). An LCA comes to a similar result, but only when mechanical methods such as sawing to obtain the stone (e.g. like with the majority of limestones) can be employed. If a stone (e.g. granite) has to be blasted, the use of explosives represents a high energy usage whose emissions can hardly be controlled (Fig. B 5.75). From the viewpoint of an LCA, the use of limestone cannot be compared with granite because the environmental impact of granite is four times that of limestone (see "Appendix", p. 262).

Production processes
Building materials are usually the result of long process chains. In the sense of a low entropy, the production should therefore be as efficient as possible. In the case of glass, for example, the processing of almost 100% of the raw materials in the end results in semi-finished products. Defective material is fed back into the manufacturing cycle, which cuts the production energy required by up to 25%.
On the other side of the equation to the reduction in entropy required for ecological reasons, we sometimes find economic aspects such as large differences in wages between individual countries or different environmental stipulations at national level. Labour-intensive fitting-out materials are frequently produced in low-wage countries. Although the price of the product is acceptable to the market, this must be weighed against the much higher emissions due to the much longer transport routes (Fig. B 5.51).
Efficiency in resources is to a large extent dependent on the method of construction, which influences – essentially also determined by the quality of the planning and the preparation of the work – the intelligent use of materials, the extent, durability and reusability of building materials, but also the careful use of materials in the construction process in order to minimise mistakes and wastage. In addition to mass production, current methods also enable customised production, i.e. the bespoke production of building components according to a specification which can respond to particular boundary conditions such as the plot, the geometry of existing structures or other requirements. The spectrum of prefabrication stretches from individual materials to components and right up to system building and complete buildings.

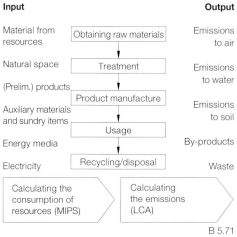

B 5.71

Calculating an MIPS

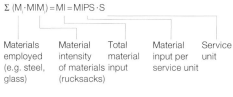

$$\Sigma\,(M_i \cdot MIM_i) = MI = MIPS \cdot S$$

| Materials employed (e.g. steel, glass) | Material intensity of materials (rucksacks) | Total material input | Material input per service unit | Service unit |

$\quad M_1 \cdot MIM_1$ e.g. steel plus rucksack
$+\,M_2 \cdot MIM_2$ e.g. glass plus rucksack
$+\,M_3 \cdot MIM_3$ e.g. PVC plus rucksack
$+\,...$

⟶ end product (1 unit, e.g. a car)

B 5.72

	Global warming potential [kg CO₂eq]	Length of time in atmosphere [a]	Increase in concentration since industrialisation
Carbon dioxide (CO_2)	1	50–200	28%
Methane (CH_4)	21	9–15	146%
Nitrous oxide (N_2O)	310	120	13%
Fluorocarbons (CF_4 u. a.)	6500	50000	from 0 ppt[1] to 72 ppt
HFCs (CHF_3 etc.)	11700	264	no data
Sulphur hexafluoride (SF_6)	23900	3200	from 0 ppt to 3–4 ppt

[1] ppt = parts per trillion

B 5.73

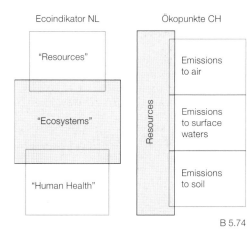

B 5.74

B 5.75

B 5.76

B 5.75   Blasting in a stone quarry
B 5.76   Private house, Moledo (P), 2000, Eduardo Souto de Moura
B 5.77   Comparing the grey energy of compact and non-compact passive houses
B 5.78   Individual and total assessment of the planning themes relevant over the life cycle plus their processing options with respect to the work phases of the architect
B 5.79   Typical cases of damage in buildings in Germany and their causes
B 5.80   Waste codes according to the German Industrial Waste Act
B 5.81   Waste streams according to the German Cradle-to-Grave Economy Act
B 5.82   Viewing platform, Helsinki (FIN), 2002, Helsinki University of Technology, Prof. Jan Söderlund

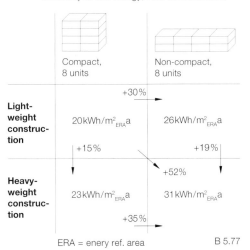

	Compact, 8 units	Non-compact, 8 units
Light-weight construc-tion	+30% → 20 kWh/m²$_{ERA}$a	26 kWh/m²$_{ERA}$a
	+15% ↓	+19% ↓
		+52%
Heavy-weight construc-tion	23 kWh/m²$_{ERA}$a +35% →	31 kWh/m²$_{ERA}$a

ERA = enery ref. area   B 5.77

Forms of construction

The discussion surrounding lightweight or heavyweight forms of construction crops up again and again in residential work in particular. Both forms of construction have their own specific merits and demerits, which do not normally permit a decision to be made in advance. Heavyweight forms of construction require about 20% more grey energy than lightweight structures (Fig. B 5.77). However, the shape of the building plays a role here (see "Urban space and infrastructure", p. 69).

In order to benefit from the advantages of both forms of construction, hybrid forms can sometimes be employed, e.g. a timber structure with a solid, stiffening concrete core.

It is true for virtually every building material that the less of it used to achieve a defined performance standard, the lower is the embodied energy over the entire life cycle. The potential for savings can often be found in safety factors far higher than those required by legislation. Constructional innovation and architectural creativity can help to relieve structures of weight and hence also visual "corpulence".

The efficient use of resources in a construction usually increases with the degree of prefabrication. The production of building components in a factory enables tighter tolerances and more slender dimensions, and results in a better-quality building with fewer deficiencies. The more careful planning and the better quality control lead to far fewer production errors and rejects (Fig. B 5.79). In this way, it is possible to avoid, for example, undesirable thermal bridges reliably (see "Building envelope", p. 90). The greater precision of the building components reduces the care and maintenance processes required over the life cycle and can lead to a longer service life.

The design of simple, functional details complying with building physics requirements results in lower operating costs and helps to maintain value, which is evident in the architecture itself (Fig. B 5.82). When the requirements regarding materials and details are clearly defined and the number of functions to be provided are limited, this has a positive effect on the outcome. Reducing the number of materials also often has a positive effect – for the design of the building as well as for the ecology. Omitting building components and building component layers reduces the need for complex, expensive maintenance procedures. And users, too, frequently perceive simply designed minimal solutions as "less stressful".

Although not common up to now, interdisciplinary prefabrication, i.e. involving more than one building trade, appears to be sensible. Small-format production methods aligned with the boundaries of the traditional building trades cause extra transport for various building processes that involve an additional consumption of resources.

Construction process and processing

Efficient processing appropriate to the material reduces the amount of waste. Close-tolerance production, e.g. with prefabricated parts, adherence to modular dimensions derived from the materials themselves or materials that adapt to suit the location (e.g. blown-in insulating materials), reduce the wastage caused by cutting to size.

In order to reduce the "inert masses", uncontaminated excavated material can be reused on the plot itself, e.g. for landscaping, although the compaction possibilities do determine the further uses quite considerably. Costs fall when waste does not have to be deposited in landfill; and there are no transport emissions either. Greater care is required if waste is to be turned into new raw materials or used for energy purposes. Since February 2007 all waste in Germany must be recycled according to the Cradle-to-Grave Economy Act (KrW/AbfG), provided this is economically viable (see p. 174).

The "Clean Building Site" campaign in Germany is based on the Industrial Waste Act (GewAbfV). In order to guarantee reuse with the highest possible quality, the producers and owners of building and/or demolition debris must collect, store and transport waste streams separately (provided they occur separately) and make them available for recycling (Figs. B 5.80 and 5.81).

Materials and building usage

As a rule, a building is tailored to a specific user, a specific location. This tailoring process uses materials to create a particular reference to the location and to underscore the identity for the user and the observer. The specific use of building materials can help a building to blend into its surroundings (Fig. B 5.76) – or to highlight it, make it stand out from its surroundings. However, the architectural intentions cannot be fully detached from the aspects of the sustainability of the materials used, their durability and ease of maintenance, the energy input, the environmental impacts and the effects on the health of the building's occupants or users.

Building materials guarantee the intended usage in physical terms and in doing so are often subjected to high stresses and strains. Complex performance profiles for building materials are derived from the usage requirements, which touch on constructional, functional, physical and architectural dimensions. Materials provide technical and functional accomplishments in order to create a permanently secure living space for human beings and to maintain buildings as a valuable object or as a cultural commodity. The diverse requirements cannot always be satisfied solely by one building material.

The physical properties of the building material determine whether it focuses on satisfying just one requirement or several requirements such as sound insulation, fire protection and thermal performance simultaneously. For example, floor

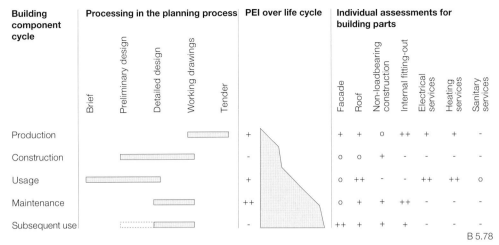
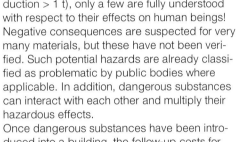
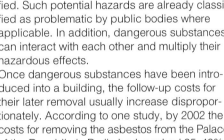

Building component cycle	Processing in the planning process					PEI over life cycle	Individual assessments for building parts						
	Brief	Preliminary design	Detailed design	Working drawings	Tender		Facade	Roof	Non-loadbearing construction	Internal fitting-out	Electrical services	Heating services	Sanitary services
Production						+	+	+	o	++	+	+	-
Construction						-	o	o	+	-	-	-	-
Usage						+	o	++	-	-	++	++	o
Maintenance						++	o	+	+	++	-	-	-
Subsequent use						-	++	+	+	+	-	-	-

B 5.78

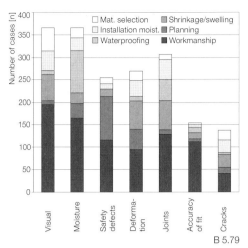

B 5.79

coverings must guarantee an abrasion resistance to match the anticipated use of the building, must withstand any liquids met with during usage or cleaning, must be light-fast, must have impact-resistant edges, etc. Good durability means low maintenance in the long-term, provided the materials selected show a certain freedom from short-term fashions and/or can achieve a high architectural quality. This durability should be backed up by a clear separation between long-lasting construction, short-lived fitting-out and upgradeable building services. Like fashions, requirements also change over the years, e.g. due to changing regulations regarding thermal performance and energy conservation. Far-sighted planning can anticipate occasional stricter requirements, e.g. regarding energy-savings and climate protection. Sometimes, though, the changes are not foreseeable, and in such cases the easy interchangeability of elements and the clear separation of building subsystems with different lifespans and functions can help to cope with unforeseen changes. The most important requirements placed on building materials in order to safeguard usage are described below.

Freedom from health risks
Building materials can emit dangerous substances during their production, installation, usage and subsequent usage phases. Freedom from health risks is therefore a fundamental requirement.

Of the approx. 20 000 substances that are used as standard in Germany (i.e. annual production > 1 t), only a few are fully understood with respect to their effects on human beings! Negative consequences are suspected for very many materials, but these have not been verified. Such potential hazards are already classified as problematic by public bodies where applicable. In addition, dangerous substances can interact with each other and multiply their hazardous effects.

Once dangerous substances have been introduced into a building, the follow-up costs for their later removal usually increase disproportionately. According to one study, by 2002 the costs for removing the asbestos from the Palace of the Republic in Berlin had reached 35–40% of the cost of an equivalent new building!

So when applying the sustainability argument to the selection of a building material, it is important to check to what extent it could trigger allergic or toxicological effects for human beings or the environment.

Dangerous substances cause very different effects. Some, e.g. heavy metals, are absorbed into the human body through the skin or from foodstuffs, even at low levels of contamination. Others are volatile, but impair the nervous system permanently. Yet others are not degradable, may enter the respiratory tract and cause cancers. The route a substance takes to enter the human body enables us to determine whether local protective measures are possible

or all traces of the material should be excluded. In doing so, national directives covering use and disposal must always be adhered to. An expert should be called in emergencies. Three methods can be used to investigate the hazard potential of a substance:

· Environmental designation and label:
Type I Environmental Product Declarations to DIN EN ISO 14024 (labels) can be attached to products provided they adhere to defined requirements. Not every label stands for comprehensive quality control or refers to the entire building products market. Users are therefore recommended to check the certified product groups, the scope of tests and the procedures of the approval bodies which analyse products and issue labels (Fig. B 5.84). The properties of the material thus determined can then be declared as a requirement in tender documents. Type II Environmental Product Declarations (DIN EN ISO 14021) also include data issued by the manufacturers themselves. In this case, there is neither a prescribed declaration nor a defined method of testing.

· Determination of hazard potential via constructions (for building materials already installed):
The effects of the majority of dangerous substances found in the existing building stock are known. It is useful here to be familiar with the state of the art in the respective country

Material groups with examples	Waste code
Conc., clay bricks, ceramic tiles/fittings	17 01
• concrete	17 01 01
Timber, glass, plastics	17 02
• plastic	17 02 03
Bitumen blends, coal tar and products containing tar	17 03
• bitumen blends containing coal tar	17 01 01
Metals (incl. alloys)	17 04
• iron, steel	17 04 05
Soil, stone, excavated material	17 05
• contaminated soil, stone	17 05 01
Insulating materials and materials containing asbestos	17 06
• insulating material containing asbestos	17 06 01
Building materials based on gypsum	17 08
• contaminated materials based on gypsum	17 08 01
Other building materials	17 09
• waste containing mercury	17 09 01

B 5.80

Group	Definition in Cradle-to-Grave Economy Act
Q1	Production or consumption residues not covered by the following definitions
Q2	Products not conforming with the standards
Q5	Substances contaminated or polluted as a result of intentional actions (e.g. cleaning residues, etc.)
Q6	Unusable elements (e.g. used batteries, catalytic converters, etc.)
Q7	Substances that have become unusable (e.g. contaminated acids, solvents, carburising agents, etc)
Q10	Residues due to mechanical and cutting operations (e.g. milling swarf, etc.)
Q12	Contaminated substances (e.g. oil contaminated with PCB, etc.)
Q13	Substances or products of all kinds whose use is prohibited by law
Q15	Contaminated substances or products occurring during land rehabilitation

B 5.81

B 5.82

Substance	Typical absorption route for humans	Effects	Typical period of use	Typical sources of emissions	Recommended measures	Limiting or guidance values
Asbestos	Inhalation	Fibrogenic (cicatrisation), carcinogenic	up to 1980 (D)	Building boards, pipes, moulded parts, mortar, render, plaster, insulating	Replacement	Preliminary measures[1]: 1000 F/m^3 (EU); refurbishment[1]: 500 F/m^3 (EU)
		materials, sealing compounds, floor coverings, textiles				
Synthetic mineral fibres	Inhalation	Fibrogenic (cicatrisation), carcinogenic, skin irritant	up to 1995 (D)	Mineral insulating materials (rock or glass wool without quality mark)	Replacement, airtight containment	no data
Dichlorodiphenyl-trichloroethane (DDT)	Foodstuffs, house dust	Damages organs and nervous system	up to 1972 (D)	Wood preservatives	Removal	10 µg/kg (WHO)[2] 1 µg/kg (D)[2] 0.5 µg/kg (USA)[2]
Dioxins, Furans	Foodstuffs	Carcinogenic	–	Fire residues, slag	Removal	no data
Flame retardants	no data	no data	still in use		[3]	
Formaldehyde	Inhalation	Irritates eyes and mucous membranes, causes headaches, carcinogenic	restricted since 1996 (D)	Wood-based board products, synthetic resins, coatings, chemical additives (e.g. in self-levelling screeds)	Removal, airtight containment, chemical binding	0.1 mg/m^3 (WHO)[1] 0.12 mg/m^3 (D)[1] Refurbishment target: 0.06 mg/m^3 (D)[1]
Total volatile organic compounds (TVOC)	Inhalation	Irritates eyes and mucous membranes, neurotoxic (sick building syndrome)	still in use	Paints, adhesives, paint removers, plastic products, wood-based products, carpeting, textiles	Airtight containment of sources, removal	0.3 mg/m^3 (D)[4]

[1] Guidance values for interior air.
[2] Per kg body weight per day.
[3] A differentiated appraisal is necessary (e.g. according to UBA text 25/01): refraining from the use of decabromodiphenyl ether and tetrabromobisphenol A, additive; reduction in tetrabromobisphenol A, reactive and tris(chloropropyl) phosphate.
[4] In new buildings, the TVOC concentration in the first year should not exceed 1–2 mg/m^3. Exceptions to this are those substances (e.g. formaldehyde) covered by special regulations.

B 5.83

Label	Licence issued by...	Licensed products	Matters checked	Testing period
Blauer Engel (blue angel)	Federal Environment Agency / RAL Deutsches Institut für Güte-sicherung e.V	Insulating materials, varnishes/glazes, wall paint, wallpaper, floor coverings, wood/wood-based products, cement/plaster/render/mortar, clay bricks and roof tiles	Depends on product group, high environmental compatibility (e.g. low dangerous substances content or high recycling proportion), serviceability, issued based on stipulations by neutral "Jury Umweltzeichen" (eco-label jury)	unlimited
Eco-Certificate for low-emissions products	eco-Umweltinstitut GmbH	Insulating materials, varnishes/glazes, floor coverings, wood-based products	Supplement to "Natureplus" label, products tested for constituents and emissions, excluding synthetic materials	14 months
EMI Code	Gemeinschaft Emissionskontrollierte Verlegewerkstoffe e.V.	Floor coverings	Emissions, classes EC 1–3, from "very low emissions" to "not low emissions", not issued when toxic constituents present	unlimited
EU "Flower"	Commission Community	Varnishes/glazes, wall paint, floor coverings (ceramic tiles)	Depends on product group, environmental impacts over life cycle (e.g. energy consumption, water/air pollution, waste, noise/soil loads if applicable), serviceability	unlimited
FSC certificate	Forest Stewardship Council A.C.	Wood/wood-based products, end products must contain min. 70%, paper min. 30% from FSC-certified operations	Certificate for production operations, raw material assessment according to 10 local, adaptable criteria in the realm of conformity with legislation, management, protection of resources, environmental impacts, sociological aspects	max. 5 years
GuT-mark for dangerous subst.	Gemeinschaft umwelt-fr. Teppichboden e.V.	Floor coverings (carpeting)	Dangerous substances content, emissions and odours, annual random tests	unlimited
IBR test mark	Institut für Baubiologie Rosenheim (IBR) GmbH	see Blauer Engel	Depends on product, primarily health-related, but also environment-related criteria, issued upon achieving a minimum number of points	2 years
Cork logo	Deutscher Kork-Verband e.V.	Cork flooring (plastic wearing course max. 0.15 mm)	Emissions, compliance with standards, serviceability	1 year
Natureplus	natureplus e.V.	Insulating materials, varnishes/glazes, wall paint, wood/wood-based products, floor coverings, cement/plaster/render/mortar, clay bricks and roof tiles	"Natural products" from min. 85% renewable and/or mineral raw materials, basic criteria (e.g. full declaration of constituents); further criteria: depends on product group, "serviceability", "health compatibility" and "environmental compatibility" over life cycle, verification of tests	3 years
Naturland	Verband für natur-gemäßen Landbau e.V.	Wood/wood-based products, Naturland operations may also use the FSC label	Certificate for operations, environmentally compatible and sustainable treatment of the ecosystems used, minimisation of dangerous substances content, serviceability	at least annual check of operations
PEFC Pan European Forest Certification	Deutscher Forst-Zertifizierungsrat (DFZR)	Wooden floor coverings, wood/wood-based products (wood from European forests)	Certificate for operations, strengthening of forestry resources and carbon life cycles, preservation and promotion of production function, biodiversity and protective functions of the forest, preservation of other socio-economic functions	unlimited
RugMark	RUGMARK/Transfair e.V.	Floor coverings (carpeting)	No child labour, guaranteed minimum wages, access to order books, unannounced inspections permitted	depends on order
Toxproof	TÜV Produkt & Umwelt GmbH	Insulating materials, varnishes/glazes, wall paint, floor coverings, wood-based products, sealants/sheeting, cement/plaster/render/mortar	Depends on product group, focus on health compatibility, especially minimising emissions	limited or unlimited, min. 1 year

B 5.84

B 5.83 Substances used in the building industry that represent health hazards (selection)
B 5.84 A selection of the type 1 Environmental Product Declarations available in Germany (building materials labels)
B 5.85 Typical distribution of costs over the life cycle (CH)
B 5.86 Electricity pylon destroyed by extreme weather conditions (D), 2004

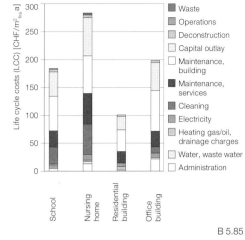

B 5.85

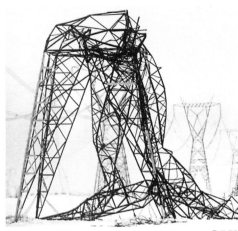

B 5.86

as it was at the time the building was erected. It is not unusual to find certain dangerous substances occurring in certain countries at certain times, e.g. phenols or cresols, which occurred in large quantities as residues from the chemicals industry in the countries of the former Eastern Bloc and were processed to form binders for floor coverings and light-weight screeds. Further examples are asbestos and synthetic mineral fibres, heavy metals such as lead or arsenic, polychlorinated biphenyls (PCB), biocides such as dichlorodiphenyltrichloroethane (DDT) or polycyclic aromatic hydrocarbons (PAH) (Fig. B 5.83).
• Hazard potential according to application (for new building materials):
Certain building materials groups are assigned a higher hazard potential. These include, in particular, coatings, adhesives, paint strippers, wood preservatives, carpeting, resilient floor coverings and insulating materials. Precise requirements for materials – maximum emissions stipulations or labels – can be formulated in the tender documents. Verification of possible final measurements for test purposes coupled with information regarding suitable procedures when exceeding target values is advisable.

Operational safety
The choice of building material is also limited by various safety requirements regarding the operation of the building. These are to large extent derived from legislation and regulations. Operational safety aspects and user comfort must in each case be harmonised with the energy-efficiency and ecological properties of the materials.

• Structural stability:
Safeguarding and maintaining the loadbearing capacity has been one of the three pillars of architecture since the time of Vitruvius (latin: *firmitas*). The structural calculations incorporate safety factors that take into account possible overloads, e.g. due to improper usage. As the climate change takes hold, climatic factors such as wind loads, quantities of precipitation due to driving rain

or snow loads may become more critical (Fig. B 5.86).
• Fire protection:
The purpose of structural fire protection is to save lives in emergencies and to maintain the fabric of the building as an economic and cultural commodity. In Germany, fire protection rules are incorporated in the Civil Code (BGB), the Criminal Code (StGB), statutory instruments such as the Building Act (BauO) or Factories Act (GewO), standards such as DIN EN 18230 or DIN 4102, and fire insurance documentation. Preventive fire protection limits the choice of suitable building materials and in many cases restricts the choice from the energy-efficiency and ecological aspects. The starting point is the DIN 4102 building materials classification in the form of fire resistance classes (F for load-bearing components, W for non-loadbearing components) or Euronorm EN 13501.
• Sound insulation:
The purpose of sound insulation is to retain the privacy, health and performance of human beings. Rules for sound insulation are specified in DIN 4109 and DIN EN 12354 plus other documents. It is often assumed that effective sound insulation, especially against airborne sound, can be achieved only through the provision of mass. But insulation against airborne sound is also equally possible with lightweight, multi-layer constructions decoupled to prevent the transmission of oscillations. Sound-absorbent materials and special lightweight, porous absorbers can help to combat undesirable acoustic effects locally.
• Moisture control:
The moisture in the air or in building materials influences the thermal comfort of human beings and hence the perceived quality of a building (see "Fundamentals", p. 55). The relative humidity should lie between 40 and 60% throughout the year. Values much higher than this can cause problems, especially with respect to mould growth if moisture can diffuse through building components and then condense. Vapour barriers, insulating materials and sorptive materials contribute to moisture control.

Care and maintenance
Architects are under a general obligation to plan economically. The architect's contract calls for him to determine the performance with the client – not only with respect to the immediate cost of building, but also with respect to the follow-up costs. The latter can prove to be a multiple of the cost of building an individual building component (Fig. B 5.85). The architect is therefore responsible for including solutions to reduce the follow-up costs in his overall concept. The costs during the usage phase are based on ongoing demands regarding cleanliness, hygiene, preservation of value, serviceability characteristics (sound attenuation, anti-slip features of floor coverings, etc.) and appearance, all of which must be satisfied. In this respect, the efficient use of finances for cleaning methods and organisation are the most important aspects. The cost of cleaning is based, however, on aspects such as energy consumption, environmental protection and the need for a healthy interior climate.

Soiling
Abrasive particles such as grains of stone or sand or splinters of glass have a negative effect on the preservation of wearing surfaces. The main source of soiling comes from dirt adhering to the soles of shoes, followed by particles in the air. Planning that takes account of cleaning requirements therefore begins by reducing the quantity of particles being transferred from outside to inside through the appropriate design of surfaces. Designing for full access by disabled people eases cleaning because cleaning machines and wheelchairs have similar dimensions.
Separating surfaces with high and low cleaning requirements is another positive move (Fig. B 5.90). The inclusion of gratings and walk-off zones (internal or external) at entrances help to reduce the cleaning requirements substantially. A distance of roughly 10 paces is sufficient to reduce the amount of incoming dirt by 80% (Fig. B 5.89).

171

Easy-care surfaces
Care and cleaning are labour-intensive operations. Besides technical plant, the floor coverings, windows, doors, partitions and linings cause high costs (Fig. B 5.88). In countries with high wages (e.g. Germany), the cleaning costs during the operation of a building are often higher than the heating costs (see "Planning and building in life cycles", p. 33, Fig. A 6.3). One aspect of economic design means being able to clean surfaces easily and with the help of machines. Smooth, seamless surfaces made from hardwearing building materials are to be recommended here (Fig. B 5.87).
Durable coatings can be applied to surfaces to resist any physical or chemical processes taking place on them and thus reduce the maintenance requirements. Reasons for their use include ensuring that dirt and water can run off easily (e.g. lotus effect, self-cleaning glass), acting as a catalytic converter (e.g. for improving the interior air, for decomposing organic substances) or as a backing for chemical substances (e.g. biocides for protecting facades). Coatings can, however, seldom be detached from their backings or otherwise recovered at the end of their useful lives. Lower costs during operation, maintenance and repairs may need to be weighed up against the higher cost of renewal. Cleaning can be helped by special material properties, e.g. the antibacterial effect of stainless steel in kitchens.
In ecological terms, easy-care means that the cleaning can be carried out efficiently and with minimal resources. The types of cleaning according to cost can be defined as follows (from low-cost to high-cost):

- dry, mechanical
- wet, mechanical
- wet, chemical
- vacuuming

The largest item on the cleaning bill when considering the materials flows is water. Wherever water is a scarce resource, ecological aspects can also become economically significant. In terms of emissions, cleaning agents have the greatest impact on the environment. Biologically degradable cleaning agents should therefore be used and their use should not be hindered by the wrong choice of material or details that are difficult to clean (Fig. B 5.90).

Easy-care floor coverings
Care and cleaning matters are easily illustrated using the example of floor coverings. When choosing colours and patterns it is important to remember that plain, bright-coloured, cold materials will easily reveal any dust and dirt, but earthy colours or patterned coverings will tend to hide any soiling.
Hard, natural or reconstituted stone floor finishes are the most economic from the cleaning point of view. Their longevity makes them advantageous in terms of both economy and ecology. Ceramic and glazed tiles are easy to clean because they absorb hardly any moisture. But their surfaces become scratched over time, particularly when subjected to heavy loads, and so their appearance suffers.
In terms of their capital outlay and running costs, resilient floor coverings are usually marginally inferior to hard floor coverings, especially in offices. However, their sound-attenuating properties cut down the noise in the workplace.

Linoleum and natural rubber floor coverings have ecological advantages. Carpeting is easy to clean, but the cost of cleaning is heavily influenced by accessibility and the stipulations of the building user. In the case of high loads, frequent, thorough cleaning and low durability, carpeting exhibits both economic and ecological disadvantages.
The care of wooden floors is more costly than that for resilient floor coverings. On the other hand, they can be resanded several times (depending on the thickness of the wearing course) and therefore can be used for many years.
An easy-care floor covering can reduce the annual cleaning costs by up to 30% (Fig. B 5.91). The higher capital outlay for such floor coverings is generally due to their better durability, which enables cost-savings over the life cycle. Durable floor coverings are therefore primarily worthwhile for unchanging, defined interior zones. In the case of a later change of use, a check must be carried out to determine whether a certain floor covering is also suitable for the new interior function.

Easy-care facades
Facade elements that require intensive cleaning are the windows and doors. Good access for cleaners is essential here, and travelling cradles may be required on large, multi-storey facades. Glass can be given a hydrophilic coating in order to reduce the cleaning requirements. A thin film of water then forms on the glass so that particles of dust and dirt can drain away better and thus minimise the cleaning cycles necessary. However, such coatings

Facade cladding material	2-storey building		10-storey building	
	Cleaning cycle [a]	Index[1] [%]	Cleaning cycle [a]	Index[1] [%]
Aluminium				
anodised surface finish (ground)	2	700	1	1600
batch-coated surface finish	2	310	2	400
continuous-coated surface finish	2	310	2	400
Copper	no data	no data	no data	no data
Zinc	3	470	no data	no data
Enamelled sheet steel	1	310	1	400
Stone				
with open-drained or sealed joints	20	100	20	100
Glass				
enamel finish on rear face	1	440	1	240
enamel/metal oxide finish on rear face	0.25	1750	0.25	960
Reconstituted stone panels with outer leaf	12	680	12	1280
Large-format precast concrete elements	12	680	12	1280
Facing brickwork outer leaf, double-leaf masonry	20	420	20	620
Wood or wood-based products[2]				
solid timber sheathing, opaque coating	5	170	–	–
solid timber sheathing, heartwood, untreated	10	20	–	–
panels made from wood-based products	10	100	–	–
Fibre-cement sheets				
large-format	2	310	2	200
small-format	10	380	no data	no data

[1] In comparison to stone (= 100%)
[2] According to information provided by the German Society for Wood Research (DGfH)

B 5.87

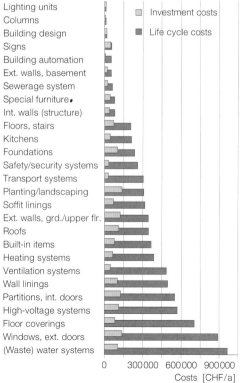

Lighting units	
Columns	
Building design	
Signs	
Building automation	
Ext. walls, basement	
Sewerage system	
Special furniture	
Int. walls (structure)	
Floors, stairs	
Kitchens	
Foundations	
Safety/security systems	
Transport systems	
Planting/landscaping	
Soffit linings	
Ext. walls, grd./upper flr.	
Roofs	
Built-in items	
Heating systems	
Ventilation systems	
Wall linings	
Partitions, int. doors	
High-voltage systems	
Floor coverings	
Windows, ext. doors	
(Waste) water systems	

Investment costs
Life cycle costs

0   300000   600000   900000
Costs [CHF/a]

B 5.88

based on organic compounds are vulnerable to scratches, and once damaged, they are difficult to renew according to the current state of the art. For this reason, special regulations regarding types of cleaning and cleaning agents apply, which may increase the costs. The growth of algae is a problem that can affect thermal insulation composite systems. Highly insulated building components reduce the surface temperature of the facade in the winter, which then approaches that of the external air. In comparison to previous building standards, the higher humidity of the air and the slower drying of the surface promotes the growth of algae. Higher moisture transport, biocides or the photocatalytic effects of specific surface coatings can diminish this effect. However, as yet, little is known about their durability.

Maintenance of surfaces
There are two contradictory materials strategies for maintaining surfaces. On the one hand, the material can have an especially resistant structure and surface that guarantees high durability and generally reduces the cost of care and maintenance. Once damaged, however, the cost of repairing such surfaces is usually high. Deficits in building maintenance are revealed in the form of the visible decay of the entire building, unless the material is visually robust (e.g. clay roof tiles, clay bricks) or an attractive patina forms.

On the other hand, the surface of the material can be allowed to exhibit a higher wear due to the usage, e.g. wooden floors, which owing to their intense texture are not perceived as unattractive and, in addition, can be resanded. If such maintenance processes are employed deliberately, the recurring renewal creates the impression of an updated, "fresh" building. Provided small-format building components and easy-to-repair surfaces are used, local damage is easily remedied. The durability of building materials is particularly important for maintenance aspects (see p. 163).

B 5.89

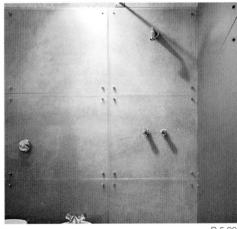

B 5.90

B 5.87   Cleaning costs for different facade claddings according to the German "Sustainable Building" guidelines
B 5.88   Life cycle and investment costs per year according to building component (CH)
B 5.89   Walkway as walk-off zone, private house, Overijse (B), 2002, Buelens Vanderlinden Architects
B 5.90   Differentiated surfaces design according to cleaning requirements, residential conversion, Pavia (I), 1998, Massimo Curzi
B 5.91   Cleaning requirements for different floor coverings according to the German "Sustainable Building" guidelines, with granite as reference material

Floor covering material	Daily cleaning [%]	Intensive cleaning [%]
Polished granite (reference material)	100	100
Reconstituted stone	102	105
Synthetic resin-bonded stone	102	100
Stone tiles, polished	102	100
Ceramic tiles, glazed	110	125
Ceramic tiles, unglazed	120	135
Natural stone, rough	120	125
Linoleum	105	130
PVC	105	130
Smooth rubber	120	115
Textured rubber	150	150
Sealed wooden floor	120	–[1]
Carpeting	90–140[2]	200

[1] Sanding and resealing
[2] Average value 110

B 5.91

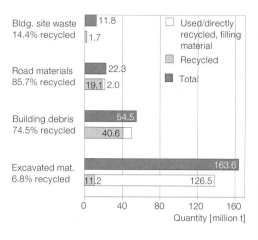

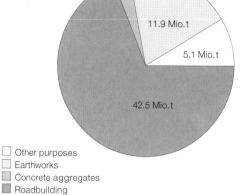

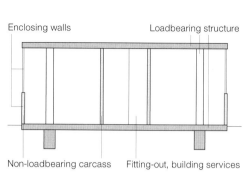

B 5.92

B 5.93

B 5.94

Subsequent usage

Every use of a material should result in a closed material life cycle, i.e. waste should be recycled. But the building industry is still far from this ideal. A start has been made in the metalworking industry, for example, but this is limited to just a few metals and metal alloys.

Waste treatment
Since February 2007 the Cradle-to-Grave Economy Act (KrW/AbfG) has specified that all waste must be recycled if economically justifiable (Fig. B 5.81). Economy is defined by the type of use and the resulting product plus the waste management, e.g. necessary for the transport processes.
By choosing a particular material, the architect specifies the raw materials that are later available to the waste management. He can therefore have an effect on the formation of material life cycles in the medium-term, or reinforce existing life cycles through the deliberate use of recyclable products (see "Urban space and infrastructure", Fig. B 2.61). Not every life cycle is equivalent, and therefore the terms "downcycling", "recycling" and "upcycling" describe the way in which materials are fed back into a material life cycle. In contrast to downcycling, recycling means that, theoretically, a permanent life cycle is rendered possible through the complete reuse of the material. Upcycling means that the material is optimised in the subsequent cycle, e.g. is freed from other "contaminating" materials.

Types of subsequent usage
The procedure for the subsequent usage is critical for the ecological value, the preservation of the raw material and the energy stored in the material. Irrespective of the aforementioned recycling options, we distinguish between the following types of subsequent usage (Fig. B 5.93):

• reuse
• recycling
• further use

Reuse designates the subsequent usage of complete building products which – after

mechanical cleaning – are hardly changed, if at all. As the damaged components have already been replaced in the previous period of use and the product has thus been optimised, the average quality of the materials in building components destined for reuse is raised. In the first application cycle, repaired components, e.g. clay tile coverings to pitched roofs, may well exhibit a higher durability than new products. Good durability and simple deconstruction encourages reuse, e.g. stone pavings. The starting point for the subsequent usage option for complete building components is the further need for such components. Standardised products improve the capacity for planning the use of integrating any elements that may be available. Economic subsequent usage should therefore be feasible with components already produced industrially. One example of this is the buildings in panel construction dating from GDR times. Panels no longer required can be used to construct new buildings at low cost and with energy-efficiency consequences (Fig. B 5.99). A component can, however, be reused only if it has not been too specifically optimised for its first life cycle, i.e. possesses a certain technical and functional neutrality. Semi-finished products, but also standardised building materials such as clay bricks or building boards, can also be used again. As the costs for proper deconstruction can clearly exceed the value of the product, deconstruction is frequently carried out according to tight schedules and second-hand products can cause warranty problems, reuse is not often employed – except in the case of components with a high or historical value, where this approach is more common (Fig. B 5.98).
Recycling is the recovery of chemical raw materials for the new production of the same materials, which also enables upcycling. Low-value products are reworked to form high-value items. The ensuing "new materials" have their very own aesthetic – clearly revealed by their production – and thus reveal the realisation of a contemporary task (Fig. B 5.97), e.g. in the form of concrete reinforced with scrap glass. New building materials are always covered by a manufacturer's warranty, which eases the use of such recycled products (Fig. B 5.95).

Composting is another form of recycling. In this case, organic building materials decompose to form humus and thus become a raw material in the production chain for organic natural products. Further use means isolating the raw materials from the products and using them for the production of new products – provided the constituents are known, the waste has been sorted beforehand and is free from any dangerous substances. Such materials recovery is ideal for standardised material compositions, large-scale industrial production and the economic use of the building material, e.g. plastics and metals, whose manufacture entails a high energy input and the use of scarce raw materials (Fig. B 5.96).
Organic building materials can be incinerated and their energy content extracted in the form of the calorific value [MJ]. Carbon dioxide is one of the main emissions and this process cancels out the positive carbon-sink effect of renewable materials. We speak of "thermal recycling", but this is not really a recycling process because the material life cycle does not continue beyond this point. Owing to the limited volume of landfill available in Germany, current legislation prescribes thermal recycling at least for all building materials made from organic substances.
One further typical form of reuse is the widespread treatment of mineral building debris: about 75% of this is downcycled to form road-building or filling materials (Fig. B 5.93).

Landfilling
The generally positive influences of subsequent usage can be illustrated by a materials flow analysis. Only if subsequent usage is impossible should landfilling be considered.
Like in almost all industrialised countries, the areas available for landfill in Germany are severely limited. This form of waste treatment therefore involves high costs and a high land consumption; furthermore, it has a negative impact on the landscape and the use of the land. And in the case of improper landfilling, pollutants can seep out uncontrolled into the environment, causing contamination of air, water and soil, eventually reaching the foodstuffs chain. In addition, there is the risk of the

B 5.95

B 5.96

fly-tipping of waste, especially where supervision is inadequate.

Since 2005 landfill waste in Germany – for safety reasons – may no longer be reactive, i.e. may not undergo any further changes to its structure. The intention behind this is to prevent uncontrolled chemical processes taking place within landfill sites. However, in most cases this calls for thermal pretreatment of the waste, which involves an additional consumption of resources. The unsorted waste with a high energy and resources content is melted in this process, which means that later recovery of the resources is impossible, or at least extremely difficult (see "Urban space and infrastructure", p. 77).

Take-back obligation
EU legislation for a general and comprehensive take-back obligation for building products is in preparation. Such an obligation will initially be restricted to the manufacturers of products or buildings. The quality of the planning and the consideration of alternative replacement and demolition processes will, however, determine or at least affect the costs of such a take-back obligation. The resulting legal consequences for architects and clients are currently unclear. Far-sighted planning is therefore already taking into account expected changes to our handling of building materials and building components, e.g. through a reversible building components structure.

Forms of construction for a material life cycle
Once all the possibilities for the further use of a building have been exhausted, demolition becomes necessary. The material life cycles in the building can then be separated again. To do this, it should be possible to separate every functional layer and every building element (Fig. B 5.94). A minimum requirement is the separation of material layers that are intended to be fed into different forms of subsequent usage. Recycling technologies are, however, undergoing an upheaval. Optimisation based on current technologies therefore appears to be more costly and less advisable than maximum separability and layers sorted according to type of material. In addition, the material composition should be known and recorded in the documentation. If – like in concrete construction – building components have been bonded together, they can only be separated at the end of their useful lives by destructive means. Although raw materials can be sorted for recovery, the energy-intensive shaping process of the building components is, however, irretrievably lost.

The possibilities for subsequent usage should therefore be especially considered for load-bearing constructions with a high energy content. This is where the consideration of industrial prefabrication techniques interfaces directly with the design of demountable constructions. (Partial) disassembly and subsequent transformation can preserve valuable building fabric or building components in many instances and in some circumstances planning activities can render possible a further cycle of usage where this is not already ensured by way of a neutral underlying structure. The preservation and the creative use of the building stock will always secure the long-term, careful use of grey energy and create enhanced environmental compatibility for the building industry.

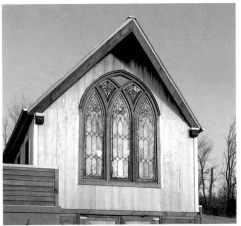

B 5.97

B 5.98

B 5.99

Strategies

B 6.1

Architects and planners have a special obligation towards the quality of our environment. Hardly any other profession intervenes so intensively in the sensory and everyday world of the human being and at the same time the global energy and materials flows. Architects therefore have a special responsibility towards the development of sustainable management. The need for better efficiency in the use of energy and resources plus the holistic mind-set surrounding sustainable development will probably generate impulses with a similar effect to those of the socio-politically motivated changes of the modern movement. The result could be new definitions of architecture and construction, so that this branch of industry can supply the contributions necessary for sustainable, viable development.

Questioning existing models
Urban planning and architecture have developed out of the context of local climatic conditions and the availability of materials and energy resources. Only a few generations have passed since the possibility of using fossil fuels enabled construction to distance itself from these boundary conditions (Fig. B 6.6). As a result, our forefathers considered high energy consumption to be the epitome of a superior culture. Statistics point to the ability of developed countries to generate and use more energy than others. The modern movement's belief that the provision of a comfortable standard of living could

be guaranteed by the virtually unlimited consumption of energy and resources – regardless of external conditions and internal requirements – occasionally spawned forms of architecture with enormous energy consumption, totally detached from the diverse interactive relationships. In the light of this, Reyner Banham was in 1967 already proclaiming the need for a new attitude in architecture because the conventional approaches were not able to solve the growing environmental problems. He illustrated the conflicting design concepts by comparing a motor boat and a sailing boat: "A motor allows practically any floating object to be turned into a steerable ship. A small, concentrated machinery package converts an undistinguished configuration into an object with function and purpose" [1]. According to Banham, architects should no longer regard a building as a structure equipped with technical apparatus, but rather should go on to develop a "climate device" which, like a sailing boat, reacts dynamically to environmental influences and gains its energy through exploiting the energy available locally (Fig. B 6.1).

The vision of the "2000 Watt Society"
Whereas just a few decades ago the discussion was about replacing materials and architecture by energy in many instances (e.g. warm-air curtains, pneumatic structures), the limits of the unbridled use of energy are now obvious to us. Limited availability and damag-

Boundary conditions

Climate

Usage

Legislation

Architecture

Energy-optimised building concepts

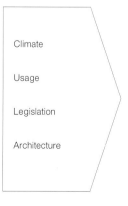

Minimisation of
energy requirements

Optimisation of
energy supplies

Evaluation

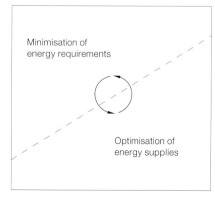

Ecology
(CO_2 pollution)

Economy
(life cycle costs)

Society
(acceptance)

Architecture
(quality of design)

B 6.2

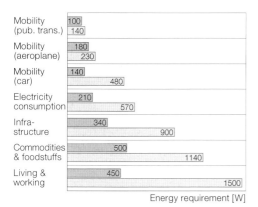

Mobility (pub. trans.)	100 / 140
Mobility (aeroplane)	180 / 230
Mobility (car)	140 / 480
Electricity consumption	210 / 570
Infrastructure	340 / 900
Commodities & foodstuffs	500 / 1140
Living & working	450 / 1500

Energy requirement [W]

▨ in the "2000 Watt Society"
☐ 4-person household in Switzerland today

B 6.3

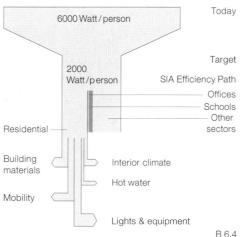

6000 Watt / person — Today

2000 Watt / person — Target

SIA Efficiency Path

Offices
Schools
Other sectors

Residential

Building materials — Interior climate

Hot water

Mobility

Lights & equipment

B 6.4

	Primary energy consumption New-build		Primary energy consumption Conversion work	
	[MJ/m²a]	[kWh/m²a]	[MJ/m²a]	[kWh/m²a]
Bldg. materials	100	27.8	60	16.7
Interior climate				
• PE$_h$	45	12.5	85	23.6
• PE$_{hil,lu}$	25	7.,0	25	7.0
Hot water	40	11.1	40	11.1
Lights/equip.	130	36.1	130	36.1
Mobility	100	27.8	100	27.8
Target value A residential	440	122	440	122

B 6.5

ing environmental impacts call for new, positive sets of targets. According to a study carried out by the Wuppertal Institute for Climate, Environment & Energy, societies will only really be fit for the future "when their methods, systems, rhythms and ordering principles are embedded in natural ordering principles" and hence human beings are therefore no longer the focus, the purpose of existence, and everything else only the subservient periphery [2]. In order to enable research findings to be implemented on the practical side of sustainable social and urban development, the Swiss Federal Institute of Technology in Zurich developed the concept of the "2000 Watt Society" back in 1998 within the framework of the "Novatlantis" project. This model project is based on the notion that the energy consumption per person represents the crucial indicator for assessing sustainability and assumes that 2000 W are necessary to guarantee economic prosperity. Owing to the fossil fuels-based energy supplies, every person, taken as a global average, currently adds more than 4 t of CO_2 to the greenhouse effect every year, which corresponds to a continuous output of 2000 W, or 17 000 kWh, annually (see "Fundamentals", p. 42). The average continuous consumption in Western Europe, on the other hand, is currently approx. 6000 W and in Switzerland about 5000 W. According to the World Climate Council, CO_2 emissions of about 1 t per person, or rather a

continuous output of just 500 W, are "environmentally compatible" in the long-term. The shortfall of about 1500 W must therefore be met by renewable energy sources. The aim of the "2000 Watt Society" model is to specify corresponding guideline values (in W) for the different sectors, e.g. living and working, commodities and foodstuffs, or mobility, in order to cut the average consumption in Switzerland and elsewhere drastically over the coming decades (Fig. B 6.3).
As about half of the current energy consumption can be attributed to the construction, operation and maintenance of buildings, the Association of Swiss Engineers & Architects (SIA) devised the "SIA Energy Efficiency Path" [3], with strategies and reference variables specially tailored to the construction industry (Fig. B 6.4). Specific target values for the path to the "2000 Watt Society" have been defined for housing, offices and schools for the areas of building materials (grey energy), interior climate, hot water, lighting and equipment, plus mobility (Fig. B 6.5).
The primary energy forms the common reference variable for all target values, which is specified in units of MJ/m²a or W/person. The "Energy Efficiency Path" has already been used as a tool for energy-efficient construction in a "2000 Watt Society" in initial pilot projects such as the "Chriesbach Forum" (see Example 15, pp. 240–42.).

Energy concepts

The early development of an energy concept is a key element in the design of buildings compatible with future demands. As Fig. B 6.2 shows, the procedure can be broken down into an analytical part (boundary conditions), a process-oriented part (concept development) and a quantitative part (evaluation). In a similar way to architectural form-finding, drawing up such a concept is a creative process that cannot be standardised. This skill represents one of the key qualifications for planners.

Analysis of boundary conditions
The starting point for the development of an energy concept is determining the boundary conditions, which can be divided into four groups (Fig. B 6.9).

Climatic boundary conditions
Our attention here focuses on the local temperature and weather conditions plus the energy potential. The course of the temperature over the year together with the respective extreme values form the framework for defining the thermal quality of the building envelope. The difference between the daytime and night-time air temperatures is an indicator of the potential for passive, natural cooling by way of the night air. The average annual temperature has an influence on the temperature level of the ground

B 6.1 The sailing boat as a "climate device": the yachts *Alinghi* and *Oracle*
B 6.2 Factors that affect the development of energy-optimised building concepts
B 6.3 Average energy requirement according to sector – now and in the "2000 Watt Society"
B 6.4 Boundary conditions according to the "SIA Energy Efficiency Path"
B 6.5 Target values for 2000 Watt-compatible construction for new-build and conversion work (residential sector)
B 6.6 A floating island housed in a pneumatic structure, sketch by Frei Otto, 1967/68

B 6.6

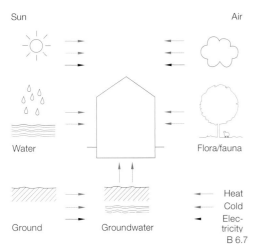

Sun   Air

Water   Flora/fauna

Ground   Groundwater   Heat
                                      Cold
                                      Elec-
                                      tricity
                                      B 6.7

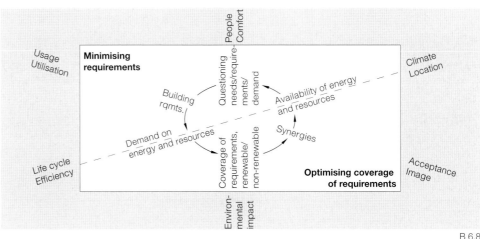

B 6.8

near the surface and hence the possible use of a shallow ground coupling. The humidity of the air forms the basis for defining humidification and dehumidification measures, and indicates the possibilities for direct adiabatic cooling. The prevailing wind speeds and directions over the seasons indicate the opportunities for natural ventilation or generating electricity from wind power. Precipitation quantities and their distribution represent the potential for evaporative cooling via ventilation systems. Accurate knowledge of the geological boundary conditions is necessary when considering using the soil or groundwater for heating or cooling the building. The quantity of solar radiation incident on the building envelope and an analysis of the sun's trajectory form the basis for passive solar use, summertime thermal performance and the calculation of the efficiency of solar thermal systems and photovoltaic installations.

Use-related boundary conditions
The energy services necessary result from an analysis of the use-related boundary conditions, which in many cases are due to the particular use of the building. These boundary conditions are, however, also influenced by the individual ideas of the owner or the user of the building. For example, requirements regarding room temperatures (e.g. living room, bedroom, office), summertime thermal performance (e.g. maximum temperatures in offices) or the quality of the air (e.g. air change rate in classrooms) are important boundary conditions for the development of an energy concept.

Technical and legal boundary conditions
The legislation covering construction work (e.g. local development plans, design guidelines, etc.) and energy conservation are gradually being woven into an ever tighter set of rules. The legislation stipulates such things as density of development, volume, roof forms, materials, etc. Information on the technical infrastructure (e.g. district heating, gas supplies, compulsory connection, etc.) plus legal requirements coupled with the type of use (e.g. ventilation in concert halls) represent further important factors.

Architectural boundary conditions
When developing an energy concept, the environmental energy potential available locally –

and hence the diverse interactions between the building and its direct environs – represents a crucial architectural boundary condition (Fig. B 6.7). The respective solar radiation available from different compass directions leads to, for example, specific requirements regarding transparent elements in the external walls, or sunshades. In addition, geometrical aspects (e.g. ratio of plot size to building volume, ratio of usable floor space to potential solar area), shadows cast by neighbouring structures or the special requirements of the client represent further important design parameters. Moreover, all these aspects should be questioned critically from the point of view of energy and sustainability.

B 6.7   Schematic presentation of local energy potential
B 6.8   Schematic diagram of the process for developing energy concepts
B 6.9   Boundary conditions and areas for action in the development of energy concepts
B 6.10 Options for coordinating energy availability and requirements
B 6.11 Building components and their usefulness for energy purposes

Boundary condition	Information	Area for action
Climate	Temperature, extreme values	Thermal quality of building envelope
	Temperature difference, day/night	Potential for natural cooling by night air
	Average annual temperature	Output potential for ground exchanger
	Relative humidity, summer/winter	Possibility of direct adiabatic cooling
	Average wind speeds	Electricity generation with wind power
	Distribution of wind directions	Wind-controlled natural ventilation
	Quantity and distribution of precipitation	Technical use of evaporative cooling
	Geological strata	Tapping the heat in the ground via boreholes
	Groundwater and surface waters	Use as heat source and for passive cooling
	Quantity of energy, solar radiation	Passive and active solar thermal usage and electricity generation
	Sun's trajectory	Optimisation of summertime thermal performance
Usage	Requirements for heated areas	Minimum and maximum temperatures
	Targets for summertime thermal performance	Room temperature and temperature range (e.g. 22°C ± 2°C; 21–28°C)
	Air quality requirements	Max. workplace concentrations, max. CO2 values
	Air humidity requirements	Relative humidity and range (e.g. 50% ± 10%)
	Lighting requirements – lux values	Sunshades and glare protection
Legislation	Development plan	Optimisation of land use up to maximum permissible development density
	Energy Conservation Act	Maximum primary energy consumption
	DIN 18599	Heat sources and sinks
	Compulsory connection	Infrastructure usage and increasing the utilisation
	Water legislation stipulations	Use of ground and groundwater as energy sources
	Legal stipulations due to usage	e.g. heat recovery if mechanical ventilation required
	Preservation of historic monuments	Preservation of identity, e.g. with internal insulation
Architecture	Neighbouring buildings and microclimatic boundary conditions	Architectural design in conjunction with use of environmental energy
	Ratio of plot size to building volume	Use of primary and secondary solar energy
	Ratio of usable floor area to potential solar area	Proportion of transparent wall surfaces according to compass direction

B 6.9

Availability	Building services					Requirements
	Energy collection	Energy conversion	Energy storage	Energy distribution	Energy output	
Crude oil	Natural gas supply	Gas-fired cond. boiler	Drinking water tank	Air-conditioning system	Radiators	Space heating
Natural gas	Crude oil tank	Oil-fired boiler	Buffer tank	Hot-water circuit	Underfloor heating	Space cooling
Mains electricity	District heating-	Electric heater	Solar storage tank	Cold-water circuit	Wall heating	Hot water
District heating	intake points	Heat pump	Combination tank	Warm-air ducts	Facade heating	Humidification
Group heating	Wood pellets bunker	Solar thermal system	Long-term heat	Cold-air ducts	Activation of building	Dehumidification
District cooling	Wood chippings bunker	Photovoltaic system	storage	Electric cables	components	External air
Solar radiation	Vegetable oil tank	Pellets burner	Boreholes	Gas pipes	Displacement ventilati-	Lighting
Wood pellets	Boreholes	Chippings burner	Latent heat storage	Heating circuit	on outlets	Electricity
Wood chippings	Groundwater	Co-generation plant	Sorption storage	Cooling water circuit	Long-range nozzles	Process heat
Vegetable oil	Heat exchanger	Compression-type	Batteries		Take-off points	Process cooling
Geothermal heat	Heat recovery	refrigeration unit	Compressed-air storage			
Groundwater		Sorption-type	Flywheel energy storage			
Surface waters		refrigeration unit	Hydrogen			
External air		Evaporative cooling				
Wind		Fuel cell				

B 6.10

Concept development

The development of an energy concept should embrace two complementary objectives (Fig. B 6.8):
Firstly, it is important to make sure that the energy requirements are kept low by employing suitable constructional measures. The building, individual constructions and materials should be harmonised at the start of the planning in such a way that the building provides a comfortable internal climate for as long as possible without the need for extensive technical installations. To do this, the components and parts of a building should not only be designed to comply with their constructional, functional and architectural specifications, but also with

the aim of gaining additional energy-efficiency benefits (Fig. B 6.11). Exploiting synergy effects and finding creative solutions for conflicting aims are the challenges here (Fig. B 6.31). A sustainable design for the technical energy supplies services forms the second conceptual focus. For this, the chain from the energy sources to the desired energy service must be traced and checked for maximum efficiency and future viability (Fig. B 6.10). Areas required for collecting energy must also be considered at an early stage, just like the provision of technical installations.
The deliberations regarding an energy concept should begin with the question of whether and to what extent specific energy services can be

omitted without users suffering any loss in quality. The systematic treatment of this "zero option" can lead to the discovery of simple technical solutions and new internal space experiences.

Clarification of design brief
The basis of the energy concept is defined in the course of clarifying the design brief (Fig. B 6.13). In doing so, the conflict of aims between low investment costs and low operating costs must be resolved. A one-sided view of keeping the initial costs as low as possible can lead to high operating costs, which have a negative effect on the overall economy of the building and can impair its long-term usability. Further-

Area, component	Primary function	Further functions
External area	Functional circulation/access, parking, recreation	Ground as heat exchanger, microclimatic improvement due to specific planting and water features, sunshading, protection from wind, minimal ground sealing, use of rainwater
Foundations	Supporting the building	Thermal mass as ventilated construction for conditioning incoming fresh air, pile foundations for exploiting geothermal heat
Ground slab	Waterproofing, structural requirements, lower termination of structure, foundations	High thermal quality due to multifunctional insulating materials capable of withstanding heavy loads, integration of heat transfer media (air/water)
External walls	Protection against weather, sound, heat and cold	High thermal insulation quality and airtightness for reducing technical systems for heating and cooling, integration of air inlets, integration of solar energy systems for electricity and heat
Windows	Daylighting, natural ventilation, view of outside world	High thermal insulation quality and airtightness for reducing technical systems for heating, daylight and energy optimisation due to arrangement, size and selectivity of glazing, solar control with sunshading and glare protection for minimal cooling loads, integration of air inlets, photovoltaic systems integrated into glazing
Roof	Protection against weather, rainwater drainage, upper termination of structure	High thermal insulation quality and airtightness for reducing technical systems for heating and cooling, microclimatic effect with green roofs, temperature amplitude damping, daylighting, integration of solar energy systems
Atrium	Usable space protected from the weather, internal circulation	Heat source or sink within the scope of passive heating/cooling strategies for adjoining rooms, climate buffer, daylighting in the case of appropriate optimisation, component in ventilation concepts as air distributor or collector (natural currents), synergy between exhaust-air and smoke/heat vents
Staircase	Internal vertical circulation, escape route	Ventilation of building by way of natural currents
Internal walls	Organisation of internal layout, separation of rooms, fire protection, structural requirements	Increasing the thermal storage capacity for temperature amplitude damping, choice of material (transparent/opaque) and surface characteristics (absorptive/reflective) in conjunction with daylight optimisation and acoustics, integration of leakage-air openings for ventilation and night-time heating of thermal masses
Suspended floors	Imposed loads, impact sound insulation, acoustics, space for building services	Use of thermal buffer effect for temperature amplitude damping by omitting soffit finishes, surface characteristics in conjunction with daylight optimisation (light reflection) and acoustics, thermal activation of building components for heating and cooling via pipes integrated into components
Floor finishes	Usable surfaces with appropriate coverings, voids for building services	Heating and cooling in the low-temperature range, optimisation of thermal and acoustic requirements

B 6.11

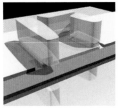
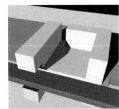
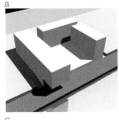
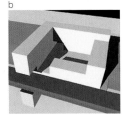

a   b

c   d   B 6.12

B 6.12   Studies of energy requirements, competition
entry for HafenCity, Hamburg (D), 2003,
Hegger Hegger Schleiff
a   Variant 1: 100%
b   Development plan: 102%
c   Variant 2: 105%
d   Variant 3: 109%
B 6.13   Themes and processing stages for the development of energy concepts according to the work
phases of the HOAI (scale of fees for architects
and engineers)
B 6.14   Established energy standards for buildings and
their definitions (EnEV = Energy Conservation
Act; KfW = Kreditanstalt für Wiederaufbau)
B 6.15   Gallery for the 21st century, design sketch,
Future Systems, 1993
B 6.16   Green Building, design sketch, Future Systems,
1990 1990

Phase 1: Clarification of design brief

• Define energy standard/benchmark

• Weigh up efficient building envelope and/or building
services

—► Energy-efficiency design strategy

Phase 2: Preliminary planning

• Optimise A/V ratio

• Optimise orientation

• Optimise solar gains

• Finalise building envelope

• Check thermal bridges

• Select energy media/heating plant

—► First estimate of energy requirement to Energy
Conservation Act

**Phases 3–4: Final design and building permission
application**

• Integrate building equipment and services into design

• Detailed design of envelope

• Determine U-values of all external components

• Reduce thermal bridges

—► Prepare Energy Conservation Act verification

**Phases 5–8: Working drawings, tender, award of
contract, construction management**

• Optimise A/V ratio

• Check eligibility of contractors

• Monitor insulating quality of building materials installed

• Monitor imperviousness

• Check energy-efficiency quality

—► Continue Energy Conservation Act verification,-
issue energy performance certificate

B 6.13

more, setting benchmarks forms the basis for
the energy design strategy plus the building
envelope and building services standards to
be aimed for. It is generally advisable to exhaust
the chances on offer systematically before investing in elaborate, expensive building services.

Preliminary planning
The foundations for an energy-efficient, sustainable building are laid during the preliminary
planning phase. Simple simulation methods
used during this phase can help to check and
optimise the design with respect to its energy
efficiency. The following targets should be considered:

• A/V ratio:
Even though building with an optimised envelope surface area is not compulsory, the
effects on the energy requirements during
usage should not be underestimated. In
smaller construction projects, some 15–20%
of the heating energy can be saved, in larger
projects up to 10% (Fig. B 6.12). Good daylighting and natural ventilation do, however,
place limits on compactness.

• Orientation of building and solar gains:
Windows, "as energy collectors", play an
important role in energy-efficiency optimisation. Shadows cast by other buildings or other
parts of the same building must be analysed
and evaluated, and every window assigned
its own shading factor. "Active energy" areas
can thus be calculated exactly and positioned
optimally. Shading factors enable the energy
gains to be quantified with respect to the
arrangement of the windows. For example,
if necessary, a building without an optimum
A/V ratio can nevertheless achieve higher
energy gains because it allows solar radiation
to enter the building at the critical places.

• Building envelope:
The thermal performance required and the
building physics properties of individual wall
constructions should be determined at an
early stage – and can be quickly investigated
with the help of energy software. Comparing
the energy-efficiency and economic properties of various types of construction can help
to target an optimum solution during the draft
design stage.

• Heating plant:
Different heating methods and fuels should
be analysed at an early stage and their different efficiencies compared. Renewable energy sources and efficient installations should
form the basis of sustainable energy supplies.

Only after the preliminary planning has been
concluded is it possible to estimate whether the
chosen approach will be able to meet the
benchmarks stipulated or the values given in
the Energy Conservation Act. In order to avoid
having to change the concept fundamentally at
a later date, an appropriate safety margin of
20–30% should be allowed for at this stage.

Final design, building permission application
During this phase, the energy-efficiency characteristics of the building design are refined on
the basis of the draft design and harmonised
with the building services.

• Building services:
Solar technology, boiler room, fuel storage,
energy storage, chimney and heating output
elements have a decisive influence on the
appearance of the interior and exterior of a
building, depending on the energy concept.

• Thermal quality of building envelope:
Specifying in detail the sequence of layers in
the envelope construction taking into account
the minimisation of transmission heat losses.
In addition, calculation of the U-values of the
various forms of construction.

• Thermal bridges:
A look at the thermal bridges reveals that
they embody a large building physics, technical and energy-efficiency optimisation
potential. The goal should be to eliminate all
thermal bridges, or to minimise them when
modernising existing buildings.

The conclusion of this stage of the design work
enables verification of the energy-efficiency
quality to be included as an essential part of
the application for building permission. For the
users of computing programs based on the
Energy Conservation Act, the preprinted forms
required at the same time form the basis for
optimising the design for energy efficiency.

*Working drawings, tender, award of contract,
construction management*
The energy-efficiency characteristics of the
final design should be conscientiously incorporated in the working drawings and all details
worked out. This applies to qualities, layer
thicknesses and the design of details to ensure
airtightness and the absence of thermal bridges.
During the tendering procedure and upon
awarding the contract, special attention should
be paid to ensuring durable, replaceable materials. Changes during the construction period
should not endanger the energy-efficiency
aspects and the results of the Energy Conservation Act analysis.
Construction on the building site exactly as
specified on the drawings is critical, e.g. when
it comes to precise, complete installation of
thermal insulation and the avoidance of thermal
bridges. Experience has shown that the quality
of junctions at roofs, windows, doors and glazing is especially significant. It is precisely at
these places that deficiencies in the airtightness can cause high ventilation heat losses.
The quality of workmanship in the various building trades can be checked using suitable
measurements, e.g. blower-door test, thermo-
graphy, as work proceeds.
Upon conclusion of the construction work, the
architect issues an energy performance certificate based on the values actually achieved
with the structure as built.

Evaluation
Energy concepts enable an objective evaluation even during early stages of the planning. Energy requirements, comfort and emissions can be determined and evaluated quite precisely with reasonable effort by way of parameters and descriptions of measures. In the sense of an overall appraisal, four dimensions – ecological, economic, social and architectural – are important:

Ecological evaluation
This considers how energy supplies and energy use may have negative consequences for the environment. The primary evaluation factor is the emission of carbon dioxide or equivalent substances. Generally accepted methods are available for performing the audit, the boundaries of which must be determined beforehand (Fig. B 6.19).

Economic evaluation
This is a check of the overall economy of measures for optimising energy efficiency, for using renewable energy sources and for the eco-efficiency of projects. In this context, considering just the capital outlay alone and how to minimise this – an approach that is still widespread – misses the point. Only in conjunction with an analysis of the day-to-day running costs, development measures and, if applicable, any revenues to be gained from the use of renewable energy is it possible to achieve an overall picture of the economics of a particular measure. The aim is to consider the costs over the entire life cycle of a building.

Social evaluation
When assessing energy concepts, it is important to consider the effects on users because their acceptance by users is, in the end, the decisive factor for the well-being of users and the proper operation of the building. Besides thermal comfort, it is primarily the visual, acoustic and olfactory comfort (e.g. perceived temperature, humidity of interior air, air movements) that influence the perceived comfort of users. In addition, options for influencing the interior climate (e.g. opening windows, individually controlled sunblinds, etc.) represent further important factors affecting the satisfaction of users.

Architectural evaluation
Energy concepts can affect the interior and exterior appearance of a building quite crucially. The concepts should characterise the architecture positively and hence lend a visible expression to a building culture that faces up to the serious socio-political challenges of our times.

Agreement on targets
A clearly formulated agreement regarding the energy-efficiency goals for a building is a practical starting point when developing an energy concept. Energy standards can provide guidelines through their unambiguous definitions of energy-efficiency requirements, methods of

Standard		Auditing level	Limiting values	Remarks
EnEV residential	D	Primary energy requirement for heating, ventilation, hot water	Depends on compactness	Minimum legal requirement in Germany
EnEV non-residential	D	Primary energy requirement for heating, ventilation, hot water, cooling, lighting	Depends on reference buildings	Minimum legal requirement in Germany
KfW-60 house	D	Primary energy parameter to EnEV	max. 60 kWh/m²a	Proof for financial assistance
KfW-40 house	D	Primary energy parameter to EnEV	max. 40 kWh/m²a	Proof for financial assistance
Minergie house	CH	Weighted energy parameter (final energy): heating, ventilation, hot water, air-conditioning	max. 42 kWh/m²a	Further requirements: e.g. building envelope, mechanical ventilation, costs
Minergie-Plus-house	CH	Weighted energy parameter (final energy): heating, ventilation, hot water, air-conditioning	25–30 kWh/m²a	Further requirements: airtightness, installed heating capacity, heating requirement, electricity requirement
Climate house	I	Heating requirement	max. 50 kWh/m²a	Climate house A: max. 30 kWh/m²a Climate house Gold: max. 10 kWh/m²a
Passive house	D	Heating requirement	max. 15 kWh/m²a	Additional requirement: max. 120 kWh/m²a primary energy requirement for heating, hot water and household electricity max. 120 kWh/m²a

B 6.14

calculation and methods of verification (Fig. B 6.14). Such definitions can be used as the foundations for more adventurous targets. For example, the target of a "zero-carbon building" can be realised by ensuring that the entire energy requirements during operation or over the entire life cycle are provided by renewable energy sources.

Assessment level
The boundaries to the energy audit are critical for the relevance of an energy concept. Clarification is required as to whether it is only the energy requirements for heating and hot water in a building during its period of use are the focus of attention, or all energy services for operation, or indeed all energy requirements – production, construction, operation and deconstruction (Fig. B 6.19). In the course of drawing up EU directives and revising the German Energy Conservation Act, energy services for lighting, cooling and ventilation have now been included for non-residential buildings in addition to the provision of heat (see p. 185). In terms of the assessment level, there are three approaches in principle:

- Energy generation and consumption are carried out completely decentrally, i.e. the building is self-sufficient in terms of energy. This generally leads to high storage costs and is only advisable for isolated sites without connections to the existing technical infrastructure.
- Energy generation is decentral, but energy consumption is safeguarded by connection to public networks. For example, the electricity grid is used as a low-losses storage medium in order to soak up surpluses of energy and to supply energy generated elsewhere as required. In the ideal case, taken over a year, every building would generate exactly the amount of electricity it needs.
- Energy generation and consumption for a building are combined in a public network. The energy generation specific to the building is completely separated from the consumption, the energy requirements are covered by suitable external energy sources (e.g. "green electricity"). A total audit is carried out for a defined region (e.g. town, city, county, country). The energy balance of a building is provided by formal means (e.g. certificates) and enables, for example, direct charging of wind energy revenues against the energy consumption of a remote building.

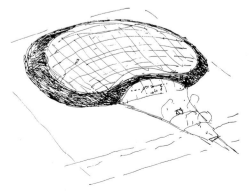

B 6.15

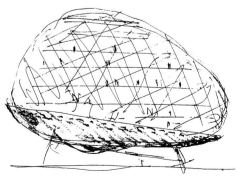

B 6.16

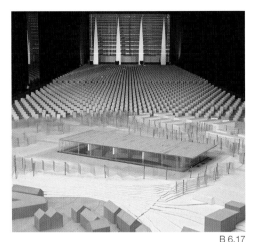

B 6.17

B 6.18

	ECA 2007 residential	ECA 2007 non-residential	Passive house	"LCA house"[1]
Obtaining raw materials				•
Prodn. of bldg. materials		•		
Construction of building				•
Space heating	•	•	•	•
Hot water	•	•	•	•
Ventilation	•	•	•	•
Cooling		•	•	•
Lighting		•		•
Household electricity		•		•
Electrical appliances				•
Deconstruction				•
Disposal				•

[1] Possible scope of audit

B 6.19

Planning aids

Simulation programs can help to achieve the aim of optimising the efficiency of a building and hence achieving maximum comfort with minimum energy consumption. Helpful software suites are available for the entire energy concept development procedure. Comprehensive thermodynamic processes within a building are illustrated in conjunction with the dynamic environmental conditions as a virtual model, which enables both the specific energy requirements of buildings and the energy-efficiency effects of alternative planning decisions to be determined quantitatively in the architectural design (Figs. B 6.17 and 6.18).

The majority of computer programs available offer specialised applications for all issues relevant to energy (Fig. B 6.20), e.g. analysis of energy requirements, comfort considerations for the interior, flow calculations or revenue prognoses for technical systems. In principle, we distinguish between static and dynamic methods of calculation.

Static simulations implement simple computational algorithms. They are used for the calculation of isolated, extreme values (e.g. heating and cooling loads), or for the simplified determination of annual energy totals (e.g. heating requirements according to passive-house stipulations or annual primary energy requirements according to the Energy Conservation Act). Dynamic simulations, on the other hand, emulate the energy flows in buildings realistically by taking into account varying internal and external loads. They determine the energy flow at defined intervals under the influence of variable parameters and consider, for example, the storage capacity of components, changing user profiles, the daily or annual solar radiation curve, etc. Besides analyses of the thermal behaviour of a building, dynamic simulations can also simulate the lighting conditions and interior air movements.

When employing such planning aids, the usefulness of the results increase with the degree of detail in the boundary conditions, which calls for a corresponding level of information in the planning process. Static simulations use generalised data to supply quick results and a rough estimate of the energy-related behaviour. Dynamic simulations can then be used for specific matters, e.g. an analysis of the shading due to neighbouring buildings, how the sizes of openings affect the incoming daylight, how sunshading affects the cooling load, how the cooling output influences the summertime room temperature, temperature stratification in an atrium, etc. Depending on the issues involved and the methods of calculation, simulation programs can be employed for analysing individual com-

Calculation/simulation	Application	Results	Design	Evaluation	Proof	CAD link	Output as images	as films
Static planning aids								
Heating load	Determination of maximum heating output in most unfavourable case for sizing output elements and heating plant	Standard heating load [W]	•	•				
Cooling load	Determination of maximum cooling load in most unfavourable case for sizing output elements and refrigeration plant	Cooling load [W]	•	•				
Annual energy requirement	Determination of annual energy quantities for various energy services according to defined methods of calculation	Heating requirement [kWh/m² a] Primary energy requirement [kWh/m² a] for heating, hot water, ventilation, lighting, cooling		•	•	•		
Dynamic planning aids								
Thermal simulation	Determination of thermodynamic behaviour of components and buildings for assessing comfort conditions, annual energy quantities and energy services	Heating load [W], cooling load [W] Air temperatures [°C] Surface temperatures [°C]		•		•	•	•
Daylighting simulation	Determination of lighting situation in rooms and buildings for optimising daylighting and artificial lighting	Duration of shading/sunshine exposure Luminance distribution Luminous intensity		•		•	•	•
Flow simulation	Determination of flows through rooms and building for assessing comfort conditions, i.e. pollutant concentrations and air velocities	Local air velocities Dynamic air change rates		•		•	•	•
Plant simulation	Determination of energy yield of building services for energy-efficiency assessment and design of components, also for optimising control systems	Yield from photovoltaic systems Yield from solar thermal systems Efficiency of heat pumps Efficiency of combined heat & power	•	•		•		
Shading simulation	Determination of shade caused by other parts of building and other buildings in urban settings for individual buildings and rooms	Lighting and shading effects over the course of a day/year				•	•	•

B 6.20

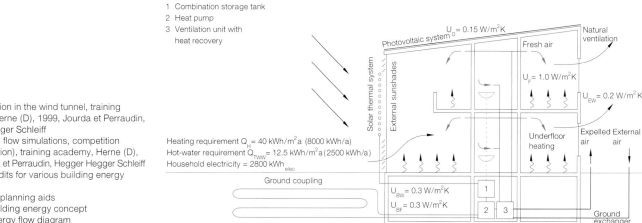

1 Combination storage tank
2 Heat pump
3 Ventilation unit with
   heat recovery

$U_D = 0.15$ W/m²K

Photovoltaic system ^{D}

Solar thermal system

External sunshades

Fresh air

Natural ventilation

$U_F = 1.0$ W/m²K

$U_{EW} = 0.2$ W/m²K

Underfloor heating

Expelled air

External air

Heating requirement $Q_H = 40$ kWh/m²a (8000 kWh/a)
Hot-water requirement $Q_{TWW} = 12.5$ kWh/m²a (2500 kWh/a)
Household electricity = 2800 kWh$_{elec}$

Ground coupling

$U_{BW} = 0.3$ W/m²K
$U_{BF} = 0.3$ W/m²K

Ground exchanger

B 6.21

B 6.17 Flow simulation in the wind tunnel, training academy, Herne (D), 1999, Jourda et Perraudin, Hegger Hegger Schleiff
B 6.18 Thermal and flow simulations, competition design (section), training academy, Herne (D), 1999, Jourda et Perraudin, Hegger Hegger Schleiff
B 6.19 Scope of audits for various building energy standards
B 6.20 Overview of planning aids
B 6.21 A typical building energy concept
B 6.22 A typical energy flow diagram

ponents, whole buildings or alternative solutions. Furthermore, the results can be used for designing or sizing building services components or for preparing proofs.

The ease of use of simulation programs is essentially determined by their user interfaces and data input options. In particular, the integration into CAD systems offers potential for synergy effects. The data output can be in the form of different parameters (e.g. heating load, cooling load, annual primary energy requirement, etc.), graphic displays of the results (e.g. room temperature over the day, annual solar energy generation, etc.) and pictorial results (e.g. luminance distribution over surfaces, temperature stratification in a room, isotherms in building components, local air velocities in the interior, etc.).

Documentation

Meaningful documentation forms the basis for communication among the members of the design team and provides information for others. Instead of simplified system sketches, abstract calculations and tables, self-explanatory graphic documentation is increasingly becoming the norm, for clarifying the package of measures and illustrating in an understandable way the path from energy services to energy sources (Figs. B 6.21 and 6.22). In addition, the documentation can create the conditions for the ongoing acquisition and evaluation of energy flows in the building.

Politics, legislation, statutory instruments

Reports and documents on the whole range of themes covering energy and materials are increasingly referring to the buzzword "sustainability", also at international level. It was in 1987 that the Brundtland Commission published a comprehensive definition of this word in connection with the new model of "sustainable development" in its concluding report. The Commission therefore designated sustainable development as that designed "to ensure that it meets the needs of the present without compromising the ability of future generations to meet their own needs" [4]. This term originated

in forestry management, where it means felling no more trees than have been replanted. Aspects of the sustainability model have now been integrated into certain normative regulations at both European and national level. Existing legislation and statutory instruments are at the moment still concentrating primarily on the environmental dimensions (Fig. B 6.23).

EU directive on the energy performance of buildings
In the course of the European harmonisation of standards, the EU member states have pledged to adopt the requirements of European Parliament directive 2002/91/EC "Energy Performance of Buildings" and accommodate this in their national legislation by January 2006. This EU directive – frequently referred to simply as the EPBD – pursues the following aims in particular:

· The holistic assessment of the energy efficiency of buildings
· Encouraging energy-efficiency upgrade measures for the existing building stock
· The provision of transparent information for consumers with respect to the energy efficiency of buildings
· Improving the energy efficiency of building services

In Germany, many of these requirements, e.g. national energy standards for new and existing buildings, the holistic assessment of the building envelope and building services plus decommissioning of outdated heating systems, have been implemented in the Energy Conservation Act (EnEV). The requirement regarding regular inspection of boilers is satisfied by the 1st Federal Immissions Protection Act (BImSchG). As, however, the EPBD requirements exceeded the previous requirements in Germany in a number of areas, the Energy Conservation Act was revised in 2005, and the following changes came into force:

· Inclusion of the energy requirements for the lighting, ventilation and air-conditioning for non-residential buildings
· Introduction of energy performance certificates when letting and selling existing buildings, houses or apartments
· The display of energy performance certificates in public and heavily frequented buildings
· Regular inspections of air-conditioning plant

Whereas the revised Energy Conservation Act entails few changes for residential buildings compared to the previous Act, the new DIN

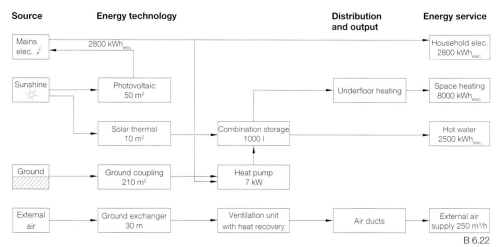

Source	Energy technology	Distribution and output	Energy service
Mains elec.	2800 kWh$_{elec.}$		Household elec. 2800 kWh$_{elec.}$
Sunshine	Photovoltaic 50 m²	Underfloor heating	Space heating 8000 kWh$_{elec.}$
	Solar thermal 10 m²	Combination storage 1000 l	Hot water 2500 kWh$_{elec.}$
Ground	Ground coupling 210 m²	Heat pump 7 kW	
External air	Ground exchanger 30 m	Ventilation unit with heat recovery	Air ducts	External air supply 250 m³/h

B 6.22

18599 "Energy efficiency of buildings" has been drawn up for non-residential buildings in order to reflect the substantially more extensive calculation and auditing methods.

Energy Conservation Act

The introduction of the Energy Conservation Act in Germany combined the stipulations of the older Thermal Insulation Act and Heating Systems Act in order to cover the more stringent requirements regarding thermal insulation and building services with a common method of analysis and common parameter for the analysis. This holistic assessment gives planners more design freedom for achieving the stipulated efficiency targets. In addition, the Energy Conservation Act provides users with greater transparency with respect to the predicted energy costs.

The Energy Conservation Act limits the maximum permissible annual primary energy requirement Qp in relation to the A/Ve ratio for all new buildings with normal interior temperatures. It expands the previous auditing framework by adding the following influencing factors (Fig. B 6.26):

- Losses in the upstream energy provision chain – the extraction, conversion and transport of energy media
- Heating requirements for hot-water provision (flat rate)

- Losses in heating plant
- Electrical auxiliary energy requirements for installations (e.g. pumps, burners, controllers)
- Energy requirements for mechanical ventilation systems
- The use of renewable energy (e.g. solar collectors)

With the choice of an energy medium (e.g. natural gas, biomass, etc.), the annual primary energy requirement of a building takes into account its environmental impacts and the upstream process chains by means of the so-called primary energy factors. In the countries of the European Union, these primary energy factors have different values depending on the requirements for extracting, converting and transporting the energy media. In Germany, for example, the primary energy factor f_p for electricity is 3.0 (this factor will, however, fall in the coming years owing to the growing contribution of renewable energy in electricity generation), 1.1 for oil and gas, and 0.2 for wood pellets. Furthermore, the Energy Conservation Act defines a "minimum standard of thermal insulation", i.e. the specific transmission heat loss H'_T related to the heat-transferring enclosing surface. This value represents the average U-value of all envelope components taking into account losses via thermal bridges. Different methods of calculation and different requirements apply to new and existing buildings:

- New buildings with normal internal temperatures ≥ 19°C must not exceed maximum values for Q_p and H'_T according to the monthly balance method.
- New buildings with normal internal temperatures ≥ 19°C and a proportion of windows ≤ 30% can be calculated according to the so-called simplified method for residential buildings.
- New buildings with low internal temperatures ≤ 19°C or small building volumes ≤ 100 m³ only have to guarantee compliance with the maximum value for H'_T, and requirements here are lower.
- Existing buildings in which refurbishment measures affect at least 20% of the area of building components facing in the same direction must comply with minimum U-values according to the building component analysis.
- Existing buildings subjected to more extensive refurbishment measures are calculated according to the monthly balance method, and the limits for new buildings may not be exceeded by more than 40%.
- For existing buildings in which the heated volume of the building is extended by more than 30 m³, the same methods of analysis and the same requirements apply to the extension as for a new building.

Irrespective of the requirements relating to refurbishment measures, the Energy Conservation Act calls for the upgrading of all non-owner-

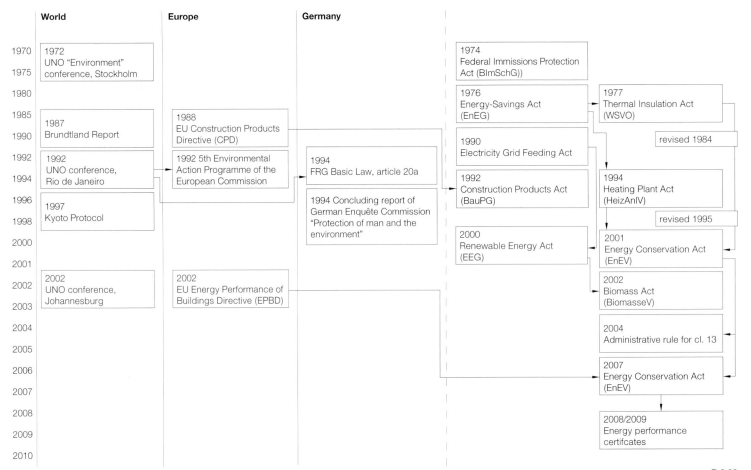

	World	Europe	Germany		
1970	1972 UNO "Environment" conference, Stockholm			1974 Federal Immissions Protection Act (BImSchG))	
1975					
1980				1976 Energy-Savings Act (EnEG)	1977 Thermal Insulation Act (WSVO)
1985	1987 Brundtland Report	1988 EU Construction Products Directive (CPD)		1990 Electricity Grid Feeding Act	revised 1984
1990					
1992	1992 UNO conference, Rio de Janeiro	1992 5th Environmental Action Programme of the European Commission	1994 FRG Basic Law, article 20a	1992 Construction Products Act (BauPG)	1994 Heating Plant Act (HeizAnlV)
1994					
1996	1997 Kyoto Protocol		1994 Concluding report of German Enquête Commission "Protection of man and the environment"		revised 1995
1998					
2000				2000 Renewable Energy Act (EEG)	2001 Energy Conservation Act (EnEV)
2001					
2002	2002 UNO conference, Johannesburg	2002 EU Energy Performance of Buildings Directive (EPBD)			2002 Biomass Act (BiomasseV)
2003					
2004					2004 Administrative rule for cl. 13
2005					
2006					2007 Energy Conservation Act (EnEV)
2007					
2008					2008/2009 Energy performance certifcates
2009					
2010					

B 6.23

occupied buildings by a certain date. Those upgrading measures refer to insulation to the topmost suspended floor, the replacement of oil- or gas-fired boilers installed prior to 1 October 1978 and the insulation of space-heating and hot-water pipes in unheated rooms.

DIN 18 599

In Germany, DIN 18599 implements the requirements of the EPBD for non-residential buildings. It is equivalent to DIN 4108 and forms the basis for calculations for new building work and refurbishment measures in the non-residential sector. The principal obligation remains the annual primary energy requirement. The calculation of this adheres to the tried-and-tested route from net energy via final energy to primary energy. The latter is, however, no longer assessed depending on area and volume, but instead primarily on the use of the building and the boundary conditions (Fig. B 6.25).

DIN 18599 is a well-formulated method of assessment with which the energy consumption for the operation of a building can be estimated at an early stage of the work and used as an aid in the rest of the planning. In order to satisfy this far-reaching claim, DIN 18599 has extended the auditing limits within the building. In future, the entire installations for conditioning and cooling the interior will be included in the energy calculations, also the artificial lighting. The energy requirement and the auxiliary energy are balanced together with the heat flows via the building envelope and the energy requirements for the systems necessary for space heating, hot-water provision and ventilation. Instead of heat gains and losses, we now calculate with heat sources and sinks. The direction of the heat flow is therefore no longer anticipated in global terms and limited to an audit of the energy requirement during the heating period. Consequently, a heat source can represent a gain or a load depending on usage and time. This change takes account of the fact that cooling represents a considerable energy requirement in the non-residential sector.

DIN 18599 is made up of 10 parts, each cover-

ing a particular theme (Fig. B 6.27). This structure guarantees that relevant partial results are available to the design process at all times. To do this, the standard takes into account interactions between the various parts, various themes, such that in the end accurate statements can be made regarding the overall efficiency.

The introduction of a multi-zone model here is a decisive new approach compared to previous methods of calculation. The building is divided into zones according to type and degree of use, building services installed and type of enclosing envelope. Each zone is treated separately in the calculations and the heat flows between zones are considered and adjusted iteratively. The separate zones are added together to give the energy requirement of the building as a whole. In order to achieve neutral boundary conditions for the diversity of uses in the non-residential sector, the final part of the standard includes standard usage profiles. Typical buildings and uses are listed here and analysed with respect to their occupancy densities, occupancy periods, internal heat sources/sinks, net energy requirements and air change rates.

The calculations supply the total primary energy requirement for the building. In the so-called reference building method, this actual value is compared with a target value, which may not be exceeded in the building being assessed.

Energy performance certificates

Up until now, the main tools of the policies for increasing efficiency in the buildings sector have been legislative measures (in Germany the Federal Immissions Protection Act, the Energy Conservation Act) plus development programmes. In order to meet the reduction obligations of the Kyoto Protocol, the member states of the European Union have resolved to develop additional measures for controlling energy demands.

Consequently, the EPBD adds a market-oriented strategy to the traditional policy tools. It creates an obligation to introduce energy performance certificates for the construction, sale or re-letting of buildings, apartments, etc. For buildings used by public authorities or to which the public has access, these certificates must be displayed in a prominent place if the building has a total usable floor space > 1000 m².

Energy performance certificates are intended to enhance the market transparency and the awareness of consumers with respect to the energy consumption of buildings and hence stimulate innovation and investment in new and existing buildings. The following rules must be adhered to:

- The energy performance certificate must specify a parameter that represents the overall energy efficiency of the building. Compar-

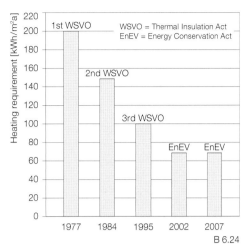

B 6.24

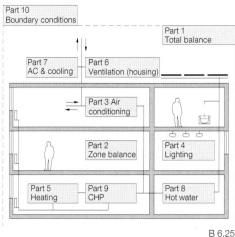

B 6.25

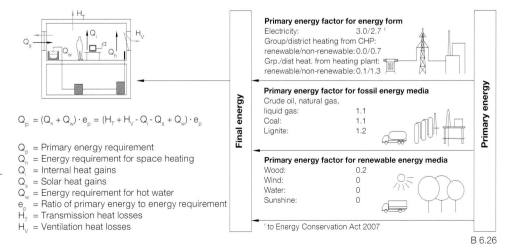

$$Q_p = (Q_h + Q_w) \cdot e_p = (H_T + H_V - Q_i - Q_s + Q_w) \cdot e_p$$

Q_p = Primary energy requirement
Q_h = Energy requirement for space heating
Q_i = Internal heat gains
Q_s = Solar heat gains
Q_w = Energy requirement for hot water
e_p = Ratio of primary energy to energy requirement
H_T = Transmission heat losses
H_V = Ventilation heat losses

B 6.23 Chronological development of demands regarding sustainability and energy efficiency in buildings
B 6.24 Average values for heating requirements
B 6.25 Scope of DIN 18599 audit
B 6.26 Scope of Energy Conservation Act audit

B 6.26

ative parameters may also be specified here for better transparency.

- Recommendations for the cost-effective improvement of the energy efficiency should also be included.
- The period of validity may not exceed 10 years.
- An energy performance certificate is only an informative document; it is not enforceable and does not constitute an obligation to carry out refurbishment measures.
- The EU member states may choose whether certificates are based on calculations of requirements or measurements of consumption.

The contents and the relevance of requirements- or consumption-based energy performance certificates are not identical. The requirements calculation concerns standardised assumptions for a standard climate and the usage conditions (e.g. room temperature 19°C, length of heating period, average air change rate) and is therefore regarded as a "theoretical consumption". Consumption-based energy performance certificates, on the other hand, take the heating costs as their starting point and therefore reflect not only the energy-efficiency quality of a building but, above all, the individual user behaviour and, if applicable, extreme climatic influences. As these influences can easily mask the true energy-efficiency quality (in the extreme case an empty house would have the highest energy efficiency!), the requirements calculation is a more meaningful way of assessing and comparing the energy efficiency of buildings.

The revised Energy Conservation Act (2007) implements the EPBD in Germany. The obligatory energy performance certificates will be introduced according to the following timetable:

- residential buildings built before 1965: 1 July 2008
- newer residential buildings: 1 January 2009

- non-residential buildings: 1 July 2009

In principle, owners may choose between consumption- or requirements-based certificates. Only residential buildings with up to four residential units built before the 1st Thermal Insulation Act came into force in 1977 needs requirements-based energy performance certificates.

New tasks for architects

The EPBD and its tools not only result in new tasks for architects, but also new responsibilities. As key players in the planning process, they must design every building according to the new energy-efficiency rules. Owing to the holistic auditing method and the balancing options between optimised building form, thermal insulation measures and the energy-efficiency quality of the building services, the architectural configuration of a building must be seen in the context of energy efficiency. If architects take on these tasks, the means of planning at their disposal can cut the energy requirements plus the costs of constructing and operating buildings quite substantially. In smaller projects, architects can carry out the work themselves using suitable computer programs, and thus expand their field of activities. In more complex construction projects, they will solve the new tasks mostly in conjunction with a building services engineer or an energy consultant. They should, however, have adequate knowledge of these aspects in order to be able to exploit fully the skills of the specialists plus the technical and architectural possibilities.

The German Energy Agency (dena) assumes that with the consequential exploitation of all economic savings potential in the residential sector, the politically motivated market incentive programmes (e.g. energy performance certificate) will result in a three-fold increase in the annual level of investment in the energy-efficiency upgrading of buildings by 2020. Issuing energy performance certificates could

encourage about 30% of private property owners to initiate refurbishment measures [5]. The creation of incentives for innovation and investment in increasing the energy efficiency of new and existing buildings could therefore make an important contribution to securing jobs in the building industry and the associated planning disciplines.

Planning process

Buildings are having to satisfy ever more complex requirements. Besides increasing demands regarding comfort, convenience, energy efficiency and environmental compatibility, safety and security requirements and the general improvement in technical standards present new challenges, which demand the involvement of specialists right from the start of a project. Users and occupants expect an unpolluted interior climate, good lighting and ventilation concepts, a reasonable view of the outside world plus adaptable, flexible interior layouts and, at the same time, low running costs. Clients and investors expect dependable schedules of costs for the construction and operation of their buildings, and even in the planning phase strive to guarantee trouble-free use of their buildings. Public authorities have a right to demand that their buildings are safe and do not cause unnecessary environmental impacts. All these requirements should be implemented with a high architectural and constructional quality, within the shortest possible time, while not exceeding the budget and often having to accept incomplete or changing framework conditions within the planning process. To do this, it is necessary to plan not only the building or structure itself, but to an increasing extent the process as well. Furthermore, clients and users are becoming more and more aware of the fact that the costs of a building's operation and maintenance play

Audit step	DIN 18599
Zoning of building according to usage, building services and building envelope	Part 1
Determination of usage-related boundary conditions and the input data necessary for the audit	Parts 1 & 10
Determination of heat sources and sinks for individual zones and rough audit of net energy requirement for heating and cooling	Part 2
Determination of heating and cooling input to be supplied by plant based on rough estimate of requirements in each zone	Part 2
Determination of net energy requirement for energy-efficient air conditioning	Part 3
Final audit of net energy requirement for heating and cooling plus allocation to various output systems	Parts 2–8
Determination of losses in output, distribution and storage for • heating plant • air-management system • cooling • hot-water provision	Part 5 Part 6 Part 7 Part 8
Breakdown of heating and cooling outputs required according to the various supply systems, and determination of absolute losses	Parts 5–8
Determination of the net and final energy requirements for lighting	Part 4
Determination of the auxiliary energy required, compilation of final energy according to energy source and calculation of primary energy requirement	Parts 5–9
Application of credit method for electricity yields from CHP	Part 9
Target-actual comparison of total primary energy requirements using reference building method	Part 10

B 6.27

B 6.27   The steps in a DIN 18599 audit
B 6.28   Linear, iterative and integrative planning
         sequences
B 6.29   Life cycle costs for different types of use
B 6.30   Course of and factors affecting total costs

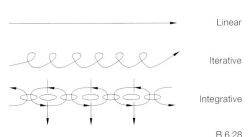

Linear

Iterative

Integrative

B 6.28

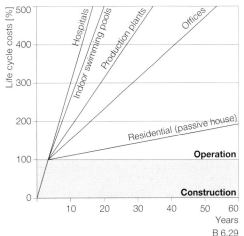

B 6.29

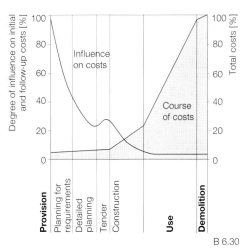

B 6.30

a significant part in the overall economy of that building and, depending on the type of use, can even exceed the capital outlay within just a few years (Fig. B 6.29). This can only be influenced effectively in the early phases of project development (Fig. B 6.30). It is therefore crucial to guarantee the cooperation of a competent, complete planning team, fully aware of its responsibilities, right from the very start of a project.

The principles of integrated planning

The aim of integrated planning is to achieve a holistic assessment of individual, separate planning aspects (Fig. B 6.28). According to the architect Niklaus Kohler, integrated planning permits "both horizontal (interdisciplinary) and vertical (life cycle-related) integration. It is therefore possible to introduce new findings and requirements into the planning process from the beginning and implement efficient optimisation techniques (feedback, simulation of variants, etc.)" [6].

In order to identify synergies between individual requirements and planning aspects at an early stage and to harmonise these, in future it will no longer be sufficient to consider interior climate, energy and mass as purely physical variables. Instead, they will have to be seen as dimensions that have to be formed in conjunction with the traditional means of architecture (e.g. form, texture, transparency, etc.), and the skilled use of precisely these means will achieve a saving in technical services. Quantifiable variables such as energy requirement, temperature level or investment costs can be defined unambiguously. However, they are often closely linked with qualitative aspects such as design, well-being or image. An integrated planning process should attempt to guarantee that both quantitative and qualitative aspects, the contributions of various disciplines and the consideration of the building and its characteristics continue to be included over the entire lifespan. Summing up, integrated planning is based on the following potential benefits [7]:

- Integration: the knowledge of engineers and the experience of specialists are incorporated in the project right from the start of the planning.

- Complexity: sustainable building aspects are assessed comprehensively.
- Iteration: design options remain open until the optimum solution has been found through interdisciplinary development and the evaluation of alternatives.
- Options: clients make decisions not only primarily on the basis of proposals presented in visual form.
- Teamwork: architects are responsible for leading the planning team, but are not the sole source of impetus during the planning work.
- Learning system: specialist planners are given an insight into the complexity of the architectural design and architects gain additional incentives for the design of the building from their growing skills in technical planning disciplines.
- Conflicts: transparency of decisions and the inclusion of the players in good time minimise tension and conflicts.

The growing degree of complexity and the specialisation in all technical areas of construction calls for the experts from various disciplines to be integrated into the design process these days; this specialisation offers potential for ever more efficient buildings. Overriding objectives, cooperation and communication are necessary for bringing the knowledge together and devising new solutions. Conflicts of aims are inevitable. For the success of the project, it is therefore crucial to recognise hindrances early on and to solve them for the sake of achieving a high-quality, sustainability-oriented overall concept. Fig. B 6.31 lists the typical conflicts of aims that can arise. Consequential analysis helps to minimise the interfacing problems and to concretise the planning targets [8].

Integrated planning demands that the players necessary are bound by contracts from an early stage (Fig. B. 6.32) because the holistic solution of sustainability requirements is only effective during the initial planning phases. This is a social process involving a division of labour. The project participants work and make decisions not in isolation, but rather within a framework of social interaction. They are affected by various interests and motivating factors plus

specific specialist knowledge, but also ingrained perceptual images. Resolving these in the sense of a learning system and combining them to form a common whole is the great chance of integrated planning.

Project structure

The nature of the relationships determined through the contracts with the client characterises the structure of a project. The traditional individual appointment of planners and contractors has proved worthwhile for different sizes of project, but calls for a high organisational effort and increased commitment on the part of the client. Appointing one architect and one contractor can reduce the client's coordination and management input, but it does lead to the planning being frozen at an early stage: changes at a later date are only possible through accepting an increase in the costs. The primarily economic interests of general contractors can lead to the ecological and social dimensions of sustainable building being given insufficient consideration.

Integrated building and operation

In order to improve the organisation of public-sector construction projects in terms of the economics, project structures in which public sector and private sector cooperate in the financing, planning, erection, operation and/or recycling of buildings have become established in recent years. In such so-called public private partnerships (PPP), the state provision of premises (e.g. schools, hospitals, etc.) has hitherto been carried out by private clients or operators and operated for a defined period of time at the start of their life cycle, usually 15–30 years. The client, as the user, pays rent over this period for the total expenditure (planning, construction, operating and maintenance costs). This means that a holistic consideration of all cost factors over the period of the contract is absolutely essential and inevitably leads to different requirements being placed on the planning, which focus on the running costs and hence low energy consumption as well. The predicted cost benefits of 10–25% therefore result from the all-embracing investigation of all phases and processes, but especially the operating phase.

Irrespective of the PPP model, the overall approach of the life cycle analysis will become a tool that promotes sustainable building and reduces the economic risks markedly. It will also contribute to minimising the ecological risks of building and raising the overall quality of a structure. The solving of the ubiquitous investor-user dilemma – the separation of the worlds of erecting and operating the building – is a prerequisite for this. Principles that fit into a life cycle approach presume integrated planning approaches and intensive cooperation among all players.

Players

The disciplines combined in the planning team and many other players are responsible, as a group, for the construction process and hence for the success of an energy-efficient, sustainable building industry. These players and their tasks are described below.

Politicians

Both the legislative and executive bodies have shown a growing awareness for the problems caused by the high environmental impacts of buildings, also with regard to overriding sustainability targets. However, despite the Kyoto Protocol, there is a lack of binding global goals. The objectives of the European Union should be assessed as positive here, but their legal implementation is proceeding exceedingly sluggishly in many countries.

The growing awareness of the need to achieve defined protective aims and the positive economic effects of sustainable management are changing the activities of this group of players.

Urban and regional planners

The plans of this group of players have a considerable influence on the use of land for buildings and infrastructure. Urban and regional planners also determine density, the mix of uses, integration and mobility plus the technical and social infrastructure of spaces and hence have a decisive influence on energy consumption and sustainability. More and more, urban planners are stipulating energy and sustainability standards within the scope of their development plans. The further stipulations of development plans, e.g. roof pitches, undeveloped areas or orientation, define the possibilities for architects to exploit local environmental energy sources (e.g. solar radiation) for buildings, and through good access to sunshine and daylight at the same time create pleasant living conditions.

Financial backers and banks

Banks are purely interested in the economic side of project developments. Project evaluations are, however, increasingly taking into account sustainability arguments because it is recognised that the long-term, secure, higher value-creation of sustainability-oriented property also means a better economic performance for those buildings.

Clients, operators

The client in the form of an individual person is replaced by institutions or the client's agents on larger projects. As the "customer", it is he who initiates the process of building activities, and can request a planning and building process geared to sustainability needs. If the client is not solely responsible for the task of erecting and reselling a property, he will be directly interested in sustainable building development. Criteria such as longevity, adaptability and low running costs are the key issues for operators. Many clients are aware of the fact that a sustainable building, considered over its lifetime, exhibits not only environmental and social benefits, but also distinct economic advantages (Fig. B. 6.33).

Architects

Owing to growing demands and the rising demand for holistic building concepts, the profile of the architect is changing from that of a universal planner to that of a coordinating team leader. As the architect is directly involved in the majority of aspects relevant to planning, he can help the client to make the right decisions at the right times. Many planners are aware, in general, of the need for integrated and sustain-

Conflicting aims	Explanation	Client	User	Architect	Energy consultant	Services engineer	Lighting engineer	Structural engineer	Acoustics engineer	Fire protection expert	Facility manager
Compactness v. daylight usage and natural ventilation	The form of the building should be developed weighing up the compactness, which has an effect mainly on the heating requirements and the capital outlay, plus a good level of incoming daylight and natural ventilation.			•	•	•	•				
Usage dynamic v. energy concept	Areas of the building with changing or unpredictable usage (e.g. atria) can trigger a much higher energy consumption due to changes of use and hence comfort requirements (e.g. heating or cooling) deviating from the energy concept.	•		•	•						
Passive cooling v. standard comfort requirements	Omitting active cooling reduces the energy consumption substantially during the operating phase, but calls for a temporarily lower standard of comfort in the summer because room temperatures occasionally exceed 26°C.	•			•	•					
Natural ventilation and passive cooling v. internal layout flexibility	Natural ventilation during the day and passive cooling through night-time ventilation often calls for a corresponding zoning layout. In order to avoid the need for a technical upgrade in the case of changing usage requirements, flexible internal layouts should be considered during the planning.	•		•	•	•					
Daylight usage and view out v. sunshades and glare protection	Choosing a system to match the requirements and combining sunshades and glare protection can rule out improper functioning and guarantee a (partial) view of the outside world.			•	•		•				
Natural ventilation v. sound insulation and fire protection	Leakage-air openings between different usage zones must be developed for natural ventilation concepts taking into account sound insulation and fire protection requirements.	•			•	•	•			•	•
Use of thermal masses v. room acoustics	The use of thermal storage masses to attenuate temperature peaks calls for a close coordination with sound attenuation or acoustic measures.			•	•	•			•	•	
Highly insulated building envelope v. transparency and efficiency of areas	Building envelopes with a high degree of thermal insulation reduce the usable floor area owing to the thicker wall constructions and limit the proportion of transparent areas. Quality of use, a link with the outside world, efficient areas and energy consumption must be harmonised in a balanced relationship through the design and energy concept.	•		•	•						
Building automation v. individuality and user acceptance	Highly automated building control systems, individual room or zone controls or manually controlled systems should be developed weighing up the costs of investment, maintenance and operation plus user acceptance.	•	•	•	•	•					•
Innovative planning team v. routine implementation	Experienced project participants should be included in the workflows and requirements of an integrated planning approach. The aims of a sustainability-oriented construction project (e.g. comfort, energy efficiency) should be described in the preamble to the tender for each building trade. Special information such as material declarations, testing or inspection methods must be worded unambiguously and requested.	•	•	•	•	•	•	•	•	•	•

B 6.31

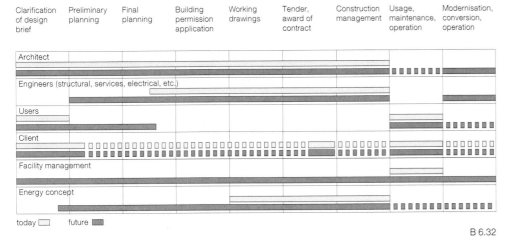

	Clarification of design brief	Preliminary planning	Final planning	Building permission application	Working drawings	Tender, award of contract	Construction management	Usage, maintenance, operation	Modernisation, conversion, operation
Architect									
Engineers (structural, services, electrical, etc.)									
Users									
Client									
Facility management									
Energy concept									

today □   future ▓

B 6.31 Typical conflicts of aims in energy-optimised planning
B 6.32 Players in the planning and usage processes, today and in the future

B 6.32

ability-oriented construction, but they often lack relevant detailed knowledge and sometimes also the ability to assert themselves. A design preference occasionally hinders the open embracing of the theme of "sustainability", the architectural innovation potential of which is currently only beginning to reveal itself.

Landscape architects and ecologists
Sustainable management has its origins in forestry. It should therefore be correspondingly anchored in the related disciplines of ecology and landscape architecture. But there are still considerable developmental reserves with respect to sustainable, energy-efficient landscaping in many areas (e.g. clearance of legacy pollution, rainwater management, design of external areas). Moreover, new topics such as the local bioenergy economy and gaining energy from the wind and the sun still have to be tackled. On the level of building planning, landscape architects can make a major contribution to improving the microclimate (e.g. water features, rainwater, shading, reflection and temperatures of surfaces).

Engineers
Engineers are professionals with a high level of specialist knowledge concerning certain individual themes of sustainable building. Integrated properly, this expert knowledge can help to discover solutions and encourage creativity with respect to the efficient use of materials and energy. Close networking between the individual disciplines is best achieved through intensive discussions among all participants right at the start of the planning process.

Building contractors, building trades
Awarding contracts according to the traditional building trades mean that the companies and subcontractors are only responsible for certain parts of the building project. The construction process is resolved into various individual tasks; some players, depending on the particular trade, have very detailed knowledge of the problems. With proper development and implementation, this knowledge can have a positive effect on the sustainability of buildings. At the same time, however, considering the whole

and the interfaces to neighbouring trades is also necessary.

Facility management
As energy prices continue to rise and the aim of sustainable building operation spreads, so facility management, the controlling tool, is becoming popular. Owing to the close relationship with the users of the building and their requirements and needs, a comprehensive assessment of all operating procedures can reduce the cost of usage permanently and maintain the value of the property in the long-term.

Users, occupants and others affected
In the case of urban and landscape planning, also large projects, the involvement of the local citizens in the relevant planning and decision-making processes has been part of everyday planning practice for a number of decades. Demands for broader forms of participation have appeared over the past 10 years in various documents concerning sustainable development (e.g. Agenda 21, Habitat II). Considering the specific needs of different groups of the population and, in particular, taking account of the interests of disadvantaged social groups represent the ideal of the responsible participation of citizens in the local community. Such participation is one of the central prerequisites for the implementation of sustainability [9]. Whereas the traditional involvement of local citizens is mainly limited to information and discussion events, the intention behind broader participation is to promote the self-regulation of processes through a diverse range of methods, e.g. round tables, mediation, future workshops or planning cells. Owing to the number of forms of participation, the first thing to clarify is which topics, which targets and which methods of participation should be used – and when. The relevant phases of discussion-type projects are similar for municipal planning and building construction projects:

• Project-planning and concept-finding phases
• Negotiation phase for discourse offers
• Discourse phase
• Transfer phase

Participation can make a serious contribution to increasing the legitimisation and acceptance of planning projects, tackling resistance and raising the quality of decisions.
Nevertheless, users, through their comfort demands and behaviour with respect to interior temperature, hot-water usage, ventilation and internal or solar gains, exert a considerable influence on the energy requirements of buildings. Here, the average consumption, depending on user profile, can lie about 15% below ("extreme saver") or about 60% above ("extreme waster") the guidelines contained in the Energy Conservation Act (Fig. B 6.34).

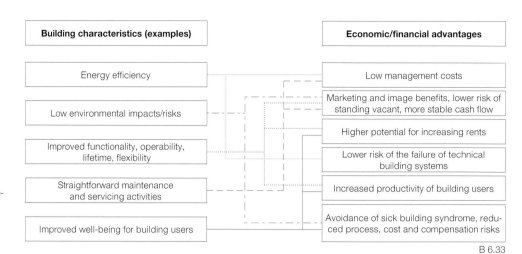

Building characteristics (examples)	Economic/financial advantages
Energy efficiency	Low management costs
Low environmental impacts/risks	Marketing and image benefits, lower risk of standing vacant, more stable cash flow
Improved functionality, operability, lifetime, flexibility	Higher potential for increasing rents
	Lower risk of the failure of technical building systems
Straightforward maintenance and servicing activities	Increased productivity of building users
Improved well-being for building users	Avoidance of sick building syndrome, reduced process, cost and compensation risks

B 6.33

B 6.33 Building characteristics and the resulting economic advantages
B 6.34 How user behaviour affects the energy requirements of residential buildings
B 6.35 Sustainable building criteria according to "Recommendation SIA 112/1, sustainable construction – buildings"

Sustainable architecture

Sustainable building is often equated with the terms "ecological building", "energy-efficient building" or "bioclimatic architecture"; but these are only parts of a development fit for the future. The sustainable building approach is more complex. The entirety of the architectural production is up for discussion, i.e. economic, ecological and social aspects must be considered in their mutual dependencies. The individual dimensions are known and have characterised architecture from its very beginnings. As can be seen in Fig. B 6.33, sustainable building brings with it numerous economic advantages in the development of the value of property [10]. Nevertheless, everyday practice is currently lagging way behind the possibilities on offer. Sustainable building opens up the chance to enrich the design repertoire of architects and create a stronger link with the key issues of society. In order to illustrate understandable facts, also measurable for many areas, the key criteria and tools of sustainable building are explained below.

Key criteria
With the intention of putting into practice the model of "sustainability" for the building and housing sector in Germany, the German Enquête Commission drew up the so-called three-pillars model, with economic, ecological

and socio-cultural targets, in its concluding report on the "Protection of man and the environment" (1998). Based on the preliminary work of the Commission, the year 2001 saw the Federal Ministry of Transport, Building & Urban Affairs publish its "Sustainable Building Guidelines" – recommendations for public buildings in order to concretise the protection aims for planning, constructing and operating buildings and to provide guidelines for planners [11]. Like the three-pillars model, the Guidelines provide an initial, valuable aid for illustrating sustainability criteria for architecture and the construction industry.
"Recommendation SIA 112/1, sustainable construction – buildings" [12] published in 2004 by the Association of Swiss Engineers & Architects (SIA) takes a similar line. The target dimensions of the three-pillar model correspond to the three areas of society, industry and environment, which in this publication are subdivided into several topics to which several criteria are assigned (Fig. B 6.35). The SIA Recommendation helps clients and planners to select the criteria specific to their projects in the sense of an agreement on targets at the start of a project and indicate measures for their implementation.

Society
The quality of the built environment reflects human notions of value and gives general ideas of culture a means of expression. Build-

ings and everything else that forms part of the built environment are so effective and omnipotent that they influence our standard of living in diverse ways. However, the corresponding criteria are often not quantifiable; they can be assessed only in qualitative or descriptive terms. But it is precisely the intangible social values such as integration, identification, participation or health that represent the essential, key factors for the sustainable, peaceful and environmentally compatible development of society.

Industry
The capital costs are often the focus of attention when making planning decisions. Primarily economy-centred activities frequently result in one-dimensional project developments that conflict with long-term thinking. The costs for the operation and maintenance of buildings can exceed the cost of investment after just a few years. Future planning practice should, however, consider the cost of building over the entire life cycle (construction, operation, deconstruction). Planning decisions must also weigh higher investment costs against lower operating and maintenance costs. High design quality has its price, but in the long-term increases the value of a property.

User behaviour	Internal temperature	Energy requirement for hot water	Air change rate	Deviations from Energy Conservation Act [1]	Household electricity requirement (incl. lighting)	Chargeable heat energy for electrical equipment
Extreme saver 10% quantile	17.0 °C	5.0 kW/m²a	0.4 /h	-14.5 %	10 kWh/m²a	2.3 kWh/m²a
Saver 30% quantile	18.5 °C	10.1 kW/m²a	0.6 /h	-2.5 %	15 kWh/m²a	3.4 kWh/m²a
Average 50% quantile	19.5 °C	15.1 kW/m²a	1.1 /h	14.2 %	20 kWh/m²a	4.5 kWh/m²a
Waster 70% quantile	21.0 °C	25.2 kW/m²a	1.5 /h	34.7 %	30 kWh/m²a	6.8 kWh/m²a
Extreme waster 90%- quantile	23.0 °C	35.3 kW/m²a	2.0 /h	59.4 %	40 kWh/m²a	9.0 kWh/m²a

[1] Deviations for a low-energy building (An = 363.52 m²) with an annual primary energy requirement of 63.1 kWh/m²a.

B 6.34

Environment

When constructing buildings and replacing components, it is primarily the materials flows of the building materials that define the ecological effects; by contrast, during operation it is the energy requirements, especially those for heating, cooling, lighting and equipment, also cleaning and maintenance. Buildings are long-lasting; assuming a new-build rate of approx. 1% for Central Europe, the energy-efficiency upgrading and ecological renewal of the existing building stock would take 100 years and more! The largest CO_2 reduction potential therefore lies in the refurbishment of the existing building stock; through the reduction in materials flows, the continued use of existing buildings makes a decisive contribution to sparing resources compared to the provision of new buildings.

Tools

Protection aims and key indicators form the prerequisites for overcoming the sustainability deficit. In order to derive concrete strategies for action from these, however, tools are required that enable the planning team to identify the effects and interactive relationships of social, economic and ecological dimensions, and deal with these in the planning and/or construction process. Numerous tools and aids, e.g. checklists, computer programs or building labels, are available for evaluating the sustainability of buildings.

The wide range of tools available is due to the many different tasks met with in the building sector (e.g. competitions, preliminary/draft/works planning, evaluation of completed buildings, etc.), which could not be dealt with by one tool alone. Fig. B 6.37 shows an overview of the tools and aids available [13, 14].

The development of building labels represents significant progress in the evaluation of sustainability. They permit a comprehensive assessment of the quality of building and planning for different levels of precision. In early phases of the work, they supply planners and clients with an evaluation of the project, from which indicators for improving the sustainability characteristics can be derived. In the case of finished projects, building certificates provide users and operators with an understandable document regarding the sustainability quality of their building. The evaluation tools available cover a wide spectrum – from very simple, qualitative assessment aids right up to precise tools with quantified data. The selection of a suitable tool must therefore always be carried out by weighing up between objective accuracy, which, however, is inevitably linked with an elaborate study, and the reliability of subjective assessments. A few of the evaluation tools available are described below.

Area	Topic	Criteria
Society	*Community*	Integration Social contact Solidarity/justice Participation
	Design	Identification/recognition Individual design/personalisation
	Usage, accessibility	Basic provisions/mixed uses Slow traffic, public transport Accessibility and usability for all
	Well-being, health	Safety/security Light Interior air Radiation Summertime thermal performance Noise/vibration
Industry	*Building fabric*	Location Structure Building layout/fitting-out
	Installation costs	Life cycle costs Financing External costs
	Operating and maintenance costs	Operation and maintenance Repairs
Environment	*Building materials*	Raw materials (availability) Environmental impact Dangerous substances Deconstruction
	Operating energy	Heating (cooling) for interior climate Heat for hot water Electricity Coverage of energy requirements
	Ground, landscape	Area of plot External facilities
	Infrastructure	Mobility Waste from operation and usage Water

B 6.35

BREEAM

The BREEAM (Building Research Establishment Environmental Assessment Method) label was developed in the early 1990s as the first assessment method for office buildings in the United Kingdom, and in the meantime is available in different versions for other types of building (e.g. department stores, supermarkets, schools, industrial buildings and houses) and for different continents (Europe, North America and Asia). The tool awards points for selected indicators; depending on the total number of points, a certificate is issued: "pass", "good", "very good" or "excellent". The indicators are divided into eight areas: management, health and well-being, energy, transport, water, materials and waste, land use and ecology, pollution. The method is especially designed for use by architects and planners. BREEAM is currently one of the most widely used building labels.

LEED

The US Green Building Council initially introduced LEED (Leadership in Energy & Environmental Design) in 1995 for the American property market. In the meantime, this assessment system is being used more and more in Europe, and especially in Asia. Similar to BREEAM, there are specific versions for different types of usage, e.g. offices, existing buildings, commercial interiors or owner-occupied homes. The award of the appropriate label ("certified", "silver", "gold", "platinum") is likewise based on the building assessment achieving a certain number of points for the corresponding catalogue of criteria. The indicators are divided into six areas: sustainable sites, water efficiency, energy and atmosphere, materials and resources, indoor environmental quality, innovation and design process.

191

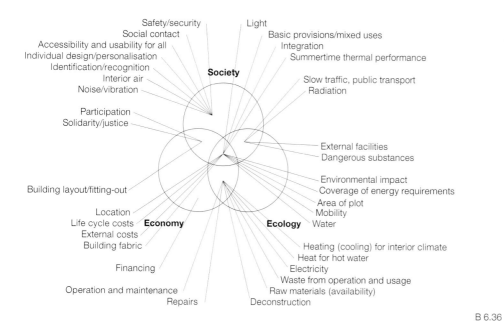

Society

Safety/security
Social contact
Accessibility and usability for all
Individual design/personalisation
Identification/recognition
Interior air
Noise/vibration
Participation
Solidarity/justice

Light
Basic provisions/mixed uses
Integration
Summertime thermal performance
Slow traffic, public transport
Radiation

Building layout/fitting-out

Economy
Location
Life cycle costs
External costs
Building fabric
Financing
Operation and maintenance
Repairs

Ecology

External facilities
Dangerous substances
Environmental impact
Coverage of energy requirements
Area of plot
Mobility
Water
Heating (cooling) for interior climate
Heat for hot water
Electricity
Waste from operation and usage
Raw materials (availability)
Deconstruction

B 6.36

Typology Object	Tools (examples)	Country	HOAI work phases
Product declarations Building products and sundries	• Type I-III environmental product declarations (see "Materials", p. 171)	D	5–7
Recommendation and exclusion criteria Building products and sundries	• Schwarz, Jutta: Ökologie im Bau. Bern/Stuttgart/Vienna, 1998		5–7
Element catalogues Building components (functional units) in as-built condition	• SIA D 0123: Construction of buildings according to ecological aspects	CH	2–5
Tendering aids Ecologically-oriented specification	• ECOBIS/WINGIS: Building Product Group Eco Information System/Building Sector Dangerous Substances & Health Aspects Information System • BKP: Data sheets according to building costs plan for tenders • ECO-DEVIS: Ecological specifications	D CH CH	3–7 3–7 5–7
Energy performance certificates Description (and evaluation) of energy efficiency of buildings	• Energy performance and energy requirement certificates according to Energy Conservation Act	D	2–8
Checklists to match purpose (e.g. energy- saving construction etc.)	• Preisig, Hansruedi, et al.: Der ökologische Bauauftrag. Munich, 2001 • Checklists for energy-related, ecological planning and building published by the Swiss Federal Office for Energy Management	CH/D CH	2–8 2–8
Building examples (best practice) Buildings featuring exemplary solutions	• SolarBau: MONITOR: "Energy-optimised building" project database of the Federal Ministry of Economics & Technology	D	2–4
Competitions (best practice) Designs with energy and sustainability evaluations	• SIA D 0200/SNARC: System for assessing the sustainability of architectural projects for the topic of the environment	CH	1–2
Guidelines Formulation of targets, principles and models	• Sustainable building guidelines • SIA D 0216: SIA energy efficiency path • SIA E 112/1: Sustainable construction – buildings	D CH CH	1–9 1–8 1–8
Holistic planning and evaluation tools Interactive tools for making decisions for different applications (e.g. competitions, life cycle analyses, etc.), partially linked to databases	• LEGEP: Integrated life cycle analysis tool ecological-economic assessment • OGIP: Planning tool for optimising the costs, energy consumption and environmental impact of buildings • VITRUVIUS: Budgeting, property valuation, project development, portfolio management,	D CH CH	2–6 2–6 2–9
Building labels, evaluations or certificates Building assessment	• BREEAM: Building Research Establishment Environmental Assessment Method • GBC (GBTool): Green Building Challenge • LEED: Leadership in Energy & Environmental Design • MINERGIE-ECO: verification method • TQB: Total Quality Building	GB CAN USA CH A	2–8 2–8 2–8 2–8 2–8

B 6.37

MINERGIE-ECO

In compliance with the criteria of "Recommendation SIA 112/1, sustainable construction – buildings", the MINERGIE-ECO has been used in Switzerland since 2006 as a verification method for offices, schools and multi-occupancy residential buildings. A revision that includes detached houses and refurbishment projects is in preparation. This building label supplements the preceding MINERGIE standard, which focused on comfort and energy efficiency, by adding the themes of health and building ecology. The assessment criteria include light, noise, interior air, raw materials, construction and deconstruction. In addition, for the energy efficiency, this label specifies that the energy consumption of the building must lie at least 25% below and the consumption of fossil energy at least 50% below the average state of the art.

In order to satisfy the requirements of the label, buildings must satisfy exclusion criteria in certain areas (e.g. no use of biocides and wood preservatives in interiors) and achieve minimum levels of compliance. In total, at least two-thirds of the criteria must comply with the specification in order to be awarded this label.

Diagnosis system for sustainable building quality (DSQ)

Taking the evaluation systems described above as a starting point, a system for assessing the sustainability of buildings was drawn up within the scope of preparing the German edition of this book (*Energie Atlas*). The diagnosis system is intended to replace the hitherto widespread description of partial aspects with an understandable presentation covering all the essential parameters of sustainability [15].

This diagnosis system has a hierarchical structure whose themes and explanations are based on the stipulations of SIA Recommendation 112/1. However, it reorganises the themes, expands the explanations and includes additional criteria and indicators. Furthermore, the criteria are assigned indicators, qualitative features and source references that ease compilation and evaluation.

One important change has been in the division of the themes according to areas. Whereas SIA Recommendation 112/1, like other sources, breaks down the sustainability aspects according to the three-pillars model, using the headings of "society", "industry" and "environment", the diagnosis system for sustainable building quality (DSQ) uses a system based on the planning-related categories of location, building and process quality (Fig. B 6.38). This is intended to simplify use by architects and planners, but this breakdown also avoids the problems of assigning criteria that touch on all three sustainability pillars, e.g. environmental pollution, location (Fig. B 6.36).

The DSQ was initially developed as a system for evaluating the sustainability of finished buildings, resulting primarily from the need to provide the case studies in Part C of this book with a single method of evaluation so that readers can easily compare the different projects. But the diagnosis system also proved to be suitable for the holistic evaluation of buildings. It provides a compact, comprehensive impression of the sustainability of a building. The definitions of targets and the explanations associated with the criteria can serve equally well as planning aids and for the comparative assessment of planning alternatives.

Besides the non-formalised verbal description and the graphic-visual illustration of buildings usual hitherto, the DSQ permits an objective, comparative assessment. We distinguish between two categories of criteria:

• The qualitative criteria, as a comprehensive "backbone" to the DSQ, cover all the areas and themes of sustainability. Using these criteria and their associated explanations as a basis, the criteria are described by way of headwords and are essentially objective.
• Supplementing these criteria are the quantified indicators (e.g. primary energy requirement in KWh/m²a), where such are available.

As significant indicators are currently hardly readily available even for model projects, the better availability of such parameters is to be hoped for in the future so that they can be used – as planning data and/or building data verified by monitoring – to enable conclusions to be drawn regarding the energy- and materials-efficiency of buildings. They can make a very important objective contribution to the ongoing professional discussions and provide incentives for more care in the use of resources and energy in the construction industry. Legally binding energy and sustainability verification, as is required by the Energy Conservation Act, energy performance certificates or life cycle assessments, for instance, will create the necessary database in the medium-term.

References:
[1] Banham, Reyner, cited in: Oswalt, Philipp: Wohltemperierte Architektur: neue Techniken des energiesparenden Bauens. Heidelberg 1995, p. 9
[2] BUND/Misereor (ed.): Zukunftsfähiges Deutschland. Ein Beitrag zu einer global nachhaltigen Entwicklung (Wuppertal Institute for Climate, Environment & Energy). Basel/Boston/Berlin, 1996
[3] Preisig, Hansruedi; Pfäffli, Katrin, et al.; Schweizerischer Ingenieur- & Architektenverein (ed.): SIA D 0216. SIA Effizienzpfad Energie. Zurich, 2006
[4] Hauff, Volker: Our Common Future, Report of the World Commission on Environment and Development. Greven 1987
[5] Gruber, Edelgard, et al.: Energiepass für Gebäude. Evaluation des Feldversuchs. Study on behalf of the German Energy Agency (dena). 2005
[6] Kohler, Niklaus: cited in: Forgber, Uwe: Teamorientierte Bauplanung. Die Vernetzung von Kompetenzdomainen in virtuellen Projekträumen. Dissertation, University of Karlsruhe, 1999
[7] Löhnert, Günter: Der integrale Planungsprozess, Teil I Grundlagen. In: EnergieEffizientes Bauen, 01/2002, p. 31.

[8] Löhnert, Günter, et al.: Zielkonflikte. In: Bürogebäude mit Zukunft. Cologne, 2005, p. 154f.
[9] Jörissen, Juliane, et al.: Zukunftsfähiges Wohnen und Bauen. Herausforderungen, Defizite, Strategien. Berlin, 2005, p. 195.
[10] Lützkendorf, Thomas, et al.: Nachhaltigkeitsorientierte Investments im Immobilienbereich. Trends, Theorie und Typologie. 2005, p. 11.
[11] Federal Ministry of Transport, Building & Urban Affairs (ed.): Leitfaden Nachhaltiges Bauen. 2001
[12] Schweizerischer Ingenieur- und Architektenverein (ed.): Empfehlung SIA 112/1. Nachhaltiges Bauen – Hochbau. Zurich, 2006
[13] Lützkendorf, Thomas, et al.: Nachhaltiges Planen, Bauen und Bewirtschaften von Bauwerken. Ziele, Grundlagen, Stand und Trends. Bewertungsmethoden und -hilfsmittel. Study on behalf of the Federal Ministry of Transport, Building & Urban Affairs. 2002
[14] Steiger, Peter: The critical path to sustainable construction. In: Construction Materials Manual. Munich, 2005, pp. 19–21
[15] The development of the diagnosis system for sustainable building quality (DSQ) was sponsored by the Deutsche Bundesstiftung Umwelt (DBU).

Area	Topic	Criteria
Location quality		Energy availability
		Basic provisions/mixed uses
		Integration
		Solidarity/justice
		Usage
		Mobility
		Noise/vibration
		Radiation
Building quality	*Access/communication*	Traffic
		Social contact
		Accessibility and usability
	Plot	Area of plot
		Open areas
	Design	Building culture
		Personalisation
	Well-being, health	Safety/security
		Sound
		Light
		Interior air
		Interior climate
	Building fabric	Structure
		Building layout/fitting-out
	Building costs	Investment costs
		Financing
	Operating and maintenance costs	Operation and maintenance
		Repairs
	Building materials	Raw materials (availability)
		Environmental impact
		Dangerous substances
		Deconstruction
	Operating energy	Building heating
		Building cooling
		Hot-water provision
		Air management
		Lighting
		Other electrical consumers
		Coverage of energy requirements
	Infrastructure	Waste from operation and usage
		Water
Process quality		Sustainable building
		Building tradition
		Participation
		Integrated planning
		Analyses
		Monitoring
		Facility management

B 6.36 Overlapping sustainability criteria according to "Recommendation SIA 112/1, sustainable construction – buildings"

B 6.37 Tools for evaluating the sustainability of planning and buildings

B 6.38 Sustainable building criteria according to the "diagnosis system for sustainable building quality" (DSQ)

B 6.38

Criterion: aim	Explanation	Sources	Qualitative features	Indicators, parameters
Location quality				
Energy availability: efficient use of energy sources and environmental energy available locally	A permanently viable, highly secure energy supply during the operating phase calls for the efficient use of the energy sources available locally. For this reason, both the local technical infrastructure (e.g. gas supply, district heating, co-generation plant) and the environmental energy available (e.g. solar radiation, groundwater, wind) must be analysed to ascertain their suitability with respect to the sustainable, efficient configuration of the energy concept.	Details of local energy suppliers, climate data	Energy supplies specific to location	• Global radiation [kWh/m²a] • Climate data relevant to location
Basic provisions/mixed uses: short distances, achieving attractive mix of uses in neighbourhood	Promoting activity in the neighbourhood plus permanent local supplies in the urban space are essential prerequisites for sustainable urban development. Mixed uses help to reduce traffic (and hence the "induced energy").	Local development plan, structure concepts	Mixed uses, measures for flexible structures	• Density [persons/km²]
Integration: creating optimum conditions for integrating different social backgrounds, cultures and generations	Communities with a social, ethnic and demographic mix have proved to be particularly stable and adaptable. Suitable building measures can promote the integration of various groups of the population. Those measures include a diverse range of housing, different housing sizes and standards, multi-purpose and community facilities, housing and business premises for rent, common infrastructures.	Development plans, land-use plans	Political and planning measures for socio-demographic integration	
Solidarity/justice: support for disadvantaged persons	The prerequisites for a society embodying justice and solidarity are that the space requirements of socially or a financially disadvantaged groups are taken more seriously and are included in the planning.	In situ visits, schemes, statistics	Vitality of neighbourhood, integration	
Usage: guaranteeing long-term economic usage appropriate to the location	The location should be equally interesting for clients, investors and users. Factors such as image, rural quality and access to open spaces, accessibility with public transport and closeness to educational, shopping and cultural amenities must be considered.	Street map, location drawing, building specification	Location and location develop ment in conjunction with usage concept	
Mobility: designing environmentally compatible mobility	Building measures and systems of incentives contribute to the shift from private cars to local public transport. The reduction and compact arrangement of car parking spaces in public areas plus the promotion of local public transport assist this development.	Location drawing with local public transport services	Measures for environmentally compatible realisation of mobility	• Distance to local public transport [m]
Noise/vibration: protection against noise and vibration from outside	Disadvantages due to external noise and vibration can be minimised through the arrangement of the internal layout, the positioning of the windows and suitable technical sound insulation measures.	Specification, sound insulation report	Internal and external sound insulation measures	
Radiation: protection against ionising and non-ionising radiation from outside	Suitable constructional measures must be taken in areas with a high radon exposure. A high intensity of non-ionising radiation (electrosmog) means that, as a precaution, the recommended maximum values (e.g. WHO: 5 kV/m) should not be exceeded.	Radon exposure map, specification, measurements	Exposure levels specific to the radiation protection measures	
Building quality				
Access/communication				
Traffic: enabling good, safe access and connections	The network of paths and roads provides the framework for developing the building and access concepts. Good links with the neighbourhood, good, unmistakable orientation possibilities and a clear layout create individual and collective feelings of safety and security.	Access concept, location drawing, ground floor plan, layout of external works with bicycle parking	Access concept, parking organisation, footpath links, positioning and design of entrance areas	• Bicycle parking [m²]
Social contact: creating meeting places to encourage communication	Nurturing social contacts promotes a feeling of responsibility, creativity and the establishment of social networks. This is helped by semi-public areas, circulation zones that encourage communication plus a well-coordinated interaction of private, semi-public and public areas in buildings and their environs.	Location drawing, layout of external works, floor plans	Quality of circulation zones, communal and exter nal areas	
Accessibility and usability: designing a well-laid-out, barrier-free building and environs	Good accessibility and a clear layout are valuable and attractive for everyone, especially those whose mobility is temporarily or permanently restricted. A barrier-free design improves communication within the building and – employed properly – increases the quality of architecture and open spaces.	Specification, access concept, location drawing, floor plans, sections, direction system	Barrier-free design (building and external works), usability (e.g. automatic doors, WCs for disabled persons, etc.)	• Barrier-free (yes/no)
Plot				
Area of plot: keeping the footprint small	Refraining from the use of undeveloped areas by recycling existing sites, the economic exploitation of the plot and compact construction render possible a sensible use of that scarce resource land. The continued use of existing buildings should take priority over new-build measures.	Specification, location drawing, floor plans	Planning measures for reducing the footprint	• Permiss./exist. plot ratio • New/exist. gross floor area [m²]
Open areas: minimising ground sealing, securing diversity of species	When designing the external works, the aim should be to preserve or create natural habitats (extensive meadows and lawns, areas left in their natural state, retention basins and biotopes, trees and hedges, green roofs and facades). Rooftop planting can replace ground sealed by construction work.	Specification, location drawing, layout of external works	Measures for preserving or creating natural habitats	• Unsealed ground [%$_{of\ plot}$] • Rooftop planting [%$_{of\ sealed\ ground}$]

Criterion: aim	Explanation	Sources	Qualitative features	Indicators, parameters
Design				
Building culture: improving orientation and identification with a locality through recognition	Recognition of developed structures and landscapes assists human orientation and conveys a feeling of safety, belonging and security. The identity of a location promotes responsibility with respect to the environment and fellow human beings. Good architecture creates the special reference to the locality, high design quality, a specific identity and obvious interactions between buildings and their environs.	Design concept, specification, location drawing, elevations	Local structures, specific identity of the locality	• Competition (yes/no)
Personalisation: creating an identity, providing personal design options	People require an identity for and the demarcation of their "territories". Architecture and open spaces make the key contribution here. Innovation is necessary for creating an unmistakable identity for a location and for solving momentary social issues. As a contribution to the building culture, however, simultaneous design freedoms for self-expression and forming an identity should be preserved.	Design concept, specification, location drawing, floor plans	Innovation, design freedoms and personalisation options	
Well-being, health				
Safety/security: reducing potential dangers, promoting a feeling of safety and security	Safety and security contribute to social and economic stability. Users should feel safe and secure both within the building (accidents, intruders, fire, industrial safety) and in its environs (assault, natural dangers), and should be protected as far as possible. Accordingly, objective potential dangers (e.g. natural dangers specific to the location, risk of slipping, tripping, fire, etc.) should be ruled out as far as possible, and contributions to the subjective perception of safety/security (e.g. good layout, good lighting, social controls, presence of other people, good visual links, etc.) are necessary.	Specification, fire protection concept, location drawing, external works, floor plans, elevations, sections, user survey	Protection against natural dangers, fire protection, safety barriers, non-slip flooring, lighting, clarity, social controls, people, visual links	
Sound: creating pleasant acoustic conditions	Noise pollution and acoustic conditions influence the well-being of people and can impair their health. Noise between usage units (e.g. airborne and impact sound) plus disturbances (noises from building services, unfavourable room acoustics) should be avoided through precautionary building physics and room acoustics measures.	Room acoustics report	Constructional sound insulation measures, room acoustics measures	• Sound insulation [dB(A)] • Reverberation time [s]
Light: creating optimum day lighting conditions, providing good artificial lighting	The daylighting conditions over the course of the day influence the human hormone balance and synchronise our "internal clock". Accordingly, daylight strategies, the orientation of the building, the proportion of windows, the depth of rooms, glare protection, the design of reflective surfaces and the colouring of the enclosing components (floors, walls, soffits) are all important design factors.	Specification (daylight simulation if applicable), sections, floor plans, elevations, section through facade	Passive and technical measures for optimum daylight usage, glare protection	• Daylight-autonomy [%]
Interior air: aiming for a high interior air quality	A poor interior climate can cause numerous bodily symptoms and lower productivity. Minimum contamination of the interior air (e.g. CO_2, cleaning agents, tobacco smells, mould, mites, etc.) should be guaranteed by way of a suitable ventilation concept backed up by corresponding user behaviour.	Specification, ventilation concept, user survey, interior air measurements	Ventilation concept and other measures for guaranteeing the interior air quality	• Ventilation: natural [$\%_{flr. area}$], mechanical [$\%_{flr. area}$]
Interior climate: guaranteeing good thermal comfort	The thermal comfort has a major influence on the human heat balance and a direct effect on the energy consumption of buildings. It should be optimised as far as possible through constructional, passive measures: e.g. generally by way of the type of construction, thermal insulation, moisture control, coordinated proportion of windows and components with thermal storage capacity; protection against overheating by way of sunshades and the possibility for night-time cooling.	Specification, draft design drawings, sunshading, floor plans, elevations, detailed drawings	Description of measures for optimising the interior air	• U-values of bldg. envelope [W/m^2K] • Operating-hours [h over 26°C/a] • Effective heat capacity [$Wh/m^2_{flr. area}$]
Building fabric				
Structure: retaining value and quality for the life of the building	Building standards and the use of resources should take into account the intended economic lifespan. The quality of the building fabric and its proper maintenance are crucial for preserving the economic value of a building and its lifespan.	Specification, detailed drawings with materials data	Measures for preserving value and quality over the lifetime of the building	• Predicted economic period-of-use [a] • Durability of • building components [a]
Building layout/fitting-out: guaranteeing good flexibility for various room and usage requirements	Fitting-out/adaptation options increase the value of a building so that it can be easily designed to take account of changing needs. The internal layout should simplify changes and, if necessary, allow for alternative usage scenarios through the creation of standardised modules and neutral layouts. During the detailed design work, the aim should be to achieve maximum separation between loadbearing structure and fitting-out.	Specification, usage concept, interior layout, floor plans, detailed drawings	Usage concept taking into account adaptation and fitting-out options, adaptable building services, separation of loadbearing structure and fitting-out elements	• Alternative usage concepts (yes/no)
Building costs				
Investment costs: activating investment taking into account the life cycle costs	Low investment costs can help to open up the property market to a wide range of the population, but – for long-lasting buildings – may not be at the expense of durability, ease of maintenance and energy requirements during operation.	Building costs calculation, life cycle costs calculation	Measures for reducing investment costs, contractual relationship between investor and user (tenant, owner-occupier etc.)	• Building costs (cost groups 300–400) [EUR] • Ratio, cost group 300/400 • Building costs [$EUR/m^2_{flr. area}$]

Criterion: aim	Explanation	Sources	Qualitative features	Indicators, parameters
Building costs (contd.)				
Financing: securing long-term financing for operating, maintenance and deconstruction costs	The costs structure should guarantee the ongoing financing of properties right up to their deconstruction. Appropriate reserves should be set up for maintenance, repairs and returning building materials to their life cycles. Buildings should recoup their costs over their period of use so that at the end there are funds available for feeding the property into a new life cycle or replacing it.	Determining the costs, contracts	Investment, maintenance and deconstruction costs, incentive schemes	
Operating and maintenance costs				
Operation and maintenance: ensuring low maintenance costs through early planning and continuous maintenance	Considered over the lifetime of a building, the operating and maintenance costs usually exceed the capital outlay. Careful planning, the choice of long-lasting, low-maintenance materials and forms of construction plus measures to reduce the energy consumption can help to lower the operating costs. A life cycle costs analysis supports the integral consideration of all cost factors and can contribute to low operating and maintenance costs.	Specification, materials concept, benchmarks, life cycle costs calculation	Measures to reduce operating and maintenance costs	• Operating costs [EUR/$m^2_{flr.\ area}$a] • Maintenance [EUR/$m^2_{flr.\ area}$a] • Energy costs [EUR/$m^2_{flr.\ area}$a]
Repairs: guaranteeing low repair costs through good accessibility and quality	The quality and lifespan of each building component should be coordinated with the intended period of use as far as possible. Components, building services, joints, connections and details should be readily accessible and designed to enable simple renewal in the case of later repairs.	Floor plans, section through facade, detailed drawings, building services drawings	Accessibility and replaceability of components, ease of repair, junction- and connection details-	
Building materials				
Raw materials (availability): good availability of primary raw materials, but primarily renewable and secondary raw materials	When choosing building materials, readily available, preferably renewable raw materials (e.g. wood), easily recycled materials and components, and secondary raw materials (recycled building materials) should be considered more and more.	Specification, materials concept, tender	Materials concept	• Proportion of -renewable-materials [% by vol.] • Proportion of secondary raw materials [% by vol.]
Environmental impact: aiming for low environmental impact during production	The production of building materials should take place with minimal environmental impact. This concerns the associated embodied energy, the CO_2 emissions but also many other factors (e.g. ozone depletion, acidification, eutrophication, photochemical ozone creation), which are the objects of a life cycle assessment.	Specification, materials concept, life cycle assessment, tender	Measures to guarantee low environmental impacts during production	• PEI of building carcass [MJ/$m^2_{flr.\ area}$]
Dangerous substances: ensuring only low amounts of dangerous substances in building materials	The careful choice of building materials and components with low or zero emissions can reduce the pollutants both indoors and outdoors quite substantially. In particular, more attention should be given to paints, sealants, wood-based board products, adhesives and metals.	Specification, materials concept, tender, user survey, interior air measurements	Measures to reduce emissions of dangerous substances from building materials	• Choice of building materials with low or zero emissions (yes/no) • Register of • building materials (yes/no) Interior air measurements (yes/no)
Deconstruction: using easily separable composite materials and constructions to enable reuse/recycling	The reuse and recycling of building materials saves raw materials and energy. Recycling requires the constructions and systems to be separated into their original components. Joints and connections should be planned taking into account easy replaceability, easy separability and good recyclability. Forms of construction with mechanical fixings are to be preferred to composite forms of construction.	Specification, materials concept, detailed drawings	Selection of building materials, recyclability, design of joints and constructions	• Deconstruction concept (yes/no)
Operating energy				
Building heating: aiming for a minimised heating requirement	The heating requirement can be considerably reduced by passive measures (compactness, building geometry, building depth, orientation, minimising shadows, airtight building envelope, thermal insulation, etc.) and by installing efficient building services.	Specification, building services concept, floor plans, elevations, detailed sections through envelope components with U-values	Passive and technical measures for reducing the heating requirement	• Heating requirement [kWh/m^2a] • Primary energy requirement [kWh/m^2a] • Final energy requirement [kWh/m^2a]
Building cooling: avoiding or minimising technical cooling requirements through constructional and building services measures	Passive measures (e.g. thermal masses, coordinated proportion of windows, form of construction, heat capacity of interior components, etc.) and constructional-technical precautions (e.g. sunshades, night-time cooling, etc.) can help to avoid overheating in the building. Active cooling should be avoided as far as possible in buildings with low internal heat loads. If cooling is necessary, it should be provided as efficiently as possible.	Specification, building services concept, sunshading concept, elevations	Specification of passive and technical measures for reducing the cooling requirement	• Primary energy requirement [kWh/m^2a] • Final energy requirement [kWh/m^2a]
Hot-water provision: reducing heating and energy requirements	A low energy requirement for hot water can be achieved through use of water-saving fittings, conceptual measures such as concentrated wet areas and minimal pipework. The actual consumption is, however, mainly influenced by user behaviour.	Specification, building materials concept, building services drawings	Measures to reduce the hot-water requirement	• Primary energy requirement [kWh/m^2a] • Final energy requirement [kWh/m^2a]

Criterion: aim	Explanation	Sources	qualitative features	Indicators, parameters
Operating energy (contd.)				
Air management: minimising electricity requirements for air management	Natural ventilation should be preferred as the optimum ventilation strategy. If mechanical air management is necessary, the system should include heat or cooling energy recovery, favourable duct cross-sections and energy-efficient motors.	Specification, building services concept, building services drawings	Constructional and technical measures for reducing electricity requirements	• Primary energy requirement [kWh/m²a] • Final energy requirement [kWh/m²a]
Lighting: minimising electricity requirements for lighting	A building design optimised for daylighting enables the energy requirement for artificial lighting to be minimised. Further lighting needs should be met by energy-efficient lighting systems, lighting concepts coordinated with activities, and brightness- and occupancy-related controls.	Specification, lighting concept	Constructional and technical measures for reducing electricity requirements	• Primary energy requirement [kWh/m²a] • Final energy requirement [kWh/m²a]
Other electrical consumers: requirements through contual and operational precautions	Important factors are reasonable comfort demands and appropriate fitting-out with operational facilities plus energy-efficient equipment and systems.	Specification	Selection of energy-efficient equipment and systems	• Primary energy requirement [kWh/m²a] • Final energy requirement [kWh/m²a]
Coverage of energy requirements: increasing the proportion of renewable energy for covering requirements	A maximum proportion of renewable energy should be used to cover the energy requirements. Options for using renewable resources available locally (e.g. geothermal heat) plus the integration of solar technology into the building envelope should be considered right at the preliminary planning phase.	Specification, energy concept	Energy concept, use of renewable energy	• Renewable energy coverage rate [%] • Solar area: solar thermal energy [m²], PV [m²]
Infrastructure				
Waste from operation and usage: setting up an infrastructure for sorting waste	Constructional precautions form the prerequisite for closing materials life cycles through the separate collection and recycling of industrial and domestic waste. Besides the functional quality of disposal systems and regular supervision, user behaviour has a considerable influence here.	Specification, floor plans	Infrastructure qualities for separating waste	
Water: reducing the consumption of drinking water	Lowering the water table can change ecosystems drastically. The treatment of drinking water and waste water is cost-intensive. Suitable measures, e.g. water-saving fittings, household appliances and WCs, the use of rainwater and grey water, and a change in user behaviour, can reduce the environmental effects substantially.	Sanitary drawings, external works	Measures for low drinking-water consumption and low waste-water quantities	• Water consumption [m³/person/a] • Rainwater/grey water usage (yes/no)
Process quality				
Sustainable building: contributing to sustainable development and to strengthening awareness among the public	Every building, whether new or refurbished, can contribute to spreading the sustainable management message through its particular features and image. The idea behind this is to develop a new planning culture whose particular characteristics and successes should be made public.	Programmes, publications	Measures for-implementing a sustainability-oriented planning process	• Sustainability-oriented benchmarks (yes/no)
Building tradition: preserving jobs, knowledge and building culture	The characteristics of good building culture, craft-like traditions and intelligent forms of construction should be nurtured and further developed in the course of the planning. Preserving the architectural or historical value of buildings contributes to the upkeep and ongoing development of regional building cultures.	Specification, detailed drawings, own view	Measures for preserving the cultural inheritance	
Participation: aiming for a high degree of acceptance through participation	The collaboration of users and others affected in the planning process promotes the acceptance and can improve the usage quality of building measures. The critical consideration of the needs and requests of later users can generate social and financial advantages. The targets, methods, scope and timing of the participation of interested parties must be defined early on.	Reports of experiences	Participation concept	• Participation concept (yes/no)
Integrated planning: optimising the sustainability potential specific to a project	The early inclusion of an integrated planning team and the provision of a sustainability-oriented design brief make vital contributions to securing the success of a project. Bringing in specialist planners in good time and with good communication plus the principles of integrated planning should be coordinated between client and architect. Corresponding benchmarks and target stipulations should be defined in the preliminary planning phase.	Specification, list of project participants, benchmarks	Project participants and their remits, description of integrated planning process	
Analyses: reducing materials flows, energy costs and operating costs	Materials flow analyses and building simulations can make a good contribution to reducing environmental impacts and operating costs. Overall and detailed analyses must be evaluated in good time with suitable simulation tools and developed further as necessary.	Building specification, results of simulations	Simulation method, optimisation levels	• Simulation-method (yes/no)
Monitoring: planning for monitoring and optimisation of the building	Building monitoring means continuous checking of interior climate influences and technical systems in order to establish the effectiveness of planned systems and draw conclusions for further planning. Monitoring contributes to identifying disruptive factors at an early stage and hence to reducing the operating costs.	Monitoring concept	Monitoring concept (e.g. measurands and duration of monitoring)	• Monitoring (yes/no)
Facility Management: advance planning and organisation of operations	Facility management (FM), as the controlling element for the building operations, contributes to minimising operational expenses and energy requirements, controlling maintenance and repair processes, and adapting the building to changing usage requirements. FM therefore ensures economic operation, the longevity of the building and its sustainable usability.	FM concept, FM contract	Concept for optimising expenditure during the phase of use	• FM concept (yes/no)

Part C   Case studies

Fig. D   Aerial photo of a school playground in
         Cornwall (GB)

Example 01

Private house

Gerra Gambarogno, CH, 1998

Architects:
Buzzi e Buzzi, Locarno
Britta Buzzi-Huppert, Francesco Buzzi
Assistant:
Gabriella Beusch
Structural engineers:
Genazzi & Stoffel e Giacomazzi, Locarno

In this small but densely built-up village on the eastern banks of Lake Maggiore, two old stone stables were made habitable again through a special refurbishment project. Important for the Ticino-based architects was to emphasize the historical context and existing structure, and deal with it sensitively. In order to create one coherent interior space, the dividing wall in the old building was demolished. The roof of the old building was removed and a geometrically precise second enclosure was inserted into the existing masonry perimeter walls like a piece of furniture. The granite walls, looking almost like ruins, serve as a thermal mass and also protect the new enclosure from the weather. In order that the box of larch wood appears like one element cast in one mould, the new roof has no overhanging eaves, which means that the joint between old and new remains exposed; a concrete slab laid to falls beneath the new enclosure drains away the incoming rainwater. The timber construction consists of 28 prefabricated elements which were delivered by helicopter and assembled within six hours.
The external cladding of larch plywood emphasizes the unity of the box. The positions and sizes of the prefitted larch wood windows, with roller shutters to provide privacy and cut out the sunlight, do not line up exactly with the existing openings in the random rubble masonry, which means that the window frames are only partially visible from outside and the original structure remains intact. Inside the building, the white-painted lining of gypsum fibreboard creates a bright, friendly atmosphere and at the same time conceals a void for pipes and cables. The bathroom and bedroom are on the lower floor; the stairs of bleached spruce with an all-glass safety barrier form a built-in cupboard. The living and dining areas plus the kitchen are on the ground floor; a low-level safety barrier to the gallery reinforces the open-plan impression.

A+U 05/2001
db 09/2001
DBZ 01/2002

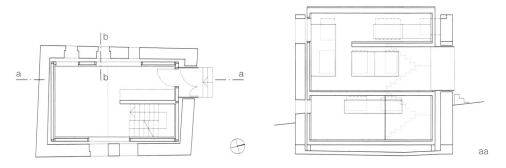

Plan of ground floor
Section
Scale 1:200
Vertical section
Scale 1:20

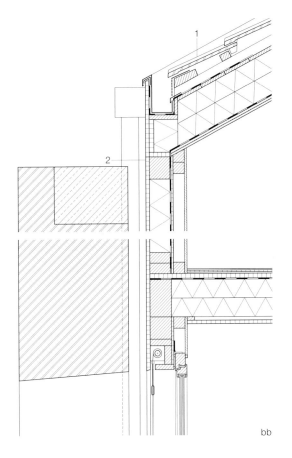

1   Roof construction:
    clay roof tiles
    30 x 50 mm counter battens
    50 x 50 mm battens
    secondary waterproofing/covering
    layer, diffusion-permeable,
    seamless, bonded to 60 x 240 mm
    rafters (ridge joint connected rigidly
    with side plates) with 2 No. 120
    mm rock wool thermal insulation
    between vapour barrier, PE sheet-
    ing, seamless, bonded to
    gypsum fibreboard soffit,
    2 No. 12.5 mm
2   Wall construction:
    20 mm 3-ply core plywood, larch
    120 mm timber-frame element,
    spruce/fir, with
    120 mm rock wool thermal
    insulation between
    PE sheeting
    12 mm OSB
    62 mm cavity for services
    12.5 mm gypsum fibreboard

bb

Theme	Qualitative features	Parameters/indicators
Location quality	*Basic provisions/mixed uses:* mountain village typical of this region *Integration:* residential area; high proportion of tourism *Solidarity/justice:* low-budget housing for local population *Usage:* accommodation for use throughout the year *Mobility:* central position in centre of village; on main tourism route	• Global radiation: 1300 kWh/m²a • Density: 134 persons/km² • Distance to local public transport: 40 m (bus)
Building quality		
Access/ communication	*Social contact:* high-density development; semi-public forecourt *Accessibility and usability:* only accessible on foot; link to intricate network of paths	• Exist. plot ratio: approx. 2.5 • Exist./new gross floor area: approx. 150 m² • Unsealed ground: approx. 15% of plot
Plot	*Area of plot:* use of area already developed *Open areas:* no ground sealing	• Sound insulation, bldg. envelope: 35 dB(A) • Sound insulation, suspend. floors: 45 dB(A)
Design	*Building culture:* respectful handling of existing building by continued use of historical external walls; preservation of uniform appearance typical of this village	• Ventilation: natural, 100% of floor area • U-values, bldg. envelope [W/m²K]:
Well-being/ health	*Safety/security:* high social controls; non-slip floor covering *Light:* maximum use of external wall openings due to frameless glazing; bright surfaces in interior; open interior layout with lighting from more than one side; energy-saving bulbs *Interior climate:* thermal mass of existing building acts as climate buffer	roof 0.2, ext. wall 0.3, window 1.6 • Projected economic period of use: 40 a • Building costs, cost groups 300–400: approx. 250 000 EUR
Building fabric	*Structure:* continued use of existing building fabric as weather protection; high precision of new structure due to prefabrication *Building layout/fitting-out:* open-plan interior layout for good variability	• Bldg. costs: 1660 EUR/m² gross floor area • Renew. raw mat.: approx. 80% by vol. • Renew. energy coverage rate: approx. 60%
Building costs	*Investment costs:* cost-savings due to omission of weather protection (existing structure)	
Operating and maintenance costs	*Operation and maintenance:* zero-maintenance inner and outer leaves of facade *Repairs:* minimised building services; simple details	• Low- or zero-emissions building materials • Deconstruction concept
Building materials	*Raw materials (availability):* wood used almost exclusively *Environmental impact:* use of materials from the region *Dangerous substances:* formaldehyde avoided *Deconstruction:* building can be separated into its constituent materials and is completely recyclable	
Operating energy	*Building heating:* compact building; good insulation to new enclosure *Coverage of energy requirements:* wood-burning stove; hot water heated by electricity	
Process quality	*Sustainable building:* comprehensive catalogue of requirements with building physics and ecological stipulations *Building tradition:* conservation of historic architecture; promotion of local craft traditions *Integrated planning:* close cooperation with building physics consultant and timber engineering company	• Sustainability-oriented benchmarks

Example 02

Private house

Satteins, A, 2002

Architect:
Walter Unterrainer, Feldkirch
Assistant:
Sabine Tschohl
Structural engineer:
Merz Kaufmann, Dornbirn

The angular form and plastic facades of this detached family home help it to stand out from its neighbours in this Vorarlberg community. The building consists of two offset blocks of different heights. The two-storey section is the main part of the house with its spacious living and dining areas on the ground floor and bedrooms and study upstairs; the single-storey section accommodates an entrance lobby, the stairs down to the basement and the garage. The entrance area serves as a link between the two sections and provides access to garage, basement and garden without having to pass through the living area. It would be possible to convert the garage into an office or add another storey (for a small apartment) to the single-storey section at a later date. The openings are arranged according to usage and compass direction. On the road side there are just two narrow windows, whereas the south-west facade includes a generous expanse of glass facing the garden.

The timber construction consisting primarily of prefabricated elements was erected on a ground slab insulated on all sides. This construction results in an energy requirement of 14.7 kWh/m²a, which meets the passive-house standard. The suspended floors and roof are highly insulated timber box assemblies. Polycarbonate twin-wall sheets were fitted in front of the 40 mm thick wood-fibre insulating boards because such sheets are easy to clean with high-pressure cleaning equipment – an aspect expressly specified by the client. Space heating requirements are provided by a controlled ventilation system with preheating of the incoming air in a ground exchanger and heat recovery. A mini-furnace, using wood logs or pellets as fuel, can be operated as well in the case of especially low temperatures. A solar thermal system, assisted by a heat pump, heats the hot water.

Graf, Anton: Neue Passivhäuser. Munich, 2003

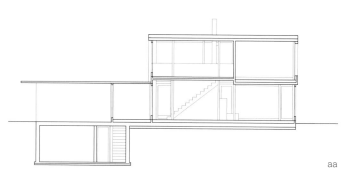

aa

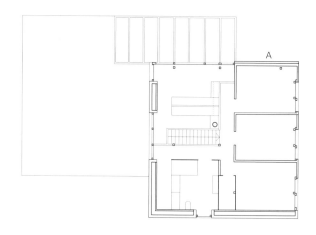

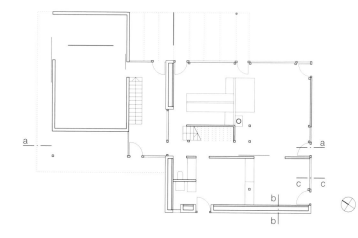

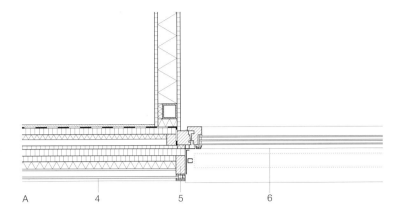

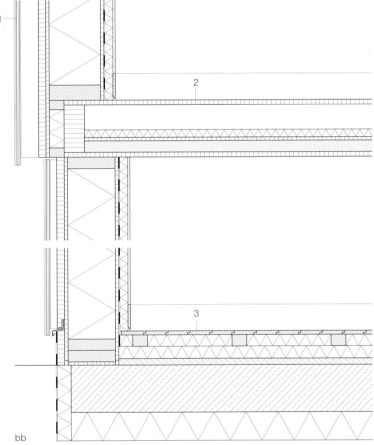

Section • Plans
Scale 1:250
Horizontal section through collector facade
Vertical sections
Scale 1:20

bb

cc

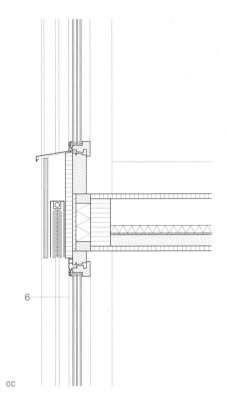

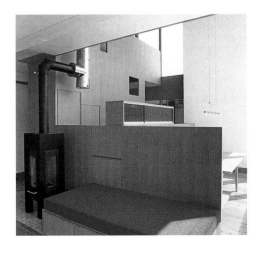

1   Facade construction, U = 0.133 kWh/m²K:
    16 mm polycarbonate twin-wall sheets on
    4 mm rubber
    100 x 30 mm battens
    40 mm wood-fibre board
    18 mm OSB
    timber frame with
    280 mm insulation between
    18 mm OSB, vapour barrier
    50 x 30 mm battens with
    50 mm flax insulation between
    12.5 mm gypsum fibreboard
2   Suspended floor construction:
    26 mm 3-ply core plywood, spruce
    250 mm glued laminated timber with
    40 mm thermal insulation between
    18 mm OSB
    60 mm chippings
    26 mm 3-ply core plywood, spruce
3   Ground floor construction:

21 mm Douglas fir floorboards
80 x 60 mm battens with
60 mm + 65 mm cellulose insulation between
34 mm levelling screed
250 mm reinforced concrete
150 mm PU foam boards as insulation
to underside
4   Wall construction, collector facade:
    120 mm insulation and collector
    40 mm wood-fibre board
    18 mm OSB
    timber construction with
    26 mm vacuum insulation panels between
    40 mm OSB
    vapour barrier
    12.5 mm gypsum fibreboard
5   Fibre-cement strips, 10 mm
    4 mm seal
6   Wood/aluminium window with
    triple glazing, U$_g$ = 0.7 kWh/m²K

Example 02

Theme	Qualitative features	Parameters/indicators
Location quality	*Energy availability:* high solar global radiation *Basic provisions/mixed uses:* exclusively residential area; connection to town centre *Integration:* various types of housing *Solidarity/justice:* presence of high vitality and perception of safety/security *Usage:* residential, office *Mobility:* rural district with little local public transport	• Global radiation: 1400 kWh/m²a • Density: 198 persons/km² • Distance to local public transport: 250 m (bus)
Building quality Access/ communication	*Traffic:* residential street, 2 garages; space for bicycles *Social contact:* good neighbourly relationships *Accessibility and usability:* ground floor designed for wheelchair users	• Exist. plot ratio: 0.25 • Gross floor area: 190 m²
Plot	*Area of plot:* footprint typical of detached family homes *Open areas:* unsealed open areas	• Unsealed ground: 80% of plot • Ventilation: mechanical, 100% of floor area
Design	*Building culture:* building volume like traditional surroundings, further development of highly efficient timber construction with innovative polycarbonate facade *Personalisation:* flexible interior layout and use of rooms	• U-values, bldg. envelope [W/m² k]: roof 0.12, ext. wall 0.13, window 0.83, grd. slab 0.12
Well-being/ health	*Sound:* above-average sound insulation, drop seals in doors; high mass in timber floors; sound-insulated leakage-air openings *Light:* high proportion of windows, living areas lit from more than one side *Interior air:* air quality constantly good due to mechanical ventilation system, individual window ventilation possible *Interior climate:* high surface temperatures due to well-insulated building envelope; external sunshades	• Building costs, cost groups 300–400: 320 000 EUR • Building costs: 1680 EUR/m² gross floor area
Building fabric	*Structure:* high building quality due to prefabrication; durable outer leaf *Building layout/fitting-out:* house can be divided into 2 apartments; optional extra storey over garage; certain rooms suitable as offices	• Proportion of renew. raw mat.: 80% by vol. • Heating requirement: 14.7 kWh/m²a
Building costs	*Investment costs:* owner-occupier *Financing:* private funds, ecological housing assistance	• Primary energy requirement (Q), heating: 25.5 kWh/m²a
Operating and maintenance costs	*Operation and maintenance:* zero-maintenance building envelope *Repairs:* roof waterproofing accessible; inspection openings for building services; horizontal cable routing behind removable skirting boards	• Renew. energy coverage rate: approx. 75% • Active solar areas: solar thermal 10 m²
Building materials	*Raw materials (availability):* timber construction with weather-resistant polycarbonate facade *Environmental impact:* complete prefabrication for optimised construction process *Dangerous substances:* use of low-risk materials *Deconstruction:* composite materials avoided; building can be separated into its constituent materials and recycled	• Barrier-free • Alternative usage concepts • Low- or zero-emissions building materials • Deconstruction concept • Rainwater/grey water usage
Operating energy	*Building heating:* excellent insulation to building envelope; ventilation system with heat recovery; high passive solar gains (passive-house standard) *Hot-water provision:* heating by solar thermal energy and exhaust-air heat pump *Air management:* short ducts; efficient fans; ground exchanger (50 m long, 180 mm dia.) *Lighting:* high daylighting component; energy-saving bulbs *Other electrical consumers:* technical equipment with best-possible energy efficiency *Coverage of energy requirements:* heating via ventilation system with heat recovery; solar thermal energy; exhaust-air heat pump; wood-burning furnace as emergency backup	
Infrastructure	*Waste from operation and usage:* separate waste room, composting on the plot *Water:* short pipes; rainwater tank for garden irrigation	
Process quality	*Sustainable building:* architect with high degree of specialist knowledge; extensive advice for client *Building tradition:* promoting the tradition of timber buildings through further development; goal: solar-heated passive house *Integrated planning:* early inclusion of structural and services engineers *Analyses:* heat requirement calculation according to passive-house project package (PHPP); simulation of solar thermal system by specialist company	• Sustainability-oriented benchmarks • Simulation method

- **Rainfall** - significant rainfall. 747mm precipitat.
annually. Frequent rain in autumn/winter - a she.
which *would help the rainwater to flow directly onto i
courtyard and irrigate the vegetation.*

- **Noise** - a significant amount of noise pollution exists
because of the busy road that run in conjunction with the
site, 60 Db average- noise insulation, the walls facing
A57 Broad lane and Bailey street are thicker and provide
a better noise insulation

- **Winds** - prevailing south-western wind, east winter
winds

Activity:

- **Flow of people** - mainly students due to the student
accommodation around it. Asian occupy a huge amount

- **Flow of cars** - traffic at weekdays usually busier than
weekends. Traffic jam occurs every day around 4:40 -
5:30 except weekends

Accesibility

- **Two entrances** - one facing Broad Lane, one facing Bailey
Street. Another two sides are not accessible. The area is
located in an open area. - The entrance to the courtyard
is located on the Bailey Street side, relatively far from
the busy Broad Lane

IDENTIFY
DISCUSS OPPORT

Residential development

Trondheim, N 2004

Architects:
Brendeland & Kristoffersen arkitekter,
Trondheim
Geir Brendeland, Olav Kristoffersen
Structural engineers:
Reinertsen Engineering, Trondheim

Housing for workers has been built in the city district of Svartlamoen since the 19th century. The first industrial premises appeared in 1947 and the district decayed over the years, until the first punks occupied empty buildings in the 1980s. The Trondheim authorities reacted to this development by abandoning plans to expand industrial operations in the area and instead build "green" housing. Sustainability, low costs and the innovative use of timber were the goals of the competition organised to find the best solution.

The result is two substantial timber buildings with living areas of 22–29 m² per person – low by Norwegian standards, where the norm is generally 50 m². The taller building contains communities of five or six people per storey and in the low-rise block there are six one-room units. To keep the overall volume small, all the stairs are in the form of external steel structures. All loadbearing components are in solid timber, which were prefabricated and erected on site in 10 days. The approx. 150 mm thick external walls are supplemented by mineral wool insulation and untreated wooden cladding. A U-value of 0.17 W/m² K was calculated for the external walls; special insulating glass was used for the windows. The 31 occupants can add their own furnishings and fittings to the unfinished interiors according to their own needs and tastes.

Arch+ 167/177, 2006
Architectural Review 12/2005
Japan Design 06/2005

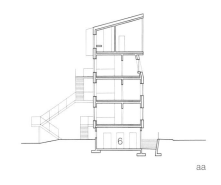

aa   bb

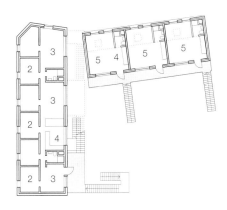

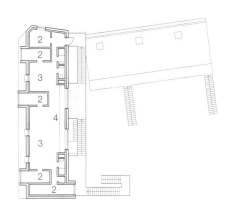

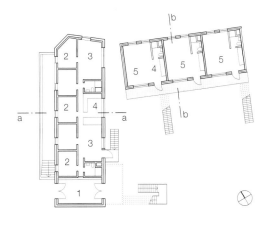

Sections · Plans
Scale 1:500

1 Entrance
2 Private area
3 Communal area
4 Kitchen zone
5 Studio apartment
6 Commercial usage

Example 03

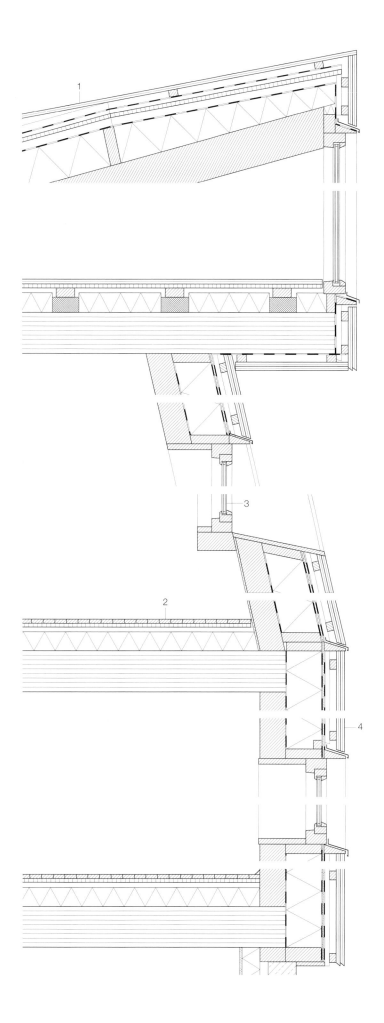

Vertical section   Scale 1:20

1   Roof construction:
    cladding, untreated pine heartwood, 22 x 148 or
    22 x 73 mm
    36 x 48 mm battens
    bituminous felt
    23 x 36 mm counter battens
    22 mm plywood
    40 mm ventilation cavity
    waterproofing
    48 x 198 mm timber rafters with mineral wool
    insulation between
    208 mm solid timber prefabricated element
2   Floor construction:
    22 mm floorboards
    20 mm cement-bonded particleboard
    48 x 125 mm timber joists with
    125 mm mineral wool insulation between
    218 mm solid timber suspended floor
3   Insulating glazing, U = 1.1 W/m²K
4   Facade construction:
    cladding, untreated pine heartwood, 22 x 148 or
    22 x 73 mm
    36 x 48 mm counter battens
    26 x 36 mm battens
    waterproofing
    9 mm plasterboard
    waterproofing
    48 x 200 mm timber studs with
    200 mm mineral wool insulation between
    vapour barrier
    144 mm solid timber wall element

Theme	Qualitative features	Parameters/indicators
Location quality	*Energy availability:* electricity from renewable energy sources *Basic provisions/mixed uses:* former district for workers' housing near an industrial district *Integration:* conversion (industrial usage), increase in quality and redefinition of location; start of long-term re-establishment of housing in the district *Solidarity/justice:* creation of low-cost housing *Usage:* different housing forms, childcare, shops, cafeteria	• Global radiation: 600 kWh/m²a • Density: 476 persons/km² • Distance to local public transport: 200 m (bus)
Building quality Access/ communication	*Traffic:* plot integrated into existing access arrangement, bicycle parking inside and around buildings *Social contact:* very high proportion of communal areas; joint kitchen and sanitary facilities *Accessibility and usability:* accommodation accessed via common inner courtyard, open stairs and covered walkways	• Exist. plot ratio:1.7 • Gross floor area: 1015 m² • Unsealed ground: approx. 60% of plot • Ventilation: natural, 100% of floor area • U-values, bldg. envelope [W/m²K]: ext. wall 0.17, glazing 1.1 • Building costs, cost groups 300–400: 1.071M EUR • Building costs: 1055 EUR/m² gross floor area • Ratio of cost groups 300/400: 80/20 • Proportion of renew. raw mat.: approx. 90% by vol. • Electrical heating (space heating, hot water): 130 kWh/m²a • Electrical requirements for lighting and other electrical consumers: 45 kWh/m²a • Renew. energy coverage rate: approx. 90% (electricity from hydroelectric plants) • Competition • Low- or zero-emissions building materials
Plot	*Area of plot:* compact form of construction and external access to minimise ground sealing *Open areas:* external areas completely unsealed	
Design	*Building culture:* striking building, constructional innovations in timber engineering *Personalisation:* occupants responsible for interior fitting-out and design of communal areas	
Well-being/ health	*Safety/security:* clear layout; high social controls *Sound:* good sound insulation due to solid timber walls *Light:* good illumination due to low room depths *Interior climate:* high thermal comfort due to untreated solid timber surfaces in interior	
Building fabric	*Structure:* solid timber construction with high quality due to prefabrication *Building layout/fitting-out:* flexible internal layouts; different apartment sizes and standards; access zones can be used as open areas	
Building costs	*Investment costs:* very low capital outlay; minimised building volume due to external access; low specific area consumption per person (22 m²), interior fitting-out omitted *Financing:* foundation established with public assistance, organised by residents, financed by rental income	
Operating and maintenance costs	*Operation and maintenance:* untreated timber surfaces; minimised building services *Repairs:* very simple building design and details to reduce cost of repairs	
Building materials	*Raw materials (availability):* timber used almost exclusively *Environmental impact:* high degree of prefabrication *Dangerous substances:* synthetic materials avoided in the interior – walls, floors and soffits of untreated larch *Deconstruction:* building can be separated into its constituent materials	
Operating energy	*Building heating:* direct electric heating *Hot-water provision:* electric heating *Other electrical consumers:* minimal technical equipment *Coverage of energy requirements:* electric heating (electricity generated almost exclusively by hydroelectric power)	
Infrastructure	*Waste from operation and usage:* waste separation as required by law; composting	
Process quality	*Sustainable building:* ecological-social pilot project, developed in conjunction with urban development plan *Building tradition:* project integrated into research project for the further development of traditional timber construction *Participation:* direct involvement of future residents	• Participation concept

Example 04

Refurbishment of a private house

Berlin, D 2003

Architect:
Thomas Hillig, Berlin
Assistant:
Thomas Kaiser
Structural engineer:
Michael Grimm, Bischofsgrün, Berlin

This gently sloping plot is located on the eastern banks of a lake in Berlin-Hellersdorf, not far from the rediscovered Lemke Villa of Ludwig Mies van der Rohe. The end house of this terrace dating from 1978 was formerly used as a guest-house/youth club. The client's original idea was to demolish the building completely and replace it with a new structure. However, as the interior layout was functional and certainly modifiable, he finally decided in favour of converting the existing building.

As the concrete internal walls are loadbearing, they could not be repositioned. Apart from the kitchen, which was transferred from the road to the garden side in the living area, the uses of the individual rooms were retained. One important component in the conversion concept was to loosen the rigid internal structure and thus make the living area more spacious. Walls were opened up and provided with sliding elements; storey-height slits for doors and windows enhance the openness.

The facades, consisting of prefabricated concrete panels with 40 mm thick polystyrene cavity insulation, were provided with a mineral thermal insulation composite system as part of the refurbishment project and in certain areas covered with a larch cladding. The complete renewal of the electrical installation, the installation of a gas-fired condensing boiler with hot-water tank and standard radiators enabled the energy consumption to be cut drastically. The new wooden windows with insulating glazing achieve a U-value of 1.3 kWh/m²a. The existing marble in the entrance and staircase was retained, the carpeting in the other rooms replaced by wood-block flooring made from smoked oak.

Architektenkammer Berlin: Architektur Berlin 04. Berlin 2004

Section • Plans
Scale 1:250
Vertical section
Scale 1:20

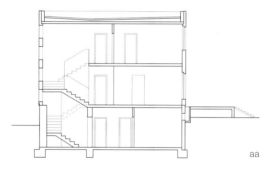

aa

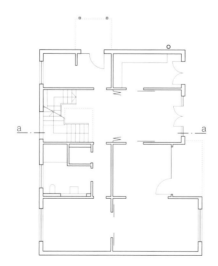

a   a

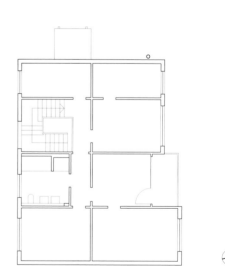

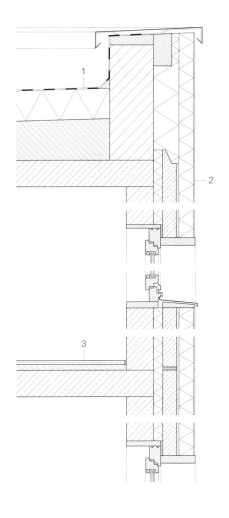

1 Roof construction:
bituminous waterproofing
160 mm polystyrene foam thermal insulation
lightweight screed laid to falls
140 mm reinforced concrete
2 Wall construction:
80 mm thermal insulation composite
system with mineral render
75 mm exposed aggregate concrete
outer leaf

50 mm cavity insulation
150 mm reinforced concrete loadbearing
inner leaf
3 Floor construction:
22 mm wood-block flooring, smoked oak
levelling mortar
30 mm screed
140 mm reinforced concrete

Theme	Qualitative features	Parameters/indicators
Location quality	*Energy availability:* natural gas supply *Basic provisions/mixed uses:* edge of town; residential area *Solidarity/ justice:* creation of low-cost housing for families *Usage:* after use as guest-house/youth club, revitalisation for residential use *Mobility:* residential access road	• Global radiation: 1000 kWh/m^{2}a • Density: 3817 persons/km^2 • Distance to local public transport: 600 m (tram, bus)
Building quality		
Access / communication	*Traffic:* garage in basement; car parking *Accessibility and usability:* access via spacious staircase; patio at ground floor level *Social contact:* better visual links to outside world	• Exist. plot ratio: 0.3 • Gross floor area, existing building: 280 m^2 • Unsealed ground: approx. 80% of plot
Plot	*Area of plot:* refraining from an extension means no increase in size of footprint *Open areas:* essentially no ground sealing to external areas	• Ventilation: natural, 100% of floor area • Building costs, cost groups 300–400:
Design	*Building culture:* sensitive treatment of building stock; energy-efficiency and architectural upgrade with low capital outlay	286 000 EUR • Building costs: 885 EUR/m^2 gross floor area
Well-being/ health	*Safety/security:* good social controls in established residential district *Light:* better use of daylight due to enlarged window areas *Interior climate:* higher surface temperatures due to supplementary insulation; highly effective thermal masses; external sunshades	• Proportion of renew. raw mat.: approx. 20% by vol.
Building fabric	*Structure:* continued use of high-quality loadbearing structure and floor coverings; retention and upgrading of external walls due to insulation and new weather protection *Building layout/fitting-out:* opening up internal layout for more flexibility	• Low- or zero-emissions building materials
Building costs	*Investment costs:* minimising the capital outlay by refraining from demolition and rebuilding	
Operating and maintenance costs	*Operation and maintenance:* use of easy-care surfaces in the interior	
Building materials	*Raw materials (availability):* prolonging the life cycles of concrete construction and high-quality floor coverings *Environmental impact:* minimising the consumption of resources by retaining the building stock *Dangerous substances:* use of natural materials internally; waxed solid wood-block flooring	
Operating energy	*Building heating:* marked reduction in heating requirement due to energy-efficiency upgrade of building envelope *Lighting:* minimising the artificial lighting requirement by increasing the window sizes *Coverage of energy requirements:* gas-fired condensing boiler	
Process quality	*Sustainable building:* optimisation of resources through use of building stock *Building tradition:* retention of cultural inheritance (panel construction) *Integrated planning:* inclusion of a landscape architect	

Example 05

Mountain refuge

St. Ilgen, A 2005

Architects:
pos architekten, Vienna
Treberspurg & Partner Architekten, Vienna
Project team:
Florian Dorninger, Jutta Leitner, Fritz Oettl,
Marie Rezac, Christian Wolfert
Structural engineers:
Robert Salzer, Hohenberg
Gerald Gallasch, Vienna
Energy concept and building physics:
Wilhelm Hofbauer, Vienna

In the Austrian Hochschwab region in the Alps there is a new self-sufficient mountain refuge in passive-house quality at an altitude of 2154 m. The location, form and internal layout of this building are matched to the extreme climatic conditions. Positioning the building on the elevated plateau means that the north-west winds, with speeds up to 200 km/h, prevent the building being engulfed in snow! The exact position was determined by analyses of the sun's trajectory. All the building materials were delivered by helicopter; the prefabricated wall elements were therefore limited to a maximum weight of 1400 kg, the roof elements 600 kg. The building consists of a plinth storey in reinforced concrete and two upper storeys in timber, and it is operated entirely with renewable energy – including drinking-water treatment and waste-water disposal. The south elevation has large expanses of glass, photovoltaic panels and solar collectors, and therefore serves as a passive and active source of solar energy. Contrasting with this, the other facades are essentially closed in order to keep thermal losses to an absolute minimum. The strict solar orientation is also reflected in the internal layout. Communal areas and bedrooms face south, whereas ancillary facilities and circulation zones are placed on the north side.

Solar collectors integrated into the facade cover an area of 64 m² and provide all the hot-water requirements. The heat recovery from the ventilation system enables the building to be self-sufficient in terms of thermal energy. About 65% of electricity needs can be met by the use of photovoltaic modules, which cover an area of 70 m²; a co-generation plant, which runs on vegetable oil, cuts in as required. Rainwater is collected in a tank in the basement and used for preparing the drinking water and other water requirements of the building. After treatment in a biological cleaning and disposal plant, the waste water can be drained into the soil without causing any harm. Dry-composting toilets prevent the unnecessary use of water.

Bauen mit Holz 9/2005
DBZ 06/2006
Intelligente Architektur 04, 2006

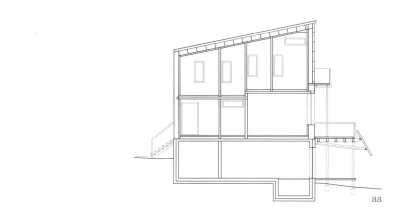

aa

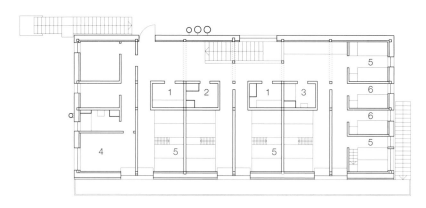

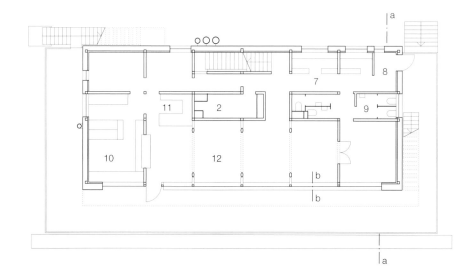

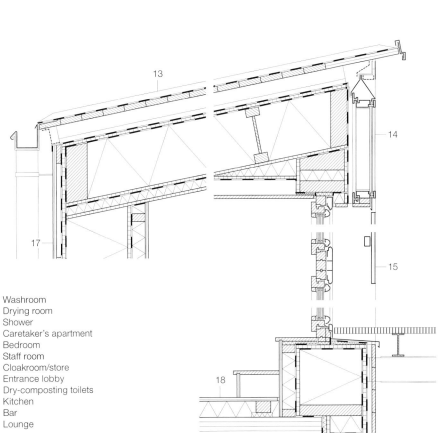

1 Washroom
2 Drying room
3 Shower
4 Caretaker's apartment
5 Bedroom
6 Staff room
7 Cloakroom/store
8 Entrance lobby
9 Dry-composting toilets
10 Kitchen
11 Bar
12 Lounge

13 Roof construction, U = 0.10 W/m²K:
   stainless steel standing seam roof covering
   separating layer, diffusion-permeable
   30 mm untreated timber decking
   100 mm ventilation cavity/battens, airtight membrane
   16 mm wood-fibre board, diffusion-permeable, hydrophobic coating
   airtight membrane
   300 mm rock wool thermal insulation between timber members
   18 mm OSB
   vapour barrier, airtight PE sheeting
   60 mm rock wool thermal insulation between battens
   fleece mat to retain fill
   15 mm 3-ply core plywood, oiled/waxed spruce
14 Solar thermal collector
15 Translucent photovoltaic panel
16 Triple glazing: 52 mm, low E coating, argon filling, U_g = 0.6 W/m²K, in wood/aluminium frame, U_w = 0.8 W/m²K
17 Facade construction, U = 0.10 W/m²K:
   19 mm larch decking
   30 mm ventilation cavity/battens
   airtight membrane
   16 mm wood-fibre board, diffusion-permeable, hydrophobic coating
   airtight membrane
   rock wool thermal insulation
   346/240 mm (lounge/standard) between timber studs
   18 mm OSB
   vapour barrier, airtight PE sheeting
   80 mm thermal insulation/battens
   15 mm 3-ply core plywood, oiled/waxed spruce
18 Floorboards, oiled/waxed spruce
19 Ready-to-lay wood-block flooring, oiled/waxed ash
20 Photovoltaic panel on galvanised steel framework

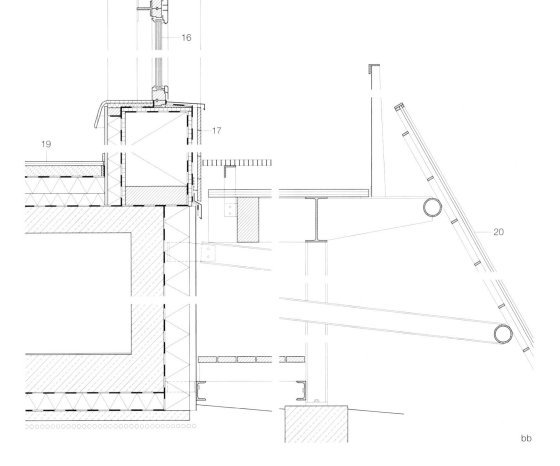

Example 05

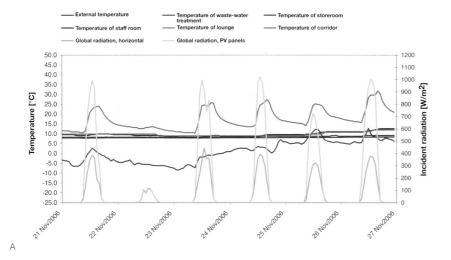

A

A   Measurements from November 2006
B   Interior zones, passive solar
C   Hot water, electricity
D   Ventilation/heat recovery

1   Solar energy
2   Hot-water tank
3   Co-generation plant, rapeseed oil
4   Battery
5   Exhaust air
6   Incoming air, 20°
7   Expelled air
8   Fresh air
9   Passive-house ventilation unit with exhaust-air heat recovery

Legend:
— External temperature
— Temperature of staff room
— Global radiation, horizontal
— Temperature of waste-water treatment
— Temperature of lounge
— Global radiation, PV panels
— Temperature of storeroom
— Temperature of corridor

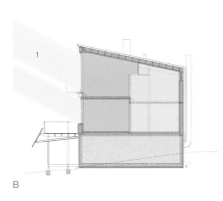

B

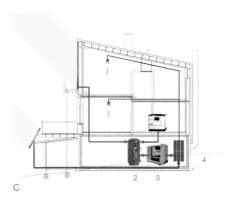

C

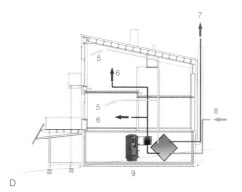

D

Theme	Qualitative features	Parameters/indicators
Location quality	*Energy availability:* 2154 m above sea level; high temperature fluctuations (min. -25°C, max. +23°C); no public infrastructure *Basic provisions/mixed uses:* self-sufficient mountain refuge, open from May to October *Solidarity/justice:* low-budget overnight accommodation Usage: guest-house with restaurant; events *Mobility:* only accessible on foot; supplies delivered and refuse collected by helicopter every 8 weeks *Noise/vibration:* very airtight form of construction and high sound insulation values to minimise wind noise	• Global radiation: 1300 kWh/m²a • Climate data relevant to location: average annual temp. -0.2°C; winds up to 200 km/h • Density: < 1 person/km² • Dist. to local public transport: 12 km (bus)
Building quality Access/ communication	*Social contact:* central common room; several beds/room; various bedroom sizes; joint sanitary facilities *Access. & usability:* forecourt; access on side facing away from wind & via terrace; common balcony	• Exist. plot ratio: 0.24 • Gross floor area, existing building: approx. 490 m²
Plot	*Area of plot:* footprint as for original building; deconstruction of old building after completion of new one *Open areas:* no ground sealing to external areas; large elevated terrace	• Gross floor area, new building: 626 m² • Unsealed ground: 90% of plot
Design	*Building culture:* re-interpretation of mountain refuge architecture in traditional timber construction; building optimised for solar energy gains; position and facade design maximise link with outside world (panoramic view)	• Sound insulation: walls > 55 dB(A), window > 35 dB(A) • Ventilation: mechanical, 100% of floor area
Well-being/ health	*Sound:* good room acoustics due to absorbent timber surfaces; high sound insulation in suspended floor, sound-insulated ventilation system *Light:* glazing quality permits large panoramic windows with optimised daylight utilisation *Interior air:* constant, good air quality due to controlled, preheated fresh air *Interior climate:* good accommodation quality due to very high airtightness and surface temperatures	• U-values, bldg. envelope [W/m²K]: roof 0.1, ext. wall 0.1, window 0.8, floor over basement 0.2 • Projected economic period of use: > 100 a
Building fabric	*Structure:* prefabricated lightweight timber structure optimised for transport and short construction time *Building layout/fitting-out:* solar-oriented usage zoning, communal rooms on south side, ancillary rooms and access on north side; flexible heated floor space, depending on number of guests	• Building costs, cost groups 300–400: approx. 2M EUR
Building costs	*Investment costs:* expensive materials transportation in mountainous area *Financing:* public assistance	• Building costs: 3200 EUR/m² gross floor area (prototype)
Operating and maintenance costs	*Operation and maintenance:* zero-maintenance facade (larch) and roof covering (stainless steel); low energy costs	• Proportion of renew. raw mat.: approx. 80% by vol.
Building materials	*Raw materials (availability):* mostly indigenous species of wood *Dangerous substances:* wooden surfaces oiled and waxed only *Deconstruction:* prefabricated construction; bldg. can be separated into its constituent materials	• Heating requirement: 11 kWh/m²a • Renew. energy coverage rate: 100% • Active solar areas: solar thermal 64 m², PV 70 m²
Operating energy	*Building heating:* compactness; passive use of solar energy (glazing); thermal insulation/passive-house standard; extract system with heat recovery *Lighting:* energy-saving bulbs *Other electrical consumers:* highest possible energy-efficiency class *Coverage of energy requirements:* solar thermal and PV systems incorporated into facade; co-generation plant (vegetable oil) as backup; log-burning boiler for kitchen; recycling of wood from existing building after deconstruction	• Low- or zero-emissions building materials • Register of building materials
Infrastructure	*Waste from operation and usage:* highly efficient grease/fat separation; less waste due to washable filters in kitchen extract system *Water:* rainwater tanks (38 m³); treated to produce drinking water; high-quality biological waste-water treatment, seepage on the plot itself; dry-composting toilets	• Deconstruction concept • Rainwater/grey water usage
Process quality	*Sustainable building:* pilot project for passive-house mountain refuge *Integrated planning:* right from start of project; project planning within the scope of a research programme *Analyses:* choice of location according to analysis of sun's trajectory; extensive simulations *Monitoring:* remote monitoring of building status, electricity load management to avoid high output requirements and to maximise battery life	• Sustainability-oriented benchmarks • Simulation method • Monitoring

District heating plant

Sexten, I, 2005

Architect:
Siegfried Delueg, Brixen
Assistants:
Thomas Malknecht, Igor Comploi
Structural engineers:
Team 4, Bruneck

Tourism and the associated service industries characterise the region around the little community of Sexten in South Tyrol. In order to preserve the rural Alpine structure of this area, harmonious, careful integration in the landscape was one of the stipulations in the design competition for the new district heating plant. The level plot is situated in an industrial estate and is bordered on the north-western and southern sides by the forested hillside and a stream. Access to the site is via the existing bridge at the north end. One of the two buildings contains the heating plant; the other is used for storing the wood chippings. The two buildings fan out towards the forest, framing an open-air storage area for further wood chippings. The location and arrangement of the buildings ensure trouble-free deliveries and short transport distances. Untreated wood chippings, sawmill by-products and logging debris from the immediate region are used exclusively as the fuel for this biomass district heating plant. The heat generated is then sent, using water as a transfer medium, via the 36 km of pipes in the district heating network to more than 300 customers in the area. The insulated steel pipes are thermally prestressed and undergo constant electronic monitoring. Pipe friction losses and a hydrostatic head of 105 m are compensated for by recirculating pumps. Some 2.4 million litres of heating oil can thus be saved every year.

Welded steel frames with rigid connections form the loadbearing structure for the heating plant building. The large-format glued laminated timber boards of the outer walls at the same time provide the bracing for the building, form a loadbearing enclosure and constitute the thermal insulation; additional, internal insulation is required only in the walls around the offices. Placing the external walls at an angle creates an optical illusion, making the buildings appear shorter than they really are. Vertical larch battens, which continue past the window and ventilation openings, reinforce the homogeneous appearance.

📖 Architektur Aktuell 10/2006
db 05/2006

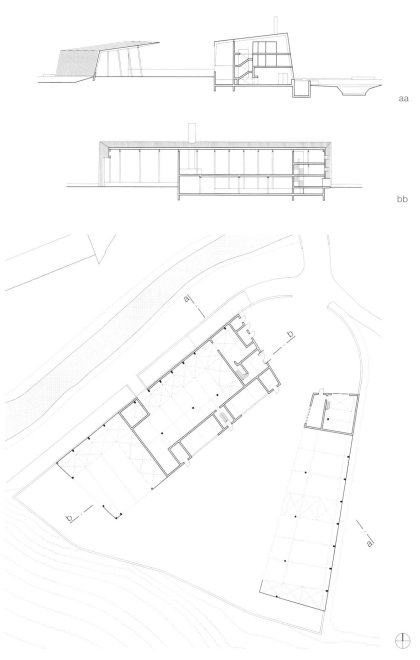

aa

bb

Sections · Plan
Scale 1:1000

Example 06

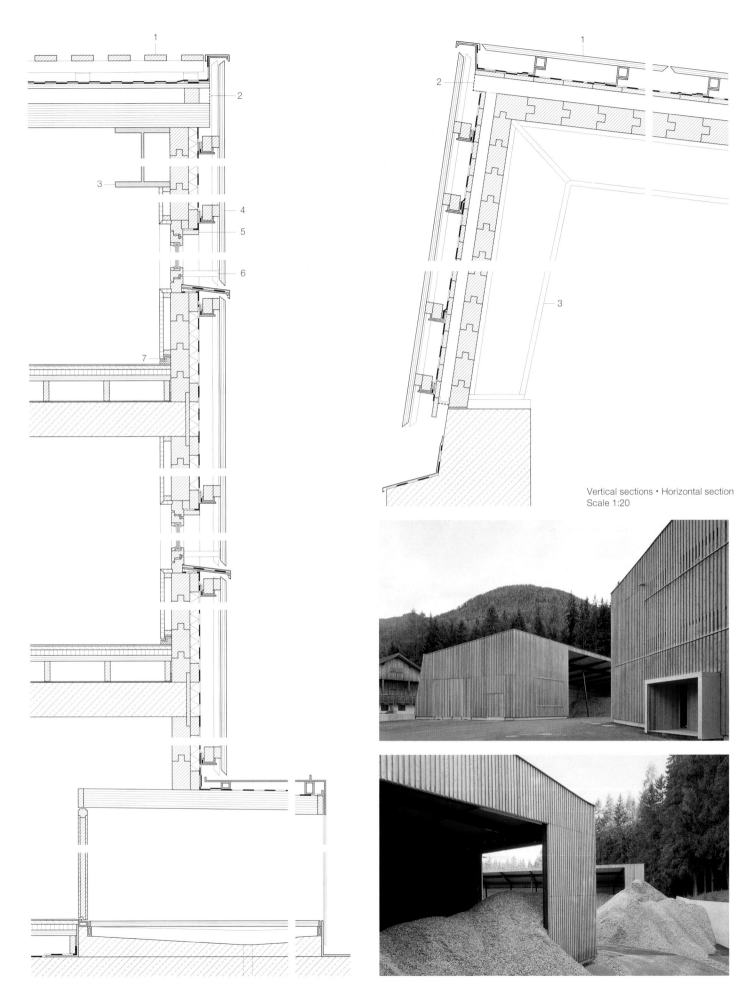

Vertical sections · Horizontal section
Scale 1:20

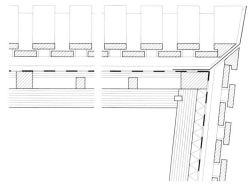

1 Roof construction:
  120 x 30 mm rough-sawn larch open decking
  60 x 40 x 2 mm steel hollow section, hot-dip galv.
  60 x 40 x 5 mm steel Z-section
  waterproofing, 2 layers of bitumen sheeting,
  airtight, diffusion-permeable
  25 mm spruce decking, 80 x 80 mm sq. sections
  128 mm solid timber roof, larch, U = 1.3 W/m²K
2 Insect screen
3 Steel I section, 300 x 550, tapering
4 Wall construction:
  120 x 30 mm rough-sawn larch cladding
  40 x 60 x 60 mm spacer blocks
  50 x 80 mm square sections
  90 x 60 x 5 mm steel angle, hot-dip galvanised
  waterproofing, 2 layers of bitumen sheeting, airtight, diffusion-permeable
  50 mm mineral wool thermal insulation
  95 mm solid timber wall, larch
  40 mm air space
  20 mm lining, spruce multi-ply board
5 Larch lining, 25 x 90 mm
6 Steel tube, Ø30 mm, hot-dip galvanised
7 Neoprene bearing

Theme	Qualitative features	Parameters/indicators
Location quality	*Energy availability:* extensive forests in the region *Basic provisions/mixed uses:* edge of settlement; industrial estate *Usage:* new plant for central heat supplies based on biomass wood chippings to replace individual heating plants *Mobility:* situated on main road	• Global radiation: 1400 kWh/m²a • Density: 23 persons/km² • Distance to local public transport: 10 m (bus); 15 km (regional trains)
Building quality		
Access/ communication	*Accessibility and usability:* arrangement of buildings creates forecourt and partially conceals open-air storage; minimal transport distances within plant *Social contact:* displays open to the public in entrance area; guided tours; assembly room fitted out to a high quality	• Plot: 6500 m² • Covered area: 2230 m² • Unsealed ground: 0% of plot (asphalt hardstanding required for storage)
Plot	*Area of plot:* footprint minimised by placing non-technical functions on upper floors *Open areas:* open area used for storing wood chippings	• U-value, boiler house walls: 1.3 W/m²K • Projected economic period of use: 50 a
Design	*Building culture:* sensitive harmonisation with the landscape; inclined facades to create the illusion of smaller surfaces; homogeneous appearance due to uniform covering to facades and roof surfaces made from larch battens attached at different pitches *Personalisation:* fitting-out determined by user	• Building costs, cost groups 300–400: 2.5M EUR • Proportion of renew. raw mat.: approx. 70% by vol.
Well-being/ health	*Interior climate:* thermal insulation to boiler house provided by solid timber facades; additional, internal insulation to offices	• Renew. energy coverage rate: 100%
Building fabric	*Structure:* materials selected taking into account efficiency and local availability *Building layout/fitting-out:* roof space suitable for conversion; flexible use of assembly room	• Competition • Low- or zero-emissions building materials
Building costs	*Investment costs:* budget typical for this type of use *Financing:* power plant belongs to local community	
Operating and maintenance costs	*Operation and maintenance:* facades of untreated larch require no maintenance *Repairs:* facades made from prefabricated elements that can be easily replaced	
Building materials	*Raw materials (availability):* use of indigenous species of wood; facades consist of structural, large-format glued laminated timber elements; steel frames for large spans; reinforced concrete adjacent to ground *Environmental impact:* biomass power plant replaces individual heating plants which hitherto had consumed 2.4 million litres of heating oil annually *Dangerous substances:* central heat generation enables high-quality flue-gas scrubbing with heat recovery for minimal air pollution in the valley *Deconstruction:* timber panel construction; entire plant can be separated into its constituent materials	
Operating energy	*Building heating:* heated rooms minimised; rooms heated via radiators fed from district heating system *Hot-water provision:* no hot-water requirements *Coverage of energy requirements:* biomass	
Infrastructure	*Waste from operation and usage:* separate ash collection/disposal *Water:* minimised water consumption for cleaning	
Process quality	*Sustainable building:* extensive stipulations in competition regarding ecological aspects; harmonious integration into the surroundings required *Building tradition:* promotion of local timber construction industry *Participation:* comprehensive involvement of citizens in project development *Integrated planning:* close cooperation with power plant engineer *Analyses:* extensive studies carried out during project development *Monitoring:* detailed monitoring by power plant operator *Facility management:* by power plant operator	• Sustainability-oriented benchmarks • Participation concept • Simulation method • Monitoring • FM concept

Example 07

Straw house

Eschenz, CH, 2005

Architect:
Felix Jerusalem, Zurich
Structural engineers:
SJB.Kempter.Fitze, Frauenfeld
Detailed design:
Création Holz, Herisau

Despite the tight budget, the architect managed to design a simple but well-thought-out house for a four-person family. Owing to the damp ground, the building is raised clear on small piles; only the heavyweight reinforced concrete core – containing bathroom, WC, kitchen units, cloakroom and basement (accessed via a hatch in the ground floor) – extends into the ground. At the same time, the concrete core divides the rectangular building into two parts: the two rooms for the children on the south side, the living room and master bedroom on the north side and above the latter – exploiting the highest part of the monopitch roof – a gallery that serves as a study. The rooms have the charm of a refined structural carcass: a sealed screed serves as the floor finish, all pipes and cables are left exposed, and in some places the walls have been left untreated. The real characteristic of the building is to be found in its construction: apart from the concrete core, the house is built entirely of pressed straw boards – a zero-emissions, recyclable building material. The floors, roof and walls consist of sandwich elements all built according to the same principle: outer layers of highly compressed straw boards for the load-bearing function, a core of lightweight straw boards for the thermal insulation. All the elements were prefabricated and then assembled on site. The building was completed in just four months.

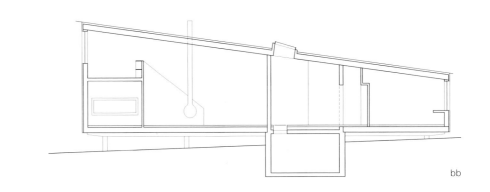

bb

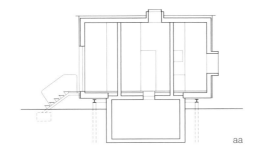

aa

Sections • Plans
Scale 1:200
Vertical section
Scale 1:20

1 Master bedroom
2 Living room
3 Entrance
4 Bathroom
5 Kitchen
6 Child's room
7 Gallery
8 Void

Detail 06/2006
Werk, Bauen und Wohnen 11/2006

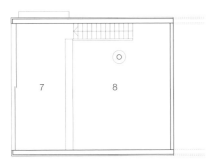

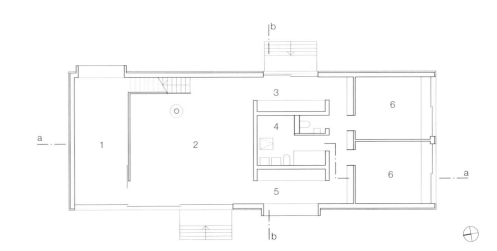

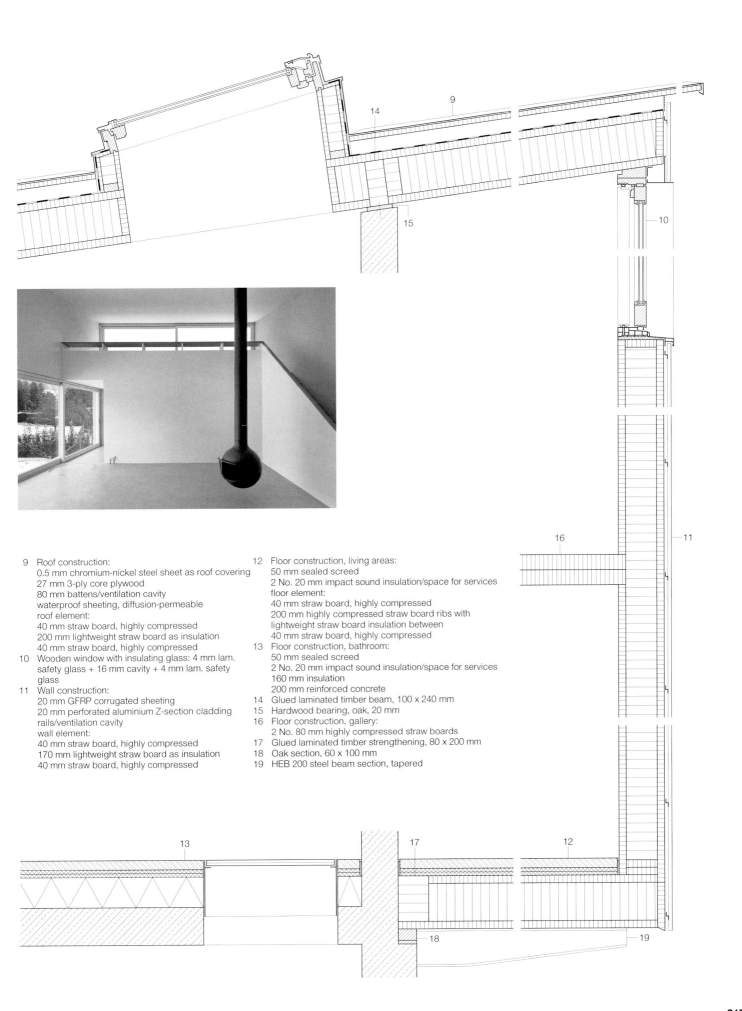

9   Roof construction:
    0.5 mm chromium-nickel steel sheet as roof covering
    27 mm 3-ply core plywood
    80 mm battens/ventilation cavity
    waterproof sheeting, diffusion-permeable
    roof element:
    40 mm straw board, highly compressed
    200 mm lightweight straw board as insulation
    40 mm straw board, highly compressed
10 Wooden window with insulating glass: 4 mm lam.
    safety glass + 16 mm cavity + 4 mm lam. safety
    glass
11 Wall construction:
    20 mm GFRP corrugated sheeting
    20 mm perforated aluminium Z-section cladding
    rails/ventilation cavity
    wall element:
    40 mm straw board, highly compressed
    170 mm lightweight straw board as insulation
    40 mm straw board, highly compressed

12 Floor construction, living areas:
    50 mm sealed screed
    2 No. 20 mm impact sound insulation/space for services
    floor element:
    40 mm straw board, highly compressed
    200 mm highly compressed straw board ribs with
    lightweight straw board insulation between
    40 mm straw board, highly compressed
13 Floor construction, bathroom:
    50 mm sealed screed
    2 No. 20 mm impact sound insulation/space for services
    160 mm insulation
    200 mm reinforced concrete
14 Glued laminated timber beam, 100 x 240 mm
15 Hardwood bearing, oak, 20 mm
16 Floor construction, gallery:
    2 No. 80 mm highly compressed straw boards
17 Glued laminated timber strengthening, 80 x 200 mm
18 Oak section, 60 x 100 mm
19 HEB 200 steel beam section, tapered

Example 07

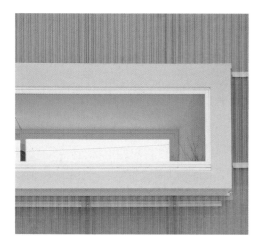

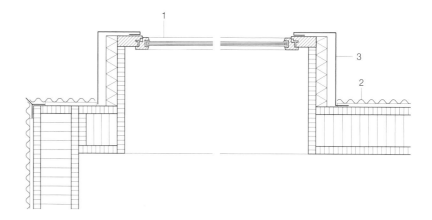

Horizontal section
Scale 1:20

1 Wooden window with insulating glass:
4 mm lam. safety glass + 16 mm cavity +
4 mm lam. safety glass
2 Wall construction:
20 mm GFRP corrugated sheeting
20 mm perforated aluminium Z-section
cladding rails/ventilation cavity
wall element:
40 mm straw board, highly compressed
170 mm lightweight straw board as insulation
40 mm straw board, highly compressed
3 Sheet steel, 2 mm
rock wool insulation, 60 mm
highly compressed straw board, 40 mm,
painted white

Theme	Qualitative features	Parameters/indicators
Location quality	*Energy availability:* natural gas supply *Basic provisions/mixed uses:* exclusively residential area *Solidarity/justice:* pilot project for developing low-budget construction and components for housing	• Global radiation: 1300 kWh/m²a • Density: 134 persons/km² • Distance to local public transport: 300 m (bus); 700 m (regional trains)
Building quality		
Access / communication	*Traffic:* connection to residential road, 2 parking spaces on the plot; good visibility *Accessibility and usability:* access via 4 steps, ramp can be added	• Exist. plot ratio: 0.2 • Gross floor area: 173 m²
Plot	*Area of plot:* minimal ground sealing due to elevated construction, preservation of natural topography *Open areas:* unsealed external areas, vegetation beneath building	• Unsealed ground: 98% of plot • Ventilation: natural, 100% of floor area
Design	*Building culture:* experimental architecture with innovative renewable materials, size adapted to the surroundings, facade with high recognition value *Personalisation:* interior and exterior design by the user	• U-values, bldg. envelope: [W/m²K] roof 0.2 [1], ext. wall 0.18 [1], window 1.1 (g-value 0.6); grd. slab 0.17 [1] • Projected economic period of use: 50 a
Well-being/ health	*Safety/security:* good social controls, numerous visual links *Sound:* high sound insulation due to new sandwich facade with components of different thickness *Light:* very high proportion of glazing, interior lit from more than one side, white interior surfaces *Interior air:* cross-ventilation possible *Interior climate:* high standard of insulation; sorptive interior surfaces; underfloor heating	• Building costs, cost groups 300–400: 370 000 EUR • Building costs: 2140 EUR/m² gross floor area (prototype)
Building fabric	*Structure:* new types of building components made from renewable raw material (prototypes) *Building layout/fitting-out:* exposed pipes and cables for simple replacement or expansion	• Proportion of renew. raw mat.: approx. 90% by vol.
Building costs	*Investment costs:* high degree of prefabrication, minimal earthworks	• Heating requirement: 15 kWh/m²a
Operating and maintenance costs	*Operation and maintenance:* zero-maintenance facade cladding; metal roof *Repairs:* minimised interior fitting-out and building services	• Barrier-free [2]
Building materials	*Raw materials (availability):* fast-growing (regrows in approx. 3 months) raw material available locally *Environmental impact:* building materials essentially compostable *Dangerous substances:* straw contains no formaldehyde *Deconstruction:* entire building can be separated into its constituent materials	• Low- or zero-emissions building materials • Deconstruction concept
Operating energy	*Building heating:* compact form of construction, MINERGIE standard, passive solar energy usage via translucent GFRP cladding *Coverage of energy requirements:* gas-fired condensing boiler, wood-burning fireplace	
Infrastructure	*Waste from operation and usage:* composting of organic waste on the plot *Water:* short pipes	
Process quality	*Sustainable building:* "green house" objective *Building tradition:* further development of traditional form of construction with renewable raw materials using new material technologies *Analyses:* comprehensive building physics and static measurements on 1:1 model	• Sustainability-oriented benchmarks • Simulation method

[1] Based on dynamic calculations by product manufacturer
[2] Provided access ramp is fitted

Combined nursing and senior citizens' home

Steinfeld, A, 2005

Architect:
Dietger Wissounig, Graz
Structural engineers:
Kurt Pock, Gerolf Urban, Spittal/Drau

The gently sloping site of this combined nursing and senior citizens' home is situated on the western border of the small town of Steinfeld in Carinthia. The building appears compact and restrained. The east-west orientation is a response to the surroundings: service areas form a buffer to the north-west, where there is a trunk road, whereas most of the apartments and communal areas face the gardens to the south-east. Inside the building, visual links and simple routing ease orientation. Generous and flexible rooms encourage communication. The supply and administrative facilities plus the events/dining hall, library and chapel – all three also open to the public – are all located on the ground floor.

The two upper floors, entirely in timber, cantilever beyond the heavyweight, set-back concrete ground floor on all four sides. Prefabricated timber-frame walls, with glued laminated timber columns and all services pre-installed, transfer the loads to the concrete plinth. The compact, highly insulated building envelope reduces transmission heat losses to the level of a passive house. Ventilation of the building is via the central glass-roofed atrium. In winter the preheating of the air in ground exchangers and the additional solar energy gains result in an average air temperature of approx. 20°C. In summer, on the other hand, the incoming external air is cooled as it passes through the ground exchanger. Shading elements above the glass roof prevent overheating in the upper section. The individual rooms are supplied with fresh air via a displacement ventilation system. Numerous individual measures like the use of rainwater for flushing toilets and watering the gardens, separate controls for heating zones, district heating and electronic control gear for the lighting mean that on the whole this building consumes about 50% less energy than comparable facilities.

Architektur Aktuell 6/2006
Baumeister 5/2006

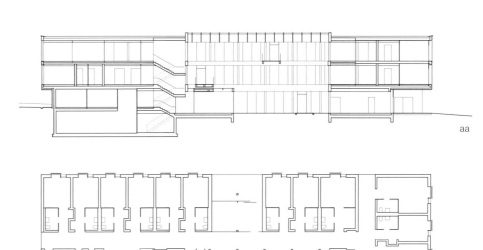

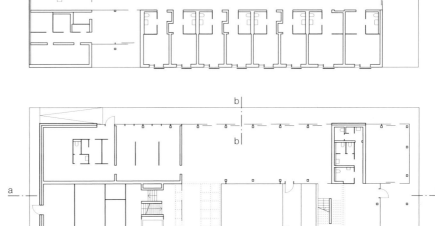

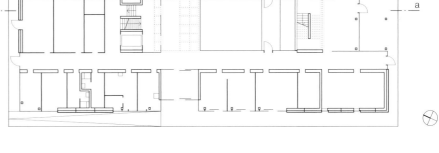

Section · Plans of ground and 1st floor
Scale 1:500

Example 08

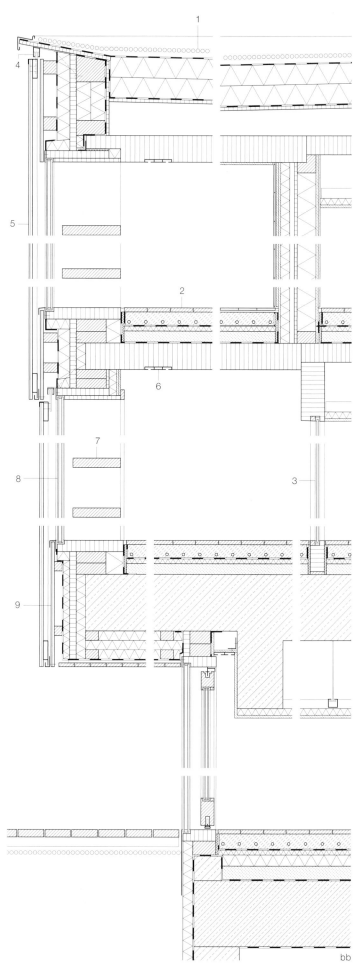

Vertical section
Scale 1:20
Energy scheme
A Winter: passive heat gains
B Summer: ventilation/cooling

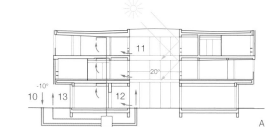

A

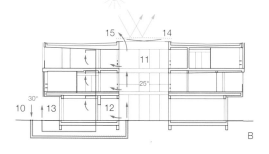

B

1　Roof construction:
　5 mm waterproof sheeting
　2 No. 110 mm PUR thermal insulation
　2 mm vapour barrier
　18 mm OSB
　20–175 mm timber firrings
　140 mm edge-glued timber elements
2　Floor construction, individual rooms:
　22 mm oak wood-block flooring
　70 mm heated screed
　separating layer, PE sheeting
　25 mm impact sound insulation
　63 mm loose fill
　separating layer, PE sheeting
　140 mm edge-glued timber elements
3　Glass wall to corridor: 20 mm tough. safety
　glass clamped in 75 x 170 mm glulam mem-
　bers (larch)
4　Track, steel channel section, 30 x 30 mm
5　Sliding element:
　80 x 20 mm vertical larch laths in 25 x 100 x
　2 mm aluminium hollow section frame
6　Track for curtains
7　Spandrel panel/rail, larch, 50 x 255 mm
8　Insulating glass, U = 0.9 W/m²K
9　Wall construction:
　tongue and groove boarding
　80 x 20 mm vertical larch laths
　35 x 50 mm counter battens
　waterproofing, diffusion-permeable
　35 x 50 mm battens with
　35 mm thermal insulation between
　36 mm wood-fibre board
　50 mm rock wool thermal insulation
10　Fresh air, ground exchanger
11　Fresh air reservoir
12　Displacement ventilation
13　Expelled air with heat recovery
14　Sunshade
15　Natural ventilation/exhaust air

Theme	Qualitative features	Parameters/indicators
Location quality	*Energy availability:* connected to district heating (biomass energy source) *Basic provisions/mixed uses:* edge of town; town centre can be reached on foot *Integration:* mixed usage; facilities suitable for different generations *Solidarity/justice:* areas accessible to the public *Usage:* home for the elderly, town library, church, rooms for public events *Mobility:* good links to existing infrastructure *Noise/vibration:* ancillary rooms positioned on road side	• Global radiation: 1300 kWh/m²a • Density: 27 persons/km² • Distance to local public transport: 20 m (bus); 1000 m (regional trains)
Building quality		
Access/ communication	*Traffic:* footpath through park; car parking *Social contact:* lobby on ground floor, café, central atrium; 2 communal rooms per storey, loggia, terraces *Accessibility and usability:* entire facility barrier-free	• Exist. plot ratio: 0.5 • Gross floor area: approx. 3730 m² • Unsealed ground: 85% of plot
Plot	*Area of plot:* 3-storey building ensures compactness; no ground sealing in atrium *Open areas:* gardens with circular paths, hardstandings with grass paving	• Ventilation: mechanical, 100% of floor area • U-values, bldg. envelope [W/m²K]: roof 0.13, walls 0.18, glazing 0.9, grd. slab 0.18
Design	*Building culture:* similar to traditional timber construction with heavyweight concrete plinth *Personalisation:* seasonal decoration of interior; users' own furniture in communal areas as well	• Projected economic period of use for facade: 65 a
Well-being/ health	*Safety/security:* high transparency from inside to outside and vice versa; central care facility; non-slip flooring; circular routes indoors and outdoors *Sound:* sound-absorbent wooden surfaces *Light:* high proportion of glazing; overhead light via atrium; artificial lighting controlled by occupancy detectors *Interior air:* constant, very high air quality due to controlled fresh/exhaust air in rooms, window ventilation possible; fresh air via atrium with ground exchanger *Interior climate:* high thermal comfort; airborne odours depending on season and planting in atrium; smell of wood in the rooms	• Building costs, cost groups 300–400: approx. 4.1M EUR • Ratio of cost groups 300/400: approx. 75/25 • Building costs: approx. 1100 EUR/m² gross floor area
Building fabric	*Structure:* high construction quality due to prefabrication *Building layout/fitting-out:* open-plan layout with numerous visual links for good orientation; communal areas suitable for various uses	• Proportion of renew. raw mat.: approx. 80% by vol. • Heating requirement: 14 kWh/m²a
Building costs	*Investment costs:* higher capital outlay for insulation standard and ventilation system recouped through savings in energy consumption *Financing:* public sector	• Renew. energy coverage rate: heating 100%
Operating and maintenance costs	*Operation and maintenance:* very easy-care surfaces, epoxy resin floors with special coating for optimum cleaning by machine *Repairs:* systematic routing, inspection hatches	
Building materials	*Raw materials (availability):* very high proportion of wood-based products; indigenous species of wood *Environmental impact:* high degree of prefabrication; untreated wooden surfaces *Deconstruction:* building structure according to "house-of-cards" principle, materials can be separated for recycling	• Barrier-free • Competition • Low- or zero-emissions building materials
Operating energy	*Building heating:* very high standard of insulation; ventilation system with heat recovery; solar gains via atrium *Building cooling:* fresh air for atrium via ground exchanger (500 m long, 800 mm dia.) *Coverage of energy requirements:* biomass via district heating	• Deconstruction concept • Rainwater/grey water usage
Infrastructure	*Water:* use of rainwater for WCs and watering gardens	
Process quality	*Sustainable building:* competition objective to achieve pilot project for combined nursing and senior citizens' home in modern timber construction with sustainable building technology; passive-house standard achieved *Building tradition:* promotion of local building trades *Integrated planning:* close involvement of specialists, external project management *Analyses:* heating requirement calculation	• Sustainability-oriented benchmarks • Simulation method

Example 09

Home for several generations

Darmstadt, D, 2003

Architects:
Kränzle + Fischer-Wasels, Karlsruhe
Klotz + Knecht, Darmstadt
Jürgen Ludwik, Reinheim (construction manager)
Structural engineers:
ISG Gesellschaft f. Ingenieurbau &
Systementwicklung, Darmstadt

On the edge of Darmstadt, this flat, block-like structure, facing the extensive park which adjoins and merges with the plot, terminates an open roadside development. The two-storey clay brick building comprises three separate maisonettes, each equipped with kitchen and bathroom so that the various generations of the client's family can live together yet independently under one roof. Grouped together within a uniform building envelope, the individually designed apartments are reached via a common internal hallway. Voids extending the full height of the building between the apartments serve as conservatories, lightwells and communal areas. Like with a building kit, the rooms can be added to horizontally or vertically, or subdivided, to suit requirements. Up to six apartments, or apartments for guests, or offices, are possible. Uniform specifications for the materials and colours of the walls, floors and soffits, concentrating the services in certain zones and neutral room proportions simplify subsequent conversions. The building is enclosed on three sides with dark grey masonry, so the house appears secluded when viewed from the road or the sides. But on the south side, facing the park, the facade is totally different, with full-height glazing providing an unobstructed view over the park landscape. Solid internal walls store the incoming solar gains and release the heat into the interior after a delay. External sunshades above the glass roofs prevent overheating in the interior. The glass facade is fitted with colourless solar-control glass which is shaded by the balcony and the extensive rooftop planting and therefore requires no further sunshading elements.

db 03/2005
DBZ 08/2006

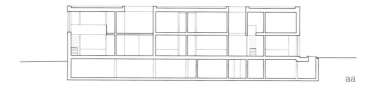

aa

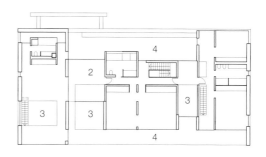

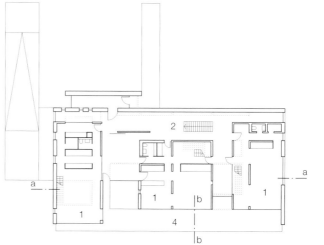

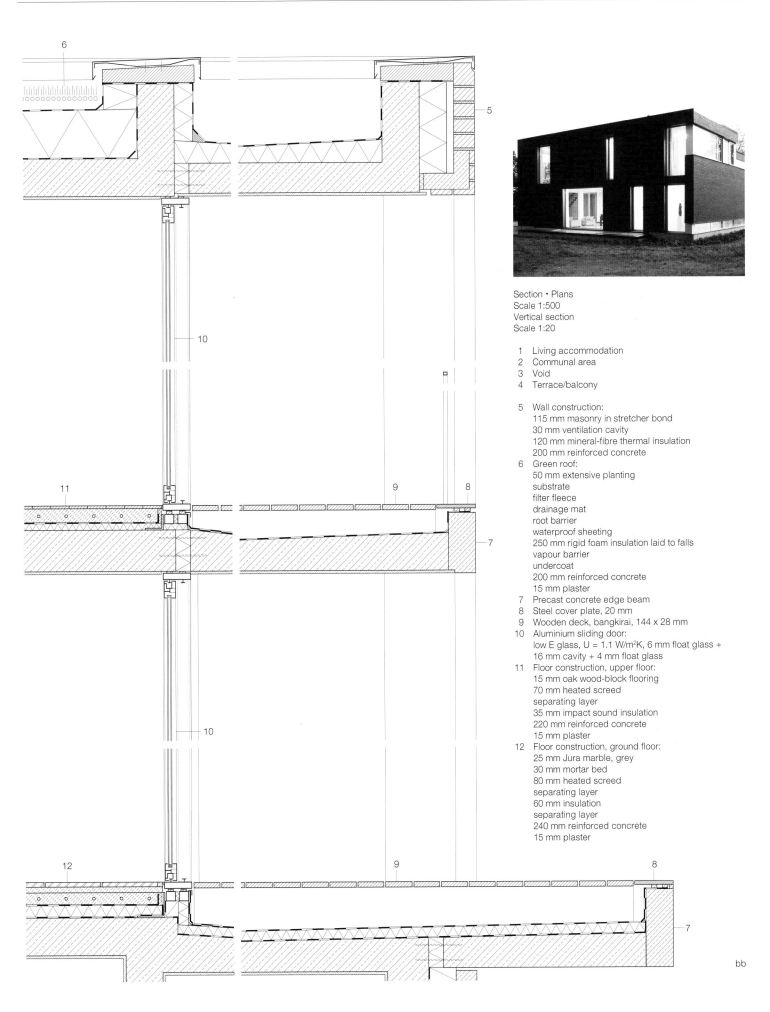

Section · Plans
Scale 1:500
Vertical section
Scale 1:20

1   Living accommodation
2   Communal area
3   Void
4   Terrace/balcony

5   Wall construction:
    115 mm masonry in stretcher bond
    30 mm ventilation cavity
    120 mm mineral-fibre thermal insulation
    200 mm reinforced concrete
6   Green roof:
    50 mm extensive planting
    substrate
    filter fleece
    drainage mat
    root barrier
    waterproof sheeting
    250 mm rigid foam insulation laid to falls
    vapour barrier
    undercoat
    200 mm reinforced concrete
    15 mm plaster
7   Precast concrete edge beam
8   Steel cover plate, 20 mm
9   Wooden deck, bangkirai, 144 x 28 mm
10 Aluminium sliding door:
    low E glass, U = 1.1 W/m²K, 6 mm float glass +
    16 mm cavity + 4 mm float glass
11 Floor construction, upper floor:
    15 mm oak wood-block flooring
    70 mm heated screed
    separating layer
    35 mm impact sound insulation
    220 mm reinforced concrete
    15 mm plaster
12 Floor construction, ground floor:
    25 mm Jura marble, grey
    30 mm mortar bed
    80 mm heated screed
    separating layer
    60 mm insulation
    separating layer
    240 mm reinforced concrete
    15 mm plaster

bb

Example 09

Theme	Qualitative features	Parameters/indicators
Location quality	*Energy availability:* natural gas supply *Basic provisions/mixed uses:* residential area; edge of town *Integration:* mixed age structure, student accommodation, home for the elderly *Usage:* home for several generations *Mobility:* basement garage accessed from main road; 4 parking spaces on the plot (also suitable for disabled persons) *Noise/vibration:* high boundary wall as noise barrier between house and road	• Global radiation: 1100 kWh/m²a • Density: 1156 persons/km² • Distance to local public transport: 200 m (bus); 3000 m (inter-city trains)
Building quality Access/ communication	*Traffic:* parking beneath building *Social contact:* common access hallway; lightwells between housing units as communal areas; areas for joint use *Accessibility and usability:* footpath to common entrance; 2 further separate entrances can be added; no barriers between inside and outside; lift can be added in lightwell	• Exist. plot ratio: 1.0 • Gross floor area: 1490 m² • Unsealed ground: approx. 70% of plot • Rooftop planting: approx. 70% of covered area
Plot	*Open areas:* no ground sealing externally; pavers with open joints to footpath and garage ramp	• Ventilation: natural, 100% of floor area
Design	*Building culture:* integration into historical built-up environment; reduced geometrical forms reminiscent of classical modernism; flexible internal layout represents a re-interpretation of multi-generation living *Personalisation:* private apartments can be arranged and decorated as required, communal areas after consultation	• U-values, bldg. envelope [W/m²K]: roof 0.26, ext. wall 0.24, window 1.4, grd. slab 0.35
Well-being/ health	*Safety/security:* high social controls due to open building structure; communal spaces and numerous visual links *Sound:* lightwells provide acoustic decoupling between individual rooms *Light:* good illumination due to high proportion of glazing plus lightwells with overhead glazing *Interior climate:* high surface temperatures, very effective thermal masses; external sunshades over roof glazing	• Heating requirement: 70 kWh/m²a • Final energy requirement, natural gas: approx. 58 500 kWh/a
Building fabric	*Structure:* minimised structure of reinforced concrete wall plates; facade with brick facing leaf and ventilation cavity *Building layout/fitting-out:* living concept with high flexibility in internal layout; building can be used with 3–6 residential units, communal spaces can be flexibly allocated to individual rooms, which means it is possible to adjust step by step to changing needs	• Barrier-free[1] • Low- or zero-emissions building materials
Building costs	*Investment costs:* use of good-quality materials with the aim of high durability and low maintenance costs; minimised building services; synergy effects due to the "house-in-house" concept	
Operating and maintenance costs	*Operation and maintenance:* zero-maintenance facade, easy-care floor coverings of stone and solid wood; metal window frames; extensive rooftop planting *Repairs:* little wear because of high building quality with very durable materials	
Building materials	*Raw materials (availability):* stone and bricks from regional operations *Environmental impact:* rooftop planting to compensate for ground sealing *Dangerous substances:* waxed wooden floors; internal walls finished with mineral paint	
Operating energy	*Building heating:* high passive solar gains; living rooms and bedrooms on south side; circulation zone and lightwells as climate buffer; underfloor heating *Lighting:* minimised artificial lighting requirements due to very high daylighting levels *Coverage of energy requirements:* gas-fired condensing boiler	
Process quality	*Sustainable building:* plot and building layout chosen to suit the lifestyles of several generations *Participation:* collaboration of the users as project developer, architect and client	• Sustainability-oriented benchmarks • Participation concept

[1] Ground floor apartments provided ramp fitted in entrance area, total building provided lift is installed (allowed for in design)

Sports hall

Tübingen, D, 2004

Architects:
Allmann Sattler Wappner, Munich
Assistants:
Dirk Bauer, Birgit Bader, Eva Hartl, Kai Homm,
Christof Kilius, Thomas Meusburger, Martin
Plock, Ulf Rössler, Steffen Schwarz
Structural engineers:
Werner Sobek Ingenieure, Stuttgart
Energy concept:
Transsolar Energietechnik, Stuttgart

This multi-function facility is located in the immediate vicinity of the sports grounds in Tübingen and the spacious leisure area along the banks of the River Neckar. The monolithic block denotes the end of the sports grounds. The hall can be used in many ways – professional training and competitions, school sports events, the latest sporting trends and popular sports – and so it was necessary to include not only the full internal volume in the concept, but also the external walls as well! All four facades have additional functions as well as just providing protection from the weather, e.g. complete solar facade, outdoor climbing wall, half-pipe. Inside, the sports arena itself, one floor lower than the surrounding ground, is naturally the central focus of the hall; the seating for spectators on all sides accommodates the change in level. The entrance level serves as a circulation and service zone, the changing rooms are located in the basement and special events can be held on the upper level. The roof to the sports hall is supported by steel girders which are supported on fair-face concrete external walls and three service cores. The minimum possible use of primary energy and the use of natural resources form the heart of the energy concept. A ground exchanger cools the incoming fresh air in summer and preheats it in winter. Refrigeration plant is used for large events when there are up to 3000 people in the building. Heat exchangers at roof level recover the heat from the exhaust air. Shimmering green solar modules with white borders cover the entire surface of the south-west elevation; the electricity generated is fed into the public grid. A flat roof with extensive planting helps to clean the air and regulate the temperature. Hot water for the radiant ceiling panels used for heating the hall during the colder months comes via a group heating network from the neighbouring swimming pool.

Baumeister 3/2005
GLAS 2/2005

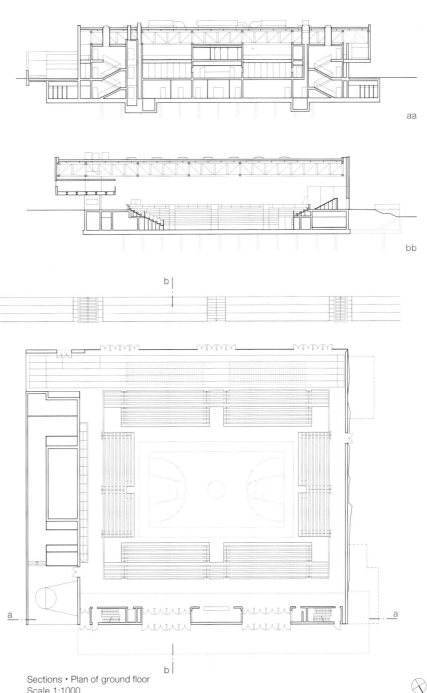

aa

bb

Sections · Plan of ground floor
Scale 1:1000

Example 10

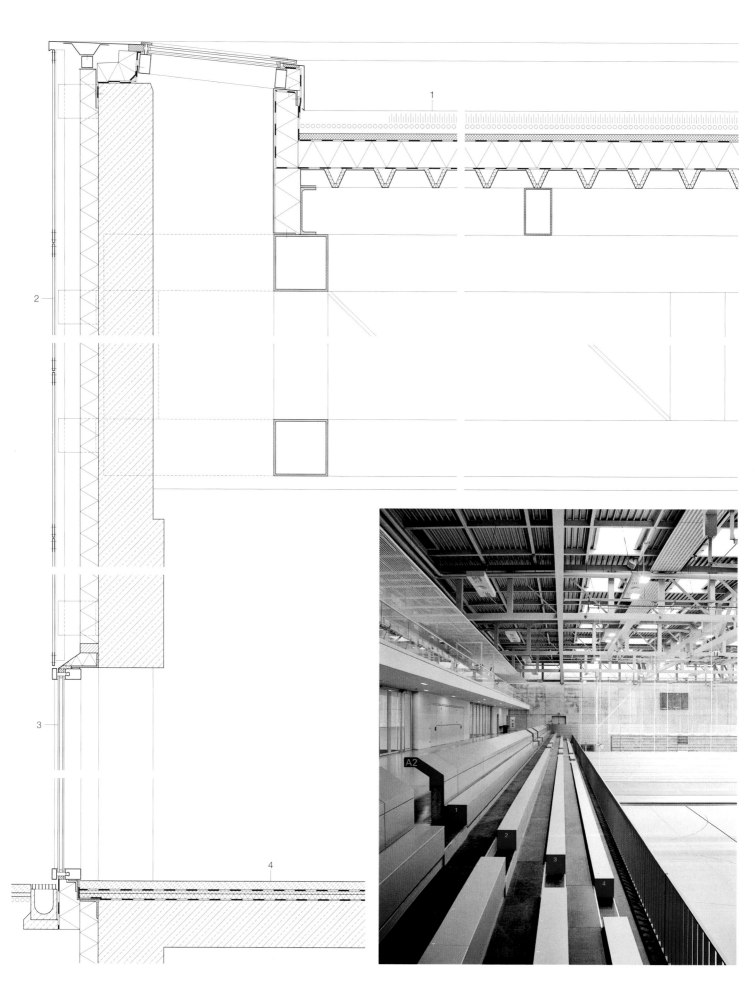

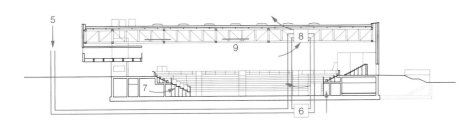

Vertical section
Scale 1:20
Energy and ventilation scheme

1 Roof construction:
   extensive rooftop planting
   substrate
   drainage and filter mat
   waterproofing, polymer-modified bitumen
   140 mm thermal insulation,
   rock wool with bitumen coating
   vapour barrier, polymer-modified bitumen
   acoustic insulation in ribs, fleece facing
   100 x 275 x 0.75 mm steel trapezoidal
   profile sheeting
2 Wall construction, photovoltaic facade:
   tough. safety glass composite supported on angle,
   supporting framework (fixed/sliding anchors)
   85 mm air space
   100 mm mineral wool with fleece facing

3 300 or 360 mm reinforced concrete
   Solar-control glass with internal glare protection, argon-filled cavity, 50% silk-screen printing on outer pane
4 Floor construction:
   50 mm cement screed
   PE sheeting
   20 mm impact sound insulation
   30 mm rigid foam
   PE sheeting
   250 mm reinforced concrete
5 Fresh air drawn in via ground exchanger
6 Heat exchanger
7 Displacement ventilation
8 Heat recovery via run-around coil
9 Radiant ceiling panels

Theme	Qualitative features	Parameters/indicators
Location quality	*Energy availability:* heating requirement covered by group heating system involving neighbouring swimming pool *Usage:* choice of location is obvious complement to existing leisure facilities (swimming pool, sports clubs, festival grounds) *Mobility:* compact arrangement of parking spaces in conjunction with adjoining facilities *Noise/vibration:* orientation of building plus positions of openings take into account noise from main road on north side	• Global radiation: 1120 kWh/m²a • Density: 775 persons/km² • Distance to local public transport: 30 m (bus); 1000 m (regional/inter-city trains)
Building quality		
Access/ communication	*Traffic:* main entrance faces secondary road with less traffic; cantilevering upper floor creates covered fore-court *Social contact:* design of external facades opens up leisure options for the whole day (skating, street-ball, climbing wall) *Accessibility and usability:* clear layout; lowering the playing level enables level entrance; ramp from ground level to basement	• Bicycle parking: 25 m² • Exist. plot ratio: 1.4 • Gross floor area, new building: 6500 m² • Unsealed ground: approx. 20% of plot • Rooftop planting: approx. 60% of covered area
Plot	*Area of plot:* footprint reduced by superimposing different types of sport and multiple uses *Open areas:* extensive rooftop planting	• Daylight autonomy: 4% • Ventilation: mechanical, 100% of floor area
Design	*Building culture:* public building represents "gateway" into town; signal effect of complete PV south facade; differentiated green colouring of different facades creates specific identity and references to surrounding landscape; roof landscape visible due to surrounding topography	• U-values, bldg. envelope[1] [W/m²K]: R 0.27, E 0.36, W 1.5, O 2.5, G 0.38
Well-being/ health	*Safety/security:* rebound walls around sports arena; smoke/fumes fan with 10-fold air change rate *Sound:* low-noise ventilation system *Light:* optimised proportions of roof and facade openings; illumination via translucent rooflights guarantees non-glare, even illumination; artificial lighting concept generates 1000 lx on playing area (TV-compatible); light-coloured surfaces to ceiling and structure (degree of reflection > 70%) *Interior air:* cross-ventilation possible; non-draughty displacement ventilation *Interior climate:* exposed thermal masses: max. summer temp. 27°C; VIP areas partly air-conditioned (cooling)	• Building costs, cost groups 300–400: 7.15M EUR • Ratio of cost groups 300/400: approx. 80/20 • Building costs: approx. 1100 EUR/m² gross floor area • Active solar areas: PV 525 m²
Building fabric	*Structure:* robust materials internally and externally *Building layout/fitting-out:* flexibility of use due to tele-scoping spectator seating; multi-functional, divisible arena	
Operating and maintenance costs	*Operation & maintenance:* low energy costs; ventilation concept cuts annual operating costs by about 36% (compared to conventional systems) *Repairs:* clear separation between loadbearing structure & fitting-out	• Competition
Operating energy	*Building heating:* compact building; entrance lobby; pre-conditioned fresh air; extract system with heat recovery; efficient radiant ceiling panels *Building cooling:* ground exchanger for basic load (everyday oper-ation); additional 180 W refrigeration unit to cover peak loads (major events) *Air management:* minimised air change rate (2.5) due to displacement ventilation; fewer fans – extract system exploits thermal currents *Lighting:* excellent daylighting; artificial lighting concept based on fluorescent tubes (basic illumination) plus additional metal halide lamps (1000 lx) *Coverage of energy requirements:* 4 ground exchangers each 50 m long – cooling output approx. 70 kW, heating output approx. 90 kW; electricity yield of PV facade min. 24 000 kWh/a; CO_2 emissions cut by approx. 40 t/a due to energy concept	
Process quality	*Integrated planning:* interdisciplinary planning team from competition onwards *Analyses:* extensive daylight and artificial light simulation; thermal-dynamic simulation	• Simulation method

[1] R: roof (heavyweight), E: external walls, W: windows, O: overhead glazing, G: ground slab

Example 11

Training academy

Herne, D, 1999

Architects:
Jourda et Perraudin, Lyon/Paris
Hegger Hegger Schleiff, Kassel
Structural engineers:
Ove Arup & Partners, London
Schlaich Bergermann & Partner, Stuttgart
Energy concept:
Ove Arup & Partners, London
HL-Technik, Munich

The Mont-Cenis Training Academy resulted in a whole city district been restructured: the 25 ha site also includes a landscaped park and a 5 ha residential estate. The glass enclosure of the academy was developed with a footprint of 16 000 m2 as a "microclimatic envelope" for passive solar energy gains, beneath which the various parts of the facility are accommodated as separate units. Photovoltaic glass modules cover about half of the roof and facade surfaces and are integral components in the design concept; apart from generating electricity, they also provide sunshading and control the amount of incoming daylight. In order to realise a "clouds effect", the modules were installed in different densities. Opening lights in the centre of the roof act as vents. The protection from the weather and the solar energy gains result in a mild climate, which makes the glass enclosure usable as an external space and reduces the energy requirements of the buildings within it. The building envelopes of the structures within the glass enclosure need to be neither airtight nor rainproof, and simple forms of construction are therefore possible. Heated areas are saved because large sections of the access zones have been transferred to the glass enclosure. The warm air that builds up beneath the glass roof can be used to save additional heating energy in winter. Loadbearing structure and facade construction are in timber, a renewable resource. The energy concept also includes a co-generation plant, which uses the methane escaping from the former mine shafts to generate electricity. As large quantities of gas are available during overcast periods of low atmospheric pressure, the plant then compensates for the low solar yields. With optimum control of the systems, the total energy requirement is approx. 32 kWh/m²a.

📖 Architectural Review 10/1999
    Hagemann, Ingo: Gebäudeintegrierte
    Photovoltaik. Cologne 2002

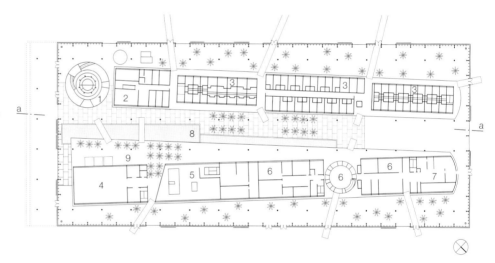

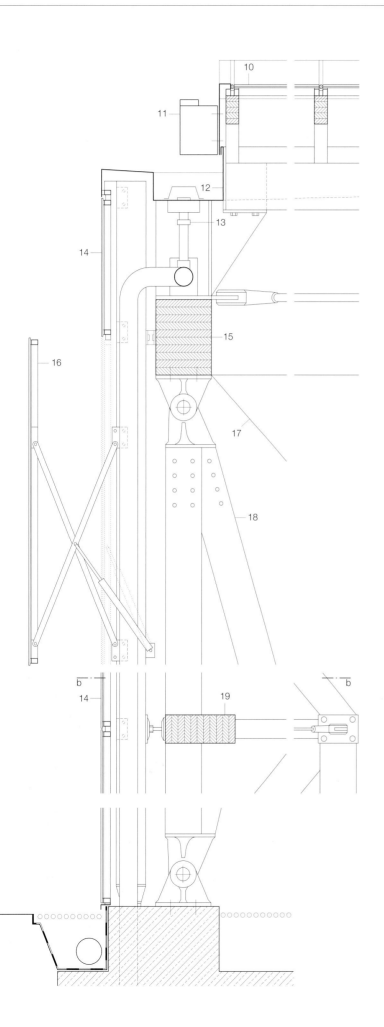

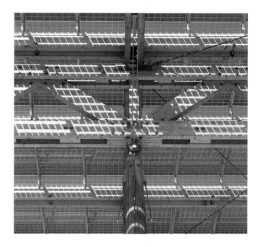

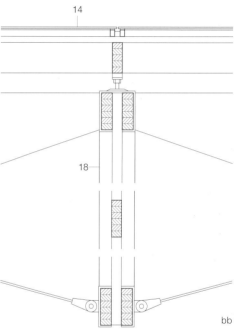

bb

Plan   Scale 1:1500
Vertical section · Horizontal section
Scale 1:20

1   Library
2   Municipal offices
3   Hotel/apartments
4   Assembly hall
5   Casino, leisure area
6   Training academy
7   Training academy offices
8   Water feature
9   Timber terrace

10   Roof glazing, laminated safety glass:
      6 mm extra-clear heat-strengthened glass
      2 mm photovoltaic cells in casting resin
      8 mm heat-strengthened glass
11   Inverter
12   Galvanised steel gutter
13   Rainwater quick-drain system
14   Facade, single glazing:
      structural sealant glazing on
      160 x 60 mm glulam facade posts
      individual photovoltaic modules in certain areas
15   Glulam edge beam, 300 x 400 mm
16   Opening lights
17   Timber roof girder
18   Timber girder to resist wind forces
19   Glulam facade rail

Example 11

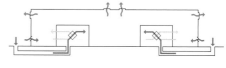

A

B

C

Schematic diagrams of
climate concept
A   Summer
B   Spring/autumn
C   Winter

Section
Scale 1:1000

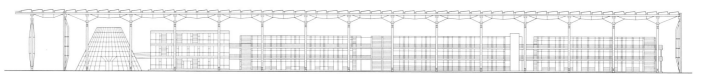

aa

Theme	Qualitative features	Parameters/indicators
Location quality	*Energy availability:* methane *Basic provisions/mixed uses:* academy, hotel, restaurant, sports facilities, community centre, public library, municipal offices *Integration:* regional training facility + local public amenities in low-income area *Usage:* symbol of structural change in region *Mobility:* bicycle parking, rented bicycles in bldg. *Noise/vibration:* less ext. noise due to climate envelope *Radiation:* sealing against methane	• Global radiation: 960 kWh/m²a • Density: 3231 persons/km² • Distance to local public transport: 100 m (bus)
Building quality Access/ communication	*Traffic:* main entrance via urban square *Social contact:* climate envelope as central, public communication space; academy guests and local citizens intermingle; networking via associated stairs and covered walkways *Accessibility and usability:* reception; 24 h public accessibility	• Bicycle parking: 80 m² • Exist. plot ratio: 0.48 • Gross floor area, climate env.: 12 326 m² internal buildings: 14 346 m²
Plot	*Area of plot:* land recycling; former colliery and coking plant *Open areas:* level, elliptical rainwater seepage, "poplar ellipse", with overflow to stream as architectural element	• Unsealed ground: approx. 40% of plot • Ventilation: natural, 100% of floor area,
Design	*Building culture:* termination of a regional green belt; high significance creates local identity in city district	climate env. mechanical 100% of floor area, bldgs.
Well-being/ health	*Safety/security:* clear design of ext. areas/climate envelope; orientation suitable for disabled persons *Sound:* absorbent int. facades *Light:* optimised window proportions; light shelves/HOEs to redirect daylight *Interior air:* ground exchangers for ventilating int. bldgs; natural ventilation of offices/seminar rooms *Interior climate:* high int. air hygiene spec.; exposed thermal masses; intermediate climate in climate envelope	• Operating hours > 26°C/a: approx. 80 h • Projected economic period of use: 50 a • Bldg. costs, cost grp. 300–400: 41.5M EUR buildings (cost group 300: 15.5M EUR;
Building fabric	*Structure:* durable materials/details *Bldg. layout/fitting-out:* separated structure, fitting-out & bldg. services	cost group 400: 5M EUR) climate envelope (cost group 300: 11.5M
Building costs	*Investment costs:* typical building costs for this type of use despite additional climate envelope *Financing:* integral photovoltaic power plant financed by local energy company	EUR; cost group 400: 9.5M EUR incl. PV) • Ratio of cost groups 300/400: 65/35
Operating and maintenance costs	*Operation and maintenance:* investment and operating costs variants analysed during the planning; low energy costs *Repairs:* use of durable materials that age gradually and naturally	• Bldg. costs: 2896 EUR/m² gross floor area • Proportion of renew. raw mat.:
Building materials	*Raw materials (availability):* structure/fit-out in untreated timber *Environmental impact:* planning w. LCA data *Dangerous substances:* checking constituents of fit-out mat. *Deconstruction:* prefab. construction	approx. 50% by vol. • Heating requirement: 56 kWh/m²a • Renew. energy coverage rate: 100%
Operating energy	*Building heating:* reduced energy requirement due to unheated climate envelope, high insulation quality for internal facades, heating via group heating network, ventilation system with heat recovery *Building cooling:* thermal masses in buildings permanently in use, night-time cooling *Hot-water provision:* central via group heating network *Air management:* local for each building, natural ventilation (except kitchen) *Lighting:* controlled via occupancy and brightness sensors *Coverage of energy requirements:* 1 MW$_{peak}$ photovoltaic system integrated into roof and facades, with 1200 kWh battery storage to cover peak loads, methane-fired 2.9 MW co-generation plant (1150kW$_{elec}$ +1740 kW$_{therm}$)	(energy-plus house) • Active solar area: PV 8400 m² • Barrier-free
Infrastructure	*Waste from operation and usage:* recyclable materials collected in basement *Water:* water-saving fittings	• Competition • Low- or zero-emissions building materials • Rainwater/grey water usage
Process quality	*Sustainable building:* model project of the federal state of North Rhine-Westphalia for sustainable, energy-efficient, barrier-free construction *Building tradition:* timber structure is reminiscent of former timber supports in mine galleries *Participation:* local citizens kept informed as part of the project; "open building site" *Integrated planning:* multi-cultural, interdisciplinary planning team with user participation during planning and construction processes *Analyses:* thermal, flow, energy requirement and daylight simulations, wind tunnel tests *Facility Management:* introduced during planning	• Sustainability-oriented benchmarks • Participation concept • Simulation method • FM concept

School

Ladakh, IND, 2001

Architects:
Arup Associates, London
Structural engineers:
Arup & Arup Associates, London
Energy concept:
Arup & Arup Associates, London

Mountains stretching into the distance and the culture of the Tibetan Buddhists characterise the district of Ladakh on the Indian side of the Himalayas. On average, the area is 3500 m above sea level. The climate is extremely dry, and even during the hottest months the temperature can drop to -10°C at night – an extreme temperature gradient. The goal of the London-based architects was to erect a school for 750 boys and girls which besides references to the religion and culture of the region would also reflect the traditional methods of building with local materials in accordance with the climatic conditions. The plan layout of the school complex is based on the form of a mandala, the size and layout on the surrounding village and monastery structures.

The economics of traditional building materials and the use of the solar energy available were optimised with the help of computer simulations and analyses. The use of solar-powered water pumps for irrigation, non-glare light management, natural cross-ventilation and passive shading resulted in virtual self-sufficiency in terms of water and energy supplies. The boarding school rooms on the north side of the complex are heated with Trombe walls – insulating glazing 100–150 mm in front of the black surface of the solid masonry walls. The radiation absorbed during the day is released slowly into the interior; ventilation openings at top and bottom ensure convection currents. All sanitary facilities were placed outside and the traditional form of the dry-composting toilet further developed – a two-chamber system with a dry pit and seepage surface behind a solar-assisted ventilation shaft. The external walls of the building are of stone with loam plaster on the inside; the internal partitions are made from loam bricks. To improve stability during earthquakes, the timber construction supporting the roof is separate from the walls. The supplies of granite, willow and poplar were obtained locally.

☐ Architectural Review 05/2002
Casabella Dec/Jan 2006/2007

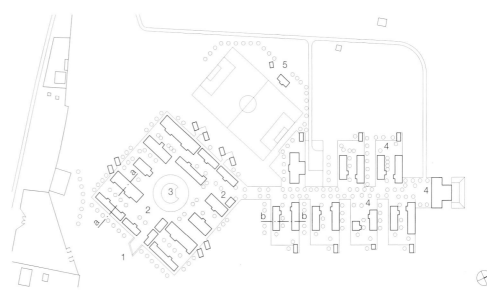

Location drawing
Scale 1:4000

1 Main entrance
2 School
3 Central assembly area
4 Boarding school

5 Central energy supply facility with water borehole and solar pump

Example 12

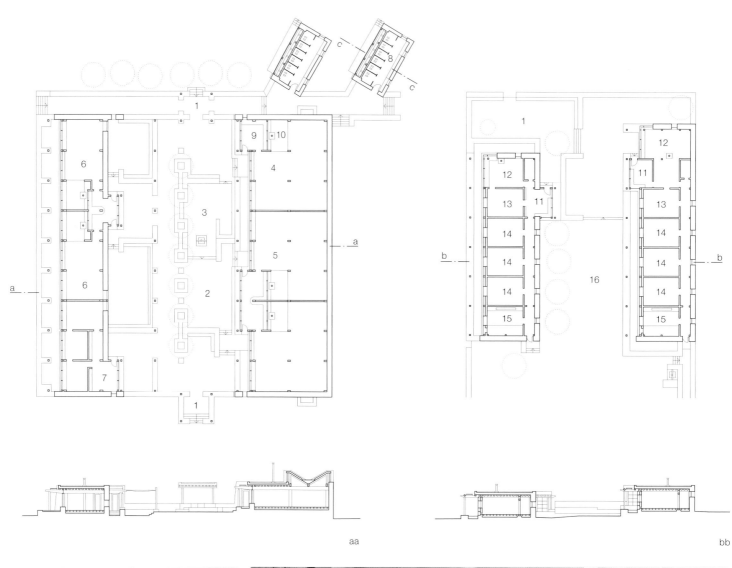

aa   bb

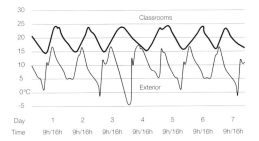

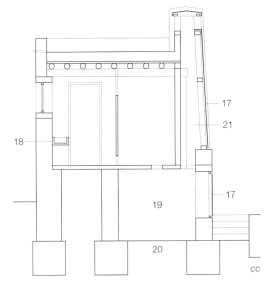

Plans · Sections
school, boarding school
Scale 1:500
Section through sanitary facilities
Scale 1:100
Temperature diagram,
classroom

1 Entrants
2 Open-air classroom
3 Playground with well
4 Nursery
5 Kindergarten
6 Classroom
7 Staff room
8 Sanitary facilities
9 Lobby with lockers
10 Heated rest room
11 Entrance lobby
12 Living room
13 Bedroom, teacher
14 Bedroom, pupil
15 Washroom
16 Internal courtyard

17 Galvanised steel sheet,
   dark paint finish
18 Communal wash basin
19 Dry pit
20 Seepage surface
21 Ventilation shaft

Theme	Qualitative features	Parameters/indicators
Location quality	*Energy availability:* 3500 m above sea level; high temperature fluctuations (down to -10°C even during summer nights); very dry and windy; hardly any public infrastructure (no electricity, water or sewage) *Basic provisions/mixed uses:* masterplan includes vocational workshops, computer workstations, kitchen and medical centre plus school and boarding school *Integration:* schooling for all social groups and all ages from kindergarten to high school; accommodation for pupils from remote villages *Solidarity/justice:* development aid project; support and vocational qualifications for low-income rural populations *Mobility:* near to main road; bus stop	· Global radiation: approx. 1800 kWh/m²a · Climate data relevant to the location: external air temp. in winter as low as -30°C · Density: 3 persons/km²
Building quality Access/ communication	*Social contact:* central assembly area; sports ground; library; open-air classrooms; playground; rest room; communal living areas	· Gross floor area, new building: 4445 m² · Unsealed ground: approx. 40% of plot
Plot	*Open areas:* vegetation guarantees protection from sun and wind; hardstandings mainly unsealed	· Ventilation: natural, 100% of floor area · Building costs, cost groups 300–400:
Design	*Building culture:* building based on the appearance of local monastery and village structures; direct reference due to the use of granite from the vicinity *Personalisation:* innovations in the contexts of "low-tech" (building materials) and "high-tech" (optimisation through simulation)	1.9M EUR · Ratio of cost groups 300/400: approx. 93/7 · Building costs: 430 EUR/m² gross floor area
Well-being/ health	*Safety/security:* seismic-resistant roof construction *Light:* large areas of south-facing glazing; even, non-glare daylight illumination of classrooms due to additional northern light; bright surfaces to walls and soffits *Interior air:* cross-ventilation in classrooms; solar-powered ventilation of sanitary facilities *Interior climate:* passive shading, internal courtyards protected from the wind	· Proportion of renew. raw mat.: 40% by vol. · Renew. energy coverage rate: 100%
Building fabric	*Structure:* selection of robust, ageing-resistant materials and forms of construction *Building layout/fitting-out:* solid construction; flexible classrooms; minimal building services; sanitary facilities in separate building	· Low- or zero-emissions building materials · Register of building materials · Rainwater/grey water usage
Building costs	*Investment costs:* low building costs; minimisation of capital outlay *Financing:* approx. 40% from donations	
Operating and maintenance costs	*Operation and maintenance:* low operating, maintenance and energy costs *Repairs:* easy-to-repair and replaceable assemblies and details; minimal plant	
Building materials	*Raw materials (availability):* primarily renewable or local building materials such as wood, loam, stone *Environmental impact:* low embodied energy *Deconstruction:* partially detachable connections	
Operating energy	*Building heating:* maximum exploitation of solar gains; classrooms face south-east; entrance lobby; Trombe wall; wood stoves *Building cooling:* thermal masses; overhanging eaves *Lighting:* no artificial lighting in classrooms *Coverage of energy requirements:* PV for water pump and electrical equipment; biomass (wood)	
Infrastructure	*Water:* water supply from groundwater (30 m deep); storage tank; dry composting toilets; grey water used for irrigation	
Process quality	*Sustainable building:* model project for sustainable development; self-sufficiency in energy supplies; conveying the idea of sustainability as part of school curriculum *Building tradition:* choice of materials, form of construction and details based on local building traditions and methods; knowledge transfer *Participation:* self-help; integration of local craftsmen and day labourers into the building process *Integrated planning:* 2-year study of conditions specific to the location; interdisciplinary in situ planning team made up of engineers and architects *Analyses:* Trombe wall; daylight and thermal-dynamic simulation	· Sustainability-oriented benchmarks · Participation concept · Simulation method

Example 13

Hotel and tourism institute

Montreal, CAN, 2005

Architects:
Lapointe Magne & Ædifica, Montreal
Michel Lapointe, Robert Magne
Assistants:
Guy Favreau, Jean-Luc Vadeboncoeur
Structural engineers:
Les Consultants Géniplus, Montreal

The building complex for the Quebec Tourism & Hotel Institute (ITHQ) contains a total floor area of 21 000 m² and was originally built in 1970. Rising from the four-storey plinth, which fills the whole area of the city-centre plot, is a seven-storey tower which creates an important landmark within the city of Montreal. Part of the ground floor is used as the entrance to an underground station and so this renowned international training centre for the tourism, hotel and restaurant industry also forms part of the public infrastructure in the city. In order to convey to the public the importance and function of this institute in a contemporary way, the interior of the building was thoroughly refurbished and the original, hermetically sealed building envelope of reinforced concrete was upgraded by adding a glass outer leaf to lend the building more transparency and depth. In addition, the use of glass elements in different colours, with different textures, now divides up the building according to its particular functions. The facilities such as restaurant, foyer and lobby on the ground floor, all open to the public, are enclosed totally in glass and are fully visible 24 hours a day. The giant letters printed on the glass to the plinth storeys ensure that the building's functions are visible to the outside world. The protruding balcony elements break up the hotel and offices areas on the longer facades of the central tower. Contrasting with this on the facade facing the Rue Saint-Denis is the alternation between clear and green glass, the appearance of which changes depending on the position of the observer. The double-leaf facade optimises the energy balance of the building: in winter the air masses in the facade cavity are heated up by solar energy gains and fed into the heating system; in summer the hot exhaust air is driven upwards by natural thermal currents and escapes via openings at the top of the facade.

Canadian Architect 05/2006

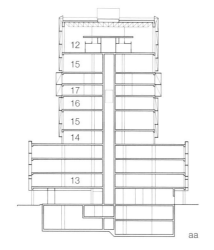

aa

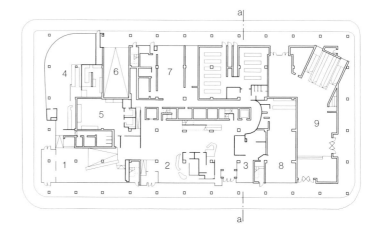

Section
Plans
ground floor
10th floor
Scale 1:1000
Horizontal section · Vertical section
double-leaf facade
Scale 1:20

1 Foyer
2 Hotel lobby
3 School lobby
4 Restaurant
5 Kitchen
6 Access to basement parking
7 Deliveries
8 Students' lounge
9 Entrance to underground station
10 Open-plan offices
11 Individual offices
12 Institute management
13 Classrooms
14 Staff room
15 Plant room
16 Banqueting halls
17 Hotel rooms

18 Facade element, cold-formed alumi-
    nium grid, 475 x 40 x 5 mm, fixed to
19 Steel angle, 50 x 50 x 3 mm
20 Clear glass, 200 x 340 mm
21 Green glass, 55 x 340 mm
22 Patent glazing fixing, 20 x 60 mm
    aluminium hollow section
23 Aluminium channel, 65 x 30 x 3mm,
    black, galvanised
24 Facade post, 100 x 65 x 5 mm steel
    hollow section, black, galvanised
25 Support for facade walkway, 50 x 50
    x 3 mm steel hollow section
26 Loadbearing construction, 150 x 75 x
    5 mm steel hollow section, black
27 Support for facade walkway, 100 x
    200 x 5 mm steel hollow section

28 Expanded metal grid, 700 x 5 mm
29 Glass door as thermal break
30 Single glazing to balcony as
    climatic separation
31 Spandrel panel to balcony, 2 No.
    10 mm lam. safety glass, clamped
    in steel sections
32 Expanded metal grid, 1350 x 5 mm
33 Balcony floor plate, 650 x 5 mm
    sheet steel
34 Balcony support beam, IPE 310
    steel section
35 Cladding to inner leaf, 5 mm sheet
    metal, painted grey
36 Thermal insulation, 140 mm
37 Reinforced concrete, 550 mm
38 Double glazing as thermal break

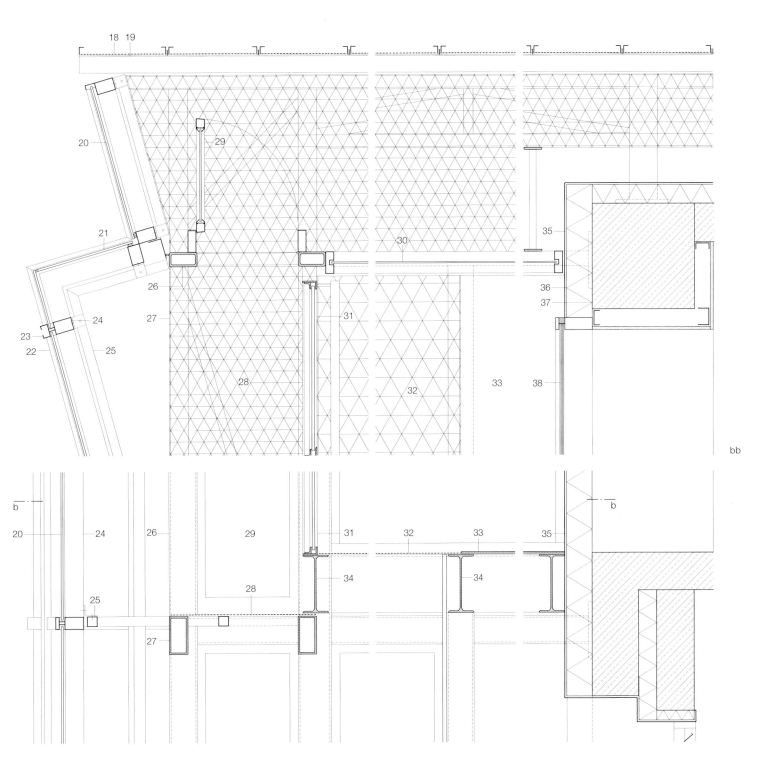

Example 13

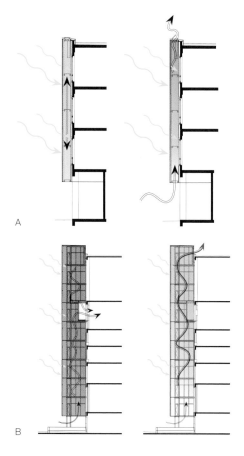

Energy scheme for double-leaf facade
A Plinth, winter/summer
B Tower, winter/summer

Theme	Qualitative features	Parameters/indicators
Location quality	*Energy availability:* natural gas supply *Basic provisions/mixed uses:* city-centre location; amenities for different user groups *Integration:* training hotel, teaching facilities, multimedia documentation centre *Usage:* PR, research and training centre for tourism, hotel and restaurant industry, PR upgrade for location *Mobility:* entrance to underground station integrated into ground floor	• Global radiation: 1200 kWh/m²a • Density: 4439 persons/km² • Distance to local public transport: 0 m (underground trains)
Building quality Access/ communication	*Traffic:* good integration into public infrastructure due to numerous entrances, facade design varies according to compass direction *Social contact:* public areas on ground floor, communication areas, workshop courses (e.g. in demonstration kitchens) *Accessibility and usability:* spacious circulation zones	• Exist. plot ratio: 5.9 • Gross floor area, existing building: 27 000 m² • Ventilation: mechanical, 100% of floor area • Unsealed ground: 0% of plot
Plot	*Area of plot:* continued usage and revitalisation of building stock	• Bldg. costs, cost grp. 300–400: 25M EUR • Building costs: 930 EUR/m² gross floor area
Design	*Building culture:* lifetime of building stock prolonged through conversion, relationships with surroundings reinforced through enhanced transparency (e.g. communication of usage)	• Energy consumption (2002, before refurb.) operating hours: 8108 h/a gas: 3 407 580 kWh/a
Well-being/ health	*Sound:* double-leaf facade cuts noise from outside *Light:* good daylighting levels due to high proportion of glazing *Interior air:* mechanical ventilation; window ventilation possible in hotel; double-leaf facade preheats incoming air *Interior climate:* increase in thermal comfort due to higher surface temperatures of existing facade	electricity: 8 873 794 kWh/a final energy requirement (heating, cooling, lighting, equipment): 455 kWh/m²a
Building fabric	*Structure:* use of building fabric dating from 1970s	• Energy consumption (2005, after refurb.) operating hours: 16 712 h/a
Building costs	*Investment costs:* cost of refurbishment approx. 50% of that for a comparable new building; lower operating costs enable opening times to be doubled, with enhanced services and turnover	gas: 2 871 690 kWh/a electricity: 8 100 000 kWh/a final energy requirement (heating, cooling, lighting, equipment): 406 kWh/m²a
Operating and maintenance costs	*Operation and maintenance:* long-lasting materials chosen for facade; easy-clean surfaces *Repairs:* modular steel construction; simple standard details	• Energy costs: 2002: 1810 EUR/m²a
Building materials	*Dangerous substances:* finishes and floor coverings with fewer dangerous substances (e.g. linoleum) *Deconstruction:* modular steel construction suitable for dismantling	2005: 1755 EUR/m²a • Renew. energy coverage rate: electricity requirement 100%
Operating energy	*Building heating:* energy-efficiency upgrade due to double-leaf facade as climate buffer; ventilation with heat recovery; energy requirement < 40% of national standard *Building cooling:* efficient compression-type refrigeration units *Air management:* fans with lower electricity consumption *Other electrical consumers:* kitchen equipment driven with alternative power (gas) *Coverage of energy requirements:* electricity (100% hydroelectric power)	
Infrastructure	*Waste from operation and usage:* recycling station on each floor; subsequent sorting within building *Water:* use of rainwater and grey water in preparation	• Barrier-free • Choice of low-emissions building materials
Process quality	*Sustainable bldg.:* energy-efficiency upgrade; increased acceptance of bldg. due to distinctive redesign; architectural discussion stimulated through exhibition in local gallery *Bldg. tradition:* further development of industrial prefabrication processes to shorten construction time *Integrated planning:* interdisciplinary planning team (e.g. involvement of restaurant consultant) *Analyses:* thermal-dynamic simulation *Monitoring:* measuring points in preparation *Facility Management:* external	• Simulation method • FM concept

University institute

Freiburg, D, 2006

Architects:
pfeifer. kuhn. architekten, Freiburg
Project team: Alwin Neuss (project manager),
Achim Schneider, Wolfgang Stocker, Johannes
Abele, Bendix Pallesen-Mustikai, Dominic Ikic,
Marcus Hannemann, Sebastian Fiedler
Structural engineers:
Mohnke Bauingenieure, Denzlingen
Energy concept:
Ingenieurbüro Kuder, Flein (building services),
Delzer Kybernetik, Lörrach (simulation)

The Department of Environmental Health Services is the second of six new buildings planned for the university's Faculty of Medicine and is located in the south-western corner of the hospital complex. These buildings are lined up along the so-called Researcher Street and will later be linked via walkways. The internal layout is based on the usage and the associated energy requirements. The supply corridor to the laboratories has been divided into accessible cells with waiting loggias along the northeast facade, which results in a flexible, open internal layout. The open-plan offices facing south-west are interrupted by the conservatories extending over three storeys. The central zone of this block is reserved for access and ventilation shafts.

Optimum use of renewable energy sources is the priority in the building's energy concept. An important element here is the air collector facade plus the conservatories on the southwest side, which collect solar energy and provide natural ventilation to the offices at the same time. During the winter, the air preheated in the collector facade is fed into the offices and extracted via the central shafts which extend up to the roof, where heat recovery takes place. During the summer, the external air, cooled in a ground exchanger, is fed via these same central shafts into the offices and extracted via the collector facade, where natural currents ensue to carry the air upwards to controlled vents at the top of the facade. After consultation with the authorities, it was decided that four air changes per hour would be adequate for the laboratories instead of the eight normally prescribed for mechanical ventilation to such rooms; however, the air change rate can be increased locally if required. This resulted in considerable energy-savings and meant that the size of the ventilation plant could be reduced.

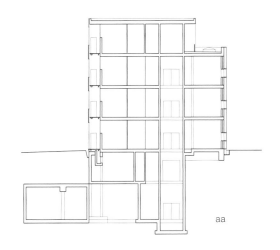

aa

Section · Plan of 1st floor
Scale 1:500

1   Supply corridor
2   Laboratory
3   Office
4   Conservatory

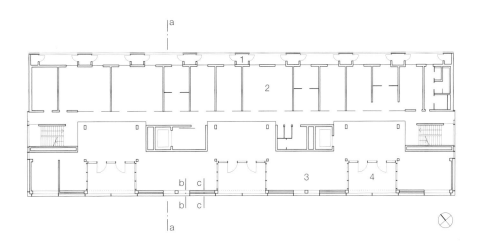

Example 14

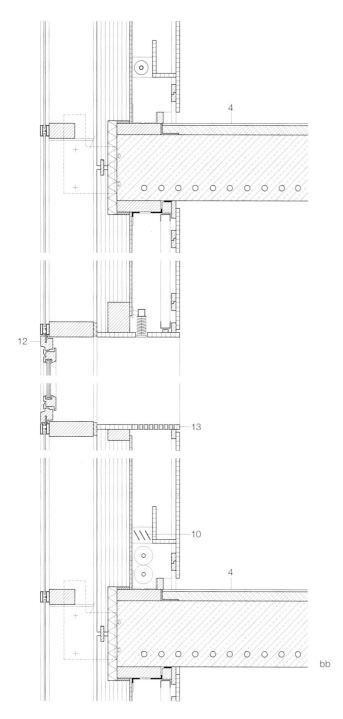

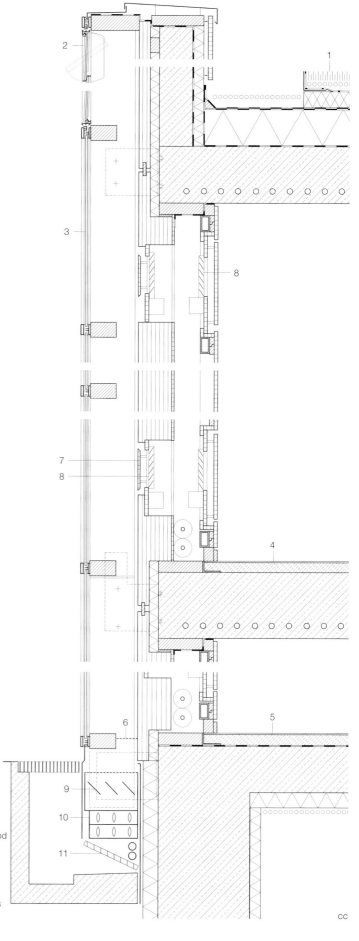

bb

cc

1 Roof construction:
  100 mm vegetation
  filter fleece, drainage mat
  storage mat, root barrier
  waterproofing, polymer-modified bitumen
  sheeting, 2 layers
  200 mm cellular glass thermal insulation
  bitumen undercoat
  300 mm reinforced concrete
2 Vent
3 Wall construction:
  post-and-rail construction with
  8 mm toughened safety glass
  260 mm cavity for air flow
  180 mm edge-glued timber elements
  12 mm OSB
  210 mm cavity for air flow
  50 mm metal stud construction
  25 mm framework
  20 mm 3-ply core plywood

4 Suspended floor construction:
  2 mm PU resin finish
  50 mm separate screed
  350 mm reinforced concrete with
  activation of concrete core
5 Ground floor construction:
  2 mm PU resin finish
  50 mm screed on separating layer
  250 mm reinforced concrete
  100 mm insulation
  100 mm 4/8 gravel
6 Ventilation grille (insect screen)
7 Fascia panel, 15 mm 3-ply core plywood
8 Vent (with motor)
9 Vent
10 Convector
11 Filter
12 Wood/ aluminium window, double
   glazed, 2 No. 4 mm tough. safety glass
13 3-ply core plywood, slotted

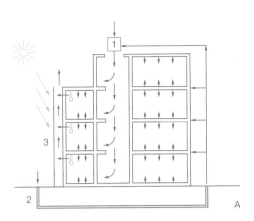

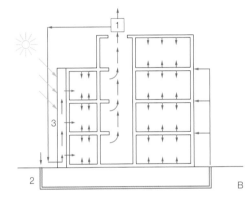

Vertical sections
Scale 1:20
Energy scheme
A Summer
B Winter

1 Heat exchanger
2 Ground exchanger
3 Collector facade

Theme	Qualitative features	Parameters/indicators
Location quality	*Energy availability:* district heating CHP; central cooling network *Usage:* site chosen in the context of the reorganisation concept of the clinical/research institute *Mobility:* central basement parking for all institute buildings (planned) *Noise/vibration:* arrangement of uses according to acoustic requirements, laboratories on road side	• Global radiation: 1160 kWh/m²a • Density: 1411 persons/km² • Distance to local public transport: 50 m (bus); 150 m (tram)
Building quality		
Access/ communication	*Traffic:* access via pedestrianised "Researcher Street"; good links to neighbouring facilities *Social contact:* circulation and access areas designed as communication zones (e.g. library, open tea kitchens)	• Bicycle parking: 40 m² • Gross floor area, new building: 5076 m²
Plot	*Area of plot:* compact structure *Open areas:* minimised ground sealing; infiltration ponds	• Rooftop planting: 90% of covered area • Ventilation: natural, 56% of floor area,
Design	*Building culture:* distinctive collector facade; multiple coding of all components and systems (function, energy, construction, appearance)	mech., 44% of floor area • U-value, bldg. envelope: H'$_T$ 0.55 W/m²K
Well-being/ health	*Safety/security:* good orientation due to clear layout; visual links to labs. (glass walls); 8-fold air change rate in the event of a fire *Sound:* suspended acoustic elements in some areas *Light:* optimised proportion of windows; good level of daylight *Interior air:* ground exchanger; natural ventilation in offices, mechanical in laboratories *Interior climate:* exposed thermal masses; summer temp. max. 26.7°C; "energy gardens"	• Operating hours > 26°C/a: 160 h • Effective heat capacity: 218.5 Wh/m²flr. area
Building fabric	*Structure:* materials chosen taking into account durability *Building layout/fitting-out:* frame construction with stiffening cores; flexible internal layout; shafts easily accessible for maintenance	• Building costs, cost groups 300–400: 7.084M EUR • Ratio of cost groups 300/400: 61/39
Building costs	*Investment costs:* life-cycle costing *Financing:* assistance from innovation fund	• Building costs: 1395 EUR/m² gross floor area
Operating and maintenance costs	*Operation and maintenance:* very low operating, maintenance and energy costs *Repairs:* low-maintenance surfaces; good access and easy replacement of components and building services	• Operating costs: 20.26 EUR/m² floor area p.a. • Energy costs: 22.77 EUR/m² floor area p.a.
Building materials	*Raw materials (availability):* wood is the preferred building material (180 mm edge-glued facade), concrete, glass	
Operating energy	*Building heating:* compact volume; passive solar gains from collector facade and "energy gardens"; pre-conditioned fresh air; extract system with heat recovery; heat pump; activation of building components; additional radiators for periods of extremely cold weather only *Building cooling:* north-south orientation with corresponding proportion of windows; high heat capacity; night-time cooling; heat pump; sorption-type refrigeration unit; activation of building components *Hot-water provision:* cold water only in the WCs *Air management:* minimised air change rate (4 instead of 8); thermal currents in air collector reduce number of extract fans needed *Lighting:* daylight sensors; occupancy detectors *Coverage of energy requirements:* ground exchanger; air collector; electricity requirements covered by "green electricity"; PV yield approx. 20 000 kWh/a	• Heating requirement: 47.6 kWh/m²a • Primary energy requirement (Q), space heating and hot water: 26.8 kWh/m²a • Q cooling: 7.5 kWh/m²a • Q air management: 12.0 kWh/m²a • Q lighting: 31.0 kWh/m²a • Active solar area: PV 145 m²
Infrastructure	*Waste from operation and usage:* connected to underground hospital supply street, automatic supply and disposal system, central waste collection depot *Water:* tanks; great water used for flushing toilets and watering gardens; waterless urinals	• Barrier-free • Competition • Rainwater/grey water usage
Process quality	*Sustainable building:* model project; ecologically oriented competition stipulations: sparing of resources (materials and energy), use of rainwater *Integrated planning:* from competition onwards *Analyses:* cyber-netic design approach; daylight simulation, thermal-dynamic simulation *Monitoring:* 12 months (relative humidity, temperature)	• Sustainability-oriented benchmarks • Simulation method • Monitoring

Example 15

Institute building

Dübendorf, CH, 2006

Architects:
Bob Gysin + Partner, Zurich
Assistants:
Rudolf Trachsel, Marco Giuliani,
Daniel Leuthold, Reto Vincenz
Structural engineers:
Henauer Gugler, Zurich
Energy concept:
3-Plan Haustechnik, Winterthur

Among the research buildings of the Swiss Federal Institute of Technology in Zurich, the one for the Water Research Institute stands out thanks to its envelope of silk-screen-printed blue glass louvres. The homogeneous envelope structure is interrupted only by the fairface concrete entrance. With a volume measuring 38 500 m³, this compact office building is regarded as one of the largest zero-energy structures in Europe. And with the help of numerous dynamic simulations (ventilation, thermal currents, shading, smoke), it was possible to keep the temperature between 20 and 26.5°C without active cooling or conventional heating.

The heart of the building is the internal atrium, which rises above the general roof level. The offices, meeting rooms and lecture theatres are arranged around this. Daylight can reach the inside of the building via the glazed roof of the atrium, which also functions as a climate buffer. During the hotter months of the year, the heat stored in heavyweight components such as concrete floors, flooring cement and loam walls dissipates at night via vents in the offices into the atrium where it can escape via the roof. During the winter, the heat stored in the building components is slowly released into the interior. The glass louvres of the outer leaf control the incoming radiation; the inner, sealed leaf made from prefabricated, highly insulated timber elements prevents the undesirable infiltration of heat and cold from outside. The fresh-air supply, the removal of pollutants and the heat balance are regulated by the central ventilation plant. The outside air passes through a ground exchanger, heat recovery and filter processes. One-third of the electricity requirement is covered by the photovoltaic installation on the roof, the remainder is drawn from the total network in this area. Rainwater is collected on the green roof and used for flushing the toilets.

Werk, Bauen und Wohnen 11/2006

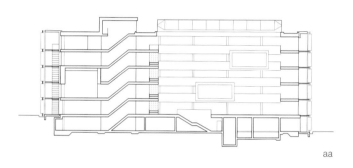

aa

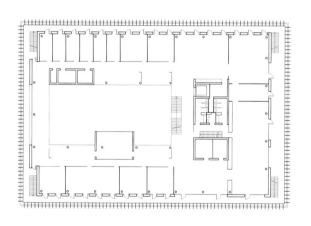

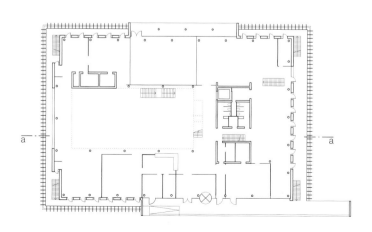

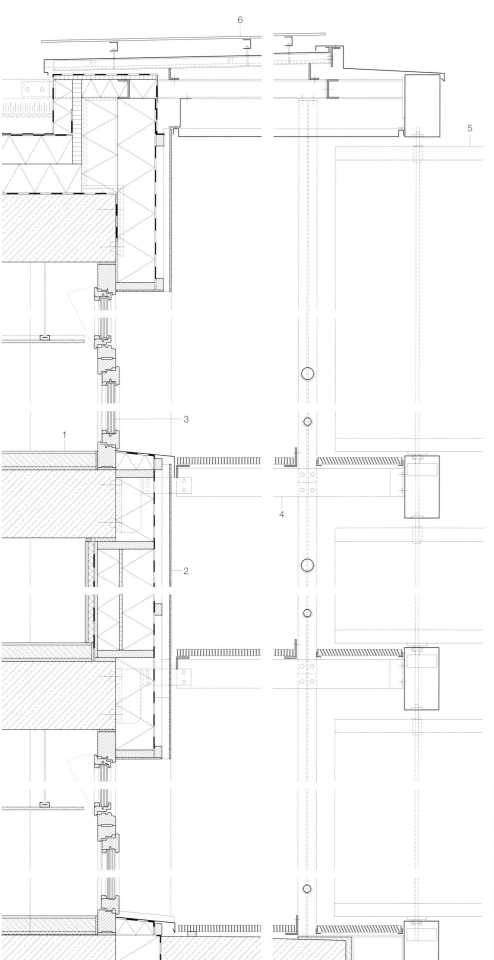

Section · Plans
ground floor
1st floor
Scale 1:750
Vertical section
Scale 1:20

1   Ground floor construction:
    10–12 mm flooring cement
    70–68 mm cement topping with glass fibre
    reinforcement
    20 mm impact sound insulation
    360 mm reinforced concrete with conventional
    reinforcement
2   Wall construction, U = 0.114 W/m²K:
    8 mm fibre-cement sheeting
    40 x 60 mm battens
    40 x 60 mm counter battens/40 mm ventilation
    cavity
    waterproof sheeting, diffusion-permeable
    180 mm mineral wool thermal insulation
    15 mm wood-fibre board, diffusion-permeable
    120 mm mineral wool insulation
    15 mm gypsum fibreboard
    vapour barrier, PE sheeting
    30 mm mineral-fibre board
    17 mm MDF acoustic board, grooved
3   Window element:
    spruce frame
    triple glazing, 6 mm float glass + 12 mm cavity +
    5 mm tough. safety glass + 12 mm cavity +
    4 mm float glass, U = 0.5 W/m²K
4   Steel flat, 150 x 10 mm, hot-dip galvanised
5   Glass louvre with silk-screen printing
6   Photovoltaic element

Example 15

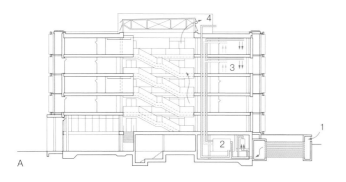

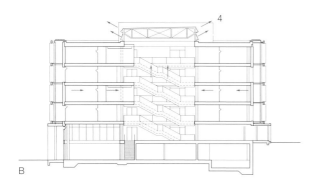

A

B

Ventilation scheme
A   Ventilating
B   Night-time cooling

1   Fresh-air reservoir,
    ground exchanger
2   Central ventilation plant

3   Expelled air with heat
    recovery
4   Natural ventilation/exhaust air

Theme	Qualitative features	Parameters/indicators
Location quality	*Energy availability:* district heating CHP (energy drawn only during periods of very low external temperatures); central cooling network *Basic provisions/mixed uses:* kindergarten on the plot for the children of employees *Usage:* choice of location is an obvious extension of the existing EAWAG and EMPA research facilities *Mobility:* fewer car parking spaces (6 spaces for visitors, no new allocations)	• Global radiation: 1300 kWh/m²a • Density: 1671 persons/km² • Distance to local public transport: 200 m (tram, planned); 700 m (regional trains)
Building quality Access/ communication	*Traffic:* grounds open to the public; good pathways to neighbouring buildings; striking main entrance *Social contact:* atrium provides orientation and space for informal meetings; restaurant; library; seminar and teaching rooms *Accessibility and usability:* all floors barrier-free, disabled WCs	• Bicycle parking: 60 m² • Gross floor area, new building: 8533 m² • Rooftop planting: 55% of covered area • Ventilation: mechanical, 100% of floor area
Plot	*Area of plot:* compact building *Open areas:* natural-type landscaped areas, indigenous vegetation; planned rehabilitation of adjoining Chriesbach stream; low proportion of ground sealing; water features	• U-values, bldg. envelope[1] [W/m²K]: R: 0.10, E: 0.11, W: 0.7, G: 0.13
Design	*Building culture:* viable sustainability concept, primary energy cut by a factor of 4 (corresponds to vision of "2000 Watt Society") *Personalisation:* open interior space for communication which helps identification	• Building costs, cost groups 300–400[2]: 13.43M EUR • Building costs: 1575 EUR/m² gross floor area
Well-being/ health	*Safety/security:* good visual links; perimeter escape balconies; sprinklers *Sound:* acoustic glass between offices/atrium, sound-attenuating office walls (perforated) *Light:* light-redirecting glass louvres; separate glare protection; offices lit from 2 sides *Interior air:* ground exchanger; mech. supply/extract air *Interior climate:* ext. sunshades; exposed thermal masses; loam walls in some areas; night-time cooling	• Heating requirement: 14.4 kWh/m²a • Primary energy requirement (Q), space heating and hot water: 2.7 kWh/m²a • Q cooling: 1.2 kWh/m²a • Q electricity: 48.6 kWh/m²a
Building fabric	*Structure:* very hardwearing floor finishes (flooring cement) and weather protection leaf (glass louvres) *Building layout/fitting-out:* frame construction; flexible office layouts; consistent separation of loadbearing structure/fitting-out/building services	• Renew. energy coverage rate: 46% • Active solar areas: solar thermal 50 m², PV 459 m²
Operating and maintenance costs	*Operation and maintenance:* very low energy and operating costs *Repairs:* easily accessible shafts, flexible building services; selection of low-maintenance materials and surfaces	• Barrier-free
Building materials	*Raw materials (availability):* recycled aggregate concrete; prefabricated timber external walls; loam partitions *Environmental impact:* low embodied energy (43 201 GJ); stipulation: 5000 MJ/m² gross floor area *Dangerous substances:* individual checks of all building materials; avoidance of solvents *Deconstruction:* deconstruction concept embodied in draft design	• Competition • Low- or zero-emissions building materials • Register of building materials • Deconstruction concept • Rainwater/grey water usage
Operating energy	*Building heating:* minimised transmission heat losses due to compactness, high standard of insulation, airtight envelope, thermal zoning (offices 20°C, circulation zones 18°C); buffer zones; no conventional heating plant (preheating of incoming air, use of waste heat from servers); extract system with heat recovery *Building cooling:* tracking sunshades; night-time cooling; high heat capacity; pre-conditioned fresh air; cooling ceilings in seminar rooms *Air management:* minimised air change rate *Lighting:* daylight sensors; occupancy detectors *Other electrical consumers:* energy-efficient appliances *Coverage of energy requirements:* 80 ground exchangers each 20 m long; yields: vacuum-tube collectors 24 000 kWh/a, PV 60 300 kWh/a	
Infrastructure	*Water:* green roof; water features; waterless urinals; no-mix WCs (rainwater usage)	
Process quality	*Sustainable bldg.:* model project; exemplary competition spec.: sparing of resources, zero-energy bldg., PV to provide 33% of electricity needs, rainwater usage *Integrated planning:* from competition onwards; early integration of general contractor *Analyses:* comprehensive simulations *Monitoring:* 2 years	• Sustainability-oriented benchmarks • Simulation method • Monitoring

[1] R: roof (average), E: external walls (average), W: windows, G: ground slab [2] Figures correspond to CHF 22.07m (Swiss building costs schedule No. 2)

Office building

Landshut, D, 2003

Architects:
Hascher Jehle Architektur, Berlin
Project team:
Thomas Weber, Thomas Breunig, Carsten
Burghardt, Andreas Dalhoff, Matthias Rempen,
Friedrich Rohdich, Ulrike von Schenk
Structural engineers:
Seeberger, Friedl & Partner, Munich
Energy concept:
Climaplan GmbH, Munich

The social security organisation for agricultural
and forestry workers purchased a 30 000 m²
plot on the edge of Landshut in order to unite
its four divisions (pensions, health insurance,
nursing insurance, employees' compensation
scheme) under one roof. The extensive building complex essentially comprises three elements: the east-west office wings at 90° to the
120 m long "thoroughfare" which widens out as
it meets the raised convex block in the eastern
corner housing entrance, meeting rooms and
library. Whereas the loadbearing structures to
the office wings consist of reinforced concrete
frames which allow the interior to be divided up
flexibly, the thoroughfare is built from timber
from local forests. The curving glued laminated
timber beams of the southern facade are carried by tree-like columns of glued laminated
timber up to 17 m tall; timber walkways at every
floor level link the office wings together. Conceived as a noise barrier and thermal buffer
zone, the natural ventilation of the building and
activation of heat thermal masses form the
main parameters for the summertime climate
concept of the glass thoroughfare. The thermal
currents are assisted by fresh-air openings at
the base of the south-facing facade and
exhaust-air vents along the northern edge of
the roof. The convex block at the eastern end
provides a certain amount of shadow to reduce
the build-up of heat, and a ventilation cavity in
the internal sunshades prevents further heat
building up within the building. Radiant panels
fitted below the walkways plus underfloor heating and convector heaters prevent cold air
descending down the facade in the winter and
thus increasing the flow velocity. On the whole,
the energy figures of the building complex are
well below the stipulations of the Energy Conservation Act.

AIT 12/2003
db 04/2005

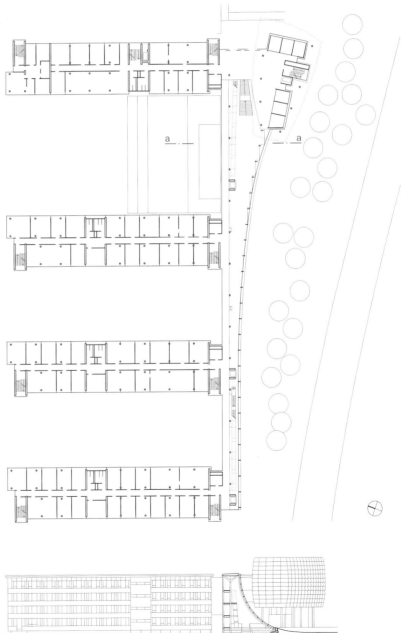

Plan of ground floor · Section Scale 1:1000

Example 16

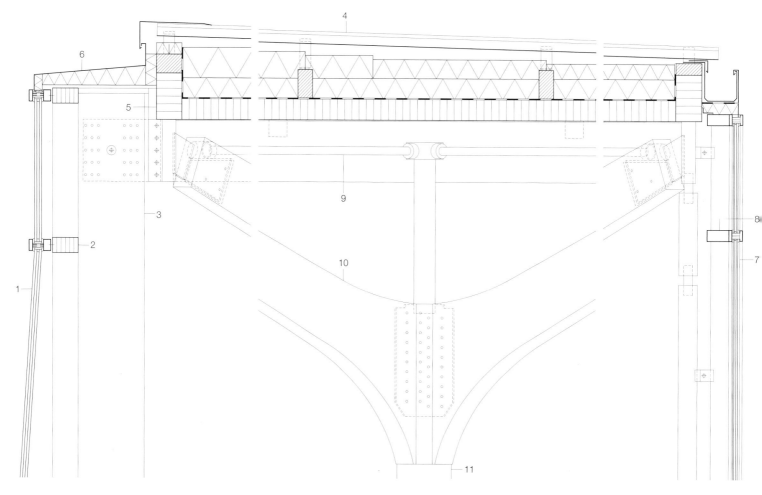

Vertical sections
Scale 1:20

1 Solar-control glazing:
   4000 x 1650 mm, fixed at 2 points top
   and bottom, lateral joints with seal but
   no patent glazing fixing
2 Glulam rail, 80 x 140 mm, inclined at
   11° to curved beams
3 Glulam curved beam, 140 x 360 mm,
   bottom section as circular arc with
   gluing in curved jigs
4 Roof construction:
   1.5 mm aluminium standing seam roof
   covering
   180–260 mm insulation laid to falls
   vapour barrier
   100 mm edge-glued timber elements
   2 No. 6 x 330 mm steel flat supports

5 Roof edge beam, glulam,
   140 x 240 mm
6 Parapet, bent aluminium sheet
7 Low E glazing
8 Post-and-rail construction, steel, with
   walkways connected to tension member (Ø101.6 mm steel hollow section)
9 Bracing, Ø44 mm steel hollow sections
10 Column head with 4 cantilever arms,
   glulam, 140 x 280–840 mm
11 Column, glulam, Ø300 mm
12 Steel plate, 300–350 x 600 x 10 mm,
   let into timber, cast into fair-face
   reinforced concrete plinth
13 Vent
14 Stainless steel with weather protection
15 Steel grille

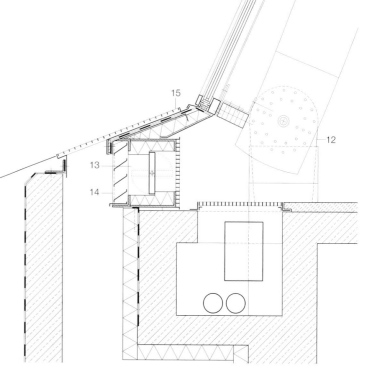

Theme	Qualitative features	Parameters/indicators
Location quality	*Usage:* attractive rural environment with adjoining urban, commercial and ex-military functions; availability of land enabled all company divisions to be united *Noise/vibration:* thoroughfare adjacent to main road to Landshut screens offices against road noise	• Global radiation: 1100 kWh/m²a • Density: 944 persons/km² • Distance to local public transport: 200 m
Building quality Access/ communication	*Traffic:* compact parking layout taking into account existing vegetation; striking design for entrance area *Social contact:* quiet int. courtyards; thoroughfare serves as foyer, main access route & canteen, provides space for informal meetings *Access. & usability:* clear bldg. layout, usability & organisation of lifts	• Bicycle parking: 80 m² • Exist. plot ratio: 0.6 • Gross floor area, new building: 18 000 m² • Unsealed ground: 65% of plot • Ventilation: natural, 95% of floor area,
Plot	*Area of plot:* revitalisation of former military barracks *Open areas:* position of building ensures that the roadside trees are preserved; diversity of species encouraged by water features and diverse planting; specific themes between office wings	mech. 5% of floor area • U-values, bldg. envelope¹ [W/m²K]: R: 0.23, E: 0.27, W: 1.4, G: 0.44
Design	*Building culture:* raised convex block and thoroughfare create significant landmarks; office wings create a reference to the neighbouring military barracks; complex geometry of southern facade and supporting structure due to extensive form-finding process	• Building costs, cost groups 300–400: 24.5M EUR • Ratio of cost groups 300/400: 73/27 • Building costs: 1360 EUR/m² gross floor
Well-being/ health	*Safety/security:* appropriate sizing of sections means that no fire compartments are necessary despite timber construction *Sound:* acoustic ceilings in conference hall and meeting rooms *Light:* good daylighting; east-west orientation of office wings; individual offices with high-level windows on corridor side *Interior air:* natural cross-ventilation in thoroughfare; window ventilation in offices; mechanical ventilation to meeting areas, canteen, kitchen *Interior climate:* offices with external sunshades; comprehensive measures guarantee thermal comfort in thoroughfare – internal sunshades with ventilation cavity; winter temp. > 18°C; prevention of descending cold air (e.g. underfloor heating, radiant ceiling panels); water feature creates pleasant microclimate in canteen area	area • Heating requirement: 60.0 kWh/m²a • Barrier-free • Competition • Rainwater/grey water usage
Building fabric	*Building layout/fitting-out:* functionally self-sufficient wings; flexible usage possible	
Building costs	*Investment costs:* economic offices layout; efficient loadbearing structure; all office wings identical	
Operating and maintenance costs	*Operation and maintenance:* energy costs cut by about 15% (compared to conventional office buildings) *Repairs:* accessible shafts	
Building materials	*Raw materials (availability):* regional timber (e.g. roof structure, loadbearing structure to thoroughfare, window, wood-block flooring) *Environmental impact:* CO₂ emissions cut by 110 t (comparison of timber and steel structures for thoroughfare)	
Operating energy	*Bldg. heating:* thermal zoning, buffer zone, solar gains in thoroughfare *Bldg. cooling:* shade from other parts of building/existing trees taken into account; exposed thermal masses; natural ventilation in thoroughfare; evaporative cooling via water feature; solar-control glazing; effective sunshades; night-time cooling	
Infrastructure	*Water:* rainwater used for watering gardens	
Process quality	*Building tradition:* promotion of regional timber building tradition *Integrated planning:* interdisciplinary development of thoroughfare – form-finding, thermodynamics, efficient loadbearing structure *Analyses:* daylighting, shading and flow simulation; thermal-dynamic simulation	• Simulation method

¹ R: roof (average), E: external walls (average), W: windows (office wings, thoroughfare), G: ground slab

Example 17

Office building

Cambridge, USA, 2003

Architects:
Behnisch, Behnisch & Partner,
Stuttgart/Venice
Project team:
Martin Werminghausen (project manager),
Maik Neumann; Tim Krebs, Claus Mihm,
Sarah Straubenmueller
Structural & building services engineers:
Buro Happold, Bath/New York
Lighting consultant:
Bartenbach Lichtlabor, Aldrans

This new headquarters for a biotechnology company is intended to allow the 920 employees and visitors to identify with the company, and combine functionality and flexibility with pleasant, communicative working conditions and modern environmental technology. Stringent urban planning stipulations led to a restrained building envelope. Prefabricated, single-leaf curtain walls alternating with double-leaf facades with accessible "loggias" as climate buffers and "live" spaces, windows that can be opened both manually and electrically for natural night-time ventilation, movable sunshading elements and coloured curtains combine energy-efficiency aspects with architectural and spatial differentiation.

A complex, graduated atrium flooded with light, which extends through all floors, forms the heart of the building. Seven computer-controlled heliostats on the roof direct the light into the atrium via a fixed bridge of mirrors. Pivoting prismatic louvres scatter the incoming daylight and prevent excessive heat infiltration through complete reflection of the direct sunlight. In the atrium, freely suspended panels split up the light into its spectral components, and vertical louvres distribute the light throughout the open area. Further reflective surfaces such as stainless steel panels and water features in the spacious lobby direct daylight deep into the interior. The atrium also serves as a giant ventilation space. Fresh air is blown into the offices via windows in the climate facade or via ventilation inlets in the ceilings, then channelled into the atrium due to the pressure difference and expelled via extractor fans fitted in the glass roof. The heating and cooling plant is operated with waste heat from the power plant located just two blocks away which is fitted with modern emissions filters. Rainwater tanks cover the requirement for cooling water and irrigation of the green roof.

📖 Architectural Review 04/2004
Steele, James: Genzyme Center.
Stuttgart, 2004

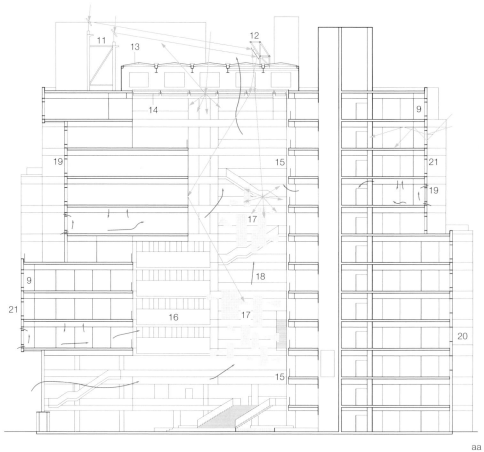

aa

1	Reading zone
2	Atrium
3	Water feature
4	Garden
5	Reception
6	Work areas
7	Lecture theatre
8	Deliveries
9	Loggia
10	Tea kitchen
11	Tracking heliostat with 1600 x 1600 mm mirror
12	Fixed bridge of mirrors
13	Rooflight with low E glazing and extractor fans
14	Prismatic tracking, pivoting louvres, perspex
15	"Light wall" made from highly reflective, computer-controlled vertical louvres
16	Stainless steel panels
17	"Chandeliers" in the form of 16 "mobiles" with a total of 768 freely moving, light-scattering tiles
18	Exhaust-air ventilation due to stack effect
19	Ventilation openings
20	Opening windows
21	Double-leaf facade

Section
Scale 1:500
Section through
atrium roof
Scale 1:250
Plans
1st floor
4th floor
Scale 1:1000

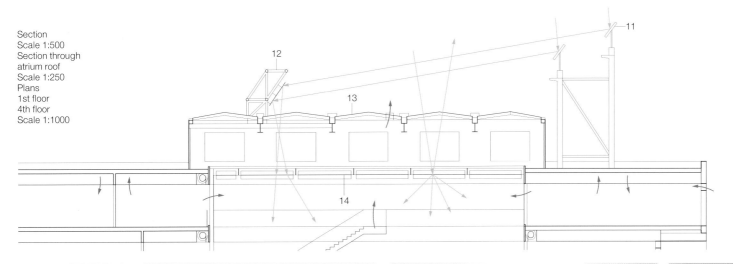

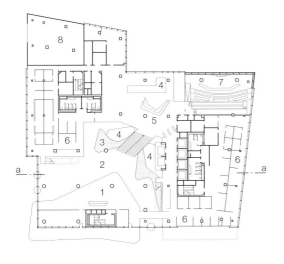

Example 17

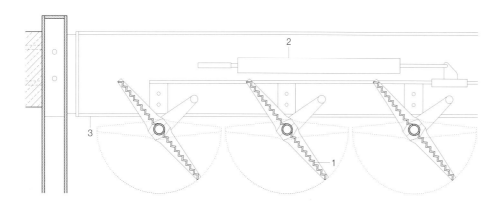

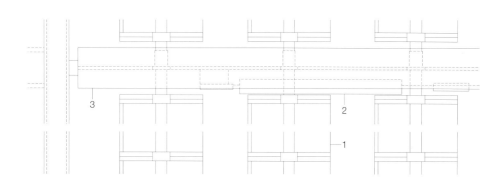

Light-redirecting louvres
Scale 1:20

1 Prismatic tracking, pivoting louvres, perspex
2 Drive for louvres
3 Steel I-beam between louvres

Theme	Qualitative features	Parameters/indicators
Location quality	*Energy availability:* district heating CHP *Basic provisions/mixed uses:* public facilities on ground floor (e.g. shops, café) *Usage:* choice of location promotes development of a new local centre; Harvard University and Massachusetts Institute of Technology (MIT) can be reached on foot *Mobility:* company vehicle fleet with 4 hybrid cars, charging point for electric cars	• Global radiation: approx. 1450 kWh/m²a • Density: 6086 persons/km² • Distance to local public transport: approx. 500 m (underground trains)
Building quality Access/ communication	*Traffic:* basement parking, for bicycles too (with changing rooms, showers) *Social contact:* numerous communication and meeting areas: company canteen on 12th floor; gardens; library; conference area; quiet zones; small café on each floor *Accessibility and usability:* good orientation and usability; spacious circulation zones	• Bicycle parking: approx. 70 m² • Exist. plot ratio: 11.2 • Gross floor area, new building: 32 500 m² • Unsealed ground: 0% of plot • Rooftop planting: 20% of covered area
Plot	*Area of plot:* recycling of a former industrial site, high utilisation of ground area (12 storeys) *Open areas:* sealed, individual roadside trees; partial rooftop planting as compensation	• Daylight autonomy[1]: 2% • Ventilation: mechanical, 100% of floor area
Design	*Building culture:* building designed to comply with stringent urban planning stipulations; differentiated facade design; interior formed as vertical city, atrium creates horizontal and vertical neighbourhoods *Personalisation:* diverse, flexible office areas (separate, combined, open-plan); high degree of identification among employees	• Building costs, cost groups 300–400[2]: approx. 107.5M EUR • Building costs[2]: approx. 3300 EUR/m² gross floor area • Active solar areas: PV 30 m²
Well-being/ health	*Safety/security:* good, clear design; access controls from 1st floor upwards *Sound:* acoustic ceilings and carpeting in offices *Light:* all offices with view of outside world; light-redirecting louvre blinds; atrium with excellent daylighting, 7 heliostats with additional light-redirecting elements ("light wall", "mobiles") *Interior air:* fresh-air supply to offices (fully air-conditioned), exhaust air via atrium; windows can be opened individually; CO₂ sensors *Interior climate:* 5% less sick leave since building first occupied	• Barrier-free • Competition • Low- or zero-emissions building materials • Rainwater/grey water usage
Building fabric	*Building layout/fitting-out:* frame construction; all storeys with different, partially flexible layouts	
Building costs	*Investment costs:* weighing up investment and operating costs (life-cycle costing)	
Operating and maintenance costs	*Operation and maintenance:* energy costs cut by 42% (compared with the US standard); easy-care floor coverings in circulation zones	
Building materials	*Raw materials (availability):* minimising transport distances (50% within 800 km radius); certified wood *Environmental impact:* building materials with higher proportion of recycled materials *Dangerous substances:* certified building materials (labels)	
Operating energy	*Building heating:* solar gains from double-leaf facade, climate buffer *Building cooling:* atrium roof with prismatic sunshading system; internal sunshades in offices; night-time cooling; cooling ceilings; decentralised absorption-type refrigeration units *Air management:* fewer fans due to thermal currents in atrium *Lighting:* high daylight autonomy; daylight sensors; luminaires (offices), metal halide lamps (atrium) *Coverage of energy requirements:* electricity requirements covered by "green electricity"	
Infrastructure	*Waste from operation and usage:* recycling of 90% of building waste *Water:* water consumption cut by 32%; waterless urinals; rainwater usage (irrigation, vegetation, cooling water)	
Process quality	*Sustainable building:* highest certification according to US Green Building Council (LEED "Platinum") *Integrated planning:* from competition onwards *Analyses:* daylighting, thermal-dynamic simulation	• Simulation method • Monitoring

[1] Related to min. 75% of office floor space; [2] Figures correspond to 140M USD gross, including interior fittings and furnishings

Conference and exhibition pavilion

Osnabrück, D, 2001

Architects:
Herzog + Partner, Munich
Thomas Herzog + Hanns Jörg Schrade
Project team:
Stefan Sinning, Kirsten Braun, Patrick Bröll,
Peter Gotsch, Matthias Lettau, Sybille Fries
Building services:
NEK Ingenieurgruppe, Braunschweig
Energy consultant:
ZAE Bayern, Garching

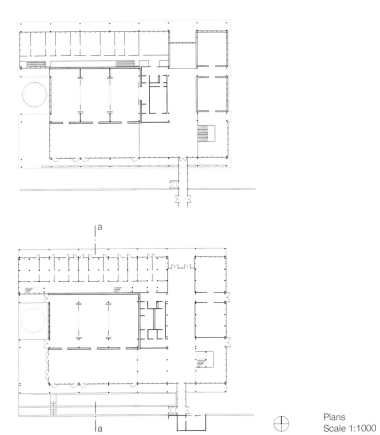

The design brief for the conference and exhibition pavilion of the German Environmental Foundation (DBU) listed optimum daylight usage, a sustainable and low-resources energy concept, flexible usage and the use of natural-based materials as the governing criteria. The heart of this timber frame building, adjoining the offices and circulation/exhibition areas, is the 6.50 m high conference room. A three-storey, stiffening reinforced concrete core, on which a photovoltaic installation and vacuum-tube collectors are mounted, houses the sanitary and technical facilities.
The transparent, ventilated membrane roof provides the weather protection. The single layer of pretensioned ETFE film can be completely reused and its anti-adhesive properties mean it is self-cleaning. Thanks to the multi-layer construction, every bay of the roof can be adapted to suit the climatic requirements of the room below. Whereas above the offices and the storeroom the inner layer is well insulated and opaque, the roof above the conference and exhibition rooms is translucent. Overhead illumination achieves a much higher luminance than light from the side. Sunshading, blackout requirements and daylight control are achieved by the pivoting louvres, which are mounted between the membrane and the glazing.
The roof construction not only contributes to saving electrical energy for artificial lighting, but also enables high passive heat gains. Nevertheless, effective shading options mean that there are no great cooling needs in summer. In winter a co-generation plant heats the new building and the existing office building. In the summer, groundwater cooling linked with the underfloor heating lowers the interior temperatures. A heat exchanger cools the outside air drawn in by the ventilation plant, or heats it up during the colder months.

Archicreation 06/2003
Rassegna 12/2006

Plans
Scale 1:1000

Section   Scale 1:750
A Schematic view of ventilation
B Schematic view of groundwater cooling
Vertical sections Scale 1:20

1 ETFE film, 1 layer, pretensioned on 4 sides
2 Galvanised steel hollow section, 120 x 80 mm
3 Aluminium louvres, can be rotated for sunshading/
  daylight control/blackout
4 Fascia plate for blackout
5 Triple glazing:
  6 mm tough. safety glass with low E coating +
  12 mm argon-filled cavity + 5 mm float glass +
  12 mm argon-filled cavity + 10 mm lam. safety
  glass with low E coating
6 Thermal insulation, 160 mm, white facing
  39 mm LVL
7 Insect screen, glass-fibre fabric, white
8 Double glazing:
  10 mm tough. safety glass + 16 mm argon-filled
  cavity + 6 mm tough. safety glass with low E
  coating
9 Sunshade, stationary aluminium plate, 3 mm,
  on Ø8 mm stainless steel cable

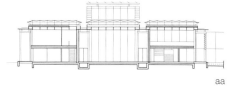

aa

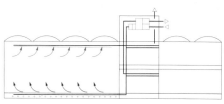

A

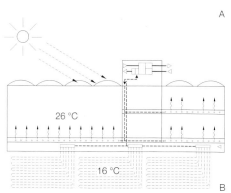

B

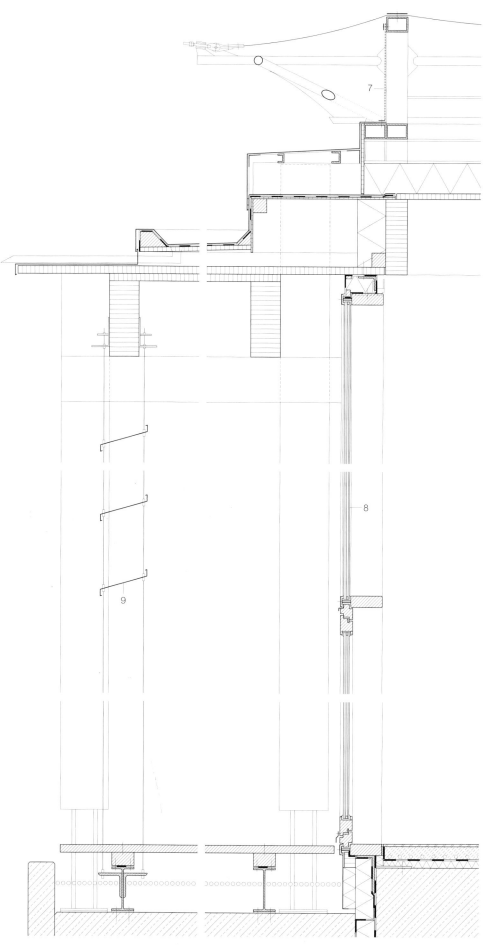

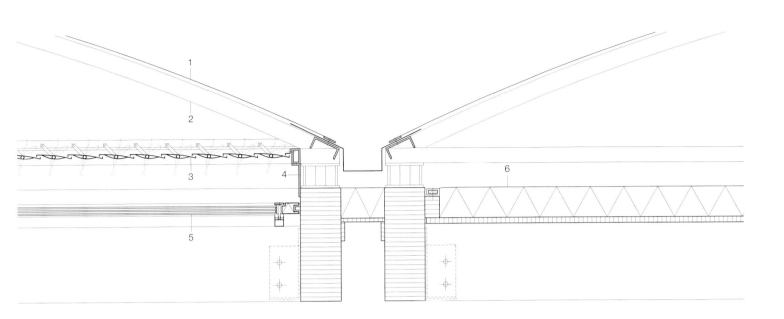

Ventilation

Besides local ventilation via individual windows, there is a mechanical ventilation system for the offices and the conference and exhibition areas. With the help of groundwater cooling, a heat exchanger can cool the incoming fresh air to approx. 23°C, even on hot days. Over much of the year, a combined supply/extract duct enables a heat recovery rate of more than 80%. In the conference and exhibition areas, the fresh air is introduced at a low level and with a low velocity, so there is always fresh, in summer also relatively cool, air just above floor level. Used, hot air rises and is extracted from beneath the ceiling – only the lower part of the great volume has to be condi-

tioned. The system can be used to remove smoke in the event of a fire. The fresh-air rate corresponds to the amount necessary for hygienic conditions; the fresh air is filtered centrally. Recirculating operation and humidification/dehumidification are unnecessary. The costs for the plant and the energy are therefore low, but the relative humidity in the interior is the same as that outside – in winter very low, in summer relatively high.

Heating and cooling

A co-generation plant heats the new building and the existing office block; considerable heat gains are achieved via direct solar radiation on the facade and,

above all, the roof. Effective shading options mean that hardly any cooling is necessary in summer. Groundwater cooling provides any cooling required: water is pumped through hoses laid below the water table not far beneath the ground slab and distributed throughout the building via the underfloor heating pipes. Water temperatures around 20°C cool the interior air temperature down to approx. 26°C. The night-time heat dissipation requires considerably lower flow rates compared to air cooling, and the room temperatures can be kept relatively low even during longer periods of hot weather.

Theme	Qualitative features	Parameters/indicators
Location quality	*Energy availability:* building services of the DBU's existing building; groundwater near the surface *Integration:* events for various groups of the population *Solidarity/justice:* events concerning the proper treatment of the environment *Usage:* choice of site supplements the existing DBU buildings; near to urban park *Mobility:* good transport and local public transport links; can be reached on foot through the park *Noise/vibration:* main rooms face onto open areas	• Global radiation: 960 kWh/m²a • Density: 1364 persons/km² • Distance to local public transport: 200 m (bus); 900 m (regional trains)
Building quality Access/ communication	*Traffic:* area open to the public; roadside car parking; entrance area readily visible *Social contact:* access, assembly and exhibition areas promote communication; defined transition to office usage; terrace with direct access to park, which can be used as a zone for relaxation *Accessibility and usability:* barrier-free design of all interior and exterior areas	• Bicycle parking: approx. 25 m² • Exist. plot ratio: 0.4 • Gross floor area, new building: 3000 m² • Unsealed ground: approx. 40% of plot • Ventilation: mechanical, 100% of floor area
Plot	*Area of plot:* compact construction, infill development for DBU site *Open areas:* differentiated open areas for high diversity of species; water features to regulate microclimate; water-permeable hardstanding for car parking	• U-values, bldg. envelope: [W/m²K] roof 0.20, ext. wall (timber studs) 0.23, ext. wall (concrete) 0.20, grd. slab 0.25 U-value dynamic calculation:
Design	*Bldg. culture:* striking landmark project for ecological & energy-efficient construction; timber structure stands out due to coloured glaze finish; innovative roof visible from distance; building integrated into landscape	post-and-rail facade: N 0.53, E/W 0.11, S 0.34; opaque membrane roof 0.25
Well-being/ health	*Sound:* good sound insulation *Light:* high daylight proportion, illumination via translucent roof glazing, good/even distribution of luminance *Interior air:* mechanical, demand-controlled ventilation system *Interior climate:* external, daylight-controlled sunshades, mechanical night-time ventilation	• Building costs, cost groups 300–400: 6.75M EUR • Building costs: 2250 EUR/m² gross floor area
Building fabric	*Structure:* durable timber frame construction; passive timber protection *Building layout/fitting-out:* room layout enables flexible usage within timber frame, conversion and partial deconstruction possible	• Heating requirement: 29 kWh/m²a • Cooling requirement: 8 kWh/m²a
Building costs	*Investment costs:* typical investment costs for this type of usage	• Electricity requirement: 18 kWh/m²a • Active solar areas: solar thermal approx.
Operating and maintenance costs	*Operation and maintenance:* reduced costs for operation and maintenance due to efficient building services *Repairs:* conscious use of known, innovative, easy-to-replace elements	5 m², PV approx. 38 m²
Building materials	*Raw materials (availability):* high proportion of renewable raw materials with natural-based usage *Environmental impact:* timber building materials with carbon-sink effect *Deconstruction:* deconstruction possible due to modular construction; avoidance of composite materials	• Barrier-free • Competition • Rainwater/grey water usage
Operating energy	*Building heating:* minimised transmission heat losses, thermal zoning, blower-door test; heated by CHP (gas); heat output via warm-air inlets and underfloor heating; extract system with heat recovery *Building cooling:* sunshades controlled by energy gains; mechanical night-time ventilation; activation of ground slab for groundwater cooling *Hot-water provision:* solar thermal-assisted hot-water provision *Air management:* minimised air change rate *Lighting:* sunshades for guaranteeing a supply of daylight to suit needs *Coverage of energy requirements:* groundwater; gas-fired co-generation plant; photovoltaics; solar thermal energy	
Infrastructure	*Waste from operation and usage:* collection in convenient waste depot, standard and special streams (e.g. toner, batteries, pallets) *Water:* gravel-filled trenches to allow rainwater seepage	
Process quality	*Sustainable building:* DBU programme; compliance with energy benchmarks *Building tradition:* further development of timber construction *Integrated planning:* interdisciplinary planning team *Analyses:* dynamic simulation (e.g. heating, cooling load, comfort); heating plant comparison; roof study using 1:7 model *Monitoring:* heating and air quality (e.g. CO_2) *Facility Management:* by operator	• Sustainability-oriented benchmarks • Simulation method • Monitoring • FM concept

Example 19

Residential and commercial development

London, GB, 2002

Architects:
Bill Dunster architects, ZEDfactory, Surrey
Structural engineers:
Ellis & Moore, London
Energy concept:
Ove Arup & Partners, London

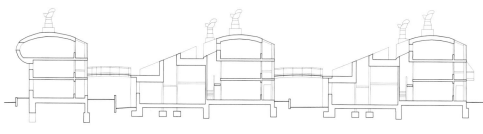

aa

"BedZED" – Beddington Zero Energy Development – is located in a southern district of London and its 82 apartments and offices form the first zero-energy settlement in the UK. Eight buildings were erected on the site of a former sewage treatment plant whose layout, form and usage are coordinated with the external climatic conditions. The basic module is a three-storey terrace house which tapers as it rises on the north-west side and can be divided into housing units of different sizes as required. The internal layout is made up of three zones: conservatories to the south-east, which act as a thermal buffer, the adjoining accommodation and offices, and special uses to the north-west. The materials of these heavyweight buildings were mainly obtained locally; renewable raw materials such as timber and stone were preferred.

Optimum exploitation of the sun as a source of heat and light is guaranteed by the fully glazed south elevation. Triple glazing and external walls with a U-value of 0.1 W/m² K ensure good insulation, a natural ventilation system with heat recovery guarantees a permanent exchange of air. More than 700 m² of photovoltaic panels provide the development with up to 11% of its electricity requirements. The remaining electricity is provided by a co-generation plant, which is fired by waste wood from the region. The plant also provides hot water. Waste water is treated microbiologically in the development's own constructed wetland and afterwards used for watering gardens and flushing toilets. Compared to conventional housing, the energy requirement could be cut by 60%. In order to develop the underlying environmentally friendly concept even further, the development was given its own mini-infrastructure: kindergarten, community centre, sports centre, cafés and car-sharing scheme save the occupants some long journeys.

📖 Architectural Review 11/2003
A+U 8/2004

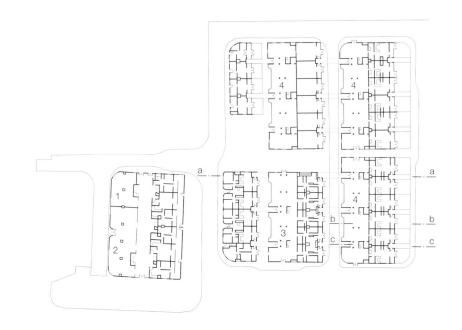

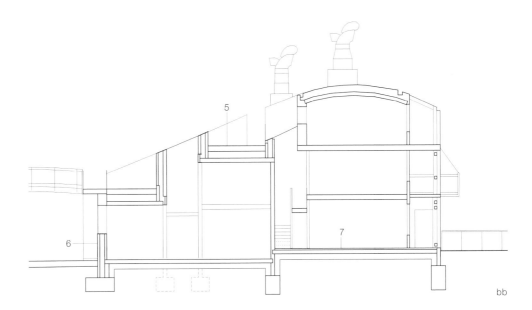

bb

Section through complete development
Scale 1:500
Plan of ground floor
Scale 1:1000
Sections through terrace house
Scale 1:200

1 Kindergarten
2 Sports centre
3 Café
4 Office

5 Roof construction:
extensive rooftop planting
substrate
drainage and filter mat
waterproofing, polymer-modified bitumen
300 mm rigid foam thermal insulation
vapour barrier, polymer-modified bitumen
225 mm precast concrete
paint finish
6 Wall construction:
102 mm facing brickwork
300 mm rock wool thermal insulation
100 mm concrete bricks
15 mm plaster
7 Ground floor construction:
60 mm screed plus floor finishes
200 mm reinforced concrete
300 mm rigid foam thermal insulation

cc

Example 19

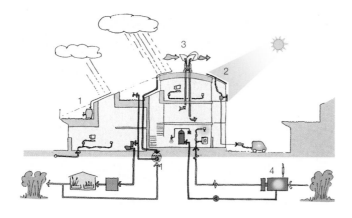

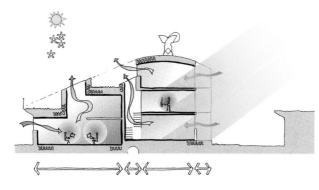

Energy scheme
A   Building services
B   Heating/cooling
1   Rainwater collection
2   Photovoltaic elements for
electric cars
3   Natural ventilation with heat
recovery
4   Co-generation plant

Theme	Qualitative features	Parameters/indicators
Location quality	*Basic provisions/mixed uses:* 82 housing units, 2400 m² commercial, kindergarten, community centre, sports centre, café, supermarket *Integration:* diverse range of housing: town houses, maisonettes, small and medium-sized apartments; premises to let for small businesses *Solidarity/justice:* 23 apartments partly state-financed, 10 apartments with low rents, 15 apartments for socially disadvantaged persons *Usage:* in conformity with location; good links to urban amenities *Mobility:* comprehensive mobility concept: number of passenger km cut by 65%, car-sharing pool, charging point for 40 electric cars	• Global radiation: approx. 800 kWh/m²a • Density: 787 persons/ha (metropolitan region; London/city 4784 persons/ha) • Distance to local public transport: 100 m
Building quality Access/ communication	*Traffic:* concentration of parking spaces, pedestrianised access to housing *Social contact:* high quality of external and circulation zones, many common areas and meeting places, differentiated design of semi-public and private areas, joint homepage for all "BedZED" residents	• Bicycle parking: 115 m² • Exist. plot ratio: 0.6 • Gross floor area, new building: 10 388 m²
Plot	*Area of plot:* recycling of former sewage treatment plant site *Open areas:* private gardens, rooftop planting	• Rooftop planting: approx. 20% of covered area
Design	*Building culture:* largest zero-carbon residential development in UK; distinctive ventilation chimneys *Personalisation:* ground-level gardens, conservatories and rooftop gardens offer individual design freedoms; high identification value for residents	• Ventilation: natural, 100% of floor area • U-values, bldg. envelope¹ [W/m²K]: R: 0.10, E: 0.11, W: 1.20, G: 0.10
Well-being/ health	*Safety/security:* clear layout; social controls *Light:* daylight optimisation, business units lit from north *Interior air:* mech. supply/extract *Interior climate:* high passive thermal insulation, exposed thermal masses	• Projected economic period of use: 120 a • Building costs, cost groups 300–400: 10.2M EUR
Building fabric	*Structure:* selection of ageing-resistant and durable materials (e.g. facing bricks, untreated oak boards) *Building layout/fitting-out:* flexible interior layouts and housing unit sizes possible	• Building costs: 1620 EUR/m² gross floor area
Operating and maintenance costs	*Operation and maintenance:* minimisation of plant, very low operating, maintenance and energy costs *Repairs:* building services readily accessible; easy-to-repair materials	• Proportion of secondary raw materials: 15% by vol. • Renew. energy coverage rate: 100% • Active solar areas: PV 777 m²
Building materials	*Raw materials (availability):* high proportion of recycled building materials and reused components; primarily building materials obtained locally (52% within 55 km radius); certified timber *Environmental impact:* no basements; CO_2 emissions cut to 675 kg/m² (< 20–30% compared to similar structures) *Dangerous substances:* all building materials checked individually *Deconstruction:* no composite materials	
Operating energy	*Building heating:* orientation; thermal zoning; conservatory; storey-height south-facing glazing; high passive thermal insulation; triple glazing; no conventional heating plant (preheated fresh air); extract system with heat recovery *Building cooling:* east/west facades essentially closed; night-time cooling *Air management:* lobbies create overpressure, no fans *Lighting:* good level of daylight *Coverage of energy requirements:* co-generation plant uses waste wood from municipal depots; 11% of electricity requirements from PV	• Low- or zero-emissions building materials • Register of building materials • Measurements of interior air • Rainwater/grey water usage
Infrastructure	*Waste from operation and usage:* target stipulation: 60% cut in household waste; central recycling depot *Water:* grey water used for flushing toilets and watering rooftop gardens; consumption of drinking water cut by 50% due to water-saving fittings and WCs, constructed wetland	
Process quality	*Sustainable building:* passive-house standard; reduction targets: passenger km 50%, heating 90%, hot water 33%, electricity 33%, water consumption 33% *Integrated planning:* interdisciplinary planning involving architects, engineers, local environmental organisation and housebuilding company *Analyses:* comprehensive simulations *Monitoring:* 5-year monitoring concept, detailed project documentation	• Sustainability-oriented benchmarks • Simulation method • Monitoring

¹ R: roof (average), E: external walls (average), W: windows, G: ground slab

Federal Environment Agency offices

Dessau, D, 2005

Architects:
sauerbruch hutton, Berlin
Matthias Sauerbruch, Louisa Hutton,
Jens Ludloff, Juan Lucas Young
Project managers:
Andrew Kiel, René Lotz
Structural engineers:
Krebs & Kiefer, Berlin
Energy concept:
Zibell, Willner & Partner, Cologne/Berlin

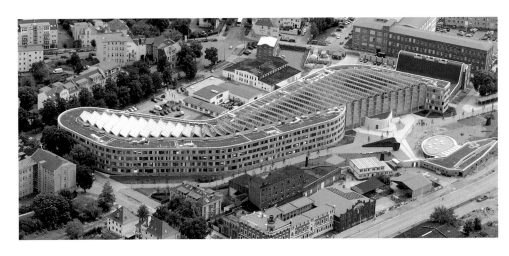

As a model project for innovative building, the 460 m long Federal Environment Agency (UBA) building wends its way demonstrably, dynamically and colourfully across the site of the former Wörlitzer railway station not far from the centre of Dessau. The large-scale format and continuity of this four-storey office building for 800 workers makes its mark on this area with its heterogeneous, small-format developments. The winding form is a response to the various urban situations and leads to differentiated qualities both internally and externally. A semicircular forum with a glass facade forms the entrance. There is space for public events and exhibitions here. Behind the facade there is an internal courtyard with planting, covered by a fully glazed roof structure with integral sunshades. In terms of its materials and colouring, the external facade emphasizes the concept of the long building: 33 shades from seven basic colours divide up the building in chromatic gradations. Continuous, prefabricated spandrel panel elements clad with larch boards alternate with set-back windows and flush glass panels with coloured printing. The window reveals are clad with powder-coated steel sheet or fitted with painted aluminium louvres. The night-time ventilation of the offices is achieved via motorised vents behind opaque glass. Besides channelling daylight into the inner row of offices, both atrium and forum help to optimise the energy and climate household: the entire building is ventilated via the roof of the central folded-plate structure, the internal courtyard functions as a thermal buffer zone. Thanks to highly insulated external walls, photovoltaic installations for generating electricity and a large ground exchanger, this office building almost achieves the energy standard of a passive house! The Federal Environment Agency building therefore fulfils the claim of amalgamating environmentally compatible construction with contemporary architecture.

Architectural Review 02/1999
Intelligente Architektur 18, 1999

Sections · Plan of ground floor
3rd floor
Scale 1:2000

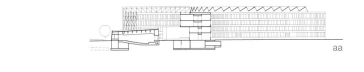

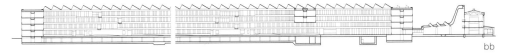

aa

bb

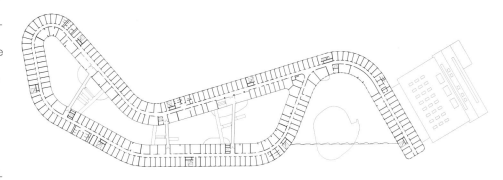

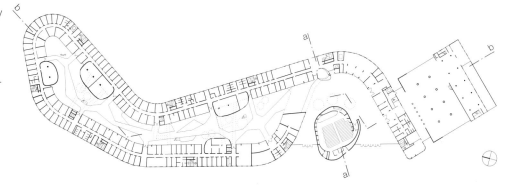

Example 20

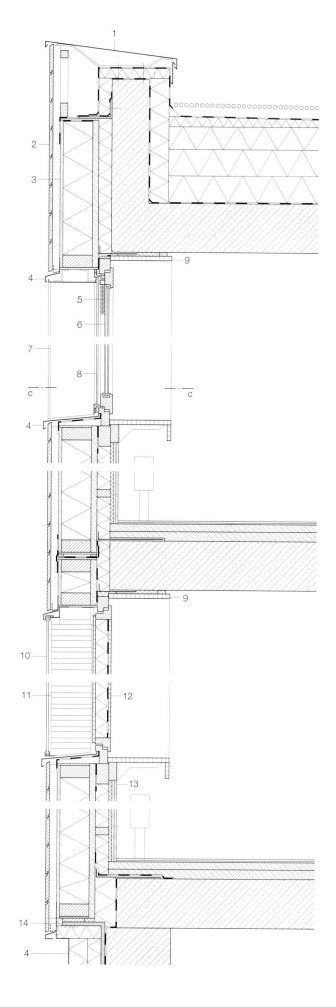

1   Tinned copper cover plate, 0.8 mm
    waterproofing, 2 layers bitumen sheet.
    72 mm mineral-fibre insulation
    vapour barrier
    200 x 650 mm reinforced concrete
2   Larch boards, 20 x 150 mm
    40 x 40 mm timber framework
    40 mm ventilation cavity
3   Panel: gypsum fibreboard, 15 mm
    100 x 160 mm glulam frame
    160 mm cellulose fibres
    29 mm cement fibreboard
4   Tinned copper flashing, 1 mm
5   Anti-glare louvres, 25 mm
6   Double glazing in wooden frame
    larch with glaze finish, U = 0.8 W/m²K
    4 mm tough. safety glass + 16 mm
    cavity + 4 mm tough. safety glass
7   Powder-coated sheet steel, 1.5 mm
8   Secondary glazing, 8 mm tough.
    safety glass

9   Window reveal, wood-based board
    product, larch with glaze finish,
    340 x 25 mm
10 Tough. safety glass, with coloured
    enamel finish, 10 mm, in
    20 mm aluminium channel section
    52 mm ventilation cavity
11 Ventilation louvres, painted aluminium
12 Motorised vent:
    14 mm coated plywood
    vapour barrier
    70 mm cellulose
    14 mm plywood with larch veneer
13 Gypsum fibreboard, 2 No. 12.5 mm
    90 mm cellulose board insulation
    27 mm resilient bar
    63 mm timber framework
14 Stainless steel L 240 x 500 x 20 mm
15 Lining, wood-based board product
    larch with glaze finish, 23 mm
    40 mm cellulose board insulation

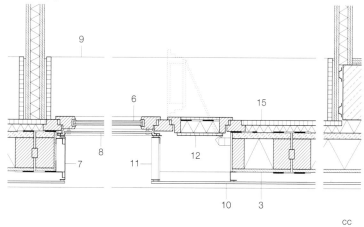

cc

Sections through external
facade
Scale 1:20
Interior ventilation scheme
A Summer's day
B Winter's day

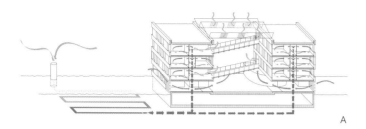

A

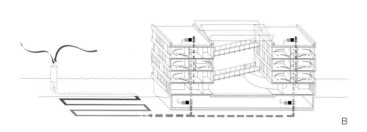

B

Theme	Qualitative features	Parameters/indicators
Location quality	*Energy availability:* district heating CHP (partly landfill gas) *Basic provisions/mixed uses:* public amenities, e.g. information centre, library, lecture theatre, cafeteria *Usage:* site chosen as a sign of structural change in the region; revitalisation of city-centre areas *Mobility:* local public transport incentives system for employees *Noise/vibration:* secondary glazing; mechanical ventilation for offices exposed to noise	• Global radiation: 1000 kWh/m²a • Density: 423 persons/ha • Distance to local public transport: 100 m (bus); 350 m (regional/inter-city trains)
Building quality Access/ communication	*Traffic:* link between main entrance and park; visitor parking at rear of building with access to basement garage; forum serves as foyer *Social contact:* park open to the public; atrium forms internal communication area – office areas well linked by bridges; distinctive direction system	• Bicycle parking: 120 m² • Exist. plot ratio: 1.5 • Gross floor area, existing building: 522 m²
Plot	*Area of plot:* recycling of former site – replacement of contaminated soil; use of building stock *Open areas:* indigenous cultivated plants combined with exotic shrubs; water features; high diversity of species	• Gross floor area, new building: 39 265 m² • Unsealed ground: 40% of plot • Rooftop planting: 30% of covered area
Design	*Bldg. culture:* ext. works design denotes former entrance to Wörlitzer Park; integration of indust. structures protected by preservation orders; high arch. quality & local identity; bldg. form generates diverse interior qualities; distinctive colour concept *Personalisation:* employees identify well with their surroundings	• Ventilation: natural, 10% of floor area, mech., 90% of floor area • U-values, bldg. envelope¹ [W/m²K]:
Well-being/ health	*Safety/security:* reception; security checks *Light:* window proportion optimised for daylight; daylight redirection; reflective surfaces in atrium *Int. air:* ground exchanger; window ventilation possible in all offices *Int. climate:* ext. sunshades; night-time ventilation; exposed thermal masses; loam walls in some areas	H'_T: 0.49, R: 0.13, E: 0.23, W: 1.2, G: 0.35 • Operating hours > 26°C/a: 200 h
Building fabric	*Structure:* materials chosen taking into account high durability *Building layout/fitting-out:* flexible layout zoning possible, access floors in some areas, separation between structure and fitting-out	• Building costs, cost groups 300–400: 56.5M EUR • Ratio of cost groups 300/400:
Operating and maintenance costs	*Operation and maintenance:* low energy costs; investment and operating cost variants investigated during planning *Repairs:* choice of low-maintenance materials and surfaces	approx. 68/32 • Building costs: 1420 EUR/m² gross flr. area
Building materials	*Raw materials (availability):* prefab. timber facade; cellulose insulation *Environmental impact:* LCA data considered; high degree of prefabrication in facade & roof *Dangerous substances:* avoidance of risky materials; individual checks of all bldg. materials during planning; very high interior hygiene level	• Heating requirement: 38.5 kWh/m²a • Primary energy rqmt., total: 76.6 kWh/m²a • Coverage rate, renewable energy²: 11%
Operating energy	*Bldg. heating:* compact building (A/V ratio 0.34); H'_{Tmax} < 53%; atrium as climate buffer; extract system w. heat recovery *Bldg. cooling:* effective sunshading; night-time cooling; high heat capacity; solar-assisted adsorption-type (computer rooms) or compression-type (lecture theatre) refrigeration units *Hot-water provision:* decentral (tea kitchens, cleaners' rooms) *Lighting:* daylight sensors; occupancy detectors *Other elec. consumers:* efficient appliances/systems *Coverage of energy requirements:* vacuum-tube collectors; PV in roof (forum); ground exchanger w. 86 000 kWh/a heating & 125 000 kWh/a cooling output	• Active solar areas: solar thermal 354 m², PV 228 m² • Barrier-free • Competition • Low- or zero-emissions building materials
Infrastructure	*Waste from operation/usage:* recyclable materials depot *Water:* green roof; tanks; gravel trenches	• Register of building materials • Interior air measurements
Process quality	*Sustainable building:* model project; exemplary competition stipulations: 50% below 1995 Thermal Insulation Act, heating requirement < 30 kWh/m²a, ecological building materials selection *Integrated planning:* inter-disciplinary team of experts during entire planning phase *Analyses:* flow, daylight and thermal-dynamic simulations; LCA *Monitoring:* 3 years, participation in "SolarBau: MONITOR" scheme	• Sustainability-oriented benchmarks • Simulation method • Monitoring

¹ H'_T: average U-value, R: roof (average), E: external walls (average), W: windows (external facade), G: ground slab
² During the first 5 years, the coverage rate for renewable energy sources is 20%; owing to depletion of landfill gas, the proportion reduces to 11% thereafter.

257

Parameters

Variable	Unit of measurement	Further units	Conversion factors
Energy	joule [J]	watt-second [Ws]	1 J = 1 Ws
		kilowatt-hour [kWh]	1 J = 2.778 x 10^{-7} kWh
		calorie [cal]	1 J = 0.239 cal
		coal equivalent [SKE]	1 J = 3.412 • 10^{-7} SKE
Pressure	pascal [Pa]	bar [bar]	1 Pa = 10^{-5} bar
		standard atmosphere [atm]	1 Pa = 9.87 • 10^{-6} atm
Volume	[cm^3]	litre [l]	1000 cm^3 = 1 l
		US barrel [US bbl]	1 l = 0.008386 US bbl (liquid)
		UK barrel [UK bbl]	1 l = 0.00611 UK bbl
		US gallon [US gal]	1 l = 0.264 US gal (liquid)
		UK gallon [UK gal]	1 l = 0.220 UK gal
Area	[m^2]	square inch [in^2]	1 m^2 = 1550 in^2
		square foot [ft^2]	1 m^2 = 10.764 ft^2
		hectare [ha]	1 m^2 = 0.0001 ha
Temperature	degree Celsius [°C]	kelvin [K]	°C = K - 273.15
		degree Fahrenheit [°F]	°C = (°F - 32)/1.8

General energy terms

Energy medium/energy source
The term energy medium actually covers the raw materials provided by nature, which owing to the convertible chemical or nuclear energy stored in them can be used to produce energy (biomass, fossil and nuclear fuels). In everyday use, however, energy sources such as solar energy, geothermal energy, wind power or water power, which are the physical media of thermal, potential or kinetic energy, are included under this heading.

Primary energy [J]
Primary energy is the energy contained in the energy media that occur naturally on the earth. Those energy media include fossil fuels such as coal, crude oil, natural gas or minerals like uranium ore and renewable energy media such as the sun, wind, water, biomass and geothermal energy. Transforming the primary energy into the net energy used by consumers at the end of the energy chain leads to losses inherent in the conversion and transmission processes.

Primary energy factor f_p [-]
The primary energy factor expresses the ratio of non-renewable primary energy input (including the losses during production, distribution and storage) to the final energy output. Typical primary energy factors are, for example, 1.1 for heating oil and natural gas, 2.7 for electricity and 0.2 for wood. The lower the primary energy factor, the more efficient is the energy provision on the basis of the corresponding primary energy medium.

Primary energy requirement Q_p [kWh/a]
When calculating the primary energy requirement for a building according to the Energy Conservation Act, the final energy requirement is determined first. The conversion losses are taken into account by the primary energy factor f_p. The relationship between final energy requirement Q_e, primary energy requirement Q_p and primary energy factor f_p is expressed by the equation $Q_p = Q_e • f_p$.

Secondary energy [J]
Secondary energy is the energy remaining after converting the primary energy medium into so-called net energy media such as electricity, heating oil, district heat or wood pellets. It is related to the source of the net energy medium.

Final energy [J]
Transporting the secondary energy to the consumer results in losses. The final energy designates the quantity of energy that is available to the end user at the place of use, e.g. in the form of electricity, wood pellets, heating oil or district heat, after deducting all conversion and distribution losses. The final energy is usually the basis for the energy costs calculation.

Final energy requirement Q_e [kWh/a]
The final energy requirement is the quantity of energy required to provide the net energy (e.g. space heating, hot water, lighting, etc.) for a building. The final energy requirement Q_e here is a theoretical value calculated according to the Energy Conservation Act. It takes into account losses in the output, distribution, storage and conversion in the building. It is specified for standard conditions (e.g. defined user behaviour, interior temperature, etc.) and separately according to the energy media used. It is determined at the system boundary of the building being assessed.

Final energy consumption [kWh/a]
In contrast to the final energy requirement Q_e, the final energy consumption designates an actual quantity of energy measured in the building. It also takes into account, for example, user behaviour and climatic fluctuations. In physical terms, however, this term is incorrect. According to the law of conservation of energy, energy in a closed system is not consumed, but only converted into another form of energy.

Net energy [J]
The net energy is the energy used in the end by the end user. For this, the final energy has to be converted, which usually involves losses. Heating, cooling, illumination, motion or sound waves are forms of net energy. The net energy defines the starting point for calculating the primary energy requirement according to the Energy Conservation Act.

Heating requirement Q_H [kWh/a]
The heating requirement is the theoretical quantity of energy that must be fed into a building during the heating period in order to cover the heat losses for the desired interior temperature. It is calculated by subtracting the solar and internal gains from the transmission and ventilation heat losses Q_v.

Energy performance certificate
According to the Energy Conservation Act 2007, from July 2008 building owners in Germany will have to obtain energy performance certificates for their existing buildings in order to present to new tenants and owners. The consumption-based certificate is based on the measured energy consumption, which depends on the behaviour of the respective user and climatic fluctuations. The requirements-based certificate is based on a calculated, theoretical energy requirement in order to be able to make objective statements – suitable for making comparisons – regarding the quality and energy efficiency of a building and its installed services. An energy performance certificate remains valid for 10 years, unless refurbishment work is carried out in the meantime.

Insulating and sealing

Thermal conductivity λ [W/mK]
The thermal conductivity is measured specifically for a material and specifies the quantity of heat passing through a 1 x 1 x 1 m cube of material per second for a temperature difference of 1 K between one side and the other. A low value indicates a material with a high thermal insulation quality. As moisture has a negative influence on the thermal conductivity, the value always refers to the material when dry.

Thermal transmittance U (U-value) [W/m^2K]
The U-value is a measure of the heat flow through a building component. It specifies the quantity of heat exchanged per second between a surface of 1 m^2 and the surrounding air during constant heating with a temperature difference of 1 K between the surface and the air. The U-value takes into account the thermal conductivities and thicknesses of the building materials plus the thermal resistances between the components and the air. In the case of inhomogeneous components, individual U-values must be calculated depending on the form of construction and then an average U-value worked out depending on the ratio of the various areas. The lower the U-value, the lower are the transmission heat losses.

U_g-value of glazing [W/m^2K]
The U_g-value is a specific U-value that designates the heat flow through one or more panes of glass. It takes into account the number of panes, the nature and number of coatings and the filling (e.g. noble gas) in any cavities between the panes.

U_f-value of window frame [W/m^2K]
In addition to the U_g-value, there is also a specific U-value for the window frame, the U_f-value. Generally, the thermal performance characteristics of the window frame are poorer than those of the glazing. The U_f-value can be improved through the choice of material, the material thickness and the quality of the seals.

U_w-value of window [W/m^2K]
The parameter for assessing the heat flow through a window is the U_w-value. It is made up of the U_g- and U_f-values, included in proportion to their areas, plus the losses due to the hermetic edge seal to the glazing and the junction between the window and the surrounding construction.

Specific transmission heat loss H_T [W/K]
Transmission heat losses are caused by heat conduction through the surfaces enclosing a heated interior space (roof, external walls, windows, doors and floor over basement) and by thermal bridges. This value therefore describes the energy-efficiency quality of a thermal enclosure. The geometry of the building and the U-values of the building components have a considerable influence on the magnitude of the transmission heat losses.

Specific transmission heat loss H'_T [W/m^2K]
The Energy Conservation Act uses H'_T to define a value for the transmission heat losses averaged over all the building envelope surfaces and related to 1 m^2 of enclosing area. This also enables a maximum permissible value to be identified depending on the volume of the building.

SI prefixes	Symbol	Factor
nano	n	10^{-9}
micro	μ	10^{-6}
milli	m	10^{-3}
centi	c	10^{-2}
deci	d	10^{-1}
deca	da	10
hecto	h	10^{2}
kilo	k	10^{3}
mega	M	10^{6}
giga	G	10^{9}
tera	T	10^{12}
peta	P	10^{15}
exa	E	10^{18}
zetta	Z	10^{21}

Ventilation heat losses Q_v [kWh/a]

Exchanging the warm interior air for colder exterior air leads to ventilation heat losses. This exchange of air is necessary for reasons of hygiene, for removing stale interior air. Leaking joints and junctions can lead to additional, uncontrolled ventilation heat losses which increase the heating requirement considerably. Controlled ventilation and heat recovery can reduce the ventilation heat losses.

Incident radiation and light

Global radiation [W/m²$_{hor}$]

The global radiation is the quantity of solar energy incident on the earth's surface – related to a horizontal surface. It consists of direct and diffuse, non-aligned radiation and depends on the solar altitude angle (which in turn is dependent on latitude and time of year) and atmospheric disturbances (clouds, particles). On very cloudy days it is practically only the diffuse component that reaches the earth's surface. In Central Europe the global radiation drops below 100 W/m² on such days. Under a cloudless sky, a value of about 700 W/m² is reached. The global radiation can also be specified as an annual total [kWh/m²$_{hor}$a]. It is then suitable, for example, for calculating the energy yields of active solar energy systems. In Germany the annual total lies between 900 and 1200 kWh/m²a.

Total energy transmittance g (g-value) [-]

The total energy transmittance defines the flow of energy through transparent building components. It is related to the entire radiation spectrum, i.e. the range of wavelengths from 300 to 2500 nm. When radiation strikes a transparent building component, one part of the energy reaches the interior immediately through transmission (primary energy transmittance). The other part is absorbed by the building components and subsequently re-emitted as infrared radiation (secondary energy transmittance). The g-value is obtained by adding together the primary and secondary energy transmittance values. With a combination of glazing and sunshades, reciprocal influences must be considered.

Solar gains Q_s [kWh/a]

Heat that contributes to heating up the interior of the building and to reducing the heating requirement – due to the incidence of solar energy on transparent and opaque building components – is designated a solar gain. The location of the building, its orientation, the inclination and size of the building components and the amount of radiation absorbed by the facade material all influence this energy input. Solar gains take place at all building components, but they are very much higher with transparent components than with other components. High solar gains can make a major contribution to reducing the heating requirement Q_H, but in summer can also lead to overheating in the building.

Equivalent U-value of windows [W/m²K]

Solar energy gains during the heating period are included in the energy-efficiency assessment of windows by way of the so-called equivalent U-value. Here, the g-value of the glazing and the radiation gain are taken into account depending on the orientation. In the case of low E glazing, a negative equivalent U-value is possible, i.e. taken as a daily average, more energy enters the interior in the form of solar radiation than is lost by transmission.

Light transmittance τ [-]

Depending on the material properties of a transparent building component, radiation is either reflected at its boundary surfaces, transmitted, or absorbed upon passing through. The light transmittance specifies the ratio of the amount of incident light with wavelengths 380–780 nm to the amount of light passing through. The higher the value, the more daylight there is in the interior. This value depends on the material, material thickness, coatings, etc.

Daylight autonomy [%]

The daylight autonomy specifies the percentage of occupied time for a room when the target illuminance for the tasks to be carried out in a room can be maintained by daylight alone. During this time, no artificial light is necessary, e.g. for illuminating a workplace. The room geometry, the proportion of opaque and transparent facade surfaces, the frame proportions of the windows and also the type of glass have an influence on the daylight autonomy

Storage

Specific heat capacity c [J/kgK]

The specific heat capacity is a variable specific to each material. It designates the quantity of heat required to raise the temperature of 1 kg of a substance by 1 K. The specific heat capacity is particularly dependent on the internal structure of a material.

Heat (storage) capacity Q_{sp} [Wh/m²K]

This value designates the ability of a building component to store thermal energy. It is the product of the specific heat capacity c, the density ρ and the thickness d of the component being assessed: $Q_{sp} = c \cdot \rho \cdot d$.

Enthalpy of fusion [kJ/kg]

The enthalpy of fusion (or heat of fusion) designates the quantity of heat required for a substance to change from the solid to the liquid state. Enthalpy of fusion is exploited by phase change materials (PCM), which upon changing between states can store energy without undergoing a change in temperature themselves. The potential energy absorption of the enthalpy of fusion over a temperature range of 4°K for 90 kg PCM, for example, corresponds to 1 m³ concrete.

Building services

Heat load ϕ_{hl} [kW]

The heat load is the output required to maintain the desired interior temperature under the most unfavourable conditions and is specific to the building. The heat load calculation is normally carried out for each room of the building separately. To do this, the transmission heat requirement (losses via the enclosing surfaces of the building) and the ventilation heat requirement are determined. Internal and solar heat gains are not included in the calculation. The heat load forms the basis for sizing the radiators and the heating plant.

Degree of efficiency [-]

The degree of efficiency designates the ratio of output (benefits) to input (work/costs) under standard conditions. It is therefore the measure for the efficiency of energy conversion and energy transmission, and for energy production systems specifies the relationship between usable and used energy. Whereas in theory only degrees of efficiency < 100% are possible, in practice degrees of efficiency > 100% have been measured, e.g. gas-fired condensing boilers. The input is related to the calorific

value of the fuel; in addition, the condensation heat of the exhaust-gas flow (gross calorific value) is used in the conversion process.

Coefficient of performance COP [-]

The COP, like the degree of efficiency, is a parameter for evaluating the efficiency of energy conversion and is primarily used for heat pumps and refrigeration plant. In the heat pump process, this value describes the ratio of usable heat output to the driving energy (e.g. electrical) input, including auxiliary energy, under standard conditions. A COP of 2.0 means that the net energy output is twice the driving energy input. This figure should be understood as an evaluation of the efficiency of the device only; it does not provide an energy-efficiency assessment of the entire installation

Annual energy efficiency ratio (AEER) β [-]

The annual energy efficiency ratio is used for assessing the energy efficiency of heat pumps. It describes the ratio of heating or cooling energy output to the driving energy (e.g. electrical) input for a heat pump over a period of one year. The AEER is therefore a measure of the total degree of efficiency of a heat pump over the course of a year.

Seasonal performance factor (SPF) e_p [-]

The seasonal performance factor describes the overall efficiency of building services installations (e.g. heating system). It expresses the ratio of net energy output to primary energy input. As renewable energy media are included in the calculation with their corresponding primary energy factors, the SPF can drop below 1.

Material parameters

Primary energy input PEI [MJ]

The primary energy input, also known as grey or embodied energy, is the energy required for the provision and use of a product. The figure includes all the energy quantities necessary for production, transport and storage (including all intermediate states/products). It serves as an indicator of a potential environmental impact by the product and can also be used to assess the technical and ecological efficiency of the provision and usage processes. The lower the value, the better the material is in ecological terms. The PEI is specified according to the energy sources used for the production – separately for renewable and non-renewable energy media. It can be expressed for materials related to weight or volume, but also for building components or complete structures.

Global warming potential (GWP 100) [kg CO₂-eq]

The accumulation of greenhouse gases in the troposphere leads to a temperature rise on the earth due to the increased reflection of infrared radiation. The global warming potential groups together all greenhouse gases in relationship to the effect of carbon dioxide (CO_2). As the damaging gases remain in the troposphere for different lengths of time, the time horizon considered must be identified; a period of 100 years is normally considered.

Durability of building components [a]

The durability describes the potential for a building material to maintain the function allocated to it, e.g. loadbearing, serviceability, for a certain period of time. This is usually specified in the form of a timespan where the lower value represents the durability with normal usage and the higher value presumes optimised planning.

Calorific value [J/kg or J/m³]

The calorific value is the unit of measurement for the thermal energy released upon the combustion of a substance. Only the usable thermal energy is considered here, i.e. without the enthalpy of condensation (or heat of condensation) of the ensuing water vapour. To enable a comparison with the calorific values of building materials, the following values for fuels can be used: wood 7–16 MJ/kg, lignite 29.9 MJ/kg, crude oil (at 25°C) 42.8 MJ/kg and natural gas (at 25°C) 3 –45 MJ/m³. If the enthalpy of condensation is included in the equation, this results in the gross calorific value of a material.

Climate data

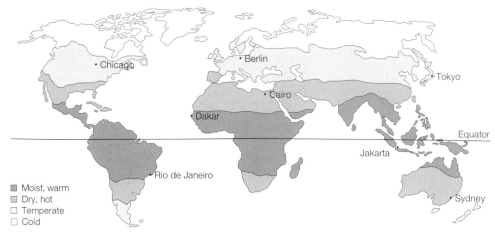

■ Moist, warm
▨ Dry, hot
□ Temperate
□ Cold

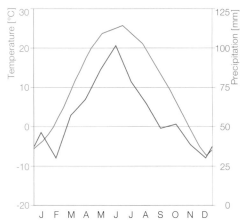

Chicago		Min.	Month	Max.	Month	Yearly average
Air temperature	[°C]	-3.3	Jan	27.3	Jul	10.5
Mean daily max. temperature	[°C]	0	Jan	27.2	Jul	13.9
Mean daily min. temperature	[°C]	-7.7	Jan	18.9	Jul	5.6
Absolute max. temperature	[°C]	18.3	Jan	40.6	Jul	40.6
Absolute min. temperature	[°C]	-30.6	Dez	9.4	Jul	-30.6
Mean relative air humidity	[%]	66.0	May	76.0	Dec	71.0
Mean precipitation	[mm]	41.0	Feb	103.0	Jun	843.0
Max. precipitation	[mm]	85.0	Feb	228.0	Jul	no data
Min. precipitation	[mm]	8.0	Feb	34.0	Jul	no data
Max. daily precipitation	[mm]	39.0	Feb	159.0	Jul	159.0
No. of precipitation days	[d]	7.0	Oct	13.0	Apr	120.0
Evaporation	[mm]	118.0	Dec	333.0	Jul	2611.0
Mean No. of sunshine hours	[h]	76.0	Dec	473.0	Jul	273.0
Radiation [1]	[Wh/m²d]	884.0	Dec	5501.0	Jul	3175.0
Mean wind speed	[m/s]	3.0	Jul, Aug	5.0	Nov–May	4.0

[1] Annual total of incoming radiation (horizontal) 1158 kWh/m²a

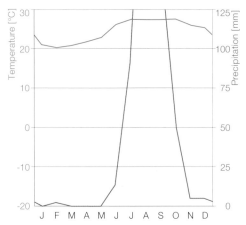

Dakar		Min.	Month	Max.	Month	Yearly average
Air temperature	[°C]	21.3	Jan	28.0	Oct	24.7
Mean daily max. temperature	[°C]	26.0	Jan	32.0	Oct	29.0
Mean daily min. temperature	[°C]	17.0	Feb	26.0	May	21.0
Absolute max. temperature	[°C]	37.0	Jul	43.0	Mar	43.0
Absolute min. temperature	[°C]	12.0	Dec	21.0	Jul	12.0
Mean relative air humidity	[%]	64.0	Dec	82.0	Sept	76.0
Mean precipitation	[mm]	< 1.0	Apr	254.0	Aug	540.0
Max. precipitation	[mm]	6.0	Mar	476.0	Aug	901.0
Min. precipitation	[mm]	0	Jan	56.0	Sept	273.0
Max. daily precipitation	[mm]	2.0	Jan	213.0	Aug	213.0
No. of precipitation days	[d]	0	Jan	13.0	Aug	38.0
Evaporation	[mm]	58.0	Jan	164.0	Jul	1370.0
Mean No. of sunshine hours	[h]	181.0	Aug	295.0	Apr	2719.0
Radiation [1]	[Wh/m²d]	4931.0	Dec	7164.0	Apr	5815.0
Mean wind speed	[m/s]	1.9	Jan	6.1	Apr	3.9

[1] Annual total of incoming radiation (horizontal) 2122 kWh/m²a

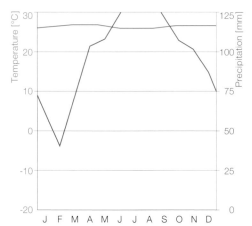

Jakarta		Min.	Month	Max.	Month	Yearly average
Air temperature	[°C]	26,1	Jan	27.2	May	26.8
Mean daily max. temperature	[°C]	28.9	Jan, Feb	31.1	Sept	30.0
Mean daily min. temperature	[°C]	22.8	Jul, Aug	23.9	Apr, May	23.3
Absolute max. temperature	[°C]	33.3	Feb, Mar, Jul	36.7	Okt	36.7
Absolute min. temperature	[°C]	18.9	Sept	20.6	Jan	18.9
Mean relative air humidity	[%]	71.0	Sept	85.0	Jan	80.0
Mean precipitation	[mm]	43.0	Aug	300.0	Jan	1799.0
Max. precipitation	[mm]	135.0	Jul	779.0	Jan	no data
Min. precipitation	[mm]	0	Jun–Sept	91.0	Feb	no data
Max. daily precipitation	[mm]	20.0	Aug	71.0	Feb	71.0
No. of precipitation days	[d]	4.0	Aug	18.0	Jan	125.0
Evaporation	[mm]	115.0	Feb	144.0	Oct	1590.0
Mean No. of sunshine hours	[h]	182.0	Feb	295.0	Aug	2975.0
Radiation	[Wh/m²d]	no data	no data	no data	no data	no data
Mean wind speed	[m/s]	1.5	Mar	1.8	Jul	1.6

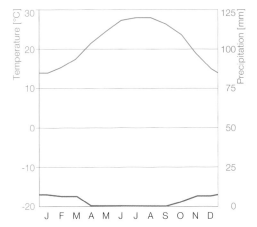

Cairo		Min.	Month	Max.	Month	Yearly average
Air temperature	[°C]	13.3	Jan	28.3	Jul, Aug	21.7
Mean daily max. temperature	[°C]	19.0	Jan	35.0	Jun, Aug	28.0
Mean daily min. temperature	[°C]	9.0	Jan, Feb	22.0	Jul, Aug	16.0
Absolute max. temperature	[°C]	30.0	Jan	47.0	May	47.0
Absolute min. temperature	[°C]	1.0	Feb	18.0	Jul	1.0
Mean relative air humidity	[%]	34.0	May	56.0	Dec	47.0
Mean precipitation	[mm]	0	Jun–Sept	8.0	Dec	24.0
Max. precipitation	[mm]	0	Jun, Jul, Sept	54.0	Dec	63.0
Min. precipitation	[mm]	0	Jan, Dec	no data	no data	3.0
Max. daily precipitation	[mm]	0	Jun, Jul, Sept	44.0	Dec	44.0
No. of precipitation days	[d]	0	Jul–Sept	3.0	Jan, Dec	10.0
Evaporation	[mm]	22.0	Jan	184.0	Jul	1170.0
Mean No. of sunshine hours	[h]	236.0	Dec, Jan	391.0	Jul	3717.0
Radiation [1]	[Wh/m²d]	no data	no data	no data	no data	5592.0
Mean wind speed	[m/s]	3.0	Jun–Dec	4.0	Jan–May	3.0

[1] Annual total of incoming radiation (horizontal) 2041 kWh/m²a

Rio de Janeiro		Min.	Month	Max.	Month	Yearly average
Air temperature	[°C]	20.2	Jul	256	Feb	22.7
Mean daily max. temperature	[°C]	23.9	Jul, Sept	29.4	Feb	26.1
Mean daily min. temperature	[°C]	17.2	Jul	22.8	Jan, Feb	20.0
Absolute max. temperature	[°C]	32.6	Jun	39.1	Jan	39.1
Absolute min. temperature	[°C]	10.2	Sept	17.6	Mar	10.2
Mean relative air humidity	[%]	75.0	Aug	81.0	Mar	78.0
Mean precipitation	[mm]	40.0	Aug	157.0	Jan	1039.0
Max. precipitation	[mm]	91.0	Jul	318.0	Jan	no data
Min. precipitation	[mm]	2.0	Aug	41.0	Nov, Dec	no data
Max. daily precipitation	[mm]	51.0	Aug	223.0	Apr	223.0
No. of precipitation days	[d]	7.0	Jul	14.0	Nov, Dec	131.0
Evaporation	[mm]	61.0	Jul	137.0	Jan	1130.0
Mean No. of sunshine hours	[h]	151.0	Oct	222.0	Jan	2350.0
Radiation [1]	[Wh/m²d]	no data	no data	no data	no data	4630.0
Mean wind speed	[m/s]	2.7	Apr, Jun, Jul	3.9	Oct	3.2

[1] Annual total of incoming radiation (horizontal) 1690 kWh/m²a

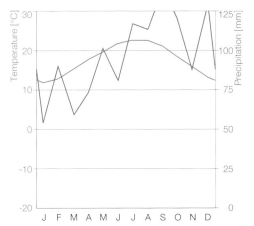

Sydney		Min.	Month	Max.	Month	Yearly average
Air temperature	[°C]	11.8	Jul	22.0	Jan	17.4
Mean daily max. temperature	[°C]	15.6	Jul	25.6	Jan, Feb	21.1
Mean daily min. temperature	[°C]	7.8	Jul	18.3	Jan, Feb	13.3
Absolute max. temperature	[°C]	25.7	Jul	45.3	Jan	45.3
Absolute min. temperature	[°C]	2.1	Jun	10.6	Jan	2.1
Mean relative air humidity	[%]	62.0	Oct	76.0	Jun	69.0
Mean precipitation	[mm]	72.0	Sept	141.0	Jun	1205.0
Max. precipitation	[mm]	282.0	Oct	643.0	Jun	2102.0
Min. precipitation	[mm]	1.0	Aug	11.0	Mar	546.0
Max. daily precipitation	[mm]	121.0	Dec	281.0	Mar	281.0
No. of precipitation days	[d]	11.0	Aug	14.0	Jan, Mar, Apr	152.0
Evaporation	[mm]	25.0	Jul	122.0	Jan	838.0
Mean No. of sunshine hours	[h]	180.0	May	229.0	Oct, Dec	2463.0
Radiation [1]	[Wh/m²d]	2919.0	Jul	6792.0	Nov	4675.0
Mean wind speed	[m/s]	3.2	Apr, May	4.1	Jan	3.7

[1] Annual total of incoming radiation (horizontal) 1706 kWh/m²a

Tokyo		Min.	Month	Max.	Month	Yearly average
Air temperature	[°C]	3.7	Jan	26.4	Aug	14.7
Mean daily max. temperature	[°C]	8.3	Jan	30.0	Aug	18.9
Mean daily min. temperature	[°C]	-1.7	Jan	22.2	Aug	10.0
Absolute max. temperature	[°C]	21.3	Jul	384	Aug	38.4
Absolute min. temperature	[°C]	-9.2	Dec, Jan	15.4	Aug	-9.2
Mean relative air humidity	[%]	60.0	Feb	80.0	Jul, Sept	72.0
Mean precipitation	[mm]	48.0	Jan	217.0	Sept	1562.0
Max. precipitation	[mm]	no data	no data	no data	no data	no data
Min. precipitation	[mm]	no data	no data	no data	no data	no data
Max. daily precipitation	[mm]	48.0	Jan	393.0	Sept	393.0
No. of precipitation days	[d]	5.0	Dec	13.0	Sept	115.0
Evaporation	[mm]	4.0	Jan	161.0	Jul	809.0
Mean No. of sunshine hours	[h]	136.0	Sept, Oct	204.0	Aug	2020.0
Radiation	[Wh/m²d]	no data	no data	no data	no data	no data
Mean wind speed	[m/s]	3.0	Dec	4.3	Mar, Apr	3.7

For the data for Berlin, please see Fig. B 1.50, p. 55.

LCA data

External cladding

The outer skin of a building characterises its external appearance. It performs diverse exchange functions between inside and outside and provides protection, especially against the weather. Included in this functional building component layer alongside the protective surfaces are also the necessary mounting constructions. High demands are placed on the safety and durability of the entire construction. External cladding forms exhibit significant differences in terms of their embodied energy and the resulting environmental impacts (see "Materials", p. 162, Fig. B 5.56). Considered in the context of the entire building, the proportion of embodied energy in the facade (see "Materials", p. 162, Fig. B 5.55) and its share of the costs are generally very high; the external cladding should therefore be given due attention during the planning.

Heavyweight external cladding forms in particular tie up a large proportion of the embodied energy in their supporting construction and fixings (see "Materials", p. 163, Fig. B 5.60). Optimising the material thickness and the weight will reduce the primary energy input in such components. Increased durability can justify the use of low-energy metals if necessary. Timber constructions act as carbon sinks and thus reduce undesirable climatic effects.

Transparent components

Transparent components consist of a transparent element and a support or bearing that does not cause any restraint. In terms of area, they represent the most costly functional layer with respect to energy efficiency (see "Materials", p. 162, Fig. B 5.56). They should therefore provide additional functions whenever possible, e.g. better daylight provision or the exploitation of solar energy media (see "Building envelope", p. 83, Fig. B 3.2).

Only seldom is glass designed as self-supporting, or to carry loads or function as bracing; but then the importance of the supporting construction increases. A high density plus higher demands regarding insulation and sealing have additional negative effects.

External cladding per m² Layers	PEI primary energy, non-renewable [MJ]	PEI primary energy, renewable [MJ]	GWP greenhouse gases [kg CO$_2$eq]	Durability [a]
Stone				
stone slabs bedded in mortar, limestone	71	3.5	5.4	80–100
limestone slab, cut, 20 mm lime-cement mortar, MG II, 15 mm				
suspended stone slabs, limestone	168	17	10	80–100
limestone slab, cut, 30 mm stainless steel fasteners (V4A), 140 mm				
Materials with mineral binders				
fibre-cement sheets	88	38	3.4	40–60
fibre-cement sheets, 8 mm timber supporting construction, 30 mm				
calcium silicate units, with ventilation cavity	320	10	33	60–80
CS units (KS Vb 20/1.8), MG II mortar, 115 mm wall ties, steel, 80 mm				
in situ concrete	680	36	55	≥ 80
in situ conc., 2% steel reinft. (FE 360 B), 100 mm concrete anchor, high-alloy steel, 120 mm				
Ceramic materials				
ceramic panels, with ventilation cavity	285	50	21	≥ 80
VFH ceramic panels, 30 mm aluminium sections, 60 mm				
facing masonry, with ventilation cavity	400	9	51	60–80
solid clay bricks (VMz 28/1.8), MG II mortar, 115 mm wall ties, steel, 80 mm				
Metal				
titanium-zinc sheet	416	43	25	70–100
titanium-zinc w. double welt stand. seams, 0.7 mm particleboard (P5), 22 mm				
corrugated aluminium sheeting	832	168	55	70–100
corrugated aluminium sheeting, 1 mm aluminium supporting construction, 30 mm				
Timber				
wooden shingles/shakes	41	226	-21	40–70
red cedar shakes, single-lap tiling, 16 mm timber supporting construction, 48 mm				
plywood	189	613	-29	40–70
building-grade veneer plywood, 16 mm timber supporting construction, 30 mm				

Transparent components per m² Layers	PEI primary energy, non-renewable [MJ]	PEI primary energy, renewable [MJ]	GWP greenhouse gases [kg CO$_2$eq]	Durability [a]
Glass				
insulating glass U$_g$ = 1.1	547	65	29	50
double glazing, argon filling, 24 mm patent glazing bar, aluminium, EPDM gasket, 40 mm				
insulating glass U$_g$ = 0.7	837	70	40	50
triple glazing, argon filling, 36 mm patent glazing bar, aluminium, EPDM gasket, 40 mm				
glass double facade	2162	353	131	50
toughened safety glass, 6 mm aluminium supporting framework, 250 mm double glazing, argon filling, 24 mm				
Synthetic materials				
plastic sheet	1099	63	52	25
4-wall sheet, polycarbonate, 40 mm patent glazing bar, aluminium, EPDM gasket				

Plaster, render and thermal insulation composite systems per m² Layers	PEI primary energy, non-renewable [MJ]	PEI primary energy, renewable [MJ]	GWP greenhouse gases [kg CO₂eq]	Durability [a]
Lime-cement plaster, internal, 2 coats	110	1.8	7.2	80
lime-cement plaster, MG P II, scraped, 15 mm primer				
gypsum plaster, internal, 2 coats	97	1.5	5.9	80
gypsum plaster, smooth, 15 mm primer				
insulating plaster	237	3.4	16	60
lime-cmt. plaster w. expanded perlite agg., 50 mm primer				
thermal insulation composite system	561	24	31	30
lime-cmt. plaster w. glass fleece reinft., 3 mm EPS, λ = 0.035 W/m²K, ρ = 30 kg/m³, 100 mm UF-based adhesive, 3.2 mm				
loam plaster, internal, 2 coats	61	0,9	3.8	80
loam undercoat, 10 mm loam finish coat, 5 mm				

Plaster, render and thermal insulation composite systems

Plaster, render and thermal insulation composite systems represent a special group among the external wall solutions. Depending on the specification, they can comprise a number of individual layers.

Plasters (internal) and renders (external) are efficient alternatives to external cladding. Insulating plaster/render and thermal insulation composite systems fulfil the functions of external cladding and insulation in one component. The addition of both layers make them comparable with other forms of construction. Their composite nature, however, results in certain disadvantages with respect to maintenance.

Insulation per m² Layers	PEI primary energy, non-renewable [MJ]	PEI primary energy, renewable [MJ]	GWP greenhouse gases [kg CO₂eq]	Durability [a]
Boards				
expanded polystyrene (EPS)	511	17	28	30
EPS board, λ = 0.040 W/m²K, ρ = 25 kg/m³, 120 mm polyvinyl acetate (PVAC) adhesive				
extruded polystyrene (XPS)	405	12	21	30
XPS board, λ = 0.040 W/m²K, ρ = 20 kg/m³, 120 mm polyvinyl acetate (PVAC) adhesive				
polyurethane PUR	349	13	17	30
PUR board, λ = 0.035 W/m²K, ρ = 20 kg/m³, 100 mm polyvinyl acetate (PVAC) adhesive				
insulation cork board ICB	15	0.24	1.1	40–60
ICB, λ = 0.040 W/m²K, 120 mm mortar-based adhesive				
wood-wool comp. board WW-C, permanent formwork	89	68	0.8	30–50
WW-C board, λ = 0.040 W/m²K, ρ = 30 kg/m³, 125 mm magnesite-bonded, mineral fibres on inside				
wood fibre insulating board WF	436	79	19	20–50
WF board, λ = 0.040 W/m²K, ρ = 160 kg/m³, 120 mm mortar-based adhesive				
cellular glass CG, external basement insulation	1030	29	49	100
cellular glass, λ = 0.040 W/m²K, ρ = 100 kg/m³, 120 mm bitumen compound				
calcium silicate board	96	3.7	16	40
CS board, λ = 0.045 W/m²K, ρ = 20 kg/m³, 120 mm polyamide fixings				
Fleeces				
mineral wool fleece	74	1.4	5.4	30–50
MW fleece, λ = 0.040 W/m²K, ρ = 20 kg/m³, 120 mm polyamide fixings				
Loose fill				
perlite fill	187	2.1	11	no data
exp. perlite, λ = 0.065 W/m²K, ρ = 100 kg/m³, 160 mm (on ground slab)				
cellulose fill	33	1.7	1.8	35–50
cellulose, λ = 0.040 W/m²K, ρ = 50 kg/m³, 120 mm (between TJI timber beams)				

Insulation

Layers of insulation consist of an insulating material and its fixings to a substrate (e.g. adhesives or mechanical fasteners). The embodied energy of insulating materials can differ by a factor of more than 10 for the same insulating performance. However, the use of insulation generally reduces the cost of energy for operating a building and increases the comfort for users. All insulating materials installed with typical thicknesses therefore recoup their costs in the form of energy-savings within a short period (see "Materials", p. 152).

The choice of an insulating material is also determined by the other requirements it has to fulfil (e.g. compressive strength below ground level). Although, for example, extruded polystyrene (XPS) generally appears to have a high energy content, in the group of compression-resistant insulating materials, for the tasks it has to fulfil it represents a comparatively good solution in terms of energy.

Roof coverings

The functional layer of the roof covering consists of the roof skin (covering or waterproofing) and the supporting structure required for this. As part of the building envelope, the energy requirements of roof coverings are similar to those of facades. Owing to the high demands placed on weather protection, good durability should be given high priority, otherwise the renewal and repair processes over the life cycle will increase the energy requirements and the costs. In the case of complex roof forms, large amounts of energy are tied up in the junctions; simple geometric structures reduce this embodied energy. The layers of wood used beneath metal roof coverings in particular cannot compensate for the CO_2 emissions associated with the layer of metal, but they do benefit from a comparatively high durability. On flat roofs, green roof solutions with extensive planting and PVC or EPDM waterproof sheeting generally involve less embodied energy than bitumen sheeting and at the same time exhibit better durability.

Roof coverings per m² Layers	PEI primary energy, non-renewable [MJ]	PEI primary energy, renewable [MJ]	GWP greenhouse gases [kg CO₂eq]	Durability [a]
Roof coverings				
flat plan tiles, titanium-zinc flashings	331	180	11	50
clay flat pan tiles, 20 mm timber battens, 24 x 48 mm, PE-HD sheathing, 0.5 mm				
concrete tiles, titanium-zinc flashings	288	155	4	50
concrete tiles, 20 mm timber battens, 24 x 48 mm, PE-HD sheathing, 0.5 mm				
titanium-zinc sheet	458	143	17	70
titanium-zinc with double-welt standing seams, 0.7 mm timber boards, 24 mm				
copper sheet	830	130	35	80
copper sheet with double-welt standing seams, 0.7 mm timber boards, 24 mm				
fibre-cement sheets, titanium-zinc flashings	689	197	26	40
corrugated fibre-cement sheets, 8 mm timber battens, 24 x 48 mm, PE-HD sheathing, 0.5 mm MDF board, 18 mm				
natural slates, copper flashings	999	138	24	70
natural slates, Old German slating, 5 mm flexible bitumen sheeting type V 13.5 mm timber boards, 24 mm				
wooden shingles, copper flashings	501	708	-44	40
wooden shingles, double-lap tiling, 24 mm timber battens, 24 x 48 mm, PE-HD sheathing, 0.3 mm timber boards, 24 mm				
Roof waterproofing systems				
flexible bitumen sheeting, with gravel	1355	38	40	25–30
gravel, 50 mm polyester fleece (PES), 2 mm flexible bitumen sheeting (PYE PY200 S5), 5 mm flexible bitumen sheeting (G200 S4), 4 mm				
EPDM sheeting, with gravel	394	28	17	25–35
gravel, 50 mm flexible EPDM sheeting, 1.2 mm perf. glass fleece, 3 mm, PE-HD vapour barrier, 0.4 mm				

Walls

The functional layer of the wall is the wall itself without its surface finishes. In terms of the overall balance, the walls tie up the second-highest amount of embodied energy, after the loadbearing structure (see "Materials", p. 162, Fig. B 5.55). The primary energy input essentially corresponds to the weight introduced into the building. Lightweight constructions should be preferred, provided these satisfy the other requirements placed on the wall (e.g. sound insulation).
Timber and metal stud walls involve less embodied energy, are easier to repair and renew, and enable simple integration of building services. Compared to timber stud walls, metal stud walls have a lower embodied energy (320 MJ/m²), but most of this is covered by non-renewable sources (307 MJ/m²). Timber stud walls, on the other hand, act as a carbon sink.

Walls per m² Layers	PEI primary energy, non-renewable [MJ]	PEI primary energy, renewable [MJ]	GWP greenhouse gases [kg CO₂eq]	Durability [a]
Solid homogeneous walls				
reinforced concrete	650	83	45	70–100
reinforced concrete (grade C 25/35) 2% steel content (FE 360 B), 200 mm				
loam bricks	96	1.2	4.2	70–90
air-dried loam bricks, ρ = 1400 kg/m³, 240 mm loam mortar				
aerated concrete bricks	410	14	65	70–90
aerated concrete bricks (PPW 4-0.6 t&g), 240 mm masonry mortar, MG III				
lightweight concrete bricks with pumice aggregate	247	5.1	26	80–90
lightwt. conc. bricks w. pumice agg. (VBL 2), 240 mm masonry mortar, MG III				
calcium silicate bricks	517	14	56	90–100
calcium silicate bricks (KSL 12/1.4), 240 mm masonry mortar, MG II				
gypsum wallboard	186	2.5	8.9	90
gypsum wallboard, 100 mm gypsum mortar, MG IV				

Walls per m² (contd.)

Layers	PEI primary energy, non-renewable [MJ]	PEI primary energy, renewable [MJ]	GWP greenhouse gases [kg CO₂eq]	Durability [a]
Solid homogeneous walls (contd.)				
vertically perforated clay bricks	599	12	79	90–100
vertically perforated clay bricks (HLz 12/1.2), 240 mm masonry mortar, MG II				
Stud walls				
timber stud wall	182	179	-5,9	40–60
plasterboard (type A), 12.5 mm timber studs, 80 x 40 mm, mineral wool, 40 mm plasterboard (type A), 12.5 mm				

Wall linings per m²

Layers	PEI primary energy, non-renewable [MJ]	PEI primary energy, renewable [MJ]	GWP greenhouse gases [kg CO₂eq]	Durability [a]
Mineral linings				
plasterboard	97	50	1.2	40–60
plasterboard (type A), 12.5 mm screw fixings, edge detail with softwood battens				
loam building board	84	2	-0.2	no data
fine loam plaster, jute fabric, 4 mm loam building board, 20 mm timber framework, screwed, 24 mm				
Timber linings				
timber boards	40	281	-26	50–90
timber boards (spruce, t&g) 19.5 mm screwed				
veneer plywood	177	540	-23	50–90
veneer plywood, 22 mm screwed				
particleboard (comparable with OSB)	40	87	-9.7	50–60
particleboard P1, 19 mm screwed				

Wall linings

With respect to their embodied energy, wall linings vary less than other building component groups, although the fixings necessary must always be taken into account together with the lining. Common materials such as wood-based board products or plasterboard represent particularly favourable options from the point of view of embodied energy. The perceived value of the material generally matches up with the embodied energy; however, better-quality surfaces are mostly also longer-lasting.

Ceilings per m²

Layers	PEI primary energy, non-renewable [MJ]	PEI primary energy, renewable [MJ]	GWP greenhouse gases [kg CO₂eq]	Durability [a]
wood-wool board	110	381	-28	30–50
wood-wool board with mineral binder, 25 mm framework of timber battens, 24 mm				
Pressed particleboard	136	109	-5.8	50
pressed particleboard with oak veneer, 19 mm framework of steel channels, galvanised, 40 mm mineral-fibre fleece, 40 mm				
Calcium silicate board	56	1.3	4.5	40
calcium silicate board, 20 mm framework of steel channels, 50 mm				
gypsum fibreboard	97	50	1.2	40–60
gypsum fibreboard, 12.5 mm framework of timber battens, 24 mm				
Plastered ceiling	56	0.8	3.3	80
gypsum plaster, 15 mm mat of reeds as background, 5 mm				
Panel ceiling, steel	375	14	22	40–70
sheet steel pans, perforated, 0.88 mm steel beams, channel sections, 840 mm grid, 7.5 mm mineral fibreboard, 40 mm PE film facing				

Ceilings

The embodied energy of ceilings and soffit finishes is mainly affected by their supporting construction as well as their surface finish. In contrast to wall linings, different systems and specifications result in very different embodied energy figures. Classical materials for interior finishes such as plaster represent efficient options in terms of their primary energy.

Owing to the greater use of materials, suspended ceilings generally result in a much higher primary energy input than ceiling types applied or attached directly to the soffit.

Screeds and subfloors

The distribution of imposed loads and sound insulation are the governing criteria for the functional layer of the screed or subfloor, which also include a separating layer and impact sound insulation. The durability of the impact sound insulation is generally less than that of the load-bearing layer.

The use of cement screeds, mastic asphalt or oriented strand boards (OSB) can result in a functional added-value if these also serve as ready-to-use surfaces or, like mastic asphalt, exhibit sound insulation advantages.

Screeds and subfloors per m² Layers	PEI primary energy, non-renewable [MJ]	PEI primary energy, renewable [MJ]	GWP greenhouse gases [kg CO$_2$eq]	Durability [a]
Mortar screeds and wet subfloors				
cement screed	203	3.8	18	50–80 [1]
cement screed (CT 20-S 50), 50 mm building paper, 0.2 mm mineral-fibre insulation, 20/15 mm				
calcium sulphate screed	71	2.2	5.8	40–60 [1]
calcium sulphate screed (CA 20-S 50), 50 mm building paper, 0.2 mm mineral-fibre insulation, 20/15 mm				
mastic asphalt	443	5.1	11	no data [1]
mastic asphalt, 25 mm building paper, 0.2 mm coconut board, 10 mm				
Dry subfloors				
gypsum fibreboard	138	10	8.2	no data [1]
gypsum fibreboard, 2 layers, 20 mm mineral-fibre insulation, 25/20 mm				
particleboard	71	88	-8.3	no data [1]
particleboard (P1), glued, 19 mm mineral-fibre insulation, 20/15 mm polyethylene (PE) fleece, 1 mm				

[1] The durability of impact sound insulation is about 50 years.

Floor coverings

Floor coverings consist of the actual wearing course plus their attachment to the substrate. Heavy loads and frequent cleaning processes (see "Materials", p. 172) place an intensive load on the floor covering and can lead to a high primary energy consumption. But even the embodied energy figures of the floor coverings themselves differ considerably, and can quickly accumulate in the case of poor durability. Stone floor finishes offer the highest durability and at the same time the lowest embodied energy. The way the floor coverings are fixed within the building is also decisive for the embodied energy. This is especially evident with resilient floor coverings and carpeting, which exhibit very high embodied energy figures owing to the use of synthetic rubber.

Solid timber products (e.g. wood-block or mosaic parquet flooring) demonstrate that a multitude of work operations and the associated increased wastage have a noticeable effect on the CO$_2$ balance.

Floor coverings per m² Layers	PEI primary energy, non-renewable [MJ]	PEI primary energy, renewable [MJ]	GWP greenhouse gases [kg CO$_2$eq]	Durability [a]
Tiles				
limestone	16	0.7	1	70–100
limest. flags, 305 x 305 mm, MG III mortar joints, 10 mm thin-bed mortar, 3 mm				
slate	43	1.1	3.5	70–100
slate flags, 300 x 300 mm, MG III mortar joints, 20 mm MG II mortar bed, 12 mm				
terracotta	137	3.2	14	40–80
terra. tiles, oiled, 300x300 mm, MG III mort. jts., 15 mm MG II mortar bed, 12 mm				
Solid timber and wood-based products				
wood-block flooring	66	447	-42	20–50
wood-block flooring, beech, oiled, 22 mm alkyd resin adhesive				
mosaic parquet	79	174	-13	20–50
mosaic parquet, oak, sealed, 8 mm alkyd resin adhesive				
real wood parquet laminate flooring	74	311	-27	20–50
real wood parquet laminate flooring, beech, 15 mm polyurethane adhesive				
laminated flooring	91	54	-2.6	10–15
laminated flooring with melamine resin coating, 8 mm polyurethane adhesive polyethylene (PE) fleece				
Resilient floor coverings				
linoleum	24	29	-0.4	15–40
linoleum (roll), 2.5 mm polyvinyl acetate (PVAC) adhesive				
rubber	702	15	21	15–40
rubber (roll) without inlay, synthetic, 4.5 mm polyurethane adhesive				

Floor coverings per m² (contd.) Layers	PEI primary energy, non-renewable [MJ]	PEI primary energy, renewable [MJ]	GWP greenhouse gases [kg CO$_2$eq]	Durability [a]
Resilient floor coverings (contd.)				
cork, waxed	22	54	-5.2	15–40
cork tiles, waxed, 6 mm latex adhesive	▫	▭	▭	
PVC	118	23	9.9	15–30
PVC (roll), 2 mm polyvinyl acetate (PVAC) adhesive	▭	▫	▭	
Textile floor coverings				
carpet, natural sisal	164	33	3.3	5–15
carpet, natural sisal, natural latex backing, 6 mm alkyd resin adhesive	▭	▫	▭	
carpet, new wool	39	27	-1.1	5–12
carpet, new wool, looped-pile, 6 mm jute felt polyvinyl acetate (PVAC) adhesive	▫	▫	▫	
carpet, fully synthetic	225	5.2	7.3	5–12
carpet, cut-pile, foam backing, 7 mm MG II mortar bed, 12 mm	▭	▏	▭	

Coatings per m² Layers	PEI primary energy, non-renewable [MJ]	PEI primary energy, renewable [MJ]	GWP greenhouse gases [kg CO$_2$eq]	Durability [a]
Mineral coatings, external				
lime coating	2	0,01	0.22	5
hydrated lime coating primer	▫	▏	▭	
silicate coating, 1-part	7.3	1.4	0.26	20–25
1-part silicate dispersion primer	▭	▫	▭	
Organic coatings, external				
alkyd resin coating	4.8	1.4	0.13	15
alkyd resin lacquer primer	▭	▫	▭	
acrylic coating	4.6	0.14	0.15	10
acrylic-based high-build glaze coat primer	▭	▏	▭	
polyurethane coating (screed sealing)	36	1.5	1.9	15–35
2-part polyurethane coating (PUR) primer	▭	▫	▭	

Coatings

Coatings consist of the actual coating itself plus in most cases the preliminary treatment of the substrate. The energy-related effects of coatings are determined, in particular, by their durability. As a "zero option", avoiding coatings altogether is an extremely efficient optimisation measure. Further optimisation options exist in the realm of health risks (see "Materials", p. 171).
On the other hand, coatings can improve the durability of building components or make them suitable for taking on additional functions (e.g. sound insulation, fire protection). For example, sealing a screed represents an energy-efficiency alternative to providing a floor finish.

Waterproofing per m² Layers	PEI primary energy, non-renewable [MJ]	PEI primary energy, renewable [MJ]	GWP greenhouse gases [kg CO$_2$eq]	Durability [a]
reaction resin waterproofing	94	3.4	5.8	80
epoxy mortar, 2 mm epoxy undercoat	▭	▫	▭	
plastic-modified thick bitumen coating	373	1.1	6.4	80
embossed synthetic sheeting for protection (HDPE) bitumen emulsion, 3 mm	▭	▏	▭	
mineral waterproofing	10	0.2	0.8	no data
cement-based waterproofing, 2 mm water glass undercoat	▫	▏	▫	
bitumen sheeting, 1 layer	294	5.6	7.4	80
bitumen sheeting (G200 S4), 4 mm bitumen undercoat	▭	▫	▭	

Waterproofing

As a functional component consisting of waterproofing layer plus preliminary treatment of substrate, waterproofing systems, exhibiting great differences in terms of their embodied energy, offer various chances to optimise the energy efficiency. However, these depend very much on the specification (e.g. hydrostatic pressure).

Statutory instruments, directives, standards

The EU has issued directives for a number of products, the particular aim of which is to ensure the safety and health of users. These directives must be implemented in the EU member states in the form of compulsory legislation and regulations.

The directives themselves do not contain any technical details, but instead only lay down the mandatory underlying requirements. The corresponding technical values are specified in associated sets of technical rules (e.g. codes of practice) and in the form of EN standards harmonised throughout Europe.

Generally, the technical rules provide advice and information for everyday activities. They are not statutory instruments, but rather give users decision-making aids, guidelines for implementing technical procedures correctly and/ or practical information for turning legislation into practice. The use of the technical rules is not compulsory; only when they have been included in government legislation or other statutory instruments do they become mandatory, or when the parties to a contract include them in their conditions. In Germany the technical rules include DIN standards, VDI directives and other publications such as the Technical Rules for Hazardous Substances.

The standards are divided into product, application and testing standards. They often relate to just one specific group of materials or products, and are based on the corresponding testing and calculation methods for the respective materials and components. The latest edition of a standard – which should correspond with the state of the art – always applies. A new or revised standard is first published as a draft for public discussion before (probably with revisions) it is finally adopted as a valid standard. The origin and area of influence of a standard can be gleaned from its designation:

- DIN plus number (e.g. DIN 4108) is essentially a national document (drafts are designated with "E" and preliminary standards with "V").
- DIN EN plus number (e.g. DIN EN 572) is a German edition of a European standard – drawn up by the European Standardisation Organisation CEN – that has been adopted without amendments.
- DIN EN ISO (e.g. DIN EN ISO 18064) is a standard with national, European and worldwide influence. Based on a standard from the International Standardisation Organisation ISO, a European standard was drawn up, which was then adopted as a DIN standard.
- DIN ISO (e.g. DIN ISO 21930) is a German edition of an ISO standard that has been adopted without amendments.

The following compilation represents a selection of statutory instruments, directives and standards that reflects the state of the art regarding building materials and building material applications as of August 2007.

General

Energy Conservation Act (EnEV) – statutory instrument dealing with energy-saving thermal performance and energy-saving installations for buildings. 2004-12
Renewable Energy Act (EEG) 2002 – legislation dealing with the restructuring of the legal side of renewable energy in the electricity sector. 2004-07
Thermal Insulation Act (WSVO) – statutory instrument dealing with energy-saving thermal performance. 1987
Revised Thermal Insulation Act. 1984
Revised Thermal Insulation Act. 1995

Part A   Positions

DIN EN ISO 9000:2000 Quality management systems – Fundamentals and vocabulary. 2005-12

Part B   Planning

Fundamentals
DIN EN 1946-2 Thermal performance of building products and components – Specific criteria for the assessment of laboratories measuring heat transfer properties – Part 2: Measurements by the guarded hot plate method. 1999-04
CEN-Bericht CR 1752 Ventilation for Buildings: Design Criteria for the Indoor Environment. 1998
DIN EN ISO 7730 Ergonomics of the thermal environment – Analytical determination and interpretation of thermal comfort using calculation of the PMV and PPD indices and local thermal comfort criteria. 2007-06
Arbeitsplatzgrenzwert (AGW) (workplace limit value). 2005
Biologischer Grenzwert (BGW) (biological limit value). 2005
DIN EN 200 Sanitary tapware. General technical specifications for single taps and mixer taps (nominal size 1/2) PN 10. Minimum flow pressure of 0.05 MPa (0.5 bar). 2005-06
DIN 4261 Small sewage treatment plants. 2002-12

Urban space and infrastructure
DIN 1986 Drainage systems on private ground. 2004-11

Building envelope
DIN 4108 Thermal insulation and energy economy in buildings. 2006-03
Energy-Savings Act (EnEG). 2005-09
VDI 2067 Economic efficiency of building installations. 2000-09
DIN 5034 Daylight in interiors. 1999-10
Places of Work Directive (ASR), in accordance with: Places of Work Act (ArbStättV). 2004-12

Building services
DIN 1946 Ventilation systems. 1999-03
DIN 1988 Codes of practice for drinking water installations (TRWI). 1988-12
DIN V 4701 Energy efficiency of heating and ventilation systems in buildings. 2003-08
DIN 4702 Boilers for central heating. 1990-03
DIN 4703 Heating appliances. 1999-12
DIN 4708 Central heat-water installations. 1994-04
DIN 4725 Floor heating, systems and components. 2001-03
DIN 4726 Warm water floor heating systems and radiator pipe connecting. 2000-01
DIN 4747 Heating plants for district heating. 2003-11
DIN V 4759 Heating installations for different sources of energy. 1986-05
DIN 5035 Artificial lighting. 2004-2007
DIN 6280-13 Generating sets – Reciprocating internal combustion engines driven generating sets – Part 13: For emergency power supply in hospitals and public buildings. 1994-12
DIN 8901 Refrigerating systems and heat pumps – Protection of soil, ground and surface water – Safety and environmental requirements and testing. 2002-12
DIN 18012 House service connections facilities – Principles for planning. 2000-11
DIN 18015 Electrical installations in residential buildings. 2004-08
DIN 18017 Ventilation of bathrooms and WCs without outside windows. 1987-02
DIN V 18160 Chimneys. 2006-01
DIN V 18599 Energy efficiency of buildings – Calculation of the net, final and primary energy demand for heating, cooling, ventilation, domestic hot water and lighting. 2007-02
DIN 44576 Electric room heating; thermal storage floor heating; characteristics of performance. 1987-03
DIN EN 307 Heat exchangers – Guidelines to prepare installation, operating and maintenance instructions

required to maintain the performance of each type of heat exchanger. 1998-12
DIN EN 1264 Floor heating – Systems and components. 1997-11
DIN EN 12097 Ventilation for buildings – Ductwork – Requirements for ductwork components to facilitate maintenance of ductwork systems. 2006-11
DIN EN 12098 Controls for heating systems. 1996-09
DIN EN 12464 Light and lighting – Lighting of work places. 2003-03
DIN EN 12665 Light and lighting – Basic terms and criteria for specifying lighting requirements. 2002-09
DIN EN 12792 Ventilation for buildings – Symbols, terminology and graphical symbols. 2004-01
DIN EN 12828 Heating systems in buildings – Design of water-based heating systems. 2003-06
DIN EN 12831 Heating systems in buildings – Method for calculation of the design heat load. 2003-08
DIN EN 13141 Ventilation for buildings – Performance testing of components/products for residential ventilation. 2004-09
DIN EN 13465 Ventilation for buildings – Calculation methods for the determination of air flow rates in dwellings. 2004-05
DIN EN 13779 Ventilation for non-residential buildings – Performance requirements for ventilation and room-conditioning systems. 2007-09
DIN EN 14134 Ventilation for buildings – Performance testing and installation checks of residential ventilation systems. 2004-04
DIN EN 14336 Heating systems in buildings – Installation and commissioning of water-based heating systems. 2005-01
DIN EN 14337 Heating systems in buildings – Design and installation of direct electrical room heating systems. 2006-02
DIN EN 14511 Air conditioners, liquid chilling packages and heat pumps with electrically driven compressors for space heating and cooling. 2004-07
DIN EN 14706 Thermal insulation products for building equipment and industrial installations. 2006-03
DIN 51731 Testing of solid fuels – Compressed untreated wood – Requirements and testing. 1996-10
VDI 3803 Air-conditioning systems – Structural and technical principles. 2002-10

Materials
DIN 4102 Fire behaviour of building materials and building components. 1998-05
DIN EN ISO 6946 Building components and building elements – Thermal resistance and thermal transmittance – Calculation method. 2003-10
DIN EN 10077 Thermal performance of windows, doors and shutters – Calculation of thermal transmittance. 2006-12
DIN EN 410 Glass in building – Determination of luminous and solar characteristics of glazing. 1998-12
DIN 4108-2 Thermal protection and energy economy in buildings – Part 2: Minimum requirements to thermal insulation. 2003-07
Industrial Waste Act (GewAbfV). 2003-01
Cradle-to-Grave Economy Act (KrW/AbfG). 1996-10
DIN EN ISO 14024 Environmental labels and declarations – Type I environmental labelling – Principles and procedures. 2001-02
DIN EN ISO 14021 Environmental labels and declarations – Self-declared environmental claims (Type II environmental labelling). 2001-12
DIN EN ISO 14040 Environmental management – Life cycle assessment – Principles and framework. 2006-10
DIN 4109 Sound insulation in buildings; requirements and testing. 1989-11
DIN 18230 Structural fire protection in industrial buildings. 1998-05
DIN EN 13501 Fire classification of construction products and building elements. 2007-05
DIN EN 12354 Building acoustics – Estimation of acoustic performance of buildings from the performance of products. 2007-06
DIN EN 13162 Thermal insulation products for buildings – Factory made mineral wool (MW) products. 2001-10
DIN EN 13167 Thermal insulation products for buildings –

Factory made cellular glass (CG) products. 2001-10

DIN EN 13169 Thermal insulation products for buildings – Factory made products of expanded perlite (EPB). 2001-11

DIN EN 14063 Thermal insulation materials and products – In-situ formed expanded clay lightweight aggregate products (LWA). 2004-11

DIN EN 13163 Thermal insulation products for buildings – Factory made products of expanded polystyrene (EPS). 2001-10

DIN EN 13164 Thermal insulation products for buildings – Factory made products of extruded polystyrene foam (XPS). 2001-11

DIN EN 13165 Thermal insulation products for buildings – Factory made rigid polyurethane foam (PUR) products. 2005-02

DIN EN 13171 Thermal insulating products for buildings – Factory made wood-fibre (WF) products. 2001-10

DIN EN 13168 Thermal insulation products for buildings – Factory made wood-wool (WW) products. 2001-11

DIN 18165-1 Fibre insulating building materials – Part 1: Thermal insulating materials. 1991-07

DIN 18165-2 Fibre insulating building materials – Part 2: Impact sound insulating materials. 1987-03

DIN EN 13170 Thermal insulation products for buildings – Factory made products of expanded cork (ICB). 2001-10

DIN EN 673 Glass in building – Determination of thermal transmittance (U-value) – Calculation method. 2003-06

ISO 14025 Environmental labels and declarations – Type III environmental declarations – Principles and procedures. 2005-07

Strategies

Energy Performance of Buildings Directive (EPBD) 2002/91/EC. 2002

Federal Immissions Protection Act (BImSchG). 1990

Construction Products Directive (CPD) 89/106/EEC. 1988

Enquête Commission: "Protection of man and the environment". 1994

Electricity Grid Feeding Act. 1990-12

Construction Products Act (BauPG). 1992

Heating Plant Act (HeizAnlV). 1994

Biomass Act (BiomasseV). 2001

"Sustainable Building Guidelines" – Federal Ministry of Transport, Building & Urban Affairs (BMVBS). 2001

SIA 112/1 "Sustainable construction – buildings". 2004

SIA D 0123 Construction of buildings according to ecological aspects. 1995

SIA D 0200/SNARC: System for assessing the sustainability of architectural projects for the topic of the environment. 2005

SIA D 0216 SIA Energy Efficiency Path. 2006

Bibliography

General

Gauzin-Müller, Dominique; Favet, Nicolas: Sustainable Architecture and Urbanism: Design, Construction, Examples. Basel/Berlin/Boston, 2002

Althaus, Dirk: Bauen heute – Bauen morgen. Architektur an der Schwelle zur postfossilen Zeit. Berlin, 2005

Behling, Sophia; Behling, Stefan: Solar Power: The Evolution of Sustainable Architecture. Munich/New York, 1996

Bundesarbeitskreis Altbauerneuerung (BAKA) e.V. (ed.): Almanach Kompetenz Bauen im Bestand. Cologne, 2006

Federal Ministry for the Environment, Nature Conservation & Nuclear Safety (BMU) (ed.): Erneuerbare Energien – Innovationen für die Zukunft. Berlin, 2004

Daniels, Klaus: Low Tech – Light Tech – High Tech. Basel/Berlin/Boston, 1998

Daniels, Klaus: The Technology of Ecological Building: Basic Principles, Examples and Ideas. Basel/Berlin/Boston, 1995

Deters, Karl; Arlt, Joachim: Leitfaden Kostendämpfung im Geschosswohnungsbau. Stuttgart, 1998

Eurosolar e.V. (ed.): The City – A Solar Power Station. The State of the Art of Solar Building and Ecological Urban Planning. Bonn, 2000

Feldhaus, Maria; Gabriel, Ingo (ed.): Vom Altbau zum Niedrigenergiehaus. Energietechnische Gebäudesanierung in der Praxis. Staufen, 2002

Frantz, Jürgen: Grüne Archen. In Harmonie mit Pflanzen leben. Das Modell der Gruppe Log ID. Frankfurt am Main, 1983

Frauns, Elke (ed.): Baukultur versus Technik? Wege zu energieeffizienten Gebäuden. Gelsenkirchen/Neuss, 2005

Gieseler, Udo; Heidt, Frank D.: Bewertung der Energieeffizienz verschiedener Maßnahmen für Gebäude mit sehr geringem Energiebedarf. Stuttgart, 2005

Glücklich, Detlef (ed.): Ökologisches Bauen. Von Grundlagen zu Gesamtkonzepten. Munich, 2005

Gonzalo, Roberto; Habermann, Karl J.: Energy Efficient Architecture: Basics for Planning and Construction. Basel/Berlin/Boston, 2006

Graf, Anton: Neue Passivhäuser. 24 Beispiele für den Energiestandard der Zukunft. Deutschland – Österreich – Schweiz. Munich, 2003

Gunßer, Christoph: Energiesparsiedlungen. Konzepte, Techniken, realisierte Beispiele. Munich, 2000

Haller, Andreas; Humm, Othmar; Voss, Karsten: Renovieren mit der Sonne. Solarenergienutzung im Altbau. Staufen, 2000

Hausladen, Gerd et al.: Climate Design: Solutions for Buildings that Can Do More with Less Technology. Munich, 2005

Hausladen, Gerhard et al.: Einführung in die Bauklimatik. Klima- und Energiekonzepte für Gebäude. Berlin, 2003

Hawkes, Dean; Forster, Wayne: Energy Efficient Buildings: Architecture, Engineering, and Environment. Stuttgart/Munich, 2002

Hegger, Manfred; Pohl, Wolfgang; Reiß-Schmidt, Stephan: Vitale Architektur. Traditionen, Projekte, Tendenzen einer Kultur des gewöhnlichen Bauens. Braunschweig/Wiesbaden, 1988

Hillmann, Gustav; Nagel, Joachim; Schreck, Hasso: Klimagerechte und energiesparende Architektur. Karlsruhe, 1981

Humm, Othmar; Gasser, Jeannette (Red.): NiedrigEnergie-Häuser. Innovative Bauweisen und neue Standards. Staufen, 1997

Jones, David Lloyd: Architecture and the Environment: Contemporary Green Buildings. Stuttgart, 1998

Knissel, Jens; Institut Wohnen & Umwelt (ed.): Energieeffiziente Büro- und Verwaltungsgebäude. Hinweise zur primärenergetischen und wirtschaftlichen Optimierung. Darmstadt, 1999

Kohler, Stephan et al.: Energieeffizienz von Gebäuden. Wüstenrot Foundation. Ludwigsburg, 2006

Königstein, Thomas: Ratgeber energiesparendes Bauen. Auf den Punkt gebracht: Neutrale Fachinformationen für mehr Energieeffizienz. Stuttgart, 2007

Krusche, Per et al.: Ökologisches Bauen/Umweltbundesamt. Wiesbaden/Berlin, 1982

Luebkeman, Chris/Arup: Drivers of Change 2006. London, 2006

Moewes, Günther: Weder Hütten noch Paläste. Architektur und Ökologie in der Arbeitsgesellschaft. Eine Streitschrift. Basel/Berlin/Boston, 1995

Moschig, Guido F.: Bausanierung. Grundlagen – Planung – Durchführung. Stuttgart/Leipzig/Wiesbaden, 2004

Musso, Florian; Schittich, Christian (ed.): In Detail: Building Simply. Munich/Basel/Boston/Berlin, 2005

O.Ö. Energiesparverband (ed.): Climasol. Leitfaden zum Thema solares Kühlen. Linz 2005

Ranft, Fred; Frohn, Bernhard: Natürliche Klimatisierung. Basel, 2003

Ray-Jones, Anna: Sustainable Architecture in Japan. The Green Buildings of Nikken Sekkei. London, 2000

Reiß, Johann; Erhorn, Hans; Reiber, Martin: Energetisch sanierte Wohngebäude. Maßnahmen, Energieeinsparung, Kosten. Stuttgart, 2002

Rötzel, Adolf: Praxiswissen umweltfreundliches Bauen. Stuttgart, 2005

Schneider, Astrid (ed.): Solararchitektur für Europa. Basel/Berlin/Boston, 1996

Schulze Darup, Burkhard; BINE-Informationsdienst (ed.): Energieeffiziente Wohngebäude. Einfamilienhäuser mit Zukunft. Cologne, 2002

Slessor, Catherine: Sustainable Architecture and High Technology. London, 1997

Steckeweh, Carl (ed.): Tendenz: nachhaltig. Info-Börse Wohnungsbau. Darmstadt, 1998

Tomm, Arwed: Ökologisch planen und bauen. Das Handbuch für Architekten, Ingenieure, Bauherren, Studenten, Baufirmen, Behörden, Stadtplaner, Politiker. Braunschweig/Wiesbaden, 2000

Voss, Karsten et al.: Bürogebäude mit Zukunft. Konzepte, Analysen, Erfahrungen. Berlin, 2006

Wines, James: Green Architecture. Cologne/London/Madrid, New York/Paris/Tokyo, 2000

Part B   Planning

Fundamentals

BINE Informationsdienst (ed.): Basis Energie 1: Klima und Energie. Bonn, 2003

BINE Informationsdienst (ed.): Basis Energie 7: Energie im Wandel. Bonn, 2000

BINE Informationsdienst (ed.): Basis Energie 15: Was ist Energie? Bonn, 2003

Federal Ministry for the Environment, Nature Conservation & Nuclear Safety (BMU) (ed.): Umweltpolitik. Erneuerbare Energien in Zahlen – nationale und internationale Entwicklung. Berlin, 2007

Federal Ministry for the Environment, Nature Conservation & Nuclear Safety (BMU) (ed.): Erneuerbare Energien – Innovationen für die Zukunft. Berlin, 2004

Fischer, Ernst Peter; Wiegandt, Klaus (ed.): Die Zukunft der Erde. Was verträgt unser Planet noch? Frankfurt am Main, 2005

Hellwig, Runa Tabea: Thermische Behaglichkeit. Unterschiede zwischen frei und mechanisch belüfteten Bürogebäuden aus Nutzersicht. Dissertation, Munich TU. Munich, 2005

Intergovernmental Panel on Climate Change (IPCC): 4th Assessment Report. Summary for Policymakers (AR4). Geneva, 2007

Meadows, Dennis et al.: The Limits to Growth. A Report for the Club of Rome's Project on the Predicament of Mankind. New York, 1972

Müller-Kraenner, Sascha: Energiesicherheit. Die neue Vermessung der Welt. Munich, 2007

Nitsch, Joachim: Leitstudie 2007. Aktualisierung und Neubewertung der Ausbaustrategie Erneuerbare Energien bis zu den Jahren 2020 und 2030 mit Ausblick bis 2050. Study carried out on behalf of the Federal Ministry for the Environment, Nature Conservation & Nuclear Safety. Berlin/Stuttgart, 2007

Nordmann, Thomas: Im Prinzip Sonne. Visionen zum Energiemarkt. Zurich, 2000

Scheer, Hermann: Solare Weltwirtschaft. Strategien für die ökologische Moderne. Munich, 2000

Schütze, Thorsten; Willkomm, Wolfgang: Klimagerechtes Bauen in Europa. Planungsinstrumente für klimagerechte, energiesparende Gebäudekonzepte in verschiedenen europäischen Klimazonen. Hamburg Polytechnic research project, with a focus on interdisciplinary research into "Planungsinstrumente für das umweltverträgliche Bauen", Department of Architecture & Civil Engineering. Hamburg 2000

Stern, Nicolas: The Economics of Climate Change. A report prepared on behalf of the UK Treasury. Cambridge, 2006

Urban space and infrastructure

Arbeitsgemeinschaft für Wärme und Heizkraftwirtschaft e.V. (AGFW): AGFW-Branchenreport. Frankfurt, 2006

Beier, Harm-Eckard: Entsiegelungswirkung verschiedener Oberbauarten. Modellhaft an einem Parkplatz in Abhängigkeit vom Witterungsverlauf. Osnabrück, 1998

Benevolo, Leonardo: The History of the City. Cambridge, 1980

BINE Informationsdienst (ed.): BINE-Info Profi-Info: Langzeitwärmespeicher und solare Nahwärme, 1/2001. Bonn, 2001

BINE Informationsdienst (ed.): BINE-Info Projektinfo: Kältespeicher in großen Kältenetzen, 10/2005. Bonn, 2005

BINE Informationsdienst (ed.): BINE-Info Projektinfo: Leistungsprognose von Windenergieanlagen, 14/2003. Bonn, 2003

Federal Ministry for Education & Research (BMBF) (ed.): Forschung für die Nachhaltigkeit – Rahmenprogramm des BMBF für eine zukunftsfähige innovative Gesellschaft. Berlin, 2005

Federal Ministry for the Environment, Nature Conservation & Nuclear Safety (BMU) (ed.): Abfallstatistik Diagramme. Berlin, 2004

Federal Ministry for the Environment, Nature Conservation & Nuclear Safety (BMU) (ed.): Fakten zur nachhaltigen Abfallwirtschaft. Berlin, 2007

Federal Ministry for Economics & Technology (BMWi); Federal Ministry for the Environment, Nature Conservation & Nuclear Safety (BMU) (ed.): Energieversorgung für Deutschland – Status Report, Energy Summit, 3 April 2006. Berlin, 2006

Centre for Resource Management: BRE Vortrag – Waste reduction in construction and recycled products. Watford 2005

Danner, Michael: INFU-Diskussionsbeiträge 25/05 – Ökologische und soziale Nachhaltigkeit beim Aufbau von Stadtteilen. Lüneburg, 2005

Faller, Peter: Der Wohngrundriss. Stuttgart, 1997

Fezer, Fritz: Das Klima der Städte. Gotha, 1995

Fisch, Manfred Norbert; Möws, Bruno; Zieger, Jürgen: Solarstadt. Konzepte, Technologien, Projekte. Stuttgart/Berlin/Cologne, 2001

Friedemann, Jens; Wiechers, Rüdiger: Städte für Menschen. Grundlagen und Visionen europäischer Stadtentwicklung. Frankfurt am Main, 2005

Gelfort, Petra et al.: Ökologie in den Städten. Erfahrungen aus Neubau und Modernisierung. Basel/Berlin/Boston, 1993

Gfeller Corthésy, Roland (ed.): Siedlungen und städtebauliche Projekte/Atelier 5. Braunschweig/Wiesbaden, 1994

Girardet, Herbert: Das Zeitalter der Städte. Neue Wege für eine nachhaltige Stadtentwicklung. Holm, 1996

Grub, Hermann; Lejeune, Petra: Emscher Landschaftspark (Region Ruhrgebiet), GrünGürtel Frankfurt, Regionalpark Rhein-Main, Grüne Nachbarschaft (Baden-Württemberg). Munich/New York, 1996

Grünwald, Reinhard; Oertel, Dagmar; Paschen, Herbert: Maßnahmen für eine nachhaltige Energieversorgung im Bereich Mobilität. Sachstandsbericht. TAB Report No. 79. Berlin, 2002

Hayden, Dolores: A Field Guide to Sprawl. New York, 2004

Herzog, Thomas: Solar Energy in Architecture and Urban Planning Munich, 1996

infas Institut f. angewandte Sozialwissenschaft; German Institute for Economic Research (DIW): Mobilität in Deutschland – Ergebnisbericht. Bonn/Berlin, 2004

Institut f. Umwelt & Energieforschung (IFEU) (ed.): Beitrag der Abfallwirtschaft zur nachhaltigen Entwicklung in Deutschland. Teilbericht Siedlungsabfälle. Heidelberg, 2005

Jessen, Johann: Lehrbausteine Städtebau. Basiswissen für Entwurf und Planung. Stuttgart, 2004

Kuhn, Tilmann E.; Institut für Umwelt und Energieforschung (IFEU): Sonnenschutz in der Fassade. Freiburg, 2002

Kennedy, Margrit; Kennedy, Declan (ed.): Handbuch ökologischer Siedlungs(um)bau. Neubau- und Stadterneuerungsprojekte in Europa. Berlin, 1998

Klotz, Arnold; Frey, Otto; Rosinak, Werner: Stadt und Nachhaltigkeit. Ein Diskurs. Vienna/New York, 2002

Knoflacher, Hermann: Stehzeuge – Fahrzeuge. Der Stau ist kein Verkehrsproblem. Vienna/Cologne/Weimar, 2001

Kreiblich, Rolf; Nolte, Roland: Umweltgerechter Verkehr. Berlin/Heidelberg/New York, 1996

Neufert, Ernst; Kister, Johannes: Bauentwurfslehre. Wiesbaden, 2005

Peter-Fröhlich, Anton et al.: Separate Ableitung und Behandlung von Urin, Fäkalien und Grauwasser. Overview of EU SCST demonstration project and results. Berlin, 2006

Ramesohl, Stephan; Wuppertal Institute for Climate, Environment & Energy (ed.): Analyse und Bewertung der Nutzungsmöglichkeiten von Biomasse. Final Report, vol. 1: Gesamtergebnisse und Schlussfolgerungen. Wuppertal, 2005

Sauer, Dirk Uwe: Optionen zur Speicherung elektrischer Energie in Energieversorgungssystemen mit regenerativer Stromerzeugung. In: Solarzeitalter, No. 4/2006

Sonderabfallgesellschaft Brandenburg/Berlin, (ed.): Kostensparen durch abfallarmes Bauen. Informationen zur Abfallvermeidung. Potsdam, 1999

Sperling, Carsten (ed.); Buchert, Matthias: Nachhaltige Stadtentwicklung beginnt im Quartier. Ein Praxis- und Ideenhandbuch für Stadtplaner, Baugemeinschaften, Bürgerinitiativen am Beispiel des sozial-ökologischen Modellstadtteils Freiburg-Vauban. Freiburg, 1999

Steierwald, Gerd (ed.): Stadtverkehrsplanung. Grundlagen, Methoden, Ziele. Berlin/Heidelberg/New York, 2005

Steinebach, Gerhard; Herz, Sabine; Jacob, Andreas: Ökologie in der Stadt- und Dorfplanung. Ökologische Gesamtkonzepte als planerische Zukunftsvorsorge. Basel/Berlin/Boston, 1993

Stich, Rudolf et al.: Stadtökologie in Bebauungsplänen. Fachgrundlagen, Rechtsvorschriften, Festsetzungen. Wiesbaden/Berlin, 1992

Sukopp, Herbert (ed.); Blume, Hans-Peter: Urban Ecology. Stuttgart/Jena/New York, 1993

Weeber, Hannes et al.: Besser wohnen in der Stadt. Konzepte und Beispiele für Familienwohnungen. Stuttgart, 2005

Weeber, Hannes; Bosch, Simone: Nachhaltig gute Wohnqualität. Beispielhafte Einfamilienhäuser in verdichteter Bebauung. Stuttgart, 2004

Weeber, Rotraut; Weeber, Hannes; Kähler, Gert: Baukultur! Informationen, Argumente, Konzepte. Zweiter Bericht zur Baukultur in Deutschland. Hamburg, 2005

Wolf, Günter; Pietzsch, Wolfgang: Straßenplanung. Düsseldorf, 2005

Building envelope

Arbeitsstätten-Richtlinien ASR 5: Lüftung. Berlin, 1979

Bergmann, Irene; Weiß, Werner: Fassadenintegration von thermischen Sonnenkollektoren ohne Hinterlüftung. Vienna, 2002

Blum, Hans Jürgen et al.: Doppelfassaden. Berlin, 2001

Compagno, Andrea: Intelligent Glass Facades. Material, Practice, Design. Basel/Berlin/Boston, 2002

Deutsches Kupfer-Institut e.V. (ed.): Architektur & Solarthermie. Dokumentation zum Architekturpreis. Darmstadt, 2002

Flagge, Ingeborg (ed.) et al.: Thomas Herzog. Architecture + Technology. Munich/London/New York, 2001

Grimm, Friedrich B.: Energieeffizientes Bauen mit Glas. Grundlagen, Gestaltung, Beispiele, Details. Munich, 2003

Hausladen, Gerhard: Climate Design: Solutions for Buildings that Can Do More with Less Technology. Munich, 2006

Herzog, Thomas; Krippner, Roland; Lang, Werner: Facade Construction Manual. Basel/Berlin/Boston, 2004

Hoffmann, C.; Voss, K.: Das Potenzial der passiven Kühlung im Gebäudebestand Bürobauten. Vorschlag einer Typologie. In: Bauphysik, No. 6/2005

Industrieverband Polyurethan-Hartschaum e.V. (IVPU) (ed.): Sommerlicher Wärmeschutz. Die wichtigsten Einflussfaktoren. Stuttgart, 2000

Kähler, Gert; Danner, Dietmar (ed.): Die klima-aktive Fassade. Leinfelden-Echterdingen, 1999

Köster, Helmut: Tageslichtdynamische Architektur. Grundlagen, Systeme, Projekte. Basel/Berlin/Boston, 2004

Pültz, Gunter: Bauklimatischer Entwurf für moderne Glasarchitektur. Passive Maßnahmen der Energieeinsparung. Angewandte Bauphysik. Munich, 2002

Reiß, Johann et al.: Solare Fassadensysteme. Energetische Effizienz – Kosten – Wirtschaftlichkeit. Stuttgart, 2005

Roth, Hans Werner: Neue Wege der Raumklimatechnik im Bürohaus. In: Intelligente Architektur/AIT Spezial, No. 01-02/2003

Schittich, Christian et al.: Glass Construction Manual, 2nd ed. Munich, 2007

Schittich, Christian (ed.): Building Skins, 2nd ed. Basel/Berlin/Boston, 2001

Schittich, Christian (ed.): Solar Architecture. Strategies, Visions, Concepts. Basel/Berlin/Boston, 2003

Association of Swiss Engineers & Architects (SIA) (ed.): SIA 382/1: Ventilation and air-conditioning systems – General principles and requirements. Zurich, 2006

Thierfelder, Anja (ed.); Carpenter, James: Transsolar Climate Engineering. Basel, 2003

Building services

Arbeitsstätten-Richtlinie ASR 7/3: Künstliche Beleuchtung. Berlin, 1993

ARCH+, No. 93/1988: Reyner Banham. Aachen, 1988

Bavarian Environment Agency (ed.): Effiziente Lichtsysteme. Energie sparen. Klima schützen. Kosten senken! Augsburg 2004

BINE-Informationsdienst (ed.); Fisch, Manfred Norbert: Wärmespeicher. Cologne, 2005

Bohne, Dirk: Ökologische Gebäudetechnik. Stuttgart, 2004

Daniels, Klaus: Advanced Building Systems: A Technical Guide for Architects and Engineers. Munich/Zurich, 2000

David, Ruth et al.: Heizen, Kühlen, Belüften & Beleuchten. Bilanzierungsgrundlagen nach DIN V 18599. Stuttgart, 2006

Eicker, Ursula: Solare Technologien für Gebäude. Stuttgart, 2001

Fraefel, Rudolf; Humm, Othmar: Heizen und Lüften im Niedrigenergiehaus. Staufen, 2000

Hagemann, Ingo Bert: Gebäudeintegrierte Photovoltaik-Systeme. Ein Beitrag zur Integration von Photovoltaik-Elementen in die Gebäudehülle. Aachen, 2002

Henning, Hans-Martin et al.: Solare Kühlung und Klimatisierung. Belüftung und Wärmerückgewinnung. Berlin, 2006

Herkel, Sebastian; Pfafferott, Jens; Zeuschner, Andreas: Thermischer Komfort im Sommer in Bürogebäuden mit passiver Kühlung. Freiburg, 2005

Hermannsdörfer, Ingrid ; Rüb, Chri: Solardesign. Photovoltaik für Altbau, Stadtraum, Landschaft. Berlin, 2005

Energy Information Centre (Baden-Württemberg) (ed.): Project documentation accompanying Baden-Württemberg Photovoltaic Architecture Prize 2001. Stuttgart, 2002

Institut für Solare Energieversorgungstechnik (ISET) (ed.): Multifunktionale Photovoltaik. Photovoltaik in der Gebäudehülle. Hamburg/Kassel 2006

Köhl, Michael; Orel, Boris: Farbige selektive Lacke für Solarfassaden. Freiburg, 2004

Laasch, Thomas; Laasch, Erhard: Haustechnik. Grundlagen – Planung – Ausführung. Wiesbaden, 2005

Baden-Württemberg Factory Inspectorate – Energy Information Centre (ed.): Sonnenwärme für Gebäude und Betrieb – Mittelgroße Solaranlagen. Stuttgart, 1999

Baden-Württemberg Factory Inspectorate – Energy Information Centre (ed.): Wasser erwärmen und heizen mit der Sonne. Stuttgart, 1997

Lüling, Claudia (ed.): Architektur unter Strom. Photovoltaik gestalten. Berlin, 2000

Lutz, Hans-Peter; Baden-Württemberg Factory Inspectorate – Energy Information Centre (ed.): Solaranlagen zur Warmwasserbereitung und Heizungsunterstützung im Eigenheim. Stuttgart, 2003

Mangold, Dirk; Müller-Steinhagen, Hans: Solar unterstützte Nahwärme und Langzeit-Wärmespeicher. In: Zeitschrift für eine nachhaltige Energiezufuhr, No. 01/2002.

Pistohl, Wolfram: Handbuch der Gebäudetechnik. Planungsgrundlagen und Beispiele. Vols. 1 & 2. Düsseldorf, 2007

Pitz-Paal, Robert: Solarthermische Kraftwerke. Wie die Sonne ins Kraftwerk kommt. In: Physik in unserer Zeit, Spezial: Solarenergie, No. 1/2004

Quaschning, Volker: Renaissance der Wärmepumpe. In: Sonne Wind & Wärme, No. 09/2006

Rexroth, Susanne (ed.): Gestalten mit Solarzellen. Photovoltaik in der Gebäudehülle. Heidelberg, 2001

RS Immo Pro (ed.): Vigas Holzvergaserkessel für wirtschaftliches und umweltschonendes Heizen. Rhede, 2007

SPIEGEL special, No. 1/2007: Neue Energien. Wege aus der Klimakatastrophe. Hamburg, 2007

Schütz, Peter: Ökologische Gebäudeausrüstung. Neue Lösungen. Vienna/New York, 2003

Stark, Thomas: Untersuchungen zur aktiven Nutzung erneuerbarer Energie am Beispiel eines Wohn- und eines Bürogebäudes. Stuttgart, 2004

Stark, Thomas; Baden-Württemberg Ministry of Economic Affairs (ed.): Architektonische Integration von Photovoltaik-Anlagen. Stuttgart, 2005

Wellpott, Edwin; Bohne, Dirk: Technischer Ausbau von Gebäuden. Stuttgart, 2006

Zimmermann, Mark: Handbuch der passiven Kühlung. Dübendorf, 1999

Materials

Addis, Dr. William: Building with Reclaimed Components and Materials. A Design Handbook for Reuse and Recycling. London, 2006

Arbeitsgemeinschaft Kreislaufwirtschaftsträger Bau (ed.): 4th Monitoring Report on Building Waste. Berlin, 2005

Baumann, Dr. Ruth et al.: Bewertung der Innenraumluft. Flüchtige organische Verbindungen – VOC. Allgemeiner Teil. Vienna, 2003

Swiss Ministry for Environment, Forests & Landscape (BUWAL) (ed.): Bewertung in Ökobilanzen mit der Methode der ökologischen Knappheit. Schriftenreihe Umwelt No. 297. Bern 1998

Austrian Ministry for Transport, Innovation & Technology (ed.): Ökoinform: Fußböden im "Haus der Zukunft". Nachhaltigkeit durch NAWARO›S. Vienna, 2006

Dworschak, Gunda; Wenke, Alfred: Der neue Systembau – Holz, Beton, Stahl. Skelett-, Tafel-, Zellenbauweise. Projektbeispiele, Konstruktion, Details, Kosten. Düsseldorf, 1999

Gesellschaft für Ökologische Bautechnik Berlin mbH (GFÖB): Instrumente für eine qualitätsabhängige Abschätzung der Dauerhaftigkeit von Materialien und Konstruktionen. Berlin, 2005

Gieseler, U.; Heidt, F.D.: Bewertung der Energieeffizienz verschiedener Maßnahmen für Gebäude mit sehr geringem Energiebedarf. Stuttgart, 2005

Graubner, Carl-Alexander; Hüske, Katja: Nachhaltigkeit im Bauwesen. Berlin, 2003

Gunßer, Christoph: Individuell bauen mit Systemen. Wohnhäuser aus Deutschland, Österreich und der Schweiz. Stuttgart/Munich, 2002

Häfele, Gottfried (ed.); Oed, Wolfgang; Sambeth, Burkhard M.: Baustoffe und Ökologie. Bewertungskriterien für Architekten und Bauherren. Tübingen/Berlin, 1996

Hegger, Manfred et al.: Construction Materials Manual. Munich/Basel, 2006

Hegger, Manfred; Drexler, Hans; Zeumer, Martin: Basics Materials. Basel/Berlin/Boston, 2007

Kasser, Ueli; Pöll, Michael; Graffe, Kathrin: Deklaration ökologischer Merkmale von Bauprodukten nach SIA 493. Erläuterung und Interpretation. Zurich, 1997

Kohler, Nikolfrom: Grundlagen zur Bewertung kreislaufgerechter, nachhaltiger Baustoffe, Bauteile und Bauwerke. Karlsruhe, 1998

Künzel, H. M. et al.: Feuchtepufferwirkung von Innenraumbekleidungen aus Holz oder Holzwerkstoffen. Stuttgart, 2006

Löfflad, Hans: Das globalrecyclingfähige Haus. Eindhoven, 2002

North Rhine-Westfalia Ministry for the Environment, Nature Conservation, Agriculture & Consumer Protection. North Rhine-Westfalia Environment & Health Campaign. Umweltzeichen für Bauprodukte. Bauprodukte gezielt auswählen – eine Entscheidungshilfe. Düsseldorf, 2004

Mittag, Martin: Baukonstruktionslehre. Ein Nachschlagewerk für den Bauschaffenden über Konstruktionssysteme, Bauteile und Bauarten. Braunschweig/Wiesbaden, 2000

Oswald, Rainer; Kottje, Johannes; Sous, Silke: Schwachstellen beim kostengünstigen Bauen. Stuttgart, 2004

Peter, Gustav; Muntwyler, René; Ladner, Marc: Baustofflehre. Bau und Energie. Leitfaden für Planung und Praxis. Zurich, 2005

Preisig, Hansruedi: Massiv- oder Leichtbauweise? Zurich, 2002

Schmidt-Bleek, Friedrich: Wieviel Umwelt braucht der Mensch? Faktor 10 – das Maß für ökologisches Wirtschaften. 1997

Schmidt-Bleek, Friedrich; Käo, Tönis; Huncke, Wolfram (ed.): Das Wuppertal-Haus. Bauen nach dem Mips-Konzept. Basel/Berlin/Boston, 1999

Schmitz, Norbert M. (Red.): Baustoffkunde für den Praktiker. Duisburg, 2004

Schneider, Klaus-Jürgen et al.: Bautabellen für Architekten. Munich, 2004

Schwarz, Jutta: Ökologie im Bau. Entscheidungshilfen zur Beurteilung und Auswahl von Baumaterialien. Bern/Stuttgart/Vienna, 1998

Sigg, René; Kälin, Werner; Plattner, Hugo: LUKRETIA – Lebenszyklus – Ressourcen – Technisierung. Zurich, 2006

Sommer, Adolf Werner: Wirtschaftliches Bauen. Kostenoptimierte Konstruktionen im Hochbau. Handbuch für Architekten und Ingenieure. Cologne, 2005

Steiger, Peter et al.: Hochbaukonstruktionen nach ökologischen Gesichtspunkten. SIA Dokumentation D 0123. Zurich, 1995

Darmstadt TU, Institute for Solid Construction, Prof. Graubner: Proceedings, Darmstadt Sustainability Symposium 2003. Darmstadt, 2003

Transsolar Energietechnik: lecture, Transsolar Climate Engineering. Basel, 2005

Waltjen, Tobias (ed.); Mötzl, Hildegund: Details for Passive Houses – A Catalogue of Ecologically Rated Constructions. Vienna/New York, 1999

Weidinger, Hans: Patina. Neue Ästhetik in der zeitgenössischen Architektur. Munich, 2003

Weston, Richard: Materials, Form and Architecture. Stuttgart, 2003

Zapke, Wilfried: Der Primärenergiegehalt der Baukonstruktionen unter gleichzeitiger Berücksichtigung der wesentlichen Baustoffeigenschaften und der Herstellungskosten. Stuttgart, 1998

Ziegert, Christof: In Balance – Das Feuchteabsorptionsvermögen von Lehmbaustoffen. Viersen-Boisheim, 2004

Zürcher, Christoph; Frank, Thomas: Bauphysik – Bau und Energie. Zurich, 2004

Zwiener, Gerd; Mötzl, Hildegund: Ökologisches Baustoff-Lexikon. Bauprodukte, Chemikalien, Schadstoffe, Ökologie, Innenraum. Heidelberg, 2006

Strategies

Bertelsmann Foundation (ed.): Prozessleitfaden Public Private Partnership. Frankfurt am Main, 2003

Federal Ministry of Transport, Building & Urban Affairs (BMVBW): Leitfaden nachhaltiges Bauen. Berlin/Bonn, 2001

BUND/Misereor (ed.): Zukunftsfähiges Deutschland. Ein Beitrag zu einer global nachhaltigen Entwicklung (Wuppertal Institute for Climate, Environment & Energy). Basel/Boston/Berlin, 1996

Deutsches Institut für Normung (DIN): DIN V 18599 preliminary standards series – Energy efficiency of buildings – Calculation of the net, final and primary energy demand for heating, cooling, ventilation, domestic hot water and lighting. Berlin, 2005

Diederichs, Claus Jürgen; Getto, Petra; Streck, Stefanie: Entwicklung eines Bewertungssystems für ökonomisches und ökologisches Bauen und gesundes Wohnen. Stuttgart, 2003

Gänßmantel, Jürgen; Geburtig, Gerd; Eßmann, Frank: EnEV und Bauen im Bestand. Berlin, 2006

Geißler, Susanne; Tritthart, Wibke: IEA TASK 23. Optimization of Solar Energy Use in Large Buildings. Vienna, 2002

Gruber, Edelgard et al.: Energiepass für Gebäude. Evaluation des Feldversuchs. Study carried out on behalf of the German Energy Agency (dena). Karlsruhe, 2005

Brundtland Commission: Our Common Future, Report of the World Commission on Environment and Development. Greven, 1987

Jörissen, Juliane et al.: Zukunftsfähiges Wohnen und Bauen. Herausforderungen, Defizite, Strategien. Berlin, 2005

Koschenz, Markus; Pfeiffer, Andreas: Potenzial Wohngebäude. Energie- und Gebäudetechnik für die 2000-Watt-Gesellschaft. Zurich, 2005

Löhnert, Günter; Herkel, Sebastian; Voss, Karsten: Bürogebäude mit Zukunft. Konzepte, Analysen, Erfahrungen. Cologne, 2005

Lützkendorf, Thomas et al.: Nachhaltiges Planen, Bauen und Bewirtschaften von Bauwerken. Ziele, Grundlagen, Stand und Trends. Bewertungsmethoden und -hilfsmittel. Brief study for the BMVBW. Karlsruhe, 2002

Lützkendorf, Thomas et al.: Nachhaltigkeitsorientierte Investments im Immobilienbereich. Trends, Theorie und Typologie. Karlsruhe, 2005

Preisig, Hansruedi et al.: Der ökologische Bauauftrag. Ein Leitfaden für die umweltgerechte und kostenbewusste Planung. Munich, 2001

Rink, Dieter; Wächter, Monika: Naturverständnisse in der Nachhaltigkeitsforschung. Frankfurt am Main, 2004

Association of Swiss Engineers & Architects (SIA) (ed.): Recommendation SIA 112/1. "Sustainable construction – buildings". Zurich, 2004

Association of Swiss Engineers & Architects (SIA) (ed.): SIA D 0216. SIA Energy Efficiency Path. Zurich, 2006

Tischer, Martin et al.: Auf dem Weg zur 100% Region. Handbuch für eine nachhaltige Energieversorgung von Regionen. Munich, 2006

U.S. Green Building Council (ed.): The LEED – New Construction & Major Renovation Version 2.2 Reference Guide. Washington, 2006

Wiese-von Ofen, Irene: Kultur der Partizipation. Beiträge zu neuen Formen der Bürgerbeteiligung bei der räumlichen Planung. Berlin, 2002

Picture credits

The authors and publishers would like to express their sincere gratitude to all those who have assisted in the production of this book, be it through providing photos or artwork or granting permission to reproduce their documents or providing other information. All the drawings in this book were specially commissioned. Photographs not specifically credited were taken by the architects or are works photographs or were supplied from the archives of the magazine DETAIL. Despite intensive endeavours we were unable to establish copyright ownership in just a few cases; however, copyright is assured. Please notify us accordingly in such instances.
The numbers refer to the figures.

Photographs

Part A Positions

A	NASA, Houston

Global change

A 1.2	Keren Su/corbis
A 1.5	Barry Howe/corbis

Energy change

A 2.1	Curtis Morton, Adelaide
A 2.5	Till Leeser, Hamburg

**Architecture and sustainability –
a difficult relationship**

A 3.2	Jan Bitter, Berlin
A 3.3	Damjan Gale, Ljubljana
A 3.4	Frank Kaltenbach, Munich
A 3.5	Paul Ott, Graz
A 3.6	Jörg von Bruchhausen, Berlin
A 3.7	Stefan Müller-Naumann, Munich
A 3.8	Frank Kaltenbach, Munich

Doing things right – on efficiency and sustainability

A 4.1a	Burgess/SPL/Agentur Focus, Hamburg
A 4.3a	Eye Of Science/Agentur Focus, Hamburg
A 4.3b	Constantin Meyer, Cologne
A 4.5a	Tobias Bindhammer, Ulm

Solar architecture

A 5.1	Dieter Leistner/artur, Essen
A 5.5	Dieter Leistner/artur, Essen
A 5.6	Robertino Nikolic/artur, Essen
A 5.7	Dieter Leistner/artur, Essen
A 5.8	Robertino Nikolic/artur, Essen

Planning and building in life cycles

A 6.1	Tomas Riehle/artur, Cologne
A 6.4	Tomas Riehle/artur, Cologne
A 6.6	Tomas Riehle/artur, Cologne

Part B Planning

B	IKONOS satellite/GeoEye, Thornton

Fundamentals

B 1.1	NASA, Houston
B 1.4	Bernd Lötsch, Vienna
B 1.5	from: Smith, Courtenay; Topham, Sean: Extreme Houses. Munich/Berlin/London/New York, 2002, p.13
B 1.6	from: Behling, Sophia & Stefan: Solar Power: The Evolution of Sustainable Architecture. Munich/New York, 1996, p. 188
B 1.31	Marine Current Turbines Ltd, Bristol
B 1.34	Richard Davis, London
B 1.35	Schlaich Bergermann und Partner, Stuttgart

Urban space and infrastructure

B 2.1	Margherita Spiluttini, Vienna
B 2.4	Darmstadt TU, GTA picture archives
B 2.9	W. Willi Engel, Berlin
B 2.10	Eduard Hueber, New York
B 2.11	Oliver Heissner, Hamburg
B 2.13	fabuloussavers.com
B 2.21	Hervé Abbadie, Paris
B 2.23	Rupert Steiner, Vienna
B 2.37	Isbrand Penner, Ettlingen
B 2.57	Darmstadt TU, FG EE picture archives
B 2.58	Thomas Ott, Mühltal
B 2.62	Der Grüne Punkt
B 2.69	Atelier 5, Bern
B 2.70a–c	Jan Gerrit Schäfer, Hanover
B 2.71	Stefan Schilling, Cologne
B 2.76	Alex S. MacLean, Cambridge

Building envelope

B 3.1	Sunways AG, Constance
B 3.4	Frank Kaltenbach, Munich
B 3.5	H. G. Esch, Hennef
B 3.6	Ruedi Walti, Basel
B 3.16	Thomas Dix/archenova, Düsseldorf
B 3.17	Lukas Roth, Cologne
B 3.18	Corinne Rose, Berlin
B 3.19	Roger Frei, Zurich
B 3.20	Christian Richters, Münster
B 3.21	Thomas Dix, Grenzach-Wyhlen
B 3.22	Jens Willebrand, Düsseldorf
B 3.23	Dieter Leistner/artur, Essen
B 3.24	Delugan-Meissl, Vienna
B 3.25	Christian Richters, Münster
B 3.26	Roland Halbe/artur, Essen
B 3.27	Greenpeace
B 3.28	Ibewert, Tröstau
B 3.33	Eduard Hueber, New York
B 3.34	Manfred Hegger, Kassel
B 3.35	Institut für Gebäude + Energie + Licht Planung, Wismar
B 3.36	Toni Küng, Herisau
B 3.37	Francesca Giovannelli, Zurich
B 3.39	Gaston Wicky, Zurich
B 3.40	Jens Willebrand, Cologne
B 3.42	Margherita Spiluttini, Vienna
B 3.43	Hinrich Reyelts, Karlsruhe
B 3.44	Beat Kämpfen, Zurich
B 3.46	Frank Dierks, Darmstadt
B 3.47	EGS-plan, Stuttgart
B 3.48	Ivar Mjell, Århus
B 3.49	Jörg Lange, Freiburg
B 3.60	Klaus Frahm/artur, Essen
B 3.61	Waltraud Krase, Frankfurt
B 3.62	Christian Kandzia, Stuttgart
B 3.63	Martin Duckek, Ulm
B 3.73	Jan Bitter, Berlin
B 3.74	Thomas Gerken, Ulm
B 3.75	Moritz Korn/artur, Essen
B 3.76	Jörg Hempel, Aachen
B 3.77	Peter Cook/view/artur, Essen
B 3.78	Dieter Leistner/artur, Essen
B 3.79	Peter Hübner, Neckartenzlingen
B 3.83	Rainer Rehfeld, Cologne
B 3.92a–b	fbta, Universität Karlsruhe
B 3.94	Oliver Schuster, Stuttgart
B 3.100	Georg Nemec, Freiburg
B 3.101	ARS, Schwerin
B 3.104	Schaudt Architekten, Constance
B 3.105	Jens Passoth, Berlin
B 3.106	Jürgen Schmidt, Cologne
B 3.107	Ferit Kuyas/Sunways AG, Constance
B 3.108	Peter Ferstl, Regensburg
B 3.109	Christian Richters, Münster
B 3.111	Constantin Meyer, Cologne

Building services

B 4.1	Manfred Hegger, Kassel
B 4.4	from: Mouchot, Augustin: Die Sonnenwärme und ihre industriellen Anwendungen. Oberbözberg, 1987, p. 199
B 4.6–8	from: Butti, Ken; Perlin, John: A Golden Thread. Palo Alto, 1980, p. 119
B 4.9	Richard Schenkirz, Leonberg
B 4.10	triolog, Freiburg
B 4.20a–c	Jenni Energietechnik AG, Oberburg
B 4.26	Westerwälder Holzpellets GmbH, Langenbach
B 4.30	Fraunhofer Institute for Solar Energy Systems, Freiburg
B 4.37	Matthias Weissengruber, Kennelbach
B 4.41	Viessmann Werke GmbH & Co. KG, Allendorf
B 4.46	Viessmann Werke GmbH & Co. KG, Allendorf
B 4.55	Wagner & Co Solartechnik GmbH, Cölbe
B 4.76	Christian Kandzia, Stuttgart
B 4.91	Denis Gilbert/VIEW/artur, Essen
B 4.92	Darmstadt TU, FG EE picture archives
B 4.96	Wolf GmbH, Mainburg
B 4.104	Thomas Mayer/www.erco.com, Lüdenscheid
B 4.105	Sunways AG, Constance
B 4.110a–b	Nigel Young, London
B 4.110c	SCHOTT Solar GmbH, Alzenau
B 4.110d	Zentrum für Sonnenenergie- und Wasserstoff-Forschung Baden Würtemberg
B 4.110e	First Solar GmbH, Berlin
B 4.114	United Solar Ovonic, Michigan
B 4.115–117	Michael Bender, Darmstadt
B 4.118	Andreas Keller, Altdorf
B 4.124	SenerTec GmbH, Schweinfurt
B 4.126	Viessmann Werke GmbH & Co. KG, Allendorf
B 4.131	Volker Quaschning, Berlin
B 4.132	Kramer Junction, USA
B 4.133	Peter Grell, Rheinfelden

Material

B 5.1	Alvar Aalto Museum, FIN-Jyväskylä
B 5.2	from: Curtis, William J. R.: Le Corbusier – Ideas and Forms. Stuttgart, 1987, p. 135
B 5.3	The Estate of R. Buckminster Fuller, Santa Babara
B 5.4	from: Werner, Ernst: Der Kristallpalast zu London. 1851, Düsseldorf, 1970
B 5.7	Francis Jonckheere, Brussels
B 5.8	James Thornett, Birmingham
B 5.9	Anne Bousema, Rotterdam
B 5.10a–c	Frank Kaltenbach, Munich
B 5.19	Wolfgang Wittmann, Munich
B 5.27	Peter Bonfig, Munich
B 5.37	Andreas Keller, Kirchentellinsfurt
B 5.38	Hugo Jehle, Stuttgart
B 5.39	Gesimat GmbH, Berlin
B 5.42	Gaston Wicky, Zurich
B 5.43	Foto Claytec, Duisburg
B 5.58	Ignacio Martinez, Hard
B 5.64	Herbert Schwingenschlögl, Vienna
B 5.65	Christian Schittich, Munich
B 5.66	Roland Halbe/artur, Essen
B 5.67	Duccio Malagamba, Barcelona
B 5.68	David Joseph, New York
B 5.75	Naoya Hatakeyama, Tokyo, from: Berg, Stephan: Naoya Hatakeyama, Ostfildern-Ruit, 2002, p. 56
B 5.76	Luis Ferreira Alves, Porto
B 5.82	Jussi Tiainen, Helsinki
B 5.86	Peter Kasper, Gundelfingen
B 5.89	Serge Brison, Brussels
B 5.90	Hélène Binet, London
B 5.96–97	Christiane Sauer, Berlin
B 5.99	Torsten Seidel, Berlin

Strategies

B 6.1	Reuters/corbis
B 6.6	Frei Otto, Leonberg-Warmbronn
B 6.12	HHS-AG, Kassel
B 6.15	from: Field, Marcus: Future Systems. Vienna, 1999, p. 58

B 6.16   from: Field, Marcus: Future Systems. Vienna, 1999, p. 192
B 6.17–18   HL-Technik, Munich

Part C Case studies

C   Jason Hawkes/corbis

p. 200 top   Wilfried Dechau, Stuttgart
p. 201   Thomas Banfi, CH-Paverne
pp. 202–204   Matthias Weissengruber, Kennelbach
pp. 205, 207   Jeroen Musch, Amsterdam
p. 206   Johan Fowelin/B. Martin, Stockholm
p. 208   Bernd Borchardt, Berlin
pp. 213–215   Günter Richard Wett, Innsbruck
pp. 216, 217,
218 bottom   Georg Aerni, Zurich
pp. 219–221   Paul Ott, Graz
pp. 222–224   Dirk Altenkirch, Karlsruhe
pp. 225–227   Jens Passoth, Berlin
pp. 228–29   Manfred Hegger, Kassel
p. 230   Monika Nikolic/artur, Essen
p. 231 top, 232 left Caroline Sohie, London
p. 231 bottom,
232 right, 233   Christian Richters, Münster
p. 234   Michel Brunelle, Montréal
p. 236   Michel Tremblay, Montréal
pp. 237, 239   Guido Kirsch, Freiburg
pp. 240–242   Roger Frei, Zurich
p. 243   Ralph Richter, Düsseldorf
p. 244   Svenja Bockhop, Berlin
p. 245   Sebastian Jehle, Berlin
p. 246   Anton Grassl, Boston
p. 247–248   Roland Halbe, Stuttgart
p. 249–250   Bertram Kober/punctum, Leipzig
p. 252   Linda Hancock, London
p. 253 left   Graham Gaunt, St. Ives
p. 253 right   Dennis Gilbert/view/artur, Essen
p. 255   Ralf-Peter Busse, Leipzig
p. 256   Frank Kaltenbach, Munich
p. 257   Paul Raftery/view/artur, Essen

Graphics

Part A   Positions

A 1.6   Deutsche BP AG: Solarstrom aus Sonnenenergie. Bochum, 2004
A 4.4   Kondratieff, Nikolai: Die langen Wellen der Konjunktur. In: Archiv für Sozialwissenschaft und Sozialpolitik, vol. 56/1926
          Nefiodow, Leo A.: Der sechste Kondratieff. Sankt Augustin, 2007
A 4.7   Die Welt, No. 8/2006, p. 20

Part B   Planning

Fundamentals
B 1.2   Meadows, Dennis et al.: The Limits to Growth. A Report for the Club of Rome's Project on the Predicament of Mankind. New York, 1972, p. 166
B 1.3   according to data from Petit, J. R.; Jouzel, J. et al.: Temperatur und CO2- Konzentration in den vergangenen 400 000 Jahren (ermittelt am Wostok-Eiskern). In: Nature, No. 369/1999
B 1.7   Stern, Nicolas: The Economics of Climate Change. A report prepared on behalf of the UK Treasury. Cambridge, 2006
B 1.8   according to data from Nitsch, Joachim: Ein globales Nachhaltigkeitsszenario. Stuttgart, 2004, p. 1
B 1.9   based on Potsdam Institute for Climate Impact Research (PIK): Tipping Points im Klimasystem. Potsdam, 2007

B 1.10   Federal Ministry for the Environment, Nature Conservation & Nuclear Safety (ed.): Erneuerbare Energien – Innovationen für die Zukunft. Berlin, 2004, p. 12
B 1.11   Federal Reserve Bank of St. Louis: Nominal Crude Oil Price (WTI), 1946 to Oct 2006. St. Louis, 2006
B 1.12   BP – Statistical Review of World Energy, IEA – World Energy Outlook: Prognosen für den Abbau nicht erneuerbarer Rohstoffe. Bochum/Paris, 2004
B 1.14   ExxonMobil: Studie "Öldorado" 2003. Zurich 2003
B 1.15–16 according to data from World Resources Institute: Die größten Klimasünder. Washington, 2003
B 1.17   German Institute for Economic Research: Klimaschutz – Das Kyoto-Protokoll. Berlin, 2004
B 1.18   ibased on Feddeck, Paul; BINE Informationsdienst (ed.): Basis Energie 15: Was ist Energie? Karlsruhe, 2003, p. 2
B 1.19   Kaltschmitt, Martin (ed.): Erneuerbare Energien. Systemtechnik, Wirtschaftlichkeit, Umweltaspekte. Berlin, 2006
B 1.20   Federal Ministry for Economics & Technology (ed.): Energie-Daten. Nationale und internationale Entwicklung. Zahlen und Fakten. Bonn, 2001
B 1.21   see B 1.10, p. 11
B 1.22   according to data from Federal Ministry for the Environment, Nature Conservation & Nuclear Safety (ed.): Entwicklung der erneuerbaren Energien im Jahr 2006 in Deutschland. Berlin/Stuttgart, 2007, p. 8
B 1.23   based on Kaltschmitt, Martin (ed.): Regenerative Energieträger zur Stromerzeugung I + II. Stuttgart, 2001
B 1.24   see B 1.10, p. 17
B 1.25   see B 1.8, p. 8
B 1.26   Nitsch, Joachim; Federal Ministry for the Environment, Nature Conservation & Nuclear Safety (ed.): Leitstudie 2007. Ausbaustrategie Erneuerbare Energien. Aktualisierung und Neubewertung bis zu den Jahren 2020 und 2030 mit Ausblick bis 2050. Berlin/Stuttgart, 2007, p. 9
B 1.27   Federal Ministry for the Environment, Nature Conservation & Nuclear Safety (ed.): Erneuerbare Energien in Zahlen – nationale und internationale Entwicklung. Berlin, 2006, p. 27
B 1.28   see B 1.22, p. 11
B 1.29   Stark, Thomas: Untersuchungen zur aktiven Nutzung erneuerbarer Energie am Beispiel eines Wohn- und eines Bürogebäudes. Stuttgart 2004, p. 33
B 1.30   see B 1.27
B 1.32   see B 1.26, p. 71
B 1.37   see B 1.10, p. 16
B 1.40–42 Daniels, Klaus: Low Tech – Light Tech – High Tech. Bauen in der Informationsgesellschaft. Basel/Berlin/Boston 1998, pp. 46, 59
B 1.43   according to data from Schütze, Thorsten; Willkomm, Wolfgang: Klimagerechtes Bauen in Europa. Planungsinstrumente für klimagerechte, energiesparende Gebäudekonzepte in verschiedenen europäischen Klimazonen. Hamburg Polytechnic research project, with a focus on interdisciplinary research. Hamburg 2000
B 1.44   Photovoltaic Geographical Information System, European Commission: Solar resource and photovoltaic electricity potential in Europe. Ispra 2006
B 1.45   see B 1.40, p. 56
B 1.46   Hausladen, Gerhard et al.: Climate Design: Solutions for Buildings that Can Do More with Less Technology. Munich, 2005, p. 183
B 1.47   Glücklich, Detlef (ed.): Ökologisches Bauen. Von Grundlagen zu Gesamtkonzepten. Munich, 2005, p. 56
B 1.48   Berkovski, Boris: Solar Electricity. New York, 1994, p. 10
B 1.49   based on Frank, W.: Raumklima und thermische Behaglichkeit. In: Berichte aus der Bauforschung,

No. 104. Berlin, 1975
B 1.50   see B 1.43
B 1.51   Behling, Sophia; Behling, Stefan: Solar Power: The Evolution of Sustainable Architecture. Munich/New York, 1996, p. 37
B 1.52   Hebgen, H.; Heck, F.: Außenwandkonstruktion mit optimalem Wärmeschutz. Gütersloh, 1983
B 1.53   Wellpott, Edwin; Bohne, Dirk: Technischer Ausbau von Gebäuden. Stuttgart, 2006, p. 13
B 1.54   Schulze Darup, Burkhard: Bauökologie. Wiesbaden/Berlin, 1996, p. 62
B 1.56   see B 1.53, p. 12
B 1.58   Hellwig, Runa Tabea: Thermische Behaglichkeit. Unterschiede zwischen frei und mechanisch belüfteten Bürogebäuden aus Nutzersicht. Dissertation, Munich Technical University. Munich, 2005
B 1.65   see B 1.58
B 1.66–67 Neufert, Ernst; Kister, Johannes: Architects' Data. Wiesbaden, 2005

Urban space and infrastructure
B 2.2   Schulze Darup, Burkhard. Nuremberg, 2002
B 2.3   Federal Ministry for Economics & Technology. Berlin, 2005
B 2.5   Herzog, Thomas: Solar Energy in Architecture and Urban Planning. Munich, 1996
B 2.6–7   Daniels, Klaus: The Technology of Ecological Building: Basic Principles, Examples and Ideas. Basel/Berlin/Boston, 1995
B 2.8   based on Gauzin-Müller, Dominique; Favet, Nicolas: Sustainable Architecture and Urbanism: Design, Construction, Examples. Basel/Berlin/Boston, 2002
B 2.12   see B 2.6
B 2.14–15   see B 2.6
B 2.18   according to data from Sukopp, Herbert (ed.); Blume, Hans-Peter: Urban Ecology. Stuttgart/Jena/New York, 1993
B 2.19   see B 2.6
B 2.20   see B 1.47
B 2.22   DIN 1986 Drainage systems on private ground. Berlin, 2004
          Beier, Harm-Eckard: Entsiegelungswirkung verschiedener Oberbauarten. Modellhaft an einem Parkplatz in Abhängigkeit vom Witterungsverlauf. Osnabrück, 1998
B 2.24   DIN 1986 Drainage systems on private ground. Berlin, 2004
B 2.26   Pistohl, Wolfram: Handbuch der Gebäudetechnik. Planungsgrundlagen und Beispiele. Vols. 1 & 2. Düsseldorf, 2007
B 2.27   see B 2.26
B 2.29   based on Schwagenscheidt, Walter: "Die Wohnung für das Existenzminimum", exhibition catalogue. In: Holz Stein Eisen, No. 9/30
B 2.31   RWE AG. Essen 2007
B 2.32   BINE Informationsdienst (ed.): Projektinfo – Leistungsprognose von Windenergieanlagen, 14/2003. Bonn, 2003
B 2.35   Greenpeace Energy. In: SPIEGEL special, No. 1/2007
B 2.38   based on Ramesohl, Stephan; Wuppertal Institute for Climate, Environment & Energy (ed.): Analyse und Bewertung der Nutzungsmöglichkeiten von Biomasse. Final report, vol. 1: Gesamtergebnisse und Schlussfolgerungen. Wuppertal 2005
B 2.41   according to data from Arbeitsgemeinschaft für Wärme und Heizkraftwirtschaft e.V.: AGFW branch report. Frankfurt 2006
B 2.42   based on Industrielle Werke Basel. Basel, 2007
B 2.43   see B 2.41
B 2.44   based on BINE Informationsdienst (ed.): www.energie-projekte.de. Karlsruhe 2006
B 2.45   based on BINE Informationsdienst (ed.): Projektinfo – Kältespeicher in großen Kältenetzen, 10/2005. Bonn, 2005
B 2.46–48 Fisch, Manfred Norbert; Möws, Bruno; Zieger, Jürgen: Solarstadt. Konzepte, Technologien, Projekte. Stuttgart/Berlin/Cologne, 2001

B 2.49   see B 2.26
B 2.50   see B 2.38
B 2.51   according to data from RWE AG: Wasser-
           Wissen. Essen 2006
B 2.53–55 see B 1.47
B 2.59   Federal Ministry for the Environment, Nature
           Conservation & Nuclear Safety: Abfallstatistik
           Diagramme. Berlin, 2004
B 2.60   Federal Ministry for the Environment, Nature
           Conservation & Nuclear Safety: Fakten zur
           nachhaltigen Abfallwirtschaft. Berlin, 2007
B 2.61   based on Duales System Deutschland GmbH.
           Cologne, 2006
B 2.63   according to data from infas Institut für ange-
           wandte Sozialwissenschaft GmbH; German
           Institute for Economic Research: Mobilität in
           Deutschland – Ergebnisbericht. Bonn/Berlin,
           2004; see also B 1.47
B 2.64   see B 1.47
B 2.65   according to data from Federal Statistical
           Office: destatis database. Wiesbaden, 2007
B 2.66   according to data from Steierwald, Gerd;
           Künne, Hans Dieter; Vogt, Walter: Stadtverkehrs-
           planung. Berlin/Heidelberg/New York, 2005
B 2.67   according to data from Grünwald, Reinhard;
           Oertel, Dagmar; Paschen, Herbert: Maßnahmen
           für eine nachhaltige Energieversorgung im
           Bereich Mobilität. Status report. TAB report
           No. 79. Berlin, 2002
B 2.68   Weeber, Hannes et al.: Besser wohnen in der
           Stadt. Konzepte und Beispiele für Familien-
           wohnungen. Stuttgart, 2005
B 2.72–73 see B 1.47
B 2.74   see B 1.66
B 2.77   see B 1.66
B 2.78   Otto Wöhr GmbH: Produktinformation.
           Friolzheim, 2006

Building envelope
B 3.9   based on Energy Conservation Act (EnEV).
           Berlin, 2007
B 3.12   based on DIN EN ISO Building components
           and building elements – Thermal resistance
           and thermal transmittance – Calculation method.
           Berlin, 2003
B 3.13   see B 3.9
B 3.14   Hegger, Manfred et al.: Construction Materials
           Manual. Munich, 2006
B 3.15   based on Sto AG. Stühlingen, 2007
B 3.31   based on Balkow, Dieter; Schittich, Christian et
           al.: Glass Construction Manual, 1st ed. Munich,
           1999
B 3.32   Langer, Heinz: tec21, No. 29-30/2001. Zurich,
           2001, p. 13
B 3.38   GLASSX AG. Zurich, 2007
B 3.45   based on Bergmann, Irene; Weiß, Werner:
           Fassadenintegration von thermischen Sonnen-
           kollektoren ohne Hinterlüftung. Vienna, 2002,
           p. 10
B 3.50   based on Association of Swiss Engineers &
           Architects (SIA) (ed.): SIA 382/1: Ventilation and
           air-conditioning systems – General principles
           and requirements. Zurich, 2006
B 3.54   DIN 4108-2 Thermal protection and energy
           economy in buildings – Part 2: Minimum
           requirements to thermal insulation. Berlin, 2003
B 3.58–59 see B 2.26, L 65
B 3.64–66 DIN 4108 Thermal protection and energy
           economy in buildings. Berlin, 2003
B 3.68–69 Hausladen, Gerhard:
           Climate Design: Solutions for Buildings that Can
           Do More with Less Technology. Munich, 2006,
           pp. 41 and 56
B 3.70   see B 2.26, L 38
B 3.71   based on Arbeitsstätten-Richtlinien ASR 5:
           Lüftung. Berlin, 1979
B 3.81   see B 1.46
B 3.82   based on Franzke, Uwe et al.; Institut für Luft- &
           Kältetechnik (ILK) (ed.): Wirtschaftlichkeit der
           dezentralen Klimatisierung im Vergleich zu
           zentralen RLT-Anlagen. Dresden, 2003, p. 11

B 3.84   based on Köster, Helmut: Tageslichtdyna-
           mische Architektur. Grundlagen, Systeme,
           Projekte. Basel/Berlin/Boston, 2004, p. 23
B 3.85   Löhnert, Günter; Herkel, Sebastian; Voss,
           Karsten: Bürogebäude mit Zukunft. Konzepte,
           Analysen, Erfahrungen. Cologne, 2005
B 3.86–87 see B 1.66
B 3.88   DIN V 4108-6 Thermal protection and energy
           economy in buildings – Part 6: Calculation of
           annual heat and energy use. Berlin, 2003
B 3.90   Lahme, Andreas: Beispiele und Vergleiche –
           Zum einfachen Berechnungsverfahren der
           Tageslichtautonomie und des Strombedarfs für
           die künstliche Beleuchtung von Räumen spe-
           ziell für die frühe Gebäudeplanungsphase.
           Braunschweig, 2002, p. 7
B 3.91   see B 1.66
B 3.95   see B 3.31
B 3.96   see B 1.66, p. 497
B 3.97–98 see B 2.26, K 97–98
B 3.99   see B 1.29, p. 198
B 3.102   see B 1.29
B 3.103   Stark, Thomas; Baden-Württemberg Ministry
           of Economic Affairs (ed.): Architektonische
           Integration von Photovoltaik-Anlagen. Stuttgart,
           2005, p. 21
B 3.110   see B 1.29

Building services
B 4.2   Treberspurg, Martin: Neues Bauen mit der
           Sonne. Ansätze zu einer klimagerechten
           Architektur. Vienna/New York, 1999
B 4.13   see B 2.26, H 41
B 4.15   according to data from BINE Informationsdienst
           (ed.): Projektinfo – Evaluierung energieeffizienter
           Wohngebäude, 5/2005. Bonn, 2005, p. 2
B 4.16   Kaltschmitt, Martin (ed.): Energie aus Biomasse:
           Grundlagen, Techniken und Verfahren. Berlin,
           2001
B 4.18   see B 2.26, H 144
B 4.19a   VIGAS Holzvergaser, RS ImmoPro GmbH.
           Rhede, 2007
B 4.19b   Rennergy Systems AG. Buchenberg, 2007
B 4.19c   ÖkoFEN. Bühl, 2007
B 4.24   based on BINE Informationsdienst (ed.): Basis
           Energie 1: Holz – Energie aus Biomasse. Bonn,
           2002, p. 2
B 4.31   Fisch, Manfred Norbert: lecture manuscript,
           Solartechnik I, ITW University of Stuttgart.
           Stuttgart, 2007
B 4.32   see B 1.29
B 4.34   see B 2.26, H 256
B 4.36   see B 4.31
B 4.40   Hilz, Wolfgang; Sonnenhaus-Institut e.V. (ed.):
           Heizkonzept im Sonnenhaus. Straubing, 2007,
           p. 2
B 4.42   see B 2.26, H 230
B 4.45   see B 2.26, H 231
B 4.47   based on BINE Informationsdienst (ed.): Basis
           Energie 10: Wärmepumpen. Bonn, 2001, p. 2
B 4.48   Quaschning, Volker: Renaissance der
           Wärmepumpe. In: Sonne Wind & Wärme;
           No. 09/2006. pp. 28-31
B 4.49   see B 4.47
B 4.51   based on BINE Informationsdienst (ed.): Basis
           Energie 19: Wärme und Strom speichern. Bonn,
           2005, p. 2
B 4.53   based on BINE Informationsdienst (ed.):
           Themeninfo – Latentwärmespeicher, 4/2002.
           Bonn, 2002, p. 2
B 4.54   based on BINE Informationsdienst (ed.):
           Projektinfo – Thermochemische Speicher,
           2/2001. Bonn, 2001, p. 2
B 4.56   BINE Informationsdienst (ed.): Profi-Info –
           Langzeit-Wärmespeicher und solare Nah-
           wärme, 1/2001. Bonn, 2001
B 4.57   based on Lutz, Hans-Peter; Baden-Württem-
           berg Factory Inspectorate – Energy Information
           Centre (ed.): Solaranlagen zur Warmwasser-
           bereitung und Heizungsunterstützung im Eigen-
           heim. Stuttgart, 2003, p. 12

B 4.58   Jenni Energietechnik AG. Oberburg, 2007
B 4.59   see B 2.26, H 150
B 4.61   see B 2.26, H 7
B 4.62–63 Hausladen, Gerhard et al.: Einführung in die
           Bauklimatik. Klima- und Energiekonzepte für
           Gebäude. Berlin, 2003, pp. 92 & 104
B 4.64   based on BINE Informationsdienst (ed.):
           Themeninfo – Thermoaktive Bauteilsysteme,
           1/2007. Bonn, 2007, p. 4
B 4.67   Zimmermann, Mark: Handbuch der passiven
           Kühlung. Dübendorf, 1999, p. 17
B 4.69–70 see B 4.67, p. 57
B 4.72–73 see B 4.67, pp. 79 & 83
B 4.75   see B 4.67, p. 63
B 4.79   based on Eicker, Ursula; Stuttgart University of
           Applied Sciences (ed.): Entwicklungstendenzen
           und Wirtschaftlichkeit solarthermischer Kühlung.
           vol. 74 – symposium, Solares Kühlen in der
           Praxis. Stuttgart, 2006, p. 11
B 4.80   Eicker, Ursula: Solare Technologien für
           Gebäude. Stuttgart/Leipzig/Wiesbaden, 2001
B 4.81   see B 2.26, L 59
B 4.84   see B 4.67, p. 103
B 4.86–87 see B 2.26, L 14 & 16
B 4.88   Paul Wärmerückgewinnung GmbH. Mülsen,
           2007
B 4.90   see B 2.26, L 59, 79, 80
B 4.95   NILAN Deutschland GmbH. Rödental, 2007
B 4.97   see B 2.26, L 99
B 4.99   see B 2.26, K 7
B 4.100   based on DIN EN 12464-1 Light and lighting –
           Lighting of work places – Part 1: Indoor work
           places. Berlin 2003
B 4.101   based on Bavarian Environment Agency (ed.):
           Effiziente Lichtsysteme. Energie sparen. Klima
           schützen. Kosten senken! Augsburg, 2004, p. 4
B 4.102   based on Hörner, Michael; Institut Wohnen &
           Umwelt GmbH (ed.): Kurzverfahren: Strom für
           Beleuchtung – Berechnungsansätze und
           Anwendung. In: proceedings, 41st Energy
           Study Group: Stromverbrauch in Bürogebäuden.
           Darmstadt, 2004, p. 27
B 4.103   see B 4.67
B 4.106   see B 4.67, p. 33
B 4.108   see B 1.29, p. 66
B 4.109–113 see B 3.103, pp. 8, 10, 20–21
B 4.120–123 based on BINE Informationsdienst (ed.):
           Basis Energie 21: Kraft und Wärme koppeln.
           Bonn, 2006, pp. 2–3
B 4.125   see B 4.120, p. 3
B 4.126a based on die Entwicklungs- und Vertriebs-
           gesellschaft Brennstoffzelle mbH (EBZ).
           Dresden, 2007
B 4.127   see B 4.58
B 4.128   see B 3.85, p. 143
B 4.129   based on Pitz-Paal, Rober: Solarthermische
           Kraftwerk. Wie die Sonne ins Kraftwerk kommt.
           In: Physik in unserer Zeit, Spezial: Solarenergie,
           No. 1/2004, p. 13
B 4.130   based on Weinrebe, Gerhard: Das Aufwind-
           kraftwerk. In: Nova Acta Leopoldina NF 91,
           No. 339/2001, pp. 117–141
B 4.134   see B 4.51, p. 3
           based on Hamelmann, Roland: Stromspeicher
           Wasserstoff. In: proceedings, 6th Flensburg
           Wind Energy Forum. 2006

Materials
B 5.6   based on Zürcher, Christoph; Frank, Thomas:
           Bauphysik – Bau und Energie. Zurich, 2004
B 5.11   see B 5.6
B 5.12   DIN 4108 Thermal insulation and energy economy
           in buildings . Berlin, 2003
B 5.14   DIN 4102 Fire behaviour of building materials
           and building components. Berlin, 1998
B 5.15   Hegger, Manfred et al.: Construction Materials
           Manual. Munich, 2006, p. 140
B 5.16   see B 3.14
B 5.17   Gieseler, U.; Heidt, F.D.: Bewertung der Energie-
           effizienz verschiedener Maßnahmen für
           Gebäude mit sehr geringem Energiebedarf.
           Stuttgart, 2005

B 5.18   DETAIL 2005/5, p. 524
B 5.20   DIN 4108-10 Thermal insulation and energy
          economy in buildings – Part 10: Application-
          related requirements for thermal insulation
          materials – Factory made products. Berlin, 2007
B 5.22   see B 5.20
B 5.23   see B 3.14
B 5.24–25 based on Schittich, Christian et al.:
          Glass Construction Manual, 2nd ed. Munich, 2007
B 5.28   see B 3.14
B 5.29–30 see B 5.24
B 5.33–36 see B 5.24
B 5.40   according to data from Sukopp, Herbert (ed.);
          Blume, Hans-Peter: Urban Ecology. Stuttgart/
          Jena/New York, 1998
B 5.41   see B 5.6
B 5.44–45 Ziegert, Christof: In Balance –
          Das Feuchteabsorptionsvermögen von Lehm-
          baustoffen. Viersen-Boisheim, 2004
B 5.46   DIN 4108-6 Thermal protection and energy
          economy in buildings – Part 6: Calculation of
          annual heat and energy use. Berlin, 2003
B 5.47   Schmidt-Bleek, Friedrich: Wieviel Umwelt
          braucht der Mensch? Faktor 10 – das Maß für
          ökologisches Wirtschaften. 1997
B 5.49   see B 3.14
B 5.50   based on Kohler, Nikolaus; et al.: Bürogebäude
          mit Zukunft. Konzepte, Analysen, Erfahrungen.
          Berlin, 2006
B 5.52–53 according to data from Hegger, Manfred;
          Fuchs, Matthias; Zeumer, Martin: research
          report, Vergleichende Nachhaltigkeitskenn-
          werte von Baustoffen und Bauteilschichten.
          Darmstadt, 2005
B 5.54   based on Nebel, Barbara: Ökobilanzierung von
          Holzfußböden. A representative study accord-
          ing to ISO 14040–43 for the German wooden
          flooring industry. Munich, 2003
B 5.55   based on die EAWAG: Forum Chriesbach – Ein
          Neubau für die Wasserforschung. Dübendorf,
          2006
B 5.56   see B 5.52
B 5.57   see B 3.14
B 5.59   Gesellschaft f. ökologische Bautechnik mbh:
          Instrumente für eine qualitätsabhängige
          Abschätzung der Dauerhaftigkeit von Materia-
          lien und Konstruktionen. Berlin, 2005
B 5.60   based on Austrian Institute for Healthy & Eco-
          logical Building (IBO): IBO database. Vienna,
          2005
B 5.61   according to data from Graubner, Carl-Alexander;
          Hüske, Katja: Nachhaltigkeit im Bauwesen.
          Berlin, 2003
B 5.63   according to data from Darmstadt TU, Energy
          Efficient Building Design Unit: e-life – Lebens-
          zyklusbetrachtung und Optimierung von
          Instandsetzungsprozessen im Wohnungsbau.
          Darmstadt, 2007
B 5.72   see B 5.47
B 5.77   based on Preisig, Hansruedi: Massivoder
          Leichtbauweise? Zurich, 2002
B 5.78   see B 1.47
B 5.79   see B 5.59
B 5.80   Industrial Waste Act (GewAbfV). 2003
B 5.81   Cradle-to-Grave Economy Act (KrW/AbfG).
          1996
B 5.83   Iaccording to data from Zwiener, Gerd; Mötzl,
          Hildegund: Ökologisches Baustoff-Lexikon.
          Bauprodukte, Chemikalien, Schadstoffe,
          Ökologie, Innenraum. Heidelberg, 2006
B 5.84   Iaccording to data from North Rhine-Westfalia
          Ministry for the Environment, Nature Conserva-
          tion, Agriculture & Consumer Protection. North
          Rhine-Westfalia Environment & Health Campaign.
          Umweltzeichen für Bauprodukte. Bauprodukte
          gezielt auswählen – eine Entscheidungshilfe.
          Düsseldorf, 2004
B 5.85   Iaccording to data from Sigg, René; Kälin,
          Werner; Plattner, Hugo: LUKRETIA – Lebens-
          zyklus – Ressourcen – Technisierung. Zurich,
          2006

B 5.87   IFederal Ministry of Transport, Building & Urban
          Affairs: Leitfaden Nachhaltiges Bauen. Berlin,
          2001
B 5.88   Isee B 5.85
B 5.91   Isee B 5.87
B 5.92–93 see B 1.47

Strategies

B 6.3–5   based on Association of Swiss Engineers &
          Architects (SIA) (ed.): SIA D 0216. SIA Effizienz-
          pfad Energie. Zurich, 2006
B 6.11   Voss, Karsten et al.: Bürogebäude mit Zukunft.
          Konzepte, Analysen, Erfahrungen. Berlin, 2006,
          p. 40
B 6.28   Löhnert, Günter: Der Integrale Planungsprozess.
          Eine Serie in vier Teilen. Teil I: Grundlagen.
          Berlin, 2007, p. 2
B 6.30   based on Diederichs, Claus Jürgen; Getto,
          Petra; Streck, Stefanie: Entwicklung eines
          Bewertungssystems für ökonomisches und
          ökologisches Bauen und gesundes Wohnen.
          Stuttgart, 2003
B 6.31–32 see B 6.11, pp. 154 and 164
B 6.33   Lützkendorf, Thomas et al.: Nachhaltigkeits-
          orientierte Investments im Immobilienbereich.
          Trends, Theorie und Typologie. Karlsruhe, 2005
B 6.34   according to data from Renner, Alexander:
          Energie und Ökoeffizienz von Wohngebäuden.
          Entwicklung eines Verfahrens zur lebenszyklus-
          orientierten Bewertung der Umweltwirkungen
          unter besonderer Berücksichtigung der Nut-
          zungsphase. Darmstadt, 2007
B 6.35   Association of Swiss Engineers & Architects
          (SIA) (ed.): Empfehlung SIA 112/1. Nachhaltiges
          Bauen – Hochbau. Zurich, 2006
B 6.37   Lützkendorf, Thomas et al.: Nachhaltiges
          Planen, Bauen und Bewirtschaften von Bau-
          werken. Ziele, Grundlagen, Stand und Trends.
          Bewertungsmethoden und -hilfsmittel. Brief
          study for the BMVBW. Karlsruhe, 2002

The Department of Architecture of Darmstadt Technical
University has taken every effort to ensure that the information provided in this book is correct and up to date.
The content of this book was prepared with the utmost
care. Nevertheless, errors and ambiguities cannot be
entirely ruled out. The Department of Architecture of
Darmstadt Technical University therefore offers no guarantee as to the relevance, correctness, completeness or
quality of the information provided herein. The Department of Architecture of Darmstadt Technical University
cannot be held liable for material or non-material damages
of any kind caused directly or indirectly by the use or dis-
use of the information given here or by the use of errone-
ous or incomplete information unless it can be proved
that the Department of Architecture of Darmstadt Technical University has acted with intent or gross negligence.

The authors and publishers would like to express their
thanks to the following persons who kindly provided
advice and assistance:

Jens Hornung, Darmstadt
Martin Huber, Stuttgart
Verena Klar, Tübingen
Jörg Lange, Freiburg
Dirk Mangold, Stuttgart
Thomas Rühle, Munich
Jürgen Schreiber, Ulm

Subject index

280